The Structure of Argument

TENTH EDITION

The Structure of
ARGUMENT

Annette T. Rottenberg

University of Massachusetts at Amherst, Emerita

Donna Haisty Winchell

Clemson University, Emerita

bedford/st.martin's
Macmillan Learning
Boston | New York

Vice President: Leasa Burton
Program Director: Stacey Purviance
Senior Program Manager: John E. Sullivan III
Director of Content Development: Jane Knetzger
Senior Development Editor: Leah Rang
Associate Editor: Cari Goldfine
Editorial Assistant: Samantha Storms
Director of Media Editorial: Adam Whitehurst
Executive Marketing Manager: Joy Fisher Williams
Director, Content Management Enhancement: Tracey Kuehn
Senior Managing Editor: Michael Granger
Content Project Manager: Matt Glazer
Senior Workflow Project Supervisor: Susan Wein
Workflow Manager: Lisa McDowell
Production Supervisor: Lawrence Guerra
Director of Design, Content Management: Diana Blume
Interior Design: Lisa Buckley
Cover Design: William Boardman
Director of Rights and Permissions: Hilary Newman
Permissions Editor: Angela Boehler
Senior Permissions Project Manager: Elaine Kosta, Lumina Datamatics, Inc.
Lumina Researcher: Richard Fox
Director of Digital Production: Keri deManigold
Advanced Media Product Manager: D. Rand Thomas
Copyeditor: Julie Dock
Composition: Lumina Datamatics, Inc.
Cover Image: Lazy_Bear/Getty Images
Printing and Binding: LSC Communications

Library of Congress Control Number: 2020939807
ISBN: 978-1-319-21475-3

Printed in the United States of America.

1 2 3 4 5 6   25 24 23 22 21 20

Acknowledgments

Text acknowledgments and copyrights appear at the back of the book on pages 471–74, which constitute an extension of the copyright page. Art acknowledgments and copyrights appear on the same page as the art selections they cover.

For information, write: Bedford/St. Martin's, 75 Arlington Street, Boston, MA 02116

Preface

Purpose

One look at today's headlines is all it takes to see that every American citizen needs to be able to think critically about what is going on in the nation and in the world. Biased reporting slants the news, and it is hard even to discern what is fact. More than ever, people of conscience need to be able to take a stand and articulate a position. They also need to be able to formulate and articulate their positions on moral and social issues even when they are not the topic of the most recent news cycle.

College has long been a place where values and beliefs are tested. Exposure to new ideas and new perspectives is a part of coming of age and of growth as students explore what role they want to play in society and in professional life. A course in argumentation is a place where students can learn the tools to critically examine ideas and where they can learn to construct their own arguments in support of their position or in defense of what they believe.

In order to get our students really thinking critically about argument, we wrote this book with these core principles:

- **We must get students to slow down and practice the art of critical reading—and listening.** We must provide them with timely, accessible readings, we must get them to analyze sustained argumentative discourse, and we must give them tools to talk about it. The vocabulary we use in this text incorporates Aristotle's ancient rhetoric, Carl Rogers's notion of common ground, stasis theory questions, and Stephen Toulmin's three principal elements of argument: claim, support, and assumption (warrant). In addition, we present the concepts of definition, language, and logic as critical tools for understanding and responding to arguments.
- **We also must get our students to *write* sustained argumentative discourse.** They must learn to apply their knowledge of claim, support, and assumption. They must learn to define key terms and to recognize, write, and support claims of fact, value, and policy. They must understand that successful arguments require a blend of *logos*, *pathos*, and *ethos*. They must appreciate the significance of audience as a practical matter.

In the rhetorical or audience-centered approach to argument, to which we subscribe in this text, success is defined as acceptance of the claim by an audience. Arguers in the real world recognize intuitively that their primary goal is not to demonstrate the purity of their logic, but to win their audiences.

To do so, students must read critically and think critically about what others have to say. The internet has redefined what research means to our students. A large part of the challenge is not to find sources but to eliminate the thousands of questionable ones. Faced with the temptation to cut and paste instead of read and understand, students need more help than ever with accurate and fair use of sources. In *The Structure of Argument*, we provide that help in the context of an increasingly digital world.

Organization

The Structure of Argument is a comprehensive argument text. Our assumption is that learning to recognize the elements of argument—claim, support, assumption, definition, language, and logic—can help students both to analyze how arguments are constructed and to structure their own.

- **Part One, "Understanding Argument,"** begins with a definition of argument to provide students a lens for critical thinking, reading, and writing. Next, it addresses the critical reading of written as well as visual and multimodal arguments. It then provides instruction on writing responses to arguments, particularly in an academic context. Selections both illustrate various arguments and offer practice for student analysis.
- **Part Two, "Writing Argument,"** introduces the different approaches to argument—Aristotelian, Rogerian, stasis theory, and Toulmin—and presents them as choices students can make to analyze or construct arguments in their own writing. It then devotes one chapter apiece to the chief elements of argument—claim, support, and assumption. Straightforward explanations simplify these concepts for students, and examples are drawn from everyday print and online sources—essays, articles, graphics, reviews, editorials, and advertisements—by both student and professional writers. Finally, Part Two introduces a chapter on how to organize an argument.
- **Part Three, "Strengthening Argument,"** details important matters of reading and writing effective argument. Chapter 10 deals with the power of word choice and addressing an audience with appropriate and purposeful language. Chapter 11 teaches students the importance of defining key terms, especially as a means of establishing common ground with an audience. Chapter 12 covers the various logical fallacies as well as how to identify and avoid logical errors in arguments.
- **Part Four, "Incorporating Research,"** takes up the process of planning, writing, and documenting arguments based on independent research. Chapter 13 focuses on planning and research, including how to narrow a topic and take notes as well as how to find and evaluate sources. Chapter 14 addresses drafting and revising written arguments as well as oral presentations. Chapter 15 covers documentation and provides sample research papers in the Modern Language Association (MLA) and the American Psychological Association (APA) documentation styles.

Features and Coverage

Three unique feature boxes enhance and reinforce the text: Argument Essentials boxes summarize and reinforce basic argument concepts, Strategies boxes provide more in-depth information on important skills such as prereading and annotating texts, and Research Skills boxes explain a variety of academic research tasks related to the argument concepts in the chapter.

Coverage of traditional rhetorical issues such as audience and purpose spans all chapters in *The Structure of Argument*, helping students grasp the importance of clear communication in a variety of situations. The text shows students how to apply concepts of rhetoric and logic to spoken, visual, online, and other multimedia arguments, and an abundance of visual arguments—including ads, photographs, screen shots, and graphics—provides visual examples and opportunities for analysis. Student essays, with documented sources, serve as models for effective writing and proper form.

For instructors who want to apply current events to their argument course, see our blog, "Argument in the Headlines." In regularly updated posts, we use argument concepts to frame issues in the news, offering ideas for instructors to help students relate the text and the course to their everyday lives. You can find the blog *Bedford Bits* at **community.macmillan.com**.

New to This Edition

In this tenth edition of *The Structure of Argument*, we offer more support for connecting argument concepts with the writing process, reorganizing and adding new chapters to help students move more clearly from analyzing arguments to writing, researching, and fine-tuning their own.

A new Chapter 1, "What Is Argument?," gets students working with argument right at the beginning of the course: defining argument, considering other perspectives, and arguing ethically. The chapter equips students with the foundational concepts of argumentation and invites them to think critically about the purposes, ethics, and needs of argument in their current educational context and the current social climate.

Part Two, "Writing Argument," and Part Three, "Strengthening Arguments," have been reorganized to more effectively lead students from planning to drafting to editing their written arguments. Approaches to argument now appear in a separate Chapter 5 to emphasize the different choices available to critical writers as they compose argument. Chapters on claims, support, and assumptions are updated with new readings on issues of language and gender bias, cultural appropriation, and the psychological benefits of having crushes that help engage students as they dive deep into these major argument concepts. A new Chapter 9, "Structuring the Argument," presents students with options for planning and organizing their arguments. Chapters dedicated to language, definition, and logic help students fine-tune their analyses and arguments with revised strategy boxes that highlight the connections between critical reading and writing, and which are optimized to support peer review or self-editing.

Updated coverage in Chapter 13, "Planning and Research," reflects how students currently consume and search for information, especially through online searches, and provides guidance on how to identify, critically evaluate, and select relevant sources. The chapter follows a new student writer through her research and note-taking process. Chapter 15, "Documenting Sources," is also revised to include more contemporary citation examples such as social media posts and online videos and podcasts, as well as a thorough update to the current APA style. Two new student papers model both MLA- and APA-style writing.

New readings within chapters keep these models current and subjects interesting. Nearly half of the readings are new and feature arguments by climate activists, podcast hosts, poets, culture critics, lawyers, prominent politicians, and more. These selections engage students in topics related to education, civic responsibility, popular culture, and public safety and policy, and pose questions for thinking critically about these contemporary issues.

New readings include

- Greta Thunberg's speech at the United Nations Climate Action Summit, "How Dare You?"
- Ocean Vuong's poetic take on his own experiences with gender awareness, "Reimagining Masculinity"
- Rachel Syme's exploration of the empowering possibilities of self-photography, "Selfie: The Revolutionary Potential of Your Own Face"

Also Available

A more robust version, *Elements of Argument*, Thirteenth Edition, is available for instructors who prefer a longer text with additional readings on contemporary and classic issues. The comprehensive text includes all of the instructional chapters on argument, critical reading, and writing—Chapters 1 through 15—as well as a readings anthology with an additional forty-eight readings organized into pro-con debates, casebooks exploring multiple perspectives, and a collection of classic arguments. See **macmillanlearning .com/college/us** for details.

Acknowledgments

This book has profited by the critiques and suggestions of many instructors over the years. We would like to thank especially those who responded to questionnaires for this edition: Mari Bailey, Phoenix College; Joshua Chase, Michigan Technological University; Geoffrey Clegg, Midwestern State University; David L. Cooper, Jefferson Community and Technical College; Joseph Corrado, Portland Community College; Sydney Darby, Chemeketa Community College; Sheilah Stokes Dobyns, Fullerton College; Curt Duffy, Los Angeles Pierce College; Hedda Fish, San Diego State University; Brandon Gainer, De Anza College; Karen K. Gibson, The State University of New York at Potsdam; Richard W. Hankins, Southwestern College; Rebecca Hope, University of Northwestern, St. Paul; Emily King, Truckee Meadows Community College; Peter Landino, Terra State Community College; Lisa A. Marzano, Palm Beach Atlantic University; Ronda K. Mehrer, Black Hills State University; Bonnie Miller, Kishwaukee College; Steven Mohr, Terra State Community College; Allison G. Murray, Long Beach City College; Salena Parker, Collin College, McKinney; Wendy Sharer, East Carolina University; Bonnie A. Spears, Chaffey College; Judith Valko, Paradise Valley Community College; and David Wilson, West Virginia University at Parkersburg. We also thank those reviewers who chose to remain anonymous.

We are grateful to those at Bedford/St. Martin's and Macmillan Learning who have helped in numerous ways large and small: John Sullivan, Leasa Burton, Matt Glazer, Hilary Newman, Angie Boehler, Richard Fox, Elaine Kosta, Thai Luong, Cari Goldfine, Samantha Storms, and, most especially, Leah Rang.

Bedford/St. Martin's Puts You First

From day one, our goal has been simple: to provide inspiring resources that are grounded in best practices for teaching reading and writing. For more than thirty-five years, Bedford/St. Martin's has partnered with the field, listening to teachers, scholars, and students about the support writers need. We are committed to helping every writing instructor make the most of our resources.

How can we help *you*?

- Our editors can align our resources to your outcomes through correlation and transition guides for your syllabus. Just ask us.
- Our sales representatives specialize in helping you find the right materials to support your course goals.
- Our learning solutions and product specialists help you make the most of the digital resources you choose for your course.
- Our *Bits* blog on the Bedford/St. Martin's English Community (**community .macmillan.com**) publishes fresh teaching ideas weekly. You'll also find easily downloadable professional resources and links to author webinars on our community site.

Contact your Bedford/St. Martin's sales representative or visit **macmillanlearning .com** to learn more.

Print and Digital Options for *The Structure of Argument*

Choose the format that works best for your course, and ask about our packaging options that offer savings for students.

Print

- *Paperback.* To order the paperback edition, use ISBN 978-1-319-21475-3.
- *Elements of Argument.* To order the comprehensive version with the readings anthology, also available in paperback format, use ISBN 978-1-319-21473-9.

Digital

- *Achieve for Readers and Writers.* Achieve puts student writing at the center of your course and keeps revision at the core, with a dedicated composition space that guides students through drafting, peer review, source check, reflection, and revision. Developed to support best practices in commenting on student drafts, Achieve is a flexible, integrated suite of tools for designing and facilitating writing assignments, paired with actionable insights that make students' progress toward outcomes clear and measurable. Achieve offers instructors a quick and flexible solution for targeting instruction based on students' unique needs. For details, visit **macmillanlearning.com/college/us/englishdigital**.

- *Popular e-book formats.* For details about our e-book partners, visit **macmillanlearning.com/ebooks**.
- *Inclusive Access.* Enable every student to receive their course materials through your LMS on the first day of class. Macmillan Learning's Inclusive Access program is the easiest, most affordable way to ensure all students have access to quality educational resources. Find out more at **macmillanlearning.com/inclusiveaccess**.

Your Course, Your Way

No two writing programs or classrooms are exactly alike. Our Curriculum Solutions team works with you to design custom options that provide the resources your students need. (Options below require enrollment minimums.)

- *ForeWords for English.* Customize any print resource to fit the focus of your course or program by choosing from a range of prepared topics, such as Sentence Guides for Academic Writers.
- *Macmillan Author Program (MAP).* Add excerpts or package acclaimed works from Macmillan's trade imprints to connect students with prominent authors and public conversations. A list of popular examples or academic themes is available upon request.
- *Mix and Match.* With our simplest solution, you can add up to fifty pages of curated content to your Bedford/St. Martin's text. Contact your sales representative for additional details.
- *Bedford Select.* Build your own print anthology from a database of more than 800 selections, or build a handbook, and add your own materials to create your ideal text. Package with any Bedford/St. Martin's text for additional savings. Visit **macmillanlearning.com/bedfordselect**.

Instructor Resources

You have a lot to do in your course. We want to make it easy for you to find the support you need—and to get it quickly.

Resources for Teaching The Structure of Argument is available as a PDF that can be downloaded from **macmillanlearning.com**. In addition to chapter overviews and teaching tips, the instructor's manual includes sample syllabi, classroom activities, and additional assignments.

How *The Structure of Argument* Supports WPA Outcomes for First-Year Composition

The following chart provides information on how *The Structure of Argument* helps students build proficiency and achieve the learning outcomes established by the Council of Writing Program Administrators, which writing programs across the country use to assess their students' work.

Rhetorical Knowledge

Learn and use key rhetorical concepts through analyzing and composing a variety of texts.	The organization of *The Structure of Argument* supports students' understanding of rhetorical strategy: ■ **Part One, "Understanding Argument,"** defines argument and gives students context for reading and writing about argument in the twenty-first century. It addresses the critical reading of written as well as visual and multimodal arguments. ■ **Part Two, "Writing Argument,"** introduces students to the Aristotelian, Rogerian, and Toulmin approaches to argumentation and to stasis theory. Detailed chapters provide in-depth coverage of the chief elements of argument: claim, support, and assumption. ■ **Part Three, "Strengthening Argument,"** details important concepts for reading and writing effective argument: language, definition, and logic. ■ **Part Four, "Incorporating Research,"** takes up the process of planning, writing, and documenting arguments based on independent research. Coverage of traditional rhetorical issues such as audience and purpose spans all chapters, helping students grasp the importance of clear communication in a variety of rhetorical situations.
Gain experience reading and composing in several genres to understand how genre conventions shape and are shaped by readers' and writers' practices and purposes.	The **55 readings (including 6 student essays)** in the book span a variety of topics, disciplines, and genres. Each selection features annotations or targeted questions that give students practice analyzing and writing for a variety of purposes and in a range of styles.
Develop facility in responding to a variety of situations and contexts calling for purposeful shifts in voice, tone, level of formality, design, medium, and/or structure.	**Chapter 5, "Approaches to Argument,"** introduces students to Aristotelian, Rogerian, and Toulmin approaches to argumentation and to stasis theory, and explains their different purposes and features to support student analysis and writing using each approach. **Chapter introductions** explain how each rhetorical element and strategy helps to achieve an author's purpose. Throughout the text, **post-reading questions** call attention to the form and function of different arguments.
Understand and use a variety of technologies to address a range of audiences.	**Chapter 3, "Critical Reading of Multimodal Arguments,"** shows students how arguments can be made using a variety of multimodal contexts, including photographs, print advertisements, political cartoons, graphics, commercials, speeches, debates, broadcast news, print news, social media, and interactive websites.
Match the capacities of different environments (e.g., print and electronic) to varying rhetorical situations.	**Chapter 3** shows students how a variety of print and electronic environments can be used to build persuasive arguments. A section in Chapter 14 on **"Oral Arguments and Presentations"** includes guidance for making rhetorical choices for spoken argument.

Critical Thinking, Reading, and Composing

Use composing and reading for inquiry, learning, critical thinking, and communicating in various rhetorical contexts.	**Parts One, Two, and Three** guide students through the process of understanding how arguments function, reading them critically, analyzing them in writing, and composing them effectively. In particular, **Chapters 3 and 4** focus on critical reading of different kinds of arguments. **Part Four** provides guidance on researching and crafting effective arguments using inquiry and critical thinking.
Read a diverse range of texts, attending especially to relationships between assertion and evidence, to patterns of organization, to the interplay between verbal and nonverbal elements, and to how these features function for different audiences and situations.	Throughout the text, diverse selections include introductions or annotations that illustrate different rhetorical elements and organizational strategies, and post-reading questions prompt students to analyze the relationship between assertion and evidence (also explored in detail in **Chapter 6, "Claims,"** and **Chapter 7, "Support"**). In addition, **Chapter 3, "Critical Reading of Multimodal Arguments,"** shows students how to analyze the relationship between verbal and nonverbal elements of multimodal texts.
Locate and evaluate (for credibility, sufficiency, accuracy, timeliness, bias, and so on) primary and secondary research materials, including journal articles and essays, books, scholarly and professionally established and maintained databases or archives, and informal electronic networks and internet sources.	**Chapter 13, "Planning and Research,"** offers practical instruction for locating and evaluating primary and secondary research materials through library resources as well as online search. **Chapter 15, "Documenting Sources,"** illustrates best practices for reviewing research. **Research Skill** boxes throughout the instructional chapters help students incorporate sources for a variety of writing activities and contexts. Of particular interest are "Using Databases," "Evaluating Expert Opinion," and "Popular vs. Scholarly Articles."
Use strategies—such as interpretation, synthesis, response, critique, and design/redesign—to compose texts that integrate the writer's ideas with those from appropriate sources.	The questions and prompts that accompany each reading ask students to interpret, respond, and critique the writer's choices. **Chapter 2, "Critical Reading of Written Arguments,"** distinguishes between content analysis and rhetorical analysis, as well as strategies for summarizing, paraphrasing, and integrating quotations to form a critical response. **Chapter 14, "Drafting, Revising, and Presenting Arguments,"** helps students compose texts that integrate the writer's ideas with those from appropriate sources. A list of helpful **sentence forms** allows students to interpret, synthesize, and respond to sources with clear purpose. **Strategies** boxes provide additional help for interpreting and responding to sources. Of particular interest are "Strategies for Summary, Paraphrase, and Quotation," "Strategies for Refuting an Opposing View," and "Strategies for Finding the Middle Ground."

Processes

Develop a writing project through multiple drafts.	**Chapter 13, "Planning and Research,"** illustrates best practices for invention, choosing a topic, initiating and conducting research, and evaluating sources. The chapter follows a student writer through her process. **Chapter 14, "Drafting, Revising, and Presenting Arguments,"** takes students through the process of reviewing research, drafting, and revision.
Develop flexible strategies for reading, drafting, reviewing, collaborating, revising, rewriting, rereading, and editing.	**Part One, "Understanding Argument,"** equips students with strategies for critical reading and analysis of arguments. **Part Two, "Writing Argument,"** gives sustained attention to the foundational elements of argument. **Chapter 5, "Approaches to Argument,"** offers students options for reading and composing arguments through different lenses. **Chapter 9, "Structuring the Argument,"** provides flexible options for planning and organizing an argument according to different purposes. **Chapter 14, "Drafting, Revising, and Presenting Arguments,"** offers guidance on developing multiple drafts and revising arguments. **Strategies** boxes such as "Strategies for Annotating a Text" and "Strategies for Critical Listening" provide additional guidance.
Use composing processes and tools as a means to discover and reconsider ideas.	Throughout each chapter, the text emphasizes the importance of rereading and rewriting to interrogate ideas. In particular, **Chapter 2, "Critical Reading of Written Arguments,"** provides strategies for evaluating arguments and ideas, and **Chapter 13, "Planning and Research,"** includes "Invention Strategies" and "Evaluating Possible Topics."
Experience the collaborative and social aspects of writing processes.	**Reading, Writing, and Discussion Questions** that follow many readings or readings chapters can be used as prompts for discussion of ideas and of the writing process. **Strategies** and **Research Skills** boxes provide additional insights into the writing and research processes and can be adapted for peer review.
Learn to give and to act on productive feedback to works in progress.	**Argument Essentials** boxes summarize key argument and writing concepts and can be used as prompts or checklists for peer feedback. **Strategies** boxes often include guided questions for analysis and can be used for peer evaluation. See, for example, "Strategies for Evaluating Arguments," "Strategies for Evaluating Appeals to Needs and Values," and "Strategies for Evaluating Word Choice."
Adapt composing processes for a variety of technologies and modalities.	**Chapter 3, "Critical Reading of Multimodal Arguments,"** shows students how a variety of technologies and modalities can be used to build persuasive arguments. **"Oral Arguments and Presentations"** in Chapter 14 prepares students for composing presentations.
Reflect on the development of composing practices and how those practices influence their work.	**Post-reading questions** and **end-of-chapter assignments** often encourage students to reflect on their knowledge, assumptions, and writing habits.

Knowledge of Conventions

Develop knowledge of linguistic structures, including grammar, punctuation, and spelling, through practice in composing and revising.	**Chapter 10, "Language,"** draws students' attention to the rhetorical effectiveness of connotation, slanting, concrete and abstract language, clichés, and figurative language. **LearningCurve activities** (available in *Achieve for Readers and Writers*) provide extensive practice with grammar, punctuation, and spelling.
Understand why genre conventions for structure, paragraphing, tone, and mechanics vary.	The text's overarching emphasis on rhetorical context and situation fosters critical thinking about genre conventions. Annotations on selected readings also highlight conventions and rhetorical choices. **Chapter introductions** for Parts Two and Three explain how each element of argument serves a writer's purpose.
Gain experience negotiating variations in genre conventions.	The variety of formats and genres represented in the **51 professional selections** gives students experience negotiating variations in genre conventions. **Part Two, "Writing Argument,"** helps students understand how to negotiate the elements of argument differently using the various argument approaches.
Learn common formats and/or design features for different kinds of texts.	Annotated selections throughout the text, including student essays, impart awareness of common formats and/or design features for different kinds of texts, and **Chapter 15, "Documenting Sources,"** provides specific instruction on formatting and design, including **MLA**- and **APA**-style student research papers with annotations highlighting the genre conventions.
Explore the concepts of intellectual property (such as fair use and copyright) that motivate documentation conventions.	A dedicated section on **"Avoiding Plagiarism"** in Chapter 14 teaches students the importance of using sources responsibly, and **Chapter 15, "Documenting Sources,"** raises awareness of different documentation conventions, specifically MLA and APA formats.
Practice applying citation conventions systematically in their own work.	**Chapter 14, "Drafting, Revising, and Presenting Arguments,"** offers guidance on avoiding plagiarism and provides sentence forms to assist source integration, and **Chapter 15, "Documenting Sources,"** shows students how to apply citation conventions of MLA and APA styles in their own writing.

Brief Contents

Contents

PART TWO Writing Argument 127

5 Approaches to Argument 129

PART THREE Strengthening Argument 267

10 Language 269

11 Definition   302

PART FOUR Incorporating Research 361

13 Planning and Research 363

The Structure of Argument

Understanding ARGUMENT

What Is Argument?

Social networking sites have changed the nature of human discourse. They provide an easy means of staying in touch with people all over the world, a means of sharing the most trivial or the most exciting news. You can tell your friends you are headed to the gym, or you can tell them you are headed for a breakup. You can debate in real time about your politics or your sports teams. You can reestablish old relationships and establish new ones. You can share pictures of your family or your cat's most recent antics.

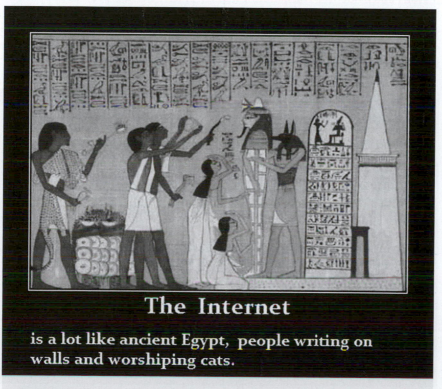

FIGURE 1.1 Meme comparing the internet to ancient Egypt.

Through social networking, we have the means of presenting a public persona like never before. Some of you may not want to "friend" or "follow" your parents because of the public persona you project online. You may not want prospective employers to see some of the comments or pictures you post on your feeds. Many college students use LinkedIn for their professional contacts and Facebook, Twitter, Instagram, or another social networking site for their personal contacts.

The very language of social networking captures its public nature. If someone writes on a wall (digital or otherwise), the message is intentionally made public. Facebook users can control who their "friends" are, but in practice a "friend" is anyone to whom you are willing to give access to your page. These are the people who can see the writing on your wall, for good or ill.

In writing in public spaces, as in other writing that you do, you have to be aware of your audience. You also have to be aware of the **rhetorical situation** — the context, purpose, and audience — of what you write and what you read. Analyze the rhetorical situation in Figure 1.2. An even simpler visual can also make a statement. For example, consider Figure 1.3. The vandalized sign makes a point different from what was originally intended. Answer the Reading, Writing, and Discussion Questions to help you analyze both figures.

Electronic media have added a whole new dimension to the study of **argumentation** — of taking a position or stating an idea and supporting it with reasons and evidence. You can now make a statement and provide support for it through documents transmitted electronically, email, Twitter, pictures, audio, video, and mixed media. This textbook will explore what argument is, why we study it, the forms that argument takes in the twenty-first century and, as the title suggests, its elements.

FIGURE 1.2 Street art rumored to be by famous street artist Banksy, quoting Raoul Vaneigem's *The Revolution of Everyday Life* (1967). Justin Ng/Avalon/Photoshot/AGE Fotostock

FIGURE 1.3 Vandalized sign. Jim Lo Scalzo/EPA/Shutterstock

Reading, Writing, and Discussion Questions

1. What argument is Figure 1.1 making about human communication? How does the composition of the meme affect your reception of the argument?

2. What exactly do you see in Figure 1.2? Who is pictured? How is the figure dressed? Why are the answers to those questions important?

3. What is the significance of the object in or on the ground in front of the subject? How does the imagery tie into the words in the mural?

4. The symbol held in the figure's hand is the emblem of the environmental activist group Extinction Rebellion, formed in October 2018 and dedicated to using nonviolent means to call attention to the global effects of climate change. Does knowing that give additional or different meaning to the words? Explain.

5. The mural appeared in April 2019 across from the Marble Arch, through which royals pass during ceremonial processions. What conclusions might you draw about the audience for whom the mural was intended? Was street art the best way to deliver the message? Why or why not?

6. What argument is the work of art making?

7. Look at Figure 1.3. What do you think the sign said before it was vandalized? What makes it clear that the vandalism was not random?

8. What point was someone trying to make in changing the sign in the way he or she did? How does the sign reflect the social and political situation?

Why Study Argument?

We all know how to argue. We've known how to argue since we were children asking our parents to let us stay up an extra half hour, play a new video game, or buy one of the candy bars so temptingly placed near the check-out line. Our support for our side of the argument may have been no more sophisticated than "Because everyone else's parents let them!" or "But I'm starving!" and our parents' rebuttal may have been no better than "Because I said so!" or "Because I said *no!*" **Argumentation** as a learned skill goes beyond verbal sparring, or fighting, to get our way.

Hopefully our skill in argumentation has improved since we were children. We still argue in support of choices we make in our personal lives. That doesn't have to mean that we *fight* with someone about those choices. It also does not mean we simply attack another point of view. The term **argument** represents forms of discourse in which a writer or speaker provides a reasoned case for their position on an issue. There may have been times you made an argument to yourself to try to clarify your thinking about what colleges to apply to or which college to attend. You may have presented to your parents or someone else your reasons for buying a new car, choosing your major, signing up for the campus meal plan, or renting your textbooks. You may have had to reason through, alone or with others, whether to accept a job offer or end a relationship. As you have grown into adulthood, you have also probably become more and more involved in arguing about your social, political, and religious views.

Unless you avoid the news entirely, you are aware that we are living in one of the most contentious times in U.S. history. Our country has been more politically divided in the opening decades of the twenty-first century than it has been at any time since the Civil War. Family members have broken with family members over liberal versus conservative beliefs, and friendships decades old have ended over who voted for whom for president.

Why study argument if people argue so much anyway? Because by and large, they are not very good at it. Too often people articulate a position without providing any support for it at all. They pass along information they see on social media without questioning its source or its truth. They blindly accept what a politician proposes without thinking through the consequences of the proposal. They vote for a political party because that's what they have always done without stopping to consider if that party still supports what is in their best interests and the best interests of the country. On campus, we see students choosing a major because it's what a parent wants instead of what they themselves want. We see them buying into prejudices without considering why. We hear them echoing others' ideas without stopping to think about them critically.

As a citizen of your town or city, your state, your country, and your world, you need to be able to analyze an argument and to construct one. You need to be able to think through what you have always believed to ascertain if it is actually what you believe or what someone else has told you to believe. You need to be able to think through those choices that will shape your education, career, livelihood, and political and social behavior. Once you make an important decision, you may have to be able to explain your reasons to your family, your friends, or yourself. An effective argument is carefully structured and fully supported.

Argument in the Twenty-First Century

Electronic media make arguments accessible, but also make them informal. Argument today is all about speed and convenience. The very names of social media sites capture the speed and brevity of the transmission of ideas: Instagram, Snapchat, Twitter, Tik Tok. Snapchat is so ephemeral that the images and messages disappear after viewing; Instagram and Facebook "stories" last only twenty-four hours. Twitter is limited to a set number of characters. Social media sites are today's equivalent of the public forum where ideas are expressed or shared, then applauded or shouted down. You may be more likely to read a news article or at least its headline if someone shares it via social media than if you have to go directly to the news outlet's own site.

Where in the past citizens thought they could believe anything they saw in the newspaper, there is a natural impulse to believe anything posted online, particularly if it supports beliefs we already hold. That impulse played right into the hands of those trying to influence the 2016 presidential election. We discovered with that election how willing Americans were to accept what they read on social media at face value and to pass it on uncritically, without considering whether the "news" was even created by a human or by a Russian bot designed to play on biases and fears.

Although online feeds may make us more blind to the source of the information we encounter, they also provide new means of making and discussing arguments, particularly in abbreviated — and often fun — forms. Consider the internet meme, which through an image and a few words presents an argument. The success of the meme is wholly dependent on knowing the context — or the time and political, social, or cultural situation that existed when the meme was created — which is the case with any argument, be it written, oral, or visual. The humor is also, of course, dependent on context.

The image in Figure 1.4 comes from the 1971 movie *Willy Wonka and the Chocolate Factory*, and the smug look on Gene Wilder's face led to the character's being dubbed "Condescending Willy." When connected with text, this image resulted in dozens of versions of the Willy Wonka meme where Willy makes fun of people for all kinds of reasons and often reveals political leanings or positions on an issue, which is the case in Figure 1.4. What is the context or issue that the meme depends on for its humor? What is the argument being made?

You may not have stopped to think about the fact that you are reading an argument when you read a meme. That's

FIGURE 1.4 Condescending Willy Wonka meme.
Photo: PictureLux/Alamy Stock Photo

where understanding the rhetorical context comes in. Consider the Willy Wonka meme. To have an argument, you must take a position on an issue. A meme doesn't explicitly state that position; your audience has to surmise that from the context. To whom is the author — via Willy Wonka — speaking? It must be those who feel that hunters should be allowed to own semi-automatic weapons, yet the author is clearly on the side of those who support restrictions on such weapons. Whoever first posted the meme is poking fun at any hunter who feels he needs a gun that holds thirty rounds. ("Why? Are the deer retaliating?") Implicit is the suggestion that there is not much sport in that. A direct statement of the point underlying the humor would be something like this: "The sale of semi-automatic weapons should be illegal in the United States." That's a big — and controversial — idea behind an image and a few words, but that is the context that gives the meme its meaning.

Abbreviated arguments like Figure 1.4 and Figure 1.5 primarily appeal to those who already agree with the politics behind them. Most likely no one would be persuaded to change his or her mind by simply seeing one of these memes. That's why they are a convenient shorthand to remind people of issues already on their minds and in the news. If you took the main idea behind either of these memes as the basis for an essay, you would have to back up that idea with convincing evidence or **support**.

FIGURE 1.5   The value of an education.

Reading, Writing, and Discussion Questions

Consider the meme in Figure 1.5.

1. What point is the meme making?
2. How do the images contribute to the argument?
3. Who is the audience for this meme? Notice the logo *Turning Point USA*. What does that organization's website reveal about its audience? Or about its purpose in creating and sharing this meme?

Abbreviated arguments like the memes and street art we've considered so far in this chapter are certainly not the only types of arguments you encounter. They just may be some of the ones you encounter most often on social media, where a post, a shared headline, or an article may alert you to breaking news. When you want to delve more deeply into a subject or issue, you may choose to access more information online, on television, or through newspapers or magazines. An article like the one below, which appeared in both print and online versions, expands on the issue of education raised by the meme in Figure 1.5.

The Financial Case for Trade School over College

MEL BONDAR

It's unfortunate that some of the best money saving tips have such a stigma attached to them.

Here's a newsflash — college isn't for everyone. Your level of intelligence doesn't necessarily equate to whether you got your bachelor's.

You have to be pretty smart to really understand how engines work or how to wire a house without electrocuting yourself.

Carpentry requires tons and tons of math.

We've held white collar jobs up on such a pedestal over the years that it's easy to forget that there's no shame in a job where you get your hands dirty.

As a matter of fact, a lot of people might be a lot happier working in a skilled trade than sitting behind a desk. The funniest part is that you're likely to make more money in many of those jobs than you could ever make in an office.

You'd also have to be living under a rock to be unaware of the college debt crisis affecting the majority of millennials. College is expensive. Over the last few decades, the cost of a college degree has tripled, completely out of proportion to standard inflation.

The average millennial has $30,000 in college loans. I know I finished up grad school with exactly that amount of debt dangling over my head and that was after not paying a penny for undergraduate and landing a few scholarships for grad school.

As a result of those $30,000 in loans, I wound up living full time on a cruise ship and a circus train for two-and-a-half years to pay them off. I was incredibly lucky to land these unique jobs that paid for room and board and allowed me to funnel nearly everything I made into paying off those debts.

Few are so lucky. For the majority of millennials, the cost of paying off their student loans has wound up holding them back from living on their own, making major purchases like buying a home and even being able to start a family.

For a lot of people, it doesn't have to be like this. I don't just mean that they should've bootstrapped themselves harder during college to come out without any debt — I mean they probably shouldn't have gone to college.

Trade schools cost a fraction of what public and private schools cost. The average cost of vocational school comes out to around $33,000 — for the *entire* education. This the average cost of a single year of college.

Additionally, people who choose vocational schools are able to enter the workforce sooner. Most programs run two years, but many can be completed in even less time. This allows you to start earning a real salary sooner.

What can you study though? Long gone are the days of trade school just being for mechanics and cosmeticians (thought both career paths are fine). These days you can study tons of different professions, including:

- Electrician
- HVAC
- Computer Networking

Mel Bondar runs the blog *brokeGIRLrich* and is a contributor to *U.S. News and World Report*, where this article appeared on April 12, 2016.

- Culinary
- Massage Therapy
- Medical Assistant
- Nursing
- Pharmacy Technician
- Welding

15   You would graduate with one to three fewer years of debt. In 2014, the average mechanic's wage was a little over $37,000 a year, which beats out most liberal arts degrees. As of 2013, the average salary for a registered nurse was nearly $69,000 a year, which far surpasses a lot of traditional degree fields.

Trade schools also are often equipped with strong job-placement programs. If you can do well in your classes there, it can be much easier to land a job than if you attend the average state school with a lackluster job-placement program.

Additionally, while most colleges try to create strong job-placement programs, if you were thinking about majoring in a smaller subject or really anything outside of the STEM or business field, schools are likely to be less equipped to help you find a job after graduation. Vocational schools pride themselves on having strong ties to the professional world in all of the program subjects they offer.

If you're not quite ready to make the leap to trade school, but think it could work for you, community colleges can be a great option for beginning your higher education. Community colleges allow you to take basic prerequisite courses for four year institutions at a fraction of the cost and many community colleges have vocational certification programs that can sometimes be completed at an even lower cost than a trade school devoted fully to certification programs.

Reading, Writing, and Discussion Questions

1. Mel Bondar is not subtle in stating her main idea. What is that main idea?
2. Is Bondar's subject appropriate for an argument in the form of an article (as opposed to the abbreviated visual arguments earlier in this chapter)? Or would it be better suited for a different format? Explain.
3. Who does Bondar's audience seem to be? What made you come to that conclusion?
4. What are some of Bondar's reasons for the opinion she holds?
5. Do you find Bondar's argument convincing? Why or why not?

The Purposes of Argument

In this book, we use the term **argument** to represent forms of discourse that attempt to change an audience's views on a controversial issue. The discourse, written or oral, is designed to achieve one of three purposes:

- To move an audience to action.
- To move an audience to change their thinking on an issue.
- To move an audience toward middle ground between two or more extreme positions on an issue.

Some arguments have two and only two sides. You might hope to move an audience to vote for or against a specific candidate or a specific amendment to your state constitution. You might hope to inspire people simply to get out and vote. You might encourage them to either see or not see Scorsese's latest film. You might have to decide whether or not to have your children vaccinated.

Other decisions are not that clear cut. Not every issue is a matter of yes or no, pro or con. If a woman decides to have an abortion, that is an either/or decision (though likely one that is not made lightly). For another person, to take a pro-life or pro-choice stance is not as black and white as those terms suggest. Some people for religious reasons would never support any woman's having an abortion under any circumstances. At the other extreme are those who approve of abortion, no matter what the circumstances. Most people actually fall in between. Some who oppose abortion in general believe that exceptions should be made when the life of the mother is at risk or the fetus is not viable or the pregnancy is the result of rape. For another example, those who hold fast to their Second-Amendment right to own guns are quick to claim that the other side wants to take them all away. Most people on the other side actually favor something much less drastic, such as gun registration or bans on certain types of military weapons. Some of the most difficult stalemates to resolve arise because each side assumes the other holds the most extreme position possible.

Most of the argumentative writing presented in this book will deal with matters of public controversy, an area traditionally associated with the study of argument. As the word *public* suggests, these matters concern us as members of a community. In the arguments you will examine, human beings are engaged in explaining and defending their own actions and beliefs and opposing or compromising with those of others. In the arguments you will write in this course, you will be doing the same.

The more personal the subject, the more emotion will enter in to how an audience responds to an argument. A woman who has made the heart-wrenching decision to terminate a pregnancy in the third trimester because the fetus is not viable is going to react emotionally to those who paint anyone who has an abortion as a baby killer. The treatment of the LGBTQ+ community may seem like a largely academic issue until someone's own son or daughter comes out. The treatment of immigrants is more emotionally charged when one's own relatives were born in another country. Even if you or your family are not directly impacted, your emotional response to a situation is relevant to how you listen to arguments about it and how you structure your own.

Whether your end goal is to move an audience to action or to change their thinking, you most likely will use a combination of logical argument and emotional appeal. If we were strictly logical creatures, facts alone might be enough to move an audience to action or to change thinking. In most cases it will also take emotional appeal to move an audience. Logic appeals to the brain; persuasive tactics appeal to the emotions.

As an example of both argument and persuasion, reading these numbers from the American Society for the Prevention of Cruelty to Animals may

FIGURE 1.6 Ad for the Shelter Pet Project.
The Humane Society of the United States, Maddie's Fund®, and the Ad Council

affect us rationally: "Each year, approximately 1.5 million shelter animals are euthanized (670,000 dogs and 660,000 cats)." Our sense of logic tells us that those are huge numbers of animals being killed because the animal shelters cannot accommodate them. That information may also affect us emotionally because we can associate those numbers with pets we own or have owned or simply because we hate the idea of any animal being euthanized. The emotional appeal, however, is even greater in an ad like the one in Figure 1.6, where the picture and the "sound" of the pet's voice add a persuasive element. We can't *see* 670,000 dogs, but we can see one cute one staring right into the camera and thus right at us. He looks healthy and well cared for, in contrast to those who die in shelters. He even speaks directly to us, explaining how carefully he leads his owner around on "her" leash since she must be afraid of getting lost, but that's okay, because he doesn't mind showing her around. The roles are reversed, of course, because we know the owner is the one who cared enough to save one dog. The hope is that others will do the same. After all, "a person is the best thing to happen to a shelter pet."

The statistics and the ad are both offered to make the point that Americans should adopt their pets from shelters in order to save lives. The numbers tell us that, but the ad adds the emotional appeal of showing just how much being adopted has meant to one dog that we can see pictured in front of us.

The Elements of Argument

Recognizing the elements of argument in what you read and hear will help you both analyze and write arguments more effectively. The elements we discuss include claim, support, assumptions, language, definition, and logic—some of which have already been mentioned in this chapter. Parts Two and Three discuss the elements at length and introduce you to some different approaches to argument that use the elements in specific ways. But here, we offer a brief introduction to some of the key terms we use throughout the book.

The **claim** answers the question "What you are trying to prove?" You are probably used to calling the main idea of an essay its **thesis** or **thesis statement**. The claim can be the thesis statement of an argumentative essay. It can also state an idea you are trying to prove in a smaller portion of the essay, like a single paragraph.

Support is the evidence you offer to back up a claim. Where the claim is a more general statement, the support is the specifics that convince a reader that the claim is true. The support may be statistics or other numerical evidence. It may be examples or case studies, analogies or precedents. Support gives you reasons to accept the claim and more hope or assurance that your reader accept it as well.

An **assumption** is an underlying belief that makes it possible for you to accept a claim based on the evidence provided. For instance, if you believe that a bakery owner should have the right to refuse service to a gay couple, you are assuming that the owner's religious beliefs should override the couple's right to be served. If you believe in capital punishment for murder, your assumption is that taking a life is wrong except when it is the state taking the life. Obviously, not everyone would agree with all of these assumptions. That is why issues like these are so controversial. You can only hope to change someone's mind, however, if you understand the assumptions underlying their beliefs.

These elements of argument will be discussed at length in Chapters 6, 7, and 8. For now, though, let's see how they appear in some brief passages about claims, the drivers of argument. There are three principal kinds of claims: claims of fact, of value, and of policy.

Sometimes the thesis of an argument is a **claim of fact**. A fact, for the most part, is not a matter for argument. It is an undisputed truth. Many facts can be confirmed by our own senses: *The sun sets in the west. Water freezes at 32 degrees Fahrenheit.* For facts that we cannot confirm for ourselves, we must rely on other sources — reference works, scientific reports, media outlets — for information: *Salmon is rich in omega 3 fatty acids. The United States budgeted $718 billion on the military in 2020.*

Unlike a simple fact, a claim of fact *asserts* that something is true — that a condition has existed, exists, or will exist. An argument built around a claim of fact must convince the reader that the statement is true, usually with the support of factual information such as statistics, examples, and testimony that most responsible observers assume can be verified.

The *claim* in this short passage is stated in the first sentence. The author then uses statistical support to convince a reader of its validity. With a factual claim like this one, the *assumption* is not particularly controversial. To accept the generalization in the first sentence, that political parties have become more partisan, one much simply accept that the statistical *support* is reliable.

> The parties have become more partisan as well. According to a recent Pew study, in 1994 about a third of Democrats were more conservative than the median Republican, and vice-versa. In 2014 the figures were closer to a *twentieth*. Though Americans across the political spectrum drifted leftward through 2004, since then they have diverged on every major issue except gay rights, including government regulation, social spending, immigration, environmental protection, and military strength. Even more troublingly, each side has become more contemptuous of the other. In 2014, 38 percent of Democrats held "very unfavorable" views of the Republican Party (up from 16 percent in 1994), and more than a quarter saw it as "a threat to the nation's well-being." Republicans were even more hostile to Democrats, with 43 percent viewing the party unfavorably and more than a third seeing it as a threat. The ideologues on each side have also become more resistant to compromise.[1]

---

[1] Steven Pinker, *Enlightenment Now: The Case for Reason, Science, Humanism, and Progress* (New York: Penguin, 2019), 371–72.

A **claim of value**, as its name suggests, makes an evaluative statement. As you read the next passage, notice that where the previous one objectively reported the increasing distance between Republicans and Democrats, this one judges the media as a threat to freedom of the press. This time the *support* is not statistical but rather takes the form of fairly broad examples: The biased press of today is a threat to freedom of the press because newsrooms do not identify their biases and make it impossible to discern truth from fiction. Underlying the argument is the *assumption* that biased news reporting is a threat to freedom of the press.

> At least the party-press of old was honest enough to identify themselves as partisans. And, for the most part, the public knew which newspaper stood with which party or candidate. Here, and throughout the modern media, the bias may usually be determined by the news-consuming public from the content put out by the newsrooms. Of course, there are also those who, when watching "the news" or reading "the news," take it at face value. And there are times when you simply cannot discern truth from fiction. But the newsrooms themselves do not transparently label or self-identify their partisanship or bias, enabling the public to weigh and filter what is being presented to it.
>
> In fact, they protest when called out and claim that they are protecting freedom of the press against their critics. But are they? Or does the threat to press freedom lie with them?[2]

A **claim of policy** asserts that specific policies should be instituted as solutions to problems. The expression *should*, *must*, or *ought to* usually appears in the statement. This is the type of claim you are using when you encourage a legislator, for example, to vote for or against a piece of legislation, when you protest that a certain speaker should not be invited to speak on campus, when you propose what should be done about the water shortage in New Jersey, or when you advocate who should be the next president of the United States. In this passage, Harriet A. Washington argues that our government must accept the responsibility for ridding American homes, schools, and businesses of toxins.

> A healthy environment—breathable air, potable water, food and game that are not imbued with heavy metals, homes that are not permeated with intellect-robbing industrial poisons, soil without deadly pesticides—is not something individuals and communities can create without the force of law and government support.
>
> To be sure, protecting the brains of exposed Americans means banishing, not reducing, the sea of dangerous pollution in which they have been forced to live, study, and work. Ending pollution means forcing powerful industries to act against their financial interests and

---

[2] Mark R. Levin, *Unfreedom of the Press* (New York: Simon and Schuster, 2019), 94.

this cannot be accomplished by individuals. It is the responsibility of our government, including the EPA and the public health professionals that advise them, to eradicate untested, under regulated poisons from residential housing, schools, and fence-line industries.[3]

A part of building a case for a claim of policy is establishing that a problem exists. Another is identifying how to solve it. Washington has spent a whole book supporting her claim that Americans, particularly those in poverty, are surrounded by deadly toxins. Here her *support* focuses on the fact that the government must address the problem because individuals can't. The *assumption* in this small portion of her argument is that the government must address threats to its citizens that they cannot abolish themselves.

The Ethics of Argument

The type of bias in the media referred to in the passage by Mark Levin in the previous section is more than just a relevant example. It is a fact of political life in the twenty-first century. You may get your news on a regular basis online. You decide what news sources you receive updates from on your phone or computer. You may be less likely than earlier generations to get your news from television or newspapers, although what you read may be the online versions of some of the same networks or publications.

The man pictured in Figure 1.7 is Walter Cronkite, a respected television journalist who anchored *CBS Evening News* for nineteen years (1962–1981), and was often called "the most trusted man in America." At that time there were only three major news networks, and televisions usually got limited channels. Today, memes will periodically make the rounds online with commentary on how news has changed. They generally combine a picture of the venerated Cronkite with the observation that he would simply read the facts of the news and let people make up their own minds, rather than touting opinions. (The observation is usually conveyed with sarcasm: "Imagine that!")

Cronkite was trusted because he did what people at that time thought a news anchor was supposed to do: He presented the news and let people decide for themselves what to think about it. His audience felt secure in assuming that Cronkite was telling the truth. In fact, it probably didn't enter their minds that he would say anything that wasn't true, or that he would push a particular agenda, as anchors—and networks—often do today.

We have long argued that the decline of television news as the objective purveyor of truth began with the advent of twenty-four-hour news channels. It is impossible—or at least repetitiously boring—to read or listen to the news twenty-four hours a day. Networks have resorted to talking *about* the news, and the most common format is to bring in several people to state their opinions

---

[3] Harriet A. Washington, *A Terrible Thing to Waste: Environmental Racism and Its Assault on the American Mind* (New York: Little, Brown Spark, 2019), 242.

FIGURE 1.7 Walter Cronkite anchoring the news desk.
Leonard McCombe/Getty Images

on the day's events. There is no longer a line between news and commentary. Networks like CNN and Fox do not even try to hide their bias. Those of us who have been around since the days of Walter Cronkite never expected to hear the blatant attacks on today's political leaders and candidates that are commonplace today. Newspapers, which have their own biases, had to establish a policy about whether or not they would call a lie a lie in their headlines. Think about that. The editorial board of a newspaper like the *Washington Post* had to decide how to report the "news" when a politician made a statement that was verifiably false. In a world where questions like this even have to be raised, the American people need more than ever to be able to analyze for themselves the arguments that they see and hear.

The speed with which an image or a statement can flash around the world has raised other ethical questions. The #MeToo movement is a good example of how rapidly an idea can spread via social media. After accusations of sexual abuse against Harvey Weinstein were made public in October 2017, actress Alyssa Milano, posting on Twitter, encouraged all women who had ever been sexually harassed or assaulted to write "Me too" as their status in order to reveal the magnitude of the problem. The phrase had originally been used by sexual harassment activist Tarana Burke, but given the rhetorical context of 2017 when Milano tweeted, half a million women wrote "Me too" within twenty-four hours. As the movement spread around the world, the numbers increased on Twitter and other social media. The movement gave these women a voice and the reassurance that they were not alone.

Unfortunately, just as a good idea can catch fire and spread, so can a destructive or unfair one. For example, in response to the #MeToo movement, some have gone too far in making sweeping accusations against all men on the basis of wrong done by a few. Emily Lindin, a writer for *Teen Vogue*, aroused the wrath of the social media world when she tweeted, "Here's an unpopular opinion: I'm actually not at all concerned about innocent men losing their jobs over false sexual assault/harassment allegations." She defended herself by writing that "false allegations VERY rarely happen, so even bringing it up borders on a derailment tactic. It's a microscopic risk in comparison to the issue at hand (worldwide, systemic oppression of half the population)." Among those joining the attack was CNN's Jake Tapper. When she accused him of "deliberate misreading," he came back at her with her own words: "I read the thread. You said 'if some innocent men's reputations have to take a hit in the process of undoing the patriarchy, that is a price I am absolutely willing to pay.' That's immoral. And it's not a price *you* would be paying, btw. It would be innocent men doing that."[4]

In our rush to absorb news and all the opinions that go with it and to share our own opinions with the click of a mouse, we need to pause long enough to stop and think if we are acting responsibly and ethically. Although online sources are quick and convenient, and many are reliable and high quality, it can be difficult to determine how trustworthy they are, especially for those who want to explore a subject in more depth. Not everything in print can be trusted to be accurate, but printed texts, if they are from reliable sources, are often held to a higher standard of accuracy than much of what appears online, in part because they are less subject to snap judgments and viral sharing.

When you are asked in later chapters to do independent research on a topic, we will discuss at length how to choose reliable sources and how to give credit to those whose ideas and words you use. The assumption behind those guidelines and behind our choice of images and readings to include in this textbook is that it is unethical to post or print images or ideas with the intention of deceiving. We assume that most readers will agree with us that it is unfair to make a judgment based on too little evidence.

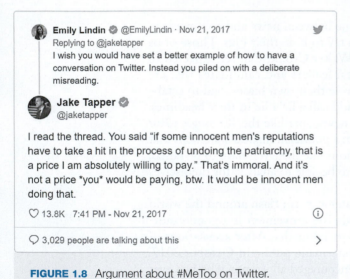

FIGURE 1.8 Argument about #MeToo on Twitter.

---

[4] Rare.us, "Writer Emily Lindin Closes Her Twitter after Sexist Tweets," *Atlanta-Journal Constitution*, November 22, 2017, http://www.ajc.com/news/national/writer-emily-lindin-closes-her-twitter -after-sexist-tweets/iBlrMp8KTQx6Zd1R8M3gZL/.

So, Why Write Arguments?

We need an educated electorate who understands that an argument is more than a sign or a simple statement: It's the complex structure of ideas behind that sign or that statement.

The more you take arguments apart to see how they work, the better able you will be to put the elements together in writing convincing arguments of your own. There is no better way to understand argumentation than to write formal, carefully structured, and well-supported arguments. Chapters 2 and 3 will ask you to analyze arguments — first written ones and then multimodal ones. Chapter 4 will guide you through the process of writing an analysis of an argument. The rest of the book will then teach you to write your own arguments, first about readings provided and finally about your own independent research.

Critical Reading of Written Arguments

Consider the cardboard sign shown in Figure 2.1. It is a brief message but the point is clear. These four words — "Jesus had two dads"—make a statement in favor of same-sex marriage. They also suggest that there is nothing immoral about it because it was Jesus's heritage. This brief statement carries a lot of meaning because of the context within which it is understood.

An argument can be summed up on a sign, in a tweet, in an ad, or on a bumper sticker. Think of the contexts that give meaning to these statements from bumper stickers. Some are funny; all have a point to make.

I don't brake for protesters.

Against abortion? Then don't have one.

Gun nuts are keeping us
from controlling nuts with guns.

From Seneca Falls to Selma to Stonewall
WE TRANSFORM AMERICA

A full response to any argument means more than understanding the message. It also means evaluating it to decide whether the message is successful, and then determining *how* the argument succeeds or fails in persuading us. In making these judgments about the arguments of others, we learn how to deliver our own. We try to avoid what we perceive to be flaws in another's arguments, and we adapt the strategies that produce clear, honest, forceful arguments.

Critical reading is essential for mastery of most college subjects, but its importance for reading and writing about argument, where meaning is often complex and multilayered, cannot be overestimated. The ability to read arguments critically is essential to advanced academic work — even in science and math — since it requires the debate of multifaceted issues rather than the memorization of facts. Just as important, learning to read arguments critically helps you develop the ability to *write* effective arguments — a process valued at the university, in the professional world, and in public life.

Prereading

You will frequently confront texts dealing with subjects unfamiliar to you, and you should have a plan of action for prereading them, that is, for getting an overview of a piece before you read. As the Strategies box demonstrates, the most important things to understand about a text before you read it include the title, genre, context, author, and target audience.

Following the Strategies box is a selection and a Practice exercise in which you can employ the prereading strategies yourself.

FIGURE 2.1 Signs can contain brief arguments.
Courtesy of Elias Kass / http://www.flickr.com/photos/eliaspunch/3032732765/

Strategies for Prereading

1. **Pay attention to the title.** The title may state the purpose of the argument in specific terms. It may also use a particular style of language — such as humorous, inflammatory, or somber — to set the tone for the argument.

2. **Understand the kind of text you are reading.** What is the *genre* of the text? In other words, what category of writing would you place it in? Does it conform to the conventions of that genre? If it is a scholarly essay, for example, does it integrate and document sources? If it is a letter, does it follow the proper formatting for its purpose?

3. **Understand the context in which the author was writing.** Where and when was the text published? Is it a response to another text, or perhaps to an event? Was there something specific that led an author to write about this subject in this way at this

particular time? What is the background of the subject?

4. **Learn about the author.** The more information you know about an author, the easier and more productive your reading will be. You should learn to read in a way that enables you to discover not just meaning in the text itself but information about the author's point of view, background, motives, and ideology.

5. **Imagine the target audience.** Was it a specific or general audience? Does the text come from a journal that publishes primarily conservative or liberal writers? What would the audience have known, if anything, about the situation that led to the writing of the text? What values and ideals are shared by the author and the audience most likely to agree with the argument? What sort of audience might be most strongly opposed to the argument, and why?

READING ARGUMENT

Seeing Prereading

The following speech transcript illustrates how useful it is to understand the context before you read.

1. **Pay attention to the title.** The full significance of the title will not become clear until you read Greta Thunberg's speech, but the tone is clearly angry and challenging: "How Dare You?"

2. **Understand the kind of text you are reading.** "How Dare You?" is the transcript of a speech. A relatively small group heard it live, but portions of it were aired widely by a variety of news networks, and the transcript is widely available online. The language is simple and direct. There is little about the speech that could not be easily understood on a single hearing.

3. **Understand the context in which the author was writing.** Thunberg is writing in the very broad context of climate change. More specifically, she is responding to the lack of progress that has been made toward preparing for the consequences of climate change. Most specifically, she delivered her speech on September 23, 2019, at the United Nations Climate Action Summit.

4. **Learn about the author.** Swedish climate activist Greta Thunberg was sixteen when she made the speech. By September of 2019, she was widely known in many countries for her fight to bring awareness to the need for a fuller and more timely response to the threat that climate change poses to the future of the planet. She gained international attention by organizing school strikes to draw attention to her position.

5. **Imagine the target audience.** The United Nations Climate Action Summit consisted of world leaders. The Summit's purpose, according to the United Nations website, was to bring together governments, the private sector, civil society, local authorities, and other international organizations "with concrete, realistic plans to enhance their nationally determined contributions by 2020."

Practice: Prereading

Use the information learned from prereading to consider Thunberg's argument.

How Dare You?
GRETA THUNBERG

My message is that we'll be watching you.

This is all wrong. I shouldn't be up here. I should be back in school on the other side of the ocean. Yet you all come to us young people for hope. How dare you!

You have stolen my dreams and my childhood with your empty words. And yet I'm one of the lucky ones. People are suffering. People are dying. Entire ecosystems are collapsing. We are in the beginning of a mass extinction, and

Greta Thunberg is a Swedish teenager who has gained international attention by speaking out about the threat climate change poses to the future of the planet and by organizing school strikes to draw attention to the problem.

all you can talk about is money and fairy tales of eternal economic growth. How dare you!

For more than 30 years, the science has been crystal clear. How dare you continue to look away and come here saying that you're doing enough, when the politics and solutions needed are still nowhere in sight.

5   You say you hear us and that you understand the urgency. But no matter how sad and angry I am, I do not want to believe that. Because if you really understood the situation and still kept on failing to act, then you would be evil. And that I refuse to believe.

The popular idea of cutting our emissions in half in 10 years only gives us a 50 percent chance of staying below 1.5 degrees [Celsius], and the risk of setting off irreversible chain reactions beyond human control.

Fifty percent may be acceptable to you. But those numbers do not include tipping points, most feedback loops, additional warming hidden by toxic air pollution, or the aspects of equity and climate justice. They also rely on my generation sucking hundreds of billions of tons of your CO_2 out of the air with technologies that barely exist.

So a 50 percent risk is simply not acceptable to us — we who have to live with the consequences.

To have a 67 percent chance of staying below a 1.5 degrees global temperature rise — the best odds given by the [Intergovernmental Panel on Climate Change] — the world had 420 gigatons of CO_2 left to emit back on Jan. 1st, 2018. Today that figure is already down to less than 350 gigatons.

How dare you pretend that this can be solved with just "business as usual" and some technical solutions? With today's emissions levels, that remaining CO_2 budget will be entirely gone within less than eight and a half years.   10

There will not be any solutions or plans presented in line with these figures here today, because these numbers are too uncomfortable. And you are still not mature enough to tell it like it is.

You are failing us. But the young people are starting to understand your betrayal. The eyes of all future generations are upon you. And if you choose to fail us, I say: We will never forgive you.

We will not let you get away with this. Right here, right now is where we draw the line. The world is waking up. And change is coming, whether you like it or not.

Thank you.

Reading, Writing, and Discussion Questions

1. Where and how in the speech does Greta Thunberg reveal her anger?
2. Does Thunberg have the knowledge to back up her anger? Explain.
3. What is the irony of Thunberg telling her audience that they will not accomplish anything because they are "not mature enough to tell it like it is"?
4. Why, according to Thunberg, does she not want to believe that these leaders really understand the urgency?
5. How do you think the audience might have reacted to Thunberg's speech?
6. Write an essay explaining how successful you think Thunberg's argument is.

Reading with an Open Mind

The next step in the critical reading process is comprehension—understanding what an author is trying to prove. Comprehending academic arguments can be difficult because they are often complex and often challenge accepted notions. Academic writing also sometimes assumes that readers already have a great deal of knowledge about a subject and therefore can require further research for comprehension.

Readers sometimes fail to comprehend a text they disagree with or that is new to them, especially in dealing with essays or books making controversial, value-laden arguments. Some research even shows that readers will sometimes remember only those parts of texts that match their points of view.[1] Or, readers may only seek out information that validates the point of view they already hold. This is called **confirmation bias**. The study of argument does not require you to accept points of view you find morally or otherwise reprehensible, but to engage with these views, no matter how strange or repugnant they might seem, on your own terms.

A common term used for slanting information in favor of or against one position over others is **spin**. We even read and hear about "spin doctors" who interpret an event in such a way that it will appear favorable toward or against one person or party. Part of learning to read critically is learning to recognize bias or spin. While spin is usually very deliberate, bias may be conscious or unconscious; unless we learn to keep an open mind and turn a critical eye on our own beliefs about an issue, we may compromise our argument with our own biases.

Reading arguments critically requires you to at least temporarily suspend notions of absolute "right" and "wrong" and to intellectually inhabit gray areas that do not allow for simple "yes" and "no" answers. Of course, even in these areas, significant decisions about such things as ethics, values, politics, and the law must be made, and in studying argument you shouldn't fall into the trap of simple relativism: the idea that all answers to a given problem are equally correct at all times. We must make decisions about arguments with the understanding that reasonable people can disagree on the validity of ideas. Read others' arguments carefully, and consider how their ideas can contribute to or complicate your own. Look for common ground between your beliefs and those of the author. Also recognize that what appears to be a final solution will always be open to further negotiation as new participants, new historical circumstances, and new ideologies become involved in the debate.

---

[1] See, for example, Shahram Heshmat, "What Is Confirmation Bias?" *Psychology Today*, April 23, 2015, https://www.psychologytoday.com/us/blog/science-choice/201504/what-is-confirmation-bias.

READING ARGUMENT

Practice: Prereading

Look ahead to the excerpt from Mark R. Levin that follows and apply the questions in the Strategies for Prereading box on page 21.

Practice: Reading with an Open Mind

The following is an excerpt from the chapter "News, Propaganda, and Pseudo-Events" in Mark R. Levin's 2019 book *Unfreedom of the Press*. As you read the passage, consider its bias. With whom do Levin's sympathies lie? How can you tell? The Reading, Writing, and Discussion Questions after the excerpt may help you answer these questions.

News, Propaganda, and Pseudo-Events

MARK R. LEVIN

Roy W. Spencer "received his Ph.D. in meteorology at the University of Wisconsin–Madison in 1981. Before becoming a Principal Research Scientist at the University of Alabama in Huntsville in 2001, he was a Senior Scientist for Climate Studies at NASA's Marshall Space Flight Center, where he and Dr. John Christy received NASA's Exceptional Scientific Achievement Medal for their global temperature monitoring work with satellites. Dr. Spencer's work with NASA continues as the U.S. Science Team leader for the Advanced Microwave Scanning Radiometer flying on NASA's Aqua Satellite."[1]

During a presentation at the Heartland Institute's Ninth International Conference on Climate Change in Las Vegas, Spencer explained that "[t]oo many people think that all areas of science are created equal and that scientists objectively look for the answers, but no, there's two kinds of scientists, male and female. Other than that they're the same as everybody else, and in many instances [in the climate sciences] more biased than your average person. . . . Spencer went on to criticize the temperature data of the National Oceanic and Atmospheric Administration (NOAA) because it has never taken into account the phenomenon of urban heat island effect."[2]

Indeed, Spencer pointed to the thermometer-related algorithms as one of the problems in measuring heat. "A lot of us still think that a lot of the warming we are seeing in the thermometer record is just urban heat island effect. In fact, Las Vegas, here, even though it's built in the desert basically . . . in the last forty years or so, night-time temperatures here have risen by ten degrees

---

Mark R. Levin hosts the FOX News program *Life, Liberty, and Levin* and is also a nationally syndicated talk-radio host. He has written five consecutive *New York Times* #1 bestsellers: *Liberty and Tyranny*, *Plunder and Deceit*, *Rediscovering America*, *Ameritopia*, and *The Liberty Amendments*, in addition to *Unfreedom of the Press*, in which this selection appears.

---

[2] Warner Todd Huston, "Dr. Roy Spencer: Science Knows 'Almost Nothing' About Global Warming," *Breitbart*, July 10, 2014, https://www.breitbart.com/politics/2014/07/10/dr-roy-spencer-science-knows-almost-nothing-about-global-warming/ (March 17, 2019).

---

[1] Roy Spencer, biography, drroyspencer.com, http://www.drroyspencer.com/about (March 17, 2019).

Fahrenheit because of urbanization. This is an effect that they can't take out of the thermometer record. Their algorithms can't take it out because you can't separate it from global warming. If you've got a long-term warming trend because of urbanization there's no way NOAA can take out that effect because it's indistinguishable from other temperature readings."[3]

In the end, Spencer argues, very little is really known about global warming, also known as climate change. "After working on global warming for the last twenty plus years, what do we know about it now? The longer you go [into the research] you get more questions than you get answers. So, what do we really know about it? Almost nothing."[4]

5   There are many more highly educated and experienced experts who raise a variety of substantive issues and questions about man-made climate change. And henceforth, none of them

_____
[3] Ibid.
[4] Ibid.

are welcome on NBC's *Meet the Press*. Moreover, like NBC, they are not likely to be taken seriously in most newsrooms or by most journalists because they dare to challenge the orthodoxy of the Democratic party–press and the progressive agenda—in which "solutions" to climate change involve new ways of expanding the government's regulatory and taxing role in society via the "urgency" of climate change, and surrendering national sovereignty to international organizations through multigovernment agreements. Thus one-sided opinion is treated as objective truth; reputable and legitimate individuals who could provide contrary factual information to the public are dismissed as science deniers and climate imposters; and the government and public are urged to engage in immediate political and social activism and demand far-reaching national solutions, such as the "Green New Deal." NBC and Chuck Todd, among other media outlets and journalists, have "interpreted" and "analyzed" the relevant facts through their progressive approach and their conclusion is final. "Period."

Reading, Writing, and Discussion Questions

1. In prereading the excerpt from Mark R. Levin's book, what did you discover that influenced your reading?

2. Where in the excerpt is Levin primarily presenting facts and where is he presenting opinions? Whose opinions?

3. The first four paragraphs are documented. That means Levin got his information from other sources, identified in the notes. What do you know about Breitbart, the source of three of those paragraphs? What type of bias might you expect from Breitbart?

4. Since Breitbart is quoting Spencer himself, the ideas in paragraphs 2–4 are Spencer's. Do those opinions reflect what you have heard from other sources about climate change? Explain.

5. How does Levin reveal his own bias in paragraph 5?

6. Did you bring to your reading your own biases about climate change? Explain.

7. Write a paragraph explaining any problems you see with Roy Spencer's view of climate change as Levin describes it.

8. Write a paragraph explaining the bias that Levin reveals in the last paragraph.

Reading for Content and Structure

Analyzing an argument—even one you don't agree with—is possible by reading for content and structure to identify how the argument is constructed. In the reading by Mark R. Levin on pages 25–26, you may not agree with Spencer's opinions about climate change or with Levin's about the Democratic party, but you can still analyze the strength of their arguments objectively. Writing about the content and elements of an argument allows you to evaluate the argument on its structural merits, rather than your emotional reaction.

Here are some suggestions about how to approach reading an argument. Remember: Your instructors will have considerations like these in mind when reading your written arguments, so they can help you with writing as well as reading an argument.

1. **Skim the reading for the main idea and overall structure.**
   - Are there subheadings or other divisions?
   - If it is a book, how are the chapters organized?
   - What is the claim or thesis statement that the piece is supporting? It will usually be in the first or second paragraph of an essay or in the introduction or first chapter of a book, but it may come at the end of the reading.

2. **Pay attention to topic sentences.** The topic sentence is usually the first sentence in a paragraph, but not always. It is the general statement that controls the details and examples in the paragraph.

3. **Don't overlook language signposts, usually transitional words and phrases:** *but, however, yet, nevertheless, moreover, for example, at first glance, more important, the first reason, next,* and so on.

4. **Consider any visuals that are included with the text.** Do they provide evidence to support the written argument? Do they set a mood or enhance the argument in other ways? (For help examining visuals, see Chapter 3.)

5. **Consider any sources that the author made use of.** Has the author indicated in any way that he or she drew any of the ideas in the piece from other people? If so, how?

The best way to read a difficult text is with pen, pencil, and highlighter in hand to **annotate** it, or mark it up by identifying and commenting on the elements we've identified above. If it is an online text, you might print a copy to hold the text in hand and annotate it, or you could use your computer's or e-reader's commenting and highlighting tools.

Remember that when you write an analysis of an argument, you can write about the content and structure to evaluate its effectiveness and evaluate the argument on its structural merits, rather than on your emotional reaction to it.

Strategies for Annotating a Text

One purpose of annotating a text is to comprehend it more fully. Another is to prepare to write about it.

1. **If you highlight as you read a text, do so sparingly.** You might consider a more targeted approach to highlighting, focusing only on thesis statements and topic sentences, for example.

2. **More useful: Make marginal notes,** perhaps underlining the portion of the text to which each note refers. Some of the most useful marginal notes will be those that summarize key ideas in your own words. Such paraphrases force you to understand the text well enough to reword its ideas, and reading the marginal notes is a quick way to review the text when you do not have time to reread all of it.

3. **Make notes on both what a piece of writing says and how it says it.** Notations about how a piece is written can focus on structural devices such as topic sentences, transitional words or phrases, and the repetition of ideas or sentence structure.

4. **Interrogate the text as you read.** Make note of surprising or interesting points, and don't be afraid to question or disagree with a point made by the author.

5. **Note similarities** that you see between the text you are reading and others you have read or between the text and your own experience.

READING ARGUMENT

Reading for Content and Structure

The following article has been annotated by a student reader to show its content and structure. After reading the article, answer the questions at the end.

A Tale of Two Airlines
CHRISTOPHER ELLIOTT

Sets up a clear comparison/contrast structure.

Similarities exist, but he will focus on differences.

In travel, as in life, there are heroes and villains. There's good and evil. And there's Southwest Airlines and Spirit Airlines.

Both are no-frills discount carriers, and both are success stories in the economic sense. But that's where the similarities end.

A brief contrast sets up Spirit as the villain and Southwest as the hero.

Spirit is known for its preponderance of fees, the risqué tone of some of its ads (as in the naughty "MILF" acronym for its "Many Islands, Low Fares" sale), and a take-it-or-leave-it attitude toward customer service. Southwest has a reputation for inclusive fares (one of the few airlines left that don't charge extra for a checked bag), a Texas-style hospitality (concerts on planes), and its famous customer-focused way.

Christopher Elliott is an author, columnist, consumer advocate, and cofounder of the advocacy group Travelers United. This article is from his Insider column in the December 2012/January 2013 issue of *National Geographic Traveler*.

A look at these airlines offers a window into the relationship between air carriers and their customers, revealing why the modern flying experience can be so infuriating.

5   For Southwest—the Dallas carrier founded in 1971—customer service is part of its corporate DNA. Consider what happened to Robert Siegel. The retired engineer and his wife, Ruth, were scheduled to fly from West Palm Beach to Philadelphia when Ruth was diagnosed with lung cancer; her doctor ordered her to cancel the trip. Even though the tickets were non-refundable, Siegel requested an exception. "Within one week, a complete credit had been posted to my credit card," he says.

Southwest: Examples of excellent customer service

    Southwest routinely waives its requirements in the interests of "Customer Service." (It also has an annoying habit of uppercasing key words, like "People.") Several years ago, one of its pilots even held the plane for a passenger so that he could make his grandson's funeral. It doesn't punish customers with ticket change fees or price its less restricted tickets so that only business travelers on an expense account can afford them. It's not perfect, of course. Southwest's prices can sometimes be significantly higher than the competition's. And its one-class service is too egalitarian for many business travelers.

What's wrong with that?

    Spirit Airlines styles itself as the anti-Southwest. The airline, based in the suburbs of Fort Lauderdale, has its roots in the trucking business, which may explain a lot: Its customers often complain that they are treated like cargo. Seems Spirit wouldn't have it any other way.

Spirit: Customers treated like cargo

    Spirit often does the exact opposite of what Southwest would. When Vietnam vet Jerry Meekins was told his esophageal cancer was terminal and advised by his doctor to cancel his flight from Florida to Atlantic City, the airline refused a refund request. Only after veterans groups intervened did the carrier cave, and only reluctantly. In an effort to not set a precedent, CEO Ben Baldanza said he personally would pay for the refund, not his airline.

    And Spirit does love fees. Fully one-third of its ticket revenue comes from fees (compared with 7.5 percent for Southwest). Spirit argues that its passengers just crave low fares, and that all of the extras are optional. But some passengers complain that the fees aren't adequately disclosed and that some are ridiculous (a $100 charge to carry—that's right, carry—a bag on a plane if you didn't prepay a lower fee online). Where Southwest's employees have a reputation for being sociable, Spirit's can be on the surly side. Baldanza once inadvertently replied directly by e-mail to a passenger this way: "Let him tell the world how bad we are. He's never flown us before anyway and will be back when we save him a penny."

Spirit has many fees . . .

Wow!

. . . but the fares are low.

10   Baldanza has a point, and it's one that drives consumers (and consumer advocates) crazy: If you can navigate the maze of fees, restrictions, and

Spirit's $9 Fare Club ($60 per year, with automatic reenrollment whether you fly or not), you can travel for impressively low fares. And stockholders love their shares of SAVE (Spirit's ticker symbol) about as much as they do Southwest's (aptly, LUV).

Each airline likes its role.

I'd say Spirit enjoys playing the villain as much as Southwest likes being the hero. Spirit certainly hasn't suffered for it financially. These two airlines represent one of travel's most enduring paradoxes: that companies offering poor customer service can succeed as well as those offering good customer service. Spirit's success defies an easy explanation, unless you have a degree in psychology. Spirit taps into the very human need to snag a deal. But understanding what makes us tick and the way we can be manipulated points to a better future for every traveler. See, Southwest and Spirit are not the only examples of travel's curious yin and yang. Whether you're staying at a hotel, renting a car, or taking a cruise, you've faced the same kinds of choices between companies. At the beginning of 2013, many of these companies find themselves at a crossroads, wondering which path to take: the embrace of a LUV or the thriftiness of a SAVE. Both clearly work in the short term. But Southwest operates on the principle that, eventually, customers will catch on.

Customers have a choice.

Then again, maybe not. If people continue to fall for the ultralow, lots-of-strings-attached rates, then the treatment of passengers like cargo might continue indefinitely. Travelers must consider more than the price when they book their ticket or make arrangements to take a cruise or rent a car. They have to take a company's service reputation into account, too. Reward the heroes of the travel industry with your business. Otherwise, the villains win.

Thesis statement

Reading, Writing, and Discussion Questions

1. The essay is a contrast between the two airlines. What specific aspects of the two does Christopher Elliott contrast?

2. What thesis or claim is Elliott supporting? What point does he make beyond the ways in which the two airlines differ? Is his essay based on a claim of fact, value, or policy?

3. What types of support does Elliott offer?

Summarizing

In order to write about another's ideas, one skill we need is the ability to summarize those ideas fairly and objectively, just as in more confrontational forms of argumentation a writer or speaker cannot build a successful case on a misunderstanding or misinterpretation of an opponent's position. At least, such a case will not hold up under careful scrutiny. The ability to summarize is also a basic research skill used in writing research papers, as discussed in Chapter 14. Summarizing is the cornerstone on which all other critical reading and writing tasks are built.

A summary can be either referential or rhetorical. A **referential summary** focuses on the content of a text, on an author's ideas about the subject. A **rhetorical summary** summarizes the text in terms of its structure and the rhetorical or structural choices the author made. As you write either type of summary, remember that it should

- be shorter than the original
- be objective instead of stating opinions
- identify the author and the work
- use present tense
- summarize the main points of the whole work or passage, not just part of it.

The following examples are summaries of "A Tale of Two Airlines" (p. 28).

Referential (Content) Summary

According to Christopher Elliott in his article "A Tale of Two Airlines," both Southwest Airlines and Spirit Airlines are successful discount carriers, but where Spirit is a "villain," Southwest is a "hero." Where Spirit has a lot of fees, risqué ads, and poor customer service, Southwest does not charge extra for checked bags, is welcoming, and takes pride in its famous customer service, even waiving its own regulations in special circumstances to help a customer. Spirit originated as a trucking line and still treats customers "like cargo." Each airline seems to like the role it plays. A customer can save money flying Spirit because of its low fares, but as long as fliers are willing to be treated like cargo to save money, they will be rewarding the villains instead of the heroes of the travel industry.

Rhetorical (Structure) Summary

In his article "A Tale of Two Airlines," Christopher Elliott *contrasts* two airlines: Southwest and Spirit. He *points out* that both are successful airlines, but then *focuses* on how the two differ in fees, tone, and customer service. Elliott *provides examples* of how Southwest goes out of its way to provide excellent customer service, even waiving its own regulations in exceptional circumstances while Spirit refuses to make exceptions. Elliott *explains* that Spirit's treatment of its customers reflects its origins as a trucking business. He *warns* that as long as customers reward Spirit by choosing its low fares in spite of its bad customer service, the villains in the world of commercial airlines will win.

RESEARCH SKILL ▶ Using Summaries in Research

When your argument requires research, there will be times when you are **taking notes** and will want to summarize what you have read instead of writing it down verbatim. That is often the case when you may want to refer to the ideas in the source, but the wording is not so special that you need to make use of it in your essay. (In Chapter 14 you will learn in detail about incorporating summary into your own writing.)

When summarizing long or difficult texts, try some of the following strategies to help you comprehend the essential points of the text.

1. **Reread the introduction and conclusion after you have read the text once or twice.** These two sections should complement each other and offer clues to the most significant issues of the text.

2. **For a difficult text, you may want to list all the subheadings (if they are used) or the topic sentences of each paragraph.** These significant guideposts will map the piece as a whole: What do they tell you about the central ideas and the main argument the author is making?

3. **Remember that when you summarize, you must put another's words into your own (and cite the original text as well).** Do not simply let a list of the subheadings or chapter titles stand as your summary. They likely won't make sense when put together in paragraph form, but they will provide you with valuable ideas regarding the central points of the text.

4. **Remember that summarizing also requires attention to overall meanings and not only to specific details.** Therefore, avoid including many specific examples or concrete details from the text you are summarizing, and try to let your reader know what these examples and details add up to.

READING ARGUMENT

Practice: Summarizing

Read and annotate the following article, using the annotations on the Christopher Elliott article (p. 28) as a model. Then answer the questions that appear at the end of the article.

Reimagining Masculinity

OCEAN VUONG

"No homo," says the boy, barely visible in the room's fading light, as he cradles my foot in his palms. He is kneeling before me—this 6'2" JV basketball second stringer—as I sit on his bed, my feet hovering above the shag. His head is bent so that the swirl in his crown shows, the sweat in the follicles catching the autumn dusk through the window. Anything is possible, we think, with the body. But not always with language. "No homo," he says again before wrapping the ace bandage once, twice, three times around my busted ankle, the phrase's purpose now clear to me: a password, an incantation, a get-out-of-jail-free card, for touch. For two boys to come this close to each other in a realm ruled by the nebulous yet narrow laws of American masculinity, we needed magic.

No homo. The words free him to hold my foot with the care and gentleness of a nurse, for I had sprained my ankle half an hour earlier playing manhunt in the McIntosh orchard. We ran, our bodies silver in the quickening dark, teenagers playing at war.

The boy—let's call him K—had helped me up, my arm slung across his shoulder as I limped toward his house, which sat just across the orchard. The war is still going on around us, the other boys' voices breaking through the brambles, and the larger war, the one in Afghanistan (for it is 2005), amplified what was at stake in the outer world, beyond the feeble sunset of childhood.

No homo.

5   I look away, as if it isn't an ankle, but roadkill, in his hands. I scan the room instead, the walls lined with baseball trophies catching the streetlight outside, which has just flickered on. Do I find him handsome? Yes. Does it matter? No.

"You're really good at hiding," he said to my foot, and though he meant at manhunt, he might as well have been talking about man*hood*. For isn't that, too, a place I have hid both in and from at once?

I was never comfortable being male—being a he—because all my life being a man was inextricable from hegemonic masculinity. Everywhere I looked, he-ness was akin to an aggression that felt fraudulent in me—or worse, in the blue collar New England towns I grew up in, self-destructive. Masculinity, or what we have allowed it to be in America, is often realized through violence. Here, we celebrate our boys, who in turn celebrate one another, through the lexicon of conquest:

> You killed it, buddy. Knock 'em dead, big guy. You went into that game guns blazing. You crushed it at the talent show. It was a blow out. No, it was a massacre. My son's a beast. He totally blew them away. He's a lady killer. Did you bag her? Yeah, I fucked her brains out. That girl's a grenade. I'd still bang her. I'd smash it. Let's spit roast her. She's the bomb. She's blowing up. I'm dead serious.

To some extent, these are only metaphors, hyperbolic figures of speech—nothing else. But there are, to my mind, strong roots between these phrases and this country's violent past. From the Founding Fathers to Manifest Destiny, America's self-identity was fashioned out of the myth of the self-made revolutionary turned explorer and founder of a new, immaculate world of possible colonization. The avatar of the pioneer, the courageous and stoic seeker, ignores and erases the Native American genocide that made such a persona possible. The American paradox of hegemonic masculinity is also a paradox of identity. Because American life was founded on death, it had to make death a kind of praxis, it had to celebrate it. And because death was considered progress, its metaphors soon became the very measurement of life, of the growth of boys. You fucking killed it.

Years later, in another life, before giving a reading, the organizer asked me for my preferred pronouns. I never knew I had a choice. "He/him" I said, after a pause, suddenly unsure. But I felt a door had opened—if only slightly—and through it I had glimpsed a path I had not known existed. There was a way out.

10   But what if I don't want to leave this room yet, but just make it bigger? Pronouns like they/them are, to my trans friends and family, a refuge—a destination secured through flight and self-agency. They/them pronouns allow an interface where one can quickly code oneself as nonnormative, in the hopes of bypassing the pain and awkwardness of explanation or the labor of legibility when simply existing can be exhausting. Would I, by changing pronouns, appropriate myself into a space others need in order to survive?

As a war refugee, I know how vital a foothold as small as a word can be. And since as a cis-presenting male, I don't need to flee he-ness

in order to be seen as myself, I will stay here. Can the walls of masculinity, set up so long ago through decrees of death and conquest, be breached, broken, recast—even healed? I am, in other words, invested in troubling he-ness. I want to complicate, expand, and change it by being inside it. And I am here for the very reasons why I feel, on bad days, I should leave it altogether: that I don't recognize myself within its dominant ranks—but I believe it can grow to hold me better. Perhaps one day, masculinity might become so myriad, so malleable, it no longer needs a fixed border to recognize itself. It might not need to be itself at all. I wonder if that, too, is the queering of a space? I wonder if boys can ever bandage each other's feet, in friendship, without a password—with only passage, between each other, without shame.

No homo, K reminds me, as he bites off the medical tape, rubs the length of my swollen ankle. He slides my white Vans back on—but not before carefully loosening the shoelaces, making room for my new damage. No homo, he had said. But all I heard, all I still hear, is *No human.* How can we not ask masculinity to change when, within it, we have become so wounded?

"You'll be fine," he says—with a tenderness so rare it felt stolen from a place far inside him. I reach for his hand.

He pulls me up, turns to leave the room. "Kill the lights," he says over his shoulder.

And I kill them.   15

I make it so dark we could be anything, even more than what we were born into. We could be human.

Reading, Writing, and Discussion Questions

1. Why does Ocean Vuong use such words as *password*, *incantation*, *get-out-of-jail-free card*, and *magic* to describe the boy's use of the phrase "No homo"?

2. What is the double meaning of the boy's statement "You're really good at hiding"?

3. Why was the author never comfortable being male?

4. Why is masculinity in America often described in terms related to death?

5. What is the main point that Vuong is trying to make about masculinity in America? Where does he himself fit into that view of masculinity? Or does he?

6. How would you describe the genre of writing that Vuong uses to make his point? What characteristics of the writing led you to your answer?

7. Write a one-paragraph rhetorical summary of "Reimagining Masculinity," focusing on choices that the author made, not just on the ideas.

8. Write a one-paragraph referential summary of "Reimagining Masculinity," focusing on content rather than on how the author structured the essay.

9. Write an essay in which you explain how Vuong uses a personal narrative to make a point about masculinity in America in "Reimagining Masculinity."

Evaluating

An **evaluation** builds on comprehension and summary by incorporating not only the argument's main point but also the reader's reaction to it. In Chapter 4, we will look more closely at how to build an effective response to an argument; in this section, we will briefly consider how to read not just for comprehension but also with a critical eye. Your overall goal is to make a careful judgment of the extent to which an argument has succeeded in making a point.

When you set out to evaluate a work, keep two points in mind:

- An argument that you disagree with is not necessarily wrong or a bad argument.
- An argument written by a published author or so-called expert is not necessarily right or a good argument.

Critically evaluating an argument means not simply reading a text and agreeing or disagreeing with it, but doing serious analytical work that addresses multiple viewpoints and considers the argument's logic, structure, and purpose before deciding on the argument's effectiveness.

Strategies for Evaluating Arguments

1. **Disagree with the author if you feel confident of the support for your view,** but first read the whole argument to see if your questions have been answered. Be cautious about concluding that the author hasn't proved his or her point.

2. **Talk about the material with classmates or others who have read it,** especially those who have responded to the text differently than you did. Consider their points of view. Defending or modifying your evaluation may mean going back to the text and finding clues that you may have overlooked.

3. **Consider the strengths of the argument,** and examine the useful methods of argumentation, the points that are successfully made (and those which help the reader to better understand the argument), and what makes sense about the author's argument.

4. **Consider the weaknesses of the argument,** and locate instances of faulty reasoning, unsupported statements, and the limitations of the author's assumptions about the world (the assumptions that underlie the argument).

5. **Consider how effective the title of the reading is,** and decide whether it accurately sums up a critical point of the essay. Come up with an alternative title that would suit the reading better, and be prepared to defend this alternative title.

6. **Evaluate the organizational structure of the essay.** The author should lead you from idea to idea in a logical progression, and each section should relate to the ones before and after it and to the central argument in significant ways. Determine whether the writer could have organized things more clearly, logically, or efficiently.

7. **Notice how the author follows through on the main claim, or thesis, of the argument.** The author should stick with this thesis and not waver throughout the text. If the thesis does waver, there could be a reason for the shift in the argument, or perhaps the author is being inconsistent. The conclusion should drive home the central argument.

8. **Evaluate the vocabulary and style the author uses.** Is it too simple or complicated? Are key terms and concepts defined? When considering style and vocabulary, keep in mind the audience the author was initially writing for.

READING ARGUMENT

Reading to Evaluate

The following article has been annotated by a student reader to demonstrate reading for content and structure as well as critical evaluation. The article is followed by a student evaluation essay.

The Internet Is a Surveillance State

BRUCE SCHNEIER

I'm going to start with three data points.

One: Some of the Chinese military hackers who were implicated in a broad set of attacks against the U.S. government and corporations were identified because they accessed Facebook from the same network infrastructure they used to carry out their attacks.

Two: Hector Monsegur, one of the leaders of the LulzSec hacker movement, was identified and arrested last year by the FBI. Although he practiced good computer security and used an anonymous relay service to protect his identity, he slipped up.

And three: Paula Broadwell, who had an affair with CIA director David Petraeus, similarly took extensive precautions to hide her identity. She never logged in to her anonymous email service from her home network. Instead, she used hotel and other public networks when she emailed him. The FBI correlated hotel registration data from several different hotels—and hers was the common name.

Examples: All three got caught because of the internet. But isn't this a good thing?

5   The internet is a surveillance state. Whether we admit it to ourselves or not, and whether we like it or not, we're being tracked all the time. Google tracks us, both on its pages and on other pages it has access to. Facebook does the same; it even tracks non-Facebook users. Apple tracks us on our iPhones and iPads. One reporter used a tool called Collusion to track who was tracking him; 105 companies tracked his internet use during one 36-hour period.

Thesis*

Examples

Increasingly, what we do on the internet is being combined with other data about us. Unmasking Broadwell's identity involved correlating her internet activity with her hotel stays. Everything we do now involves computers, and computers produce data as a natural by-product. Everything is now being saved and correlated, and many big-data companies make money by building up intimate profiles of our lives from a variety of sources.

Topic sentence: Internet activity is combined with other sources.

Facebook, for example, correlates your online behavior with your purchasing habits offline. And there's more. There's location data from your cell phone, there's a record of your movements from closed-circuit TVs.

This is ubiquitous surveillance: All of us being watched, all the time, and that data being stored forever. This is what a surveillance state looks like, and it's efficient beyond the wildest dreams of George Orwell.

Repeats thesis. Reference to 1984.

Sure, we can take measures to prevent this. We can limit what we search on Google from our iPhones, and instead use computer web browsers that allow us to delete cookies. We can use an alias on Facebook. We can turn our cell phones off and spend cash. But increasingly, none of it matters.

Topic sentence: Counter measures

10   There are simply too many ways to be tracked. The internet, email, cell phones, web browsers, social networking sites, search engines: these have

But (transition): They don't work.

Bruce Schneier is an expert in technological security and privacy and the former Chief Technology Officer of Resilient, an IBM company, a fellow at Harvard's Berkman Klein Center for Internet and Society, and author of *Liars and Outliers: Enabling the Trust Society Needs to Survive* (2012) and *Data and Goliath: The Hidden Battles to Collect Your Data and Control Your World* (2015). This article appeared on CNN on March 16, 2013.

become necessities, and it's fanciful to expect people to simply refuse to use them just because they don't like the spying, especially since the full extent of such spying is deliberately hidden from us and there are few alternatives being marketed by companies that don't spy.

Topic sentence

This isn't something the free market can fix. We consumers have no choice in the matter. All the major companies that provide us with internet services are interested in tracking us. Visit a website and it will almost cer-

Examples

tainly know who you are; there are lots of ways to be tracked without cookies. Cell phone companies routinely undo the web's privacy protection. One experiment at Carnegie Mellon took real-time videos of students on campus and was able to identify one-third of them by comparing their photos with publicly available tagged Facebook photos.

Topic sentence

Maintaining privacy on the internet is nearly impossible. If you forget even once to enable your protections, or click on the wrong link, or type the

Example

wrong thing, you've permanently attached your name to whatever anony-mous service you're using. Monsegur slipped up once, and the FBI got him. If the director of the CIA can't maintain his privacy on the internet, we've got no hope.

Topic sentence

In today's world, governments and corporations are working together to keep things that way. Governments are happy to use the data corporations collect—occasionally demanding that they collect more and save it longer—to spy on us. And corporations are happy to buy data from governments.

What do the people want?

Together the powerful spy on the powerless, and they're not going to give up their positions of power, despite what the people want.

Language a bit over-the-top? Exaggeration?

Fixing this requires strong government will, but they're just as punch-drunk on data as the corporations. Slap-on-the-wrist fines notwithstanding, no one is agitating for better privacy laws.

So, we're done. Welcome to a world where Google knows exactly what   15
sort of porn you all like, and more about your interests than your spouse does. Welcome to a world where your cell phone company knows exactly where you are all the time. Welcome to the end of private conversations, because increasingly your conversations are conducted by email, text, or social networking sites.

Argument assumes that data mining is a bad thing — is it? And we have hardly fought against it.

And welcome to a world where all of this, and everything else that you do or is done on a computer, is saved, correlated, studied, passed around from company to company without your knowledge or consent; and where the government accesses it at will without a warrant.

Welcome to an internet without privacy, and we've ended up here with hardly a fight.

Giving Up Our Privacy: Is It Worth It?

WHITNEY CRAMER

Whitney Cramer
ENGL 203-017
Dr. Winchell
September 15, 2017

Giving Up Our Privacy: Is It Worth It?

The internet is many things to many people. It provides a quick way to find information, an easy way to shop from the comfort of home or dorm room, and a way to stay in touch with friends and family. Most of us would probably not think of the internet as a means of surveillance—that is, until we read Bruce Schneier's essay "The Internet Is a Surveillance State," posted to *CNN* on March 16, 2013. Primarily through his use of examples, Schneier builds a convincing case that by using the internet, we have given up our privacy without even a fight, but he fails to acknowledge what some of his other examples reveal: that there are times when we *want* the internet to be a surveillance state.

Schneier opens his essay with examples of three people who have been caught in indiscretions at least and in crimes at most by means of the internet. Chinese hackers who targeted the American government and corporations were caught because they accessed Facebook on the same network. Hector Monsegur, another hacker, was caught by the FBI when he made one mistake and revealed his identity. Paula Broadwell's affair with the director of the CIA was discovered because she emailed him using public networks. But aren't these exactly the types of crimes and indiscretions that we should want revealed? Schneier writes, "If the director of the CIA can't maintain his privacy on the internet, we've got no hope." But do we want the director of the CIA to use his internet privacy to hide his wrongdoing?

Part of the reason we have no hope is that governments and corporations have joined forces to track us. Schneier cites Google, Apple, and Facebook as examples of companies that track users. Facebook, for example, combines what it knows about your online activity with information about your offline buying habits. Governments use what corporations collect, and corporations use what the government collects, for a price. Perhaps most unsettling, cell phones and closed-circuit TV's can be used to track your movements. Big Brother knows where you are and what you are doing (Schneier 39).

Schneier gives examples of things we can do to protect our privacy, but he admits that none of them matter. We could turn off our cell phones and our computers, but we have become so used to them that we would rather give up our privacy than give up our electronics. We could limit what we search, use aliases, and use cash rather than credit, but since the spying is not obvious, it is easy to ignore. And there is the other side of the issue—the good that internet surveillance does. In spite of his opening examples, Schneier fails to acknowledge that for those who are doing no wrong, internet surveillance may be annoying, but it may be worth the loss of privacy to protect the innocent against those who use the internet to commit crimes.

Work Cited

Schneier, Bruce. "The Internet Is a Surveillance State." *CNN,* 16 Mar. 2013, www.cnn.com/2013/03/16/opinion/schneier-internet -surveillance/index.html. Reprinted in *Elements of Argument: A Text and Reader,* 13th ed., edited by Annette T. Rottenberg and Donna Haisty Winchell, Bedford/St. Martin's, 2021, pp. 36–38.

ARGUMENT ESSENTIALS

Examining Written Arguments

The following steps will help you understand any written argument.

1. **Preread the text** to gain background information on the title, genre, context, author, and audience.
2. **Read with an open mind,** noting any bias in the coverage of the topic.
3. **Read the text for content and structure.**
   - Pay attention to the organization and how the argument is shaped.
   - Read actively: Mark up the text and ask questions as you read.
   - Look for visuals that may enhance the argument.
   - Summarize the main point of the argument in your own words.
   - Referential summaries focus on content.
   - Rhetorical summaries focus on strategy.
4. **Evaluate the argument's effectiveness.**
   - Keep an open mind to opposing views.
   - Objectively consider the argument's strengths and weaknesses.
   - Consider the appropriateness of the title.
   - Determine how effective the argument's organization is.
   - Decide how well the argument supports its main claim or thesis.
   - Evaluate the use of language and the definitions of key terms.

Assignments for Critical Reading of Written Arguments

Reading and Discussion Questions

1. The chapter opens with some examples of bumper stickers as argument. What are some bumper stickers that you have seen, and what points were they making?

2. Protest signs also make arguments in just a few words. What examples have you seen? You can find numerous examples on Google or Flickr or in any news article covering a protest or demonstration.

3. Where an essay or an image is published can, in itself, make a statement. Are you aware of certain publications that have a political bias? Consider how even advertisements are geared for the target audience of any given magazine. Locate two ads for the same product or type of product but published in different magazines. How are the ads targeted to the different audiences?

4. Where do you in your daily life read written arguments? Where in newspapers, for example, are arguments published? Where do you find them online?

5. Locate a print or online editorial. Use what you have learned in this chapter to examine it for content, structure, and rhetorical strategies.

Writing Suggestions

1. Choose a print or online editorial, and write an essay analyzing the author's rhetorical strategies.

2. Choose two editorials or argumentative essays on different sides of the same issue and write an essay comparing the authors' rhetorical strategies.

3. Write a paragraph in which you explain whether or not you agree with Whitney Cramer's analysis of Bruce Schneier's article "The Internet Is a Surveillance State."

RESEARCH ASSIGNMENT ▷ **Summarizing**

Do a database search to find a long magazine or journal article (at least 1,200 words) on a topic that interests you: sports, politics, the environment, entertainment, education, or the like.

1. Use the advice in this chapter to preread and then read the article. If possible, print it out and mark up the text.

2. On a separate sheet of paper, list each of the article's subheadings or main ideas, and then summarize each section's point in your own words.

3. Follow the Research Skill box on page 32 and the Strategies for Evaluating Arguments box on page 36 to write a paragraph that briefly and objectively summarizes the article. Your paragraph may be either referential or rhetorical— you should be able to identify which type of summary you are writing and explain what makes it so.

Critical Reading of Multimodal Arguments

Of course, not all arguments are written. In addition to the critical reading skills discussed in Chapter 2, special scrutiny is needed when listening to and viewing arguments in other media. We use the term **multimodal** in the title of this chapter because now we turn to arguments that use words in combination with another medium or that use a mode other than the printed word to get a message across — visual, audiovisual, and digital media.

In reading written texts, we used three steps to help uncover the essential elements of argument:

- Prereading
- Reading for content and structure
- Evaluation

The same general principles apply in looking at multimodal arguments, but we will change them a bit depending on the types of arguments we consider in this chapter: visual, audiovisual, and online.

Visual Rhetoric

Not every visual image makes a statement or presents an argument. Some, however, do so in a way that the printed word alone cannot. If an image arouses emotion or brings to mind a controversial issue, it is making some kind of statement to you. What statement, for example, does Figure 3.1 make to you? What details lead to that statement or support an argument?

The reading strategies below are general guidelines for reading all visuals.

- **Prereading.** With a visual, prereading includes noticing who took or otherwise created the picture or graphic, but often more important are the context and purpose. It may also be relevant where the visual was published, if it was, and when. Print ads, especially, are targeted for a particular audience. The same ad, in different versions, often appears in different publications. With a political cartoon, the political context is critical to understanding the humor. Graphics are often meant to convey information or data about a particular issue.
- **Reading for content.** To "read" a visual means to see what is there—pictures and text. Published images are usually carefully planned to convey a message by means of who or what is shown.
- **Reading for rhetorical strategies.** As a viewer, consider the composition of the visual. Why did the photographer place things where he or she did? Why are some objects in sharp focus and others not? Why, in an ad, is the text a certain size and placed in a certain location? How does the eye move about the ad? Why is the logo or product placed where it is? In a cartoon, what does the physical appearance suggest about the characters? In a graphic, what data are being highlighted?
- **Evaluation.** Consider how effective the visual is in achieving its purpose. How does a photograph make you feel? Does an ad make you want to purchase a product? Does the cartoon make you consider a new perspective? Does a graphic aid your understanding of a complex issue?

The following pages discuss additional considerations for specific types of visuals: photographs, print advertisements, political cartoons, and graphics.

Photographs

You've probably seen powerful still images in photographic journalism: soldiers in battle, destruction by weather disasters, beautiful natural landscapes, inhumane living conditions, the great mushroom clouds of early atomic explosions. These photographs and thousands of others encapsulate arguments of fact, value, and policy: *The tornado devastated the town. The Grand Canyon is our most stupendous national monument. We must not allow human beings to live like this.* Sometimes captions are used to help get the photograph's message across.

FIGURE 3.1 Homeless family. Bruce Ayres/The Image Bank/Getty Images

READING ARGUMENT

Examining Photographs

The photograph below by Erik McGregor was taken at a candlelight vigil at Prospect Park in Brooklyn, New York, on August 5, 2019. McGregor describes the purpose of the vigil: "to mourn the lives lost during recent mass shootings in Brownsville, Dayton, El Paso, and Gilroy, denouncing the surge in gun violence throughout the city and country, and calling on lawmakers at the federal level to enact real gun reform." Thirty people had died in mass shootings within an eight-day span. The speaker at the podium is New York Representative Alexandria Ocasio-Cortez. Although she is an American citizen by birth, Ocasio-Cortez has been a lightning rod for some attacks by conservatives in part because of her Puerto Rican ancestry and also because of her outspokenness. Not all the shooting victims were minorities, but some were targeted because of their ethnicity.

Each pair of shoes represents a life lost in a mass shooting. Lighting candles for the dead, as has been done here, is a well-established tradition in many cultures. The variety of types and styles of shoes reflects the fact that these victims are not just numbers but unique individuals. The circle of shoes is completed by the people standing behind Ocasio-Cortez, and the circle gives the shot its focus. The framing of the shot suggests unity, and unity against gun violence was the theme of the event.

Candlelight Vigil for Mass Shooting Victims
ERIK McGREGOR

ZUMA Press, Inc./Alamy Stock Photo

The next pair of photographs feature the same person, Greta Thunberg, the teenaged environmental activist from Sweden who has gained international fame for her fight against climate change. Translated, her sign reads, "The School Strike for the Climate." The first photograph was taken at the beginning of the school strikes that Thunberg initiated as a means of drawing attention to the future threat that climate change poses for people her age. She has argued that being in school is not as important as fighting for the future of the planet. Therefore, she called upon others to join her in skipping classes each Friday to protest outside the Swedish parliament building. The picture, dated August 28, 2018, emphasizes her solitude at first. She is huddled into a slight recess in the stark wall of the building, legs drawn up with her arms around them, looking small and alone and unhappy.

Friday School Strikes, August 2018
MICHAEL CAMPANELLA

Michael Campanella/Getty Images

The second picture shows the change in just one year. It was taken in August 2019 at one of many international events protesting the lack of progress that is being made in the fight to slow climate change. Thunberg is standing erect, holding her sign, and she is backed by dozens if not

hundreds of people joining her in protest. She is in the front, symboliz-
ing her leadership of the movement. She is not quite centered in the shot;
instead she is joined by another young woman speaking to her, and someone
else has placed her hands on Thunberg's shoulders in an almost protective
way. Thunberg is not very tall, but her small stature belies her power. The
image makes very clear that Thunberg is no longer alone, literally or in her
fight for the future of the planet.

Together, with the same figure and the same sign in both shots, the two
pictures make the argument that one person can change the world.

Fridays for the Future, Six Months Later
MARCO MERLINE

SOPA Images/Getty Images

Practice: Examining Photographs

Analyze the images that follow on pages 47–48, keeping in mind the reading
strategies listed above.

The View from the Other Side

NORMA JEAN GARGASZ

Norma Jean Gargasz/Alamy Stock Photo

A Standoff over Immigration

JOSEPH PREZIOSO

JOSEPH PREZIOSO/Getty Images

Little Boy Holds Hand of Crying Classmate
COURTENEY COKO MOORE

Courtney Coko Moore/Facebook

Reading, Writing, and Discussion Questions

1. What visual details contribute to the success of Norma Jean Gargasz's picture of a man looking through the border wall from Mexico?

2. In Joseph Prezioso's photograph, the sign around the neck of the protester on the left says, "(Making a Profit) Caging Babies Is Immoral!" She was one of a group of protesters who marched in August 2019 from churches in various New England states to Dover, New Hampshire, where ninety-five immigrants were being detained by U.S. Immigration and Customs Enforcement (ICE) at the Strafford County Detention Center. The woman on the right was among the counter protesters. How would you describe the looks on the women's faces and their body language? What values are at odds in their confrontation? How does the angle of the camera contribute to the statement made in the image?

3. The photo by Courtney Coko Moore was taken on the first day of second grade for the two boys. The boy on the left has autism and had started crying because of all the noise and chaos as they waited for the doors to open. What visual elements contribute to the impact of the picture? Why do you think the picture went viral in August 2019?

Print Advertisements

Alluring photographs from advertisers — car companies, restaurants, sporting goods manufacturers, clothiers, jewelers, movie studios — promise to fulfill our dreams of pleasure. On a very different scale, animal-rights groups show photographs of brutally mistreated dogs and cats, and children's rights advocates publish pictures of sick and starving children in desolate refugee camps.

But photographs are not the only visual images used by advertisers. Other kinds of illustrations—as well as signs and symbols, which over the years have acquired connotations, or suggestive significance—are also used as instruments of persuasion. The flag or bald eagle, the shamrock, the crown, the cross, the hammer and sickle, the rainbow, and the swastika can all arouse strong feelings for or against the ideas they represent. These symbols may be defined as abbreviated claims of value. They summarize the moral, religious, and political principles by which groups of people live and often die. In commercial advertisements, we recognize symbols that aren't likely to enlist our deepest loyalties but, nevertheless, may impact our daily lives: the apple with a bite in it, the golden arches, the Starbucks mermaid, the Nike swoosh, and a thousand others.

In fact, a closer look at commercial and political advertising, which is heavily dependent on visual argument and is something we are all familiar with, provides a useful introduction to this complex subject. We know that advertisements, with or without pictures, are short arguments, often lacking fully developed support, whose claims of policy urge us to take an action: Buy this product or service; vote for this candidate or issue. The claim may not be directly expressed, but it will be clearly implicit. In print, on television, or on the internet, the visual representation of objects, carefully chosen to appeal to a particular audience, can be as important as, if not more important than, any verbal text.

Consider these questions as you analyze print advertisements:

1. Who is the sponsor?
2. What does the sponsor want me to do or believe?
3. Is there sufficient text to answer questions I may have about the claim?
4. Are the visual elements more prominent than the text? If so, why?
5. Does the arrangement of elements in the message tell me what the sponsor considers most important? If so, what is the significance of this choice?
6. Does the visual image lead me to entertain unrealistic expectations? (Can using this shampoo make my hair look like that shining cascade on the model? Does the picture of the candidate for governor, shown answering questions in a classroom of eager, smiling youngsters, mean that he has a viable plan for educational reform?)

ARGUMENT ESSENTIALS
Visual Rhetoric

Use these four steps as basic guidelines for analyzing visual rhetoric:

- **Preread.** Consider who created the visual, what the context was, and whether and where it was published.
- **Read for content.** With visual rhetoric, this means "reading" both the pictures and the written text.
- **Read for rhetorical strategies.** Consider the placement and focus of text and visuals. In general, what draws your eye?
- **Evaluate.** How does the image make you feel? What mood does it create? Is it effective in achieving its goal?

READING ARGUMENT

Examining Print Advertisements

The print advertisement below has been annotated with careful attention paid to the questions listed on page 49. The ad is followed by a brief analysis that shows prereading, reading for content, reading for rhetorical strategies, and evaluation.

Stop Climate Change before It Changes You
WORLD WILDLIFE FUND

Frightening visual more prominent than text; intended to show that humans are threatened by climate change

No evidence to support claim

Claim (that humans will turn into fish if we don't stop climate change) is exaggerated.

Message is clear: Stop Climate Change.

Sponsor is WWF: World Wildlife Fund.

The advertisement is for the WWF, or World Wildlife Fund, a nonprofit environmental organization. The ad appeared in Belgium in 2008.

The creepy-looking visual is more prominent than the text. The front and top of the person's head are well lit, to show that a human face has turned into a fish face. The message here is that we could all be living under water if the sea level rises. The text is brief and direct: "Stop climate change before it changes you." The text is located at the bottom of the ad, and it reinforces the image's message: Humans are threatened by climate change. The friendly-looking panda and WWF logo are small and are placed at the very bottom of the ad.

The ad is certainly attention-getting, and you really need to look at it for a minute to figure out what is going on. However, the human with a fish face is quite unrealistic, and the scare tactic used in the ad seems too heavy-handed. This ad may work for readers who already believe that climate change must be stopped. In that case, the ad is simply reinforcing readers' existing worldview as a way to generate support for the WWF. But the ad would probably be less effective in convincing more conservative readers because it lacks any evidence to support the claim that climate change is threatening the human species.

Practice: Examining Print Advertisements

Practice your analytical skills by applying the four steps—prereading, reading for content, reading for rhetorical strategies, and evaluation—to the following ads. Be sure to keep in mind the questions on page 49.

It Only Takes a Moment to Make a Moment
AD COUNCIL

My Future Is What I Make It
L'OREAL

Image courtesy of The Advertising Archives

Political Cartoons

Knowing the context of a political cartoon is essential to both understanding it and appreciating its humor. These cartoons age quickly. You can go back to historical cartoons and appreciate them only if you know the context in which they were created. If today's political cartoons are not created and published quickly, they will have lost their currency and their humor. Remember that if the cartoon is an argument, it has a claim. Consider what the claim is and how the artist used both drawing and text to articulate that claim. Often the picture will provide the support. Since political cartoons are generally judgmental, there will be values on which that judgment is based; puzzling out those values may help you understand the cartoon.

READING ARGUMENT

Examining Political Cartoons

In the cartoon below, the sign tells us that the men constitute the Citizenship Test Forum, which suggests that they are there to discuss what a citizenship test should consist of. All of the members of the committee appear to be white men, who actually look pretty much like one another. Their ties are loosened, and the ends are tucked into their shirt fronts as if to keep them out of the way of serious work. Even their clothes are almost identical. So here we have a very uniform group of white men positioned to make a decision about what others should know or do in order to become citizens. The very appearance of the men suggests a lack of diversity, and the text drives home the point if the picture doesn't: "The IMPORTANT thing is that we only accept the people who'll FIT IN!"

The cartoonist, "Fran," uses irony to make her point. Those taking a citizenship test don't do so to prove that they will fit in. They are tested, rather, on the history and government of the country in which they are applying for citizenship. They will bring diversity, and in many instances won't look very much like these committee members. Fran pokes fun at those who want everybody to be like them and questions the right of a group of white men, in their comfortable uniformity, to make the rules for citizenship. The cartoon has an important and timely message, given recent controversy over immigration.

Citizenship Test Forum

FRAN

The IMPORTANT thing is that we only accept the people who'll FIT IN!

Practice: Examining Cartoons

The following two cartoons are totally different in context yet deal with the same broad issue. Explain the point that each is making about that issue, supporting your analysis with details from the cartoons.

I Understand the Ten Commandments

PETER STEINER

"I understand the Ten Commandments. But what is this Second Amendment he keeps going on about?"

Sorry, Sir, You've Been Red-Flagged
CHIP BOK

Graphics

Graphics are charts, graphs, diagrams, and other visuals that provide an alternative to presenting information as text. They can offer a concise, efficient way of getting information across easily and quickly. A bar graph can show at a glance if sales are higher or lower in the fourth quarter than in the third. A pie chart can make clear how much of the national budget is spent on defense. A map can show emerging centers of population growth.

Different types of graphics serve different purposes. It's important to read accurately the type of graphic you are examining. Always look at the title of the graphic, which should be descriptive, and for labels and keys that will help you understand the information being presented. Color will often serve to make contrasts more striking and simply to make the graphic more visually appealing. Of course, you should always take note of who created or sponsored the graphic as you consider what argument it is making.

READING ARGUMENT

Examining Graphics

The following graphic on tobacco has been annotated for you.

Tobacco's Shifting Burden

THEWORLD.ORG

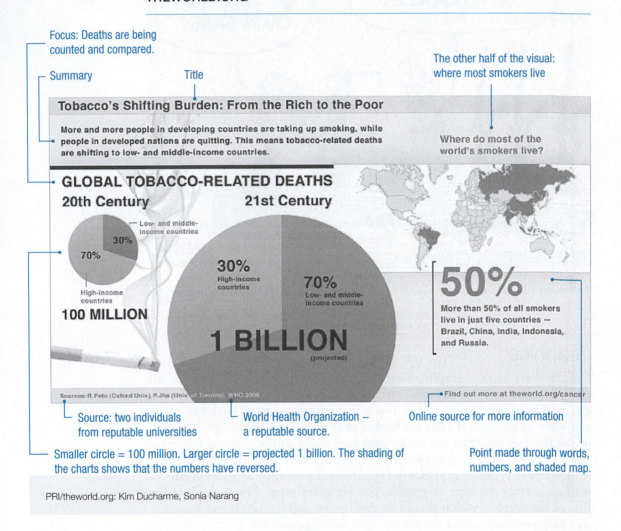

Focus: Deaths are being counted and compared.

Summary

Title

The other half of the visual: where most smokers live

Tobacco's Shifting Burden: From the Rich to the Poor

More and more people in developing countries are taking up smoking, while people in developed nations are quitting. This means tobacco-related deaths are shifting to low- and middle-income countries.

Where do most of the world's smokers live?

GLOBAL TOBACCO-RELATED DEATHS

20th Century

Low- and middle-income countries

30%

70%

High-income countries

100 MILLION

21st Century

30% High-income countries

70% Low- and middle-income countries

1 BILLION
(projected)

50%

More than 50% of all smokers live in just five countries — Brazil, China, India, Indonesia, and Russia.

Sources: R. Peto (Oxford Univ.), P. Jha (Univ. of Toronto), WHO 2009

Find out more at theworld.org/cancer

Source: two individuals from reputable universities

World Health Organization — a reputable source.

Online source for more information

Smaller circle = 100 million. Larger circle = projected 1 billion. The shading of the charts shows that the numbers have reversed.

Point made through words, numbers, and shaded map.

PRI/theworld.org: Kim Ducharme, Sonia Narang

Practice: Examining Graphics

Analyze this graphic sponsored by the Union of Concerned Scientists, and answer the questions that follow.

Where Your Gas Money Goes

UNION OF CONCERNED SCIENTISTS

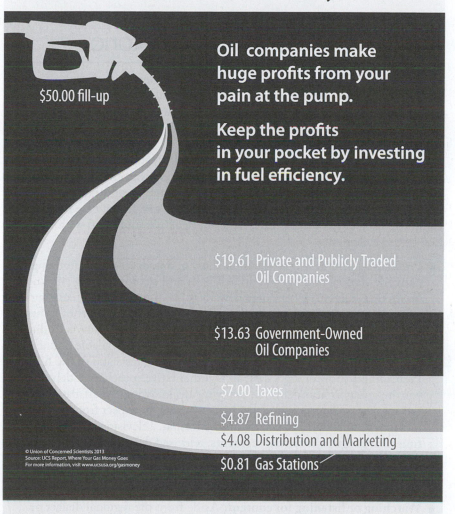

Union of Concerned Scientists

1. "Read" the graphic. What is it saying?
2. The ad was sponsored by the Union of Concerned Scientists. What might you speculate about that group? What does your research reveal about it?
3. Does the group have a purpose in the ad beyond explaining where your gas money goes? If so, what is it?
4. What are some conclusions you can draw from the ad?

Audio and Audiovisual Rhetoric

Where in our daily lives do we see examples of argumentation that go beyond print? We see them on television news networks and on talk shows that deal with politics and social issues. We hear news and opinions through videos we see on Facebook and YouTube and listen to them in podcasts, political speeches, and debates.

Audio allows all that the human voice adds, from a regional dialect to a tinge of nervousness; television and video allow all that the visual dimension adds, from body language to hair style to movement and pacing. In other words, audiovisual combines sound and motion. And, in the case of television commercials, we see most of the features of print ads amplified with the addition of these elements.

- **Prereading.** Prereading a television show or a podcast means noticing the network, station, or organization behind it and acknowledging any known biases that suggests. With some news organizations, it won't take long for a liberal or conservative bias to become obvious. The sponsors of a show may be relevant. For talk shows, a practical part of prereading is finding out who the guests will be. That information is often available online in advance. What are the affiliations of the various guests and of the host? Prereading a show or a podcast, an argumentative speech, or a debate that you are going to hear delivered orally means knowing the affiliation of the speaker or debaters and what biases you might expect from each. It includes familiarizing yourself with the format. Television shows sometimes have regular recurring segments; televised debates follow a format that is explained at the beginning of the telecast. Podcasts may feature speakers that represent two or more political perspectives or may take the form of a single long interview that lasts for the entire episode.
- **Watching or listening for content.** Aside from the regional dialect or the tinge of nervousness, the body language or the hairstyle, what is being said? Televised news incorporates photographs, graphics, and video clips along with the script. By way of all that, what are viewers being told? As you hear different speakers on a podcast or in a speech or a debate, can you start to recognize their positions on the issues?

- **Watching or listening for rhetorical strategies.** As you watch a segment of a television show or listen to a podcast, a speech, or a debate, are you aware of any errors in logic? Does the speaker or debater support his or her claims? Are there unspoken assumptions with which you do not agree? How is bias revealed? Is the content or delivery slanted for a particular audience? In analyzing commercials for rhetorical strategies, consider how speech, music, and special effects might appeal to a viewer.
- **Evaluation.** How effective is a speaker or debater in building a convincing case for the intended audience? How effective is a television segment, speech, or podcast in delivering its content? How effective is it in presenting a legitimate exchange of opinions and not a shouting match? How effective is the commercial in selling a product or service?

From television news shows that go well beyond reporting the news to expressing opinions about it, it is only a small step to political commentary shows that from their inception were meant to be a sounding board for different opinions on contemporary politics. Some of these shows have been around for decades. *Meet the Press* is the longest-running television series in the history of American broadcasting; it has been on the air for more than sixty years. The most intelligent and responsible programs usually consist of a panel of experts—politicians, journalists, scholars—led by a neutral moderator (or one who, at least, allows guests to express their views). Other examples of these programs are *Face the Nation* with Margaret Brennan, *This Week with George Stephanopoulos* (cohosted by Martha Raddatz), *Fox News Sunday* with Chris Wallace, and *State of the Union with Jake Tapper*.

More clearly biased news shows include the conservative *Hannity* on the Fox News Channel and the liberal *The Rachel Maddow Show* on MSNBC. Variations on these are some very popular political comedy shows like *The Daily Show with Trevor Noah*, *Full Frontal with Samantha Bee*, and *Last Week Tonight with John Oliver*. Radio also has its share of news and call-in hosts who are known for their political bias, such as conservative Rush Limbaugh and liberal Stephanie Miller.

Television and radio were long the standard means of hearing about controversy in our city, state, nation, and world, along with newspapers and news magazines, of course. One of the major ways these older outlets have changed is that they have had to make their content available digitally in order to survive.

Television Commercials

Television commercials have come of age since their first appearance in 1941 with an ad for Bulova watches. The cost of that ad? Nine dollars. Of course, we all know what a big business commercials are today. The cost of a thirty-second commercial during the Super Bowl hit $5.6 million in 2020. Television commercials can be analyzed much like print ads.

You can preview a commercial, or watch it to get the general idea before breaking it down into component parts for analysis. Consider the context, including the intended audience, at what time of day the ad airs, and during what shows or types of shows it airs. Consider text and visuals, as you did with print ads, but also consider the action in the commercial and to what extent sound adds to its overall appeal. To read for rhetorical strategies, consider what audience the commercial targets and how it appeals to that audience, and evaluate how effective the commercial is at achieving its purpose.

READING ARGUMENT

Examining Television Commercials

In 2012, Toyota changed its slogan to "Let's Go Places," replacing "Moving Forward," which had been its slogan since 2004, and did a series of commercials around the new theme. The new tagline was introduced on December 31, 2012, in launching the redesigned 2013 Avalon sedan. The stills presented here show the approach the company took in one of them. Look at the images and read the analysis that accompanies each one to understand how Toyota employed audiovisual rhetoric in its commercial.

Let's Go Places

TOYOTA

Voiceover: *Let's go places.*

This is one of numerous shots that show Toyotas moving through different types of landscape—mountains, residential neighborhoods, snowy woods, and so on. These are some of the physical places we can go. The varied landscape suggests that wherever you go, you can do it in a Toyota. Different locales appeal to different viewers, depending on where they live or where they would like to travel. The first series of rapid shots shows the landscape but not the car.

A second shows the landscape as seen from behind the car. The movement of the camera from in front of the car to behind it gives the impression of the car outracing the camera in the rush to go places.

Voiceover: *Not just the ones you can find on a map. But the ones you can find in your heart!*

The ad goes for emotional appeals, including shots of familiar points in the lives of everyday people. Some of them are common events like a trip out for ice cream with the family or a camping trip to the lake, and some are major events like going to the prom, bringing a new baby home, or being in a wedding.

Voiceover: *Let's go beyond everything we know and embrace everything we don't. And once we have reached our destination, let's keep going, because inspiration does not favor those that sit still. It dances with the daring and rewards the courageous with ideas that excite, challenge, and even inspire.*

With these words, the focus shifts to Toyota's tough four-wheel drive vehicles to show how they can function in rough terrain. Toyotas are even shown painted like race cars. One vehicle "dances with the daring" by launching off a ramp into the air. The whole ad campaign stresses moving instead of sitting still. The text tells us that our destination is beyond everything we know and suggests new, tougher challenges, like making the car fly through the air. The music, "It's My Life" by Tim Myers, builds from soft piano notes at the beginning to a crescendo as the car takes to the air. This portion of the ad goes beyond the comfort of earlier familiar scenes to appeal to the daredevil in most of us.

Voiceover: *Ideas that take you to a place that you never imagined. Ideas big enough and powerful enough to make the heart skip a beat and in some cases even two. Toyota. Let's go places.*

The Tundra CrewMax 5.7L V8 is towing far beyond its published towing capacity in a one-time, short-distance event. Never tow beyond a vehicle's published towing capacity. Always consult Owner's Manual.

By the end of the ad, Toyota is appealing to viewers' pride in America. One place that you probably would not have imagined a Toyota going is the "parade route" along which the retired space shuttle *Endeavour* was pulled from Los Angeles International Airport to a downtown museum. The words "Born in America" across the front of the Toyota Tundra stress that although Toyota is a Japanese automaker, the Tundra is made in San Antonio. And the places that the shuttle has been advance the idea of humankind's ultimate journeys. The shuttle dwarfs all around it, just as its destinations dwarf most of our dreams of places we would like to go. However, the ad encourages its viewers not to place limits on themselves when they dream. A final shot of a globe reinforces the notion that there is no place, on this planet at least, that one cannot go in a Toyota.

Practice: Examining Television Commercials

Choose a current or recent television commercial to analyze as the Toyota commercial was analyzed above. Select a few screenshots to support your analysis.

Podcasts

The term *podcast* came from combining the terms *iPod* and *broadcast*. A podcast is a series of audio files that a consumer can download to a mobile device or computer and listen to at his or her leisure. Podcasts can be about anything from fitness to UFOs, based on the interests of those who record them and those who choose to listen. Not every podcast is an argument, nor is it about controversial issues. Many are simply meant to be informative or comedic. A podcast succeeds to the extent that it achieves its purpose(s) and can attract an audience of subscribers. Some podcasters are famous enough to be household names; many are unknowns hoping to become known.

READING ARGUMENT

Examining Podcasts

When it comes to politics and social issues, there are a range of podcasts for any taste. Some feature a podcaster interviewing a single guest. More often a moderator guides a discussion among several guests or regular contributors. Many podcasts have a clear political bias or slant and are most likely to appeal to listeners who share that perspective and who listen to have their ideas reinforced. You can listen for the content or speakers' delivery to identify bias and, after hearing a few episodes, you can identify their political leanings.

The podcast episode from which the following conversation was taken is called *Left, Right, Center*, and, as its title suggests, it features a panel who discuss a different topic each episode, approaching it from a range of different political perspectives. The portion of the particular episode transcribed here is about immigration rules.

The moderator, Josh Barro, who identifies himself as a conservative, introduces the issue of the day, which is an administration ruling that will make it harder for immigrants to get a green card. Barro defines a key term, *public charge*. An immigrant becomes a public charge when he or she is dependent on the government. Barro uses a hypothetical case to suggest that the new rule will favor immigrants who are middle class or higher. He introduces his first guest, Randy Capps, with a question about the subjectivity of predicting which immigrants may or may not become public charges. Capps is not identified as being either left- or right-leaning, but he is identified as director of research at the Migration Policy Institute, so we might assume that he is sympathetic to the plight of immigrants.

As a conservative, Barro sets up the conversation in an objective way, but later he tries to emphasize the positives of the proposed change, a move expected of someone supporting the administration proposing it. He describes it as a reinterpretation of an existing law that merely counts a few more things, like some forms of Medicare, as part of what might make an immigrant dependent on the government. He clearly states that he does not see the new proposal as an abuse of administrative power.

Capps reveals his more liberal slant in his concern that the policy leaves a great deal of discretion to the immigration officer. Although most immigrants applying for a green card would not have previously received the types of benefits that have made them dependent on the government, predicting whether they will or not based on what might happen in the future is very speculative and could exclude a large number of people. Even the conservative Barro has to admit that the amount of discretion given an immigration official is worrisome.

Tim Carney, a conservative from the *Washington Examiner*, enters the conversation to criticize liberals who celebrate the desire of immigrants to come to the United States and make it on their own financially yet don't support the proposal that they must prove before they get their green card that they will be able to do so. The segment concludes with Helaine Olen, a liberal from the *Washington Post*, attacking the administration's entire immigration policy as chaotic because it doesn't balance what types of workers the United States needs to bring in with the needs of those who want to come in.

Recession Fears, Immigration Rules, and "Electability"
LEFT, RIGHT, CENTER

Date: August 16, 2019

Josh Barro: The Trump administration has issued a rule that will, starting in October, make it significantly harder to get a green card. Like before, potential permanent residents will have to show that they're not likely to become a public charge, dependent on the government. But the definition of who's a public charge will be greatly broadened. People who are likely to qualify for certain government benefits like food stamps and Medicaid may be considered public charges even if they or other members of their household have significant labor income.

But an immigrant household that makes at least 250 percent of the federal poverty level, which is about $64,000 for a family of four, will be strongly presumed not to be likely to be a public charge, so this is a rule that is designed to strongly favor immigrants who are already solidly in the middle class or affluent before they become permanent residents of the United States. To discuss what this rule will do and whether it's actually within the Trump administration's legal authority to implement, we're joined now by Randy Capps. Randy is the director of research at the Migration Policy Institute.

So, the first question I have about this rule is that it seems vague in certain ways. It sets out a lot of things that might make you a public charge or might make you not a public charge, but they're not bright-line rules. They're factors that an immigration officer is supposed to weigh in deciding whether or not to issue a green card. So, I guess the question is do we know how big an effect this rule is likely to have? How do we know that when this rule is applied how many people will be denied green cards who otherwise would have gotten them?

Randy Capps: It really depends on the discretion of the immigration officer. The rule, as you said, mentions a list of factors: age, educational attainment, English proficiency, income, employment, and health insurance coverage, the factors an immigration officer can weigh and some of them are positive and some of them are negative, and some of them are heavily weighted, and some of them are not. But there's a lot of factors in the role, and there's no standard as to how many things have to count for or against someone for them to get a green card.

Josh Barro: The law does say, not in very precise terms, that you should not be granted your permanent residency if you are likely to be a public charge. What this is doing simply in part is just expanding the class of benefit programs that count as public charge. So, Medicaid used to not really count, and now some Medicaid services do. And this wouldn't go after refugees or asylum seekers. Should we still have this idea that if you're persecuted you're welcome and even if you're gonna be on welfare? And we still have this idea that there are all sorts of programs including CHIP and programs for young people that they're not going to be kicked out because they took some welfare or public aid when they were teenagers. So, you say it's drastic, but it's taking what is the law and interpreting it differently. I'm very sensitive to presidents abusing power, but this doesn't look like an abuse of power to me.

Randy Capps: The reality is that there's almost no immigrants who can get these benefits before they become green card holders. Certainly, if they're applying from outside the United States, they're not going to have access to U.S. benefits, and they're barred legally under the Personal Responsibility Act from getting food stamps and Medicaid — unless they're children, and children are exempted from the rule — before they get a green card. So, the universe of people who are going to be excluded because they already used benefits is going to be very small. The big exclusion is the forward looking test — the age, the education, the English language proficiency, income, assets and all of these things. The issue there is that it's very broad. Now, the law does specify that the federal government can use these factors to make people inadmissible or ineligible for a green card, but it doesn't specify how. What the rule does, I think, is expands the scope so much that a really wide variety of people could be excluded under these terms.

Josh Barro: I'm a conservative. I see two sorts of conflicting poles here. One is that yes, U.S. immigration law should make it so that immigration is helping Americans. Immigration law is not there to serve the rest of the world — it's our law, it's there to serve us. There's something to be said that people shouldn't come here to use our welfare. So, those two principles in one direction. But the way you're describing it does bug me to think that there are federal bureaucrats who can look at it and with somebody not having used welfare, do some sort of math and say, "I think you're going to go on welfare, and I think you're going to go on Medicaid." That is a discretion of federal agents that I find worrisome.

Tim Carney (*Washington Examiner*, Right): In a congressional debate, assuming we had a functional Congress that could pass laws, you would have a debate over things like, should we care about income? Because one of the Trump administration defenses of this is no matter how poor you are, no matter where you're coming from, if you work hard enough you should be able to basically avoid becoming a public charge. If we're looking at what your income is the day that you land, then that's not addressing that. . . . The way that a lot of liberals say immigration is great is by pointing to the fact that people who come here want to come and be self-starters. And so if you oppose a public charge rule, then saying that is a lie. You're saying, "Oh no, we do want anyone to show up here even if we don't think that they're going to be able to contribute to the economy."

Helaine Olen (*Washington Post,* **Left):** I think there's another thing that needs to be taken into account here, too, and that is what jobs do we need filled? One of the things Trump has talked about a lot is bringing in more high-skilled people, which is a valid point. But at the same time, what we're seeing right now is that the jobs that are going wanting are actually not particularly high-skilled jobs. . . . Again, could they raise the salaries and get more Americans? Potentially, but probably not as many as we would like to think. So, this also begs the bigger question of how are we going to reform our immigration policy so that we get what we need in this country while still trying to help people out as we have traditionally done. . . . And doing things like this, what Donald Trump is proposing, is just sort of, in the end, kind of incoherent, frankly.

Practice: Examining Podcasts

Intelligence Squared is an organization that stages debates and discussions "to promote a global conversation that enables people to make informed decisions about the ideas that matter." Use the questions at the end to examine this excerpt from the *Intelligence Squared* podcast from August 30, 2019.

How the Information Age Crashed Our Democracy
TOM BALDWIN AND NINA SCHICK, INTELLIGENCE SQUARED

Baldwin: It's this abusive relationship between media and politics on the one hand and that information age on the other that is at the heart of the crisis in our democracy now.

Schick: So, obviously, people might counter and say, you know, fake news or political propaganda or the misuse of media is as old as politics itself. This is not a new phenomenon. So, what in particular do you see in the past decade or the last thirty years or in your experience that has really changed it? You know, why is this in particular a very dangerous time for our democracies?

Baldwin: . . . There's so much more news. There's just this expansion in the first instance, the same expansion, I think, also created a kind of insurgence in the media. Because there's so much more, it meant that, you know, once something had appeared on a 24/7 cable TV channel, it was no longer new for the newspapers to write about, so they had to write something different, something more speculative. The need to generate constant drama and controversy out of actually quite mundane moments of politics, I think, added to the stress and strain of the system, and then you get to the political response to this media insurgency, which is to try and spin your way out of it, to try and control the flow of information, to try and manage it. And it's the two things together which I think undermined trust in the media and in politics. It helped unpick the seams of truth, and that opened up space, I think, for people online, below the line, in terms of newspaper comments, in blogs, to begin to question some of the bonds which kept democracy together.

Reading, Writing, and Discussion Questions

1. How is the format of *Intelligence Squared* different from the format of the excerpt from *Left, Right, Center*? Why might that appeal to a different audience?
2. What is Nina Schick's role in the podcast?
3. Explain Tom Baldwin's point about how newspapers were changed by the emergence of 24-hour news networks.
4. How does Baldwin argue that changes in the media have undermined our democracy?
5. What do the language choices reveal about each speaker? Do you think their language differs from how they would write the same information in a book or report? Why?

Speeches and Debates

Good speeches on controversial issues are some of the best examples of argument. Unlike the brief sound bites that we hear on the evening news or in response to a microphone thrust in a politician's face as she leaves a building, a carefully prepared speech is the closest we come in the twenty-first century to formal rhetoric. Of course, those in the highest offices have speechwriters, but whoever writes public addresses for candidates or governmental officials must be skilled at moving an audience to act or at least to change an opinion.

ARGUMENT ESSENTIALS
Audiovisual Rhetoric

Use these four steps as basic guidelines for analyzing audiovisual rhetoric:

- **Preread.** Notice a television or radio show's network or station and its sponsors, and consider any possible bias. Consider the organization or company behind a commercial and the affiliations of a speaker.
- **Watch or listen for content.** Consider what you are being told when you listen to the news. Consider what product, service, candidate, or idea a speaker or a commercial is encouraging you to accept.
- **Watch or listen for rhetorical strategies.** Consider if and how any bias is being revealed. With speeches or debates, consider how the speaker is trying to appeal to a specific audience. With commercials, consider the questions used in analyzing visual rhetoric plus any added by sound, motion, and special effects.
- **Evaluate.** Consider how effective a news show is in delivering the news in a fair manner or how effective a talk show is in allowing varied opinions to be heard. Consider whether a speaker's content and strategies are appropriate for his or her audience. Consider how effective a commercial is in selling its product, service, candidate, or idea.

Candidates also prepare carefully for debates, but the success of the debate depends largely on the moderator. A weak moderator might allow each candidate to deliver set speeches no matter what the question or allow the whole event to become a verbal sparring match, which can be entertaining but may not clarify the candidates' positions on a wide range of issues. A strong moderator can hold the candidates to a clear response and rebuttal format that covers a lot of ground in a short time.

Listening to a speech — or reading one — requires focus on the ideas to the exclusion of the distraction of physical appearance. It requires listening for claim and support. It requires keeping in mind the audience for whom the speech is or was intended. (You will learn more in Chapter 10 about making language serve the needs of argument.) For now, consider how well speeches fit the contexts in which they were delivered and how convincing you find their arguments to be.

READING ARGUMENT

Examining Speeches

The following speech was delivered by Senator Elizabeth Warren in 2015. It has been annotated to show argument strategies in speech.

Remarks at the Edward M. Kennedy Institute for the United States Senate

ELIZABETH WARREN

Paul Zimmerman/Getty Images

Thank you. I'm grateful to be here at the Edward M. Kennedy Institute for the United States Senate. This place is a fitting tribute to our champion, Ted Kennedy. A man of courage, compassion, and commitment, who taught us what public service is all about. Not a day goes by that we don't miss his passion, his enthusiasm, and—most of all—his dedication to all of our working families.

As the Senior Senator from Massachusetts, I have the great honor of sitting at Senator Kennedy's desk—right over there. The original, back in Washington, is a little more dented and scratched, but it has something very special in the drawer. Ted Kennedy carved his name in it. When I sit at my desk, sometimes when I'm waiting to speak or to vote, I open the drawer and run my thumb across his name. It reminds me of the high expectations of the people of Massachusetts, and I try, every day, to live up to the legacy he left behind.

Senator Kennedy took office just over fifty years ago, in the midst of one of the great moral and political debates in American history—the debate over the Civil Rights Act. In his first speech on the floor of the Senate, just four months after his brother's assassination, he stood up to support equal rights for all Americans. He ended that speech with a powerful personal message about what the civil rights struggle meant to the late President Kennedy:

> His heart and soul are in this bill. If his life and death had a meaning, it was that we should not hate but love one another; we should use our powers not to create conditions of oppression that lead to violence, but conditions of freedom that lead to peace.

A plea for peace and unity

"We should use our powers not to create conditions of oppression that lead to violence, but conditions of freedom that lead to peace." That's what I'd like to talk about today.

5 A half-century ago, when Senator Kennedy spoke of the Civil Rights Act, entrenched, racist power did everything it could to sustain oppression of African Americans, and violence was its first tool. Lynchings, terrorism, intimidation. The 16th Street Baptist Church. Medgar Evers. Emmett Till. When Alabama Governor George Wallace stood before the nation and declared during his 1963 inaugural address that he would defend "segregation now, segregation tomorrow, segregation forever," he made clear that the state would stand with those who used violence.

Examples of historical violence and discrimination against African Americans in America

But violence was not the only tool. African Americans were effectively stripped of citizenship when they were denied the right to vote. The tools varied—literacy tests, poll taxes, moral character tests, grandfather clauses—but the results were the same. They were denied basic rights of citizenship and the chance to participate in self-government.

Warren starts using the three aspects of black treatment that will organize her remarks: three tools used against African Americans—violence, voting, and economic injustice.

The third tool of oppression was to deliberately deny millions of African Americans economic opportunities solely because of the color of their skin.

I have often spoken about how America built a great middle class. Coming out of the Great Depression, from the 1930s to the late 1970s, as GDP went up, wages went up for most Americans. But there's a dark underbelly to that story. While median family income in America was growing—for both white and African-American families—African-American incomes were only a fraction of white incomes. In the mid-1950s, the median income for African-American families was just a little more than half the income of white families.

And the problem went beyond just income. Look at housing: For most middle class families in America, buying a home is the number one way to build wealth. It's a retirement plan—pay off the house and live on Social Security. An investment option—mortgage the house to start a business. It's a way to help the kids get through college, a safety net if someone gets really sick, and, if all goes well and Grandma and Grandpa can hang on to the house until they die, it's a way to give the next generation a boost — extra money to move the family up the ladder.

For much of the twentieth century, that's how it worked for generation   10
after generation of white Americans — but not black Americans. Entire legal structures were created to prevent African Americans from building economic security through home ownership. Legally-enforced segregation. Restrictive deeds. Redlining. Land contracts. Coming out of the Great Depression, America built a middle class, but systematic discrimination kept most African-American families from being part of it.

State-sanctioned discrimination wasn't limited to homeownership. The government enforced discrimination in public accommodations, discrimination in schools, discrimination in credit — it was a long and spiteful list.

Economic justice is not — and has never been — sufficient to ensure racial justice. Owning a home won't stop someone from burning a cross on the front lawn. Admission to a school won't prevent a beating on the sidewalk outside. But when Dr. King led hundreds of thousands of people to march on Washington, he talked about an end to violence, access to voting AND economic opportunity. As Dr. King once wrote, "the inseparable twin of racial injustice was economic injustice."

The tools of oppression were woven together, and the civil rights struggle was fought against that oppression wherever it was found — against violence, against the denial of voting rights, and against economic injustice.

The battles were bitter and sometimes deadly. Fire hoses turned on peaceful protestors. Police officers setting their dogs to attack black students. Bloody Sunday at the Edmund Pettus Bridge.

But the civil rights movement pushed this country in a new direction.   15

- The federal government cracked down on state-sponsored violence. Presidents Eisenhower, Kennedy, and Johnson all called out the National Guard, and, in doing so, declared that everyone had a right to equal protection under the law, guaranteed by the Constitution. Congress protected the rights of all citizens to vote with the Voting Rights Act.
- And economic opportunities opened up when Congress passed civil rights laws that protected equal access to employment, public accommodations, and housing.

In the same way that the tools of oppression were woven together, a package of civil rights laws came together to protect black people from violence, to ensure access to the ballot box, and to build economic opportunity. Or to say it another way, these laws made three powerful declarations: Black lives matter. Black citizens matter. Black families matter.

Fifty years later, we have made real progress toward creating the conditions of freedom — but we have not made ENOUGH progress.

Warren's claim

Fifty years later, violence against African Americans has not disappeared. Consider law enforcement. The vast majority of police officers sign up so they can protect their communities. They are part of an honorable profession that takes risks every day to keep us safe. We know that. But we also know — and say — the names of those whose lives have been treated with callous indifference. Sandra Bland. Freddie Gray. Michael Brown. We've seen sickening videos of unarmed, black Americans cut down by bullets, choked to death while gasping for air — their lives ended by those who are sworn to protect them. Peaceful, unarmed protestors have been beaten. Journalists have been jailed. And, in some cities, white vigilantes with weapons freely walk the streets. And it's not just about law enforcement either. Just look to the terrorism this summer at Emanuel AME Church. We must be honest: Fifty years after John Kennedy and Martin Luther King, Jr. spoke out, violence against African Americans has not disappeared.

1. Examples of how fifty years later, there is still violence

And what about voting rights? Two years ago, five conservative justices on the Supreme Court gutted the Voting Rights Act, opening the floodgates ever wider for measures designed to suppress minority voting. Today, the specific tools of oppression have changed — voter ID laws, racial gerrymandering, and mass disfranchisement through a criminal justice system that disproportionately incarcerates black citizens. The tools have changed, but black voters are still deliberately cut out of the political process.

2. Examples of today's discrimination

20   Violence. Voting. And what about economic injustice? Research shows that the legal changes in the civil rights era created new employment and housing opportunities. In the 1960s and the 1970s, African-American men and women began to close the wage gap with white workers, giving millions of black families hope that they might build real wealth.

3. Examples of today's economic injustice

But then, Republicans' trickle-down economic theory arrived. Just as this country was taking the first steps toward economic justice, the Republicans pushed a theory that meant helping the richest people and the most powerful corporations get richer and more powerful. I'll just do one statistic on this: From 1980 to 2012, GDP continued to rise, but how much of the income growth went to the 90 percent of America — everyone outside the top 10 percent — black, white, Latino? None. Zero. Nothing. One hundred percent of all the new income produced in this country over the past 30 years has gone to the top ten percent.

Today, 90 percent of Americans see no real wage growth. For African-Americans, who were so far behind earlier in the 20th century, this

Effective use of statistics for support.

means that since the 1980s they have been hit particularly hard. In January of this year, African-American unemployment was 10.3 percent—more than twice the rate of white unemployment. And, after beginning to make progress during the civil rights era to close the wealth gap between black and white families, in the 1980s the wealth gap exploded, so that from 1984 to 2009, the wealth gap between black and white families tripled.

Examples, expert opinion, causal relationships as support

The 2008 housing collapse destroyed trillions in family wealth across the country, but the crash hit African-Americans like a punch in the gut. Because middle class black families' wealth was disproportionately tied up in home-ownership and not other forms of savings, these families were hit harder by the housing collapse. But they also got hit harder because of discriminatory lending practices—yes, discriminatory lending practices in the twenty-first century. Recently several big banks and other mortgage lenders paid hundreds of millions in fines, admitting that they illegally steered black and Latino borrowers into more expensive mortgages than white borrowers who had similar credit. Tom Perez, who at the time was the Assistant Attorney General for Civil Rights, called it a "racial surtax." And it's still happening—earlier this month, the National Fair Housing alliance filed a discrimination complaint against real estate agents in Mississippi after an investigation showed those agents consistently steering white buyers away from interracial neighborhoods and black buyers away from affluent ones. Another investigation showed similar results across our nation's cities. Housing discrimination alive and well in 2015.

Violence, voting, economic justice.

She has looked at past and present. Now she will look to the future.

We have made important strides forward. But we are not done yet. And now, it is our time.   25

Warren acknowledges that she cannot fully appreciate what black Americans have suffered.

I speak today with the full knowledge that I have not personally experienced and can never truly understand the fear, the oppression, and the pain that confronts African Americans every day. But none of us can ignore what is happening in this country. Not when our black friends, family, neighbors literally fear dying in the streets.

Listen to the brave, powerful voices of today's new generation of civil rights leaders. Incredible voices. Listen to them say: "If I die in police custody, know that I did not commit suicide." Watch them march through the streets, "hands up don't shoot"—not to incite a riot, but to fight for their lives. To fight for their lives.

This is the reality all of us must confront, as uncomfortable and ugly as that reality may be. It comes to us to once again affirm that black lives matter, that black citizens matter, that black families matter.

Once again, the task begins with safeguarding our communities from violence. We have made progress, but it is a tragedy when any American cannot trust those who have sworn to protect and serve. This pervasive and persistent distrust isn't based on myths. It is grounded in the reality of unjustified violence.

Solutions to violence

30   Policing must become a truly community endeavor — not in just a few cities, but everywhere. Police forces should look like, and come from, the neighborhoods they serve. They should reach out to support and defend the community — working with people in neighborhoods before problems arise. All police forces — not just some — must be trained to de-escalate and to avoid the likelihood of violence. Body cameras can help us know what happens when someone is hurt.

We honor the bravery and sacrifice that our law enforcement officers show every day on the job — and the noble intentions of the vast majority of those who take up the difficult job of keeping us safe. But police are not occupying armies. This is America, not a war zone — and policing practices in all cities — not just some — need to reflect that.

Next, voting.

Solutions to voting discrimination

It's time to call out the recent flurry of new state law restrictions for what they are: an all-out campaign by Republicans to take away the right to vote from poor and black and Latino American citizens who probably won't vote for them. The push to restrict voting is nothing more than a naked grab to win elections that they can't win if every citizen votes.

Two years ago the Supreme Court eviscerated critical parts of the Voting Rights Act. Congress could easily fix this, and Democrats in the Senate have called for restoration of voting rights. Now it is time for Republicans to step up to support a restoration of the Voting Rights Act — or to stand before the American people and explain why they have abandoned America's most cherished liberty, the right to vote.

Specific suggestions for change

35   And while we're at it, we need to update the rules around voting. Voting should be simple. Voter registration should be automatic. Get a driver's license, get registered automatically. Nonviolent, law-abiding citizens should not lose the right to vote because of a prior conviction. Election Day should be a holiday, so no one has to choose between a paycheck and a vote. Early voting and vote by mail would give fast food and retail workers who don't get holidays off a chance to proudly cast their votes. The hidden discrimination that comes with purging voter rolls and short-staffing polling places must stop. The right to vote remains essential to protect all other rights, and no candidate for president or for any other elected office — Republican or

Democrat—should be elected if they will not pledge to support full, meaningful voting rights.

Solutions to economic injustice

Finally, economic justice. Our task will not be complete until we ensure that every family—regardless of race—has a fighting chance to build an economic future for themselves and their families. We need less talk and more action about reducing unemployment, ending wage stagnation and closing the income gap between white and nonwhite workers.

And one more issue, dear to my heart: It's time to come down hard on predatory practices that allow financial institutions to systematically strip wealth out of communities of color. One of the ugly consequences of bank deregulation was that there was no cop on the beat when too many financial institutions figured out that they could make great money by tricking, trapping, and defrauding targeted families. Now we have a Consumer Financial Protection Bureau, and we need to make sure it stays strong and independent so that it can do its job and make credit markets work for black families, Latino families, white families—all families.

Yes, there's work to do.

Extended example/personal anecdote

Back in March, I met an elderly man at the First Baptist Church in Montgomery, Alabama. We were having coffee and donuts in the church basement before the service started. He told me that more than fifty years earlier—in May of 1961—he had spent eleven hours in that same basement, along with hundreds of people, while a mob outside threatened to burn down the church because it was a sanctuary for civil rights workers. Dr. King called Attorney General Bobby Kennedy, desperately asking for help. The Attorney General promised to send the Army, but the closest military base was several hours away. So the members of the church and the civil rights workers waited in the sweltering basement, crowded together, listening to the mob outside and hoping the U.S. Army would arrive in time.

After the church service, I asked Congressman John Lewis about that night. He had been right there in that church back in 1961 while the mob gathered outside. He had been in the room during the calls to the Attorney General. I asked if he had been afraid that the Army wouldn't make it in time. He said that he was "never, ever afraid. You come to that point where you lose all sense of fear." And then he said something I'll never forget. He said that his parents didn't want him to get involved in civil rights. They didn't want him to "cause trouble." But he had done it anyway. He told me: "Sometimes it is important to cause necessary trouble."   40

Closes with memorable quotation

The first civil rights battles were hard fought. But they established that Black Lives Matter. That Black Citizens Matter. That Black Families Matter. Half a century later, we have made real progress, but we have not made ENOUGH progress. As Senator Kennedy said in his first floor speech, "This is not a political issue. It is a moral issue, to be resolved through political means." So it comes to us to continue the fight, to make, as John Lewis said, the "necessary trouble" until we can truly say that in America, every citizen enjoys the conditions of freedom.

Reiterates her claim

Thank you.

Practice: Examining Speeches

Using the annotations on the Elizabeth Warren speech as a model, read and annotate the speech by former president Barack Obama (p. 297).

Strategies for Critical Listening

Listening is hearing with attention. It is a skill that can be learned and improved. Here are some of the characteristics of critical listening most appropriate to understanding and responding to arguments that are delivered through live speech or recorded on audio or video.

1. **Concentrate.** If you are distracted, you cannot go back as you do with the written word to clarify a point or recover a connection. As you listen, try to avoid being distracted by facts alone. Look for the overall patterns of the speech. Take notes using an outline of the material being covered.

2. **Pay attention to the claim and support.** Avoid focusing on the speaker's appearance and delivery. Research shows that listeners are likely to give greater attention to the dramatic elements of speeches than to the logical ones. But you can enjoy the sound, the appearance, and the drama of a spoken argument without allowing these elements to overwhelm what is essential to the development of a claim.

3. **Avoid premature judgments about what is actually said.** Good listeners try not to allow their prejudices to prevent careful evaluation of the argument. This doesn't mean accepting everything or even most of what you hear. This precaution is especially relevant when the speakers and their views are well known and the listener has already formed an opinion about them, favorable or unfavorable.

Online Environments

Many of us spend a good part of our lives online. What role does argumentation play in our digital lives? Any of us can get into an argument online, but can argument in online environments be studied as a rhetorical act? How does our study of writer, subject, and audience apply when our audience can range from our best friend to someone we may never meet face-to-face? How do claim, support, and assumption apply to a website or a blog? What is the writer–audience relationship like when we can communicate online behind a mask of anonymity? The prose may be informal — at times, it is the digital world's own unique shorthand — but an online argument is still grounded in the elements of argument that shape written discourse.

What the online world can also offer us that books, newspapers, and even television and radio can't — except for an occasional call-in show — is interactivity, and hyperlinks literally let us decide what direction our reading of a text will take.

- **Prereading.** In the context of electronic environments, prereading can be seen as familiarizing yourself with a new way of interacting. If you have never used Twitter or Instagram, prereading is the step where you learn what exactly Twitter or Instagram *is* and how to use it. You might sample a few posts to see if the feed or channel covers topics of interest to you. You might explore a website to see who sponsors it and what content it has to offer.
- **Reading for content.** This step is most relevant to blogs, forums, and websites — all of which you read or watch because you need the information or simply have an interest in the subject, and all of which are more fully developed than most Facebook posts. With social networking sites, the content is about as free of structure as a stream-of-consciousness novel. Social networking sites are your window into the lives of others; therefore, much of the content is the content of their lives, plus their views on what is happening in the world around them, which are often presented as commentary on an article, video, meme, or other argumentative artifact that they share with their friends and followers.
- **Online interaction.** Online environments let readers participate in ways that a static text cannot. On a social network, you can post a question, conduct a poll, make a joke, or simply tell all of your friends what your day has been like. You can comment on a blog or start your own. You can click from link to link to link in an endless chain of connections, controlling the twists and turns of your search. *Interactivity* is one of the two features that have helped the internet revolutionize communication. The other is *hypertextuality*, or the ability to read different levels of a text by means of hyperlinks. There is no single linear way to read a website.

■ **Evaluation.** Evaluation of online communication has to take place in the context of its purpose. Much of it is informal and certainly not polished prose. At the other extreme are websites that businesses depend on for their success, which must be professional in their design and content.

Networking Sites

In educational settings, closed networks are a means of linking students within one class or across several for the purpose of managing learning and providing a place to exchange ideas. Your school may use Blackboard, Canvas, or Moodle as a convenient place to make announcements, explain assignments, and get students communicating with one another. Such systems allow the teacher or students to post to a class discussion board and respond to one another.

On a much larger scale, the term *World Wide Web* is apt in that it is like a spider web. At any given juncture, there are multiple ways to branch off, and the strands of the web form a structure that is unbelievably complex and intricate. Online social networks are like that too. You may follow someone on Instagram because you had a single friend in common or because of a common interest. They may be people that you might never have even struck up a conversation with in person, but your web branches in many directions for many different reasons. Sometimes that social web brings you together online with people with political and social views very different from your own. (They could be some of your best friends.) And since people like to share online the latest meme or the latest attack on liberals or the latest dig at the NRA, you may find yourself on opposite sides of a computer screen from people whose views are diametrically opposed to your own. And then the debate begins.

More common, however, is probably the "bubble" that is created by our social networks, which has been well documented. Because we tend to follow and connect with people with similar interests, our feeds weed out or suppress other perspectives, which gives the false impression that our views are more widely shared than they actually are. As a result, online environments have the danger of becoming an endless loop of false validation.

READING ARGUMENT

Examining Networking Sites

The social media exchange on page 80 shows how even friends can find themselves at odds over a controversial issue. Read the text and analysis, and answer the questions that follow.

"Peaceful" Act of Compassion

WILLIAM WHARTON

William Wharton
William Wharton
June 21, 2013
Another "peaceful" act of compassion from the
religion of "peace"!

**REUTERS/Alamy
Stock Photo**

Taliban behead boy aged 10 over "spying":
Two children killed after taking food from police.
June 21, 2013
www.dailymail.co.uk
- Killed as a warning to villagers not to cooperate
  with Afghan government
- The boys named Khan and Hameedullah were killed on Sunday
- Their bodies and severed heads were left in their village

 👍 Like   💬 Comment   Share

Sam Lane
Sam Lane
June 21, 2013
Unfortunately, Bill, stories like this just foster hate.

William Wharton
June 21, 2013
I don't hate Muslims. My son's best friend is a Muslim and I love
that child like my own. But her religion teaches things that
facilitate such actions as these.

Sam Lane
June 21, 2013
Kinda like the Old Testament?

William Wharton
June 21, 2013
Sam, you know as well as I that such a comparison is utterly false.

Sam Lane
June 21, 2013
I really don't. Crazy stuff in Old Testament that we are told to do.
But we know not to. Most Muslims don't kill people. And even if
Muslims are the enemy . . .
Matthew 4:44 and Romans 12:17-21.

William's sarcasm reveals his actual opinion:

Claim: Islam is not a religion of peace.

Support: The Muslims who killed these children had no compassion.

Assumption: A religion of peace does not kill children with no compassion.

William's claim is valid only if the particular Muslims who killed the children were acting in a way representative of the teachings of their religion. To prove that this is the case, William offers the example of his son's best friend, whose religion "teaches things that facilitate such actions as these." Whether or not you accept William's judgment of Islam depends largely on whether your own experience plus your knowledge of Islam convinces you that what these individuals did was in keeping with the dictates of their religion.

Reading and Discussion Questions

1. What is Sam's claim, support, and assumption? Is his claim valid?
2. How different is Sam's reasoning about Christianity from William's reasoning about Islam?
3. Is there any validity to Sam's comparing the actions of Taliban members to the teachings of the Old Testament?

ARGUMENT ESSENTIALS

Online Environments

Prereading. Familiarize yourself with the particular online environment that is new to you. Explore what it has to offer in content and in function.

Reading for content. Social networking sites provide primarily a source of information about your "friends" and their responses to the world around them. Blogs, feeds, threads, and websites may be worth exploring for information you might need or simply have an interest in.

Online interaction. Online environments let readers participate in ways that a static text cannot. Interactivity is one of the two features that have helped the internet revolutionize communication. The other is hypertextuality, or the ability to read different levels of a text by means of hyperlinks.

Evaluation. Evaluation of online communication has to take place in the context of its purpose.

RESEARCH SKILL ▶ Evaluating Online Sources

In your search for reliable online information, you may not always find it easy to determine who is responsible for a source. A good first step is to check the domain name. Next, ask yourself some questions about the domain as well as the author of the material. Be aware that nonprofit sites are not necessarily free of bias, commercial sites may offer plenty of useful information, and sites with the .edu extension are not always approved by the institution.

- ***.com:*** A commercial site, including corporate-sponsored sites such as nike.com, as well as news sites, such as cnn.com, and personal sites. Do you recognize the name as a brand, news source, or other corporate entity? If not, do a search on the site's name to see if you can find any information about it (keeping in mind, of course, that those sites must also be evaluated). If the site is personal, what can you find out about the author?

- ***.gov:*** A government-sponsored site, maintained by one of the many government agencies, such as whitehouse.gov, supremecourt.gov, and dol.gov (Department of Labor). Although most

government agencies should provide unbiased information, elected officials — from the White House to your local town government — may be selective or biased in the information they provide. What do you know about the party affiliation or political agenda of the source of your information?

- ***.edu:*** A site sponsored by an educational institution, such as clemson.edu. Although an educational institution may be hosting the website, schools often allow professors and students to put up personal pages that may or may not be scholarly or trustworthy. Who is the author of the information, and what do you know about this person?

- ***.org:*** A site sponsored by a nonprofit group, such as heart.org (American Heart Association) or sierraclub.org. Nonprofit organizations often have a particular focus to promote: consumer protection, civil liberties, health, environment, and the like. In addition, they may be sponsored or supported by groups that have particular agendas (check the "About Us" section). Is it possible that the information provided on the site is biased in favor of the sponsor's goals?

Interactive Websites

One of the most useful features of the internet is the ability to find information about almost any subject in a matter of minutes — if not seconds. We'll discuss more fully in Chapter 13 how to evaluate websites; for now, we will focus only on how the interactive feature of websites plays into their attempt to make an argument.

READING ARGUMENT

Examining Interactive Websites

In the following example, we have applied our usual categories to a website — Prereading, Reading for Content, and Evaluation — but we have replaced the category Reading for Rhetorical Strategies with the category Online Interaction to explore the interactive features of the site.

embracerefugees.org

AD COUNCIL

- **Prereading.** It is clear from the site's web address that it is an organization's site. The name "embracerefugees.org" suggests that the site exists to aid refugees, eliciting the image of putting welcoming arms around them. We know from the news that refugees in the twenty-first century have not always been welcomed. The largest groups of refugees in recent years have been from Syria, Iraq, South Sudan, Burma, and, in the West, the Caribbean. Syrian refugees are feared in Eastern Europe and the United States because of the threat of terrorism. The copyright for the site is by the Ad Council, which produces public service advertising. A long list of resources suggests that embracerefugees.org has done substantial research into its subject.

- **Reading for Content.** The home page of the site immediately captures the eye with a picture of five children. One looks a bit uneasy, but four of them are smiling at the camera. The largest text tells us, "Refugees are no different from us." While our inclination might be to think, "Yes, they are!" the next sentence reminds us that all people are alike in that they don't want to live in fear. Next comes a definition of "refugee."

- **Online Interaction.** The image and words mentioned already are all that appear on the home page. How you proceed to read the site depends on how you move through it from here. There are two ways to maneuver through the site. A downward arrow and the words "Learn about the Refugee Experience" indicate that you can scroll down for more information, but dots along the right-hand margin also let you click to go to the same information in any order, if you prefer. Hovering over each reveals these topics: Refugee Journey, Their Stories, Investment, Watch Stories, Community, and Get Involved.

"Their Stories" presents a collage of photographs of different individuals and groups from all over the world, surrounding text that argues, "Refugees Are Resilient." Hovering over each image gives you a brief description and a link to go one level deeper into the site to read a longer description. Each has links to let you share via Facebook, Twitter, or LinkedIn.

"Investment" tries to dispel the myth that refugees are a burden on the countries they enter. Each of the circles at the bottom is a link with information about how refugees give back to the nations they enter: Are Eager to Work, Strive for Independence, Yield Dividends, Spark New Ideas, and Invigorate Our Economy. For each, as for each story above, a link to the source of the information is provided.

"Watch Stories" first reminds us that there are nearly 20 million refugees worldwide and that "59% of Americans believe that the US should do more to help refugees or should continue to offer assistance at the current level." Then comes a screen entitled "What's in Your Bag?" with four videos that you can move among by clicking on the arrows. The first shows four Americans who were told that they had five minutes to fill a bag with whatever they would take if that was all that they could take from their homes. The other three are stories by refugees who found themselves in similar positions when they had to flee their homes but who have succeeded in spite of those circumstances.

"Community" is another collage of individuals that reveals their success in America, with links to more information.

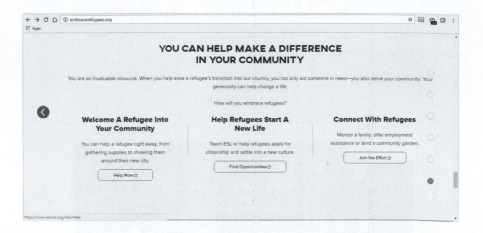

"Get Involved" is a call to action, and provides links that you can click on to find ways of contributing to the move to embrace refugees.

- **Evaluation.** The site is well designed for ease of movement from one level to another. It makes good use of hypertextuality. The color photographs are visually appealing, and you become an active reader whenever you click on a link to find more information. It moves from trying to establish common ground between you and the refugees to defining the term "refugee" to drawing you into the stories of refugees through photographs and additional text, plus videos. A range of types of appeal are designed to make you sympathize with the refugees, and at the end, there are opportunities to find out how to get involved in improving their plight.

Assignments for Critical Reading of Multimodal Arguments

Reading and Discussion Questions

1. Analyze the photograph in Figure 3.1 on page 43. There is no caption other than a title. What caption would you write for it?

2. Find a picture that you believe makes a statement without words. Be prepared to explain your reading of it.

3. Locate a political cartoon, and be prepared to explain to your classmates the assumption or assumptions behind it.

4. Locate a graphic or an annotated map and be prepared to discuss the information it provides and the effectiveness with which it presents that information.

5. Watch (and *listen to*) one of the afternoon television talk shows in which guests discuss a controversial social problem. (Your cable provider's guide, streaming services like Hulu, and online listings often list the subject or a brief description of the episode. Past topics include when parents abduct their children, when children kill children, and when surgery changes patients' lives.) Analyze the discussion, considering the major claims, the most important evidence, and the declared or hidden assumptions. How much did the oral format contribute to the success or failure of the arguments?

6. Watch an episode of either *The Daily Show with Trevor Noah* or *Last Week Tonight with John Oliver*, and discuss how the show, successfully or not, tries to use humor to make serious points about political and/or social issues.

7. Locate an advertisement that you find visually and/or verbally interesting. Using the questions on page 49 as a guide, what sorts of observations can you make about your ad? Exchange ads with a classmate, and discuss whether the two of you respond in the same way to each ad.

Writing Suggestions

1. Choose a photograph, and write an essay explaining how content and structure work together to make an argument.

2. Choose a print ad to analyze, and present your observations in an essay. Be sure to organize your specific observations about the ad around a clear thesis statement.

3. Write a paragraph analyzing a political cartoon.

4. Write a paragraph explaining any bias you see in a news report by CNN or Fox News.

5. Listen to one episode of one of these podcasts: *Left, Right, Center*; *Intelligence Matters*; *Hidden Brain*; *Freakonomics*; or *Intelligence Squared*. Write a review, telling how much you learned about the subject(s) of discussion. Be specific about the features of the show that were either helpful or not helpful to your understanding.

6. Read the speech by Jimmy Carter, "Why I Believe the Mistreatment of Women Is the Number One Human Rights Abuse" (p. 414). Write an essay in which you explain what Carter's main points are about discrimination and violence against women and what support he offers for those main points.

RESEARCH ASSIGNMENT   **Evaluating Online Sources**

Conduct an online search to answer the question "Is vaping more dangerous than smoking cigarettes?" or another question of your choice. Find one source each with domain extensions *.com, .gov, .edu,* and *.org,* for a total of four sources. For each source, answer the following questions:

1. Who is the sponsor of the website? What does the "About Us" section of the site reveal about the sponsor's mission? What else can you find out about the sponsor?

2. Who is the author of the material? Research this person to find any political or corporate affiliations he or she may have.

3. What is the main purpose of the site? Is the group looking for support or donations? Is it attempting to drive advertising? Is it trying to sell a product? Is it scholarly? Does it seem purely informational? How might its purpose affect its content?

Write a paragraph explaining which site you found to be the most reliable and which you determined to be the least reliable, based on the answers to your questions above.

Writing Argument Analysis

Part Two will discuss how to write your own arguments, including how to write arguments to fulfill course assignments. Before we move on to discuss the writing of arguments, consider in what academic contexts you might be called upon to write an analysis of someone else's argument.

The ability to write argument analysis is considered so predictive of success in college that if you took the SAT after March 2016, the optional essay assigned was argument analysis. The prompt would appear in the format below, followed by a short passage to analyze:

As you read the passage below, consider how [the author] uses evidence, such as facts or examples, to support claims.

- Evidence, such as facts or examples, to support claims.
- Reasoning to develop ideas and to connect claims and evidence.
- Stylistic or persuasive elements, such as word choice or appeals to emotion, to add power to the ideas expressed.

Write an essay in which you explain how [the author] builds an argument to persuade [his/her] audience that [author's claim]. In your essay, analyze how [the author] uses one or more of the features listed above (or features of your own choice) to strengthen the logic and persuasiveness of [his/her] argument. Be sure that your analysis focuses on the most relevant features of the passage. Your essay should not explain whether you agree with [the author's] claims, but rather explain how the author builds an argument to persuade [his/her] audience.[1]

---

[1] College Board, "SAT Practice Tests." Inside the Test, accessed October 1, 2019, https://collegereadiness.collegeboard.org/sat/inside-the-test/essay.

This is how the College Board explains what the essay measures:

- Reading: A successful essay shows that you understood the passage, including the interplay of central ideas and important details. It also shows an effective use of textual evidence.
- Analysis: A successful essay shows your understanding of how the author builds an argument by:

  Examining the author's use of evidence, reasoning, and other stylistic and persuasive techniques
  Supporting and developing claims with well-chosen evidence from the passage

- Writing: A successful essay is focused, organized, and precise, with an appropriate style and tone that varies sentence structure and follows the conventions of standard written English.[2]

In your classes, any time you are asked to write on similar topics, you will be writing argument analysis. You will also be writing argument analysis any time you read a similar passage and are asked to evaluate its argument. Sometimes the source to be analyzed will be longer than the short passages provided on the SAT. At other times, the arguments may not be written, but may be oral, like a political speech, or visual, like an art work.

If you take the GMAT exam in preparation for pursuing an MBA or similar degree, this is the type of essay required on the exam:

In the Analysis of an Argument section you will discuss how well reasoned you find a given argument. To do so, you will analyze the line of reasoning and the use of evidence in the argument. . . . Your ideas will need to be organized and fully developed.[3]

It should be more than clear by now how seriously educational institutions take the ability to analyze arguments. In your classes, you may be required to write formal analysis essays, or you may write impromptu essay responses on tests or exams. In theory, there are two parts of argument analysis: content analysis and rhetorical analysis. In practice, the two are virtually inseparable. *Content analysis* is the study of ideas, of what an author says. *Rhetorical analysis* is the study of strategy, of how the author presents the argument. Writing an analysis of an argument almost inevitably requires considering rhetorical strategies in the context of the ideas being discussed.

---

[2] Ibid.

[3] "GMAT: Analytical Writing Assessment Section," Graduate Management Admission Council (GMAC), accessed September 22, 2019, https://www.mba.com/exams/gmat/about-the-gmat-exam/gmat-exam-structure/analytical-writing-assessment.

Writing the Thesis (Main Claim)

When you write an analysis of an argument that you have read, listened to, or seen, you have two major options for your thesis, the main claim of your argument. You may choose to make a factual, nonjudgmental statement about the argument, or you may choose to evaluate it. If you examined the most recent McDonald's commercial and wrote an essay explaining what tactics were used to try to persuade consumers to eat at McDonald's or to try McDonald's newest sandwich, you would be supporting a factual claim, or a **claim of fact**. In contrast, if you evaluated the ad's effectiveness in attracting adult consumers, you would be supporting an evaluative claim, or a **claim of value**. It's the difference between *explaining* Geico's use of a talking gecko in its ads and *praising* that marketing decision. What this means, of course, is that an analysis of a commercial or any other type of argument that you see or read will itself have a claim of fact or a claim of value as its thesis.

What about a **claim of policy**, the third type of claim introduced in Chapter 1? In analyzing an argument, it would be rare to have a thesis that expressed what should or should not be done. Claims of policy are future oriented. They do not look back and express what should have been done in the past, but instead look forward to what should be done in the future. You might write an essay about what McDonald's should do in its future ads, but you would not really be writing an analysis.

Think how claims of fact and claims of value might serve as thesis statements for essays *about* arguments. For our examples, we have drawn on two famous historical arguments. Abraham Lincoln's Gettysburg Address is the subject of an essay by Charles Adams, "Lincoln's Logic," which supports a claim of value:

> Lincoln's address did not fit the world of his day. It reflected his logic, which was based on a number of errors and falsehoods.

Writing the Claim for Analysis

	CLAIM OF FACT	CLAIM OF VALUE
Analyzing one argument	Analyze it objectively.	Evaluate it.
Analyzing two or more arguments	Compare and contrast objectively.	Evaluate them in relation to each other.

An objective analysis of the speech, based on a claim of fact, might explain the oration in the context of its time or Lincoln's use of poetic language.

Consider how your thesis looks different when you are making a *statement* about a document than when you are making a *judgment*:

Claims of fact: (statement)	The Declaration of Independence bases its claim on two kinds of support: factual evidence and appeals to the values of its audience.
	As a logical pattern of argument, the Declaration of Independence is largely deductive.
Claims of value: (judgment)	Jefferson's clear, elegant, formal prose remains a masterpiece of English prose and persuades us that we are reading an important document.
	The document's impact is lessened for modern readers because several significant terms are not defined.

In these examples based on the Gettysburg Address and the Declaration of Independence, we have been looking at one document at a time and thus at a single argument. At times, you will want to compare two (or more) arguments, synthesizing their ideas. Again, there are two basic types of thesis that you might choose to support: those that *objectively analyze* the points of comparison or contrast between the two, and those that *evaluate* the two in relationship to each other. If you wrote claims about how the two pieces compare, they might look like these:

Claims of fact:	Where Jefferson based his argument primarily on logical appeal, Lincoln depended primarily on emotional appeal.
	Because Lincoln's purpose was to dedicate a cemetery, he left implicit most of his references to the political situation that was on the minds of his listeners. Because Jefferson knew he was justifying rebellion for King George III but also for the future, he spelled out explicitly why the colonies were breaking with England.
Claims of value:	Lincoln's address is a period piece that recalls a dark chapter in American history, but Jefferson's Declaration has had a much greater impact as an inspiration for other reform movements worldwide.
	Different as the two historical documents are, both the Gettysburg Address and the Declaration of Independence were effective in achieving their respective purposes.

Planning the Structure

When your purpose in writing argument analysis is to support a factual claim, you will most likely use a very simple and direct form of organization called *defending the main idea*. In all forms of organization, you need to defend your main idea, or claim, with support; in this case, the support will come from the argument or arguments you are writing about.

At times, your claim may set up the organization of your essay, as was the case with the first example about the Declaration of Independence:

> The Declaration of Independence bases its claim on two kinds of support: factual evidence and appeals to the values of its audience.

The body of an essay with this thesis would most likely have two main divisions: one about factual evidence, providing examples, and the other about appeals to values, also providing examples. The subject and the length of the essay would determine how many paragraphs there would be in each of the main divisions.

Example: Claim Announces Organization

Introduction with Thesis (Main Idea)

Support from the text (Declaration of Independence) Factual evidence and examples

Support from the text (Declaration of Independence) Appeals to values

Conclusion

The other thesis about the Declaration of Independence does not suggest such an obvious structure. An essay based on that thesis would need to explain how the Declaration is an example of deductive reasoning, most likely by first establishing what generalization the document is based on and then what specifics Jefferson uses to prove that the colonists' situation fits that generalization.

Remember that when you compare or contrast two arguments, there will be two basic patterns to choose from for structuring the essay. One, often called **point-by-point comparison**, discusses the first point about Subject A and Subject B together before moving on to the second point, where again both subjects are discussed:

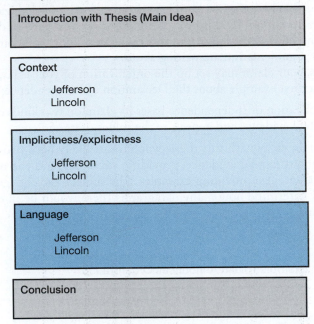

Example: Point-by-Point Comparison

> **Introduction with Thesis (Main Idea)**
>
> **Context**
> > Jefferson
> > Lincoln
>
> **Implicitness/explicitness**
> > Jefferson
> > Lincoln
>
> **Language**
> > Jefferson
> > Lincoln
>
> **Conclusion**

The second, often called **parallel order comparison**, focuses roughly half the essay on Subject A and then the other half on Subject B. The points made in each half should be parallel and should be presented in the same order:

Example: Parallel Order Comparison

> **Introduction with Thesis (Main Idea)**
>
> **Jefferson**
> > Context
> > Implicitness/explicitness
> > Language
>
> **Lincoln**
> > Context
> > Implicitness/explicitness
> > Language
>
> **Conclusion**

Remember that the subject and length of the essay will determine how many paragraphs each part of the outline will take.

ARGUMENT ESSENTIALS
Planning the Structure

- **Analyzing one argument:** Organize essay according to supporting points.
- **Analyzing two or more arguments:** Organize essay according to a point-by-point comparison pattern or to a parallel order comparison pattern.

Providing Support

In analyzing any argument, you will need to understand the argument and to make it clear to your readers that you do. You cannot write a clear explanation or a fair evaluation if you do not have a clear understanding of your subject. You will need to look closely at the piece to recall what specific words or ideas led you to the thesis statement that you have chosen to support.

Your support for your thesis will come from the text or texts you are writing about in the form of summary, paraphrase, or quotations. The ability to summarize, paraphrase, and quote material from your source is necessary in writing about arguments, but it is also essential in writing your own arguments, especially those that require research.

Summarizing

A summary involves shortening the original passage as well as putting it into your own words. It gives the gist of the passage, including the important points, while leaving out details. What makes summarizing difficult is that it requires you to capture often long and complex texts in just a few lines or a short paragraph. To summarize well, you need to imagine yourself as the author of the piece you are summarizing and be true to the ideas the author is expressing, even when those ideas conflict with your personal point of view. You must then move smoothly from being a careful reader to being a writer who, in your own words, re-creates another's thoughts.

We summarize for many reasons: to let our boss know the basics of what we have been doing or to tell a friend why she should or should not see a movie. In your classes, you are often asked to summarize articles or books, and even when this is not an explicit part of an assignment, the ability to summarize is usually expected. That is, when you are instructed to analyze an essay or to compare and contrast two novels, central to this work is the ability to carefully comprehend and re-create authors' ideas. If you summarized the Declaration of Independence, one of the works used in the examples in this chapter, your summary might look like this:

> The stated purpose of the Declaration of Independence is to explain why the colonists felt it necessary to reject government by England and establish a new government. The document's list of the "repeated injuries and usurpations" by the King of England comprises the majority of the document. The colonists' petitions for redress have been answered by additional injuries. Unanswered appeals to the colonists' "British brethren" have forced them to separate from them and declare them "Enemies in War, in Peace Friends." The document closes with the declaration that the colonies are "Free and Independent States" owing no allegiance to the British crown.

See "Summarizing" (p. 31) in Chapter 2 for a more detailed treatment of summary.

Paraphrasing

Paraphrasing involves restating the content of an original source in your own words. It differs from summarizing in that a paraphrase is roughly the same length as the passage it paraphrases instead of a condensation of a longer passage. You can use paraphrasing when you want to capture the idea but there is nothing about the wording that makes repeating it necessary. You may also use it when the idea can be made clearer by rephrasing it or when the style is markedly different from your own. Here is an example:

> Randolph Warren, a victim of the thalidomide disaster himself and founder and executive director of the Thalidomide Victims Association of Canada, reports that it is estimated 10,000 to 12,000 deformed babies were born to mothers who took thalidomide. (40)

There is no single sentence on page 40 of the Warren article that both provides the estimate of the number of affected babies and identifies Warren as one of them. Both the ideas were important, but neither of them was worded in such a unique way that a direct quote was needed. Therefore, a paraphrase was the logical choice. In this case, the writer correctly documents the paraphrase using Modern Language Association (MLA) style.

ARGUMENT ESSENTIALS
Providing Support

Support your claim with information from your source(s) in the form of

- **Summary** — a shortened version of the original, in your own words
- **Paraphrase** — a version of the original in your own words that is about the same length as the original
- **Quotation** — exact words from the original, placed in quotation marks

Provide documentation, usually the author and page number, whenever you use someone else's words or ideas.

Quoting

You may want to quote passages or phrases from your sources if they express an idea in words more effective than your own. In reading a source, you may come across a statement that provides succinct, irrefutable evidence for an issue you wish to support. If the author of this statement is a professional in his or her field, someone with a great deal of authority on the subject, it would be appropriate to quote that author. Suppose, during the course of a student's research for her paper, she found several sources that agree that women in the military who are denied combat experience are, as a result, essentially being denied a chance at promotion to the highest ranks. Others argue that such considerations should not be a deciding factor in assigning women to combat. To represent the latter of these two positions, the student might choose to use a quotation from an authority in the field, using APA style:

> Elaine Donnelly, president of the Center for Military Readiness, wrote, "Equal opportunity is important, but the armed forces exist to defend the country. If there is a conflict between career opportunities and military necessity, the needs of the military must come first" (as qtd. in "Women in the Military," 2000).

It is especially important in argumentative writing to establish a source's authority on the subject under discussion. The most common way of doing this is to use that person's name and position of authority to introduce the quotation, as in the previous example. It is correct in both MLA and APA styles to provide the author's name in parentheses at the end of the quoted material, but that type of documentation precludes lending to the quote the weight of its having come from an authority. Most readers will not know who Donnelly is just by seeing her name in parentheses. Your writing will always have more power if you establish the authority of each author from whose work you quote, paraphrase, or summarize. To establish authority, you may refer to the person's position, institutional affiliation, publications, or some other similar "claim to fame."

Here is another example, using MLA style:

> According to Alicia Oglesby, assistant director of school and college counseling at Bishop McNamara High School in Maryland and co-author of *Interrupting Racism: Equity and Social Justice in School Counseling*, "Students who feel supported by diversity, equity, and inclusion efforts are more likely to feel safe. But because the majority often takes safety for granted, these efforts must be intentional, systemic, and honest" (49).

Notice that once the name of the author being cited has been mentioned in the writer's own text, it does not have to be repeated in the parentheses.

RESEARCH SKILL ⟩ Incorporating Quotations into Your Text

There are three primary means of linking a supporting quotation to your own text. Remember that in each case, the full citation for the source will be listed alphabetically by the author's name in the list of works cited at the end of the paper, or by title if no author is given. The number in parentheses is the page of that source on which the quotation appears. The details of what appears in parentheses are covered in Chapter 15 in the discussion of APA (American Psychological Association) and MLA (Modern Language Association) documentation styles.

- **Make a brief quotation a grammatical part of your own sentence.** In this case, you do not separate the quotation from your sentence with a comma, unless there is another reason for the comma, and you do not capitalize the first word of the quotation, unless there is another reason for doing so. There may be times when you have to change the tense of a verb, in brackets, to make the quotation fit smoothly into your text or when you need to make other small changes, always in brackets.

Examples:
APA style
James Rachels (1976), University Professor of Philosophy at the University of Alabama at Birmingham and author of several books on moral philosophy, explained that animals' right to liberty derives from "a more basic right not to have one's interests needlessly harmed" (p. 210).

MLA style
James Rachels, University Professor of Philosophy at the University of Alabama at Birmingham and author of several books on moral philosophy, explains that animals' right to liberty derives from "a more basic right not to have one's interests needlessly harmed" (210).

- **Use a traditional speech tag such as "he says" or "she wrote."** This is the most common way of introducing a quotation. Be sure to put a comma after the tag and to begin the quotation with a capital letter. At the end of the quotation, close the quotation, add the page number and any other necessary information in parentheses, and then add the period.

Students are sometimes at a loss as to what sorts of verbs to use in these tag statements. Try using active, descriptive verbs, such as terms from this list or others like them. Remember that in writing about a printed or electronic text, it is customary in APA style to use past or present perfect tense; in MLA style, write in present tense unless there is a compelling reason to use past tense.

argue	implore
ask	insist
assert	proclaim
conclude	question
continue	reply
counter	respond
declare	state
explain	suggest

Examples:
APA style
James Rachels (1976), University Professor of Philosophy at the University of Alabama at Birmingham and author of several books on moral philosophy, wrote, "The right to liberty — the right to be free of external constraints on one's actions — may then be seen as derived from a more basic right not to have one's interests needlessly harmed" (p. 210).

MLA style
James Rachels, University Professor of Philosophy at the University of Alabama at Birmingham and author of several books on moral philosophy, writes,

continued

"The right to liberty — the right to be free of external constraints on one's actions — may then be seen as derived from a more basic right not to have one's interests needlessly harmed" (210).

- **Use a colon to separate the quotation from a complete sentence that introduces it.** This can help add variety to your sentences.

Examples:
APA style

For example, the Zurich Zoo's Dr. Heini Hediger (1985) protested that it is absurd to attribute human qualities to animals at all, but he nevertheless resorted to a human analogy: "Wild animals in the zoo rather resemble estate owners. Far from desiring to escape and regain their freedom, they are only bent on defending the space they inhabit and keeping it safe from invasion" (p. 9).

MLA style

The late Ulysses S. Seal III, founder of the Conservation Breeding Specialist Group and of a "computer dating service" for mateless animals, acknowledges the subordinate position species preservation plays in budgeting decisions: "Zoos have been established primarily as recreational institutions and are only secondarily developing programs in conservation, education, and research" (74).

Integrating Your Sources

Chapter 15 will provide additional information about documenting sources, but you should start now documenting your use of others' work, even when the only sources you use are essays from this textbook. The single most important thing to remember is why you need to inform your reader about your use of sources. Once it is clear from your writing that an idea or some language came from a source and thus is not your own original thought or language, full documentation provides the reader with a means of identifying and, if necessary, locating your source. If you do not indicate your source, your reader will naturally assume that the ideas and the language are yours. It is careless to forget to give credit to your sources. It is dishonest to intentionally take credit for what is not your own intellectual property. Note, though, that the convention is for authors of magazine articles and websites not to provide page numbers for their sources in the way that you will be expected to do.

The following Strategies for Summary, Paraphrase, and Quotation box provides the general guidelines for documenting your use of sources.

Strategies for Summary, Paraphrase, and Quotation

1. **Give credit for any ideas you get from others**, not only for wording you get from them.
2. **Identify the author and the location of ideas that you summarize.** A summary is the condensing of a longer passage into a shorter one, using your own words.
3. **Identify the author and the location of ideas that you paraphrase.** A paraphrase is a rewording of another author's idea into your own words. A paraphrased passage is roughly the same length as the original.

4. **Identify the author and the location of language that you quote.** A quotation is the copying of the exact wording of your source and is placed in quotation marks. You cannot change anything inside quotation marks, with these exceptions:

- If there is a portion of the quotation that is not relevant to the point that you are making and that can be omitted without distorting the author's meaning, you may indicate an omission of a portion of the quotation with an ellipsis (. . .). If there is a sentence break within the portion you are omitting, add a fourth period to the ellipsis to so indicate.

- If you need to make a very slight change in the quote to make the quote fit grammatically into your own text or to avoid confusion, and if the change does not distort the author's meaning, you may make that slight change and place the changed portion in square brackets ([ ]). This method is used primarily to change the tense of a quoted passage to match that of your text or to identify a person identified in the quotation only by a pronoun.

5. **Make use of in-text or parenthetical documentation.** While a complete bibliographical listing for each work summarized, paraphrased, or quoted in your text is included in a Works Cited or References list at the end of your paper, each is also identified exactly at the point in the text where you use the source. If you are using the MLA system of documentation, the system most commonly used in the humanities, immediately following the sentence in which you use material from a source, you need to add in parentheses the author's name and the page number on which the material you are using appeared in the original source. However, since the credibility of your sources is critical in argumentative writing, it is even better to name the source in your own sentence and to identify the position or experience that makes that person a reliable source for the subject being discussed. In that case, you do not need to repeat the author's name in the parentheses. In fact, anytime the author's name

is clear from the context, you do not need to repeat it in the parentheses.

Acceptable: The mall has been called "a common experience for the majority of American youth" (Kowinski 3).

Better: According to William Severini Kowinski, author of *The Malling of America*, "The mall is a common experience for the majority of American youth" (3).

In the APA system, the system most commonly used in the social sciences, in-text or parenthetical documentation is handled a bit differently because the citation includes the year of publication. The most basic forms are these:

The mall has been called "a common experience for the majority of American youth" (Kowinski, 1985, p. 3).

Kowinski (1985) writes, "The mall is a common experience for the majority of American youth" (p. 3).

6. **These examples show only the most basic forms for documenting your sources.** Some works will have more than one author. Sometimes you will be using more than one work by the same author. Usually websites do not have page numbers. Long quotations need to be handled differently than short ones. For all questions about documenting your use of sources not covered here, see Chapter 15.

Note: Unless your instructor indicates otherwise, use the page numbers on which your source appears *in this textbook* when summarizing, paraphrasing, or quoting from it instead of going back to the page numbers of the original. Also, unless your instructor indicates otherwise, use this model for listing in your Works Cited page a work reprinted here:

Ingram, James W., III. "Electoral College Is Best Way to Choose U.S. President." *Elements of Argument: A Text and Reader*, 13th ed., edited by Annette T. Rottenberg and Donna Haisty Winchell, Bedford/St. Martin's, 2021, pp. 101–3.

Reading and Practicing Argument Analysis

READING ARGUMENT

Examining a Written Argument

Use the annotations and the questions at the end to analyze the following essay.

Electoral College Is Best Way to Choose U.S. President
JAMES W. INGRAM III

The Electoral College is once again under siege. Critics arguing that it is obsolete and undemocratic have greatly overestimated the benefits of electing presidents by popular vote plurality.

> Ingram's statement of his main claim.

One key reason the founders of the United States of America created the Electoral College was the possibility that once George Washington retired or died, no other candidate could garner majority support from such a diverse nation. Their concern was well-founded.

> Ingram's thesis refers to plurality, but here he refers to majority.

Of the 49 presidential elections the United States has held since 1824, when many states began allowing the public to choose electors, a full 18 contests have not given any candidate a popular vote majority.

> But someone did win the popular vote, just not by a majority. Majority = more than 50% of the votes.

The electoral vote has only reversed a popular vote majority once, in 1876, an election called into question by vote fraud. In 1888, when the person who won the electoral vote had a smaller share of the popular vote, no candidate won a popular majority.

> But someone who had more popular votes lost to the winner of the electoral college.

5   Likewise in 2000 and 2016, the most recent elections in which critics claim the Electoral College subverted the people's will, neither Hillary Clinton nor Al Gore won popular vote majorities. Clinton won 48 percent compared to Donald Trump's 46 percent; Gore won 48.4 percent to George W. Bush's 47.9 percent. Clinton and Gore outpolled their opponents, but the majority supported someone else for president.

> What difference does it make if they did not win the majority? They received more popular votes. Good statistics, but they work against Ingram's argument.

The Electoral College usually amplifies the people's voice, electing the candidate who wins most states and votes. This allows the winner to claim a mandate and lead the country.

James Ingram teaches political science at San Diego State University and helped reform the mayoral systems of Los Angeles and San Diego. His article appeared in the *San Diego Union Tribune* on January 13, 2017.

But there is another option — require the president to gain a plurality of the popular vote.

Had the founders required presidents to gain a majority of the popular vote rather than of the Electoral College, over 30 percent of our presidential elections would have been decided by the U.S. House. In both 2000 and 2016, the Republican House majorities surely would have chosen the Republican candidate, the same one who won the electoral vote.

The House should not decide the election.

The problem with House selection is that this raises questions of legitimacy. In 1824, no one won an Electoral College or a popular vote majority. When the House chose John Quincy Adams over plurality winner Andrew Jackson, the latter denounced the "corrupt bargain," undermining Adams' presidency.

Every presidential election which lacked a popular majority featured significant third party candidates. Gary Johnson in 2016, Ralph Nader in 2000, and Ross Perot in 1992 and 1996 are prominent examples.

Third-party candidates highlight neglected issues, but increase the   10
probability nobody wins a majority. The problem with electing the candidate who achieves only a popular vote plurality is that someone supported by a small minority of people and states could win, provided everyone else has even fewer votes.

The earlier examples seem to dispute this.

By mandating an Electoral College majority rather than a popular vote plurality, the Constitution requires a presidential candidate to win more states. Since over half of the U.S.'s population lives in the nine largest states, plurality rules would instead allow presidents to win with only a small minority of states.

What's more important, how many states vote for the winner or how many people?

But since the nine most populous states have only 240 of the needed 270 electoral votes, the current system requires candidates to be competitive in more states. Clinton won almost 3 million more votes than Trump, but she won merely 19.75 states and D.C., while Trump won 30.25 states (they split Maine).

Alexander Hamilton defended the Electoral College in Federalist Paper No. 68, stating it was intended to ensure presidents would have "the esteem and confidence of the whole Union, or of so considerable a portion of it as would be necessary." Hamilton called it "unsafe to permit less than a majority" of the states' electors to select the president.

Hamilton is referring to the majority of electors, not voters.

Our present system has only elected the candidate who won fewer states thrice, in 1824, 1960 and 1976. The two main candidates tied in the number of states won in 1848 and 1880, but both times the contestant with more popular support won the electoral vote. In every other presidential plebiscite, the winner carried a majority of states.

If presidents only needed plurality support, the victor might regularly be the   15
candidate who won fewer states. This would weaken presidential leadership.

The Electoral College prevents smaller states from being ignored in presidential elections. The states' diversity should be just as fully represented as other dimensions of diversity in our multicultural republic.

Electing presidents by popular vote is a bad idea. The only big countries using this method are France, Mexico and Russia. Russia selected Vladimir Putin through popular vote majority. Are these three countries really better governed than America?

Raises the question: Are Russian elections really legitimate elections?

If our Electoral College mechanism for choosing presidents is imperfect, it is because human beings have never devised a perfect system. But in 11 score and 7 years we have chosen 45 presidents to lead our country. What isn't broken doesn't need fixing.

That begs the question whether we chose the best presidents. And Ingram hasn't proven that the system isn't broken.

Reading, Writing, and Discussion Questions

1. What is the difference between a plurality and a majority? Why are the definitions of those two terms critical to James Ingram's argument?
2. Reread the second sentence of the essay. What is the benefit of electing the President by popular vote plurality? Why does Ingram contend that that the plurality suggestion is highly overrated?
3. Where does Ingram most effectively make use of statistics to make his point?
4. In paragraph 5, Ingram states that in the 2000 and 2016 elections, "Clinton and Gore outpolled their opponents, but the majority supported someone else for president." Is that statement true or false? Explain.
5. In paragraph 7, Ingram writes, "Had the founders required presidents to gain a majority of the popular vote rather than of the Electoral College, over 30 percent of our presidential elections would have been decided by the U.S. House." Why is this an either/or fallacy? In other words, are there only two options? (See Chapter 12 for help identifying fallacies.)
6. What is Ingram's reason for believing that it is best that the president be elected by a majority of the states?
7. Do Ingram's statistics support his contention that a small minority could decide the election if popular vote were the deciding factor? Explain.
8. Do you agree with Ingram's belief that "[e]lecting presidents by popular vote is a bad idea"? Why or why not? Does it matter in your reasoning that the only large countries doing so are France, Mexico, and Russia?
9. Write an essay explaining how Ingram builds his argument in his essay.
10. Write an essay in which you explain why you agree or disagree with Ingram's argument.

Practice: Analyzing a Multimodal Argument

Read the captioned graphics on pages 104–5, and answer the questions that appear at the end.

The Science Facts about Autism and Vaccines
HEALTHCARE MANAGEMENT

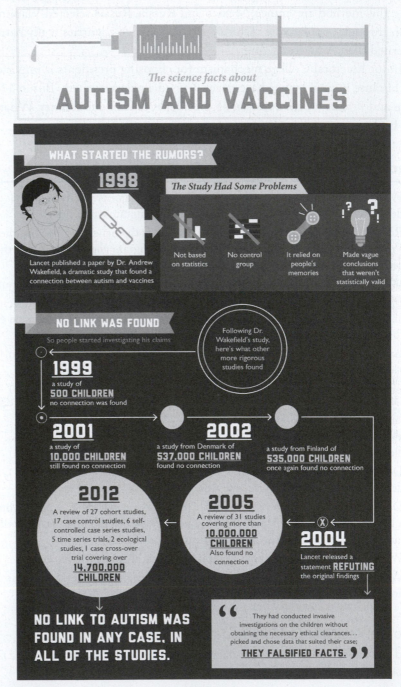

The science facts about
AUTISM AND VACCINES

WHAT STARTED THE RUMORS?

1998

The Study Had Some Problems

Not based on statistics

No control group

It relied on people's memories

Made vague conclusions that weren't statistically valid

Lancet published a paper by Dr. Andrew Wakefield, a dramatic study that found a connection between autism and vaccines

NO LINK WAS FOUND

So people started investigating his claims

Following Dr. Wakefield's study, here's what other more rigorous studies found

1999
a study of
500 CHILDREN
no connection was found

2001
a study of
10,000 CHILDREN
still found no connection

2002
a study from Denmark of
537,000 CHILDREN
found no connection

a study from Finland of
535,000 CHILDREN
once again found no connection

2012
A review of 27 cohort studies, 17 case control studies, 6 self-controlled case series studies, 5 time series trials, 2 ecological studies, 1 case cross-over trial covering over
14,700,000 CHILDREN

2005
A review of 31 studies covering more than
10,000,000 CHILDREN
Also found no connection

2004
Lancet released a statement **REFUTING** the original findings

NO LINK TO AUTISM WAS FOUND IN ANY CASE, IN ALL OF THE STUDIES.

"They had conducted invasive investigations on the children without obtaining the necessary ethical clearances... picked and chose data that suited their case; **THEY FALSIFIED FACTS.**"

NowSourcing, Inc. and healthcare-management-degree.net

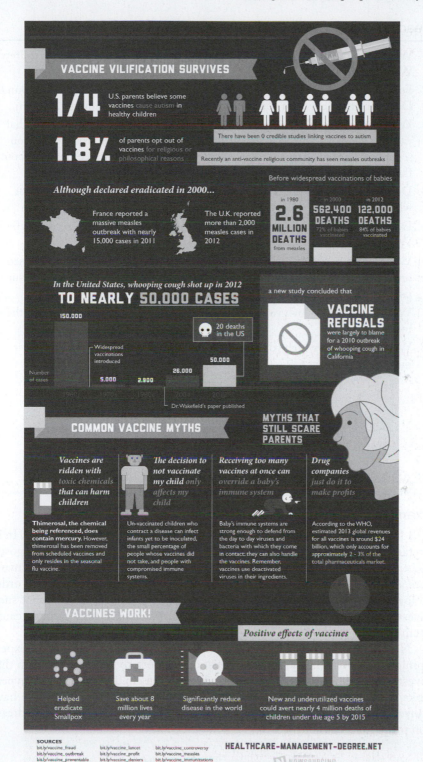

VACCINE VILIFICATION SURVIVES

1/4 U.S. parents believe some vaccines cause autism in healthy children

1.8% of parents opt out of vaccines for religious or philosophical reasons

There have been 0 credible studies linking vaccines to autism

Recently an anti-vaccine religious community has seen measles outbreaks

Before widespread vaccinations of babies

Although declared eradicated in 2000...

France reported a massive measles outbreak with nearly 15,000 cases in 2011

The U.K. reported more than 2,000 measles cases in 2012

in 1980 **2.6 MILLION DEATHS** from measles

in 2000 **562,400 DEATHS** 72% of babies vaccinated

in 2012 **122,000 DEATHS** 84% of babies vaccinated

In the United States, whooping cough shot up in 2012

TO NEARLY 50,000 CASES

150,000

Widespread vaccinations introduced

Number of cases

5,000 **2,900** 26,000 50,000

20 deaths in the US

Dr. Wakefield's paper published

a new study concluded that

VACCINE REFUSALS
were largely to blame for a 2010 outbreak of whooping cough in California

COMMON VACCINE MYTHS

MYTHS THAT STILL SCARE PARENTS

Vaccines are ridden with *toxic chemicals that can harm children*

Thimerosal, the chemical being referenced, does contain mercury. However, thimerosal has been removed from scheduled vaccines and only resides in the seasonal flu vaccine.

The decision to not vaccinate my child *only affects my child*

Un-vaccinated children who contract a disease can infect infants yet to be inoculated, the small percentage of people whose vaccines did not take, and people with compromised immune systems.

Receiving too many vaccines at once can *override a baby's immune system*

Baby's immune systems are strong enough to defend from the day to day viruses and bacteria with which they come in contact; they can also handle the vaccines. Remember, vaccines use deactivated viruses in their ingredients.

Drug companies *just do it to make profits*

According to the WHO, estimated 2013 global revenues for all vaccines is around $24 billion, which only accounts for approximately 2 - 3% of the total pharmaceuticals market.

VACCINES WORK!

Positive effects of vaccines

Helped eradicate Smallpox

Save about 8 million lives every year

Significantly reduce disease in the world

New and underutilized vaccines could avert nearly 4 million deaths of children under the age 5 by 2015

SOURCES
bit.ly/vaccine_fraud
bit.ly/vaccine_outbreak
bit.ly/vaccine_preventable
bit.ly/vaccine_facts
bit.ly/vaccine_lancet
bit.ly/vaccine_profit
bit.ly/vaccine_deniers
bit.ly/vaccine_parents
bit.ly/vaccine_controversy
bit.ly/vaccine_measles
bit.ly/vaccine_immunizations
bit.ly/vaccine_anti

HEALTHCARE-MANAGEMENT-DEGREE.NET

NOWSOURCING

NowSourcing, Inc. and healthcare-management-degree.net

Reading, Writing, and Discussion Questions

1. What were the problems with the research reported in *Lancet* by Dr. Andrew Wakefield in 1998?

2. Follow the timeline from 1999 to 2012. What have subsequent studies found? Does the graphic build a convincing argument for those findings? Explain.

3. What are some of the consequences of the belief that some people have that vaccines cause autism? What specific support for the existence of those consequences does the graphic offer? How do the visuals reinforce the text about these consequences?

4. Do you find the arguments against the vaccine myths convincing? Why or why not?

5. Do you find the overall argument being made in this infographic convincing? Why or why not?

6. Write a paragraph in which you support one conclusion you can draw based on the evidence presented in the infographic and use specifics from it to support your topic sentence.

7. Write an essay in which you analyze the argument that is being made in the infographic.

8. Write an essay in which you evaluate the effectiveness of the infographic in making its argument.

READING ARGUMENT

Examining an Argument Analysis

The following article is an example of argument analysis in simple form. In it, Stefan Andreasson, who teaches comparative politics, analyzes one proposed solution to the negative impact fossil fuels have on the environment. Investors are encouraged to sell off investments in fossil fuel companies in order to lower the demand for fossil fuels. Andreasson, however, argues that such divestment will not reduce greenhouse gas emissions but may actually cause them to rise.

Notice that Andreasson uses extensive and carefully documented expert opinion, much of it in the form of statistical support, to back up his claim that divestment will not solve the problem. Andreasson cited his support as hyperlinks in the original publication, which is common for the genre. (We have converted the sources to endnotes here.) In the last four paragraphs, Andreasson proposes a solution.

Fossil Fuel Divestment Will Increase Carbon Emissions, Not Lower Them

STEFAN ANDREASSON

A global campaign encouraging individuals, organizations and institutional investors to sell off investments in fossil fuel companies is gathering pace. According to 350.org, eleven trillion dollars (U.S.) has already been divested worldwide.[1]

But, while it may seem a logical strategy, divestment will not lower demand for fossil fuels, which is the key to reducing greenhouse gas emissions. In fact, it may even cause emissions to rise.

At first sight, the argument for divestment seems straightforward. Fossil fuel companies are the main contributors to the majority of CO_2 emissions causing global warming.[2] Twenty fossil fuel companies alone have contributed thirty-five percent of all energy-related carbon dioxide and methane emissions since 1965.[3]

The argument goes that squeezing the flow of investment into fossil fuel companies will either bring their demise, or force them to drastically transform their business models. It makes sense for investors, too, as they avoid the risk of holding "stranded assets"—fossil fuel reserves that will become worthless as they can no longer be exploited.

5   For companies heavily invested in coal—the most polluting fossil fuel—this rings true. Although new coal plants are still being constructed in countries such as China, India, and Indonesia, predictions by major energy agencies and industry alike indicate a steep decline in its contribution to the global energy supply.[4] With cleaner alternatives readily available, coal is no longer considered a safe long-term investment—and widespread divestment will only add to this sentiment.

When it comes to oil and natural gas, however, the picture looks quite different. Oil is used for a much wider range of products[5] and processes than is coal, while the cleaner reputation of natural gas gives it significant appeal as a "bridge fuel" to a zero carbon economy, whether rightly or not.[6] As a result, the push for oil and gas divestment is likely to have unintended consequences.

Divestment Troubles

The primary targets of the divestment movement are international oil companies (IOCs)—private corporations that are headquartered in Western countries and listed on public stock exchanges. ExxonMobil, Chevron, Royal Dutch Shell, BP, and Total are among the private oil "supermajors."

Recent research suggests that divestment can reduce the flow of investment into these companies.[7] But even if the divestment movement were successful in reducing the economic power of these companies, IOCs currently only produce about ten percent of the world's oil.[8]

The rest is mostly produced by national oil companies (NOCs)—state-owned behemoths such as Saudi Aramco, National Iranian Oil

Stefan Andreasson is a senior lecturer in comparative politics at Queen's University in Belfast. He has published widely in journals such as *Political Studies*, *Political Geography*, *Business & Society*, *Third World Quarterly*, *Democratization*, and *Commonwealth & Comparative Politics*. This article appeared in *The Conversation* on November 25, 2019.

Company, China National Petroleum Corporation and Petroleos de Venezuela, located mostly in low and middle income countries.

10   Given that NOCs are less transparent about their operations than are IOCs,[9] and that many of them are also headquartered in authoritarian countries, they are less exposed to pressure from civil society. As a result, they are "dangerously under-scrutinized," according to the Natural Resource Governance Institute.[10]

As they are state-owned, they are also not directly exposed to pressure from shareholders. Even the imminent public listing of Saudi Aramco will only offer one and half percent of the company,[11] and this will mainly come from domestic and emerging markets, which tend to impose much less pressure to value environmental issues. Environmental groups have urged Western multinational banks not to invest in the Saudi company.[12]

This means that while global demand for natural gas[13] and oil[14] is still rising, and investments are insufficient to meet future demand,[15] divestment pressures are unlikely to impact the business plans of NOCs. As a result, instead of reducing global fossil fuel production, the divestment movement will simply force IOCs to cede market share to NOCs.

If anything, this would cause CO_2 emissions to rise. The carbon footprints of NOCs per unit of fuel produced are on average bigger than those of IOCs.[16]

IOCs are also generally better placed and more willing than are NOCs to reduce the carbon intensity of their products and support the transition to renewable energy. They have, for example, led the way among oil companies in research into capturing and storing carbon, even if results have so far proven elusive.

15   In a nutshell, the divestment movement will not reduce demand for oil and gas. It will transfer the supply of fossil fuel to companies that are more polluting, less transparent, less sensitive to societal pressures, and less committed to addressing the climate crisis.[18]

Missing the Mark

The divestment movement is understandably enjoying widespread appeal in a time of climate emergency. But by targeting the low-hanging fruit that are IOCs, the movement misses the more complex question of how to actually reduce the global demand for fossil fuels.

To achieve that goal, we'd be better off creating a regulatory environment that forces both IOCs and NOCs to redirect their energies. For example, eliminating fossil fuel subsidies[19] and putting a price on carbon[20] would make heavily investing in renewables — already cheaper to produce than fossil fuels[21] — more attractive for all energy companies.

Such changes could also generate nearly three trillion dollars (U.S.) by 2030 for governments worldwide.[22] These funds could be used to massively scale up renewables,[23] prioritize the development of energy storage to address the intermittent nature of such power, and improve energy efficiency in industry, transport[ation], and housing — which will make fossil fuels increasingly redundant.

While IOCs now produce much less fossil fuel than they used to, they still have a huge amount of expertise[24] that could be applied to the energy transition.[25] In my view, rather than transferring power to less environmentally conscious NOCs, we should make use of them.

20   As for those with shares in fossil fuel companies: exercise your powers as a shareholder to pressure them to support the energy transition as constructively and ethically as possible. Your influence matters.

Notes

1. Monica Tyler-Davies, "A New Fossil Free Milestone: $11 Trillion Has Been Committed to Divest from Fossil Fuels," *350.org*, September 8, 2019, http://350 .org/11-trillion-divested/.

2. "Scientific Consensus: Earth's Climate Is Warming," Global Climate Change: Vital Signs of the Planet, NASA, last modified January 28, 2020, http://climate.nasa.gov /scientific-consensus/.

3. Matthew Taylor and Jonathan Watts, "Revealed: The 20 Firms behind a Third of All Carbon Emissions," *The Guardian*, October 9, 2019, http://www.theguardian .com/environment/2019/oct/09/revealed -20-firms-third-carbon-emissions.

4. McKinsey, *Global Energy Perspective 2019: Reference Case*, January 2019, https://www .mckinsey.com/~/media/McKinsey/Industries /Oil%20and%20Gas/Our%20Insights/Global %20Energy%20Perspective%202019 /McKinsey-Energy-Insights-Global-Energy -Perspective-2019_Reference-Case-Summary .ashx.

5. "What Are Petroleum Products, and What Is Petroleum Used For?," Independent Statistics and Analysis, U. S. Energy Information Administration, last modified May 31, 2019, https://www.eia.gov/tools/faqs/faq.php?id =41&t=6.

6. Aled Jones, "The EU Wants to Fight Climate Change—So Why Is It Spending Billions on a Gas Pipeline?," *The Conversation*, February 9, 2018, https://theconversation.com/the-eu -wants-to-fight-climate-change-so-why-is-it -spending-billions-on-a-gas-pipeline-91442.

7. Theodor Cojoianu et al., "The Economic Geography of Fossil Fuel Divestment, Environmental Policies and Oil and Gas Financing," *SSRN*, April 22, 2019, https://papers .ssrn.com/sol3/papers.cfm?abstract_id =3376183.

8. Paul Stevens, "International Oil Companies: The Death of the Old Business Model," *Chatham House*, May 5, 2016, https://www .chathamhouse.org/publication/international -oil-companies-death-old-business-model.

9. Fiona Harvey, "Secretive National Oil Companies Hold Our Climate in Their Hands," *The Guardian*, October 9, 2019, https://www .theguardian.com/environment/2019/oct/09 /secretive-national-oil-companies-climate.

10. National Resource Governance Institute, "National Oil Companies, with $3.1 Trillion in Assets, Are Dangerously Under-scrutinized," press release, April 25, 2019, https:// resourcegovernance.org/news/national-oil -companies-31-trillion-assets-are-dangerously -under-scrutinized.

11. Mark Shackleton, "Saudi Aramco's $1.5 Trillion IPO Flies in the Face of Climate Reality," *The Conversation*, November 8, 2019, https://theconversation.com/saudi-aramcos -1-5-trillion-ipo-flies-in-the-face-of-climate -reality-126544.

12. Jillian Ambrose, "Banks Warned over Saudi Aramco by Environmental Groups," *The Guardian*, October 17, 2019, https://www .theguardian.com/business/2019/oct/17 /banks-warned-over-saudi-aramco-by -environmental-groups.

13. International Energy Agency, *Gas 2019*, June 2019, https://www.iea.org/gas2019/.

14. International Energy Agency, *Oil 2019*, March 2019, https://www.iea.org/oil2019/.

15. International Energy Agency, "Global Energy Investment Stabilised above USD 1.8 Trillion in 2018, but Security and Sustainability Concerns are Growing," May 14, 2019, https:// www.iea.org/newsroom/news/2019/may /global-energy-investment-stabilised-above -usd-18-trillion-in-2018-but-security-.html.

16. Luke Fletcher et al., *Beyond the Cycle: Which Oil and Gas Companies Are Ready for the Low-Carbon Transition?*, CDP, November 2018, https://www.cdp.net/en/investor /sector-research/oil-and-gas-report.

17. Ensieh Shojaeddini et al., "Oil and Gas Company Strategies Regarding the Energy Transition," *Progress in Energy* 1, no.1 (July 2019), https://doi.org/10.1088/2516-1083/ab2503.

18. Naghmeh Nasiritousi, "Fossil Fuel Emitters and Climate Change: Unpacking the Governance Activities of Large Oil and Gas Companies," *Environmental Politics* 26, no. 4 (2017): 621–647, https://doi.org/10.1080/09644016.2017.1320832.

19. Jan Corfee-Morlot, Michael I. Westphal, and Rachel Spiegel, "4 Ways to Shift from Fossil Fuels to Clean Energy," *World Resources Institute*, January 15, 2019, https://www.wri.org/blog/2019/01/4-ways-shift-fossil-fuels-clean-energy.

20. "What Is Carbon Pricing?," *S&P Global*, 2019, https://www.spglobal.com/en/research-insights/articles/what-is-carbon-pricing.

21. James Ellsmoor, "Renewable Energy Is Now the Cheapest Option—Even Without Subsidies," *Forbes*, June 15, 2019, https://www.forbes.com/sites/jamesellsmoor/2019/06/15/renewable-energy-is-now-the-cheapest-option-even-without-subsidies/#3ba480995a6b.

22. Jan Corfee-Morlot, Michael I. Westphal, and Rachel Spiegel, "4 Ways to Shift from Fossil Fuels to Clean Energy," *World Resources Institute*, January 15, 2019, https://www.wri.org/blog/2019/01/4-ways-shift-fossil-fuels-clean-energy.

23. Sgouris Sgouridis et al, "Comparative Net Energy Analysis of Renewable Electricity and Carbon Capture and Storage," *Nature Energy* 4, (2019): 456–465, https://www.nature.com/articles/s41560-019-0365-7.

24. Kamel Bennaceur, "How the Oil and Gas Industry Is Contributing to Sustainability," *Journal of Petroleum Technology* 71, no. 3 (2019), https://pubs.spe.org/en/jpt/jpt-article-detail/?art=5152.

25. Matthew Bach, "The Oil and Gas Sector: From Climate Laggard to Climate Leader?," *Environmental Politics*, 28.1 (November 2019): 87–103, https://doi.org/10.1080/09644016.2019.1521911.

Practice: Analyzing an Argument Analysis

The following article analyzes the argument that banning plastic bags is good for the environment. The analysis is more complex because the argument is more complex. As author Ben Adler points out, the solution is just not that simple. Use the questions that follow the article to analyze Adler's analysis.

Are Plastic-Bag Bans Good for the Climate?

BEN ADLER

Like cigarettes, plastic bags have recently gone from a tolerated nuisance to a widely despised and discouraged vice. In May 2016, the New York City Council passed a 5-cent-per-bag fee on single-use bags handed out by most retailers. Two weeks ago, the Massachusetts State Senate passed a measure that would ban plastic bags from being dispensed by many retail businesses and require a charge of 10 cents or more for a recycled paper or reusable bag. The Massachusetts proposal may not become law this year, but it's the latest sign that the plastic bag industry is losing this war. Already in Massachusetts, 32 towns and cities

---

Ben Adler is a senior editor at *City & State NY* and was previously an editor at *Newsweek* and *Reuters*. As a reporter, he covered environmental policy and politics for *Politico*, *The Nation*, and *Grist*, where this article appeared on June 2, 2016.

have passed bag bans or fees. So have at least 88 localities in California, including the cities of Los Angeles and San Francisco, plus cities and towns in more than a dozen other states and more than a dozen other countries.

The adverse impacts of plastic bags are undeniable: When they're not piling up in landfills, they're blocking storm drains, littering streets, getting stuck in trees, and contaminating oceans, where fish, seabirds, and other marine animals eat them or get tangled up in them. As longtime plastic bag adversary Ian Frazier recently reported in *The New Yorker*, "In 2014, plastic grocery bags were the seventh most common item collected during the Ocean Conservancy's International Coastal Cleanup, behind smaller debris such as cigarette butts, plastic straws, and bottle caps." The New York City Sanitation Department collects more than 1,700 tons of single-use carry-out bags every week, and has to spend $12.5 million a year to dispose of them.

Bag bans cut this litter off at the source: In San Jose, California, a plastic bag ban led to an 89 percent reduction in the number of plastic bags winding up in the city's storm drains. Fees have a smaller, but still significant, effect. Washington, DC's government estimates that its 5-cent bag tax has led to a 60 percent reduction in the number of these bags being used, although that figure is contested by other sources.

Is Plastic Really Worse Than Paper?

But advocates of these laws and journalists who cover the issue often neglect to ask what will replace plastic bags and what the environmental impact of that replacement will be. People still need bags to bring home their groceries. And the most common substitute, paper bags, may be just as bad or worse, depending on the environmental problem you're most concerned about.

That's leading to a split in the anti-bag movement. Some bills, like in Massachusetts, try to reduce the use of paper bags as well as plastic, but still favor paper. Others, like in New York City, treat all single-use bags equally. Even then, the question remains as to whether single-use bags are necessarily always worse than reusable ones.

Studies of bags' environmental impacts over their life cycle have reached widely varying conclusions. Some are funded by plastic industry groups, like the ironically named American Progressive Bag Alliance. Even studies conducted with the purest of intentions depend on any number of assumptions. How many plastic bags are replaced by one cotton tote bag? If a plastic bag is reused in the home as the garbage bag in a bathroom waste bin, does that reduce its footprint by eliminating the need for another small plastic garbage bag?

If your chief concern is climate change, things get even muddier. One of the most comprehensive research papers on the environmental impact of bags, published in 2007 by an Australian state government agency, found that paper bags have a higher carbon footprint than plastic. That's primarily because more energy is required to produce and transport paper bags.

"People look at [paper] and say it's degradable, therefore it's much better for the environment, but it's not in terms of climate change impact," says David Tyler, a professor of chemistry at the University of Oregon who has examined the research on the environmental impact of bag use. The reasons for paper's higher carbon footprint are complex, but can mostly be understood as stemming from the fact that paper bags are much thicker than plastic bags. "Very broadly, carbon footprints are proportional to mass of an object," says Tyler. For example, because paper bags take up so much more space, more trucks are needed to ship paper bags to a store than to ship plastic bags.

Looking Beyond Climate Change

Still, many environmentalists argue that plastic is worse than paper. Climate change, they say, isn't the only form of environmental degradation to worry about. "Paper does have its own environmental consequences in terms of how much energy it takes to generate," acknowledges Emily Norton, director of the Massachusetts Sierra Club. "The big difference is that paper does biodegrade eventually. Plastic is a toxin that stays in the environment, marine animals ingest it, and it enters their bodies and then ours."

10　　Some social justice activists who work in low-income urban neighborhoods or communities of color also argue that plastic bags are a particular scourge. "A lot of the waste ends up in our communities," says Elizabeth Yeampierre, executive director of UPROSE, an environmental and social justice–oriented community organization in Brooklyn. "Plastic bags not only destroy the physical infrastructure," she says, referring to the way they clog up storm drains and other systems, "they contribute to emissions." And she points out that marine plastic pollution is a threat to low-income people who fish for their dinner: "So many frontline communities depend on food coming from the ocean." That's why her group supported New York City's bag fee even though it's more of a burden on lower-income citizens. A single mom, or someone working two jobs, is more

likely to have to do her shopping in a rush on the way home from work than to go out specifically with a tote bag in hand. But for UPROSE, that concern is outweighed by the negative impacts of plastic bags on disadvantaged communities.

Increasingly, environmentalists are pushing for laws that include fees for all single-use bags, and that require paper bags to be made with recycled content, which could lower their carbon footprint. The measure now under consideration in Massachusetts, for example, would mandate that single-use paper bags contain at least 40 percent recycled fiber. That's the percentage the Massachusetts Sierra Club has advocated for at the state level and when lobbying for municipal bag rules.

It's Complicated

But what if reusable bags aren't good either? As the Australian study noted, a cotton bag has major environmental impacts of its own. Only 2.4 percent of the world's cropland is planted with cotton, yet it accounts for 24 percent of the global market for insecticides and 11 percent for pesticides, the World Wildlife Fund reports. A pound of cotton requires more than 5,000 gallons of water on average, a thirst far greater than that of any vegetable and even most meats. And cotton, unlike paper, is not currently recycled in most places.

The Australian study concluded that the best option appears to be a reusable bag, but one made from recycled plastic, not cotton. "A substantial shift to more durable bags would deliver environmental gains through reductions in greenhouse gases, energy and water use, resource depletion and litter," the study concluded. "The shift from one single-use bag to another single-use bag may improve one environmental outcome, but be offset by another environmental impact."

But studies conducted in Australia or Europe have limited applicability in the US, particularly when you're considering climate impact, because every country has a different energy mix. In fact, every region of the US has a different energy mix.

15   "There's no easy answer," says Eric Goldstein, New York City environment director for the Natural Resources Defense Council, which backed NYC's bag fee. "There are so very many variables. Here's just one tiny example: Does the paper for paper bags come from a recycled paper mill on Staten Island or a virgin forest in northern Canada? As far as I know, nobody has done the definitive analysis, which would necessarily need to have a large number of caveats and qualifications. Also, this question is something like asking, 'Would you prefer to get a parking ticket or a tax assessment?' It depends on the specifics, but it's better to avoid both wherever possible."

Goldstein is confident that if people switch to reusable bags, even cotton ones, and use them consistently, that will ultimately be better for the environment.

The ideal city bag policy would probably involve charging for paper and plastic single-use bags, as New York City has decided to do, while giving out reusable recycled-plastic bags to those who need them, especially to low-income communities and seniors. (The crunchy rich should already have more than enough tote bags from PBS and Whole Foods.)

The larger takeaway is that no bag is free of environmental impact, whether that's contributing to climate change, ocean pollution, water scarcity, or pesticide use. The instinct to favor reusable bags springs from an understandable urge to reduce our chronic overconsumption, but the bags we use are not the big problem.

"Eat one less meat dish a week—that's what will have a real impact on the environment," says Tyler. "It's what we put in the bag at the grocery store that really matters."

Reading, Writing, and Discussion Questions

1. Before discussing possible solutions to a problem, it is important to establish that a problem exists. What are some of the most convincing details that Ben Adler presents to establish how big a problem plastic bags are?

2. What are some of the alternatives that cities have come up with? Do you feel that Adler does a good job of explaining the difficulty of choosing the best alternative to plastic bags? Explain.

3. What evidence does Adler offer that plastic bags are a problem that needs to be dealt with?

4. Adler follows the convention of newspaper articles in that he does not use parenthetical documentation to indicate where he got his information. Still, it is clear that he has researched his subject. How, exactly, can you tell?

5. How does Adler identify his sources and establish them as authorities on the subject? Where do such claims to authority lead into direct quotations? Where does Adler summarize or paraphrase from a source, rather than quote?

6. Why is there no simple solution to the problem of what people use to carry their groceries home?

7. Do you feel that Adler does a good job of analyzing the complexity of the situation? Explain.

8. Write an essay analyzing Adler's essay. Support either a claim of fact or a claim of value.

9. Locate another article on the issue of banning plastic bags and write an analysis of it.

READING ARGUMENT

Examining an Argument and an Analysis of It

Lesley Wexler and Jennifer K. Robbennolt's essay is followed by a student analysis of their argument.

#MeToo and Restorative Justice: Realizing Restoration for Victims and Offenders
LESLEY WEXLER AND JENNIFER K. ROBBENNOLT

The #MeToo movement has hastened a modern-day reckoning with sexual assault and sex discrimination. Claims of sexual misconduct have surfaced in all walks of life and disrupted business as usual in settings as disparate as Hollywood board rooms and Supreme Court confirmation hearing chambers. Some high-level and high-profile individuals who have been accused of wrongdoing have been fired or suspended, and many have resigned. Others have remained in their jobs or even ascended to positions of greater power.

When civil rights activist Tarana Burke founded Just Be Inc. and crafted the related Me Too concept more than a decade ago, before the days of pervasive social media and hashtag designations, she did not plan a worldwide campaign that would change the way individuals and companies deal with sexual misconduct in the workplace. Instead Burke, who worked with mostly poor women and girls of color who had suffered sexual violence, intended to create a nonprofit organization to provide resources for victims of sexual harassment and assault. It would, she hoped, offer opportunities for radical healing. In a 2017 interview, Burke described her multilayered vision of healing: victims use "Me Too" as a way of creating connections and sharing empathy; the community recognizes victims and their needs; perpetrators move toward discussions of accountability, transparency, and vulnerability; and everyone considers

Lesley Wexler and Jennifer K. Robbennolt are both professors of law at University of Illinois College of Law, and Robbennolt is also a professor of psychology there. This article is an adaptation of an article, "#MeToo, Time's Up, and Theories of Justice," written by these two authors and Colleen Murphy, that appeared in the *Illinois Law Review*.

how "collectively, to start dismantling these systems that uphold and make space for sexual violence."[1]

Amid the discussion of how to address #MeToo claims, there have been calls — most publicly in actress Laura Dern's Golden Globes acceptance speech — for the use of "restorative justice" to address the needs of both victims and harassers. But these calls have not been explicit about what sort of restoration is contemplated. Exactly what restorative justice might look like in Hollywood or any other setting remains unclear.

One possible interpretation of the phrase speaks exclusively to the "restoration," the return as best as possible to the rightful, pre-incident state, of those who have experienced sexual harassment and assault. But a broader understanding of restorative justice focuses on not only the restoration and reintegration of victims but of wrongdoers — and also addresses the implications of the wrongdoing for the community as a whole.

5   Restorative justice processes share a number of core commitments, including participation of offenders and victims in the process; narration of the wrongful behavior and its effects; acknowledgement of the offense and acceptance of responsibility for it by the offender; joint efforts to find appropriate ways to repair the harm done; and reintegration of the offender into the broader community.[2] How might these key components of restorative justice — including acknowledgement, responsibility-taking, harm repair, non-repetition, and reintegration — play out in the context of #MeToo? In this article, we begin to explore some of the insights of restorative justice in this context.

Acknowledgement

Those who are injured by someone, including those injured by sexual harassment and other forms of sexual violence, often want acknowledgment of their experiences, the specifics of the wrongful behavior, and how they were affected. Acknowledgement affirms the victim's experience, can convey that the victim was not overreacting or to blame, and signals community support for the victim.

Failure to acknowledge the wrongful behavior is not only insulting but can result in further offense. Consider, for example, snowboarder Shaun White's initial response to questions about a settled sexual harassment lawsuit, including a disparaging characterization of the event as "gossip." His statement that "I am who I am, and I'm proud of who I am. And my friends . . . love me and vouch for me. And I think that stands on its own," did not acknowledge either the harm or the victim.[3]

In similar ways, apologies that are conditional ("if I . . ."), cast doubt on the consequences ("if anyone was offended"), or refer only generally to "actions" or "behavior" do not acknowledge the specific harmful behavior in question or demonstrate an understanding of its wrongfulness or effects. Actor Jeffrey Tambor, for example, responded to accusations of

---

[1] Daisy Murray, *"Empowerment Through Empathy" — We Spoke to Tarana Burke, the Woman Who Really Started the "Me Too" Movement*, Elle (Oct. 23, 2017).

[2] For a review of restorative justice, see Carrie Menkel-Meadow, *Restorative Justice: What Is It and Does It Work?*, 3 Ann. Rev. L. & Soc. Sci. 161 (2007).

[3] Rich Juzwiak, *Shaun White Apologizes After Referring to Sexual Harassment Allegations Against Him as "Gossip"*, Jezebel (Feb. 14, 2018).

misconduct with the following statement: "I am deeply sorry if any action of mine was ever misinterpreted by anyone as being sexually aggressive or if I ever offended or hurt anyone."[4] This sort of vague apology, in addition to failing to clearly acknowledge the behavior or the harm, can also appear to fault the person who was harmed for being overly sensitive or misinterpreting what transpired.

Responsibility-taking

Many victims want offenders to go beyond acknowledgement, to accept responsibility for having caused harm. Responsibility-taking can be difficult even under the best of circumstances, with concerns for self-image, reputation, future employment, vulnerability, and potential legal consequences looming large.

10   But responsibility-taking is a central feature of restorative justice. Indeed, most restorative justice programs are specifically designed to be available only in cases in which the offender has acknowledged having engaged in the wrongful acts at issue. Responsibility-taking is also the central feature of apologies and is central to their potential.

As we have seen many times, some offenders accused of sexual misconduct are very quick to deny any wrongdoing — and many are even more reluctant to acknowledge exactly what they did. Take, for example, actor Kevin Spacey's apology, which first denied any memory of sexual misconduct, then expressed remorse for deeply inappropriate behavior if it happened, and then seemingly deflected any responsibility

by discussing the challenges of living as an openly gay man. While Chef Mario Batali claimed to accept responsibility, his fleeting and vague reference to his "many mistakes" was hardly better, though it was accompanied by a tasty cinnamon roll recipe.[5] Contrast this with the apology given by television show writer Dan Harmon, which included a very specific acknowledgement of the variety of ways in which he had created a toxic work environment for his victim, including gaslighting and retaliation, and the ways in which it had affected her.[6] If someone accused of sexual assault or sexual harassment cannot or will not acknowledge and take responsibility for his or her active, voluntary role in perpetrating abuse, restorative justice simply will not follow.

Harm repair

Restorative justice incorporates the notion that the offender should repair the harm caused by the wrongful behavior and contemplates dialogue and joint decision-making about how best to accomplish that repair. The notion of joint decision-making is complicated in the context of sexual assault and harassment. Take, for instance, agent Adam Venit's request to actor and former NFL player Terry Crews, the man he assaulted, that "they talk in person to come together . . . and be an amazing force for positivity and change in our culture." Crews was not comfortable with this proposal or even accepting Venit's apology until six months later, when Venit took the additional

---

[4] Caitlin Flynn, *Jeffrey Tambor's Response to New Sexual Misconduct Allegation is So Offensive to Sexual Violence Victims* (Nov. 16, 2017), http://www.refinery29.com/2017/11/181477 /jeffrey-tambor-sexual-harassment-response-trace-lysette.

[5] Emily Stewart, *Mario Batali's Sexual Misconduct Apology Came with a Cinnamon Roll Recipe*, Vox.com (Dec. 16, 2017) https://www.vox.com/2017/12/16/16784544/mario-batali -cinnamon-roll-apology.
[6] Harmontown, http://www.harmontown.com/2018/01 /episode-dont-let-him-wipe-or-flush/.

step of resigning from his high-level position.[7] While some victims may be comfortable with direct communication with their assaulter, others will not. Thus, when victims and perpetrators are willing to discuss repair, representatives and neutrals may be particularly valuable in facilitating mutual understanding.

One aspect of this repair is often financial compensation. Victims might look for money damages as concrete compensation for tangible economic losses, as acknowledgement of their experience, as evidence of responsibility-taking, or as reaffirmation of their self-worth.

Some victims of sexual misconduct might be hesitant to seek individual compensation, viewing money as incommensurate with the harm they have suffered. Others might be hesitant to claim compensation because of concerns about how they will be viewed—and critiqued—by others. Take for example, the pre #MeToo criticisms of Andrea Constand, the former director of operations for the woman's basketball team at Temple University, as a gold digger for seeking civil damages from comedian Bill Cosby or the widespread praise of musician Taylor Swift for seeking only symbolic and not monetary damages from her assaulter.[8] Communities ought to be cognizant of these social pressures on victims. Expecting the self-sacrifice of victims, and in particular that of lower-status victims, and demanding that their interests extend only to protecting each other and not to seeking

financial redress for their harm is part of the stereotyping and denial of their interests that fosters harassment and assault in the first place.

Other forms of repair are also appropriate. Apologies, for instance, can serve to repair some aspects of the harm. And community service, particularly if it relates to the underlying harm, can be a valuable effort toward repair.

Non-Repetition

Part of affirming the dignity and status of the harmed individual is taking steps to avoid perpetuating similar wrongdoing in the future. Victims are often motivated to take action against offenders, to seek restorative or other forms of "justice," in the hope of preventing others from experiencing similar harm. Important, too, are efforts by those who *enabled* the wrongful conduct to take responsibility for their part in supporting or failing to prevent or stop the wrongful behavior and to forge systemic change.

But many of the statements we have seen from public figures accused of sexual harassment have failed to outline how their behavior will change in the future. Even those who acknowledge their past misdeeds seem to have little concrete to offer on this front. Moreover, vows to stop engaging in wrongful behavior must be more than promises. One risk is that offenders will be, in the words of Donna Coker, a professor at the University of Miami's School of Law who specializes in domestic violence policy and law, "quick to apologize, slow to change." While an apology may happen at a particular moment in time, the larger project of amends-making in which it is embedded is often an ongoing endeavor. Such an endeavor must include both non-repetition of the offender's own behavior and evidence of how the offender will make

15

---

[7] Tyler Coates, *Terry Crews Shared an Apology Letter from the Talent Agent who Allegedly Groped Him*, GQ (Sept. 14, 2018), https://www.esquire.com/entertainment/tv/a23148698/terry-crews-adam-venit-apology-letter.

[8] Lesley Wexler, *Ideal Victims and the Damage of a Damage Free Victory*, VERDICT (Sept. 27, 2017), https://verdict.justia.com/2017/09/29/ideal-victims-damage-damage-free-victory.

helpful contributions to changing the structures and culture that enabled the bad behavior. Our colleague at the University of Illinois College of Law, Professor Jay Kesan, for example, has made such promises in the academic setting, acknowledging to his victims and the larger community the harms of his past actions, binding himself to specific norms of appropriate behavior, and promising to make positive contributions to the #MeToo conversation.[9] Only time will tell the sincerity of such promises. As they say, the proof is in the pudding.

Redemption and reintegration

Another tenet of restorative justice is the reintegration of the offender back into the relevant community. The restorative justice notion of "earned redemption" anticipates both that offenders will be held accountable for their behavior and that they will be enabled to "earn their way back into the trust of the community."[10] Note, however, that reintegration has been somewhat controversial in the context of sexual violence and retaliation. Concerns for the reintegration of the victim who might have voluntarily or involuntarily excluded herself from the workplace or social community should be seen as particularly pressing. Actress Hilarie Burton, for instance, described how she "has refused to audition and refused to work for show runners she does not already know." She explained that "[t]he fear of being forced into another one of these situations was crippling. I never wanted to be the lead female on any show ever, ever, ever again."[11] While a car thief or a burglar who is truly remorseful and truly understands his crime might be able to return to a job or be restored to a prior position, would we or should we say the same of those who have raped or assaulted, given the high personal toll they have exacted from their victims? While actor Bryan Cranston might speak for some in his willingness to see Harvey Weinstein restored if Weinstein were willing to do the work described above,[12] others are less sure.

What is required for those called out by #MeToo to rebuild their moral and social identities may depend, in part, on the nature of their offense — its severity, intentionality, and pervasiveness. Attention to these nuances is important in order to avoid moral flattening, the temptation to conflate crimes and behaviors that are meaningfully different. But insufficient attention to building a foundation for redemption can cause efforts at reintegration or "comebacks" to fall flat. As actress and early Weinstein accuser Ashley Judd has noted, "There's an appropriate sequence. Accountability, introspection, restitution, then redemption. You don't get to skip the stages that lead to redemption."[13]

Finally, it is important to consider the role of forgiveness in reintegration. Neither

20

---

[9] Donna Coker, *Transformative Justice: Anti-Subordination Processes in Cases of Domestic Violence, in* Restorative Justice and Family Violence 128, 148 (Heather Strang & John Braithwaite eds., 2002).

[10] Gordon Bazemore, *Restorative Justice and Earned Redemption: Communities, Victims, and Offender Reintegration,* 41 Am. Behav. Sci. 769, 770 (1998).

[11] Daniel Holloway, *"One Tree Hill" Cast, Crew Detail Assault, Harassment Claims Against Mark Schwahn* (Nov. 17, 2017), http://variety.com/2017/tv/news/one-tree-hill-mark-schwahn-harassment-assault-1202617918/.

[12] *Bryan Cranston: "There May Be a Way Back For Weinstein,"* BBC News (Nov. 13, 2017), http://www.bbc.com/news/av/entertainment-arts-41973917/bryan-cranston-there-may-be-a-way-back-for-weinstein.

[13] Quoted in Anna Silman, *7 Actresses on Whether the Men of #MeToo Should Get a Path to Redemption,* The Cut, May 1, 2018.

reintegration nor forgiveness must mean reinstatement to a former role or position or that a victim must reconcile with an offender. Despite the common refrain, "forgive and forget," forgiveness does not imply forgetting. Indeed, remembering is crucial, essential so that offenders can learn and others can protect themselves as necessary. Finally, pressuring a victim to forgive can inflict additional harm, which for people who have been assaulted is particularly troublesome as it magnifies their original loss of agency. In claiming their autonomy, victims must be able to choose for themselves whether to forgive.

Of course, restorative justice is not the only approach to resolving #MeToo claims. Many victims might not seek justice at all or prefer only traditional retributive justice. We write not to undermine those choices, but because we believe the potential of restorative justice has been underexplored in discussions of #MeToo. It provides one among many valuable tools for a path forward.

Restorative Justice and the #MeToo Movement
DESTINÉE MILLER

Destinée Miller
English 1020
Prof. Barrett
5 November 2019

Restorative Justice and the #MeToo Movement

In January 2018, the Golden Globes ceremony became a tribute to victims of sexual harassment and sexual assault, following accusations of sexual misconduct against Hollywood producer Harvey Weinstein. The #MeToo movement had led hundreds of women in and out of the entertainment industry to go public with their stories, prompting a nationwide discussion about how to ensure justice. Many of the celebrities at the ceremony wore black in solidarity with the women, and a number of those presenting the awards and receiving them took time to highlight the movement in their remarks. One of those whose words stood out at the ceremony was actress Laura Dern, who went beyond praising the victims and condemning the perpetrators to issue a plea for restorative justice.

In their article "#MeToo and Restorative Justice: Realizing Restoration for Victims and Offenders," Lesley Wexler and Jennifer K. Robbennolt define restorative justice in the context of sexual assault or harassment as a practice that "focuses on not only the restoration and reintegration of victims but of wrongdoers—and

An opening anecdote

Defines a key term in the context in which the authors are using it, considering the victim, the wrongdoer, and the community

Miller's thesis

also addresses the implications of the wrongdoing for the community as a whole" (115). Wexler and Robbennolt show that the path to restorative justice requires certain commitments, and they draw their summary of the steps in restorative justice from Carrie Menkel-Meadow's article "Restorative Justice: What Is It and Does It Work?": "participation of offenders and victims in the process; narration of the wrongful behavior and its effects; acknowledgment of the offense and acceptance of responsibility for it by the offender; joint efforts to find appropriate ways to repair the harm done; and reintegration of the offender into the broader community" (115). These steps provide the authors a framework for analyzing the #MeToo movement in the context of restorative justice through social accountability and victim visibility. At the same time, however, they call into question the effectiveness of restorative justice within the scope of the entertainment industry, identifying its shortcomings under the weight of grossly uneven power dynamics in Hollywood.

Wexler and Robbennolt highlight the benefits of restorative justice as a two-fold process in ensuring justice for victims of sexual assault—that unlike simply receiving justice that will return a victim to their pre-assault self (as well as possible), this type of restitution seeks to ensure that the entire community is set to rights. Victims of sexual violence need to have what happened to them and how it affected them acknowledged. Wexler and Robbennolt use examples from the world of sports and entertainment to distinguish between sincere acceptance of guilt and insulting conditional apologies like Jeffrey Tambor's: "I am deeply sorry if any action of mine was ever misinterpreted by anyone as being sexually aggressive or if I ever offended or hurt anyone" (116). This example from an actor who plays some well-known comedic characters shows how widespread the problem is and appeals to the reader's desire for accountability from not only this actor but from society at large, a condition that restorative justice attempts to satisfy.

Miller acknowledges that Wexler and Robbennolt are cautious because they are not sure how the process applies to Hollywood.

However, the authors are very cautious in applying the core commitments of restorative justice to the #MeToo movement, acknowledging from the beginning that it is unclear exactly what restorative justice would look like in the context of Hollywood. As they work through the steps in the process of restorative justice, they address some of the roadblocks to success when the process is applied to victims of sexual harassment and assault, such as reluctance to admit to guilt and vague, empty apologies on behalf of offenders. One such case involves actor Kevin Spacey, who "expressed remorse for deeply inappropriate behavior if it happened" (116). This example reminds readers of the complexity of sexual harassment issues and the difficulty of holding offenders accountable, especially on the universal stage of the entertainment industry. The authors in turn emphasize that restorative justice is dependent upon culture and society as key components in encouraging and upholding accountability.

Wexler and Robbennolt go on to emphasize the importance of acknowledgement to victims of sexual assault—victims want those who have harmed them not only to acknowledge their guilt but to take responsibility for it. However, as the authors explain, "responsibility-taking can be difficult even under the best of circumstances, with concerns for self-image, reputation, future employment, vulnerability, and potential legal consequences looming large" (116). Here, the authors present to readers the difficulties of acknowledging sexual harassment within the very public entertainment industry—that usually when the restorative justice process is used with any crime, the process cannot continue if the perpetrator is not willing to participate. By highlighting both the benefits and drawbacks of restorative justice, the authors allow readers to make their own decisions regarding the potential solution.

The final steps of the restorative justice process include non-repetition of the offense and the redemption and reintegration of the offender into the greater community—steps that highlight restorative justice's dual focus on supporting both the victim and the offender. Through their explanation of these steps, Wexler and Robbennolt again emphasize how much restorative justice's success depends on the actions and decisions of both parties: "what is required for those called out by #MeToo to rebuild their moral and social identities may depend, in part, on the nature of their offense—its severity, intentionality, and pervasiveness" (118). The authors conclude with the same caution with which they began. They offer restorative justice as one means of resolving #MeToo claims, one tool among many for readers to consider to help victims of sexual assault move forward and to hold their offenders accountable.

Strong link between this example and Miller's thesis.

5

One of the difficulties or roadblocks referred to earlier

Strong analytical statement

Reiterates the authors' caution in applying restorative justice to claims of assault and harassment.

Works Cited

Wexler, Lesley, and Jennifer K. Robbennolt. "#MeToo and Restorative Justice." *Elements of Argument*, 13th ed., edited by Annette T. Rottenberg and Donna Haisty Winchell, Bedford/ St. Martin's, 2021, pp. 114–19.

Practice: Examining an Analysis of Two Arguments

The following student essay is an analysis of two essays that appear in this text: James W. Ingram III's "Electoral College Is Best Way to Choose U.S. President" (p. 101) from earlier in this chapter and John R. Koza's "States Can Reform Electoral College—Here's How to Empower Popular Vote" (p. 260) in Chapter 9. The essay uses parallel order to compare the two related arguments.

As you read, annotate the essay to identify the main claim and the ways the student structures her argument by analyzing two readings.

How to Pick a President: Electoral College vs. National Popular Vote

SABRA STAPLETON

Sabra Stapleton
English 1020
Prof. Barrett
14 January 2020

How to Pick a President:

Electoral College vs. National Popular Vote

In essay "Electoral College Is Best Way to Choose U.S. President," professor of political science James W. Ingram III defends the Electoral College as the most appropriate and safest method of choosing the nation's president. In "States Can Reform Electoral College—Here's How to Empower Popular Vote," computer scientist John R. Koza defends the popular vote as the most democratic and inclusive method of choosing the president. Each author supports American democracy but emphasizes the strengths of his preferred system for electing the President of the United States.

Ingram begins his argument in support of the Electoral College by emphasizing one of the biggest problems with the popular vote system of electing the U.S. president: the difficulty with which a candidate wins a popular vote majority in a two-party system. He uses the past to emphasize his point, recalling that after George Washington left office, there was the fear that no candidate could receive the majority of votes (101). Ingram writes, "The Electoral College usually amplifies the people's voice, electing the candidate who wins most states and votes. This allows the winner to claim a mandate and lead the country" (101). The same is not true if a president is elected by less than half of the popular votes cast.

Electing the president by popular vote, he argues, would compromise the authority and effectiveness of the executive branch—that "if presidents only needed plurality support, the victor might regularly be the candidate who won fewer states" (102). Ingram shows his belief in American democracy by focusing his argument on protecting the executive branch and on the historical development of the system.

Ingram also argues that in the absence of a popular vote, the next step in the system would be biased. With a popular vote, if no candidate won the majority of popular votes, the president would be elected by the House of Representatives. Thus the party in control of the House of Representatives would almost certainly select the candidate affiliated with that party, gaining further power and, as Ingram asserts, actually weakening our democracy (101–2). Ingram chooses to strengthen his argument for the Electoral College by emphasizing the possibility of a transfer of power—from the public to the House—taking advantage of potential reader anxieties about increased government control. At the conclusion of his argument, Ingram blames any issues with the Electoral College on its inherently flawed creators. He writes, "If our Electoral College mechanism for choosing presidents is imperfect, it is because human beings have never devised a perfect system. . . . What isn't broken doesn't need fixing" (103).

By focusing on what he sees as the problem with the popular vote, Ingram strengthens his argument that the Electoral College encourages candidates to adopt a more diverse and inclusive mindset in developing their campaign strategy. The values of diversity and inclusion are shared by Koza, but he argues in support of the popular vote. Koza is concerned with issues of voter diversity, believing that the Electoral College forces presidential candidates to focus on the needs and interests of only a few of the most populous states. To introduce his argument, Koza criticizes the winner-take-all laws enforced by most U.S. states, appealing to the reader's potential desire for a sense of equality or diversity. He writes that in the 2016 U.S. presidential election, "candidates concentrated ninety-four percent of their campaign events in just twelve closely divided 'battleground' states, while giving little or no attention to states with seventy percent of the nation's population" (260). Koza emphasizes how the current system encourages candidates to pursue individual states rather than individual votes. He argues instead for a solution that forces candidates to consider rural issues. Before proposing his solution to this problem, Koza criticizes the Electoral College for its long-term practice of encouraging first-term presidents to grant post-election benefits, "including grants, disaster declarations, and various exemptions" (261), to battleground states.

5   Unlike Ingram, who believes the current system is an acceptable and timeless mechanism of American democracy, Koza proposes an alternative: the National Popular Vote interstate compact. The compact would make "every vote, in every state, politically relevant in every presidential election" (261). A state could choose to have all of its electoral votes go to the candidate winning the national popular vote. With this solution, the popular vote will have become the means of electing the president without having to change the Constitution, since each state already has the power to decide how to allocate its electoral votes. Koza asserts that the compact would solve the problem of candidates ignoring the interests of less populous states, appealing to voters who value diversity. At the same time, however, he appeals to the power and legitimacy of the Constitution; his solution establishes a middle ground. In so doing, Koza makes the popular vote plurality seem more feasible to the reader.

Both Ingram and Koza speak to readers' anxieties about the lack of diversity and equality in the presidential election process, with Ingram defending the current Electoral College system and Koza supporting a new popular vote plurality system. But while Ingram believes the current system to be as close to achieving these goals as possible, Koza offers a more personal and individual alternative that appeals to the reader's desire for actual solutions to the problems that face voters across the nation.

Works Cited

Ingram, James W., III. "Electoral College Is Best Way to Choose U.S. President." Rottenberg and Winchell, pp. 101–3.

Koza, John R. "States Can Reform Electoral College—Here's How to Empower Popular Vote." Rottenberg and Winchell, pp. 260–62.

Rottenberg, Annette, and Donna Haisty Winchell, editors. *Elements of Argument: A Text and Reader.* 13th ed., Bedford/St. Martin's, 2021.

Assignments for Writing Argument Analysis

Reading and Discussion Questions

1. Choose an editorial from your campus or local newspaper and evaluate it. How successful an argument does it make?

2. Which essay do you find most effective in this chapter? Why? Be specific and support your answer with examples from the text.

3. Think of some television commercials that have caught your eye. What tactics are used to try to convince you to buy a product or service?

Writing Suggestions

1. Choose an editorial from your campus or local newspaper, and write an objective analysis of it. Your thesis statement will be a claim of fact.

2. Locate two editorials or two articles that take different stands on the same controversial issue. Write an analysis in which you objectively compare the two as examples of argumentation.

3. Locate two editorials or two articles that take different stands on the same controversial issue. Write an essay in which you argue which of the two is a more effective argument and why.

4. In a paragraph, explain the organizational pattern used by either Destinée Miller in "Restorative Justice and the #MeToo Movement" (p. 119) or Sabra Stapleton in "How to Pick a President: Electoral College vs. National Popular Vote" (p. 122) and evaluate how effective the organizational choice is—whether it should have been organized differently and why.

5. Write a paragraph in which you explain what claim you would support if you were writing about James W. Ingram III's "Electoral College Is Best Way to Choose U.S. President" (p. 101) and John R. Koza's "States Can Reform Electoral College—Here's How to Empower Popular Vote" (p. 260) together. Would you come to the same conclusion as Sabra Stapleton in "How to Pick a President: Electoral College vs. National Popular Vote" (p. 122)? Would you have argued the same point differently? Explain what approach you would take.

RESEARCH ASSIGNMENT ▸ **Incorporating Quotations**

Read each of the following passages. Then for each, write one or two sentences that analyze the passage and incorporate a quotation as evidence. Also incorporate in your sentence(s) the author's name and the title of the work. Choose a different way of incorporating the quote each time so that all three ways are represented: (1) as a grammatical part of your own sentence, (2) with a speech tag such as "he says" or "she writes," and (3) with a complete sentence and a colon.

Put the page number in parentheses, and punctuate correctly according to MLA style.

Passage 1

The school district [in Washington, D.C.] Michelle Rhee inherited in 2007 was in freefall. Not only had student enrollment plummeted and test scores scraped the bottom of any national rankings, but also many principals had lost control of their schools. Rhee's response to the latter was to eject (or offer voluntary retirement to) nearly fifty principals who had tolerated those conditions.

Her yardstick for progress was basic. In the first year, a principal entering an out-of-control school must succeed in "locking down" the school: seize control of the hallways, bathrooms, lunchrooms, and the nearby city blocks during school dismissal and ensure calm and respect in the classrooms. If principals succeed with that first-year lockdown but test scores still look miserable, they generally got a pass. The second and third years, however, measurable "teaching and learning" was supposed to kick in. If that didn't happen, the principal was "non-reappointed," the district's euphemism for getting fired. Not surprisingly, a lot of principals stumbled along that path, which means a lot of non-reappointments—and a lot of interviews for new principals.

(Source: Richard Whitmire, *The Bee-Eater* (San Francisco: Jossey-Bass, 2011), 131–32.)

Passage 2

Back in the 1970s, organic food had no such positive image. Many dismissed it as a fringy fad served cold with an eat-your-spinach sermon. How could organic taste good? Indeed, taste was the key challenge. Organic advocates couldn't popularize a cuisine simply by declaring it spiritually and ecologically superior. The world, like my mother, was not waiting for or willing to eat inedible soul food. To win acceptance, it had to be truly delectable.

(Source: Gary Hirshberg, "Organics—Healthy Food, and So Much More," in Karl Weber, ed., *Food, Inc.: How Industrial Food Is Making Us Sicker, Fatter and Poorer—And What We Can Do about It*, ed. Karl Weber (New York: Participant Media, 2009), 49.)

Writing
ARGUMENT

Approaches to Argument

In argument, as in all forms of communication, a *person* (the writer or speaker) presents a text *about something* (the subject) and *for someone* (the audience). These three main components can be viewed as a triangle:

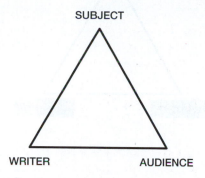

Dating back to 400 B.C.E., with the work of Aristotle and other Greek philosophers, the study of argument has evolved over the centuries as scholars continually examine what makes an argument most effective. Although they may use different words and emphasize different ideas, the approaches to argument given in this book—those of Aristotle as well as those of American psychologist Carl Rogers and British philosopher Stephen Toulmin—share important similarities and overlapping concepts, and the components of the communication triangle are evident in all three. However, even though the basic relationships among writer, audience, and subject remain in place, today's world presents both arguers and audiences with new challenges and new opportunities in creating and understanding argument texts.

As you read an argumentative text, it is useful to have a range of approaches to choose from in reaching a full understanding of the author's ideas and strategies. In fact, you may draw on your knowledge of more than one approach to argumentation in analyzing the same text. When you write an argument, you will most likely stick to one approach, but it can be useful to have a repertoire of approaches to choose from.

Aristotelian Rhetoric

Aristotle wrote a treatise on argument that has influenced its study and practice for well over two thousand years. He used the term *logos* to refer to logical appeals and the term *pathos* to refer to emotional appeals. In an ideal world, logic alone would be enough to persuade. Aristotle acknowledged, however, that in the less-than-ideal real world, effective arguments depend not only on *logos* and *pathos* but also on the writer's or speaker's credibility, which he called *ethos*. Together, *ethos*, *logos*, and *pathos* were the primary focus of Aristotle's *Rhetoric*, which is where the term *rhetorical* comes from. Rhetoric is concerned with how the writer persuades the audience.

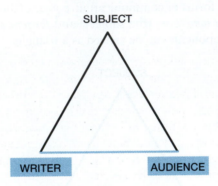

Ethos

Aristotle considered *ethos* to be the most important element in the arguer's ability to persuade the audience to accept a claim. He named intelligence, character, and goodwill as the attributes that produce credibility. Today we might describe these qualities somewhat differently, but the criteria for judging writers' credibility remain essentially the same. Writers must convince their audience that

- they are knowledgeable and as well informed as possible about the subject,
- they are not only truthful in the presentation of evidence but also morally upright and dependable,
- they have good intentions and have considered the interests and needs of others as well as their own.

A reputation for intelligence, character, and goodwill is not often earned overnight. And it can be lost more quickly than it is gained. Once writers or speakers have betrayed an audience's belief in their character or judgment, they may find it difficult to persuade that audience to accept subsequent claims, no matter how sound the data and reasoning are. The late ABC news correspondent Cokie Roberts was once reprimanded for faking a live shot outside the Capitol in Washington from the warmth of an ABC studio a few blocks away as she reported on the State of the Union Address, even though her location had nothing to do with the substance of her report. NBC anchor Brian Williams suffered a much more significant fall from grace when he was discovered to have lied about being in a helicopter that was shot down in Iraq during his coverage of the war there. He received a six-month suspension, and there were suggestions that his career would never recover, but it eventually did. A person does not have to be found guilty of a crime or a major indiscretion to have his or her integrity questioned. All it takes, usually, is being caught in a lie or a misrepresentation. An exception has been President Donald Trump, who retained a following in spite of repeated falsehoods made in public addresses and on Twitter; his supporters find trust in his self-presentation and methods rather than the accuracy of his claims.

Logos

Logos refers to the logic of an argument: the evidence or proof that supports a writer's claim. Aristotle taught that there are two types of proof to offer in support of an argument: the example and the enthymeme. In simplest terms, this meant induction and deduction. **Induction** is the process of generalizing from specifics (examples). Aristotle was less concerned with providing a large number of examples than with providing one particularly apt one. **Deduction** is the process of applying a generalization to a specific instance.

The **syllogism** is the foundation of deductive reasoning in which a major premise and a minor premise lead to a logical conclusion.

Syllogism:
Major premise: All mammals are warm blooded.
Minor premise: Dolphins are mammals.
Conclusion: Dolphins are warm blooded.

The syllogism above is *deductive* because it leads from a generalization about all mammals to a specific instance, dolphins. Because premises in a syllogism are generally certain, the conclusions are rarely disputable. Aristotle defined an **enthymeme** as a syllogism in which the conclusion is probable, but not certain, because it deals with human affairs, not scientific fact.

Aristotle's Enthymeme:
Major premise: Mass murderers are narcissists.
Minor premise: Seung-Hui Cho was a mass murderer.
Conclusion: Seung-Hui Cho was a narcissist.

Today we use the term *enthymeme* to refer to a syllogism in which one of the premises is *implied* rather than stated outright.

Modern Enthymeme:
Major premise (implied): Bombs that detonate are lethal.
Minor premise: The bomb is going to detonate in one minute.
Conclusion: Let's get out of here!

Pathos

Pathos is appeal to the emotions. An audience can be moved by the logic of an argument alone, but more often emotional appeal combines with logic and ethical appeal to sway the audience. Appeals to the emotions and values of an audience are an appropriate form of persuasion unless (1) they are irrelevant to the argument or draw attention from the issues being argued or (2) they are used to conceal another purpose. The most popular emotional appeals are to pity and to fear. A picture of a starving child in Africa is a legitimate emotional appeal unless the picture leads donors to send money that goes largely to administrative costs and not to the children who need help. It is legitimate to arouse fear of the consequences of texting while driving if the descriptions are accurate. It is not legitimate to scare a family into buying an insurance policy they cannot afford by appealing to their fear of ruinous medical bills if the insurance would not provide the promised relief.

An argument becomes personal when it hits close to home. We can sometimes look objectively at society's problems until our own children are threatened or our own livelihood is in jeopardy. Then emotion enters the picture and often outweighs logic.

Some individuals and groups are quick to take advantage of human willingness to show compassion to others. Our emotional response to an event like the COVID-19 pandemic or the devastation that Hurricane Dorian caused in the Bahamas in 2019 may be to contribute to those who have suffered loss or injury. Unfortunately, in our emotional vulnerability we have to guard against those who are only out for personal gain and may collect gifts that will never reach the victims.

Ancient Rhetoric Today

How can we apply the teachings of Aristotle in the digital age? We can use the same vocabulary and study the same writer-subject-audience relationships, but we must also take into account the many cultural and technological changes that have occurred in the past two thousand years.

Writers — but more commonly speakers — in Aristotle's world of the fourth century B.C.E. were very limited in audience and in subject matter. As far as the rhetorical relationship is concerned, inventions like the printing press, and later the telegraph, gave writers access to a wider and wider range of audiences; more recent developments such as blogs, Facebook, and Twitter have increased exponentially the audiences a writer can reach. Moreover, today's audiences have more access to background information about authors, enabling readers to consider a writer's *ethos* for themselves. In addition, readers are more active participants in today's rhetorical relationships: They are encouraged to think critically about and respond to the arguments they encounter, and they can do so instantly and publicly in online forums.

The amount of information available at the click of a mouse has also exploded. That means that the relationship between writer and subject has also changed with the times. Technological advances have raised expectations about what an arguer should know about a subject. Living in the information age as we do, writers must be able to find, understand, evaluate, and manage information from a seemingly endless range of sources—and then synthesize that information into a coherent argument.

Technology has also greatly influenced the audience-subject relationship. In the limited world of ancient Greece, it was relatively easy to predict what an audience would know about a subject. There was more of a shared worldview than has existed in more recent times. In ancient Greece, rigid rules dictated the organization of a speech, and the examples were drawn from well-known narratives, true or fictional. Today it is much more difficult for a writer to place himself or herself in someone else's position and try to see a subject from that person's point of view because of the diversity of the people and experiences that the writer comes into contact with. And, just as writers do, readers also have more access to information than ever before. Readers, therefore, can—and do—form opinions based on their own chosen sources, which may contradict the evidence presented by the writer.

Because of its emphasis on *ethos*, or on the character of the speaker, the Aristotelian approach to reading or writing argument may be a good choice when it is significant who is doing the writing. In the following op-ed, Captain Chesley B. "Sully" Sullenberger, for example, brings to his words the authority of a public figure and a hero. The opposite could also be true if an audience had reason to suspect the veracity of a speaker or writer because of his or her past actions. Quite often we may not even know anything about the author of journalistic writing, but you will see in the research portion of this book that establishing the authority of an author whose ideas we draw upon, whatever the subject, is an essential part of building the strongest possible case for one's position. Part of your *ethos* as a writer comes from identifying your sources, giving them the credit they deserve, and establishing yourself as a trustworthy person by presenting their ideas and yours fully and fairly.

ARGUMENT ESSENTIALS
Aristotelian Rhetoric

Three means of appealing to an audience:

- *Ethos* — appeal based on the writer's or speaker's credibility
- *Logos* — logical appeal
- *Pathos* — emotional appeal

Two types of proof:

- Inductive reasoning — drawing a general conclusion based on specific examples
- Deductive reasoning — drawing a specific conclusion based on general rules

READING ARGUMENT

Seeing Aristotelian Rhetoric

The editorial that follows has been annotated to show key features of Aristotelian rhetoric used by the author.

We Saved 155 Lives on the Hudson. Now Let's Vote for Leaders Who'll Protect Us All.

CHESLEY B. "SULLY" SULLENBERGER III

Ethos: Sully references the incident that made many call him a hero.

Sully's thesis: Leadership is needed in a crisis, including a national one.

Pathos: Readers feel sympathy for the elderly and the very young.

Ethos: Sully exhibits humility by pointing out that the favorable outcome was the work of many.

Logos: Sully sets up an analogy between being responsible for a plane and for a country.

Logos:

Major premise: You get what you project.
Minor premise: I projected calm and confidence to the passengers.
Conclusion: The passengers responded with calm and confidence.

Nearly 10 years ago, I led 154 people to safety as the captain of US Airways Flight 1549, which suffered bird strikes, lost thrust in the engines, and was forced to make an emergency landing on the Hudson River. Some called it "the Miracle on the Hudson." But it was not a miracle. It was, in microcosm, an example of what is needed in emergencies—including the current national crisis—and what is possible when we serve a cause greater than ourselves.

On our famous flight, I witnessed the best in people who rose to the occasion. Passengers and crew worked together to help evacuate an elderly passenger and a mother with a nine-month-old child. New York Waterway took the initiative to radio their vessels to head toward us when they saw us approaching. This successful landing, in short, was the result of good judgment, experience, skill—and the efforts of many.

But as captain, I ultimately was responsible for everything that happened. Had even one person not survived, I would have considered it a tragic failure that I would have felt deeply for the rest of my life. To navigate complex challenges, all leaders must take responsibility and have a moral compass grounded in competence, integrity, and concern for the greater good.

I am often told how calm I sounded speaking to passengers, crew, and air traffic control during the emergency. In every situation, but especially challenging ones, a leader sets the tone and must create an environment in which all can do their best. You get what you project. Whether it is calm and confidence—or fear, anger, and hatred—people will respond in kind. Courage can be contagious.

Capt. "Sully" Sullenberger is a safety expert, author, and speaker on leadership and culture. He is best known for what has been called the "Miracle on the Hudson," when he and his crew safely landed US Airways Flight 1549 on New York's Hudson River, saving all 155 lives onboard on January 15, 2009. This op-ed was originally published in the *Washington Post* on October 29, 2018.

5 Today, tragically, too many people in power are projecting the worst. Many are cowardly, complicit enablers, acting against the interests of the United States, our allies and democracy; encouraging extremists at home and emboldening our adversaries abroad; and threatening the livability of our planet. Many do not respect the offices they hold; they lack—or disregard—a basic knowledge of history, science, and leadership; and they act impulsively, worsening a toxic political environment.

As a result, we are in a struggle for who and what we are as a people. We have lost what in the military we call unit cohesion. The fabric of our nation is under attack, while shame—a timeless beacon of right and wrong—seems dead.

This is not the America I know and love. We're better than this. Our ideals, shared facts, and common humanity are what bind us together as a nation and a people. Not one of these values is a political issue, but the lack of them is.

This current absence of civic virtues is not normal, and we must not allow it to become normal. We must rededicate ourselves to the ideals, values, and norms that unite us and upon which our democracy depends. We must be engaged and informed voters, and we must get our information from credible, reputable sources.

For the first 85 percent of my adult life, I was a registered Republican. But I have always voted as an American. And this critical Election Day, I will do so by voting for leaders committed to rebuilding our common values and not pandering to our basest impulses.

10 When I volunteered for military service during wartime, I took an oath that is similar to the one our elected officials take: "I do solemnly swear that I will support and defend the Constitution of the United States against all enemies, foreign and domestic." I vowed to uphold this oath at the cost of my life, if necessary. We must expect no less from our elected officials. And we must hold accountable those who fail to defend our nation and all our people.

After Flight 1549, I realized that because of the sudden worldwide fame, I had been given a greater voice. I knew I could not walk away but had an obligation to use this bully pulpit for good and as an advocate for the safety of the traveling public. I feel that I now have yet another mission, as a defender of our democracy.

We cannot wait for someone to save us. We must do it ourselves. This Election Day is a crucial opportunity to again demonstrate the best in

Logos: Sully sets up a syllogism that reflects the opposite: If you project the worst, you get the worst. He supports his premise with examples.

Pathos: An appeal to patriotism and community.

Links back to his idea that the leader projects the tone for the nation. He relies on his established *ethos* to make an implicit argument that readers should follow his lead.

Ethos: He deserves respect for volunteering to serve during war.

Ethos: He used his fame to advocate for the safety of the traveling public and the country.

Pathos: Appeals to the readers' emotions, asking if they would be proud to tell their grandchildren what they did.

each of us by doing our duty and voting for leaders who are committed to the values that will unite and protect us. Years from now, when our grandchildren learn about this critical time in our nation's history, they may ask if we got involved, if we made our voices heard. I know what my answer will be. I hope yours will be "yes."

Practice: Aristotelian Rhetoric

Using the comments on the op-ed by Sullenberger on pages 134-36 as a model, analyze the following blog post using Aristotle's terminology. Then answer the questions at the end of the essay.

I Am Adam Lanza's Mother

LIZA LONG

Three days before 20-year-old Adam Lanza killed his mother, then opened fire on a classroom full of Connecticut kindergartners, my 13-year-old son Michael (name changed) missed his bus because he was wearing the wrong color pants.

"I can wear these pants," he said, his tone increasingly belligerent, the black-hole pupils of his eyes swallowing the blue irises.

"They are navy blue," I told him. "Your school's dress code says black or khaki pants only."

"They told me I could wear these," he insisted. "You're a stupid bitch. I can wear whatever pants I want to. This is America. I have rights!"

5   "You can't wear whatever pants you want to," I said, my tone affable, reasonable. "And you definitely cannot call me a stupid bitch. You're grounded from electronics for the rest of the day. Now get in the car, and I will take you to school."

I live with a son who is mentally ill. I love my son. But he terrifies me.

A few weeks ago, Michael pulled a knife and threatened to kill me and then himself after I asked him to return his overdue library books. His 7- and 9-year-old siblings knew the safety plan—they ran to the car and locked the doors before I even asked them to. I managed to get the knife from Michael, then methodically collected all the sharp objects in the house into a single Tupperware container that now travels with me. Through it all, he continued to scream insults at me and threaten to kill or hurt me.

That conflict ended with three burly police officers and a paramedic wrestling my son onto a gurney for an expensive ambulance ride to the

Liza Long, from Boise, Idaho, is an author, musician, mental health advocate, and mother of four who blogs under the name The Anarchist Soccer Mom. This particular post, which appeared originally on her blog in 2012, quickly went viral in the wake of the Newtown elementary school shootings. Her son since that time has been diagnosed with bipolar disorder and received the proper medication, and she has written a book entitled *The Price of Silence: A Mom's Perspective on Mental Illness*.

local emergency room. The mental hospital didn't have any beds that day, and Michael calmed down nicely in the ER, so they sent us home with a prescription for Zyprexa and a follow-up visit with a local pediatric psychiatrist.

We still don't know what's wrong with Michael. Autism spectrum, ADHD, Oppositional Defiant or Intermittent Explosive Disorder have all been tossed around at various meetings with probation officers and social workers and counselors and teachers and school administrators. He's been on a slew of antipsychotic and mood altering pharmaceuticals, a Russian novel of behavioral plans. Nothing seems to work.

10   At the start of seventh grade, Michael was accepted to an accelerated program for highly gifted math and science students. His IQ is off the charts. When he's in a good mood, he will gladly bend your ear on subjects ranging from Greek mythology to the differences between Einsteinian and Newtonian physics to Doctor Who. He's in a good mood most of the time. But when he's not, watch out. And it's impossible to predict what will set him off.

Several weeks into his new junior high school, Michael began exhibiting increasingly odd and threatening behaviors at school. We decided to transfer him to the district's most restrictive behavioral program, a contained school environment where children who can't function in normal classrooms can access their right to free public babysitting from 7:30–1:50 Monday through Friday until they turn 18.

The morning of the pants incident, Michael continued to argue with me on the drive. He would occasionally apologize and seem remorseful. Right before we turned into his

school parking lot, he said, "Look, Mom, I'm really sorry. Can I have video games back today?"

"No way," I told him. "You cannot act the way you acted this morning and think you can get your electronic privileges back that quickly."

His face turned cold, and his eyes were full of calculated rage. "Then I'm going to kill myself," he said. "I'm going to jump out of this car right now and kill myself."

That was it. After the knife incident, I told 15 him that if he ever said those words again, I would take him straight to the mental hospital, no ifs, ands, or buts. I did not respond, except to pull the car into the opposite lane, turning left instead of right.

"Where are you taking me?" he said, suddenly worried. "Where are we going?"

"You know where we are going," I replied.

"No! You can't do that to me! You're sending me to hell! You're sending me straight to hell!"

I pulled up in front of the hospital, frantically waving for one of the clinicians who happened to be standing outside. "Call the police," I said. "Hurry."

Michael was in a full-blown fit by then, 20 screaming and hitting. I hugged him close so he couldn't escape from the car. He bit me several times and repeatedly jabbed his elbows into my rib cage. I'm still stronger than he is, but I won't be for much longer.

The police came quickly and carried my son screaming and kicking into the bowels of the hospital. I started to shake, and tears filled my eyes as I filled out the paperwork — "Were there any difficulties with . . . at what age did your child . . . were there any problems with . . . has your child ever experienced . . . does your child have . . ."

At least we have health insurance now. I recently accepted a position with a local college, giving up my freelance career because when you have a kid like this, you need benefits. You'll do anything for benefits. No individual insurance plan will cover this kind of thing.

For days, my son insisted that I was lying — that I made the whole thing up so that I could get rid of him. The first day, when I called to check up on him, he said, "I hate you. And I'm going to get my revenge as soon as I get out of here."

By day three, he was my calm, sweet boy again, all apologies and promises to get better. I've heard those promises for years. I don't believe them anymore.

25   On the intake form, under the question, "What are your expectations for treatment?" I wrote, "I need help."

And I do. This problem is too big for me to handle on my own. Sometimes there are no good options. So you just pray for grace and trust that in hindsight, it will all make sense.

I am sharing this story because I am Adam Lanza's mother. I am Dylan Klebold's and Eric Harris's mother. I am James Holmes's mother. I am Jared Loughner's mother. I am Seung-Hui Cho's mother. And these boys — and their mothers — need help. In the wake of another horrific national tragedy, it's easy to talk about guns. But it's time to talk about mental illness.

According to *Mother Jones*, since 1982, 61 mass murders involving firearms have occurred throughout the country. Of these, 43 of the killers were white males, and only one was a woman. *Mother Jones* focused on whether the killers obtained their guns legally (most did). But this highly visible sign of mental illness should lead us to consider how many people in the U.S. live in fear, like I do.

When I asked my son's social worker about my options, he said that the only thing I could do was to get Michael charged with a crime. "If he's back in the system, they'll create a paper trail," he said. "That's the only way you're ever going to get anything done. No one will pay attention to you unless you've got charges."

I don't believe my son belongs in jail. The   30 chaotic environment exacerbates Michael's sensitivity to sensory stimuli and doesn't deal with the underlying pathology. But it seems like the United States is using prison as the solution of choice for mentally ill people. According to Human Rights Watch, the number of mentally ill inmates in U.S. prisons quadrupled from 2000 to 2006, and it continues to rise — in fact, the rate of inmate mental illness is five times greater (56 percent) than in the non-incarcerated population.

With state-run treatment centers and hospitals shuttered, prison is now the last resort for the mentally ill — Rikers Island, the LA County Jail, and Cook County Jail in Illinois housed the nation's largest treatment centers in 2011.

No one wants to send a 13-year-old genius who loves Harry Potter and his snuggle animal collection to jail. But our society, with its stigma on mental illness and its broken healthcare system, does not provide us with other options. Then another tortured soul shoots up a fast food restaurant. A mall. A kindergarten classroom. And we wring our hands and say, "Something must be done."

I agree that something must be done. It's time for a meaningful, nation-wide conversation about mental health. That's the only way our nation can ever truly heal.

God help me. God help Michael. God help us all.

Reading, Writing, and Discussion Questions

1. Why is the essay called "I Am Adam Lanza's Mother"? (After all, she isn't.) What is her purpose in telling her story?

2. Where in the essay does Liza Long most clearly state her thesis?

3. What type of appeal is Long using when she recounts the details of Michael's violence and threats of violence?

4. Where does she make use of logical appeal?

5. Does Long come across as a credible person? In other words, what sort of *ethos* does the essay convey?

6. Imagine or research the online responses to Long's blog post, and formulate your own response.

Rogerian Argument

Carl Rogers was a twentieth-century humanistic psychologist who translated his ideas about therapy into communication theory. As a therapist, he believed that the experience of two people meeting and speaking honestly to each other would have a healing effect. In later years, he became convinced that the same principles of nondirective, nonconfrontational therapy that emphasized attentive listening could work not only for couples and small groups but also for large groups, even nations, to create more harmonious relationships.

Such nonconfrontational communication between individuals or among groups is hampered, Rogers believed, by the fact that there is no longer anything approaching a shared worldview. In the past, those like Copernicus and Galileo who saw reality differently were often condemned or even killed. Rogers wrote, "Although society has often come around eventually to agree with its dissidents . . . there is no doubt that this insistence upon a known and certain universe has been part of the cement that holds a culture together."[1] In the Rogerian approach to argumentation, effective communication requires both understanding another's reality and respecting it.

Rogers's approach to communication is based on the idea of mutual elements or **common ground**. A writer or speaker and an audience who have very different opinions on a highly charged emotional issue need a common ground on which to meet if any productive communication is going to take place. In the midst of all of their differences, they have to find a starting point on which they agree. In 1977, Maxine Hairston summed up five steps for using Rogerian argumentation that incorporate the two essentials of the

---

[1] Carl Rogers, "Do We Need 'a' Reality?" *A Way of Being* (New York, Houghton Mifflin, 1980), 103.

approach—being able to (1) summarize another's position with understanding and clarity and (2) locate common ground between two different positions:

1. Give a brief, objective statement of the issue under discussion.
2. Summarize in impartial language what you perceive the case for the opposition to be; the summary should demonstrate that you understand their interests and concerns and should avoid any hint of hostility.
3. Make an objective statement of your own side of the issue, listing your concerns and interests but avoiding loaded language or any hint of moral superiority.
4. Outline what common ground or mutual concerns you and the other person or group seem to share; if you see irreconcilable interests, specify what they are.
5. Outline the solution you propose, pointing out what both sides may gain from it.[2]

Rogerian argument places more emphasis on the relationship between audience and subject than other rhetorical theories do. It emphasizes the audience's view of the subject and places it in juxtaposition to the writer's. Understanding another's ideas with the clarity and lack of a judgmental attitude that Rogers proposed requires taking on, temporarily, that other's point of view—walking a mile in his shoes—and seeing the subject with his eyes.

As shown on the communications triangle below, the Rogerian approach seeks to find common ground between the writer's and audience's relationship to the subject.

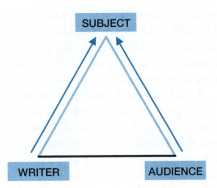

In an essay written using the Rogerian approach to argumentation, the thesis or claim will be one that reconciles opposing positions—at least as far as that is possible with the sorts of emotionally charged subjects that call for a nonconfrontational approach in the first place.

---

[2] Maxine Hairston, "Carl Rogers's Alternative to Traditional Rhetoric," *College Composition and Communication* (December 1976): 375–76.

Consider the example of management and striking union members. The situation can quickly degenerate into shouting matches and violence with little progress toward resolution. The union can make demands, which the management turns down, and the shouting matches begin again. Rogers would advocate the seemingly simple method of the two sides listening to each other with understanding. Management has to be able to explain the union's position in a way that the union members feel is fair before it can present its own. And then the reverse. This approach is time consuming, but it can keep the discussion from dissolving into anger and impasse. The resolution—parallel to the thesis of an essay employing the Rogerian method—will most likely be a compromise between the two positions.

In writing an essay using the Rogerian method, the test of the writer's *ethos*, or ethics, is how fairly she sums up her opponent's views. A common tactic for unethical writers is to attack an opponent for something he never said. This puts the opponent in the position of trying to defend a position that he does not believe and sidetracks the whole argument—which is exactly what the unscrupulous writer is trying to do.

The Rogerian approach is most useful in analyzing or writing about those topics that are tied to our most strongly held commitments, beliefs, and values. In the previous example, management and workers have very good reasons for holding the opposing positions that they do. For workers, their livelihoods and their ability to support their families are at risk; for management, the very survival of a company may be at risk, or at least its financial welfare. Even more controversial are arguments over issues that threaten individuals' moral or ethical values. That is why abortion remains a heated issue decades after Roe v. Wade. It's why American voters have sacrificed other values in the hope of seating a Supreme Court opposed to abortion. It is why LGTBQ+ rights are still controversial in the early twenty-first century. Debates about gun control are heated because gun owners feel that their Constitutional rights are at risk.

In cases like these, the most we may be able to hope for is a compromise or a move toward middle ground. Ironically, that is often all that opponents on an issue really want. Because we often assume our opponents on these controversial issues hold the most extreme position and they assume the same about us, even getting a conversation started can be difficult. The Rogerian approach is useful when a move toward middle ground is a good starting point and may be all that we can hope for.

ARGUMENT ESSENTIALS
Rogerian Argument

- Presents opponent's views accurately and objectively.

- Presents writer's views fairly and objectively.

- Explains what common ground exists between the two positions.

- Thesis statement presents a compromise between the two positions.

READING ARGUMENT

Seeing Rogerian Argument

The essay that follows has been annotated to show the key features of Rogerian argument used by the author.

Gun Debate: Where Is the Middle Ground?

MALLORY SIMON

Opening example

Amardeep Kaleka will never forget the moment when his father laid on the ground and prayed.

Satwant Singh Kaleka had been shot five times while wrestling a gunman in a Sikh temple in Oak Creek, Wisconsin. His turban was knocked off, and two kids and a priest crawled up beside him. Together, they prayed.

Amardeep Kaleka went to the temple and stared at that spot.

His father did not survive. He died along with five others.

"It felt like he was praying and putting something into the zeitgeist and imprinting it," he told CNN. His son hoped it would lead to a changing tide on gun violence.

As he began his meditation that day, Amardeep made a vow: He would do whatever he could to ensure nobody ever went through what his family had.

"It just came over me that you can't stay silent," he said. "You can't continue to allow violence like this to happen haphazardly at a church, at a school, any place."

That was August 2012.

Related example

Four months later, twenty children and six adults were gunned down in Newtown, Connecticut.

That school massacre has led many people, including Kaleka, 33, to question where we go from here as a country. Or if we will ever get there at all.

Looking for common ground

It led him to stand up at a gathering here on Thursday, CNN's *Guns Under Fire: An AC360° Town Hall Special*, and ask a panel of advocates with polar opposite views if they could agree on anything. If there was actually any middle ground.

5

10

Mallory Simon is a cross-platform manager at CNN. This piece appeared on CNN on January 31, 2013.

Mallory Simon, "Gun Debate: Where Is the Middle Ground?" *CNN.com*, January 31, 2013.

"After meeting with so many senators, so many gun proponents and gun control advocates, it seems like they're recycling the same jargon all the time," he said, explaining his reason for the question. "So I was just hoping, let's get to the common ground."

The panel included National Rifle Association board members, the president of the Brady Campaign to End Gun Violence, law enforcement representatives, and other participants voicing viewpoints across the spectrum.

Was there a consensus?

15   Sort of.

"There's a lot of common ground," Sandra Froman, a member of the NRA board of directors and a former president of the group, said at the town hall. "We don't want people who are insane to have guns, we don't want terrorists to have guns. Part of this national dialogue is coming together."

Expert representing one position: There is common ground.

So everyone agreed: Something has to happen. The devil is in the details.

Common ground

"I think the common ground clearly exists from a policy standpoint when talking about background checks," said Dan Gross, president of the Brady Campaign to End Gun Violence.

Expert representing another position: There is common ground.

But it isn't that simple. It never is when it comes to gun control.

20   "The NRA is not against background checks," Froman said. "We support making sure they are enforced. We're not supporting more background checks of law-abiding citizens."

Her remarks signaled a slight change in the NRA's stance.

In a heated back and forth, the two debated whether it was truly harmful to force everyone who wants to purchase a gun—whether at a gun store, a gun show, or in a private sale—to go through a background check.

Froman talked about how the current background check system was broken, noting that an "instant check" in Colorado can actually take about ten days.

Example

"We have to get it working before we add any more checks," she said, noting that requiring everyone to undergo a check would take a lot of resources and money.

25   Philadelphia Police Commissioner Charles Ramsey spoke from his experience, saying whatever it took, whatever the price tag, it would be worth it to stem the violence.

Appeal to the need for security

"Please, don't worry about the cost. I'll spend the money," he said, a line that drew massive applause from the crowd at George Washington University. "It's a much greater cost than human lives. We have to do something. The status quo is not acceptable."

When Kaleka, the son of one of the Sikh shooting victims, rose to ask his question about finding a middle ground, he wasn't just talking about policy. He also meant in our collective way of thinking. A filmmaker, Kaleka has made a documentary about violence in America. There are too many facets to the problem, he says.

"It's a culture of violence. And that has to do with guns, that has to do with mental illness, it has to do with stigmatizing people, it has to do with the media, everything about our culture."

Many appeared to think he was right.

"Everybody's got to step up on this," Ramsey said. "That's prosecutors,   30
the courts, everyone. If we're serious about this, it can't just be a series of laws that are passed."

Much of the discussion inside the town hall went beyond politics and legislation. One heated debate focused on whether armed guards should be posted at schools.

That's a proposal that's been discussed by former congressman Asa Hutchinson.

_{Emotional appeal/appeal to needs and values}

"What is more important than the education and the safety of those children?" he asked, noting that if malls have armed security, so should schools. "I believe an armed security presence is very important."

It's an idea that Veronique Pozner thinks about. Her son Noah was killed in the shooting at Sandy Hook Elementary in Newtown.

"I think there might be a certain power in deterrence," she said. "In the   35
case of Newtown, it's clear that the perpetrator did choose the path of least resistance, the most vulnerable defenseless victims. He didn't head for the high school where he could have been tackled."

_{Appeal to need for security}

While she said she wasn't sure an armed guard would have saved her son, she did say it made her feel more comfortable dropping off her other children at the new school for Sandy Hook children, a building that does have armed guards.

Colin Goddard, who survived the Virginia Tech shooting, said he understood the desire to protect children, but he didn't understand why arming guards is the go-to solution.

"I just don't understand why the first idea put forth is something that might help at the last second," he said, to massive applause from the audience. "We can do things in advance to keep a dangerous person and a gun from coming together in the first place."

That's the conversation that usually leads to a debate about mental health. It is an area President Barack Obama has pledged resources to; he and many others hope to keep guns out of the hands of the mentally ill.

40   The difficulty comes in figuring out who poses a threat.

A possible area for compromise

"We look at behavior and what's going on in the person's life, the social dynamics and what are the personality issues that make that person think acting out dangerously is a way to handle their problems," said Mary Ellen O'Toole, a former FBI special agent and criminal profiler.

Froman, the NRA board member, said she'd like to see more sharing of resources to ensure a database of the mentally ill would prevent them from having access to guns.

But Liza Long, whose blog post *I Am Adam Lanza's Mom* went viral after the Newtown shooting, said perhaps we were thinking about this all wrong. What if it wasn't just about identifying threats, but actually making a change.

"We spend a lot of time talking about keeping guns out of the wrong hands," she said. "What if we could put those resources to making people less dangerous."

45   For Kaleka, at the end of the day, progress on enforcing background checks would be a step in the right direction.

A positive move on which different sides might agree

He recognizes that no solution will make everyone happy. But he wishes every advocate, no matter their point of view, would think about the issue as if they were in his shoes.

"When you are a survivor or a victim or someone close to you dies, it's everyday you think about it," he said. "Gun advocates or scholars or people making money about it, they probably think about it 10 percent of how much we think about it. We go to the bathroom and think about it. We take a cold shower one day, and we start to cry. We wake up in the middle of the night with night sweats, and we have to live with it. Every breath is taken with some thought of violence and safety."

He thinks it is time the country does the same: that its citizens think about the issue with every breath.

"I can never go another moment in my life without thinking about it. My wife, my brother, my mother, the people of Newtown, they will not go a moment for the rest of their life without thinking about it," he said. "Personally I think the tide is changing, the zeitgeist is moving towards justice. Hopefully, once we stop the fear mongering on both sides we can finally get to the point of what makes sense."

Understanding of the need to work toward common ground

50   His greatest hope: That the will to do something about the violence does not die along with those who never had to.

Practice: Rogerian Argument

Use a Rogerian approach to analyze the following essay. Use the comments on the preceding essay as a model. Then answer the questions that appear at the end of the essay.

Teaching Trigger Warnings: What Pundits Don't Understand about the Year's Most Controversial Higher-Ed Debate

SARAH SELTZER

When Kyla Bender-Baird was an undergraduate a decade ago, a gender studies lecture she was attending ended with an incident she'll never forget: a visiting professor played a rape victim's graphic 911 call. Then the class was dismissed and, she says, everyone went home dazed and had "messed-up dreams" that night.

Although the professor apologized at the next session for failing to place the recording in appropriate context and give students adequate time to process it, Bender-Baird kept the incident in mind when she became a PhD candidate at the CUNY Graduate Center, teaching sociology courses to undergraduates. Now, she includes a note at the end of her syllabus that reads, in part:

> It is my goal in this class to create a safe environment in which we examine our assumptions . . . Discomfort can be part of the learning process as we are challenged to shift our paradigms. I invite you to sit with this discomfort. However, if the discomfort starts to turn to distress, I want you to take care of yourself. You can withdraw from an activity or even leave the classroom.

Since Bender-Baird added this text to her syllabus, only one student has walked out of her class, simply slipping out when she opened a discussion about "reclaiming the N-word."

Whether the student felt triggered by the word or simply couldn't bear having the same conversation yet again, the incident ended there.

Bender-Baird doesn't use the label "trigger warning" for her disclaimer, since it's unobtrusively placed at the end of her list of resources and segues into contact information for the counseling center. Yet it falls under the umbrella of cautionary notes encompassed by that loaded phrase, which has increasingly become the chief symbol of a tug-of-war on American campuses. "Trigger warning"—arising from PTSD psychology and popularized in feminist spaces on the Internet—refers to an advance notice for any content, usually violent, that might prompt a flashback, panic attack, or episode for survivors of trauma.

Intellectual heavyweights have decried   5
trigger warnings in widely circulated pieces. In a *New York Times* op-ed published in March, Judith Shulevitz bemoaned the focus on "safety" on campus: "While keeping college-level discussions 'safe' may feel good to the hypersensitive, it's bad for them and for everyone else," she wrote. Much of the academic Internet seemed to agree, particularly after the

Sarah Seltzer is a freelance journalist, essayist, and fiction writer in New York and an editor at *Lilith* magazine. This essay appeared on May 27, 2015, on *Flavorwire*.

publication of an op-ed by four Columbia University students arguing that Ovid's *Metamorphoses* was triggering and that classes needed to respect diverse identities. The backlash was intense on all sides of the political spectrum: right-wing columnist Kathleen Parker called students "swaddled," while feminist Lori Horvitz worried they were "coddled." Biology professor Jerry A. Coyne said the students' request smacked of "Big Brotherhood" and "cocooning." The real world doesn't come with trigger warnings, he said. On the other side, radical writers like Malcolm Harris have argued that the real problem is the Western canon itself: "Why should students have to endure gender- and race-based contempt from their required reading list?" he asks.

The debate has mostly been framed as students vs. faculty, hand-holding vs. freedom, political correctness vs. mind-expanding curricula. But educators who choose to utilize these warnings in their classrooms often see more nuance in the issue. "We have to take [students demanding trigger warnings] seriously . . . because being more acutely aware of how students are responding to challenging material is just better and more responsible pedagogy," wrote Aaron R. Hanlon last week. Faculty in this camp say that they're committed to academic and intellectual freedom, but also to honoring students' experiences, in particular the often silent presence of rape survivors — a trauma-prone group — among the college-aged population. Rather than debating whether to teach troubling material, as much of the anti-trigger warning contingent fears, they say they've moved on to asking how to do so in a respectful way.

Trigger warnings arose out of the psychological concept of Post-Traumatic Stress Disorder "triggers" — experiences or events that cause a trauma survivor to re-experience an incident, go into avoidance mode, or "numb out." While the theory evolved in the wake of the Vietnam War, the use of "trigger warnings" is very much a result of the feminist Internet, and the atmosphere of the twenty-first-century political climate. In a recent piece about trigger warnings, Jeet Heer noted that today's students are products of a post-9/11, War on Terror mentality. "PTSD is, in a crucial sense, a theory of memory: It posits that for certain people the memory of a trauma always exists, lying just below the surface," he wrote. "A theory of this sort will naturally lead to a heightened vigilance." Heer failed to mention the growing media and government attention to the campus rape epidemic, but that, too, is part of the trauma-saturated cultural picture in 2015.

Though, in recent years, "trigger" has become one of those frequently used terms that begin to lose meaning, understanding PTSD helps us understand why a classroom setting can be so fraught for some. "People who go through a trauma, the main thing they're reacting to is a loss of control," says NYC psychotherapist Bea Arthur (no relation to the *Golden Girls* actress). "Any other opposing force is going to be hard to accept, especially if it's an authority figure."

Caroline Heldman, a professor in Occidental University's politics department, learned about trigger warnings the hard way the better part of a decade ago, when students began experiencing PTSD-related episodes in her classes. "There were a few instances where students would break down crying and I'd have to suspend the class for the day so someone could get immediate mental health care," she says. In a sense, Heldman says, she introduced trigger warnings in order to keep the long tail of trauma outside the doors of learning rather than ushering it in.

10   "Trigger warnings allow me to have a conversation, to say, 'This is not a class about your personal life,'" Heldman told me. "This actually helps to make the class more academic. And it has the benefit of letting students prepare for what might come."

From a trauma-suffering student's perspective, the opportunity for preparation is key. "What happens if I'm warned that something has images of domestic violence or abuse in advance? I have five seconds to take a deep breath, to say to myself, ok, this is not real," grad student Angela Bennett-Segler wrote in a blog post that several friends in academia flagged for me. "I never shy away. Why? Because stories are powerful. Because they empowered me."

Haylin Belay is a brand-new graduate of Columbia University who has been diagnosed with PTSD. She says she seeks out individual accommodations from professors, checking in intermittently if she thinks material is going to be triggering. "It's far less disruptive," says the anthropology major. "In those classes, I'm able to participate more fully." She notes that when these systems are deployed most effectively—via a private back-and-forth with a professor, in communications ranging from frequent to rare—other students aren't affected at all, since their curriculum isn't disrupted. As for whether such a system is tenable in the real world, beyond the university setting, Belay compares it to an experience she had at a recent health education job, where she politely asked her supervisor to steer her away from discussions on the topic of rape and was accommodated.

Some instructors, particularly those who are survivors of rape or other trauma, also benefit from warnings, hoping they'll create a larger culture of compassion. "Part of the reason I give warnings is that I hope that they'll give me a few seconds of prep time, as well," one friend, a poet who teaches graduate-level writing and preferred to remain anonymous, told me. "It sucks to read through an essay and just abruptly read a student's usage of rape as an analogy for, like, soccer." Indeed, when professors inveigh against trigger warnings by complaining that they give students too much power over the classroom, they are glossing over this potential dynamic of students re-traumatizing professors.

A close reading of the text of actual trigger warnings, or similar disclaimers, on college syllabi reveals little in the way of coddling. In fact, most of these statements put the onus directly on students to deal with trauma, while acknowledging that professors understand the material might be unpleasant. "Over the course of the semester, we will be examining topics that may be emotionally triggering for trauma survivors," Heldman's syllabus reads in part. "If you are a trauma survivor, please develop a self-care plan for the semester so that you can effectively engage the course material and participate in class." According to Heldman, "It doesn't infantilize students, but treats them like they can handle information and process it. It makes me very comfortable introducing content I might otherwise be leery of introducing." It also reminds students that others in the classroom may be suffering from any number of causes, she says, preparing them to enter the real world with more empathy.

Dr. Mo Pareles, a postdoctoral fellow in   15
Medieval Literature at Northwestern University, uses a similarly straightforward disclaimer for her Medieval Humans and Beasts class: "I will not give trigger warnings, except to say here that the literature in this course contains a good deal

of nontrivial sexism, racism, violence, and so forth," it reads. "However, although shock value is certainly a legitimate pedagogical tool, nothing is included in the syllabus for that purpose."

"There is so much violence and bigotry in the material I teach that I can't really catalog it all," Pareles explained to me. "So this trigger warning is my way of saying that being upset is a valid reaction to some of what you'll encounter."

Compare these warnings to the standard spoken introduction that Josh Lambert, a visiting assistant professor of English at University of Massachusetts–Amherst, has used in Holocaust-related courses, and you'll find something similar. Lambert sent me his old notes, which read in part: "We'll be dealing with some harsh images and subjects. These are topics about which many people are understandably sensitive, and yet in this class I specifically want to deal with some texts that are excessive, or strange, or humorous, or difficult to take, or offensive," he told his students. "We should be respectful of everyone in the room, and keep in mind that some people in the room lost relatives in the Holocaust."

When it comes to the Holocaust, a gentle heads up may sound like common sense rather than censoriousness. The struggle taking place on campuses now is, in part, a way of asking faculty to see rape and racialized or gendered violence on a continuum with such self-evidently difficult topics. Unfortunately, outside of activist circles, where such questions are ceaselessly analyzed, many faculty members or students might not even recognize the depiction of rape in art or literature they assign—as in the Columbia students' complaint that *The Metamorphoses* was taught without any explanation that it depicted rape. Conversely, students who think themselves fluent in the language

of social justice might not understand why reading a book containing a depraved sexual assault isn't endorsing that depravity. This is exactly where more dialogue between professors and students might help, not hurt.

"Students who don't distinguish between conversations about racism and actual racism, for instance, are probably misunderstanding what 'triggers' actually are," says Carrie Nelson, a writer who worked as a TA in film classes at the New School when she was a graduate student. "Professors should teach students the nuances that distinguish feeling triggered and feeling uncomfortable or offended. But, of course, that involves a degree of extra work that underpaid university professors—rightfully—may not want to put in."

Columbia graduate Belay cites an example [20] of a professor who gives the same lecture twice, once with potentially disturbing accompanying slides and once without, as a particularly thoughtful response to student needs. Regardless of whether faculty members are willing to go to such lengths, she says, "We're not asking for syllabi to be rewritten or classes to be struck from the curriculum. I find that just as alarming as other people do. We're asking for accommodations." By understanding PTSD in the classroom as a disability, Belay makes a huge distinction between hurtful topics and triggering topics. She notes that students have said troubling things about subjects like welfare in classes she's attended—a potentially uncomfortable moment, but not necessarily a triggering one. When she was upset by comments like that, she had a voice to counter them. She contrasts this with the experience of actually having a PTSD reaction, when a student might feel paralyzed and unable to speak at all, and might disengage entirely.

When you read the warnings used by these teachers, it seems that they might achieve two goals: giving traumatized students time to prepare, but also asking all students to willingly engage. This second idea attempts to explicitly avoid the trigger warning "slippery slope" that concerns so many thinkers. The bottom of that slope is a passel of squeamish, conservative, or immature students gleefully manipulating the idea of triggers as a way of shirking intellectual growth—how far is the distance from, "I can't read Ovid because it depicts rape" to, "I can't read Sappho because it's gay"? Opening class by saying, "It's up to you to come up with a plan to handle upsetting stuff," might actually dissuade any students acting in bad faith from trying to use the concept of triggers to take over the classroom.

Moments of overreach are likely inevitable in any environment where entitled students roam—though, again, not always in precisely the way outside observers might assume. Faculty members relayed anecdotes to me including an objection to the word "breast" because it might offend breast cancer survivors, and another situation in which the lone male in a classroom said his position as such made him uncomfortable hearing the word "rape." Students who act in bad faith will probably do so no matter what. Still, this kind of "we can't read Gatsby" incident, strewn throughout every comment section of every article on the subject, explains many educators' understandable fear that the culture of trigger warnings will lead to a chilling atmosphere on campus.

Students and faculty who use trigger warnings acknowledge legitimate concerns about the state of academia—while maintaining that thinking about how to teach with sensitivity is very different from squelching autonomy.

"Online, the conversation got ugly," says Bender-Baird. "Trigger warnings became the depository for a lot of things that are going wrong in academia, like corporatization and the expansion of administrative control over classrooms. The students and their emotional and psychological needs get completely lost in the conversation." By the same token, Pareles says, it's crucial to discuss "the erosion of academic freedom and the marketing of college as a consumer item," where students' demands are justified by their (or their family's) enormous investment. Yet to use those issues as a way to avoid the trigger question entirely, she says, means that faculty are ironically insulating themselves from painful material—namely, the real-world power dynamics involved in trauma.

If presented in a careful way, these warnings (as most often worded) can do the opposite of babying students; they open up the lines of communication between students and professors, ask students to take responsibility for their own reactions, and prevent disingenuous students from making every class discussion a venue for airing their own alleged grievances. As for situations in which students are demanding trigger warnings or asking administrators to make them mandatory, not a single person I spoke to, student or professor, supports administrative interference on this matter. They simply say that professors—whether through content warnings or in some other way—should let students know that they're approachable and responsive and understand the existence of trauma in the population they teach. In this kind of environment, perhaps some outlandish curricular demands would be handled in one office-hours conversation rather than in the national news.

25   Similarly, the phrase "trigger warning" itself—whose meaning in the culture has morphed from vocabulary specific to the realm of therapy to an overused symbol of an "oversensitive" cadre—might be more distracting than useful. Faculty might be better off folding content notes into resource sections on syllabi, or into their introductory notes, without employing the term. Alternately, Belay says, rather than mandating trigger warnings, universities could systematically enable students with PTSD to communicate with professors via backchannels, making the entire process more streamlined and less public.

Whatever the individual solutions are, at least grappling with the subject beyond the pro/con debate might lead to growth and new approaches to teaching. "To be honest, I feel that the debate on trigger warnings is actually a blind," Pareles says. "No one is going to be forced to use trigger warnings, but thinking about them forces the question: How much do people who have not experienced sexual assault, racism, transphobia, and so on have to consider how profoundly these experiences continue to harm people in their own community?"

Reading, Writing, and Discussion Questions

1. How does Sarah Seltzer define trigger warnings?
2. What are some of the positions that others have taken on the issue of trigger warnings?
3. In what sense is Seltzer's essay an example of Rogerian argument? What compromise does she offer?
4. How does Seltzer support her opinion about trigger warnings?

Stasis Theory

Another concept from the classical age of Greek and Roman rhetoric that can still be applied to arguments today is that of **stasis theory**. Aristotle and another Greek philosopher, Hermagoras, wrote about stasis theory, and their ideas were refined by the Roman philosophers Cicero, Quintilian, and Hermogenes. Stasis theory provided citizens preparing a legal case a means of exploring the case and of achieving stasis, or arriving at agreement as to the point at issue.

The Stasis Questions

Consider first how a series of questions could provide a structured way of thinking about an alleged crime:

- **Questions of Fact or Conjecture:** What happened? Did the accused do it?
- **Questions of Definition:** What crime was it?

- **Questions of Quality:** Was it right or wrong? Was it justified? What was the motivation?
- **Questions of Procedure:** What should be done about it? What is the proper court to hear the case?

These questions have been recast into more general questions that can be applied to any issue about which there is disagreement. It is important to achieve stasis in order to argue effectively because you have to know precisely what is at issue. For example, the term "gun control" is so broad that it is necessary to define the term before trying to argue for or against it. If one party is arguing in favor of taking all guns away from all American citizens, that party will not agree with someone who is arguing that "controlling" guns means enforcing stricter laws about the types of guns that can be sold or about the waiting period for buying a gun. There is a difference between which guns are controlled and how gun ownership is controlled that will make formal debate about the issue pointless until some definitions are clarified. A starting point could be to decide, for example, whether or not American citizens should be allowed to own semiautomatic weapons, but even then, the definition of "semiautomatic" would have to be agreed upon.

The stasis questions are frequently used in writing courses as a means of exploring a subject. Different textbooks and different scholars word the questions a bit differently, and some list four questions, while others list five. This list of four is fairly standard as a set of questions for exploring argumentative topics:

- **Questions of Fact:** What are the facts of the issue?
- **Questions of Definition:** What is the meaning or nature of the issue?
- **Questions of Quality:** What is the seriousness or value of the issue?
- **Questions of Policy:** What is the plan of action about the issue?

READING ARGUMENT

Seeing Stasis Theory

Used as a means of invention, the stasis questions can generate a wealth of information. You will most likely use only a portion of the ideas generated by the invention exercise, but you may also discover ideas that you might not have thought about otherwise.

Take a subject like the Electoral College in the United States, and see what ideas might come to mind in working through the questions:

- **Questions of Fact: What are the facts about the Electoral College?**
  On September 6, 1787, the Constitutional Convention approved a proposal to create a group of Electors to select the president and vice president of the new United States. Each of the fifty states has a number of Electors equal to its number of members of Congress, and the District of Columbia has the same number of Electors as the least populous state. There are now 538 Electors. Since the 1880s, all states except Maine and

Nebraska pledge all of their Electors to the presidential candidate who wins the most popular votes in that state. A majority of 270 electoral votes is needed to elect the president. When Americans cast their votes every four years, they are actually voting not for a candidate but for Electors representing that candidate.

What has happened in some recent elections? In 2016, Donald Trump defeated Hillary Clinton, winning 306 electoral votes to Clinton's 232, but winning only 62,984,825 popular votes compared to Clinton's 65,853,516. In 2012, Barack Obama defeated Mitt Romney, winning 332 electoral votes to Romney's 206, and winning 65,446,032 popular votes to Romney's 60,589,084. Obama won the popular vote in 26 states and the District of Columbia, and Romney won the popular vote in 24 states. In 2000, George W. Bush defeated Al Gore Jr., winning 271 electoral votes to Gore's 266, and winning 50,456,062 popular votes to Gore's 50,996,582.

Electoral votes are not cast until December after a presidential election in November. Each state sends a Certificate of Votes recording how the Electors voted to the Senate, where the votes are counted on the sixth of January. There is no Constitutional requirement that Electors vote according to the popular vote, but some states require their Electors to do so, making it binding by state law or by pledges to the political parties.

- **Questions of Definition: What is the meaning or nature of the Electoral College?**

The Electoral College is not a place but a process—the process by which the president and vice president of the United States are chosen. The Constitution refers to Electors but not to a college of Electors. The concept was written into federal law in 1845 as a "college of Electors." The Electoral College was originally a compromise between the election of a president by a vote in Congress and election by a popular vote of qualified citizens. The question of what constituted qualified citizens was complicated in the eighteenth century by the existence of slavery in some states. Technically, a vote for Clinton or Trump, Bush or Gore was not a vote for any of those individuals but a vote for an Elector chosen to vote for one of them. The Electors from each state do not meet as a group until December after a presidential election in November.

- **Questions of Quality: What is the seriousness or value of the Electoral College?**

Some question whether in the twenty-first century the Electoral College is preferable to popular vote as the method of choosing president and vice president. Is a procedure fair if it is possible for a candidate to win the popular vote but not win the election because of Electoral College votes? The writers of the Constitution felt that a small group of Electors would make a wiser political decision than the general public. Small states also feared the power of larger states. Would states with a small number of popular votes be largely ignored if popular vote were used? Are some states currently disadvantaged by the winner-take-all system in forty-eight states that can make almost 50 percent of voters feel that their votes are wasted because all of that state's electoral votes go to the candidate who wins the majority of the popular vote?

- **Questions of Policy: What is the plan of action about the issue?**
  Should the Electoral College be abolished? Should it be replaced by popular vote? Should the Electoral College continue to exist, but the winner-take-all method of distributing electoral votes be abolished?

Practice: Stasis Theory

Using the analysis of the Electoral College above as a guide, apply the four stasis questions to one of the following topics. Push yourself to write more than a sentence or two in response to each question. What you write can be a combination of questions and statements.

> Shelter-in-place orders and social distancing
> Late-term abortion
> Hazing
> Open carry
> Body cameras for police
> Good Samaritan laws
> Social media censorship

Stasis Theory Claims

The stasis questions can help lead to decisions regarding what to say about a topic. Each of the four questions leads most directly to a certain type of claim, or thesis statement, and a certain type of argument.

Questions of Fact	lead to	**Claims of Fact**	and	**Analysis.**
Questions of Definition	lead to	**Claims of Definition**	or	**Definition Arguments.**
Questions of Quality	lead to	**Claims of Value**	or	**Evaluation Arguments.**
Questions of Policy	lead to	**Claims of Policy**	or	**Proposal Arguments.**

Keep in mind that many arguments are not a pure form of any of these types of argument. Establishing facts and definitions is often a part of building a sound evaluation or proposal argument. Evaluation is often a part of establishing the need for a proposed change.

In the section on the Toulmin Method, you will read more about claims of fact, value, and policy, and the whole of Chapter 6 is devoted to the writing of these three types of claims. Chapter 11 discusses the need for clear definition in any argument and those topics that may require an entire essay of definition.

RESEARCH SKILL Narrowing Your Research

Given the freedom to choose your own topic for an argument based on independent research, the stasis questions can help you discover what you want to say about it. You can generate more starting points for your research than you will be able to pursue, but in the abundance of ideas you produce, you may find the one that will be the most fruitful avenue of research. In this box, the stasis questions explore the general topic of sexual assault in the military.

- **Questions of Fact:** What are the facts of the issue?

  For facts, you might choose to go to newspapers as a starting point to find objective reporting on details of the issue. Searching newspaper databases, such as Newspaper Source Plus or CQ Researcher, may mean trying different combinations of search terms. In our example case, we also wanted recent information, so these numbers are based on sources published since 2015.

  - Searching the terms "sexual assault" and "military" produces 1,164 sources.
  - Adding the term "number" to the search produces 134.
  - Restricting the search to U.S. newspapers produces a more manageable 46.

- **Questions of Definition:** What is the meaning or nature of the issue?

  For sources that go beyond reporting facts to interpreting them, you might choose to go to a general resource like Google as a starting place to look for articles. The number of hits there, however, may be too large to be useful.

  - A search for "sexual assault in the military" produces 78,000,000 hits.
  - Limiting the search to academic articles still produces 240,000.

Going to an academic database — in this case Academic OneFile — is one way to limit the number of sources immediately.

- Searching the terms "sexual assault" and "military" produces 72 sources.
- Limiting the search again to sources since the beginning of 2015 produces 26.
- Limiting the search to the United States produces 11.

- **Questions of Quality:** What is the seriousness or value of the issue?

  When you move into the area of making value judgments about an issue, you can move into sources such as editorials.

  - Adding the document title "editorial" to the keywords "sexual assault" and "military" leads to a manageable 40 sources, all of them newspaper articles.
  - Limiting the search again to editorials since 2015 leads to 3 sources.

- **Questions of Policy:** What is the plan of action about the issue?

  Looking through databases in one college library reveals a specialized database called the Military and Government Collection, which seems like a possible source for information about proposals for solving the problem of sexual assaults in the military. This database also uses keywords to search.

  - Searching the keywords "sexual assault" and "military" produces 118 sources.
  - Limiting the search to the United States narrows the number to 1, which seems useful since it as an article from 2015 that discusses new rules from the Department of Defense regarding rape cases.

This is only one example of how a search might proceed using the stasis questions as a discovery technique. Every search will be different.

The Toulmin Model

Although Aristotle and Rogers, centuries and worlds apart, have both made significant contributions to rhetorical theory, the Toulmin model presents what we believe is a more helpful argumentative model for reading and writing arguments in a systematic manner. The late Stephen Toulmin provided the vocabulary about argumentation that gives this book its original structure.[3]

Toulmin's model, proposed in 1958 in *The Uses of Argument*, was designed to analyze courtroom arguments. Our hope is that you will find it useful in analyzing the arguments that you read and in planning the arguments you will write. Only after his model had been introduced to rhetoricians by Wayne Brockriede and Douglas Ehninger did Toulmin discuss its rhetorical implications in *Introduction to Reasoning* (1979). That link to rhetoric laid the foundation for the Toulmin model as a way of teaching how to write arguments. It is a model that can be applied to the reading or writing of any argument. Of the six key terms in Toulmin's model, we draw heavily on three: claim, support, and assumption (also sometimes called a warrant).

The Toulmin model addresses all three legs of the communication triangle, connecting writer, subject, and audience.

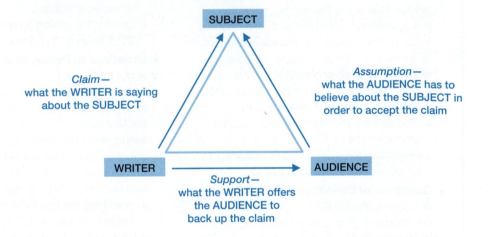

The Claim

The **claim** (also called a proposition) answers the question "What are you trying to prove?" It will generally appear as the thesis statement of an essay, although in some arguments it may not be stated directly. There are three principal kinds of claims (discussed more fully in Chapter 6): claims of fact, of value, and of policy. **Claims of fact** assert that a condition has existed,

---

[3] Stephen Toulmin, *The Uses of Argument* (Cambridge: Cambridge University Press, 1958).

exists, or will exist and are based on facts or data that the audience will accept as being objectively verifiable.

- The diagnosis of autism is now far more common than it was twenty years ago.
- Fast foods are contributing significantly to today's epidemic of childhood obesity.
- Climate change will affect the coastlines of all continents.

All these claims must be supported by data. Although the last example is an inference or an educated guess about the future, a reader will probably find the prediction credible if the data seem authoritative.

Claims of value attempt to prove that some things are more or less desirable than others. They express approval or disapproval of standards of taste and morality. Advertisements and reviews of cultural events are one common source of value claims, but such claims emerge whenever people argue about what is good or bad, beautiful or ugly.

- *Fleabag* does an excellent job of depicting grief and mental health issues.
- Abortion is wrong under any circumstances.
- The right to privacy is more important than the need to increase security at airports.

Claims of policy assert that specific policies should be instituted as solutions to problems. The expression *should*, *must*, or *ought to* usually appears in the statement.

- The Electoral College should be replaced by popular vote as the means of electing a president.
- Attempts at making air travel more secure must not put in jeopardy the passengers' right to privacy.
- Existing laws governing gun ownership should be more stringently enforced.

Policy claims call for analysis of both fact and value.

Practice

1. Classify each of the following as a claim of fact, value, or policy.
    a. Solar power could supply 20 percent of the energy needs now satisfied by fossil fuel and nuclear power.
    b. Violence in video games produces violent behavior in children.
    c. Both intelligent design and evolutionary theory should be taught in the public schools.
    d. Some forms of cancer are caused by viruses.
    e. Dogs are smarter than cats.
    f. The money that our government spends on foreign aid would be better spent solving domestic problems like unemployment and homelessness.

    g. Wherever the number of unauthorized immigrants increases, the crime rate also increases.

    h. Movie sequels are generally inferior to their originals.

    i. Tom Hanks is a more versatile actor than Tom Cruise.

    j. Adopted children who are of a different ethnic background than their adoptive parents should be raised with an understanding of the culture of their biological parents.

    k. Average yearly temperatures in North America are already being affected by climate change.

    l. Human activity is the primary cause of climate change.

2. Which claims listed above would be most difficult to support?

3. What type or types of evidence would it take to build a convincing case for each claim?

The Support

Support consists of the materials that the arguer uses to convince an audience that his or her claim is sound. These materials include evidence and motivational appeals to needs and values. The **evidence** or data consists of facts, statistics, and testimony from experts. The **appeals to needs and values** are the ones that the arguer makes to the values and attitudes of the audience to win support for the claim. These appeals (also known as *emotional* or *motivational* appeals) are the reasons that move an audience to accept a belief or adopt a course of action. (See Chapter 7 for a detailed discussion of support.)

The Assumption

Certain **assumptions** underlie all the claims we make. In the Toulmin model, the term *warrant* is often used for such an assumption, a belief or principle that is taken for granted. It may be stated or unstated. If the arguer believes that the audience shares the assumption, there may be no need to express it. But if the audience seems doubtful or hostile, the arguer may decide to state the assumption to emphasize its importance or argue for its validity. The assumption, stated or not, enables the reader to make the same connection between the support and the claim that the author does. In other words, you have to accept the assumption in order to accept the author's claim based on the evidence provided.

    Claim: The popular vote should replace the Electoral College as the means of electing the president.

    Support: The popular vote gives each voter one vote for president.

    Assumption: The president should be elected by a system that gives each voter one vote.

Claim: A picture ID should be required for eligibility to vote.

Support: Picture IDs would cut down on voter fraud.

Assumption: A requirement that cuts down on voter fraud should be implemented.

Claim: In the United States, 1 in 68 children has an autism spectrum disorder.

Support: That number is based on the latest report from the Centers for Disease Control.

Assumption: The latest report from the Centers for Disease Control is a reliable source of information on the incidence of autism spectrum disorders in the United States.

Claim: The 2019 movie version of *Little Women* is a much better movie than the 1994 version.

Support: The new movie is much more realistic.

Assumption: A more realistic movie is better than one that is less realistic.

One more important characteristic of the assumption deserves mention. In most cases, the assumption is a more general statement of belief than the claim. It can, therefore, support many claims, not only the one in a particular argument. For example, the assumption that being safe is worth a small loss of privacy expresses a broad assumption or belief that we take for granted and that can underlie claims about many other practices in American society. (For more on assumptions, see Chapter 8.)

Toulmin and the Syllogism

You will see some similarities between Toulmin's three-part structure of claim, support, and assumption and the classical deductive syllogism articulated by Aristotle. In fact, a comparison of the two may help in understanding the assumption.

The syllogism is useful for laying out the basic elements of an argument, and it lends itself more readily to simple arguments. It is a formula that consists of three elements: (1) the major premise, (2) the minor premise, and (3) the conclusion, which follows logically from the two premises. The following syllogism summarizes a familiar argument.

Major premise: Advertising of things harmful to our health should be legally banned.

Minor premise: Cigarettes are harmful to our health.

Conclusion: Therefore, advertising of cigarettes should be legally banned.

Cast in the form of the Toulmin model, the argument looks like this:

Claim: Advertising of cigarettes should be legally banned.

Support (Evidence): Cigarettes are harmful to our health.

Assumption: Advertising of things harmful to our health should be legally banned.

Or in diagram form:

SUPPORT ——————————————→ **CLAIM**

Cigarettes are harmful   Advertising of cigarettes
to our health.   should be legally banned.

ASSUMPTION

Advertising of things harmful to our
health should be legally banned.

ARGUMENT ESSENTIALS
The Toulmin Model

Claim — the proposition that the author is trying to prove. The claim may appear as the thesis statement of an essay but may be implied rather than stated directly.

- *Claims of fact* assert that a condition has existed, exists, or will exist and are based on facts or data that the audience will accept as being objectively verifiable.

- *Claims of value* attempt to prove that some things are more or less desirable than others; they express approval or disapproval of standards of taste and morality.

- *Claims of policy* assert that specific plans or courses of action should be instituted as solutions to problems.

Support — the materials used by the arguer to convince an audience that his or her claim is sound; those materials include evidence and motivational appeals.

Assumption — an inference; a belief or principle that is taken for granted in an argument.

In both the syllogism and the Toulmin model, the principal elements of the argument are expressed in three statements. You can see that the claim in the Toulmin model is the conclusion in the syllogism — that is, the proposition that you are trying to prove. The evidence (support) in the Toulmin model corresponds to the minor premise in the syllogism. And the assumption in the Toulmin model resembles the major premise of the syllogism.

While the syllogism is essentially static, with all three parts logically locked into place, the Toulmin model suggests that an argument is a *movement* from support to claim by way of the warrant (assumption), which acts as a bridge. Toulmin introduced the concept of warrant by asking, "How do you get there?" (His first two questions, introducing the claim and support, were "What are you trying to prove?" and "What have you got to go on?")

READING ARGUMENT

Seeing the Toulmin Model

The following essay has been annotated to show the key features of the Toulmin model used by the author.

To Be a Good Doctor, Study the Humanities

ANGIRA PATEL

A three-year-old was newly diagnosed with a brain tumor called a medullo-blastoma. The pediatric oncologist, aware of the steep odds against the child's survival, explained the diagnosis and counseled the family. The doctor performed a bone marrow biopsy while singing the alphabet to soothe the child. Eventually, she comforted the family when their child died, tears in her eyes. As a medical student who was new to witnessing death, I could feel the grief of both the family and the physician. Later, as a doctor in training, I actively cared for a child with congenital heart disease as he died of multi-system organ failure. Eventually, when I became the doctor in charge, I determined the treatment course and was responsible for guiding the conversation when a patient's death was imminent.

Recently, I told these stories in an introductory undergraduate religion class that asked the students to consider how best to support a patient who is dying. Do you cry with the patient? Is it acceptable to be detached? Is it OK to resume your life and laugh a few hours later? Further: How, where, and from whom do you learn these skills? Most of the students were science majors and hoping to become doctors. They understood the general idea that how you experience death and dying changes over time, and is not the same process for everyone. But they also wanted to know what makes a good doctor.

As a philosophy major in college before medical school, I believe I learned what it means to be a good doctor equally from my humanities classes as from my science classes. Studying the humanities helps students develop critical-thinking skills, understand the viewpoints of others and different cultures, foster a just conscience, build a capacity for empathy, and become wise about emotions such as grief and loss. These are all characteristics that define a good doctor.

The National Academies of Sciences, Engineering, and Medicine recently released a report arguing for the integration of STEM with the arts and the humanities. Given the projected increase in STEM jobs, the need

Patel uses her opening example to support her claim, which comes later. The examples are also an appeal to the emotions, which is a type of support.

The paragraph traces her evolution as a doctor and her increasing awareness of the emotion involved, helping establish her claim to authority.

Patel summarizes her experience, then offers supporting examples of what she learned that helped her become a good doctor.

Patel states one of her underlying assumptions, that these qualities developed in humanities classes make one a good doctor.

Support: An example of a prominent organization that agrees with her claim

Angira Patel is an assistant professor of pediatrics and medical education and a member of the Center for Bioethics and Medical Humanities at Northwestern University's Feinberg School of Medicine; a pediatric cardiologist at the Ann & Robert H. Lurie Children's Hospital of Chicago; and a Public Voices Fellow through The OpEd Project. Her essay appeared in *Pacific Standard* on May 23, 2018.

for a workforce to fill them, and the prospect of a well-paying job, it's not surprising that students are encouraged to pursue STEM fields.

At the same time, the important role of humanities in medicine is emphasized in scores of programs in the United States and around the world, including Stanford University, Northwestern University's Feinberg School of Medicine, the University of California–San Francisco, and King's College London. Meanwhile, some medical schools are reworking their curricula, and peer-reviewed journals such as *Medical Humanities* and the *Journal of Medical Humanities* publish work that emphasizes the importance of the humanities for doctors.

This emphasis on the humanities in medical school trains future doctors to become proficient in the social and cultural context of health care, beyond what they learn from the hard sciences. Both skills are necessary to promote and improve the health of a society that depends on scientific innovation but also needs desperately to tackle the social determinants of health.

The research suggests that this focus needs to start earlier, in future physicians' undergraduate years.

Only 3.5 percent of medical school applicants major in humanities, but their acceptance rate is higher (50 percent) than the overall rate (41 percent).

A 2009 study found that, once they reach medical school, students who majored in humanities as college students perform just as well as, if not better than, their peers with science backgrounds. Furthermore, a 2010 study assessed the medical school performance of humanities and social science majors who omitted traditional science classes in college, versus those who had a traditional pre-medical preparation. Both groups of students performed at an equivalent level in medical school based on clerkship grades. Another study suggested that formal art observation training can improve a medical student's capacity to make accurate observations of physical findings in a patient.

A more recent study from earlier this year shows that medical students who are exposed to the humanities demonstrate higher levels of positive skills and qualities such as empathy, tolerance for ambiguity, wisdom, emotional appraisal, self-efficacy, and spatial reasoning—all important in being a competent, good doctor.

The same study found that humanities exposure is inversely correlated with negative qualities that can be detrimental to physician well-being, such as intolerance to ambiguity, physical fatigue, emotional exhaustion, and cognitive weariness.

Humanities majors may be more likely to pursue residencies in primary care and psychiatry—both areas where there is tremendous need.

Support: Other examples of schools and publications that emphasize the role of humanities in medicine. The underlying assumption is that these schools and publications know what makes a good doctor.

Claim

Statistical support

The next three paragraphs of examples support her claim. The underlying assumption is that these studies were carefully conducted and, therefore, that the conclusions reached are valid.

5

10

Humanities exposure can arguably benefit patients by making better doctors and it may also be beneficial for the individual physician.

In this era of increasing dissatisfaction within the medical profession, a doctor also needs the tools to develop and nurture her own humanity so that she can continue her work, healthy in mind and body. Patients deserve a doctor who is thoughtful, professional, compassionate, understanding, humble, collaborative, wise, and knowledgeable. And while there are many factors in the development of a physician, humanities education is one important avenue toward making better doctors.

15   As you read this, students have secured positions in the freshman class of 2019 and are deciding what to study in college. Presumably, some aspiring doctors will look into the STEM fields. I suggest that all students should look to the humanities.

Assumption: The study of humanities gives a doctor the means of developing her own humanity.

Practice: The Toulmin Model

Analyze the following article using Toulmin's three key terms: claim, support, and assumption. Use the Angira Patel essay as a model. Then answer the questions that appear at the end.

Embryo Selection May Help Prevent Some Inherited Disorders
STEVEN REINBERG

When a twenty-seven-year-old woman wanted to have a baby using in vitro fertilization, there was one major problem—she was a carrier of Gerstmann-Straussler-Sheinker syndrome.

This rare, degenerative neurological condition is usually diagnosed in mid-life and is always fatal. Not wanting to risk having her child become a victim of the syndrome, she turned to a technique that tests embryos for certain mutated genes and only uses those embryos that don't carry the mutation for implantation.

"This disease was found in five generations in this family, and we stopped passing these bad genes to the next generation," said study co-author Svetlana Rechitsky, laboratory director at the Reproductive Genetics Institute in Chicago.

According to Dr. Ilan Tur-Kaspa, lead researcher and president and medical director of the Institute for Human Reproduction in Chicago, "These new cases can be prevented now by pre-implantation genetic diagnosis." Although this is the first report on using this method for a so-called prion disorder, it could also help prevent diseases like Huntington's and familial forms of Alzheimer's disease, he said.

Prion diseases involve abnormal foldings of the prion protein in the brain. The most commonly known one, which is not inherited,

Steven Reinberg, a health journalist, is a senior staff reporter for healthday.com, where this article appeared on February 3, 2014.

is bovine spongiform encephalopathy, or "mad cow" disease.

The report was published online February 3 in the journal *JAMA Neurology*.

The process started with a simple in vitro fertilization procedure. Eggs from the woman were removed and fertilized. Then came the tricky part.

Doctors removed single cells from the embryos, and because the syndrome is caused by a single gene mutation, they looked at DNA to find embryos that didn't have the mutated gene.

"We can identify which embryo is healthy, and which embryo has the bad gene," Rechitsky explained.

10   Two of the disease-free embryos were implanted, and the woman had twins delivered by cesarean section a little more than 33 weeks later. The remaining normal embryos were frozen for later use.

At twenty-seven months, the twins had normal communication, social, and emotional skills, the researchers reported.

One expert noted the importance of the finding.

"Most of the genetic disorders identified by pre-implantation genetic diagnosis are caused by either single genes — such as cystic fibrosis, Huntington's disease, sickle cell anemia, Down syndrome, Trisomy 18 (Edwards syndrome) and chromosomal translocations — and most have no treatment or cure," said Christine Metz, director of Maternal-Fetal Medicine Research at the Feinstein Institute for Medical Research in Manhasset, New York. "Thus, it is important for young parents to know and understand their risks for inherited diseases prior to conception."

In addition, pre-implantation genetic diagnosis is beginning to be used to reduce the transmission of mutant cancer genes, such as the BRCA1/BRCA2 genes, which are tied to breast cancer, and the MLH1, MSH2, and APC genes that are linked to colon cancer, she said.

"Over several generations, we can hope to   15 improve human health by reducing the transmission of several hereditary disorders," Metz said.

Rechitsky acknowledged that some people have ethical problems with the potential for this technology to be used to tailor babies to parents' desires. However, in the twenty-five years they have been doing the procedure it hasn't been a problem, she said.

"We had the first successful pregnancy in 1990," Rechitsky said. "Over the years, we have performed over 4,000 procedures for single-gene disorders. It has become a more widely accepted approach to prevent hereditary disease," she explained.

As to tailoring babies, "we have never ever had any requests like this," she said. Moreover, many of the things parents might want to select for like intelligence, involve many genes, not just one. "We don't know even how to approach this," she noted.

Dr. Avner Hershlag, chief of the Center for Human Reproduction at North Shore University Hospital in Manhasset, New York, said, "Like any sophisticated technique, reproductive technology can be abused. There are ethical issues."

Hershlag said that "the most ethical   20 approach is that it should be used for identifying disease only, and for selecting embryos that are free of disease. I don't want it to ever head into that murky, questionable line between what is right and what is wrong. It is absolutely right to diagnose a disease in an embryo and to use embryos that don't have disease."

Reading, Writing, and Discussion Questions

1. How does the procedure that Steven Reinberg describes stop the inheritance of diseases?
2. Why might some people find the procedure unethical? What is Dr. Hershlag's defense against that charge?
3. Is Reinberg's claim in the article the same as the claim that Dr. Hershlag is making?
4. What types of support for his claim does Reinberg offer?
5. What assumption must a reader be willing to accept in order to accept Reinberg's claim?

Assignments for Approaches to Argument

Reading and Discussion Questions

1. How are the Aristotelian and the Toulmin approaches to argumentation different? How are they similar?
2. Do you believe that presidential debates are good examples of argumentation? Explain.
3. When you write essays and reports for your classes, how do you establish your credibility? In contrast, how do students lose their credibility with the instructors who read their work?
4. What are some situations you have been in—or have read or heard about—in which people's opinions were so far apart that the best you could hope for was compromise rather than total victory for one side or the other?
5. What are some of the controversial issues in the field of your major or a major that you are considering? Analyze one or more of them using Toulmin's terms: claim, support, and assumption.
6. Think of some situations in which each of these approaches to argument might be the best approach and why: Aristotelian, Rogerian, Stasis theory, Toulmin model.

Writing Suggestions

1. Write an essay in which you discuss how technological advances have changed an audience's ability to evaluate a speaker's *ethos*.
2. Write an essay in which you discuss how both Aristotelian and Rogerian argument are useful in contemporary politics.
3. Write an essay in which you identify some of the issues about which it is most difficult to achieve common ground, and explain why.
4. Write an essay in which you explain why different underlying assumptions make it so difficult to reach a compromise on the issue of gun control.

RESEARCH ASSIGNMENT

For a topic you have chosen for a research paper or one that is the object of controversy in your major field or in a field in which you might major, do some preliminary research, using the Stasis Questions as a starting point. Write 1–2 paragraphs on each question, similar to the answers about the Electoral College (pp. 152–154), but also write down where you found the information. The Research Skill: Narrowing Your Research box (p. 155) gives some examples of where you might look for information, using the Stasis Questions as a guide. At the end, write a paragraph about a direction your further research might take, given what you learned in your preliminary research.

- **Questions of Fact:** What are the facts of the issue?
- **Questions of Definition:** What is the meaning or nature of the issue?
- **Questions of Quality:** What is the seriousness or value of the issue?
- **Questions of Policy:** What is the plan of action about the issue?

Claims

Wastat are you trying to prove? Your claim, or proposition, represents your answer to this question. A **claim** is the statement that a writer makes about a subject and thus is most closely aligned with the writer-subject leg of the communications triangle.

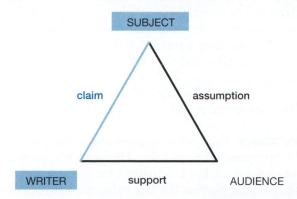

Your **main claim** is a conclusion you reach when you are trying to decide what to say about a subject. You are by now familiar with the concept of a **thesis** statement, or the single statement that summarizes the main claim of your essay and may also indicate the organization of the piece. The thesis of an argument that you read or write must be arguable, and there may be other claims in an argumentative essay that also need to be supported. They may appear as the topic sentences of some of the body paragraphs in the essay, but they won't necessarily be so easy to identify in a single statement. Therefore, it is important to understand what a claim is so you can locate and evaluate it in arguments you read, and so you can clearly state it in the arguments you write.

Claims can be classified as claims of fact, claims of value, and claims of policy, although at times there is a fine line between one type of claim and another.

Claim of fact	States that a condition exists, has existed, or will exist, based on factual evidence.	■ *Excess sun exposure causes skin cancer.* ■ *Environmental policies have slowed the depletion of the Earth's ozone layer.*
Claim of value	States that something is desirable or undesirable based on moral or aesthetic principles.	■ *The most relaxing vacations are spent on the beach.* ■ *Bathing suits have gotten too skimpy.*
Claim of policy	States that a specific course of action should be implemented.	■ *Sunscreen products should be more closely regulated.* ■ *Stricter emissions policies are needed for trucks.*

Claims of Fact

A fact is, for the most part, not a matter for argument but rather an undisputed truth. A claim of fact *asserts* that something is true — that a condition has existed, exists, or will exist. An argument based on a claim of fact tries to convince the reader that the claim is true, using the support of factual information such as statistics, examples, and testimony. (See Chapter 7 for a detailed discussion of support.)

Why, you may wonder, would a claim of fact need to be proven, if we all agree on facts? There are several reasons.

Different Interpretations. Facts, while indisputable at their most basic level, may not always be interpreted the same way. Different interpretations lead to different points of view on a subject. Scientists, for example, may look at the same data yet disagree about whether the data indicate a warming of the planet.

> **Claim:** Based on the available evidence, the earth has been undeniably growing warmer for the past fifty years.

> **Claim:** The earth's temperatures have remained flat for the past twenty years.

Causal Relationships. A claim of fact may assert a causal relationship based on facts. For example, some researchers may claim that soda consumption is responsible for the rise in the nation's obesity rates, while others may blame the higher obesity rates on Americans' increasingly sedentary lifestyles. Just as different interpretations of facts can lead to different perspectives, a different understanding of cause can lead to a different claim.

> **Claim:** Soda and other sugary drinks are the leading cause of obesity in the United States.

> **Claim:** Americans are overweight because they eat too much and exercise too little.

Predictions. A prediction uses known facts to make a claim about the future. Based on available evidence, an analyst may predict that holding teachers accountable for their students' standardized test scores will improve our educational system. This prediction may be disputed by others, who assert that the available evidence indicates the opposite outcome is likely. A prediction can be tested in the future to determine its validity. But even in the future, the results will be subject to interpretation and potential disputes about cause.

> **Claim:** An increased emphasis on standardized testing will lead to higher graduation rates among high school students.

> **Claim:** Too much emphasis on standardized testing will decrease student and teacher morale, leading to higher dropout rates among high school students.

New Data. Scientists and scholars in all fields are constantly working not only to interpret existing data, but also to uncover new data. Such new data may change our understanding of history, physics, or biology and cause us to reevaluate our conclusions. In the health field in particular, researchers regularly uncover new information that may complicate or contradict earlier findings. When new data emerge in a field, the public may require some convincing to accept a new theory over the prevailing viewpoint, such as when the Environmental Protection Agency listed secondhand smoke as a major carcinogen in 1992.

> **Claim:** Although it was once generally believed that cigarette smoke was harmful only to the smoker, researchers now conclude that secondhand smoke poses serious health hazards for nonsmokers as well.

Not all claims are so neatly stated or make such unambiguous assertions. Because we recognize that there are exceptions to most generalizations, we often qualify our claims with words such as *generally*, *usually*, *probably*, and *as a rule*. It would not be true to state flatly, for example, *College graduates earn more than high school graduates.* This statement is generally true, but we know that some high school graduates who are electricians or city bus drivers or sanitation workers earn more than college graduates who are schoolteachers or nurses or social workers. In making such a claim, therefore, the writer should qualify it with a word that limits the claim—a **qualifier**. However, watch out for words that overstate your claim. Words like *always*, *every*, *all*, and *never* allow for no exceptions.

Remember: Labeling a statement a claim of fact does not make it true. The label simply means that it is worded as though it were a true statement. It is up to the writer to provide support to prove that the statement is indeed true.

ARGUMENT ESSENTIALS
Claims of Fact

- Claims of fact assert that a condition has existed, exists, or will exist.
- Claims of fact are supported by factual information such as statistics, examples, and testimony.
- Claims of fact may take one of several forms:
  - A statement in favor of a particular interpretation of data
  - A suggestion of a causal relationship
  - A prediction
  - A case for the acceptance of new evidence
- Claims of fact may be limited by qualifiers such as *generally* and *probably*.

RESEARCH SKILL ▸ Using Databases

Once you have in mind a general subject to research, what is the first step you should take as you move toward deciding what to say about it or what main claim or thesis to argue?

If your response is to go to Google, you may be right. In your daily life, if you need to look up some factual information, you can find it quickly on Google or another similar search engine. But for most assignments for your classes, the answer is no, and you will need specific types of high-quality, reliable sources.

For one thing, remember that Google finds any reference to your search term and doesn't discriminate based on quality. Anyone can post on the internet, so there is no control over accuracy. You will also be inundated with far more sources than you could ever look at.

If you had checked Google for information about Aristotle when this book went to press, you would have found these numbers:

"Aristotle" — 23,800,000 results
"Aristotle" and "argument" — 70,000 results
"Aristotle's argument" — 530,000 results
"Aristotle" and "rhetoric" — 603,000 results
"Aristotle's rhetoric" — 164,000 results

Wikipedia will be near the top of the list for many subjects, but you shouldn't plan to use Wikipedia as a source for college work. It lacks the authority your professors will expect because most have multiple authors, and the content is not always checked for accuracy.

Where, then, should you start? At the library, by prowling the shelves? Don't rule out electronic sources. Instead, find out what databases your school has access to and which of those databases are most appropriate for your research.

For example, a good general database for academic subjects is Academic OneFile. There, a search for information about Aristotle yields these results:

"Aristotle" — 1,158 results (subject search);
13,906 results (keyword search)
"Aristotle" and "argument" — 0 results (subject);
214 results (keyword)
"Aristotle" and "rhetoric" — 9 results (subject);
219 results (keyword)

As you can see, by the end of this search you are reaching a manageable number of sources to explore. With these smaller numbers of results, a quick look at the titles will eliminate some and let you know which ones are worth investigating.

You will learn more about finding sources in Chapter 12.

READING ARGUMENT

Seeing a Claim of Fact

The following essay has been annotated to highlight claims of fact.

Spinster, Old Maid or Self-Partnered: Why Words for Single Women Have Changed through Time
AMY FROIDE

In a recent interview with *Vogue*, actress Emma Watson opened up about being a single 30-year-old woman. Instead of calling herself single, however, she used the word "self-partnered."

I've studied and written about the history of single women, and this is the first time I am aware of "self-partnered" being used. We'll see if it catches on, but if it does, it will join the ever-growing list of words used to describe single women of a certain age.

Women who were once called spinsters eventually started being called old maids. In 17th-century New England, there were also words like "thornback"—a sea skate covered with thorny spines—used to describe single women older than 25.

Attitudes toward single women have repeatedly shifted—and part of that attitude shift is reflected in the names given to unwed women.

The Rise of the "Singlewoman"

5   Before the 17th century, women who weren't married were called maids, virgins, or "puella," the Latin word for "girl." These words emphasized youth and chastity, and they presumed that women would only be single for a small portion of their life—a period of "pre-marriage."

But by the 17th century, new terms, such as "spinster" and "singlewoman," emerged.

What changed? The numbers of unwed women—or women who simply never married—started to grow.

In the 1960s, demographer John Hajnal identified the "Northwestern European Marriage Pattern," in which people in northwestern European countries such as England started marrying late—in their 30s and even 40s. A significant proportion of the populace didn't marry at all. In this region of Europe, it was the norm for married couples to start a new household when they married, which required accumulating a certain amount of wealth. Like

---

Marginal notes:

- Froide opens with a brief, contemporary event, then leads into a brief response that establishes her authority.
- Froide's thesis, a claim of fact
- Froide lists examples of early terms for single women to highlight the assumption that singleness was a temporary state.
- A key causal reason supporting Froide's claim: The terms changed when more women remained single.

Amy Froide is a professor of history at the University of Maryland, Baltimore County, with a focus on early modern British and women's history and specifically economic, social, and financial history. Her essay was published online at *The Conversation* on December 1, 2019.

today, young men and women worked and saved money before moving into a new home, a process that often delayed marriage. If marriage were delayed too long—or if people couldn't accumulate enough wealth—they might not marry at all.

Now terms were needed for adult single women who might never marry. The term spinster transitioned from describing an occupation that employed many women—a spinner of wool—to a legal term for an independent, unmarried woman.

Single women made up, on average, 30 percent of the adult female population in early modern England. My own research on the town of Southampton found that in 1698, 34.2 percent of women over 18 were single, another 18.5 percent were widowed, and less than half, or 47.3 percent, were married.

Many of us assume that past societies were more traditional than our own, with marriage more common. But my work shows that in 17th-century England, at any given time, more women were unmarried than married. It was a normal part of the era's life and culture.

The Pejorative "Old Maid"

In the late 1690s, the term old maid became common. The expression emphasizes the paradox of being old and yet still virginal and unmarried. It wasn't the only term that was tried out; the era's literature also poked fun at "superannuated virgins." But because "old maid" trips off the tongue a little easier, it's the one that stuck.

The undertones of this new word were decidedly critical.

"A Satyr upon Old Maids," an anonymously written 1713 pamphlet, referred to never-married women as "odious," "impure," and repugnant. Another common trope was that old maids would be punished for not marrying by "leading apes in hell."

At what point did a young, single woman become an old maid? There was a definitive line: In the 17th century, it was a woman in her mid-20s.

For instance, the single poet Jane Barker wrote in her 1688 poem, "A Virgin Life," that she hoped she could remain "Fearless of twenty-five and all its train, / Of slights or scorns, or being called Old Maid."

These negative terms came about as the numbers of single women continued to climb and marriage rates dropped. In the 1690s and early 1700s,

Margin notes:

In the case of *spinster*, the meaning of the term itself changed.

The term *old maid* was critical, but so were the other terms of the late 17th and early 18th centuries.

An example from the time offers support for Froide's claim of fact in the previous paragraph.

Line numbers: 10   15

English authorities became so worried about population decline that the government levied a Marriage Duty Tax, requiring bachelors, widowers, and some single women of means to pay what amounted to a fine for not being married.

Still Uneasy about Being Single

Today in the U.S., the median first age at marriage for women is 28. For men, it's 30.

What we're experiencing now isn't a historical first; instead, we've essentially returned to a marriage pattern that was common 300 years ago. From the 18th century up until the mid-20th century, the average age at first marriage dropped to a low of age 20 for women and age 22 for men. Then it began to rise again.

20   There's a reason *Vogue* was asking Watson about her single status as she approached 30. To many, age 30 is a milestone for women—the moment when, if they haven't already, they're supposed to go from being footloose and fancy-free to thinking about marriage, a family, and a mortgage.

Even if you're a wealthy and famous woman, you can't escape this cultural expectation. Male celebrities don't seem to be questioned about being single and 30.

While no one would call Watson a spinster or old maid today, she nonetheless feels compelled to create a new term for her status: "self-partnered." In what some have dubbed the "age of self-care," perhaps this term is no surprise. It seems to say, I'm focused on myself and my own goals and needs. I don't need to focus on another person, whether it's a partner or a child.

If the old terms are outdated, there is still a need for something to call women of 30 or older who are single.

To me, though, it's ironic that the term "self-partnered" seems to elevate coupledom. Spinster, singlewoman, or singleton: None of those terms openly refers to an absent partner. But self-partnered evokes a missing better half.

It says something about our culture and gender expectations that despite her status and power, a woman like Watson still feels uncomfortable simply calling herself single.

Froide's conclusion introduces a new line of thought that suggests that "singleness" is still not culturally accepted.

Even for the rich and famous, the simple term *single* does not seem to be adequate.

Practice: Claim of Fact

Review the print advertisement below, and answer the questions that follow.

Paper Because

DOMTAR PAPER

Domtar Paper Company

Reading, Writing, and Discussion Questions

1. How is the claim qualified?
2. How does this ad use text and picture to reinforce each other?
3. How valid do you feel the text is? (Have you observed scenes like the one depicted in the ad, or perhaps been part of such a scene?)
4. How clear is the connection between what the ad says about social media and what is being advertised? What *is* being advertised?

Claims of Value

Unlike claims of fact, which state that something is true and can be validated by reference to the data, claims of value make a judgment. They express approval or disapproval. They attempt to prove that some action, belief, or condition is right or wrong, good or bad, beautiful or ugly, worthwhile or undesirable.

Claim: Democracy is superior to any other form of government.

Claim: Killing animals for sport is wrong.

Claim: The Sam Rayburn Building in Washington is an aesthetic failure.

Some claims of value are simply expressions of taste, likes and dislikes, or preferences and prejudices. The Latin proverb *De gustibus non est disputandum* means that we cannot dispute taste. If you love the musical *Wicked*, there is no way for anyone to prove you wrong.

Many claims of value, however, can be defended or attacked on the basis of standards that measure the worth of an action, a belief, a performance, or an object. As far as possible, our personal likes and dislikes should be supported by reference to these standards. Value judgments occur in any area of human experience, but whatever the area, the analysis will be the same. We ask the arguer who is defending a claim of value: *What are the standards or criteria for deciding that this action, this belief, this performance, or this object is good or bad, beautiful or ugly, desirable or undesirable? Does the thing you are defending fulfill these criteria?*

There are two general areas in which people often disagree about matters of value: aesthetics and morality.

Aesthetics

Aesthetics is the study of beauty and the fine arts. Controversies over works of art — the aesthetic value of books, paintings, sculpture, architecture, dance, drama, and movies — rage fiercely among experts and laypeople alike. They may disagree on the standards for judging or, even if they agree about standards, may disagree about how successfully the art object under discussion has met these standards. The Rogerian approach to conflict resolution can be particularly useful in resolving disagreements over the standards for judging. Agreeing on those standards is the first step toward resolving the conflict and is a necessary step before seeking agreement on how well the standards have been met.

Consider a discussion about popular music. Hearing someone praise the singing of Manu Chao, a hugely popular European singer also playing to American crowds, you might ask why he is so highly regarded. You expect Chao's fans to say more than "I like him" or "He's great." You expect them to give reasons to support their claims. They might show you a short review from a respected newspaper that says, "Mr. Chao's gift is simplicity. His music owes a considerable amount to Bob Marley . . . but Mr. Chao has a nasal, regular-guy voice, and instead of the Wailers' brooding, bass-heavy undertow, Mr. Chao's band delivers a lighter bounce. His tunes have the singing directness of nursery rhymes."[1] Chao's fans accept these criteria for judging a singer's appeal.

You may not agree that simplicity, directness, and a regular-guy voice are the most important qualities in a popular singer. But the establishment of standards itself offers material for a discussion or an argument. You may argue about the relevance of the criteria, or you may agree with the criteria but argue about the success of the singer in meeting them. Perhaps you prefer complexity to simplicity. Or even if you choose simplicity, you may not think that Chao has exhibited this quality to good effect.

It is probably not surprising, then, that despite wide differences in taste, professional critics more often than not agree on criteria and whether an art object has met the criteria. For example, almost all movie critics agree that *Citizen Kane* and *Gone with the Wind* are superior films. They also agree that *Plan 9 from Outer Space*, a horror film, is terrible.

Morality

Value claims about morality express judgments about the rightness or wrongness of conduct or belief. Here disagreements are as wide and deep as in the arts—and more significant. The first two examples on page 175 reveal how controversial such claims can be. Although a writer and reader may share many values—among them a belief in democracy, a respect for learning, and a desire for peace—they may also disagree, even profoundly, about other values. The subject of divorce, for example, despite its prevalence in our society, can produce a conflict between people who have differing moral standards. Some people may insist on adherence to absolute standards, arguing that the values they hold are based on immutable religious precepts derived from God and biblical scripture. Since marriage is sacred, divorce is always wrong, they say, whether or not the conditions of society change. Other people may argue that values are relative, based on the changing needs of societies in different places and at different times. Since marriage is an institution created by human beings at a particular time in history to serve particular social needs, they may say,

---

[1] Jon Pareles, *New York Times*, July 10, 2001, B1.

it can also be dissolved when other social needs arise. The same conflicts between moral values might occur in discussions of abortion or suicide.

Nevertheless, even where people agree about standards for measuring behavior, a majority preference is not enough to confer moral value. If in a certain neighborhood a majority of heterosexual men decide to harass a few gay men and lesbians, that consensus does not make their action right. In formulating value claims, arguers should be prepared to ask and answer questions about the way in which their value claims, as well as those of others, have been determined. Lionel Ruby, an American philosopher, sums it up in these words: "The law of rationality tells us that we ought to justify our beliefs by evidence and reasons, instead of asserting them dogmatically."[2]

> **ARGUMENT ESSENTIALS**
> ## Claims of Value
>
> - Claims of value make a judgment.
> - Claims of value should be supported by reference to standards that measure the worth of an action, belief, performance, or object.
> - Claims of value most often are about aesthetics or morality.

READING ARGUMENT

Seeing a Claim of Value

The following essay has been annotated to highlight claims of value.

The NFL's Protest Crisis
SAMUEL CHI

The National Football League has a real crisis on its hands.

No, this isn't about concussions, domestic violence or even the ridiculously infamous "Deflategate." This is about the national anthem—whether to stand, kneel or raise a fist while giant American flags are being unfurled from end zone to end zone.

The anthem crisis maybe isn't an existential one—yet—to the NFL, but it has the potential to mushroom into something much bigger than being merely about Colin Kaepernick and a few other protesters. This crisis threatens to pit the league against its very own paying customers.

A catchy opening

Establishing what the crisis is not to more firmly focus on what it is: the national anthem

Notes the scope of the issue: The crisis may turn out to be the response of the NFL's customers.

Samuel Chi (1969–2017) was a sports journalist, a college football analyst, proprietor of BCSGuru.com, senior editor at *RealClearPolitics*, and managing editor at *RealClearSports*. Only months before his death from pancreatic cancer, he started a new career at Breitbart news. Samuel Chi, "The NFL's Protest Crisis," *CNN*, September 16, 2016. Copyright © 2016 by Turner Broadcasting Systems, Inc. All rights reserved. Used under license.

---

[2] Lionel Ruby, *The Art of Making Sense* (New York: Lippincott, 1968), 271.

You see, strangely, a league that has no compunction about fining players for wearing the wrong socks, shoes or twerking after a touchdown is suddenly silent about whether its employees must stand during the playing of the national anthem. "The Shield" that would not allow players to commemorate slain police officers in Dallas has no firm policy on whether it's OK or not if someone in an NFL uniform decides to chill during the singing of the Star-Spangled Banner.

Contrast with things that *are* deemed inappropriate

The NBA, generally considered the most player-friendly and progressive of the North American pro sports leagues, actually has a rule about the anthem (and it's pretty unequivocal): "Players, coaches and trainers are to stand and line up in a dignified posture along the sidelines or on the foul line during the playing of the National Anthem." And that goes for both the U.S. and Canadian anthems, since it has a team based in Toronto.

Contrast with how the NBA responds to the national anthem

But when Kaepernick, the San Francisco 49ers' backup quarterback, decided that he would no longer honor the flag, NFL Commissioner Roger Goodell limply made a statement saying the league merely "encourages" players to be "respectful" during the anthem, but there was no mention of requiring players to stand. If Kaepernick's protest left the door ajar, Goodell's response served to blow it from the hinges as a stampede of players decided to use the occasion to demonstrate whatever grievances they have against their own country.

Chi's disapproval is clear in his use of the word "limply." He is making a value judgment.

Kaepernick's stated reason for his protest is that minorities in the U.S. are being oppressed. But more specifically, he claimed that he could not stand for the flag while the police are murdering civilians and getting away with it. He also displayed his disdain for law enforcement by wearing socks featuring pigs in police hats during practice (and so far appears to have received no discipline from the league for impermissible gear).

Chi establishes that he understands why Kaepernick has done what Chi disapproves of. He also provides another instance of Kaepernick's ignoring the rules.

Whether anyone agrees with Kaepernick's sentiments, however, should be irrelevant to the NFL. This isn't a free speech issue as many sympathetic to Kaepernick's cause have claimed it to be. If Kaepernick made disparaging remarks toward gays, minorities or any ethnic group, he would've been fined and/or suspended. In fact, he was docked over $5,000 by the league in 2014 for allegedly uttering the N-word during a game toward Lamarr Houston of the Chicago Bears (although he was later judged not to have used the slur).

This isn't about the First Amendment. While Congress shall make no law infringing on your freedom of expression, your employer damn well can impose what kind of conduct it expects when you're on company time while wearing company gear. The NFL—just like the NBA—has every right to demand that its players stand erect and make no fuss while the national anthem is playing.

If Congress does not have a law against Kaepernick's type of disrespect, the league can have rules.

5

10   By being derelict on this matter, though, Goodell risks his league alienating a healthy chunk of its paying customers—the fans and sponsors. The commissioner, already with an antagonistic relationship with the players and their union over what many see as his disciplinarian overreach, probably decided that he didn't want to pick another fight. Maybe he wished that this whole anthem business would go away quickly, especially had the shaky Kaepernick been cut by the 49ers.

Claim: By not enforcing rules, Goodell has made the matter worse.

But by suggesting that there are no rules, Goodell guaranteed that this issue would engulf his league—for the entire season and possibly beyond. And make no mistake, there's already a strong racial undercurrent in this chasm—so far, the protesting football players are black, and the most visceral reaction toward the protesters has come from the league's majority white fan base. The NFL has unwittingly allowed itself to become the biggest platform in America's summer of discontent, pitting certain minority groups against the police and their supporters.

Chi's clearest statement of the problem

What Goodell has done is not even condoned by some of the owners, who are ostensibly his bosses. And it is simply bad business. The NFL, already beset by problems with player safety and discipline, risks further erosion of its fan base, as reflected both in attendance and especially television ratings.

Chi's claim of value: This is "simply bad business."

What the all-powerful commissioner should have told his players is this: Protest all you want, but do it on your own time and dime.

Practice: Claim of Value

Movie reviews by definition support claims of value. Analyze the following review, focusing on its claim and support for that claim.

Black Panther

ODIE HENDERSON

In 1992, a little Black kid on a makeshift basketball court in Oakland, California, disrupts his game to glance up at the sky. Figuratively, he's looking at the loss of hope, a departure represented by glowing lights drifting away into the night. As we learn later, those lights belong to a futuristic flying machine returning to the mysterious African country of Wakanda, the setting of *Black Panther*. The young man was once told by his father that Wakanda had the most wonderful sunsets he would ever see, so he cradles that perceived vision of beauty through his darkest

Odie Henderson has two blogs, *Big Media Vandalism* and *Tales of Odienary Madness*, and also has contributed to *Slate*'s blog *The House Next Door* since 2006. He writes for MovieMezzanine, Movies without Pity, *Salon*, and RogerEbert .com, where this review was posted on February 15, 2018.

hours. When he finally sees the sun go down over Wakanda, it provokes a haunting emotional response.

That same response will be felt by viewers of *Black Panther*, one of the year's best films, and one that transcends the superhero genre to emerge as an epic of operatic proportions. The numerous battle sequences that are staples of the genre are present, but they float on the surface of a deep ocean of character development and attention to details both grandiose and minute. Wakanda is a fully fleshed-out, unapologetically Black universe, a world woven into a tapestry of the richest, sharpest colors and textures. Rachel Morrison's stunning cinematography and Ruth Carter's costumes pop so vividly that they become almost tactile. You can practically feel the fabric of the hat worn by Angela Bassett as it beams in the sunlight on the day her son becomes king.

Bassett is just one of numerous familiar and up-and-coming actors of color who bring their A-games to *Black Panther*. Forest Whitaker, Sterling K. Brown and *Get Out* star Daniel Kaluuya are just a few of the others. The entire cast creates characters with complexities rarely afforded minorities in cinema; these people are capable of contradictory human responses that have lasting consequences. Their feelings are deep, instantly relatable, and colored with the shades of grey not often explored in blockbuster entertainment. When the villain still manages to make your eyes tear up despite trying to murder the hero in the previous scene, you know you're in the presence of great acting and storytelling.

The villain in question, nicknamed Killmonger, is played by Michael B. Jordan. Someday, the team of Jordan and writer/director Ryan Coogler will be mentioned with the same reverence reserved for Scorsese and De Niro.

The duo have done three films together, and though this is the first where Jordan is in a supporting role, they still convey a cinematic shorthand that's representative of their trusted partnership. A film like this is only as good as its villains, and Jordan deserves a place in the anti-hero Hall of Fame alongside such greats as Gene Hackman's Little Bill Daggett from *Unforgiven*. Like Hackman, Jordan lures you in with his likeable comic swagger before revealing the shocking levels of his viciousness. He is hissable, but his character arc is not without sympathy nor understanding.

Coogler is the perfect fit for this material. It hits all the sweet spots he likes to explore in his films. So much gets written about which prominent directors should helm a superhero film next, but relatively few would be allowed to leave such a personal mark on a product so slavishly devoted to fan feelings. Coogler turns the MCU into the RCU—the Ryan Coogler Universe—by including everything we've come to expect from his features in the script he co-wrote with Joe Robert Cole. Like Oscar Grant in *Fruitvale Station*, T'Challa (Chadwick Boseman) is a typical Coogler protagonist, a young Black man seeking his place in the world while dealing with his own personal demons and an environment that demands things from him that he is unsure about giving. Like Donny in *Creed*, T'Challa exists in the shadow of a late father once known for a greatness he also wishes to achieve through similar means.

Coogler extends these same character traits to his muse Jordan's Killmonger who, true to comic book lore form, has a "two sides of the same coin" relationship with the hero. Even their plans apply this theory. T'Challa wants to keep Wakanda away from the rest of the world, protecting his country by using its advanced

5

technology solely for its denizens. Killmonger wants to steal that technology and give it to others, specifically to underprivileged Black folks so they can fight back and rule the world.

Additionally, the dual, reflective imagery of T'Challa and Killmonger is beautifully drawn to the surface in a scene where both men undergo the same spiritual journey to visit the fathers they long to see. But these similar journeys are polar opposites in tone, as if to prove the adage that one man's Heaven is another man's Hell. These scenes have a way of burrowing into your skin, forcing you to reckon with them later.

Coogler's universe also isn't male-dominated. In each of his films, there are women who advise and comfort the male leads while still having their own lives and agency. In *Fruitvale Station*, it's Octavia Spencer's Mrs. Grant; in *Creed*, it's Tessa Thompson's artistic girlfriend. *Black Panther* really ups the stakes, presenting us with numerous memorable, fierce and intelligent women who fight alongside Black Panther and earn their own cheers. Lupita Nyong'o is Nakia, the ex for whom T'Challa still carries a torch. Letitia Wright is Shuri, T'Challa's sister and the equivalent of James Bond's Q; she provides the vibranium-based weapons and suits Black Panther uses. And Danai Gurira is Okoye, a warrior whose prowess may even outshine T'Challa's because she doesn't need a suit to be a badass. All of these women have action sequences that drew loud applause from the audience, not to mention they're all fully realized people. Okoye in particular has an arc that replays Black Panther's central ideological conflict in microcosm.

For all its action sequences (they're refreshingly uncluttered, focusing on smaller battles than usual) and talk of metals that exist only in the mind of Stan Lee, *Black Panther* is still Marvel's most mature offering to date. It's also its most political, a film completely unafraid to alienate certain factions of the Marvel base. It's doing a great job upsetting folks infected with the Fear of a Black Planet on Twitter, to be sure. To wit, Wakanda has never been colonized by White settlers, it's the most advanced place in the universe and, in a move that seems timely though it's been canon since 1967, Wakanda masquerades as what certain presidents would refer to as a "shithole nation." Coogler really twists the knife on that one: In the first of two post-credits sequences, he ends with a very sharp response about what immigrants from those nations can bring to the rest of the world.

Speaking of endings, Coogler is a man who knows how to end a movie. His last shot in *Creed* is a tearjerking thing of beauty, and the last scene (pre-credits that is) in *Black Panther* made me cry even harder. As in *Creed*, Coogler depicted young brown faces looking in awe at a hero, something we never see in mainstream cinema. "Black Panther"'s last scene is a repeat of the scene I described in my opening paragraph: In the present day, a little Black kid on a makeshift basketball court in Oakland, California disrupts his game to glance up at the sky. Figuratively, he's about to gain some hope, an addition represented by a humanitarian hero with much to teach him and his fellow basketball players. The young man stares in awe, realizing that his life, and the lives of those around him will be changed.

It's an ending rife with meta, symbolic meaning. Starting this weekend, a lot of brown kids are going to be staring at this movie with a similar sense of awe and perception-changing wonder. Because *the main superhero, and almost everyone else, looks just like them.* It was a long time coming, and it was worth the wait.

Reading, Writing, and Discussion Questions

1. What single sentence best sums up Odie Henderson's claim of value?
2. What sorts of evidence does Henderson offer in support of his claim?
3. What are some of the specific details that you find most convincing?
4. What was Henderson's organizational plan for the essay?
5. Do you feel that Henderson makes a convincing case for his thesis? Is your opinion related to your having seen the movie or not? Explain.

Claims of Policy

Claims of policy argue that certain conditions should exist. As the name suggests, they advocate adoption of policies or courses of action because problems have arisen that call for solution. Almost always, *should* or *ought to* or *must* is expressed or implied in the claim.

Claim: Voluntary prayer should be permitted in public schools.

Claim: A dress code ought to be introduced for all public high schools.

Claim: A law should permit sixteen-year-olds and parents to "divorce" each other in cases of extreme incompatibility.

Claim: Mandatory jail terms must be imposed for drunk driving violations.

Claim-of-policy arguments often begin by attempting to convince the audience that a problem exists. This will require a factual claim that offers data proving that present conditions are unsatisfactory. Claims of value may also be necessary to support the claim of fact. The policy itself is usually introduced after the problem is established; the policy is presented as a viable solution to the problem.

Consider this policy claim: *The time required for an undergraduate degree should be extended to five years.* Immediate agreement with this policy among student readers would certainly not be universal. Some students would not recognize a problem. They would say, "The college curriculum we have now is fine. There's no need for a change. Besides, we don't want to spend more time in school." First, then, the arguer would have to persuade a skeptical audience that there is a problem — that four years of college is no longer enough because the stock of knowledge in almost all fields of study continues to increase. The arguer would provide data to show that students today have many more choices in history, literature, and science than students had in those fields a generation ago and would also emphasize the value of greater knowledge and more schooling compared to the value of other goods the audience cherishes, such as earlier independence. Finally, the arguer would offer a plan for implementing the policy. The plan would have to consider initial psychological resistance, revision of the curriculum, costs of more instruction, and costs of lost production in the workforce. Most important, this policy would point out the benefits for both individuals and society if it were adopted.

In this example, we assumed that the reader would disagree that a problem existed. In many cases, however, the reader may agree that there is a problem but disagree with the arguer about the way to solve it. Most of us, no doubt, agree that we want to reduce or eliminate the following problems: misbehavior and vandalism in schools, drunk driving, crime on the streets, child abuse, pornography, pollution.

But how should we go about solving those problems? What public policy will give us well-behaved, diligent students who never destroy school property? safe streets where no one is ever robbed or assaulted? loving homes where no child is ever mistreated? Some members of society would choose to introduce rules or laws that punish infractions so severely that wrongdoers would be unwilling or unable to repeat their offenses. Other members of society would prefer policies that attempt to rehabilitate or reeducate offenders through training, therapy, counseling, and new opportunities.

> **ARGUMENT ESSENTIALS**
> ## Claims of Policy
>
> - Claims of policy argue for an action or a change in thinking.
> - Claims of policy express or imply that something should or must be done.
> - Claims of policy usually depend on a factual claim that establishes that present conditions are unacceptable.

READING ARGUMENT

Seeing a Claim of Policy

The following essay has been annotated to highlight claims of policy.

College Life versus My Moral Code
ELISHA DOV HACK

Many people envy my status as a freshman at Yale College. My classmates and I made it through some fierce competition, and we are excited to have been accepted to one of the best academic and extracurricular programs in American higher education. I have an older brother who attended Yale, and I've heard from him what life at Yale is like.

He spent all his college years living at home because our parents are New Haven residents, and Yale's rules then did not require him to live in the dorms.

Background that reveals his respect for Yale and his connection to it through his brother

Elisha Dov Hack was a member of the Yale College freshman class of 1997. This article appeared on September 9, 1997, in the *New York Times*. The case brought by Hack and four other Jewish students remained in court until all but Hack had graduated. Hack went on to marry — and live off campus — before his 2003 graduation in engineering sciences.

But Yale's new regulations demand that I spend my freshman and sophomore years living in the college dormitories.

I, two other freshmen, and two sophomores have refused to do this because life in the dorms, even on the floors Yale calls "single sex," is contrary to the fundamental principles we have been taught as long as we can remember—the principles of Judaism lived according to the Torah and 3,000-year-old rabbinic teachings. Unless Yale waives its residence requirement, we may have no choice but to sue the university to protect our religious way of life.

Bingham Hall, on the Yale quadrangle known as the Old Campus, is one of the dorms for incoming students. When I entered it two weeks ago during an orientation tour, I literally saw the handwriting on the wall. A sign titled "Safe Sex" told me where to pick up condoms on campus. Another sign touted 100 ways to make love without having sex, like "take a nap together" and "take a steamy shower together."

That, I am told, is real life in the dorms. The "freshperson" issue of the *Yale Daily News* sent to entering students contained a "Yale lexicon" defining *sexile* as "banishment from your dorm room because your roommate is having more fun than you." If you live in the dorms, you're expected to be part of the crowd, to accept these standards as the framework for your life.

Can we stand up to classmates whose sexual morality differs from ours? We've had years of rigorous religious teaching, and we've watched and learned from our parents. We can hold our own in the intellectual debate that flows naturally from exchanges during and after class. But I'm upset and hurt by this requirement that I live in the dorms. Why is Yale—an institution that professes to be so tolerant and open-minded—making it particularly hard for students like us to maintain our moral standards through difficult college years?

We are not trying to impose our moral standards on our classmates or on Yale. Our parents tell us that things were very different in college dormitories in their day and that in most colleges in the 1950s students who allowed guests of the opposite sex into their dorm rooms were subject to expulsion. We acknowledge that today's morality is not that of the 1950s. We are asking only that Yale give us the same permission to live off campus that it gives any lower classman who is married or at least twenty-one years old.

Yale is proud of the fact that it has no "parietal rules" and that sexual morality is a student's own business. Maybe this is what Dean Richard H. Brodhead meant when he said that "Yale's residential colleges carry . . . a moral meaning." That moral meaning is, basically, "Anything goes." This morality is Yale's own residential religion, which it is proselytizing by force of its regulations.

We cannot, in good conscience, live in a place where women are permitted to stay overnight in men's rooms, and where visiting men can traipse

5

through the common halls on the women's floors — in various stages of undress — in the middle of the night. The dormitories on Yale's Old Campus have floors designated by gender, but there is easy access through open stairwells from one floor to the next.

Floors designated by gender are not the solution.

The source of conflict

10   The moral message Yale's residences convey today is not one that our religion accepts. Nor is it a moral environment in which the five of us can spend our nights, or a moral surrounding that we can call home.

Yale sent me a glossy brochure when it welcomed me as an entering student. It said, "Yale retains a deep respect for its early history and for the continuity that its history provides — a continuity based on constant reflection and reappraisal." Yale ought to reflect on and reappraise a policy that compels us to compromise our religious principles.

Uses Yale's own advertising against it

Follow Up

What happened to the lawsuit to which Hack refers? It was tied up in court until 2001, when all of the students involved except Hack had graduated. The students lost the legal battle at all levels, primarily because their case depended on their proving that having to live in a residence hall constituted discrimination based on religion. The university successfully argued that the residence requirement was not discriminatory. Hack graduated from Yale in 2003. All five students chose to live in apartments during their first two years while paying full housing fees for dorm rooms they never occupied.

Practice: Claim of Policy

Read the following essay and answer the questions at the end.

How to Avoid Cultural Appropriation at Coachella
JESSICA ANDREWS

Since it launched in October of 1999, Coachella's become something of a cultural force. The music and arts festival draws almost 100,000 people per day, according to *Goldenvoice*, including today's top performers and street-style stars. But every year, the thorn in the festival's side is appropriative fashion. From the overtly racist to the blindly ignorant, some Coachella attendees see festival fashion as the opportunity — knowingly or unknowingly — to demean cultures for Instagram likes.

Jessica Andrews is the Deputy Director of Fashion at Refinery29, a media and entertainment company for young women. Before that she was Fashion Features Editor at *Teen Vogue*. She has her own blog, Glamazons, and writes for *ELLE*, *Vanity Fair*, the *New York Times*, and *Essence*. This article appeared online at *Teen Vogue* on April 13, 2018.

Bindis, feathered headpieces, dashikis, war paint: Coachella street style is mired in cultural appropriation. And it's the kind that reeks of privilege. For South Asian women, bindis are a cultural symbol that represents the third eye, a sacred site of wisdom and spiritual development. For some Coachella attendees, it's just a pretty forehead accessory.

A feathered headdress is nothing more than an eye-catching look for many festival-goers, but as Adrienne Keene writes on *Native Appropriations*, "eagle feathers are presented as symbols of honor and respect and have to be earned," and they're traditionally worn by male chiefs in sacred ceremonies. But that doesn't mean anything to those Coachella attendees who don't respect other cultures. When you can't see the humanity in people who are different from you, you find no fault in treating their sacred cultural symbols as something to be worn and discarded.

Even when people feign ignorance, there's little excuse. In the past, I've worn a Pocahontas costume for Halloween. It's a mistake I regret, and I'll never do it again knowing how hurtful it is. With appropriation being such a huge conversation these days, it's easier than ever to educate yourself about cultural symbols. If you still choose to regard one as a disposable trend, it's because you simply don't respect the people behind it.

5   Like fashion, appropriative hairstyles are now ubiquitous at Coachella. Cornrows or box braids are not a "hot new festival trend"; black women have been wearing them for centuries. When outlets cover the hairstyle as if it started with Kylie Jenner, it's not appreciation; it's erasure. Those celebratory headlines are yet another reminder that black hairstyles are only acceptable when they're removed from actual black people.

Unbeknownst to some Coachella attendees, there's a stigma associated with cornrows and braids when black people wear them. These hairstyles are still being banned in schools — as recently as 2016 — and they're often deemed too unprofessional for work. The same hairstyle is celebrated when other races wear it. When Kylie sports cornrows at Coachella, it's considered "edgy" and "cool." When black people wear cornrows, they get passed over for jobs, and are asked to leave their classrooms.

And white women wearing braids at Coachella is not the same as black women straightening their hair, no matter what Whoopi Goldberg says on *The View*. Appropriation and assimilation are two very different ideals. In a world where high schools ban students for wearing natural hair, people are fired for defending their Afros, and celebrities are compared to dogs for wearing Afros, black women feel undue pressure to straighten their hair just to get by. In some circles, wearing braids, locs, or Afros is still a revolutionary act for black women — not a passing fad that comes around once a year at festival season.

There are myriad ways to dress up at Coachella without offending an entire group of people. As you're packing your outfit for a fun-filled weekend in Palm Springs, remember that sacred cultural symbols are not a fashion trend. Black hairstyles are not "lewks to try" when you want to feel "edgy," only to discard them once you're bored and ready to retreat back to your privileged bubble.

Stripping a cultural object of its significance and donning it like a costume is the very height of disrespect. It's not just ignorant; it's dehumanizing and incredibly painful. Go to Coachella, dance in the sun, watch Beyoncé perform, Instagram every moment, and have a blast — just don't do it at everyone else's expense.

Reading, Writing, and Discussion Questions

1. What claim of policy is Jessica Andrews supporting in her essay? Can you find one or more sentences where she most clearly articulates her claim?
2. What was Andrews's organizational plan in the piece?
3. Do you feel that Andrews builds a convincing case for her thesis? Why or why not?
4. What is the difference between appropriation and assimilation, and how does that relate to points that Andrews is making?
5. What other examples can you think of where appropriation of certain aspects of another culture might be offensive or perhaps has already been discarded for that reason?

Strategies for Reading and Writing Claims

READ: Claims

All Claims

Keep the author's audience and purpose in mind. Ask:

- Whom was the author writing for, and why?
- What was the author trying to convince that audience of?
- What did he or she want them to do?
- Would it be clear to the audience how the issue pertains to them?

Claims of Fact

- Consider whether the author has provided sufficient supporting evidence to back up his or her claim.
- Consider whether the author has used qualifiers such as *generally*, *usually*, *always*, and *never*. Evaluate if the qualifiers help clarify the writer's argument or weaken it.
- Consider whether the author has considered opposing viewpoints and, if necessary, refuted them.

WRITE: Claims

All Claims

Keep your audience and purpose in mind. Ask:

- Whom are you writing for, and why?
- What are you trying to convince them of?
- What do you want them to do?
- How will readers know the issue should be important to them and that they should listen to your argument?

Claims of Fact

- Find supporting evidence to back up your claim.
- Use qualifiers such as *generally*, *usually*, and *probably* to limit a claim; avoid using words such as *always*, *every*, *all*, and *never*, which do not allow for exceptions.
- Acknowledge viewpoints or claims that oppose your own, and refute them in a way that shows respect but also proves that your claim is more persuasive.

continued

READ: Claims

Claims of Value

- If the author is writing about an aesthetic issue, consider whether he or she has made clear the criteria by which the aesthetic judgment is being made.
- If the author is writing about a moral issue, consider whether he or she has used ideas or language that would alienate or offend those holding opposing views on the subject.
- Consider whether the author has provided strong evidence and good reasons for any claim of value.

Claims of Policy

- Consider whether the author has built a convincing case that a problem exists.
- Consider whether the claim of policy is worded in such a way that is inclusive to all readers, no matter what their position.
- Consider whether the author has acknowledged other possible solutions and explained convincingly why his or her proposal is superior.
- Consider whether the author has made clear what he or she wants the audience to do about the situation, whether to do something or simply to consider the situation from the author's perspective.

WRITE: Claims

Claims of Value

- Be sure you understand and have successfully established the criteria used to measure standards in the field of aesthetics you are writing about: sports, dance, music, photography, and so on.
- When writing about a moral issue, be careful to be respectful of readers who may espouse opposing views on the subject, and use language that will be convincing, not dismissive.
- As much as possible, provide strong evidence and good reasons for your claims of value, and avoid dogma.

Claims of Policy

- Begin by proving that the problem exists: employ a claim of fact with supporting evidence. (You may also need to include a claim of value to convince readers that something must be done.)
- Use special care to frame your claim of policy in a way that readers — especially those with a high level of emotional involvement in the topic — will not immediately reject.
- Acknowledge viewpoints or claims that oppose your own, and refute them in a way that shows respect but also proves that your claim is superior.
- Have realistic expectations about what you hope to achieve — what your audience can actually do about the situation. Sometimes you may argue for people to vote a certain way, sign a petition, or write letters to officials. At other times, the most you might hope to accomplish is to get your audience to consider the situation from your perspective.

Assignments for Claims

Reading and Discussion Questions

1. Find several recent print ads and explain what their claims are.

2. Notice that Amy Froide's essay "Spinster, Old Maid or Self-Partnered: Why Words for Single Women Have Changed through Time" does not take a side in whether or not singleness is a positive state; she just concludes that it is meaningful to our society. Choose a similar current controversial issue, and brainstorm some claims of fact about it.

3. Locate a movie review online or in hard copy that has a clear claim and is based on clear evaluative criteria. Choose a review that is an essay, not just a single paragraph. Bring it to class, and share it with your class or group. By looking at a range of different reviews, come to some conclusions about the sorts of criteria used in making judgment calls about movies and what sort of claims provide good thesis statements for reviews. What are some other characteristics that all or most good movie reviews share?

4. Consider one or more of your school's policies that you would like to see changed. In your opinion, what is wrong with the policy as it currently stands? What exactly would you recommend be done to improve the situation?

Writing Suggestions

1. Choose a controversial issue in the field in which you are majoring or one in which you might major. Practice differentiating among the three types of claims by writing a claim of fact, a claim of value, and a claim of policy on that issue.

2. Choose one of the claims of fact you wrote for #2 under Reading and Discussion Questions above, and write an essay supporting it.

3. Choose a recent print ad, and write an essay explaining how text and pictures work together in it to support a claim.

4. Write a review of a recent movie. Your thesis will be a claim of value.

5. Write a review of a recent play, concert, art exhibit, or similar cultural event. Your thesis will be a claim of value.

6. Using Elisha Dov Hack's essay as a model, write an essay suggesting a change at your school. Write it in the form of a letter to your school's newspaper or to the appropriate school official. Your thesis will be a claim of policy.

7. Some sports teams have long used Native American mascots or symbols, but that practice has come under scrutiny in recent years. Do you feel that these uses were signs of disrespect that were appropriately banned, or do you think arguments against them went too far in the attempt to be politically correct? Write an essay defending your position.

RESEARCH ASSIGNMENT   **Acknowledging Reliable Authorities**

The following is a list of quotations and the names of those who are quoted. Do some research to find out what gives the person quoted the authority to speak knowledgeably on the subject of the quotation. Then work the information you found into a lead-in to the quotation, as in the example.

Example

"We are promoting human rights by building homes for people who don't have them."—Jimmy Carter

"We are promoting human rights by building homes for people who don't have them," explains former president Jimmy Carter, who has been involved with Habitat for Humanity International since 1984 and who, with his wife, leads its Jimmy and Rosalynn Carter Work Project one week each year.

1. "Innovation has nothing to do with how many R&D dollars you have. When Apple came up with the Mac, IBM was spending at least 100 times more on R&D. It's not about money. It's about the people you have, how you're led, and how much you get it."—Steve Jobs

2. "If gun laws in fact worked, the sponsors of this type of legislation should have no difficulties drawing upon long lists of crime rates reduced by such legislation. That they cannot do so after a century and a half of trying—that they must sweep under the rug the southern attempts at gun control in the 1870–1910 period, the northeastern attempts in the 1920–1939 period, the attempts at both Federal and State levels in 1965–1976—establishes the repeated, complete, and inevitable failure of gun laws to control serious crime."—Orrin G. Hatch

3. "That the networks and other 'media elites' have a liberal bias is so blatantly true that it's hardly worth discussing anymore. No, we don't sit around in dark corners and plan strategies on how we're going to slant the news. We don't have to. It comes naturally to most reporters."—Bernard Goldberg

4. "You built a factory and it turned into something terrific or a great idea—God bless! Keep a hunk of it. But part of the underlying social contract is you take a hunk of that and pay forward for the next kid who comes along."—Elizabeth Warren

5. "It takes more courage to send men into battle than to fight the battle yourself."—Colin Powell

6. "I want to state upfront, unequivocally and without doubt: I do not believe that any racial, ethnic, or gender group has an advantage in sound judging. I do believe that every person has an equal opportunity to be a good and wise judge, regardless of their background or life experiences."—Sonia Sotomayor

Support

When you read or listen to a well-constructed argument, you should be aware of what the claim is. What you look for next is reasons to believe that claim. When you write your own arguments, you need to put yourself in the position of your readers or listeners and consider what reasons you can give them for accepting your claim. Support for a claim represents the answer to the question "What have you got to go on?"[1] All claims in an argument—whether of fact, of value, or of policy—must be supported. Sometimes an author will use his or her own experience as support for a claim. At other times, authors may conduct interviews, field research, lab experiments, or surveys to obtain support for their position. As a student, you will most likely turn primarily to print and electronic sources for your support. (See Chapter 13 for a full discussion of finding sources.)

The emphasis in providing support is on the relationship between writer and audience—the rhetorical leg of the communications triangle:

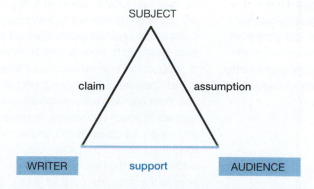

```
                    SUBJECT


      claim                      assumption



  WRITER          support          AUDIENCE
```

---

[1] Stephen Toulmin, *The Uses of Argument* (Cambridge: Cambridge University Press, 1958), 98.

You are presenting **evidence** to an audience in hopes of convincing that audience to see the subject in the same way you do. You may remember from the discussion of Aristotelian rhetoric in Chapter 5 that arguments rely on *ethos*, *logos*, and *pathos* for their effectiveness. You must present your evidence and yourself in such a way that your audience finds you trustworthy (*ethos*). You also have to consider what evidence your audience will find convincing—what examples, statistics, and opinions will appeal to them logically (*logos*). You are using emotional appeal (*pathos*) in conjunction with other types of appeal when you appeal to your audience's needs and values.

Strategies for Reading and Writing Support

READ: Support

- Consider what sort of audience the argument was addressed to. Does the author seem to be writing for a general audience, such as those who read a major newspaper, or for a more specialized audience that would already know the subject fairly well, such as those who would read a scholarly journal in a limited field? Does the author seem to be writing for those who already agree with the main claim, those who are hostile to it, or those somewhere in between?

- As you're reading, highlight or annotate the text to identify different types of support the author used. Consider whether the types the author chose are the most effective. Would a different type of support have been more convincing? Should there have been more variety or a better balance of evidence and appeals to needs and values to convince the audience?

WRITE: Support

- In deciding how much support you need for your claim, it is always a good idea to assume that you are addressing an audience that may be at least slightly hostile to that claim. Those who already agree with you do not need convincing.

- Keep a mental, if not a written, list of the different types of support you use in an essay. Few essays will use all of the different types of support, but being aware of all the possibilities will prevent you from forgetting to draw on one or more types of support that may advance your argument. In that checklist of types of support, don't forget that there are two main categories: evidence and appeals to needs and values. Appeals to needs and values will generally require the reinforcement that comes from more objective forms of evidence, but the two in combination can often provide the strongest case for your claim.

Evidence

When authors provide evidence in support of their claim, they primarily use facts, examples, statistics, opinions (usually the opinions of experts), and images.

Factual Evidence

In Chapter 6, we defined facts as statements possessing a high degree of public acceptance. Some facts can be verified by experience alone.

- Eating too much will make us sick.
- We can get from Hopkinton to Boston in a half hour by car.
- In the Northern Hemisphere, it is colder in December than in July.

The experience of any individual is limited in both time and space, so we must accept as fact thousands of assertions about the world that we ourselves can never verify. Thus we accept the existence of black holes in space because we trust those who can verify their existence.

Facts can provide important support for a claim, as shown in the example here. The claim has been underlined.

Nuclear energy has a wide-ranging value proposition. Nuclear energy

- produces large amounts of electricity at industry-leading reliability and efficiency levels
- is affordable and has forward price stability that will continue to fuel the nation's economy
- provides more than half of all carbon-free electricity in the United States
- maintains grid stability through nonstop operation of reactors
- contributes to the fuel and technology diversity that is one of the bedrock characteristics of a reliable and resilient electric sector
- is an economic driver through high-paying jobs and taxes in the communities and states where nuclear plants are located.[2]

Factual evidence appears most frequently as examples and statistics, which are a numerical form of examples.

Examples

Examples are the most familiar kind of factual evidence. In addition to providing support for the truth of a generalization, examples can enliven otherwise dense or monotonous prose. In the following paragraph, the writer supports the claim (underlined in the topic sentence) by offering a series of specific examples.

You can hardly go anywhere these days and not see or hear an advertisement for college. Throughout Concourse B at Denver International Airport, nearly every other advertisement greeting passengers is for a higher-education institution: Colorado State University, the University of Wyoming, Colorado Mesa College, and the University of Northern Colorado. Airline magazines are filled with promotions for executive MBA programs. At least once an hour on the all-news radio station in Washington, D.C., listeners hear about the degree in cybersecurity offered by a University of Maryland campus. Sunday newspapers are filled with details on certificate programs in the latest hot job fields, such as social media and sustainability. Anyone checking email on Google will see ads pop up for the creative writing program at Southern New Hampshire University or the political management degree at George Washington University.[3]

---

[2] "Nuclear Energy: Just the Facts," *Nuclear Energy Institute*, last modified September 2019, www.nei.org/CorporateSite/media/filefolder/resources/fact-sheets/just-the-facts-2019-09.pdf.

[3] Jeffrey J. Selingo, *College (Un)Bound: The Future of Higher Education and What It Means for Students* (New York: New Harvest, 2013), 6.

Hypothetical examples, which create imaginary situations for the audience and encourage them to visualize what might happen under certain circumstances, can also be effective. The following paragraph illustrates the use of hypothetical examples. (The author is describing megaschools—high schools with more than two thousand students—and her claim is underlined.)

> [I]n schools that big there is inevitably a critical mass of kids who are neither jocks nor artists nor even nerds, kids who are nothing at all, nonentities in their own lives. . . . The creditable ballplayer who might have made the team in a smaller school. . . . The artist who might have had work hung in a smaller school. . . . [T]he disaffected and depressed boy who might have found a niche, or a friend, or a teacher who noticed, falls between the cracks. Sometimes he quietly drops out. Sometimes he quietly passes through. And sometimes he comes to school with a gun.[4]

All claims about vague or abstract terms would be boring or unintelligible without examples to illuminate them. For example, if you claim that a movie contains "unusual sound effects," you will certainly have to describe some of the effects to convince the reader that your generalization can be trusted.

Statistics

Statistics express information in numbers. In the following example, statistics have been used to support the authors' claim, which has been underlined.

> To the kids growing up in a housing project on Chicago's south side, crack dealing was a glamour profession. For many of them, the job of gang boss—highly visible and highly lucrative—was easily the best job they thought they had access to. Had they grown up under different circumstances, they might have thought about becoming economists or writers. But in the neighborhood where J. T.'s gang operated, the path to a decent legitimate job was practically invisible. Fifty-six percent of the neighborhood's children lived below the poverty line (compared to a national average of 18 percent). Seventy-eight percent came from single-parent homes. Fewer than 5 percent of the neighborhood's adults had a college degree; barely one in three adult men worked at all. The neighborhood's median income was about $15,000 a year, well less than half the U.S. average. During the years that Venkatesh lived with J. T.'s gang, foot soldiers often asked his help in landing what they called "a good job": working as a janitor at the University of Chicago.[5]

---

[4] Anna Quindlen, "The Problem of the Megaschool," *Newsweek*, March 26, 2001, 68.

[5] Steven D. Levitt and Stephen J. Dubner, *Freakonomics: A Rogue Economist Explores the Hidden Side of Everything* (New York: William Morrow, 2005), 105.

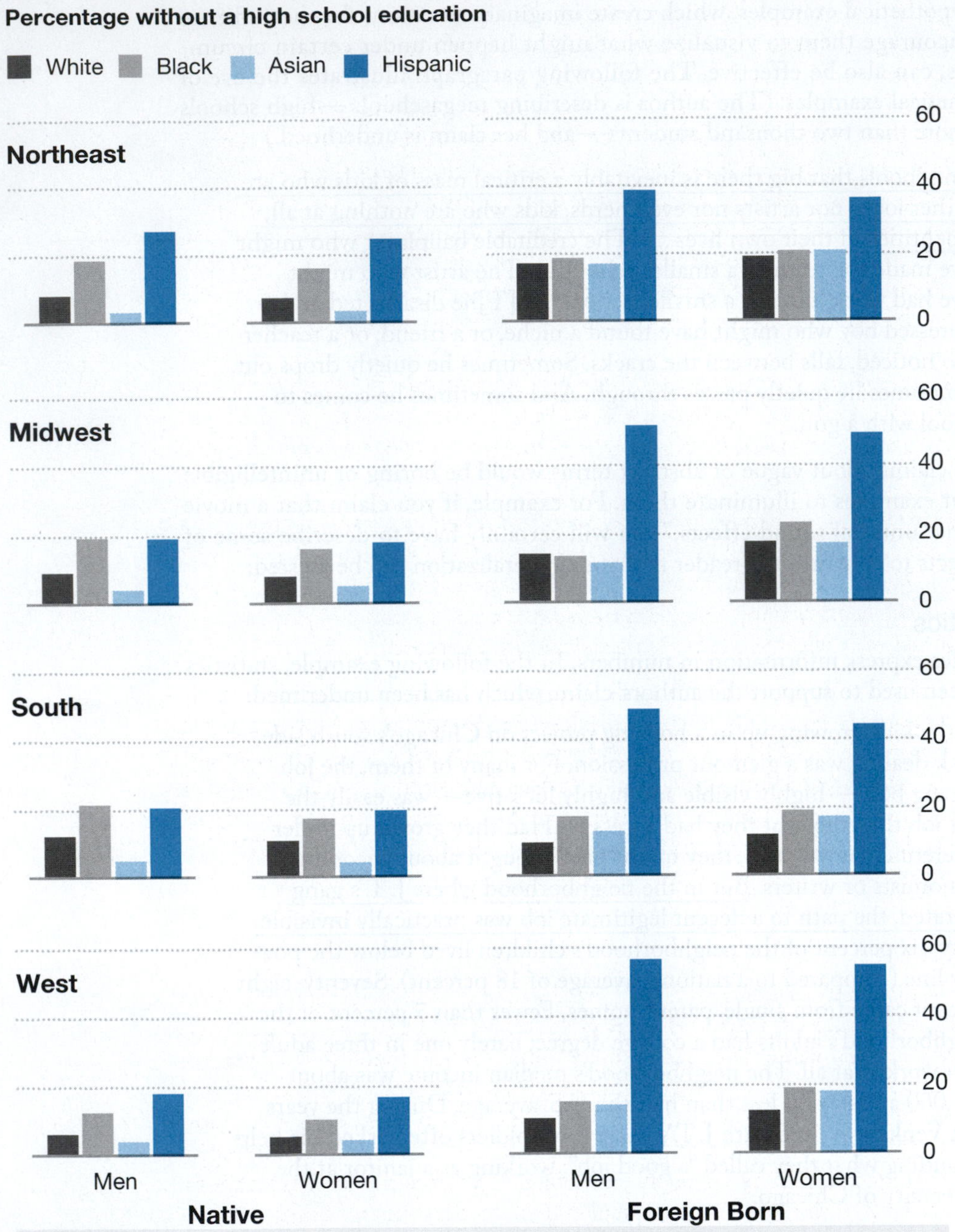

Percentage without a high school education

FIGURE 7.1 Without a High School Education. U.S. Census Bureau.
http://www.census.gov/dataviz/visualizations/035/

Statistics are more effective in comparisons that indicate whether a quantity is relatively large or small and sometimes even whether a reader should interpret the result as gratifying or disappointing. For example, if a novice gambler were told that for every dollar wagered in a state lottery, 50 percent goes back to the players as prizes, would the gambler be able to conclude that the percentage is high or low? Would he be able to choose between playing the state lottery and playing a casino game? Unless he had more information, probably not. But if he were informed that in casino games, the return to the players is over 90 percent and in slot machines and racetracks the return is around 80 percent, the comparison would enable him to evaluate the meaning of the 50 percent return in the state lottery and even to make a decision about where to gamble his money.[6]

Comparative statistics are also useful for measurements over time. For instance, the following statistics show what comparisons based on BMI, or body mass index, reveal about how Miss America contestants have changed over the years.

> Miss America contestants have become increasingly thinner over the past 75 years. In the 1920s, contestants had BMIs in the normal range of 20–25. . . . Since 1970, nearly all of the winners have had BMIs below the healthy range, with some as low as 16.9, a BMI that would meet part of the diagnostic criteria for anorexia nervosa.[7]

Diagrams, tables, charts, and graphs can make clear the relations among many sets of numbers. Such charts and diagrams enable readers to grasp the information more easily than if it were presented in paragraph form. For example, Figure 7.1 shows bar graphs used by the Census Bureau to explore the issue of high school education attainment among selected groups. Figure 7.2 (p. 198) is a graphic compiled by the Congressional Budget Office to show the 2018 U.S. Federal Budget.

Images

Evidence does not always have to be verbal. Images can also provide support for an argument. Before there were photographs, paintings and even crude cave drawings provided evidence of the cultures that produced them. A man named Mathew Brady captured the reality of war through his photos of the Civil War and thus earned the title the Father of Photojournalism. Crime scene photos and video surveillance tapes provide evidence on screen and in real life. In April 2013, the Boston Marathon bombers were identified through photos from more than one source, some of them first circulated via reddit.com and Facebook.

---

[6] Curt Suphee, "Lotto Baloney," *Harper's,* July 1983, 201.

[7] S. Rubenstein and B. Caballero, "Is Miss America an Undernourished Role Model?" in *JAMA,* 1569, (2000): 1569, quoted in Jillian Croll, "Body Image and Adolescents," *Guidelines for Adolescent Nutrition Services,* ed. J. Stang and M. Story (2005), June 9, 2007. http://www.epi.umn.edu/let /pubs/adol_book.shtm.

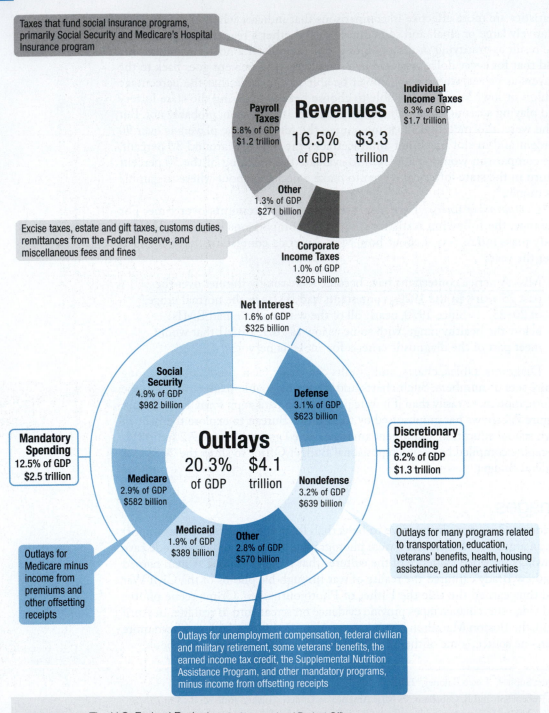

Taxes that fund social insurance programs, primarily Social Security and Medicare's Hospital Insurance program

Payroll Taxes
5.8% of GDP
$1.2 trillion

Revenues
16.5% of GDP $3.3 trillion

Individual Income Taxes
8.3% of GDP
$1.7 trillion

Other
1.3% of GDP
$271 billion

Excise taxes, estate and gift taxes, customs duties, remittances from the Federal Reserve, and miscellaneous fees and fines

Corporate Income Taxes
1.0% of GDP
$205 billion

Net Interest
1.6% of GDP
$325 billion

Social Security
4.9% of GDP
$982 billion

Defense
3.1% of GDP
$623 billion

Mandatory Spending
12.5% of GDP
$2.5 trillion

Outlays
20.3% of GDP $4.1 trillion

Discretionary Spending
6.2% of GDP
$1.3 trillion

Medicare
2.9% of GDP
$582 billion

Nondefense
3.2% of GDP
$639 billion

Medicaid
1.9% of GDP
$389 billion

Other
2.8% of GDP
$570 billion

Outlays for Medicare minus income from premiums and other offsetting receipts

Outlays for many programs related to transportation, education, veterans' benefits, health, housing assistance, and other activities

Outlays for unemployment compensation, federal civilian and military retirement, some veterans' benefits, the earned income tax credit, the Supplemental Nutrition Assistance Program, and other mandatory programs, minus income from offsetting receipts

FIGURE 7.2 The U.S. Federal Budget. U.S. Congressional Budget Office

FIGURE 7.3 A police shooting. Tulsa Police Department via AP

Figure 7.3 is from a police video taken from a helicopter by the Tulsa Police Department on September 16, 2016. Terence Crutcher, left, held his arms up as he walked next to his stalled SUV before he was shot and killed by one of the police officers. The video has brought into question whether the officer was justified. Videos such as the one this still is taken from and those taken routinely now by dash-cams can provide critical support in such a situation.

Images are also critical as evidence in scientific research. Proof of a hypothesis often takes the form of plants and animals viewed in the wild or in the lab, of cells viewed through a microscope, or of distant objects viewed through a telescope. The photo shown in Figure 7.4 was released by NASA in December 2013, as possible evidence of liquid water active on Mars.

FIGURE 7.4 Martian surface. NASA/JPL-Caltech/University of Arizona

Before you begin to write, you must determine whether the evidence you have chosen to support your claim is sound. Can it convince your readers?

- **Are the facts up to date?** The importance of up-to-date information depends on the subject. For many of the subjects you write about, recent research and scholarship will be important, even decisive, in proving the soundness of your data. "New" does not always mean "best," but in fields where research is ongoing — education, psychology, technology, medicine, and all the natural and physical sciences — you should be sensitive to the dates of the research.

- **Is the factual evidence sufficient?** The amount of factual evidence you need depends on the complexity of the subject and the length of your paper. Given the relative brevity of most of your assignments, you will need to be selective. For the claim that indoor pollution is a serious problem, one supporting fact would obviously not be enough. For a 750- to 1,000-word paper, three or four supporting facts would probably be sufficient. The choice of evidence should reflect different aspects of the problem: in this case, different sources of indoor pollution — gas stoves, fireplaces, kerosene heaters, insulation — and the consequences for health.

- **Are the facts relevant?** All the factual evidence should, of course, contribute to the development of your argument. Also keep in mind that not all readers will agree on what is relevant. Is the unsavory private life of a politician relevant to his or her performance in office? If you want to prove that a politician is unfit to serve because of his or her private activities, you may first have to convince some members of the audience that private activities are relevant to public service.

Examples

- **Are the examples representative?** This question emphasizes your responsibility to choose examples that are typical of all the examples you do not use. If you were trying to build a case about the economic impact of illegal immigrants in the United States but took your statistics from Maine, Vermont, Montana, North Dakota, and West Virginia, your sample would not be representative because these states have the smallest numbers of illegal immigrants, estimated to be less than 0.5 percent of the population for each of the five states.

- **Are the examples consistent with the experience of the audience?** The members of your audience use their own experiences to judge the soundness of your evidence. If your examples are unfamiliar or extreme, they will probably reject your conclusion. If most members of the audience find that your examples don't reflect their own attitudes, they may question the validity of the claim.

Statistics

- **Do the statistics come from trustworthy sources?** You should ask whether the reporter of the statistics is qualified and likely to be free of bias. Among the generally reliable sources are polling organizations such as Gallup, Roper, and Louis Harris and agencies of the U.S. government such as the Census Bureau and the Bureau of Labor Statistics. Other qualified sources are well-known research foundations, university centers, and insurance companies that prepare actuarial tables.

- **Are the terms clearly defined?** The more abstract or controversial the term, the greater the necessity for clear definition. *Unemployment* is an example of a term for which statistics will be difficult to read if the definition varies from one user to another. For example, are seasonal workers employed or unemployed during the off-season? Are part-time workers employed?

- **Are the comparisons between comparable things?** Folk wisdom warns us that we cannot compare apples and oranges. Population statistics for the world's largest city, for example, should indicate the units being compared. Greater London is defined in one way, greater New York in another, and greater Tokyo in still another. The population numbers will mean little unless you can be sure that the same geographical units are being compared.

- **Has any significant information been omitted?** Consider an example: A company called Lifestyle Lift has advertised a procedure as a revolutionary approach to facial rejuvenation. What the website does not mention is that as a result of a probe in Florida, the company was ordered by Florida's attorney general in June 2013 to stop calling its procedures revolutionary and that a similar probe in New York "found evidence that company employees were posing as satisfied customers." Florida's attorney general ordered the company to make clear whether its satisfied customers were compensated for their testimonials. The Lifestyle Lift company still advertises its procedures as groundbreaking in spite of the fact that they are tried and true plastic surgery methods done with local instead of general anesthesia.

Images

- **Is the image relevant?** The photograph or other image should advance your argument. If it doesn't, it is not effective support. If it does, it must deserve the trust put in it as legitimate support. In the 2012 movie *Promised Land*, unscrupulous businessmen posing as environmental activists try to prove that fracking is killing livestock in the surrounding area by showing the locals a photograph of dead cows. They lose local support, however, when a closer look at the photo reveals that it was taken in a completely different part of the country.

- **Are you confident the photograph has not been altered?** It is so easy these days to photoshop or otherwise alter images that we can hardly trust what our eyes tell us.

- **Does the image depend too much on emotional appeal?** Emotional appeal is a legitimate form of appeal if it complements, instead of replaces, logic. We have all seen pictures of starving children and abused animals used to move us to donate money to alleviate their suffering. That is a legitimate use of emotional appeal as long as the money really goes to help the suffering children or animals. A little research can reveal what percentage of money donated to a given charity actually reaches those in need.

Expert Opinion

Based on their reading of the facts, experts express opinions on a variety of controversial subjects: whether capital punishment is a deterrent to crime; whether legalization of marijuana will lead to an increase in its use; whether children, if left untaught, will grow up honest and cooperative; whether sex education courses will result in less sexual activity and fewer illegitimate births. The interpretations of the data are often profoundly important because they influence social policy and affect our lives directly and indirectly.

For the problems mentioned above, the opinions of people recognized as authorities are more reliable than those of people who have neither thought about nor done research on the subject. But opinions may also be offered by student writers in areas in which they are knowledgeable. If you were asked, for example, to defend or refute the statement that work has advantages for teenagers, you could call on your own experience and that of your friends to support your claim. You can also draw on your experience to write convincingly about your special interests.

One opinion, however, is not always as good as another. The value of any opinion depends on the quality of the evidence and the trustworthiness of the person offering it. Clayton M. Christensen and Henry J. Eyring are both experts on the subject of education. Christensen held a named professorship in Business Administration at the Harvard Business School, and Eyring has been director of Brigham Young University's MBA program and is currently the president of BYU–Idaho. In spite of their own credentials, when they wrote their book *The Innovative University: Changing the DNA of Higher Education from the Inside Out* (2011), they were careful to establish the expertise of those whose ideas they drew upon:

> No one could doubt that U.S. Education Secretary Margaret Spellings meant business. In upbraiding the nation's universities and colleges, the 2006 report of her commission on the future of higher education used the language of business:
>
> > What we have learned over the last year makes clear that American higher education has become what, in the business world, would be called a mature enterprise: increasingly risk-averse, at times self-satisfied, and unduly expensive. It is an enterprise that has yet to successfully confront the impact of globalization, rapidly evolving technologies, an increasingly diverse and aging population, and an evolving marketplace characterized by new needs and paradigms. . . .
>
> The Spellings Commission was not a lone voice of criticism in 2006. That same year two distinguished academics, Derek Bok and Harry Lewis, both of Harvard, published books critical of higher education.[8]

What happens when authoritative sources disagree? Such disagreement is probably most common in the social sciences. They are called the "soft" sciences precisely because a consensus about conclusions in these areas is more difficult to reach than in the natural and physical sciences. The following two paragraphs show experts disagreeing over the reason for rises in college tuition costs.

> Suppose we asked the president of a public university to explain what he or she sees. Very likely that president would point out the fact that tuition and fees tend to rise very rapidly after decreases in growth in the overall economy. Your attention would be drawn to the rapid tuition increases following the episodes of negative GDP growth in 1982 and 1991 and the very slow GDP growth in 2001. Even the decade of falling tuition in the 1970s was interrupted by the oil shock years around 1974.

---

[8] Clayton M. Christensen and Henry J. Eyring, *The Innovative University: Changing the DNA of Higher Education from the Inside Out* (Hoboken, NJ: Jossie-Bass, 2011), 4–5.

The university president would say something like this: "When the overall economy slows down, state tax collections fall, and states cut appropriations for universities. As a result public universities have to resort to large tuition increases to make up for lost public funding."

If we asked Representatives Boehner and McKeon to comment on the data, they would focus on an entirely different phenomenon. In *The College Cost Crisis* they say "the facts show tuition increases have persisted regardless of the circumstances such as the economy or state funding, and have far outpaced inflation year after year, regardless of whether the economy has been stumbling or thriving." Essentially, they are looking at the fact that after 1980 the "real" growth in college tuition and fees always has been positive. This means that tuition and fees always have grown more rapidly than the CPI (Consumer Price Index). Representatives Boehner and McKeon also claim they know why this has happened. They place the blame squarely on "wasteful spending by college and university management."[9]

But even in the natural and physical sciences, where the results of observation and experiment are more conclusive, we encounter heated differences of opinion. A popular argument concerns the extinction of the dinosaurs. Was it the effect of an asteroid striking the earth? or widespread volcanic activity? or a cooling of the planet? All these theories have their champions among the experts. A debate of more immediate relevance concerns the possible dangers of genetically modified foods, as distinguished from foods modified by traditional breeding practices. Jeffrey M. Smith, director of the Institute for Responsible Technology and author of *Seeds of Deception: Exposing Industry and Government Lies about the Safety of the Genetically Engineered Foods You're Eating* (2003) and *Genetic Roulette: The Documented Health Risks of Genetically Engineered Foods* (2007), presents a different perspective on the issue:

> In addition to unintended changes in the DNA, there are health risks from other aspects of GM crops. When a transgene starts to function in the new cell, for example, it may produce proteins that are different from the one intended. The amino acid sequence may be wrong, the protein's shape may be different, and molecular attachments may make the protein harmful. The fact that proteins act differently in new plant environments was made painfully clear to developers of GM peas in Australia. They cancelled their ten-year, $2 million project after their GM protein, supposedly identical to the harmless natural version, caused inflammatory responses in mice. Subtle, unpredicted changes in molecular attachments might have similarly triggered deadly allergic reactions in people if the peas were put on the market.[10]

---

[9] Robert B. Archibald and David H. Feldman, *Why Does College Cost So Much?* (New York: Oxford, 2010), 9.

[10] Jeffrey M. Smith, *Genetic Roulette: The Documented Health Risks of Genetically Engineered Foods* (St. Louis: Yes!, 2007).

In 2000, at a hearing before the U.S. Senate Committee on Foreign Relations, Subcommittee on International Economic Policy, Export and Trade Promotion, Roger N. Beachy made the following statement. Beachy produced the world's first genetically modified tomato and in 2009–2011 was President Obama's director of the National Institute for Food and Agriculture.

> Agricultural producers in the U.S. have a growing awareness of their duties as keepers of the environment; many are actively reducing the use of harmful agrichemicals while maintaining highly efficient production of safe foods. Plant scientists and agriculturists have developed better crops and improved production methods that have enabled farmers to reduce the use of insecticides and chemicals that control certain diseases. Methods such as integrated pest management, no-till or low-till agriculture have been tremendously important in this regard. Some of the success has come through the judicious application of biotechnology to develop new varieties of crops that resist insects and that tolerate certain herbicides. For example, biotechnology was used to develop varieties of cotton and corn that are resistant to attack by cotton bollworm and corn borer. These varieties have allowed farmers to reduce the use of chemical insecticides by between 1.5 and 2 million gallons, while retaining or increasing crop yields. Crops that are tolerant to certain "friendly" herbicides have increased no-till and low-till agriculture, reducing soil erosion and building valuable topsoil to ensure the continued productivity of our valuable agricultural lands.[11]

How can you choose between authorities who disagree? If you have applied the tests discussed so far and discovered that one source is less qualified by training and experience or makes claims with little support or appears to be biased in favor of one interpretation, you will have no difficulty in rejecting that person's opinion. If conflicting sources prove to be equally reliable in all respects, then you should continue reading other authorities to determine whether a greater number of experts support one opinion rather than another. Although numbers alone, even of experts, don't guarantee the truth, nonexperts have little choice but to accept the authority of the greater number until evidence to the contrary is forthcoming. Finally, if you are unable to decide between competing sources of evidence, you may conclude that the argument must remain unsettled. Such an admission is not a failure; after all, such questions are considered controversial because even the experts cannot agree, and such questions are often the most interesting to consider and argue about. In some cases, you may be able to synthesize or combine the authorities' ideas into a new idea that you state as a claim, then bring together the differing perspectives as support.

---

[11] "World Renowned Plant Scientist Dr. Roger N. Beachy Testifies before U.S. Senate Committee to Explain the Role of Agricultural Biotechnology in the Battle against Poverty and Hunger in Developing Countries," *agbioworld.org*, July 12, 2000.

RESEARCH SKILL ▶ Evaluating Expert Opinion

Before you begin to write, you must determine whether the expert opinion you have chosen to support your claim is convincing.

- **Is the source of the opinion qualified to give an opinion on the subject?** Certain achievements by the interpreter of the data — publications, acceptance by colleagues — can tell us something about his or her competence. The answers to questions you must ask are not hard to find: Is the source qualified by education? Is the source associated with a reputable institution — a university or a research organization? Is the source credited with having made contributions to the field — books, articles, research studies? If the source is not clearly identified, you should treat the data with caution.

  In addition, you should question the identity of any source listed as "spokesperson" or "reliable source" or "an unidentified authority." Even when the identification is clear and genuine, you should ask if the credentials are relevant to the field in which the authority claims expertise. All citizens have the right to express their views, but this does not mean that all views are equally credible or worthy of attention.

- **Is the source biased for or against his or her interpretation?** Even authorities who satisfy the criteria for expertise may be guilty of bias. Bias arises as a result of economic reward, religious affiliation, political loyalty, and other interests. The expert may not be aware of the bias; even an expert can fall into the trap of ignoring evidence that contradicts his or her own intellectual preferences. Before accepting the interpretation of an expert, you should ask: Is there some reason why I should suspect the motives of this particular source?

  This is not to say that all partisan claims lack support. They may, in fact, be based on the best available support. But whenever special interest is apparent, there is always the danger that an argument will reflect this bias.

- **Has the source bolstered the claim with sufficient and appropriate evidence?** An author might claim, "Statistics show that watching violence on television leads to violent behavior in children." But if the author gave no further information — neither statistics nor proof that a cause-effect relation exists between televised violence and violence in children — the critical reader would ask, "What are the numbers? Who compiled them?"

  Even those who are reputed to be experts on the subjects they discuss must do more than simply allege that a claim is valid or that the data exist. They must provide facts to support their interpretations.

ARGUMENT ESSENTIALS
Evidence

- Evidence can take the form of facts, or statements possessing a high degree of public acceptance.
- Evidence can take the form of examples, which provide specific support for a generalization and enliven prose.
- Evidence can take the form of statistics, or information expressed in numbers.
- Evidence can take the form of images, or nonverbal support for an assertion.
- Evidence can take the form of expert opinion, or the interpretations of facts by people recognized as authorities on or at least knowledgeable about the subject.

READING ARGUMENT

Seeing Evidence

The following student essay on organic food has been annotated to highlight the use of evidence. At the time she wrote this essay, Kristen Weinacker was an undergraduate at Clemson University.

"Safer? Tastier? More Nutritious?" The Dubious Merits of Organic Foods

KRISTEN WEINACKER

Kristen Weinacker
ENGL 203
Dr. Winchell
October 23, 2017

"Safer? Tastier? More Nutritious?" The Dubious
Merits of Organic Foods

Causal connections

Organic foods are attractive to some consumers because of the principles behind them and the farming techniques used to produce them. There is a special respect for organic farmers who strive to maintain the ecological balance and harmony that exist among living things. As these farmers work in partnership with nature, some consumers too feel a certain attachment to the earth (Wolf 1–2). They feel happier knowing that these foods are produced without chemical fertilizers, pesticides, and additives to extend their shelf life (Pickrell; Agricultural Extension Service 5). They feel that they have returned to nature by eating organic foods that are advertised as being healthy for maintaining a vigorous lifestyle. Unfortunately, research has not provided statistical evidence that organic foods are more nutritious than conventionally grown ones.

Claim of fact

The debate over the nutritional benefits has raged for decades. Defenders of the nutritional value of organic foods have employed excellent marketing and sales strategies. First, they freely share the philosophy behind their farming and follow up with detailed descriptions of their management techniques. Second, organic farmers skillfully appeal to our common sense. It seems reasonable to believe that organic foods are more nutritious since they are grown without chemical fertilizers and pesticides. Third, since the soil in which these crops are grown is so rich and healthy, it seems plausible that these crops have absorbed and developed better nutrients. As Lynda Brown asserts in her book *Living Organic,* "Organic farmers believe that growing crops organically provides the best possible way to produce healthy food" (26). Brown provides beautifully illustrated and enlarged microscopic photographs to show the more developed structure of organic foods compared to conventional products to convince the consumer to believe that organic foods are more nutritious (27). Fourth, many consumers view the higher price tags on organic foods and assume that they must be more nutritious. Generalizations permeate the whole world of organic foods. These marketing strategies persuade the consumer that organic foods are healthier than conventional foods without providing any factual comparisons.

    In their book *Is Our Food Safe?* Warren Leon and Caroline Smith DeWaal compare organic and conventionally produced foods. They strongly suggest that consumers buy organic foods to help the environment (68). They believe that organic foods are healthier than conventional ones. However, statistics supporting this belief are not provided. The authors even warn consumers that they need to read product labels because some organic foods may be as unhealthy as conventional ones (68–69). An interesting poll involving 1,041 adults was conducted by ABC News asking, "Why do people buy organic?" Analyst Daniel Merkle concluded that 45 percent of the American public *believes* that organic products are more nutritious than conventionally grown ones. Also, 57 percent of the population maintains that organic farming is beneficial for the environment. According to the pollsters, the primary reason why people bought organic foods is the belief that they are healthier because they have less pesticide residue. However, there has never been any link established between the nutritional value of organic foods and the residue found on them. Clever marketing strategies have made the need for concrete data really not of prime importance for the consumer to join the bandwagon promoting organic foods.

    This pervasive belief among the American public that organic foods are probably healthier than conventionally grown foods was

Expert opinion

Causal connection: Consumers believe organic foods are healthier because of these marketing strategies.

Expert opinion

Statistics

Expert opinion

Suspected causal connections, but not supported by statistical evidence

Expert opinion

Causal connections cannot be drawn.

Another expert opinion that causal connections cannot be drawn

reiterated in my telephone interview with Mr. Joseph Williamson, an agricultural county extension agent working with Clemson University. When asked if organically grown foods are more nutritious than those grown conventionally, he replied that they probably were for two reasons. First, organic crops tend to grow more slowly. Therefore, the nutrients have more time to build up in the plants. Second, organic plants are usually grown locally. The fruits and vegetables are allowed to stay on the plants for a longer period of time. They ripen more than those picked green and transported across miles. He contends that these conditions promote a better nutrient buildup. Unfortunately, the extension agent acknowledges that statistical evidence is not available to support the claim that organic products are more nutritious.

An article entitled "Effect of Agricultural Methods in Nutritional Quality: A Comparison of Organic with Conventional Crops" reports on conclusions drawn by Dr. Virginia Worthington, a certified nutrition specialist. Worthington examines why it is so difficult to ascertain if organic foods are more nutritious. First, "the difference in terms of health effects is not large enough to be readily apparent." There is no concrete evidence that people are healthier eating organic foods or, conversely, that people become more ill eating conventionally grown produce. Second, Dr. Worthington notes that variables such as sunlight, temperature, and amount of rain are so inconsistent that the nutrients in crops vary yearly. Third, she points out that the nutrient value of products can be changed by the way products are stored and shipped. After reviewing at least thirty studies dealing with the question if organic foods are more nutritious than conventionally grown ones, Dr. Worthington concludes that there is too little data available to substantiate the claim of higher nutritional value in organic foods. She also believes that it is an impossible task to make a direct connection between organic foods and the health of those people who consume them.

After being asked for thirty years about organic foods by her readers and associates, Joan Dye Gussow, writer for *Eating Well* magazine, firmly concludes that there is "little hard proof that organically grown produce is reliably more nutritious." Reviewing seventy years' worth of studies on the subject, Gussow has no doubt that organic foods should be healthier because of the way

5

they are produced and cultivated. Gussow brings up an interesting point about chemical and pesticide residue. She believes that the fact that organic foods have been found to have fewer residues does not make them automatically more nutritious and healthier for the consumer. As scientific technologies advance, Gussow predicts that research will someday discover statistical data that will prove that organic foods have a higher nutritional value compared to conventionally grown ones.

In order to provide the public with more information about the nature of organic foods, the well-known and highly regarded magazine *Consumer Reports* decided to take a closer look at organic foods in their January 1998 magazine, in an article entitled "Organic Foods: Safer? Tastier? More nutritious?" By conducting comparison tests, their researchers discovered that organic foods have less pesticide residue, and that their flavors are just about the same as conventionally grown foods. These scientists came to the conclusion that the "variability within a given crop is greater than the variability between one cropping system and another." *Consumer Reports* contacted Professor Willie Lockeretz from the Tufts University School of Nutrition Science and Policy. He told researchers that "the growing system you use probably does affect nutrition. . . . But it does it in ways so complex you might be studying the problem forever." Keeping in mind these comments made by Dr. Lockeretz, *Consumer Reports* believes it would be an impossible task to compare the nutritional values of organic and conventional foods. Therefore, researchers at *Consumer Reports* decided not to carry out that part of their comparison testing.

> More expert opinion

Although statistical evidence is not available at this time to support the claim that organic foods are more nutritious than conventionally grown ones, there is a very strong feeling shared by a majority of the general public that they are. We are called back to nature as we observe the love that organic farmers have for the soil and their desire to work in partnership with nature. We are easily lured to the attractive displays of organic foods in the grocery stores. However, we must keep in mind the successful marketing techniques that have been used to convince us that organic foods are more nutritious than conventionally grown ones. Although common sense tells us that organic foods should be more nutritious, research has not provided us with any statistical data to prove this claim.

> Restatement of thesis

Works Cited

Agricultural Extension Service. *Organic Vegetable Gardening.*
    University of Tennessee, PB 1391.

Brown, Lynda. *Organic Living.* Dorling Kindersley, 2000.

"Effect of Agricultural Methods on Nutritional Quality: A Comparison
    of Organic with Conventional Crops." *Alternative Therapies* 4,
    1998, pp. 58–69, 18 Feb. 2003, www.purefood.org/healthier101101
    .cfm.

Gussow, Joan Dye. "Is Organic Food More Nutritious?" *Eating Well*,
    May/June 1997, 27 Mar. 2003, www.prnac.net/rodmap-nutrition
    .html.

Leon, Warren, and Caroline Smith DeWaal. *Is Our Food Safe?* Three
    Rivers, 2002.

Merkle, Daniel. "Why Do People Buy Organic?" *ABC News* Polls, 3 Feb.
    2000, abcnews.go.com/onair/DailyNews/poll_2000203.html.

"Organic Foods: Safer? Tastier? More Nutritious?" *Consumer
    Reports*, Jan. 1998, www.consumerreports.org/main/detailsv2
    .jsp?content%3%ecnt_id+18959&f.

Pickrell, John. "Federal Government Launches Organic Standards."
    Science News, vol. 162. no. 17, www.sciencenews.org/blog
    /food-thought/federal-government-launches-organic-standards.

Williamson, Joseph. Telephone interview. 28 Feb. 2013.

Wolf, Ray, ed. *Organic Farming: Yesterday's and Tomorrow's
    Agriculture.* Rodale, 1977.

Reading, Writing, and Discussion Questions

1. Looking back over the annotations, what types of support did you find noted
   most often?

2. What is unusual about the use of causal connections in this particular piece?
   How does that contribute to Kristen Weinacker's thesis?

3. Does Weinacker come across as a reliable and credible writer (*ethos*)? Why or
   why not?

Practice: Evidence

Read the following essay on sports fans and annotate the author's use of evidence, using the annotations on the previous essay by Weinacker as a model. Then answer the questions following the essay.

Are Sports Fans Happier?

SID KIRCHHEIMER

Let the madness begin!

March is the time when vasectomies increase by 50 percent thanks to the much-anticipated opportunity for patients to "recover" in front of their TVs.

March is also the time when workplaces do some real number-crunching: on the expected loss in employee productivity (estimated at 8.4 million hours and $192 million last year); on money bet on office pools (a hefty chunk of the $2.5 billion in total sports wagering each year); and even on the number of times workers hit the so-called "Boss Button" (computer software that instantly hides live video of games with a phony business spreadsheet), which was activated more than 3.3 million times during the first four days of last year's tournament.

But mostly, the NCAA Basketball Championship—better known as "March Madness" or "The Big Dance"—is a time that gives us something to cheer about beyond the game itself. If history and science hold true, no matter the outcome of the three-week tournament that begins in March, most of the millions who will follow its hard-court action will emerge as winners. "That's because in the long run it's really not the games that matter," says Daniel Wann, Ph.D., a professor of psychology at Murray State University in Kentucky and author of *Sports Fans: The Psychology and Social Impact of Spectators.* "Being a fan gives us something to talk about, to share and bond with others. And for the vast majority of people, it's psychologically healthier when you can increase social connections with others."

After conducting some 200 studies over the past two decades, Wann, a leading researcher on "sports fandom," finds consistent results: people who identify themselves as sports fans tend to have lower rates of depression and higher self-esteem than those who don't. Blame it on our primal nature. "Sports fandom is really a tribal thing," says Wann, a phenomenon that can help fulfill our psychological need to belong—providing similar benefits to the social support achieved through religious, professional, or other affiliations. "We've known for decades that social support—our tribal network—is largely responsible for keeping people mentally sound. We really do have a need to connect with others in some way."

But when it comes to opportunities to connect, the Big Dance may have a foothold over other sporting events. "The beauty of March Madness is that it attracts people of all levels of sports fandom—and for different reasons," says Edward Hirt, Ph.D., a professor of psychology at Indiana University who researches how fanship affects social identity.

Some watch, whether or not they usually follow sports, because they are alumni or have another previous affiliation to these "tribal networks"—the 60-plus participating college teams. Others connect on the spot, perhaps

5

Sid Kirchheimer is a health and medical writer and editor who has written for AARP since 2000 and for WebMD since 2002. He is the author of *The Doctors Book of Home Remedies II*. This article appeared in the March 13, 2012, edition of the *Saturday Evening Post*.

because it's easier to form emotional allegiances with gutsy amateur athletes who compete with heart and soul (and while juggling mid-term exams) rather than for the paychecks collected by millionaire pros.

Also consider the unique nature of the tournament itself—a series of back-to-back games over the course of several weeks with little to no idle time in between during which a casual fan might lose interest. "I have not seen any empirical evidence to support that March Madness is necessarily better than other sports events" for promoting mood and mindset enhancements. "But theoretically I expect it could be," says Wann.

"There are only a couple of events—the Super Bowl also comes to mind—that seem to transcend typical fandom into being akin to a national holiday . . . a reason for people to get together. But with the Super Bowl, everything leads to one game—and most of the time it's an anticlimactic one that's over by half-time."

10   With March Madness, however, Wann notes, "there's a longer, more drawn out event that provides more opportunities to engage in social opportunities and connections. And bonds tend to be stronger with a longer passage of time."

Do the math: More games + more time = more opportunities to share for better bonding. "Because upsets are a normal occurrence, and you get runs by Cinderella teams knocking off the perennial favorites, there's enough uncertainty and unpredictability in this tournament to get people excited—and keep them excited," adds Hirt. "Early games affect later decisions; there's a cascading effect, as opposed to a

one-time pick . . . and that allows for the pride that comes with someone with no sports expertise being able to win the office pool."

Maybe that's why despite a short-term productivity loss many experts believe that March Madness actually benefits the workplace in the long term. Bonds formed in office pools and post-game water-cooler chatter build morale and inspire teamwork. At afterwork get-togethers in front of the tube, buddies can share chicken wings—and their emotions. "You have guys hugging each other, cursing at the ref, and bonding by sharing a sense of commonality," says Hirt. "Where else can guys express their emotions like that?"

And those other relationships? Although studies show that two to four percent of marriages are negatively affected when one spouse is an ardent fan (think of the so-called "football widow"), sports fandom has a positive or neutral effect on nearly half of relationships, says Wann. "It gives many couples something to do together or allows one to have time to go off and do their own thing."

Even if you watch in solitude, March Madness and other sporting events provide a diversion from the woes of everyday life—if only for a few hours. "Older people, especially when widowed or physically incapacitated, are more likely than others to relate to televised events," says Stuart Fischoff, Ph.D., senior editor of the *Journal of Media Psychology* and a California State University, Los Angeles, professor emeritus of psychology. "Watching sports helps us get outside ourselves."

With the thrill of victory, many fans experi-   15
ence bona fide joy—complete with hormonal

and other physiological changes such as increased pulse and feelings of elation. And with defeat, the overwhelming majority may initially feel sadness and disappointment, but usually rebound within a day or two, studies show.

However, lest we present too rosy a picture, it must be said that sports fandom can also be a health hazard. In a 2008 study published in the *New England Journal of Medicine*, researchers found that on days when Germany's soccer team played in the World Cup, cardiac emergencies more than tripled for German men and nearly doubled for women. Of course, European soccer fans are an extreme bunch; but even in the U.S., although visits to hospital emergency rooms tend to decrease during a much-anticipated sports game, there's a higher-than-usual surge immediately after the game ends. The explanation: To see a game's final outcome, some die-hard fans delay making that trip to the ER.

And, of course, no story about March Madness would be complete without mention of gambling. The odds of predicting all game winners are about 9.2 quintillion to one. Yet when it comes to sports betting, nothing turns John Q. Fan into Jimmy the Greek more than the NCAA tournament. Workplace camaraderie is one reason. But there's another important factor.

Bragging rights.

With Super Bowl pools there's just a series of boxes with different scores. If you're lucky enough to pick the right one, you win. "But it's a more complex task in filling out all the March Madness brackets, and a seductive pleasure in trying to predict the upsets," says psychologist Edward Hirt.

Another reason why nearly twice as much money is wagered on March Madness than the Super Bowl: More than in other events, NCAA tournament fans simultaneously root for more than one team, triggering a greater likelihood of making multiple bets.

With other sports championships you have to wait a week or at least several days between games, but this sports soap opera—with its David versus Goliath battles—continues night and day, providing a stronger hook.

So let the games begin. Whatever the final outcome, odds are good that the overall advantage—for mind, body, and spirit—is definitely in your court.

Reading, Writing, and Discussion Questions

1. Write an essay in which you explain the types of support that Sid Kirchheimer makes use of the most in his essay "Are Sports Fans Happier?" You will need to provide examples of the types of support that he uses.
2. Do you find Kirchheimer's essay effective? Why, or why not? If you were going to write an evaluative essay about "Are Sports Fans Happier?" what would its thesis be?
3. How does Kirchheimer appeal to the needs and values of his readers?

Appeals to Needs and Values

Good factual evidence is usually enough to convince an audience that your factual claim is sound. Using examples, statistics, and expert opinion, you can prove, for example, that women do not earn as much as men for the same work. But even good evidence may not be enough to convince your audience that unequal pay is wrong or that something should be done about it. In making value and policy claims, an **appeal to the needs and values** of your audience is absolutely essential to the success of your argument. If you want to persuade the audience to change their minds or adopt a course of action—in this case, to demand legislation guaranteeing equal pay for equal work—you will have to show that assent to your claim will bring about what they want and care deeply about.

If the audience concludes that the things you care about are very different from what they care about, if they cannot identify with your goals and principles, they may treat your argument with indifference, even hostility, and finally reject it. But you can hope that decent and reasonable people will share many of the needs and values that underlie your claims. Finding these shared needs and values is what Carl Rogers was advocating when he said that the way to improved communication is to try to express your audience's position fairly and to look for common ground between their position and yours. The appeal to these needs and values was what Aristotle called *pathos*.

Appeals to Needs

The most familiar classification of needs was developed by the psychologist Abraham H. Maslow in 1954.[12] These needs, said Maslow, motivate human thought and action. In satisfying our needs, we attain both long- and short-term goals. Because Maslow believed that some needs are more important than others, he arranged them in hierarchical order from the most urgent biological needs to the psychological needs that are related to our roles as members of a society (Fig. 7.5).

For most of your arguments, you won't have to address the audience's basic physiological needs for nourishment or shelter. The desire for health, however, now receives extraordinary attention. Appeals to buy health foods, vitamin supplements, drugs, exercise and diet courses, and health books are all around us. Many of the claims are supported by little or no evidence, but readers are so eager to satisfy the need for good health that they often overlook the lack of facts or authoritative opinion. The desire for physical well-being, however, is not so simple as it seems; it is strongly related to our need for self-esteem and love.

---

[12] Abraham H. Maslow, *Motivation and Personality* (New York: Harper and Row, 1954), 80–92.

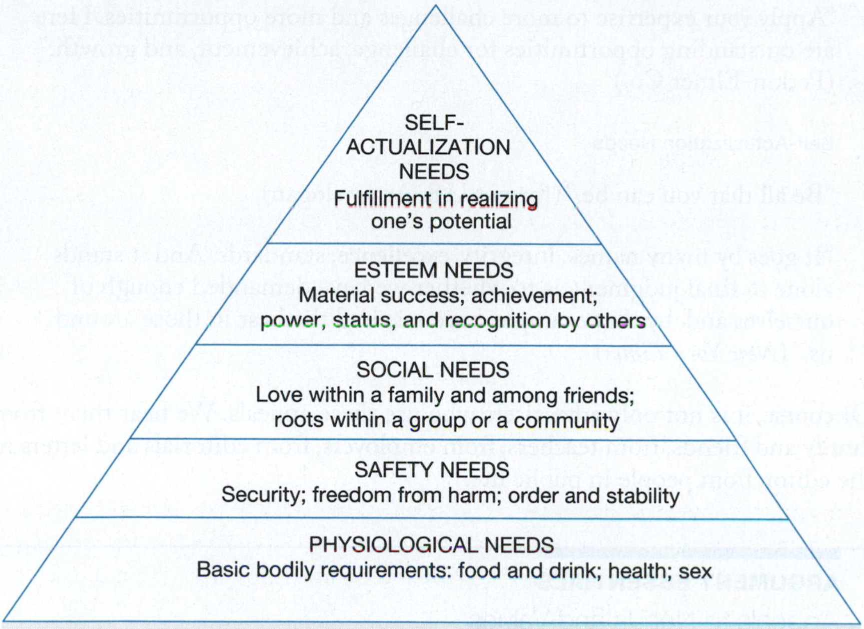
SELF-
ACTUALIZATION
NEEDS
Fulfillment in realizing
one's potential
ESTEEM NEEDS
Material success; achievement;
power, status, and recognition by others
SOCIAL NEEDS
Love within a family and among friends;
roots within a group or a community
SAFETY NEEDS
Security; freedom from harm; order and stability
PHYSIOLOGICAL NEEDS
Basic bodily requirements: food and drink; health; sex

Figure 7.5 Maslow's Hierarchy of Needs

Appeals to our needs to feel safe from harm, to be assured of order and stability in our lives, are also common. Insurance companies, politicians who promise to rid our streets of crime, and companies that offer security services all appeal to this profound and nearly universal need. (We say "nearly" because some people are apparently attracted to risk and danger.) Those who monitor terrorist activity are attempting both to arouse fear for our safety and to suggest ways of reducing the dangers that make us fearful.

The last three needs in Maslow's hierarchy are the ones you will find most challenging to appeal to in your arguments. It is clear that these needs arise out of human relationships and participation in society. Advertisers make much use of appeals to these needs.

Social Needs

"Whether you are young or old, the need for companionship is universal." (ad for dating app)

"Share the Fun of High School with Your Little Girl!" (ad for a Barbie doll)

Esteem Needs

"The power to be your best." (Apple)

"Apply your expertise to more challenges and more opportunities. Here are outstanding opportunities for challenge, achievement, and growth." (Perkin-Elmer Co.)

Self-Actualization Needs

"Be all that you can be." (former U.S. Army slogan)

"It goes by many names: integrity, excellence, standards. And it stands alone in final judgment as to whether we have demanded enough of ourselves and, by that example, have inspired the best in those around us." (*New York Times*)

Of course, it is not only advertisers who use these appeals. We hear them from family and friends, from teachers, from employers, from editorials and letters to the editor, from people in public life.

ARGUMENT ESSENTIALS

Appeals to Needs and Values

- In making value and policy claims, it is essential to appeal to the needs and values of your audience, but first you must identify what those needs and values are.
- Needs can be viewed on a hierarchy developed by psychologist Abraham Maslow.
- Values are the principles by which we judge what is good or bad, beautiful or ugly, worthwhile or undesirable.

Appeals to Values

Needs give rise to values. If we feel the need to belong to a group, we learn to value commitment, sacrifice, and sharing. And we then respond to arguments that promise to protect our values. It is hardly surprising that **values**, the principles by which we judge what is good or bad, beautiful or ugly, worthwhile or undesirable, should exercise a profound influence on our behavior. Virtually all claims, even those that seem to be purely factual, contain expressed or unexpressed judgments.

For our study of argument, we will speak of groups or systems of values because any single value is usually related to others. People and institutions are often defined by such systems of values.

Values, like needs, are arranged in a hierarchy; that is, some are clearly more important than others to the people who hold them. Moreover, the arrangement may shift over time or as a result of new experiences. In 1962, for example, two speech teachers prepared a list of what they called "Relatively Unchanging Values Shared by Most Americans."[13] Included were "puritan and pioneer standards of morality" and "perennial optimism about the future." Now, an appeal to these values might fall on a number of deaf ears.

You should also be aware of not only changes over time but also different or competing value systems that reflect a multitude of subcultures in the United States. Differences in age, sex, race, ethnic background, social environment, religion, even in the personalities and characters of its members, define the groups we belong to. Such terms as *honor, loyalty, justice, patriotism, duty, responsibility, equality, freedom,* and *courage* will be interpreted very differently by different groups.

All of us belong to more than one group, and the values of the several groups may be in conflict. If one group to which you belong—say, peers of your own age and class—is generally uninterested in and even scornful of religion, you may nevertheless hold to the values of your family and continue to place a high value on religious belief.

How can a knowledge of your readers' values enable you to make a more effective appeal? Suppose you want to argue in favor of a sex education program in the high school you attended. The program you support would not only give students information about contraception and venereal disease but also teach them about the pleasures of sex, the importance of small families, and more inclusive sexual orientations. If the readers of your argument are your classmates or your peers, you can be fairly sure that their agreement will be easier to obtain than that of their parents, especially if their parents think of themselves as conservative. Your peers are more likely to value experimentation, tolerance of alternative sexual practices, freedom, and novelty. Their parents are more likely to value restraint, conformity to conventional sexual practices, obedience to family rules, and foresight in planning for the future.

Knowing that your peers share your values and your goals will mean that you need not spell out the values supporting your claim; they are understood by your readers. Convincing their parents, however, who think that freedom, tolerance, and experimentation have been abused by their children, will be a far more challenging task. In one written piece you have little chance of changing their values, a result that might be achieved only over a longer period of time. So you might first attempt to reduce their hostility by suggesting that even if a community-wide program were adopted, students would need parental permission to enroll. This might convince some parents that you share their values regarding parental authority and primacy of the family. Second, you

[13] Edward Steele and W. Charles Redding, "The American Value System: Premises for Persuasion," *Western Speech*, no. 26 (Spring 1962): 83–91.

might look for other values to which the parents subscribe and to which you can make an appeal. Do they prize maturity, self-reliance, responsibility in their children? If so, you could attempt to prove, with authoritative evidence, that the sex education program would promote these qualities in students who took the course.

But familiarity with the value systems of prospective readers may also lead you to conclude that winning assent to your argument will be impossible. It would probably be fruitless to attempt to persuade a group of lifelong pacifists to endorse the use of nuclear weapons. The beliefs, attitudes, and habits that support their value systems are too fundamental to yield to one or two attempts at persuasion.

Strategies for Evaluating Appeals to Needs and Values

If your argument is based on an appeal to the needs and values of your audience, the following questions will help you evaluate the soundness of your appeal.

- **Have the values been clearly defined?** Because value terms are abstractions, you must make their meaning explicit by placing them in context and providing examples. If a person values his Second Amendment rights, does that mean he is opposed to any restrictions on gun ownership? Does another's opposition to abortion extend to cases of rape and incest?

- **Are the needs and values to which you appeal prominent in the reader's hierarchy at the time you are writing?** Gun control becomes a focus in the media and on people's minds whenever a mass shooting occurs. The need for election reform is a hot topic every four years but fades from memory in between.

- **Is the evidence in your argument clearly related to the needs and values to which you appeal?** Remember that readers must see some connection between your evidence and their goals. Statistics can be impressive, for example, but your audience must see their relevance.

READING ARGUMENT

Seeing Appeals to Needs and Values

The following essay on genetics has been annotated to highlight appeals to needs and values. Read the selection, and answer the questions that follow. The annotations in paragraphs 5–9 point out threats to human needs and values posed by reprogenetics. The annotations in paragraphs 11–14 sum up the author's response.

Building Baby from the Genes Up

RONALD M. GREEN

The two British couples no doubt thought that their appeal for medical help in conceiving a child was entirely reasonable. Over several generations, many female members of their families had died of breast cancer. One or both spouses in each couple had probably inherited the genetic mutations for the disease, and they wanted to use in-vitro fertilization and preimplantation genetic diagnosis (PGD) to select only the healthy embryos for implantation. Their goal was to eradicate breast cancer from their family lines once and for all.

Appeal to physiological need for health

In the United States, this combination of reproductive and genetic medicine—what one scientist has dubbed "reprogenetics"—remains largely unregulated, but Britain has a formal agency, the Human Fertilization and Embryology Authority (HFEA), that must approve all requests for PGD. In July 2007, after considerable deliberation, the HFEA approved the procedure for both families. The concern was not about the use of PGD to avoid genetic disease, since embryo screening for serious disorders is commonplace now on both sides of the Atlantic. What troubled the HFEA was the fact that an embryo carrying the cancer mutation could go on to live for 40 or 50 years before ever developing cancer, and there was a chance it might never develop. Did this warrant selecting and discarding embryos? To its critics, the HFEA, in approving this request, crossed a bright line separating legitimate medical genetics from the quest for "the perfect baby."

Appeal to values: Was it right to reject an embryo that would develop into a person who might never get the disease or live 40 to 50 years without it?

Like it or not, that decision is a sign of things to come—and not necessarily a bad sign. Since the completion of the Human Genome Project in 2003, our understanding of the genetic bases of human disease and non-disease traits has been growing almost exponentially. The National Institutes of Health has initiated a quest for the "$1,000 genome," a 10-year program to develop machines that could identify all the genetic letters in anyone's genome at low cost (it took more than $3 billion to sequence the first human genome). With this technology, which some believe may be just four or five years away, we could not only scan an individual's—or embryo's—genome, we could also rapidly compare

Ronald M. Green is Eunice and Julian Cohen Professor Emeritus for the Study of Ethics and Human Values at Dartmouth College, a member of the Department of Community and Family Medicine at Dartmouth's Geisel School of Medicine, the author of *Babies by Design: The Ethics of Genetic Choice* (2007) and *Kant and Kierkegaard on Time and Eternity* (2011), and co-editor of *Suffering and Bioethics* (2014). This article was published on April 11, 2008, in the *Washington Post*.

thousands of people and pinpoint those DNA sequences or combinations that underlie the variations that contribute to our biological differences.

With knowledge comes power. If we understand the genetic causes of obesity, for example, we can intervene by means of embryo selection to produce a child with a reduced genetic likelihood of getting fat. Eventually, without discarding embryos at all, we could use gene-targeting techniques to tweak fetal DNA sequences. No child would have to face a lifetime of dieting or experience the health and cosmetic problems associated with obesity. The same is true for cognitive problems such as dyslexia. Geneticists have already identified some of the mutations that contribute to this disorder. Why should a child struggle with reading difficulties when we could alter the genes responsible for the problem?

Many people are horrified at the thought of such uses of genetics, seeing   5
echoes of the 1997 science-fiction film *Gattaca*, which depicted a world where parents choose their children's traits. Human weakness has been eliminated through genetic engineering, and the few parents who opt for a "natural" conception run the risk of producing offspring—"invalids" or "degenerates"— who become members of a despised underclass. *Gattaca*'s world is clean and efficient, but its eugenic obsessions have all but extinguished human love and compassion.

These fears aren't limited to fiction. Over the past few years, many bioethicists have spoken out against genetic manipulations. The critics tend to voice at least four major concerns. First, they worry about the effect of genetic selection on parenting. Will our ability to choose our children's biological inheritance lead parents to replace unconditional love with a consumerist mentality that seeks perfection?

Second, they ask whether gene manipulations will diminish our freedom by making us creatures of our genes or our parents' whims. In his book *Enough*, the techno-critic Bill McKibben asks: If I am a world-class runner, but my parents inserted the "Sweatworks2010 GenePack" in my genome, can I really feel pride in my accomplishments? Worse, if I refuse to use my costly genetic endowments, will I face relentless pressure to live up to my parents' expectations?

Third, many critics fear that reproductive genetics will widen our social divisions as the affluent "buy" more competitive abilities for their offspring. Will we eventually see "speciation," the emergence of two or more human populations so different that they no longer even breed with one another? Will we re-create the horrors of eugenics that led, in Europe, Asia and the United States, to the sterilization of tens of thousands of people declared to be "unfit" and that in Nazi Germany paved the way for the Holocaust?

Appeal to need for health, physical and cognitive

Appeal to need for love and community

Appeal to need for self-actualization

Appeal to values—threat of increased social division and a return to the horrors of the Holocaust

Finally, some worry about the religious implications of this technology. Does it amount to a forbidden and prideful "playing God"?

Appeal to religious values

10 To many, the answers to these questions are clear. Not long ago, when I asked a large class at Dartmouth Medical School whether they thought that we should move in the direction of human genetic engineering, more than 80 percent said no. This squares with public opinion polls that show a similar degree of opposition. Nevertheless, "babies by design" are probably in our future—but I think that the critics' concerns may be less troublesome than they first appear.

Will critical scrutiny replace parental love? Not likely. Even today, parents who hope for a healthy child but have one born with disabilities tend to love that child ferociously. The very intensity of parental love is the best protection against its erosion by genetic technologies. Will a child somehow feel less free because parents have helped select his or her traits? The fact is that a child is already remarkably influenced by the genes she inherits. The difference is that we haven't taken control of the process. Yet.

Author responds with faith in parental love.

Knowing more about our genes may actually increase our freedom by helping us understand the biological obstacles—and opportunities—we have to work with. Take the case of Tiger Woods. His father, Earl, is said to have handed him a golf club when he was still in the playpen. Earl probably also gave Tiger the genes for some of the traits that help make him a champion golfer. Genes and upbringing worked together to inspire excellence. Does Tiger feel less free because of his inherited abilities? Did he feel pressured by his parents? I doubt it. Of course, his story could have gone the other way, with overbearing parents forcing a child into their mold. But the problem in that case wouldn't be genetics, but bad parenting.

Author responds that there will be no threat to self-actualization.

Granted, the social effects of reproductive genetics are worrisome. The risks of producing a "genobility," genetic overlords ruling a vast genetic underclass, are real. But genetics could also become a tool for reducing the class divide. Will we see the day when perhaps all youngsters are genetically vaccinated against dyslexia? And how might this contribute to everyone's social betterment?

Author responds that some divisions could be reduced.

As for the question of intruding on God's domain, the answer is less clear than the critics believe. The use of genetic medicine to cure or prevent disease is widely accepted by religious traditions, even those that oppose discarding embryos. Speaking in 1982 at the Pontifical Academy of Sciences, Pope John Paul II observed that modern biological research "can ameliorate the condition of those who are affected by chromosomic diseases," and he lauded this as helping to cure "the smallest and weakest of human beings . . . during their

Author responds that religions tend to accept modification for disease cures or prevention but not for other reasons.

intrauterine life or in the period immediately after birth." For Catholicism and some other traditions, it is one thing to cure disease, but another to create children who are faster runners, longer-lived, or smarter.

But why should we think that the human genome is a once-and-for-all-finished, untamperable product? All of the biblically derived faiths permit human beings to improve on nature using technology, from agriculture to aviation. Why not improve our genome? I have no doubt that most people considering these questions for the first time are certain that human genetic improvement is a bad idea, but I'd like to shake up that certainty.

Genomic science is racing toward a future in which foreseeable improvements include reduced susceptibility to a host of diseases, increased life span, better cognitive functioning, and maybe even cosmetic enhancements such as whiter, straighter teeth. Yes, genetic orthodontics may be in our future. The challenge is to see that we don't also unleash the demons of discrimination and oppression. Although I acknowledge the risks, I believe that we can and will incorporate gene technology into the ongoing human adventure.

Human genetic improvement is not a bad thing.

Claim

15

Reading, Writing, and Discussion Questions

1. Remember that the annotations here focus only on appeals to needs and values because that is the focus of this portion of the chapter. That does not mean that those are the only types of support in the essay. What other types of support did you notice? To begin with, what type of support does the first paragraph provide?

2. The annotations make the organization of most of the essay fairly obvious. Explain the organizational pattern.

3. If you were going to write an essay analyzing Ronald M. Green's use of support, what would your thesis be?

4. Green builds a case for the use of genetic engineering in some cases. What are some of the reasons that people oppose it? How does Green respond to those critics?

5. Write an essay explaining whether or not you believe that it was acceptable for the HFEA to approve the request made by two British couples in Ronald M. Green's "Building Baby from the Genes Up." Use specific evidence from the essay to support your opinion.

Practice: Appeals to Needs and Values

In the following essay, Sarah Griffiths looks at what happens inside our brains when we have a crush. Read the essay, and use the questions that follow it to consider what Griffiths is saying about our needs and values.

Why Having a Crush Is Good for You
SARAH GRIFFITHS

We've all played the lead role in a teen drama laden with angst, sweaty palms, a racing heart, and an inability to concentrate on anything or anyone else but the object of our desire. And just as every Hollywood scenario depicts, crushes can be excruciatingly embarrassing in high school, but can also affect us in adulthood. So it might seem difficult to imagine that all this cringe-worthy behavior has a purpose and is actually good for us—at least most of the time.

Adults can also be taken unaware when cupid strikes, suddenly becoming self-conscious around someone attractive at work or swooning over a celebrity, even when they're happily married. Why this happens is a bit of a mystery. "Crushes have more to do with fantasy than with reality," psychologist and author Dr. Carl Pickhardt has written. "They tell much more about the admirer than the admired."

In its purest sense, a crush is a form of parasocial relationship; a one-sided relationship where you have feelings for someone else but those feelings are not reciprocated, according to Dr. Anna Machin, an evolutionary anthropologist at the University of Oxford's Department of Experimental Psychology. "The research into the brain isn't there yet, so we still don't know whether crushes generate the same [neural] patterns as when someone is genuinely in love," she said. Despite this, she added, the feeling of infatuation or love that crushes produce is real.

What Goes On in Our Heads?

It's thought that when we're in love or lust, the stress and reward systems in our brain are working overtime, and the same is possibly true of having a crush. Nerve cells in the brain release a chemical called norepinephrine that stimulates the production of adrenaline, and give us the feeling of arousal that causes our palms to sweat and our hearts to pound. The feel-good chemical dopamine is also released, making us excitable and talkative, and perhaps explains why we sometimes blurt out unimaginably embarrassing things. This is charmingly described as "word vomit" in the cult film *Mean Girls*, and exemplified by the mortifying line, "I carried a watermelon" in *Dirty Dancing*.

"If we were to reduce down what love is, in a neural sense, it's a neurochemical reward, so the feelings you have are a mixture of chemicals . . . and dopamine is your go-to reward chemical in life," said Dr. Machin. "When you're in love or you have a crush, you'll still get your dopamine reward for that, even if your feelings are not reciprocated." It's this process that seems to account for our slightly obsessive behavior when we have a crush—think Cameron in *Ten Things I Hate about You*—because thinking of an unintended brief encounter can make us feel happy, and that's addictive.

The limbic area of the brain is thought to be involved both in love and crushes. When examined in an MRI scanner, someone in love will typically have high activity in an area of the limbic system called the caudate nucleus. That's important, because it links to the neocortex, which handles the more cognitive or sensible

5

Sarah Griffiths is a freelance science journalist. Her essay appeared on the Relationships vertical of Medium.com on December 3, 2018.

aspects of love, Dr. Machin explained. Perhaps, this is the area we refer to if we trust our head more than our hearts when it comes to finding a partner. But it means that rather than slavishly following our amorous fantasies, our rational mind regulates the limbic brain's desire for dopamine. While it wins out most of the time, because the limbic system is associated with addiction, getting over a crush can be tough, and some of us hold a torch for years.

Why Do We Have Crushes Anyway?

Is there a higher purpose for having a crush, beyond just making us feel good? Dr. Machin believes they play a strong evolutionary role. "Parasocial relationships in adolescence are a very valuable experience," she explained. "They are something that's part of our development because they allow an adolescent to start to explore relationships and their own sexuality and understand what attracts them in a safe way, because they're not going to get hurt in the same way as they might in a real relationship."

Whereas many of us have dated the wrong "type" of person, and had our hearts broken as a result, crushes can help ensure this doesn't happen. "This person [the crush] is the right person because you idolize them," Dr. Machin said. "They're going to be who you want them to be, therefore, it's very safe. It's a training ground for proper relationships in the real world." Harry Styles, then, might be building a generation's romantic resilience. "In adolescence, crushes are a healthy thing and teenagers shouldn't feel embarrassed," she added.

In adulthood, things are more complicated. It's important to distinguish between imagining what a relationship could be like, and having a crush with the intention of exploring a real relationship. Dr. Gary W. Lewandowski Jr., a writer and relationship scientist at Monmouth University in New Jersey, said that our evolutionary history suggests we are not a monogamous species. So crushes could be a way to help identify a future or additional partner to meet our needs—or they could be the sign of adults who are simply stuck in adolescence and unable to have a real relationship. "A crush could be a gateway behavior that eventually leads to cheating," said Dr. Lewandowski.

What Are the Upsides to This Embarrassing Behavior?

Left as daydreams, crushes are usually harmless. Research shows that people with crushes often feel like they are in a real relationship, which could be a way to decrease loneliness, and may even boost our confidence. Crushes could help reinvigorate stale relationships by revealing what they are lacking, and give people insight into how to improve their love lives. And even the most unlikely or strange crushes could be enlightening. "People aren't always good at knowing what they want, so a crush may actually be insight into something you don't like and didn't realize or didn't want to admit," Dr. Lewandowski said.

How do you cope with a crush as a teenager or an adult? "I'd encourage people to recognize that they are idealizing their crush," said Dr. Lewandowski. Perhaps take the advice of Cher from *Clueless* and send yourself flowers and love letters—because ultimately, you can't control who you have a crush on, so you may as well have fun.

10

Reading, Writing, and Discussion Questions

1. How does Sarah Griffiths define the term *crush*?

2. What happens in our brains when we have a crush? What needs does that brain activity meet for us?

3. According to Dr. Anna Machin, what needs does a crush fulfill for us?

4. According to Dr. Gary W. Lewandowski Jr., what needs does a crush fulfill for us?

5. Based on what Griffiths says, that a crush is physiological, should there be no guilt involved, even if one is married? In your answer, explain what values are addressed.

6. Write an essay explaining how effective you think Griffiths is in supporting the claim that having a crush is good for a person.

Assignments for Support

Reading and Discussion Questions

1. Consider what types of evidence you find most convincing in an argument. Is the best type of evidence dependent on the topic and the context? Explain.

2. Look for examples in the media of the misuse of evidence. Explain why the evidence is misleading.

3. Use examples to explain which news shows depend on factual evidence and which depend largely on opinion. Do both have a useful role to play in our society? Explain.

4. In the aftermath of the many recent school shootings, there has been talk of passing laws requiring teachers to carry weapons on school and college campuses. What needs of the people were those who proposed the law appealing to? How could opponents of such laws have used similar types of appeal to argue their case?

5. Consider presidential debates you have seen or other televised coverage of candidates during the months leading up to an election. What are some specific examples of how the candidates try to appeal to the voters' needs and values?

6. The average American citizen is usually ignorant of much of the reality of what goes on in the Islamic world. When Americans take a stand on issues such as U.S. involvement in Syria, to what extent do you believe they are basing that stand on solid supporting evidence?

Writing Suggestions

1. Analyze different television commercials for the same product or similar products. Write an essay supporting a conclusion you are able to draw about the types of appeal used in the commercials.

2. Write a letter about a problem on your campus to the person who is in a position to correct the problem. Provide convincing evidence that a problem exists, and in suggesting a solution to the problem, keep in mind the needs and values of your audience as well as those of others on campus.

3. There has been a debate recently about whether comic book movies should be considered art. Whether or not they are, there is ample evidence for their success at the box office. Write an essay proving that they are, if nothing else, a financial success, and provide a variety of types of support.

4. The nature of the senior year in high school in America has changed in the last few decades. Consider one or more of the current alternatives, such as the International Baccalaureate or dual enrollment in high school and college, to support a conclusion about how the senior year has changed where academics are concerned.

RESEARCH ASSIGNMENT **Finding Support**

1. Do some preliminary research on the following topics:
   - The link between autism and vaccines
   - The effects of social media on relationships
   - The movement to drop standardized tests as a requirement for college admissions
   - The environmental impact of plastic water bottles

2. For each of the topics above, track down one or more sources that use each type of evidence and emotional appeal discussed in the chapter:
   - An example
   - A statistic
   - An expert opinion
   - An image
   - An appeal to a need
   - An appeal to a value

3. Evaluate the sources you have found, using the Research Skill boxes on pages 200 and 205.

Assumptions

We now come to the third element in the structure of the argument—the underlying **assumption**, or **warrant**. Claim and support, the other major elements we have discussed, are more familiar in ordinary discourse, but there is nothing mysterious or unusual about the idea of an underlying assumption. All our claims, both formal and informal, are grounded in assumptions that the audience must share with us if our claims are to prove to be acceptable.

The arrows in the following diagram illustrate that writer and audience must be looking at the subject with the same underlying beliefs in order for the argument to be persuasive.

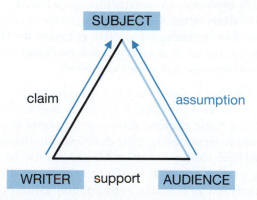

General Principles

The following exercise provides a good starting point for this chapter. Do the assigned task by yourself or in a small group.

Practice: Assumptions

A series of catastrophic environmental events has virtually wiped out human life on Earth. The only known survivors in your vicinity are the eleven listed below. There are resources to sustain only seven. Choose seven of the following people to survive. List them in the order in which you would choose them, and be prepared to explain the reasons for your selection: that is, why you chose these particular persons and why you placed them in this certain order.

- Dr. D.—thirty-seven, Ph.D. in history, college professor, in good health (jogs daily), hobby is botany, enjoys politics, married with one child (Bobby).
- Mrs. D.—thirty-eight, M.A. in psychology, counselor in a mental health clinic, rather obese, diabetic, married to Dr. D., has one child.
- Bobby D.—ten, cognitively deficient with IQ of 70, healthy and strong for his age.
- Mrs. G.—twenty-three, ninth-grade education, cocktail waitress, worked as a prostitute, married at age sixteen, divorced at age eighteen, one son (Joseph).
- Joseph G.—three months old, healthy.
- Mary E.—eighteen, trade school education, wears glasses, artistic.
- Mr. N.—twenty-five, starting last year of medical school, music as a hobby, physical fitness buff.
- Mrs. C.—twenty-eight, daughter of a minister, college graduate, electronics engineer, single now after a brief marriage, member of Zero Population Growth.
- Mr. B.—fifty-one, B.S. in mechanics, married with four children, enjoys outdoors, much experience in construction, quite handy.
- Father Frans—thirty-seven, Catholic priest, active in civil rights, former college athlete, farming background, often criticized for liberal views.
- Dr. L.—sixty-six, doctor in general practice, two heart attacks in the past five years, loves literature and quotes extensively.

There may have been a great deal of disagreement over which survivors in the above scenario to select. If so, the reason for that disagreement was that in making their choices, different members of your group or of your class as a whole were basing their decisions on different assumptions. Some of you may have chosen not to let Mrs. G. survive because she seemed to have nothing particularly vital to offer to the survival of the group as a whole. If you analyzed your claim, support, and assumption in that case, they would look something like the following. Notice the assumption in particular.

Claim: Mrs. G. should not be allowed to survive.

Support: She has no skills vital to the survival of the group.

Assumption: Those chosen to survive must have skills vital to the survival of the group.

Another way of looking at the assumption is to ask yourself this question: *What would I have to believe in order to accept that claim, given the support I have to go on?*

Others may have felt that Mrs. G. should be allowed to survive along with her child, the infant in the group. The reasoning would look like this:

Claim: Mrs. G. should be allowed to survive.

Support: She has an infant son.

Assumption: Those with infants should be allowed to survive.

That assumes, of course, choosing to allow the infant, Joseph G., to survive. If that was not the case, the assumption behind letting Mrs. G. survive would be invalid.

Did you decide to let Baby Joseph survive? If so, what was your reasoning? How would you fill in the blanks?

Claim: Joseph G. should be allowed to survive.

Support: _____

Assumption: _____

Or if you thought the opposite — that the infant should not be one of the seven allowed to survive — what was your reasoning?

Claim: Joseph G. should not be allowed to survive.

Support: _____

Assumption: _____

You may have felt that an infant had very little chance of survival and therefore his spot should be given to someone more likely to survive. Or you may have thought that the future of the civilization depended on the survival of the young. Or you may just not have liked the thought of killing an infant.

There are few easy answers in this exercise, but behind each choice is an underlying assumption. If you chose to kill off Dr. L., it was probably because he had had two heart attacks and was less likely than others to survive. You might have decided that the young Mr. N., a physical fitness buff and a medical student, would be more vital to the survival of the others. Out of compassion, you might have wanted to save Bobby D., or you might have concluded that a cognitively deficient ten-year-old with an IQ of 70 had the least to offer the rest of the group.

Obviously, this is an exercise with no right answer. What it can teach us, however, is to consider the assumptions on which our beliefs are based. There are reasons you might have chosen certain individuals to survive that could be stated as general principles:

Those who are in the best physical condition should be allowed to survive.

Those with the most useful skills should be allowed to survive.

Those who are mentally deficient should not be allowed to survive.

Those who are most likely to reproduce should be allowed to survive.

Fortunately, this is merely an intellectual exercise. Whenever you take a stand in a real-life situation, though, you do so on the basis of certain general principles that guide your choices. Those general principles that you feel most strongly about exist as part of your intellectual and moral being because of what you have experienced in your life thus far. They have been shaped by your observations, your personal experience, and your participation in a culture. Some of the general principles behind your thoughts and actions may be these:

> Cheating is always wrong.
>
> I have a right to express my opinion.
>
> Premarital sex is wrong.
>
> Morality changes with the times.
>
> Killing under any circumstances is wrong.
>
> Killing is wrong except in self-defense.
>
> Killing is wrong except in war.
>
> Cruelty to animals is wrong.
>
> Government intrudes too much in my daily life.

All of these are broad statements that could apply in any number of different circumstances. That's why we refer to them as **general principles**. Your stated assumptions may not always be this broad, but at times they will be. Because the observations, experiences, and cultural associations on which these principles are based vary from one individual to another, your audience may not always agree with your assumptions. The success of many arguments depends on identifying at least one assumption, or warrant, that opposing sides share so you can establish common ground. (This is especially true in the case of Rogerian Argument [p. 139].) The success of any argument depends on at least understanding your own assumptions and those of your audience.

Widely Held Assumptions

Some assumptions are so widely accepted that they do not need to be stated or require any proof of their validity. If an argument claims that every new dorm on campus should have a sprinkler system, it probably does not even need to state that assumption. If it did, it would be something like this: *Measures that would increase the likelihood that dorm residents would survive a fire should be implemented in all dorms.*

Other examples of claims and support that depend on widely held assumptions:

Claim: Michael should get a smoke detector.

Support: His new apartment doesn't have a working smoke detector.

Assumption: Every apartment needs a working smoke detector.

Claim: I should drive you home.

Support: You've been drinking, and I haven't.

Assumption: The one who hasn't been drinking should do the driving.

Claim: Ping's mother won't let him visit at Daniel's house.

Support: Daniel's parents keep guns that are not locked up in their home.

Assumption: People shouldn't let their children visit where guns are not kept locked up.

Notice that an assumption is a broad generalization that can apply to a number of different situations, while the claim is about a specific place and time. It should be added that in other arguments the assumption may not be stated in such general terms. However, even in arguments in which the assumption makes a more specific reference to the claim, the reader can infer an extension of the assumption to other similar arguments. In the sprinkler system example, the assumption mentions dorms in particular. But it is clear that such warrants can be generalized to apply to other arguments in which we accept a claim based on an appeal to our very human need to feel secure.

Often, multiple assumptions underlie a claim. If your house catches on fire, you call 911. If your car is stolen, you call the police (or 911). We teach these responses even to young children, who in some cases have saved their own lives and those of others by knowing what to do.

Claim: I should call 911.

Support: I just saw a stranger sneaking around my house.

Assumption: If you see a stranger sneaking around your house, you should call 911.

Another possible assumption underlying this claim, and one that gets at the heart of why we call 911, is this one:

Assumption: Calling 911 and summoning the police will bring me protection.

Unfortunately, we live in a culture where not all groups feel that they can assume that calling 911 will bring a rapid response and protection by the police. Black Lives Matter exists because some African Americans do not feel that police officers' dedication to protect and serve applies the same to them as to white citizens. Thus not all audiences will agree with the assumption that calling 911 and summoning the police will bring them protection.

What about other assumptions that are controversial? Why is it so difficult for those who oppose abortion, for example, to communicate with those who favor choice, and vice versa? Anyone who believes that abortion is the murder of an unborn child is basing that argument on the assumption that a fetus is a child from conception. Many on the other side of the debate do not accept that assumption and thus do not accept the claim. Obviously, disagreements on such emotionally charged issues are very difficult to resolve because the underlying assumptions are based on firmly held beliefs that are resistant to change. It is always better to be aware of your opponent's assumptions, however, than to simply dismiss them as irrelevant.

The British philosopher Stephen Toulmin, who developed the concept of *warrants*, dismissed more traditional forms of logical reasoning in favor of a more audience-based, courtroom-derived approach to argumentation. He refers to warrants as "general, hypothetical statements, which can act as bridges" and "entitle one to draw conclusions or make claims."[1] The word *bridges* to denote the action of the warrant, or assumption, is crucial. We use the word *assumption* to emphasize that in an argument it guarantees a connecting link—a bridge—between the claim and the support. This means that even if a reader agrees that the support is sound, the support cannot prove the validity of the claim unless the reader also agrees with the underlying assumption.

The following dialogue offers another example of the relationship between the assumption and the other elements of the argument.

> *"Put down your phone, and concentrate on driving!"*
> *"Aw, I always text when I'm driving."*
> *"Well, you shouldn't. It's not safe."*

If we put this into outline form, the assumption in the argument is clear.

Claim: You shouldn't text on your phone while you are driving.

Support: Texting on a phone while driving is not safe.

Assumption: You shouldn't do unsafe things while driving.

We can also represent an argument in diagram form, which shows the assumption as a bridge between the claim and the support.

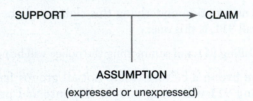

SUPPORT ⟶ CLAIM

ASSUMPTION
(expressed or unexpressed)

The argument above can then be written like this:

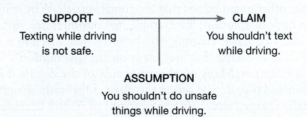

SUPPORT ⟶ CLAIM
Texting while driving   You shouldn't text
is not safe.   while driving.

ASSUMPTION
You shouldn't do unsafe
things while driving.

---

[1] Stephen Toulmin, *The Uses of Argument* (Cambridge: Cambridge University Press, 1958), 98.

Claim and support (or lack of support) are relatively easy to uncover in most arguments. One thing that makes the assumption different is that it is often unexpressed and therefore unexamined by both writer and reader because they take it for granted. In the argument about texting while driving, the assumption was stated. Consider another example where the assumption is implied, not stated. What is the implied assumption in the following?

> The technological revolution in how information is distributed and consumed holds the promise to scale higher education to serve more students and cut costs. At the same time, the rush to embrace technology as a solution to every problem has created tension on campuses over whether the critical role higher education plays in preparing the whole person to be a productive citizen in a democratic society is at risk. Indeed, in an increasingly complex world, the foundation of learning — a liberal arts education — is more important than ever.[2]

The claim is that traditional higher education has the potential to be transformed by technology. The implied assumption — the warrant — is that increasing the number of students receiving a quality liberal arts education in a cost-effective way will lead to a better society.

ARGUMENT ESSENTIALS
Assumptions

- An assumption guarantees a connecting link — a bridge — between the claim and the support. This means that even if a reader agrees that the support is sound, the support cannot prove the validity of the claim unless the reader also agrees with the underlying assumption.
- The success of any argument depends on understanding your own assumptions, those of your audience, and those of opposing parties. It is always better to be aware of your opponent's assumptions, however, than to simply dismiss them as irrelevant.
- Some assumptions are so widely accepted that they do not need to be stated or require any proof of their validity. A possible danger is that such assumptions will be taken for granted and go unexamined by both writer and reader.
- There can be more than one assumption for a single claim or text, so it is important to examine an argument from multiple perspectives.

---

[2] Jeffrey J. Selingo, *College (Un)Bound: The Future of Higher Education and What It Means for Students* (New York: New Harvest, 2013), xvii.

Recognizing and Analyzing Assumptions

There is no simple formula for locating assumptions. And, yes, there can be more than one assumption in a single text because different portions of the text may be based on separate assumptions. Once you have read a selection, it is a good idea to locate the thesis statement or try to put the thesis into your own words. Then look at the evidence the author offers in support of that thesis. The assumption will be a statement that shows the connection between the claim and support.

We have already noted that sometimes the assumption is unstated. Arguers might neglect to state their assumptions for one of two reasons: (1) as in our earlier examples, they may believe that the assumption is obvious and need not be expressed; (2) they may want to conceal the assumption in the hope that the reader will overlook its weakness.

"Obvious" Assumptions

Here are a few more examples of assumptions that seem so obvious that they need not be expressed:

> Mothers love their children.
> A good harvest will result in lower prices for produce.
> Killing innocent children is wrong.
> First come, first served.

These statements seem to embody beliefs that most of us would share and that might be unnecessary to make explicit in an argument. The last statement, for example, is taken as axiomatic, an article of faith that we seldom question in ordinary circumstances. Suppose you hear someone make the claim, *I deserve to get the last ticket to the concert.* If you ask why he is entitled to a ticket that you also would like to have, he may answer in support of his claim, "Because I was here first." No doubt you accept his claim without further argument because you understand and agree with the assumption that is not expressed: *If you arrive first, you deserve to be served before those who come later.*

But even those assumptions that seem to express universal truths invite analysis if we can think of claims for which these assumptions might not, after all, be relevant. "First in line," for example, may justify the claim of a person who wants a concert ticket, but it cannot in itself justify the claim of someone who wants a vital medication that is in short supply.

Moreover, offering a rebuttal to a long-held but unexamined assumption can often produce an interesting and original argument. If someone exclaims, "All this buying of gifts! I think people have forgotten that Christmas celebrates the birth of Christ," she need not express the assumption—that the buying of gifts violates what ought to be a religious celebration. It goes unstated by the speaker because it has been uttered so often that she knows the hearer will supply it. But one writer, in an essay titled "God's Gift: A Commercial Christmas," argued that contrary to popular belief, the purchase of gifts—which means the expenditure of time, money, and thought on others rather than oneself—is not a violation but an affirmation of a religious Christmas spirit.[3]

Intention to Deceive

The second reason for refusal to state the assumption lies in the arguer's intention to disarm or deceive the reader, although the arguer may not be aware of this. For instance, failure to state the assumption is common in advertising and politics, where the desire to sell a product or an idea may outweigh the responsibility to argue explicitly. The advertisement in Figure 8.1 was famous not only for what it said but for what it did not say.

FIGURE 8.1 Famous Virginia Slims campaign

---

[3] Robert A. Sirico, *Wall Street Journal*, December 21, 1993, A12.

The text on the ad reads, "Virginia Slims remembers when the business world first called upon women to serve" over a picture of businessmen eating and conversing at a long conference table while a woman waits on them. The focus of the ad is the modern (for the 1980s) woman, carefree and confident. What is the unstated assumption in the ad? The manufacturer of Virginia Slims hoped we would agree that being permitted to smoke cigarettes was a significant sign of female liberation. But many readers would insist that proving "You've come a long way, baby" requires more evidence than women's freedom to smoke (or "serve" the business world). Also, knowing what we now know about the dangers of smoking undermines the notion that smoking is a sign of women's progress. The shaky assumption weakened the claim.

Strategies for Recognizing Assumptions

READ: Recognizing Assumptions for Analysis

- In written arguments, locate the one sentence that best states the author's claim. If the argument is unwritten (such as a print advertisement), or if there is no single sentence that sums up the claim, try to express the claim in a single sentence of your own.

- Think about what audience the author was targeting. How is that audience likely to respond to the claim? The most important question to ask about the audience regarding assumptions is this one: What assumption or assumptions must the audience make to be able to accept the claim? The answer to that question will be the assumption or assumptions on which the piece is based.

- Remember that the assumption is the link between claim and support. Ask yourself what the claim is, what support the author is offering, and what assumption connects the two. Do that for each of the author's major supporting statements.

- The author may not need to state his or her assumption directly if it is a universally accepted truth that most reasonable readers would agree with. It should be clear to you as a reader, however, what the assumption is.

WRITE: Recognizing Assumptions in Your Own Arguments

- In your writing, be sure that there is a single sentence that clearly states your main claim or that the main claim is clearly implied.

- Consider your audience when interrogating your own assumptions. What assumption or assumptions must your audience make to be able to accept your main claim and any other claims in your argument? How is your audience likely to respond to your claims and the assumptions on which they are based?

- For each of your supporting statements, ask yourself what the claim is, what support you have offered, and what assumption connects the two. If the assumption is one that your audience may disagree with, state it clearly and try to establish common ground.

- If you leave any of your assumptions unstated, be sure that they are based on such universally accepted truths that most reasonable readers will agree with them.

READING ARGUMENT

Recognizing Assumptions

The following essay differs from most that you have read in this book because of its tone. Thomas R. Wells offers a solution to the problems posed by anti-vaxxers, those who oppose letting their children be vaccinated, but he does so with more than a hint of irony.

Let the Anti-Vaxxers Have Their Way

THOMAS R. WELLS

The authority of scientific experts is in decline. This is unfortunate since experts—by definition—are those with the best understanding of how the world works, what is likely to happen next, and how we can change that for the best. Human civilization depends upon an intellectual division of labor for our continued prosperity, and also to head off existential problems like epidemics and climate change. The fewer people believe scientists' pronouncements, the more danger we are all in.

> **Claim:** We are in increasing danger.
> **Support:** The authority of scientific experts is in decline.
> **Assumption:** The fewer people believe scientists' pronouncements, the more danger we are all in.
>
> Wells's major claim (though ironic)

Fortunately I think there is a solution for this problem. Unfortunately, it looks like some people are going to have to die.

I

How did we get to this place? Two interacting mechanisms: the paradox of expertise and the rise of consumocracy.

By definition, experts are the best source of knowledge and policy advice. (If someone knows better than the official experts, that just means they are the real expert.) So expertise should be a highly valuable, respected resource. But it isn't because of the paradox of expertise, that experts lose credibility for getting things right as well as for getting things wrong.

5   First, consider what happens when experts give correct advice and we believe it and act on it in time. In that case the problem they warned us about will be prevented or much reduced. But then, because nothing really bad happened, the casual observer will conclude that yet again the experts

> When experts predict bad things and those things are avoided or their impact reduced, the assumption is that the experts were wrong or exaggerating.

Thomas R. Wells teaches philosophy at Tilburg University in the Netherlands. In his personal blog, *The Philosopher's Beard*, he writes for the general public about how philosophy intersects with politics and economics. This essay was posted on *3 Quarks Daily* on June 3, 2019.

were wrong or exaggerating. The problem here is that the better experts are at identifying and fixing problems before they appear, the harder it is for them to show the value of their contribution: the terrible things that would have happened without their intervention.

Second, consider what happens when we follow experts' advice that turns out to be mistaken. This is bound to happen sometimes. The fact that experts represent the best understanding anyone in the world has about some topic doesn't mean that that understanding can't be wrong (as medical science got ulcers wrong for decades). It just means that we don't have any good reason to believe that anyone else knows better. It can also be that scientific knowledge is correct in general, but doesn't have the resolution to give accurate predictions about every case (such as who the economic losers will be from the free trade policies that make the world much richer on average). In either case, excuses aren't considered. Science got it wrong: the experts are blamed for the problems they failed to prevent and the credibility of their future claims is reduced.

> When the experts are wrong and something bad happens, the assumption is that the experts failed to prevent it.

‖

Besides the built in self-undermining character of expertise there is also the phenomenon of consumocracy: the increasingly popular notion that we have the right to believe whatever it pleases us to believe and anyone who tries to tell us we're wrong can go to hell.

This is driven partly by our human psychology directing us towards the things that promise to make us feel good. What the people who have dedicated their lives to scientific research have to say is difficult to comprehend and often bone-achingly dull compared to a YouTube video by a Flat Earther that makes you feel like you can do science from your couch. There are various kinds of psychic reward available here. There may be a pleasure in believing outrageous things and arguing with other people about them on the internet; or in believing you know something that other people don't; or in membership of a community of fellow believers. Conspiracy theories are particularly fun to believe in because they make complicated and unpleasant events immediately comprehensible by making them all about you, the consumer of news events. The world isn't so big and scary and difficult after all! It's just a conspiracy by an all powerful government agency (or alien, or God) that cares deeply about your opinion!

> **Assumption:** We want to feel good—what Wells calls psychic reward. Sometimes what makes us feel good is believing outrageous things like conspiracy theories.

Although the pursuit of purely psychic rewards has always been a vulnerability of human reasoners, it has only become full blown consumocracy thanks to a cultural shift. As Kurt Andersen explains very eloquently in his *Fantasyland*, we are dealing with an outgrowth of the same individualism that fueled the rational enlightenment against unjustified authority and gave us modern science (the motto of Britain's Royal Society was "On no-one's authority"). The flip side of establishing the right of individuals to follow the evidence wherever it leads is the right of individuals to believe whatever they want for whatever half-assed reasons they find compelling. Of course this is ridiculous. Facts are not matters of personal preference, like pizza toppings. They are or they aren't. And whether they are has nothing to do with what we would like.

> The right to follow the evidence can lead to following it to a false conclusion.

10   When consumocracy combines with the paradox of expertise, we get the anti-civilizational phenomenon of mass idiocy: vast numbers of people turning their backs on what humanity actually knows in favor of homespun stories that they enjoy more. That includes such dangerous stories as the idea that vaccines cause autism. The main response from those who still believe in science has been to stop the idiots from acting on their beliefs by backing up the epistemic authority of expertise with political force, such as by making vaccination compulsory. However, I do not think this is sustainable in a democracy since it does nothing about the core mechanisms that continue to undermine faith in expertise.

> **Paraphrase:** People have the right to be idiots.

> Now Wells turns to his main point about vaccinations. **Assumption:** If people do not have faith in the experts, you cannot force them to act in their own best interest.

I have a different solution. We should let some people die for their mistakes so that the full price of idiocy is once again clear to everyone.

> Wells's shocking solution

III

Should I vaccinate my child against measles?

When we are deciding who or what to believe on this question we are making an epistemic gamble. The most obvious thing to figure out is what outcome is most likely. Scientific experts are objectively the most likely of anyone to be correct, and so it might seem that the rational person should always bet with the scientific experts rather than against them. However, the most important feature of a gamble is not the probabilities of the different outcomes but the stakes: how much might I win or lose?

Here, the actions of the government become important. If it intervenes to enforce the advice of experts, then the worst possible outcomes are forestalled. Vaccination rates stay high and measles outbreaks remain easily contained. Unfortunately, by reducing the life and death stakes—by protecting parents from reality—the government has also reduced parents' interest in finding out who really has the best knowledge of how vaccines or measles

> Here Wells applies the paradox of expertise to vaccination.

actually work. The stakes in this epistemic wager now come down to the parent's own internal psychic rewards, for example the pleasure of fantasizing themself a hero in the resistance movement against arrogant scientific dogma. This is a bet the anti-vaxxer can't lose.

It may not be irrational for an individual to select their beliefs in this way. Nevertheless, once large numbers of people start making choices based on what they would prefer to believe is true, protecting them from the real world consequences of being an idiot quickly becomes politically unsustainable. This is because their behavior undermines the authority of the scientific expertise that holds together the system in which their dissent from reality is made possible. At some point the system will collapse dramatically, like a political constitution overwhelmed by the careless opportunism of politicians who took stability for granted.

How can we break this cycle of increasing consumocracy and declining credibility of experts? Telling people to trust scientists doesn't fly (although I have tried it elsewhere[1]). Forcing people to go along with what the experts say just makes them more complacent in their idiocy. I think we should consider letting the stakes rise again. Society won't recover its respect for the value of scientific expertise unless it has vivid and recent memories of what happens when we don't follow the correct advice of experts. Sometimes a tragedy can do more good than harm. From time to time, we should step aside and let the idiots have their way.

So if parents don't want to vaccinate their children because of what they think they found out in their Facebook research, let them experience the full consequences of that decision. Some of their children will die, and this is sad because those children will be paying the price for their parents' fantasies. Some other children will die despite their parents' faith in vaccines (because they were too young to be fully protected, or had immune-system problems) and this is also sad. But it is that sadness which would provide the reality check that nothing else seems capable of providing. It may seem callous to think of children's lives in this calculating way, but societies trade off innocent lives for other values all the time (or we would have made the speed limit 20 mph). In this case there is something much more important at stake than saving commuters a few minutes a day. For if we cannot recover our ability to trust the experts then much worse things than a few measles outbreaks will follow.

15

---

[1] "Democracy Is Not a Truth Machine," *Philosophersbeard.org*, 5 December 2011, http://www.philosophersbeard.org/2010/11/democracy-is-not-truth-machine.html.

Margin notes:

If enough people ignore the experts, the system falls apart.

The assumption behind his argument: sometimes we have to let people see what happens when the experts are ignored.

Wells's concluding assumption is that everyone loves their children and wants them to live happy and healthy lives (common ground), so letting some children die because of their parents' idiocy may be the only way to make anti-vaxxers accept reality.

RESEARCH SKILL	Focusing a Research Topic

When you have a research assignment, you might start with a topic idea that is too broad for the length of the paper you have been assigned. That does not mean that you have to abandon the idea completely. Instead, you can narrow the topic to one that is more manageable, given the length of the paper you will be writing.

1. Try using some of these approaches to identify a part of your broad topic that might be appropriate:

	Instead of	Try
Narrow according to *time*:	The U.S. space program	The U.S. space program in the twenty-first century
Narrow according to *place*:	Wind power	Wind farms in California
Narrow to one *aspect*:	Abortion	Late-term abortion
Narrow to one *part*:	Affordable health insurance	Insurance for businesses with fewer than fifty employees
Narrow to one *group*:	Immigration reform	Immigration reform and college students
Narrow to a single *problem*:	Standardized testing	Cultural bias in standardized testing

2. You may get some additional ideas by applying to your broad topic the traditional reporter's questions: *who*, *what*, *where*, *when*, and *why*.

3. You may get still different information if you look at your broad subject in terms of *relationships*: How do parts *compare* and *contrast*? What can you discover about *causes* and *effects*? How is the *definition* of your key term different from that of similar terms?

Once you narrow your topic, you can start working toward a thesis. As you do, you will want to consider your purpose and your audience. Part of analyzing your audience should involve trying to understand what their *relationship* is with the subject and what assumptions underlie their beliefs about it. Once you have in mind a claim to support in your writing, think about the underlying assumptions. Then consider what assumptions might underlie the claim of someone who disagrees with you.

READING ARGUMENT

Analyzing Assumptions

The following essay has been annotated to highlight claims, support, and assumptions.

The Case for Torture
MICHAEL LEVIN

It is generally assumed that torture is impermissible, a throwback to a more brutal age. Enlightened societies reject it outright, and regimes suspected of using it risk the wrath of the United States.

I believe this attitude is unwise. There are situations in which torture is not merely permissible but morally mandatory. Moreover, these situations are moving from the realm of imagination to fact.

Suppose a terrorist has hidden an atomic bomb on Manhattan Island which will detonate at noon on July 4 unless . . . (here follow the usual demands for money and release of his friends from jail). Suppose, further, that he is caught at 10 A.M. of the fateful day, but—preferring death to failure—won't disclose where the bomb is. What do we do? If we follow due process—wait for his lawyer, arraign him—millions of people will die. If the only way to save those lives is to subject the terrorist to the most excruciating possible pain, what grounds can there be for not doing so? I suggest there are none. In any case, I ask you to face the question with an open mind.

Torturing the terrorist is unconstitutional? Probably. But millions of lives surely outweigh constitutionality. Torture is barbaric? Mass murder is far more barbaric. Indeed, letting millions of innocents die in deference to one who flaunts his guilt is moral cowardice, an unwillingness to dirty one's hands. If you caught the terrorist, could you sleep nights knowing that millions died because you couldn't bring yourself to apply the electrodes?

Once you concede that torture is justified in extreme cases, you have admitted that the decision to use torture is a matter of balancing innocent lives against the means needed to save them. You must now face more realistic cases involving more modest numbers. Someone plants a bomb on a jumbo jet. He alone can disarm it, and his demands cannot be met (or if they can, we refuse to set a precedent by yielding to his threats). Surely we can, we must, do anything to the extortionist to save the passengers. How can we tell three hundred, or one hundred, or ten people who never asked to be put in danger, "I'm sorry, you'll have to die in agony, we just couldn't bring ourselves to . . ."

Here are the results of an informal poll about a third, hypothetical, case. Suppose a terrorist group kidnapped a newborn baby from a hospital.

5

Introduction: statement of opposing view

Claim of policy: rebuttal of opposing view

Support: hypothetical example to test the reader's belief

These questions are assumptions that he rejects. His responses are assumptions he can accept.

The assumptions on which the essay is based

Support: hypothetical example

Support: informal poll

Michael Levin is a professor of philosophy at the City University of New York and author of *Why Race Matters* (1997). This essay is reprinted from the June 7, 1982, issue of *Newsweek*.

I asked four mothers if they would approve of torturing kidnappers if that were necessary to get their own newborns back. All said yes, the most "liberal" adding that she would administer it herself.

I am not advocating torture as punishment. Punishment is addressed to deeds irrevocably past. Rather, I am advocating torture as an acceptable measure for preventing future evils. So understood, it is far less objectionable than many extant punishments. Opponents of the death penalty, for example, are forever insisting that executing a murderer will not bring back his victim (as if the purpose of capital punishment were supposed to be resurrection, not deterrence or retribution). But torture, in the cases described, is intended not to bring anyone back but to keep innocents from being dispatched. The most powerful argument against using torture as a punishment or to secure confessions is that such practices disregard the rights of the individual. Well, if the individual is all that important—and he is—it is correspondingly important to protect the rights of individuals threatened by terrorists. If life is so valuable that it must never be taken, the lives of the innocents must be saved even at the price of hurting the one who endangers them.

Better precedents for torture are assassination and preemptive attack. No Allied leader would have flinched at assassinating Hitler, had that been possible. (The Allies did assassinate Heydrich.) Americans would be angered to learn that Roosevelt could have had Hitler killed in 1943—thereby shortening the war and saving millions of lives—but refused on moral grounds. Similarly, if nation A learns that nation B is about to launch an unprovoked attack, A has a right to save itself by destroying B's military capability first. In the same way, if the police can by torture save those who would otherwise die at the hands of kidnappers or terrorists, they must.

There is an important difference between terrorists and their victims that should mute talk of the terrorists' "rights." The terrorist's victims are at risk unintentionally, not having asked to be endangered. But the terrorist knowingly initiated his actions. Unlike his victims, he volunteered for the risks of his deed. By threatening to kill for profit or idealism, he renounces civilized standards, and he can have no complaint if civilization tries to thwart him by whatever means necessary.

10   Just as torture is justified only to save lives (not extort confessions or recantations), it is justifiably administered only to those *known* to hold innocent lives in their hands. Ah, but how can the authorities ever be sure they have the right malefactor? Isn't there a danger of error and abuse? Won't we turn into Them?

Margin notes:

Defense of the claim:
a) Not punishment but protection of the innocent

The warrant for this particular line of defense

b) Precedents for torture

Basically, the same assumption, reworded

c) Denial that terrorists have rights

Assumptions

Questions like these are disingenuous in a world in which terrorists proclaim themselves and perform for television. The name of their game is public recognition. After all, you can't very well intimidate a government into releasing your freedom fighters unless you announce that it is your group that has seized its embassy. "Clear guilt" is difficult to define, but when 40 million people see a group of masked gunmen seize an airplane on the evening news, there is not much question about who the perpetrators are. There will be hard cases where the situation is murkier. Nonetheless, a line demarcating the legitimate use of torture can be drawn. Torture only the obviously guilty, and only for the sake of saving innocents, and the line between Us and Them will remain clear.

There is little danger that the Western democracies will lose their way if they choose to inflict pain as one way of preserving order. Paralysis in the face of evil is the greater danger. Some day soon a terrorist will threaten tens of thousands of lives, and torture will be the only way to save them. We had better start thinking about this.

Practice: Recognizing and Analyzing Assumptions

Read the following argument by Robert A. Sirico. Then summarize the argument in a paragraph. The questions at the end can guide your reading and writing.

An Unjust Sacrifice
ROBERT A. SIRICO

An appeals court in London has made a Solomonic ruling, deciding that eight-week-old twins joined at the pelvis must be separated. In effect, one twin, known as Mary, is to be sacrificed to save the other, known as Jodie, in an operation the babies' parents oppose.

The judges invoked a utilitarian rationale, justified on the basis of medical testimony. The specialists agreed that there is an 80 to 90 percent chance that the strong and alert Jodie could not survive more than a few months if she continued to support the weak heart and lungs of Mary, whose brain is underdeveloped.

This is a heartbreaking case, and the decision of the court was not arrived at lightly. But even the best of intentions, on the part of the state or the parents, is no substitute for sound moral reasoning. Utilitarian considerations like Mary's quality of life are not the issue. Nor should doctors' expert testimony, which is subject to error, be considered decisive.

Robert A. Sirico, a Roman Catholic priest, is cofounder of the Action Institute for the Study of Religion and Liberty in Grand Rapids, Michigan. This article appeared in the September 28, 2000, issue of the *New York Times*.

Here, as in the case of abortion, one simple principle applies: There is no justification for deliberately destroying innocent life. In this case, the court has turned its back on a tenet that the West has stood by: Life, no matter how limited, should be protected.

5 While this case is so far unique, there are guidelines that must be followed. No human being, for instance, can be coerced into donating an organ—even if the individual donating the organ is unlikely to be harmed and the individual receiving the organ could be saved. In principle, no person should ever be forced to volunteer his own body to save another's life, even if that individual is a newborn baby.

To understand the gravity of the court's error, consider the parents' point of view. They are from Gozo, an island in Malta. After being told of their daughters' condition, while the twins were in utero, they went to Manchester, England, seeking out the best possible medical care. Yet, after the birth on August 8, the parents were told that they needed to separate the twins, which would be fatal for Mary.

They protested, telling the court: "We cannot begin to accept or contemplate that one of our children should die to enable the other one to survive. That is not God's will. Everyone has a right to life, so why should we kill one of our daughters to enable the other one to survive?"

And yet, a court in a country in which they sought refuge has overruled their wishes. This is a clear evil: coercion against the parents and coercion against their child, justified in the name of a speculative medical calculus.

The parents' phrase "God's will" is easily caricatured, as if they believed divine revelation were guiding them to ignore science. In fact, they believe in the merit of science, or they would not have gone to Britain for help in the first place.

10 But utilitarian rationality has overtaken their case. The lawyer appointed by the court to represent Jodie insisted that Mary's was "a futile life." That is a dangerous statement—sending us down a slippery slope where lives can be measured for their supposed value and discarded if deemed not useful enough.

Some might argue that in thinking about the twins, we should apply the philosophical principle known as "double effect," which, in some circumstances, permits the loss of a life when it is an unintended consequence of saving another. But in this case, ending Mary's life would be a deliberate decision, not an unintended effect.

Can we ever take one life in favor of another? No, not even in this case, however fateful the consequences.

Reading, Writing, and Discussion Questions

1. What is Robert A. Sirico's main claim?
2. What support does he offer for that claim?
3. What assumptions underlie your opinion about the twins?
4. What assumptions underlie Sirico's beliefs? Do you agree with those assumptions? Why or why not?
5. Sirico's belief in the sanctity of human life appears to be absolute, even when it will most likely lead to the death of both twins. Write an essay in which you give examples of how your value system underlies your political views.

Assignments for Assumptions

Reading and Discussion Questions

1. Should students be given a direct voice in the hiring of faculty members? On what assumptions about education do you base your answer?

2. Discuss the assumption in this statement from the *Watchtower* (a publication of the Jehovah's Witnesses) about genital herpes: "The sexually loose are indeed 'receiving in themselves the full recompense, which was their due for their error' (Romans 1:27)." Is it valid?

3. In 2010, a judge in Saudi Arabia had to make the decision whether or not a man could be intentionally paralyzed as punishment for having paralyzed another man in a fight. His victim had requested this punishment. What would the judge's assumption be if he chose to order the punishment? What would it be if he decided not to honor the victim's request?

4. In view of the increasing interest in health in general, and nutrition and exercise in particular, do you think that universities and colleges should impose physical education requirements? If so, what form should they take? If not, why not? What assumption underlies your position?

5. What are some of the assumptions underlying the preference for natural foods and medicines? Can *natural* be clearly defined? Is this preference part of a broader philosophy? Try to evaluate the validity of the assumption.

6. The author of the following passage, Katherine Butler Hathaway, became a hunchback as a result of a childhood illness. Here she writes about the relationship between love and beauty from the point of view of someone who is deformed. Discuss the assumptions on which the author bases her conclusions.

   I could secretly pretend that I had a lover . . . but I could never risk showing that I thought such a thing was possible for me . . . with any man. Because of my repeated encounters with the mirror and my irrepressible tendency to forget what I had seen, I had begun to force myself to believe and to remember, and especially to remember, that I would never be chosen for what I imagined to be the supreme and most intimate of all experience. I thought of sexual love as an honor that was too great and too beautiful for the body in which I was doomed to live.

Writing Suggestions

1. Diagram three of the decisions you made about survivors of the imaginary catastrophe in the opening assignment (p. 227). Show claim, support, and assumption.

2. Both state and federal governments have been embroiled in controversies concerning the rights of citizens to engage in harmful practices. In Massachusetts, for example, a mandatory seatbelt law was repealed by voters who considered the law an infringement of their freedom. (It was later reinstated.) Write an essay in which you explain what principles you believe should guide government regulation of dangerous practices.

3. Henry David Thoreau writes, "Unjust laws exist: Shall we be content to obey them, or shall we endeavor to amend them, and obey them until we have succeeded, or shall we transgress them at once?" Write an essay in which you explain under what circumstances you would feel compelled to break the law, or why you feel that you would never do so.

RESEARCH ASSIGNMENT ▶ **Focusing a Research Topic**

1. Think of three different ways to narrow each of the following broad topics:
   - The effects of stress
   - Eating disorders
   - Presidential elections
   - Genetic engineering
   - Athletes and drugs
   - College admissions tests
   - Suicide in the military
   - Social networking

2. For each broad topic, select one of the narrower topics you came up with. For that narrower topic, identify some widely held assumptions. Then explain what underlying assumptions that are not so widely held might make it difficult to reach agreement.

Structuring the Argument

Some of what you learn in college will come through memorization of facts or mastering of procedures. More of it will require **synthesis**, the bringing together and analyzing of ideas and the formulation of opinions. Any time you are asked to express an opinion and support it, you are being asked to write an argument, even if your **purpose** for writing will differ from one situation to another. Presenting a reasoned argument for what you believe is a skill that you will use throughout your life, as a student, a parent, a follower of a particular religion, a Democrat, Republican, or Independent, an employee. Your college classes are a place to practice reasoned argument and the delivery of it in a thoughtful, well-organized way.

This chapter builds on the elements of argument covered so far in Part Two (Chapters 5–8): argument approaches, claim, support, and assumptions. In Part Three (Chapters 13–15), we will discuss how to write an argument based on independent research. For now, we want to talk about writing an argument based on course material, as on an exam or in an assigned essay, and offer some options for structuring your argument and for writing introductions and conclusions.

Think of the types of assignments that require a response in the form of an argument. You may not think of literary analysis, for example, as argumentation, but if you are defending an opinion you have about the literary work, you are writing an argument. Your **thesis** will be a claim of fact or a claim of value. Consider these other types of assignments in different disciplines that call for an argumentative response supporting a claim of fact, value, or policy.

Political Science: Do you support the National Popular Vote Interstate Compact as a replacement for the winner-take-all way of allocating electoral votes currently used in forty-eight states? Why or why not?

Biology: Can environmental factors affect DNA? Explain.

Education: How would you respond to parents who argue that having children with special needs mainstreamed into regular classes takes the teacher's time and attention away from other students?

Sociology: Should sports teams continue to use Native American imagery and names? Why or why not?

Chemistry: What threats are there to the continued effectiveness of antibiotics?

Media Studies: Why is there such a discrepancy between the financial success of a film and its critical success?

The topic will usually dictate the type of claim you will support in writing an argument. The audience for your writing is a bit artificial in that you are writing to an instructor or professor who knows more about the subject than you do. There is the temptation to think, "I don't need to say that. He knows it already!" Remember, though, that your goal is to build a case for your claim. You need to draw in any information from your textbooks or lectures that will help you do that. The more specific your support, the more convincing your argument will be. You will also need to be aware of the assumptions underlying your claims and of your audience's potential reaction to them.

Organizing the Argument

The first point to establish in organizing your argument is your **purpose**. Is your intention to make readers aware of some problem? to offer a solution to the problem? to defend a position? to refute a position held by others? The way you organize your material will depend to a great extent on your goal.

Let's look at various ways of organizing an argumentative paper, based on your purpose in writing. Here are four possibilities:

- **Defending the thesis** — If your purpose is to convince your audience of the validity of your position, or to believe or act in a certain way

- **Refuting an opposing view** — If your purpose is to show that your position is stronger than another position on the issue

- **Finding the middle ground** — If your purpose is to mediate between two different positions

- **Presenting the stock issues** — If your purpose is to present a solution to a need and the advantages of the proposed solution

The graphics in this chapter represent the basic divisions of essays using these organizational patterns. Do not take the number of blocks in the graphics too literally. Except in long essays, your introduction and your conclusion will generally each be a single paragraph. The length of your essay and your specific subject will determine how many paragraphs comprise the blocks in the body of your essay.

Defending the Thesis

All forms of organization will require you to defend your thesis, or main idea, but one way of doing this is simple and direct. Early in the paper, state the thesis that you will defend throughout your argument, which will be a statement of your position, what you want your audience to think or do. You can also indicate here the two or three points you intend to develop in support of your claim, or you can raise these later as they come up. Suppose your thesis is that widespread vegetarianism would solve a number of problems. You could phrase it this way: *If the majority of people in this country adopted a vegetarian diet, we would see improvements in the economy, in the health of our people, and in moral sensitivity.*

You would then develop each of the improvements in your list with appropriate data. However, if you find that listing your two or three main ideas in the claim leads to too much repetition later in the paper, you can introduce each one as it arises in your discussion of the topic. Your claim would remain more general: *If the majority of people in this country adopted a vegetarian diet, there would be noticeable improvement.*

Let's put this example in the context of how it might look in the organizer. Later in the chapter we will present a number of suggestions for developing introductions and conclusions. If you need help developing the body paragraphs, which primarily offer support for the main claim or thesis, look back at Chapter 7.

Defending the Thesis

Introduction

Thesis (Main Claim)

Evidence

Conclusion

Introduction: Opening statistics about the number of people in the United States who now consider themselves vegetarians.

Thesis (Main Claim): If the majority of people in this country adopted a vegetarian diet, there would be noticeable improvement.

Evidence: Improvements in the economy, in the health of our people, and in moral sensitivity.

Conclusion: A call to action to try a vegetarian diet.

Defending the thesis is effective for factual claims as well as policy claims, in which you urge the adoption of a certain policy and give the reasons for its adoption. It is most appropriate when your claim is straightforward and can be readily supported by direct statements.

Refuting an Opposing View

Refuting an opposing view means revealing its faults it in order to weaken, invalidate, or make it less credible to a reader. Since all arguments are dialogues or debates—even when the opponent is only imaginary—refutation of another point of view is always implicit in your arguments. As you write, keep in mind the issues that an opponent may raise. You will be looking at your own argument as an unsympathetic reader may look at it, asking yourself the same kinds of critical questions and trying to find its weaknesses in order to correct them. In this way, every argument you write becomes a form of refutation. There may be situations in which you accept a portion of the opposing view, but not all of it. This is called a **concession**.

A claim for this type of essay might take this form:

On the topic of _____, X claims that _____.
However, _____.

Example: Some people claim that vaccinations cause autism. However, there is no valid scientific proof of that connection.

A general outline might look like the following, which would be further developed in multiple paragraphs and with adequate support for the claims.

Introduction: A brief definition of autism and discussion of when it starts to manifest itself in children.

Summary of Opposing View: The publication of a study in 1998 led some people to believe that the MMR (measles-mumps-rubella) vaccine causes autism.

Refutation of Opposing View: Not only has the data in that study been found to be false, but no other study has established a link between vaccinations and autism.

Conclusion: A call for stricter enforcement of school vaccination requirements.

Refuting an Opposing View

Introduction

Summary of Opposing View

Refutation of Opposing View

Conclusion

Strategies for Refuting an Opposing View (Counterargument)

1. **Read the argument carefully,** noting the points with which you disagree. You must be familiar with your opponent's argument in order to refute it.

2. **Summarize an opposing view at the beginning of your paper** if you think your audience may be sympathetic to it or unfamiliar with it. Give readers enough information to understand what you plan to refute. Be respectful of the opposition's views. You do not want to alienate readers who might not agree with you at first.

3. **If your argument is long and complex, choose only the most important points to refute.** Otherwise, the reader who does not have the original argument on hand may find a detailed refutation hard to follow. If the argument is short and relatively simple — a claim supported by only two or three points — you may decide to refute them all, devoting more space to the most important ones.

4. **Refute the principal elements in the argument of your opponent (sometimes referred to as *counterarguments*).**

   a. Question the evidence. (See Chapter 7, Support.) Question whether your opponent has proved that a problem exists.

   b. Question the assumptions or warrants that underlie the claim. (See Chapter 8, Assumptions.)

   c. Question the logic or reasoning of the opposing view. (Refer to the discussion of fallacious reasoning in Chapter 12, Logic.)

   d. Reject the proposed solution to a problem, pointing out that it will not work.

5. **Be prepared to do more than refute the opposing view.** Supply evidence and good reasons in support of your own claim.

READING ARGUMENT

Seeing Opposing Views

The following essay is an example of an argument that refutes opposing views.

The Rich Get Richer, the Poor Go Hungry

SHARON ASTYK AND AARON NEWTON

Astyk and Newton begin with opposing views, followed by the refutation.

What is the most common cause of hunger in the world? Is it drought? Flood? Locusts? Crop diseases? Nope. Most hunger in the world has absolutely nothing to do with food shortages. Most people who go to bed hungry, both in rich and in poor countries, do so in places where markets are filled with food that they cannot have.

A concession

Despite this fact, much of the discourse about reforming our food system has focused on the necessity of raising yields. Though it is true that we might need more food in coming years, it is also true that the world produces more food calories than are needed to sustain its entire population.

The authors' refutation of the claim that raising yields is a good solution to reforming the food system—and their thesis.

The problem is unequal access to food, land, and wealth, and any discussion must begin not from fantasies of massive yield increases, but from the truth that the hunger of the poor is in part a choice of the rich.

Refutation of the idea that food shortages cause famines; instead, inequity and politics do. Astyk and Newton support their claim with examples.

Inequity and politics, not food shortages, were at the root of almost all famines in the twentieth century. Brazil, for example, exported $20 billion worth of food in 2002, while millions of its people went hungry. During Ethiopian famines in the 1980s, the country also exported food. Many of even the poorest nations can feed themselves—or *could* in a society with fairer allocation of resources.

It can be hard to grasp the degree to which the Western lifestyle is implicated. We don't realize that when we buy imported shrimp or coffee we are often literally taking food from poor people. We don't realize that our economic system is doing harm; in fact, the system conspires to make it nearly impossible to figure out whether what we're doing is destructive or regenerative.

A summary of what we (the audience) have been told, then a refutation of it

We have been assured that "a rising tide lifts all boats," that it is necessary for us to make rich people richer, because that will, in turn, enrich the poor. The consequences have been disastrous—for the planet and for the people whose food systems have been disrupted, who never had a chance to be lifted by any tide.

5

Sharon Astyk is a former academic, a writer, and a farmer in New York state. She is the author of *Depletion and Abundance: Life on the New Home Front* (2008) and coauthor, with Aaron Newton, of *A Nation of Farmers: Defeating the Food Crisis on American Soil* (2009). Newton is a coordinator of the Elma C. Lomax Research and Education Farm, an organic farm in North Carolina where future farmers are trained. This selection is from *A Nation of Farmers*.

Journalist Jeremy Seabrook, in his book *The No-Nonsense Guide to World Poverty*, describes First World efforts to eliminate poverty and hunger this way:

> It is now taken for granted that relief of poverty is the chief objective of all politicians, international institutions, donors, and charities. This dedication is revealed most clearly in a determination to preserve [the poor]. Like all great historical monuments, there should be a Society for the Preservation of the Poor; only, since it is written into the very structures of the global economy, no special arrangements are required. There is not the remotest chance that poverty will be abolished, but every chance that the poor themselves might perish.

It is hard for many of us to recognize that the society we live in helps create poverty and insecurity, but it is true. Our economy is based on endless growth. We're told that if the rich get richer, it makes other people less poor. Think about it for a moment—about how crazy that is. Wouldn't it make much more sense to enrich the poor directly, to help them get land and access to resources?

Opposing view and refutation

Historically, rural people have been quite poor, but often, despite their poverty, could grow enough food to feed themselves. Over recent decades, however, industrial agriculture and widespread industrialization have moved large chunks of the human population into cities, promising more wealth. But rising food and energy prices (rising because of this move and this urban population's new demands for energy and meat) have left people unable to feed their families.

Multinational food companies have also worked their way into the food budgets of the poor. Faith D'Aluisio and Peter Menzel are the authors of *Hungry Planet.* "Few of the families we met [in the developing world] could afford a week's worth of a processed food item at one time," they report in the *Washington Post,* "so the global food companies make their wares more affordable by offering them in single-serving packets."

10   Around the world, industrial agriculture has consolidated land ownership into the hands of smaller and smaller populations. Rich nations dumped cheap subsidized grain on poor nations. Local self-sufficiency was destroyed. Now, as the price of food has risen dramatically, those created dependencies on cheap grain, which doesn't exist anymore, mean that millions are in danger of starvation.

Real alleviation of poverty and hunger means reallocating the resources of our world into the hands of people who need them most. This is not only ethically the right thing to do, it is necessary. There is no hope that newly industrializing nations will help us fight climate change if it means a great inequity between their people and those of the United States. Russia, India, and China have all said so

The authors claim that this is what the world needs instead of the failed attempts at helping the poor. "Real" announces their solution is preferable to the other solutions, which they have refuted.

explicitly. The only alternative to the death of millions in a game of global chicken is for everyone to accept that the world cannot afford rich people—in any nation.

One solution to the problem

What is the best strategy of reallocation? One—that is, for those of us who live in nations where there is plenty of land and food so that we don't have to rely on the exports of poor nations—would be to enable the world's farmers to eat what they grow and to have sufficient land to feed themselves and their neighbors.

Most of the world's poorest people are urban slum dwellers (often displaced farmers) or landpoor farmers, agroecologist Peter Rosset notes. Both groups are increasing, in large degree because of economic policies that favor food for export and allow large quantities of land to be held in the hands of the richest.

"The expansion of agricultural production for export, controlled by wealthy elites who own the best lands, continually displaces the poor to ever more marginal areas for farming," Rosset writes in *Food Is Different*. "They are forced ... to try to eke out a living on desert margins and in rainforests. As they fall deeper into poverty ... they are often accused of contributing to environmental degradation."

In this system, poor people who depend on the land, and who best understand the urgency of preserving it, are forced by necessity to degrade and destroy it—and they, rather than we, are held responsible. But a large part of the responsibility rests on the way we eat. This is an important point, because it acknowledges that there are things that we in wealthy nations can do to enable poorer people to eat better—or even to eat at all.

Solutions

One way to do this is simply to grow our own food, to rely not on foods grown thousands of miles away but on foods grown at local farms and gardens. We also can concentrate on creating food sovereignty in poor nations. We can cut back on global food trade, importing primarily high-value, fair-traded dry goods that take little energy to transport, and place limits on food speculation, which drives up prices so that multinational corporations can get richer at the expense of the poor.

Most of all, we can recognize that self-sufficiency is as urgent in the rich world as in the poor. Globalization's demise is coming. The rising costs of transportation and the trade deficit in the United States make it inevitable that we will increasingly be looking to meet our basic needs locally.

When we grow our own food, or buy it directly from local farmers, we take power away from multinationals. We make it harder for them to extract wealth and the best land of other nations—and if they don't need that land, local farmers may be able to use it for their own needs.

In the conclusion, Astyk and Newton summarize the advantages of their solutions locally and globally.

We also put power in the hands of our neighbors, many of whom are also victims of globalization. There are 49 million people in the United

15

States who can't consistently afford a basic nutritious diet. It turns out that the things that make us poor—lack of education, lack of access to land and home, and the industrial economy—are precisely the things that make other people poor. By creating local food systems, we can enrich our immediate neighbors as we stop impoverishing our distant ones.

Finding the Middle Ground

Although an argument, by definition, assumes a difference of opinion, we know that opposing sides frequently find accommodation somewhere in the middle, which is the Rogerian Argument approach discussed in Chapter 5 (p. 139). As you mount your own argument about a controversial issue, you need not confine yourself to support of any of the differing positions. You may want to acknowledge that there is some justice on all sides and that you understand the difficulty of resolving the issue. Your thesis or main claim will be your accommodation of two or more of the different views, or a position that satisfies all parties as much as possible.

A claim for this type of essay might take this form:

On the topic of _____, X claims that _____.

In contrast, Y argues that _____.

They agree that _____, a view that deserves consideration.

Example: In the aftermath of so many mass shootings, gun enthusiasts still often oppose any restrictions on gun ownership. In contrast, gun control advocates believe the federal government should impose some restrictions. One innovative proposal that already has passed in some states and has received a good bit of bipartisan support is a policy called Extreme Risk Protection Order, also known as a Gun Violence Restraining Order or sometimes "red flag laws."

An argument that finds middle ground might be structured as follows, with multiple well-developed paragraphs supporting the thesis:

Introduction: Introduction of the opposing sides in the argument but of a shared interest in the safety of children.

Presentation of Various Viewpoints: Views held by those on both sides of the issue of gun control.

Proposal of Middle Ground: Extreme Risk Protection Orders as possible middle ground.

Conclusion: A summary of the current status of ERPOs and the next needed steps.

Finding the Middle Ground

Introduction

Presentation of Various Viewpoints

Proposal of Middle Ground

Conclusion

Strategies for Finding the Middle Ground

Consider these guidelines for an argument that offers a compromise between or among competing positions:

1. **Explain the differing positions** early in your essay. Make clear the major differences separating the two (or more) sides.

2. **Point out, whenever possible, that the differing sides already agree** to some exceptions to their stated positions. Such evidence may prove that the differences are not so extreme as their advocates insist.

3. **Make clear your own moderation and sympathy,** your own willingness to negotiate.

4. **Acknowledge that opposing views deserve to be considered,** if you favor one side of the controversy.

5. **Provide evidence that accepting a middle ground can offer marked advantages** for the whole society. Whenever possible, show that continued polarization can result in violence, injustice, and suffering.

6. **Be as specific as possible** in offering a solution that finds a common ground, emphasizing the part that you are willing to play in reaching a settlement.

READING ARGUMENT

Seeing the Middle Ground

The following essay is an example of an argument that seeks to find the middle ground on a topic.

Innovative Gun Control Idea Gains Support

JACK BEYRER

Beyrer establishes the background and his entry point: There has been debate between two positions, but this proposal might change the argument. The next three paragraphs explain the proposal.

In the post-Parkland era, gun control continues to resurface in the news cycle as an issue of importance. While nearly seven out of ten Americans want serious change in gun policy, national legislation hasn't reflected this opinion. But one innovative proposal at the state level may change the terms of the debate.

A policy called Extreme Risk Protection Order, also known as a Gun Violence Restraining Order or sometimes a "red flag law," has garnered

---

When he wrote this article, Jack Beyrer was a student at Wake Forest University and was interning at RealClearPolitics, where this article was posted June 22, 2019. He previously edited the *Wake Forest Review*, the conservative newspaper and magazine on campus.

significant bipartisan support. ERPOs are currently in place in sixteen states and are up for a vote in seven more.

In simple terms, an ERPO sets up a process for reporting to authorities a fellow citizen who displays distressing behavior.

After a legal hearing where the so-called respondent is often not present, some combination of a judge, law enforcement, and a medical professional decide if there is enough evidence to confiscate the respondent's firearm.

5   After a set period of time, the person subject to the order can have his firearm returned. This "cooling off" period can make all the difference, according to Dr. Garen Wintemute, a professor at University of California, Davis. "A temporary reduction in risk achieved by firearm recovery and purchase prohibition also allows an opportunity to reduce risk by other means, including medical or mental health treatment or social service intervention," said Wintemute, who is director of UC-Davis' Violence Prevention Research Program.

Support for the proposal: expert opinion

It's an approach being tried across the country. Maryland alone issued 258 ERPOs from October 2018 through March of this year. According to analyses by Everytown Research, Indiana's suicide rate fell by 7.5 percent in the ten years subsequent to its ERPO law taking effect, and in Connecticut one suicide was averted for every eleven guns removed.

Paragraphs 6 and 7 offer statistical support for the proposal.

A study by Everytown also found that 51 percent of mass shooters from 2009 to 2017 displayed actionable warning signs before they committed violence. This has caught the attention of Republicans and Democrats alike: Sens. Lindsey Graham, Dianne Feinstein and Marco Rubio have since initiated ERPO-related bills.

Early polling suggests that this approach is a popular middle ground between protecting the rights of gun owners and keeping firearms out of the hands of the mentally unstable. A Hart Research poll of 1,200 likely voters found 89 percent support for ERPOs on a federal level, including 86 percent of Republicans and 84 percent of gun owners.

Here Beyrer clearly establishes ERPOs as a popular middle ground.

The policy is not without its critics. Colorado-based libertarian Jay Stooksberry has written about complaints that emerged—both practical and constitutional—when a red flag law took effect in his home state.

Beyrer addresses criticism of the proposal.

10   "There's a variety of objections to this," Stooksberry told RealClearPolitics. "I live in a community that's very enthusiastic about their firearms and they take them very seriously and they have quite the arsenals. That means overloading the existing sheriff department's evidence lockers."

There are other practical problems, too, he said. Due to a Colorado policy that hearings for ERPOs must be held within fourteen days of their filing, courts without enough judges suffer severe backlog.

Rally for Our Rights founder Lesley Hollywood and other gun rights activists raise the question of whether expedited legal processes give those cited adequate time to prepare for a hearing. "How do you even get an attorney?" she told RCP. "How do you build a defense, how do you do a mental health evaluation within fourteen days?"

The *ex parte* nature of these hearings creates Sixth Amendment concerns. Alex Yablon, a journalist for The Trace, an online outlet covering gun violence, noted that because the initial hearing often happens without the respondent present, "some people have said that's an abuse of people's civil rights, and you shouldn't lose this right to own a gun without being present."

Enthusiasm for enforcing red flag laws differs among law enforcement agencies, often depending on attitudes about guns within their jurisdictions. Sheriff Steve Reams of rural Colorado's Weld County, once proclaimed that he would go to jail rather than serve an ERPO. "It's a matter [of] doing what's right," he told CNN in March [2019].

The National Rifle Association also levied its own constitutional criticisms, issuing this official statement to RCP: "The NRA supports risk protection orders that respect due process rights and ensure those who are found dangerous receive the mental health treatment they so dearly need. Unfortunately, none of the bills signed into law include such safeguards and therefore lack our support."   15

Despite these criticisms, the bulk of evidence points to ERPOs as an effective policy option, Yablon told RCP. "Even the NRA's opposition to this is more measured than it is for a lot of other things, like universal background checks," he said. "They do say they could conceive of some way in which they could support an ERPO bill rather than opposing the very idea of it. I would expect this to be a continuing part of the gun discourse."

He added that he has yet to see a credible account of someone's civil rights being abused by these laws. "Due process is built into these bills," he said. "I understand why people are concerned about that and it makes sense for civil libertarians to be skeptical of things like this. But I think that those might not bear out when you look at the details of this."

In practice, this seems to be the case: Maryland turned down slightly less than half of the ERPO petitions sought as of March 2019, as they did not meet the evidence standards needed for firearm seizure. "Orders are not only being issued appropriately," Montgomery County Sheriff Darren Popkin told the *Capital Gazette*, "but saving lives."

The bulk of evidence supports the effectiveness of the policy. Both sides could accept it. The NRA could support some form of ERPOs; civil libertarians might find their concerns are unfounded.

Presenting the Stock Issues

Presenting the stock issues, or stating the problem before the solution, is a type of organization borrowed from traditional debate format. It works for policy claims when an audience must be convinced that a need exists for changing the status quo (present conditions) and for introducing plans to solve the problem. You begin by establishing that a problem exists (need). You then propose a solution (plan), which is your thesis. Finally, you show reasons for adopting the plan (advantages). These three elements—need, plan, and advantages—are called the *stock issues*.

For example, suppose you wanted to argue that measures for tighter restrictions on vaping should be introduced at once. You would first have to establish a need for such measures by defining the problem and providing evidence of damage. Then you would present your claim, a means for improving conditions. Finally, you would suggest the benefits that would follow from implementation of your plan. Notice that in this organization your claim usually appears toward the middle of your paper, although it may also appear at the beginning.

A sentence form such as the following can guide you in writing an appropriate thesis:

_____ is a problem, but
_____ can help resolve it.

Example: Traffic congestion around the stadium on game days is a problem, but temporarily limiting University Avenue to eastbound traffic would allow for a smoother and faster flow of traffic.

A rough outline of an argument supporting that claim of policy might take this approach:

Introduction: Description of typical game day traffic around the stadium.

Establishment of Problem (Need): Traffic congestion around the stadium on game days is a problem.

Proposal of Solution (Plan): University Avenue could temporarily be limited to eastbound traffic on game days.

Explanation of Advantages: Traffic could flow faster and more smoothly.

Conclusion: A call for the campus police to implement this change.

Presenting the Stock Issues

Introduction

Establishment of Problem (Need)

Proposal of Solution (Plan)

Explanation of Advantages

Conclusion

READING ARGUMENT

Seeing the Stock Issues

The following essay is an example of an argument that presents the stock issues on a topic.

States Can Reform Electoral College — Here's How to Empower Popular Vote

JOHN R. KOZA

Hillary Clinton and President-elect Donald Trump rarely agree, but in 2001 Clinton called for a bill for a national popular vote for president, while Trump referred to the current system of electing the President in 2012 as "a disaster for a democracy . . . a total sham and a travesty."

Need (a problem exists)

The reason why five of our nation's 45 incoming presidents have entered office after losing the national popular vote (while winning the Electoral-College vote) is that most states have winner-take-all laws that award all the state's electoral votes to the candidate receiving the most popular votes in that state. Given that there have now been eight consecutive presidential elections with an average national-popular-vote margin of less than 5 percent, it is safe to predict that the nation will continue to experience elections ending in this unhealthy way.

These state winner-take-all laws are also the reason why the 2016 presidential candidates concentrated 94 percent of their campaign events in just 12 closely divided "battleground" states, while giving little or no attention to states with 70 percent of the nation's population. Candidates have no reason to pay attention to the concerns of states where they are safely ahead or hopelessly behind (and therefore have nothing to gain and nothing to lose). The result of presidential candidates focusing on a mere 12 states is not just that babies don't get kissed in the

Consequences of the current system

spectator states. There are real consequences to the current system and they are not trivial. Presidential candidates and sitting first-term presidents shape important policies with an eye to winning the 12 critical states that decide the election.

The 2016 candidates, for example, catered to Michigan, Wisconsin, Ohio, and Pennsylvania in fashioning their positions on trade treaties. In 2001, President George W. Bush imposed steel quotas, despite his party's

John R. Koza is a computer scientist and a former consulting professor at Stanford University. He published a board game involving Electoral College strategy in 1966 and is lead author of the book *Every Vote Equal: A State-Based Plan for Electing the President by National Popular Vote*. This article originally appeared on *The Hill* on November 20, 2016 — two days after Donald Trump had been elected President of the United States.

long-standing preference for free trade. President Barack Obama bragged that the Small Business Administration gave its largest grant in history to a ricotta cheese factory in—you guessed it—Ohio.

5   Recent books such as *Presidential Pork; Presidential Swing States: Why Only Ten Matter; The Two Million Voters Who Will Elect the Next President; The Particularistic President;* and *The Rise of the President's Permanent Campaign* provide innumerable examples of battleground states receiving a wide variety of presidentially-controlled benefits, including grants, disaster declarations, and various exemptions.

Fortunately, the Founding Fathers provided us with a way to change the current method of electing the president so that the candidate receiving the most popular vote in all 50 states always wins the White House.

This makes every vote, in every state, politically relevant in every presidential election.

The U.S. Constitution empowers each state to choose the method of awarding its electoral votes ("Each State shall appoint, in such Manner as the Legislature thereof may direct, a Number of Electors . . . .").

Despite attempts by defenders of the current system to suggest that the Founders designed or preferred the current state-by-state winner-take-all method of awarding electoral votes, winner-take-all is not in the U.S. Constitution, was not debated by the Constitutional Convention, was never mentioned in the Federalist Papers, and was used in only three states in the nation's first presidential election in 1789.

10   The National Popular Vote interstate compact provides a way to guarantee the presidency to the candidate who receives the most popular votes in all 50 states and the District of Columbia. The compact will go into effect after being enacted by states possessing a majority of the electoral votes—that is, enough to elect a president (270 of 538).

Under the compact, when the Electoral College meets in mid-December, the candidate who received the most popular votes in all 50 states (and the District of Columbia) would receive all the electoral votes from all the enacting states (and thereby become president).

So far, 11 states possessing 165 electoral votes have enacted the National Popular Vote bill into law. Enactment by states possessing an additional 105 electoral votes is necessary to bring the compact into effect. The bill has made significant progress in this direction by already passing one legislative chamber in 12 additional states with 96 electoral votes.

The bill was most recently approved by a bipartisan 40–16 vote in the Republican-controlled Arizona House, 28–18 in the Republican-controlled Oklahoma Senate, 37–21 in the Democratic-controlled Oregon House, and

The Constitution leaves it up to each state to choose its method for awarding its electoral votes. Therefore, the **plan** that Koza proposes is allowed by the Constitution.

The **plan**—and Koza's **thesis** or main claim: States possessing a majority of the electoral vote should pass the National Popular Vote interstate compact so that the candidate who received the most popular votes in all 50 states would receive all the electoral votes from participating states and would become President.

The **advantage**, according to Koza, is that the candidate who received the most popular votes nationwide would be elected.

unanimously by legislative committees in Georgia and Missouri. A total of 2,794 state legislators have endorsed it.

When the state legislatures convene in 2017, they should enact the National Popular Vote compact in order to ensure that we have a 50-state campaign for President in 2020 and that the president is the candidate receiving the most popular votes in all 50 states and the District of Columbia.

*Restatement of **advantage** in the Conclusion*

ARGUMENT ESSENTIALS
Organizing the Argument

In writing an argument based on course material, as on an exam or in an assigned essay:

- Consider your purpose, determine your argument approach, and choose an organizational pattern accordingly. Some options include the following:
  - Defending the thesis
  - Refuting an opposing view
  - Finding the middle ground
  - Presenting the stock issues
- Introduce your subject with more than the single sentence that is your main claim. Move your readers smoothly into your subject.
- Clearly state the argument's main claim or thesis, typically within the introduction.
- Use the body paragraphs to provide support for the main claim and other claims made in the argument.
- A direct statement of the assumption underlying each claim may not be necessary, but be aware of your assumptions and your audience's likely reaction to them.
- Conclude your argument with more than a single sentence and use the conclusion to highlight the significance of your subject.

Introductions and Conclusions

Writing the Introduction

Having found a claim you can defend and an organizational pattern, you must now think about how to begin. An introduction to your subject should consist of more than just the claim. It should invite the reader to give attention to what you have to say. It should also point you in the direction you will take in developing your argument.

Consider the kind of argument you intend to present. Does your paper make a factual claim? Does it address values? Does it recommend a policy or action? Is it a rebuttal of some current policy or belief? The answers to those questions will influence the way you introduce the subject.

If your thesis makes a factual claim, you may be able to summarize it briefly. *Whether we like it or not, money is obsolete. The currency of today is not paper or coin, but plastic.* Refutations are easy to introduce in a brief statement: *Contrary to popular views on the subject, America is not as competitive in the cyber world as its citizens would like to believe.* With rare exceptions, however, you should always develop your introduction beyond one sentence, getting your audience into the subject, and not merely stating your thesis.

A claim that defends a value is usually best preceded by an explanatory introduction. *Sending troops to Iraq was the best decision Bush could have made at the time* is a thesis that can be stated as a simple declarative opening sentence. However, readers who disagree may not read any further than the first line. Someone defending this type of claim is likely to be more persuasive if he or she presents the thesis less directly:

> "When 9/11 happened I thought I'm not hearing from Muslims like ourselves . . . I'd only hear from the old men and the conservative women. So I started writing opinion pieces. I wanted to get another voice out there to show that, look, 9/11 doesn't represent all Islam."[1]

One way to keep a thesis from alienating the audience is to begin with a question.

> How do you know you can trust what you read? Start by recognizing that there is no such thing as completely unbiased news. No one can report any news story without . . . adopting a point of view that makes it possible to stitch together all the elements and tell a story.[2]

For any subject that is highly controversial or emotionally charged, especially one that strongly condemns an existing situation or belief, you may sometimes want to express your indignation directly. Of course, you must be sure that your indignation can be justified. The author of the following introduction, a physician and writer, openly admits that he is about to make a case that may offend readers.

---

[1] Mona Eltahawy, quoted in Ron Rosenbaum, "The Next Revolution," *Smithsonian*, May 2013, 30.

[2] Post Editors, "Balancing Act," *Saturday Evening Post*, May/June 2013, 46.

Is there any polite way to introduce today's subject? I'm afraid not. It must be said plainly that the media have done about as sorry and dishonest a job of covering health news as is humanly possible.[3]

If your claim advocates a policy or makes a recommendation, it may be a good idea, as in a value claim, to provide a short background.

Competitive foods in schools are the soft drinks, sugary snacks, and chips that we were not allowed to buy in the school cafeteria but that today's public school students are. These foods that are largely lacking in nutrition contribute to the overall problem of obesity among children and youth. We may not be able to control what young children eat at home or what teenagers eat when they are out with their friends, but we can control what they eat while at school. For the good of the next generation, all competitive foods should be banned from the public schools.

There are also other ways to introduce your subject. One is to begin with an appropriate quotation or indirect quotation.

"I am not skilled enough or energetic enough to craft a persona. I just have to be who I am," admitted Pete Buttigieg.[4]

Or you may begin with an anecdote:

As a child, Kamala accompanied her parents to civil rights marches in Oakland. She's been making strides for justice — and breaking down barriers — ever since.[5]

Or you may begin with a statement meant to capture your readers' attention — maybe even shock them a bit — in order to make them read on.

North Korea's Supreme Leader Kim Jong Un was the world's youngest head of state — and behaved like it.[6]

---

[3] Michael Halberstam, "TV's Unhealthy Approach to Health News," *TV Guide*, September 20–26, 1980, 24.

[4] Chelsea Janes and Michael Scherer, "Pete Buttigieg, the Young and Openly Gay Midwest Mayor, Finds a Voice in Crowded Democratic Presidential Field," *Washington Post*, March 17, 2019, www.washingtonpost.com/politics/pete-buttigieg-the-young-and-openly-gay-midwest -mayor-finds-a-voice-in-crowded-democratic-presidential-field/2019/03/16/839f4f3c-474c -11e9-90f0-0ccfeec87a61_story.html.

[5] Nancy Pelosi, "Kamala Harris: California's Triple Threat," *Time*, April 29–May 6, 2013, 64.

[6] Barbara Demick, "Kim Jong Un: Asia's Nuclear Bully," *Time*, April 29–May 6, 2013, 68.

Writing the Conclusion

You may have heard the advice to tell your readers in the introduction what you are going to say, then say it in the body of your paper, and then in your conclusion tell them what you have said. That doesn't mean to repeat your thesis statement word for word, although you will want to return to your thesis idea. The essays that you will be writing will likely be short enough that a reader will notice if you repeat ideas, and especially wording, unnecessarily. In a long essay, there may be a need to summarize key points at the end, but not in shorter essays.

Here are a few other things to avoid in conclusions (though of course there may always be some rare exceptions):

- Don't begin with "In conclusion," "In summary," "To conclude," or some other similar but unnecessary transition.
- Don't switch into first person with "I think," "I feel," or another similar personalization.
- Don't start a new topic.
- Don't let a concluding quotation replace your own concluding thoughts.
- Don't have a one-sentence conclusion.
- Don't use vague platitudes such as "Only time will tell" or "History will be the judge."

Here are some strategies to consider as you conclude your paper:

- Answer the question "So what?" What is the significance of your argument? Point out how the future may be affected or what other implications there might be.
- Issue a call for action. Make clear to your readers what they can do about the situation.
- Generalize about your subject's broader applications or what the next step might be.
- Bring all of your ideas into a coherent whole. Make clear how all of the pieces fit together.
- Use a relevant quotation in conjunction with, but not in place of, your own concluding ideas.

In any case, you will want to return to your thesis idea and be sure your conclusion encompasses the whole essay, not just part of it. The conclusion establishes the impression that your readers are left with, and you want it to be a good one.

Assignments for Structuring Arguments

Reading and Discussion Questions

1. Go back to the sample assignments for different subjects, listed at the beginning of the chapter (p. 248), or develop your own list from your other classes. For each assignment, consider which organizational pattern would work best for an essay and explain why.

2. What are some of the controversial topics in your major area or in an area in which you might major? Choose one topic and decide how you could approach it in writing, using at least two of the different organizational patterns covered in this chapter.

3. What is a topic current on your campus or in your community that might best be written about by presenting the stock issues?

4. What is an issue current in United States or international politics that might best be written about by finding the middle ground? By refuting an opposing view? Why would one of those organizational patterns work better for some topics than the other?

Writing Suggestions

1. It may seem ironic that in America, obesity is a problem among the poor. Write an essay in which you explain that seeming paradox.

2. Write an essay in which you defend your position on the Electoral College as the means of selecting the American president.

3. Choose one of the issues you came up with in #3 or #4 in the Reading and Discussion Questions and write an argument expressing and defending your opinion on the topic.

4. Choose an issue that is currently causing controversy on your campus or in your community and write an essay in which you take a stand on the issue.

RESEARCH ASSIGNMENT

For a topic you have chosen for a research paper, or one that is the object of controversy in your major field or in a field in which you might major, do some preliminary research to find at least four sources. As you evaluate each source, write a paragraph that describes the structure of the argument. Does the source use one of the organizational patterns outlined in this chapter? Does it combine patterns?

When you have analyzed the structure of each source, write a final paragraph in which you identify similarities or differences between the sources. Do you notice any common structures for sources from the same type of publication, such as a popular periodical?

Strengthening
ARGUMENT

PART 3

Language

Words play such a critical role in argument that they deserve special treatment. An important part of successful writers' equipment is a large and active vocabulary, but no single chapter in a book can give this to you; only reading and study can widen your range of word choices. Even in a brief chapter, however, we can point out how words influence the feelings and attitudes of an audience, both favorably and unfavorably.

The Power of Words

Nowhere is the power of words more obvious and more familiar than in advertising, where the success of a product may depend on the feelings that certain words produce in the prospective buyer. Even the names of products have significance. Although most manufacturers agree that a good name won't save a poor product, they also recognize that the right name can catch the attention of the public and persuade people to buy a product at least once.

Careful thought and extensive research, for example, go into the naming of automobiles, a "big ticket" item for most consumers. What reasoning might have gone into the naming of the models, old and new, listed below? What response do the names Mercedes-Benz and Rolls-Royce evoke?

Blazer	Jaguar	Outback	Tesla
Fusion	Land Rover	Passport	Trailblazer
Grand Prix	Malibu	Prius	Tundra
Grand Safari	Matrix	Quest	Vanquish
Impala	Mustang	Rendezvous	Versailles
Infinity	Nova	Speedster	Vixen

Even scientists recognize the power of words to attract the attention of other scientists and the public to discoveries and theories that might otherwise remain obscure. A good name can even enable the scientist to visualize a new concept. One scientist says that "a good name," such as *quark*, *black hole*, *big bang*, *chaos*, or *great attractor*, "helps in communicating a theory and can have a substantial impact on financing."[1] Certainly the subatomic particle that gives mass to matter attracts more attention when called the *God particle* than when referred to as the *Higgs boson*.

Emotive Language

One kind of language responsible for shaping attitudes and feelings is emotive language, language that expresses and arouses emotions. Understanding it and using it effectively are indispensable to the arguer who wants to move an audience to accept a point of view or undertake an action.

It is not hard to see the connection between the use of words in conversation and advertising and the use of emotive language in the more formal arguments you will be reading and writing. Emotive language can reveal your approval or disapproval, assign praise or blame—in other words, make a judgment about the subject. Keep in mind that unless you are writing purely factual statements, such as scientists write, you will find it hard to avoid expressing judgments. Neutrality does not come easily, even where it may be desirable, as in news stories or reports of historical events. For this reason, you need to attend carefully to the statements in your argument, making sure that you have not disguised judgments as statements of fact. In Rogerian argument, you need to remain neutral as you summarize your opponent's argument as well as your own.

Of course, in attempting to prove a claim, you will not be neutral. You will be revealing your judgment about the subject—first in the selection of facts and opinions and the emphasis you give to them, and second in the selection of words.

Like the choice of facts and opinions, the choice of words can be effective or ineffective in advancing your argument, moral or immoral in the honesty with which you exercise it. This chapter offers some insights into recognizing and evaluating the use of emotive language in the arguments you read, as well as into using such language in your own arguments where it is appropriate and avoiding it where it is not. Your decisions about language determine the voice you project in your writing. You do not use the same voice in everything you write, but in formal written arguments you will want to be especially mindful of using a voice appropriate for your intended audience.

READING ARGUMENT

Seeing Emotive Language

In the Stihl ad and its annotations that follow, the word *confidence* elicits positive emotion, as does referring to Stihl stores as *the family* in the fine print. Words like *proud*, *independent*, and *dedication* appeal to a sense of pride and integrity in most people, as does describing Stihl's customers as *hard-working* and *passionate about a job done right*. Their Stihl *real tools* are contrasted favorably with others' *toys that need to be replaced*. The person who uses Stihl tools may wear cuff links

---

[1] Stephen S. Hall, "Scientists Find Catchy Names Help Ideas Fly," *New York Times*, October 20, 1992, C1.

(a suit) to work, but likes to roll up his or her sleeves after returning from work. This customer comes across through that language as a person who is successful in business but one who is also down to earth and hands-on. Notice, too, how the ad avoids using pronouns or other terms that might associate the tool with traditional ideas of masculinity (by a particular definition). In the next section, we will have more to say about the use of the words *investment* and *portfolio*.

Consumer Confidence

STIHL

Confidence elicits positive emotion, especially set in large, bold, capitalized print.

CONSUMER CONFIDENCE.
SOMETHING YOU'LL ALWAYS FIND IN THE STIHL PORTFOLIO.

Portfolio is part of a metaphor for wealth and power that also includes *Wall Street*, *cuff links*, and *investment*.

You won't find STIHL in Lowe's®, The Home Depot® or on Wall Street. We keep it in the family. You will find us where there's a proud commitment to customer service—at over 8,000 independent STIHL dealers nationwide. In 2008, their dedication helped us achieve our 17th consecutive year of record growth. You'll also find us in the hands of millions of hard-working folks who are truly passionate about a job done right. Who use real power tools, not toys that need to be replaced. People who like to roll up their sleeves when the cuff links are off. Who know a sharp investment when they see one. Invest in a STIHL today. You can count on us to help you do more. Visit STIHLUSA.com

Proud, independent, dedication, and *hard-working* appeal to consumer values and integrity.

Real tools are contrasted with *toys that need to be replaced*.

Number 1 Worldwide

Practice: Emotive Language

Locate in the following speech by President Trump examples of emotive speech and what emotions that language is designed to arouse in his listeners.

Remarks on the Shootings in El Paso, Texas, and Dayton, Ohio

DONALD J. TRUMP

Good morning. My fellow Americans, this morning our Nation is overcome with shock, horror, and sorrow. This weekend, more than 80 people were killed or wounded in two evil attacks.

On Saturday morning, in El Paso, Texas, a wicked man went to a Walmart store, where families were shopping with their loved ones. He shot and murdered 20 people and injured 26 others, including precious little children.

Then, in the early hours of Sunday morning in Dayton, Ohio, another twisted monster opened fire on a crowded downtown street. He murdered 9 people, including his own sister, and injured 27 others.

The First Lady and I join all Americans in praying and grieving for the victims, their families, and the survivors. We will stand by their side forever. We will never forget.

5   These barbaric slaughters are an assault upon our communities, an attack upon our Nation, and a crime against all of humanity. We are outraged and sickened by this monstrous evil, the cruelty, the hatred, the malice, the bloodshed, and the terror. Our hearts are shattered for every family whose parents, children, husbands, and wives were ripped from their arms and their lives. America weeps for the fallen.

We are a loving nation, and our children are entitled to grow up in a just, peaceful, and loving society. Together, we lock arms to shoulder the grief, we ask God in Heaven to ease the anguish of those who suffer, and we vow to act with urgent resolve.

I want to thank the many law enforcement personnel who responded to these atrocities with the extraordinary grace and courage of American heroes.

I have spoken with Texas Governor Greg Abbott and Ohio Governor Mike DeWine, as well as Mayor Dee Margo of El Paso, Texas, and Mayor Nan Whaley of Dayton, Ohio, to express our profound sadness and unfailing support.

Today we also send the condolences of our Nation to President Obrador of Mexico, and all the people of Mexico, for the loss of their citizens in the El Paso shooting. Terrible, terrible thing.

I have also been in close contact with   10
Attorney General Barr and FBI Director Wray. Federal authorities are on the ground, and I have directed them to provide any and all assistance required, whatever is needed.

At the time he delivered this speech, Trump was serving as the 45th president of the United States. He was responding on Monday, August 5, 2019, to the deadly weekend shootings in El Paso, Texas, and Dayton, Ohio, that killed thirty-one people. On Sunday, the El Paso police chief had reported that it was likely that the shooter there had posted a white nationalist, anti-Hispanic manifesto online before the attack. The twenty-two victims at the Walmart in El Paso were from both sides of the U.S.–Mexico border.

The shooter in El Paso posted a manifesto online consumed by racist hate. In one voice, our Nation must condemn racism, bigotry, and White supremacy. These sinister ideologies must be defeated. Hate has no place in America. Hatred warps the mind, ravages the heart, and devours the soul. We have asked the FBI to identify all further resources they need to investigate and disrupt hate crimes and domestic terrorism, whatever they need.

We must recognize that the internet has provided a dangerous avenue to radicalize disturbed minds and perform demented acts. We must shine light on the dark recesses of the internet and stop mass murders before they start. The internet, likewise, is used for human trafficking, illegal drug distribution, and so many other heinous crimes. The perils of the internet and social media cannot be ignored, and they will not be ignored.

In the two decades since Columbine, our Nation has watched with rising horror and dread as one mass shooting has followed another, over and over again, decade after decade. We cannot allow ourselves to feel powerless. We can and will stop this evil contagion. In that task, we must honor the sacred memory of those we have lost by acting as one people. Open wounds cannot heal if we are divided. We must seek real, bipartisan solutions. We have to do that in a bipartisan manner. That will truly make America safer and better for all.

First, we must do a better job of identifying and acting on early warning signs. I am directing the Department of Justice to work in partisan — partnership with local, State, and Federal agencies, as well as social media companies, to develop tools that can detect mass shooters before they strike. As an example, the monster in the Parkland high school in Florida had many red flags against him, and yet nobody took decisive action. Nobody did anything. Why not?

Second, we must stop the glorification of violence in our society. This includes the gruesome and grisly video games that are now commonplace. It is too easy today for troubled youth to surround themselves with a culture that celebrates violence. We must stop or substantially reduce this, and it has to begin immediately. Cultural change is hard, but each of us can choose to build a culture that celebrates the inherent worth and dignity of every human life. That's what we have to do.

Third, we must reform our mental health laws to better identify mentally disturbed individuals who may commit acts of violence and make sure those people not only get treatment, but, when necessary, involuntary confinement. Mental illness and hatred pulls the trigger, not the gun.

Fourth, we must make sure that those judged to pose a grave risk to public safety do not have access to firearms and that, if they do, those firearms can be taken through rapid due process. That is why I have called for "red flag" laws, also known as extreme-risk protection orders.

Today I am also directing the Department of Justice to propose legislation ensuring that those who commit hate crimes and mass murders face the death penalty and that this capital punishment be delivered quickly, decisively, and without years of needless delay.

These are just a few of the areas of cooperation that we can pursue. I am open and ready to listen and discuss all ideas that will actually work and make a very big difference. Republicans and Democrats have proven that we can join together in a bipartisan fashion to address this plague. Last year, we enacted the STOP School

Violence and Fix NICS Acts into law, providing grants to improve school safety and strengthening critical background checks for firearm purchases. At my direction, the Department of Justice banned bump stocks. Last year, we prosecuted a record number of firearms offenses. But there is so much more that we have to do.

20   Now is the time to set destructive partisanship aside — so destructive — and find the courage to answer hatred with unity, devotion, and love. Our future is in our control. America will rise to the challenge. We will always have, and we always will win. The choice is ours and ours alone. It is not up to mentally ill monsters; it is up to us.

If we are able to pass great legislation after all of these years, we will ensure that those who were attacked will not have died in vain.

May God bless the memory of those who perished in Toledo. [May God bless the memory of those who perished.]* And may God protect them. May God protect all of those from Texas to Ohio. May God bless the victims and their families. May God bless America.

Thank you very much. Thank you.

NOTE: The President spoke at 10:08 a.m. in the Diplomatic Reception Room at the White House. In his remarks, he referred to Patrick Wood Crusius, suspected gunman in the shooting at a Walmart store in El Paso, TX, on August 3; Connor Stephen Betts, suspected gunman in the shooting in the Oregon District of Dayton, OH, on August 4, and his sister Megan, who was killed in the shooting; and Nikolas J. Cruz, suspected gunman in the shooting at Marjory Stoneman Douglas High School in Parkland, FL, on February 14, 2017.

----

* White House correction.

Reading, Writing, and Discussion Questions

1. In the opening paragraphs, some of the words selected to elicit a negative emotional response are *wicked* and *twisted monsters*, and the use of *murdered* instead of the more objective verb *shot*. Where else in the speech do you see such emotive language?

2. Where in the speech do you see language selected to elicit a positive emotional response?

3. Given the occasion for the speech, is the emotive language appropriate for the context? Explain.

4. Rewrite paragraphs 2–5, using as objective language as possible.

Connotation

The **connotations** of a word are the meanings we attach to it apart from its explicit definition. Because these added meanings derive from our feelings, connotations are one form of emotive language. For example, the word *rat* denotes or points to a kind of rodent, but the attached meanings of "selfish person," "evil-doer," "betrayer," and "traitor" reflect the feelings that have accumulated around the word. In the Stihl ad (p. 271), the text reads, "Consumer Confidence. Something you'll always find in the Stihl portfolio." Consumers are described as hard-working folks "who know a sharp investment when they see one," and are encouraged to "invest in a Stihl today." References to portfolios and investments call forth images of Wall Street and the stock exchange, of wealth and the power that goes with it. It is unusual to refer to the buying of a tool as an investment, but that is exactly how the Stihl family want you to see that purchase: if you purchase a Stihl, you will reap the rewards of many years of dependable use from the product.

Definitions of controversial terms, such as *poverty*, may vary so widely that writer and reader cannot always be sure that they are thinking of the same thing (see Chapter 11 for more on using definitions to argue effectively). A similar problem arises when a writer assumes that the reader shares his or her emotional response to a word. Emotive meanings originate partly in personal experience. The word *home*, defined merely as "a family's place of residence," may suggest love, warmth, and security to one person; it may suggest friction, violence, and alienation to another. The values of the groups to which we belong also influence meaning. Writers and speakers count on cultural associations when they refer to our country, our flag, and heroes and enemies we have never seen. The arguer must also be aware that some apparently neutral words trigger different responses from different groups—words such as *cult*, *revolution*, *police*, and *beauty contest*.

Various reform movements have recognized that words with unfavorable connotations have the power not only to reflect but also to shape our perceptions of things. In 2007, the NAACP went so far as to hold a "funeral for the N—word." The women's liberation movement also insisted on changes that would bring about improved attitudes toward women. The movement condemned the use of *girl* for a female over the age of eighteen and the use in news stories of descriptive adjectives that emphasize the physical appearance of women. And the homosexual community succeeded in reintroducing the word *gay*, a word current centuries ago, as a substitute for words they considered offensive. Some communities and individuals have begun intentionally stating their choice of gendered or non-gendered pronouns (*she/her/hers* or *they/their*, for example) to declare their identities.

Members of certain occupational groups have invented terms to confer greater respectability on their work. The work does not change, but the workers hope that public perceptions will change

— if janitors are called *custodians*;

— if garbage collectors are called *sanitation engineers*;

— if undertakers are called *morticians*;

— if people who sell makeup are called *cosmetologists*.

Events considered unpleasant or unmentionable are sometimes disguised by polite terms, called **euphemisms**. For example, many people refuse to use the word *died* and choose *passed away* instead. Some psychologists and physicians use the phrase *negative patient care outcome* for what most of us would call *death*. Even when referring to their pets, some people cannot bring themselves to say *put to death* but substitute *put to sleep* or *put down*. In place of a term to describe an act of sexual intercourse, some people use *slept together* or *went to bed together* or *had an affair*.

Polite words are not always so harmless. If a euphemism disguises a shameful event or condition, it is morally irresponsible to use it to mislead the reader into believing that the shameful condition does not exist. An example of such usage was cited by a member of Amnesty International, a group monitoring human rights violations throughout the world. He objected to a news report describing camps in which the Chinese government was promoting *reeducation through labor*. This term, he wrote, "makes these institutions seem like a cross between Police Athletic League and Civilian Conservation Corps camps." On the contrary, he went on, the reality of *reeducation through labor* was that the victims were confined to "rather unpleasant prison camps." The details he offered about the conditions under which people lived and worked gave substance to his claim.[2]

Perhaps the most striking examples of the way that connotations influence our perceptions of reality occur when people respond to questions posed by pollsters. Sociologists and students of polling know that the phrasing of a question, or the choice of words, can affect the answers and even undermine the validity of the poll. In one case, pollsters first asked a selected group of people if they favored continuing the welfare system. The majority answered no. But when the pollsters asked if they favored government aid to the poor, the majority answered yes. Although the terms *welfare* and *government aid to the poor* refer to essentially the same forms of government assistance, *welfare* has acquired for many people negative connotations of corruption and shiftless recipients.

In 2013, Michael Dimock, director of the Pew Research Center for the People & the Press, provided an excellent example of how much difference the wording of a survey question can make. It had just been made public that the Department of Justice had subpoenaed the phone records of AP journalists. The following pie charts show how three different polling organizations worded their questions about the action by the Justice Department—and the responses. Dimock called his report "a case study in the challenges pollsters face in a breaking news environment when public attention and information is relatively limited."[3]

---

[2] Letter to the *New York Times*, August 30, 1982, p. 25.

[3] Michael Dimock, "Polling When Public Attention Is Limited: Different Questions, Different Results," pewresearch.org. Original charts provided by Pew Research Center.

Three Questions on the Department of Justice/AP Issue

Do you approve or disapprove of the Justice Department's decision to subpoena the phone records of AP journalists as part of an investigation into the disclosure of classified information? (Data from Pew Research)

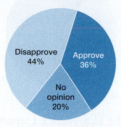

The AP reported classified information about U.S. anti-terrorism efforts and prosecutors have obtained AP's phone records through a court order. Do you think this action by federal prosecutors is or is not justified? (Data from *Washington Post*/ABC News)

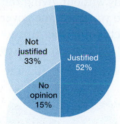

As you may know, after the AP ran news stories that included classified information about U.S. anti-terrorism efforts, the Justice Department secretly collected phone records for reporters and editors who work there. Do you think that the actions of the Justice Department were acceptable or unacceptable? (Data from CNN/ORC)

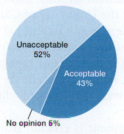

Fox News Question and Context

Fox News began its own survey two days later and concluded it one day later than the other polling organizations. The slight delay in timing raises the possibility that opinions in this fourth poll had shifted over time—even just a few days.

Does it feel like the federal government has gotten out of control and is threatening the basic civil liberties of Americans, or doesn't it feel this way to you? (Data from Fox News)

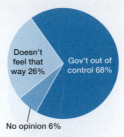

As you may have heard, the U.S. Justice Department secretly seized extensive telephone records of calls on both work and personal phones for reporters and editors working for the Associated Press in the spring of 2012. At the time, the news organization, using government leaks, had broken a story about an international terrorist plot. The government obtained the phone records without giving the news organization prior notice, as is customary. Do you think the government was probably justified in taking these actions or does this sound more like the government went too far? (Data from Fox News)

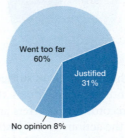

Polls concerning rape address another highly charged subject. Dr. Neil Malamuth, a psychologist at the University of California at Los Angeles, says, "When men are asked if there is any likelihood they would force a woman to have sex against her will if they could get away with it, about half say they would. But if you ask them if they would rape a woman if they knew they could get away with it, only about 15 percent say they would." The men who change their answers aren't aware that "the only difference is in the words used to describe the same act."[4]

The wording of an argument is crucial. Because readers may interpret the words you use on the basis of feelings different from your own, you must support your word choices with definitions and with evidence that enables readers to determine how and why you made them.

---

[4] *New York Times*, August 29, 1989, C1.

READING ARGUMENT

Practice: Seeing Connotation

Bathroom Politics: Preserving the Sanctity of the "Ladies' Room"
PAMELA POWERS HANNLEY

In the 1950s the Ladies' Room was a place of refuge, a wall-papered lounge with a couch, polished mirrors, fresh flowers, and often an attendant armed with fresh towels, perfume, and mints. As men have always suspected, we didn't go there just to use the facilities; the Ladies' Room was a safe gathering place.

We went there to talk, to primp, to smoke, to cry, to adjust a poor wardrobe choice, to sneak away from a bad dinner date, or just to sneak away. The Ladies' Room was a place where women could be women — a place with no men watching, commenting, judging.

The Politicization of Bathrooms
In the early 1970s, at the height of the feminist era, "Ladies" Rooms came under fire. We feminists were not "ladies" who needed fainting couches in restrooms because we didn't have the fortitude to work an 8-hour day without a nap or a good cry. "Ladies" were well-behaved women; we early feminists were anything but ladylike. As a result, "Ladies" Rooms became the Women's Rooms — or Womyn's Rooms — and the couches all but disappeared.

In November 2016, Pamela Powers Hannley won election to the Arizona House of Representatives from District 9. To assume her duties there, she gave up her position as managing editor for the *American Journal of Medicine*, but she stays active in her chosen career of public health by working part-time for the *Journal* and by serving in the Arizona House as the ranking Democrat on the Health Committee. This entry was posted on May 6, 2014, on *Tucson Progressive*.

Reading, Writing, and Discussion Questions

1. The term *facilities* is a euphemism for a restroom. What connotations does Pamela Powers Hannley argue are associated with the term *Ladies' Room*?
2. Why did feminists object to the connotations associated with Ladies' Rooms?
3. What was the new name for Ladies' Rooms, and what changes did the new term bring with it?
4. Write down some words that, for you, have positive connotations. Then write some that have negative connotations for you.

Slanting

Slanting, says one dictionary, is "interpreting or presenting in line with a special interest." The term is almost always used in a negative sense. It means that the arguer has selected facts and words with favorable or unfavorable connotations to create the impression that no alternative view exists or can be defended. For some questions, it is true that no alternative view is worthy of presentation, and emotionally charged language to defend or attack a position that is clearly right or wrong would be entirely appropriate. We aren't neutral, nor should we be, about the tragic abuse of human rights anywhere in the world or even about infractions of the law such as drunk driving or vandalism, and we should use strong language to express our disapproval of these practices.

Most of your arguments, however, will concern controversial questions about which people of goodwill can argue on both sides. In such cases, your own judgments should be restrained. Slanting will suggest a prejudice—that is, a judgment made without regard to all the facts. Unfortunately, you may not always be aware of your bias or special interest; you may believe that your position is the only correct one. You may also feel the need to communicate a passionate belief about a serious problem. But if you are interested in persuading a reader to accept your belief and to act on it, you must also ask: If the reader is not sympathetic, how will he or she respond? Will he or she perceive my words as "loaded"—one-sided and prejudicial—and my view as slanted?

R. D. Laing, a Scottish psychiatrist, defined *prayer* in this way: "Someone is gibbering away on his knees, talking to someone who is not there."[5] This description probably reflects a sincerely held belief. Laing also clearly intended it for an audience that already agreed with him. But the phrases *gibbering away* and *someone who is not there* would be offensive to people for whom prayer is sacred. Consider the effect on an audience of such statements as these:

- Any senator who would vote for this bill is ignoring the most basic rights of humanity.
- It is selfish for gun owners to think only of their own desires.
- The children had the misfortune of being raised by a single mother.
- Drug company executives who refuse dying children the compassionate use of experimental drugs have no conscience.
- The current level of airport security is an insult to the law-abiding citizens who are delayed by it.
- No one who values human life would text while driving.

You can slant an argument by means of the facts you choose to include or leave out as well as by means of word choice.

- During the search for Malaysia Airlines Flight 370, one reporter made headlines with the report that one of the pilots had been having marital difficulties. What he did not offer was any proof whatsoever that the pilot's personal life had any bearing on the plane's disappearance.
- A defense sometimes offered when a young person is accused of a crime is that he is a straight-A student, a fact that is irrelevant to his guilt or innocence.

---

[5] "The Obvious," in David Cooper, ed., *The Dialectics of Liberation* (Harmondsworth, U.K./Baltimore, MD: Penguin Books, 1968), 17.

- The fact that a defendant does not testify in her own defense is often assumed to be a sign of guilt when there may be a number of reasons why she does not take the stand. That fact may override, for some, other facts that are clearly in evidence.
- An argument might be made that an individual has never been indicted for abusing his wife. Other records may reveal, however, that the police have been called to the home on numerous occasions to investigate domestic violence but no charges have been filed.
- In the movie *The Hunt* (2012), a kindergarten teacher is accused of molesting a little girl because she describes the teacher's anatomy in language it is assumed she would not know otherwise. What the viewers don't know is that she has heard her older brother and his friends using such language while looking at sexually explicit pictures.

RESEARCH SKILL Evaluating Language in Sources

The sources you use are in a sense "witnesses" on behalf of your argument. Some sources are believable and trustworthy, just as some witnesses are. However, your argument is weakened by any hint that your sources are unreliable. Be sure that your sources do not weaken your argument by

- using so many words with negative connotations that there seems to be a clear and unfair bias;

- using such inflammatory language that ideas get lost in the emotion;
- using language that builds on hidden assumptions;
- using language that would be offensive to your intended audience.

Practice: Slanting

Locate specific examples of slanted language in the first of these two excerpts. What effect does the word choice have in the first piece? How does it compare to the word choice in the second passage, on the same topic?

1. The Founding Fathers did not want every man armed in order to shoot Bambi or Thumper, although they had nothing against doing so. The Founding Fathers wanted every man armed in order to shoot soldiers or police of tyrannical regimes who suppress the rights of free men.[6]
2. To "keep and bear arms" for hunting today is essentially a recreational activity and not an imperative of survival, as it was 200 years ago; "Saturday night specials" and machine guns are not recreational weapons and surely are as much in need of regulation as motor vehicles.[7]

---

[6] Roger McGrath, "A God-Given Natural Right," *Chronicles*, October, 2003, 425.

[7] Warren Burger, "The Right to Bear Arms," *Parade*, January 14, 1990, 419.

Figurative Language

Figurative language consists of words that produce images in the mind of the reader. Students sometimes assume that vivid picture-making language is the exclusive instrument of novelists and poets, but writers of arguments can also avail themselves of such devices to heighten the impact of their messages.

Figurative language can do more than render a scene. It shares with other kinds of emotive language the power to express and arouse deep feelings. Like a fine painting or photograph, it can draw readers into the picture where they partake of the writer's experience as if they were also present. Such power may be used to delight, to instruct, or to horrify. In 1741, the Puritan preacher Jonathan Edwards delivered his sermon "Sinners in the Hands of an Angry God," in which people were likened to repulsive spiders hanging over the flames of Hell to be dropped into the fire whenever a wrathful God was pleased to release them. The congregation's reaction to Edwards's picture of the everlasting horrors to be suffered in the netherworld included panic, fainting, hysteria, and convulsions. Subsequently Edwards lost his pulpit in Massachusetts, in part as a consequence of his success at provoking such uncontrollable terror among his congregation.

Language as intense and vivid as Edwards's emerges from very strong emotion about a deeply felt cause. In the following paragraph from his 1963 "Letter from Birmingham Jail," Martin Luther King Jr. uses figurative language to express his disappointment with the attitude of America's churches toward the treatment of black Americans.

> There was a time when the church was very powerful—in the time when the early Christians rejoiced at being deemed worthy to suffer for what they believed. In those days the church was not merely a thermometer that recorded the ideas and principles of popular opinion; it was a thermostat that transformed the mores of society. Whenever the early Christians entered a town, the people in power became disturbed and immediately sought to convict the Christians for being "disturbers of the peace" and "outside agitators." But the Christians pressed on, in the conviction that they were "a colony of heaven," called to obey God rather than man. Small in number, they were big in commitment. . . . Things are different now. So often the contemporary church is a weak, ineffectual voice with an uncertain sound. So often it is an archdefender of the status quo.[8]

---

[8] April 16, 1963.

You are familiar with some of the most common figures of speech. You know that you can occasionally add creativity and sensory appeal to your writing by means of metaphors and similes. A famous simile—a comparison using *like* or *as*—comes from the acceptance speech that George H. W. Bush gave before the Republican convention in 1988:

> For we are a nation of communities, of thousands and tens of thousands of ethnic, religious, social, business, labor union, neighborhood, regional and other organizations, all of them varied, voluntary, and unique.
>
> This is America: the Knights of Columbus, the Grange, Hadassah, the Disabled American Veterans, the Order of Ahepa, the Business and Professional Women of America, the union hall, the Bible study group, LULAC, "Holy Name"—a brilliant diversity spread like stars, like a thousand points of light in a broad and peaceful sky.

Had Bush simply left out the word *like* in the last sentence, he would have been using a **metaphor**.

Another quote from the same speech illustrates another use of language that comes in handy at times in writing an argument: the **analogy**. An analogy is like a metaphor or simile in that it compares; but it is generally more complex, drawing parallels between two things that are similar in some ways but dissimilar in others. At times, an analogy is useful in explaining something unknown or less well known in terms of something else the audience is more familiar with.

In this particular analogy, Bush was comparing the economy to a patient. In comparing the economy to a human being, he was also making use of **personification**:

> My friends, eight years ago this economy was flat on its back— intensive care. We came in and gave it emergency treatment: Got the temperature down by lowering regulation, got the blood pressure down when we lowered taxes. Pretty soon the patient was up, back on his feet, and stronger than ever.
>
> And now who do we hear knocking on the door but the doctors who made him sick. And they're telling us to put them in charge of the case again. My friends, they're lucky we don't hit them with a malpractice suit!

The rules governing the use of figurative language are the same as those governing other kinds of emotive language. Is the language appropriate? Is it too strong, too colorful for the purpose of the message? Does it result in slanting or distortion? What will its impact be on a hostile or indifferent audience? Will they be angered, repelled? Will they cease to read or listen if the imagery is too disturbing?

READING ARGUMENT

Practice: Figurative Language

Read the following excerpt from W. E. B. Du Bois's treatise *The Souls of Black Folk*. Analyze the figurative language used in the essay, and answer the questions that follow.

Of Our Spiritual Strivings
W. E. B. Du BOIS

Between me and the other world there is ever an unasked question: unasked by some through feelings of delicacy; by others through the difficulty of rightly framing it. All, nevertheless, flutter round it. They approach me in a half-hesitant sort of way, eye me curiously or compassionately, and then, instead of saying directly, How does it feel to be a problem? they say, I know an excellent colored man in my town; or, I fought at Mechanicsville; or, Do not these Southern outrages make your blood boil? At these I smile, or am interested, or reduce the boiling to a simmer, as the occasion may require. To the real question, How does it feel to be a problem? I answer seldom a word.

And yet, being a problem is a strange experience, — peculiar even for one who has never been anything else, save perhaps in babyhood and in Europe. It is in the early days of rollicking boyhood that the revelation first bursts upon one, all in a day, as it were. I remember well when the shadow swept across me. I was a little thing, away up in the hills of New England, where the dark Housatonic winds between Hoosac and Taghkanic to the sea. In a wee wooden schoolhouse, something put it into the boys' and girls' heads to buy gorgeous visiting-cards — ten cents a package — and exchange. The exchange was merry, till one girl, a tall newcomer, refused my card, — refused it

peremptorily, with a glance. Then it dawned upon me with a certain suddenness that I was different from the others; or like, mayhap, in heart and life and longing, but shut out from their world by a vast veil. I had thereafter no desire to tear down that veil, to creep through; I held all beyond it in common contempt, and lived above it in a region of blue sky and great wandering shadows. That sky was bluest when I could beat my mates at examination-time, or beat them at a foot-race, or even beat their stringy heads. Alas, with the years all this fine contempt began to fade; for the words I longed for, and all their dazzling opportunities, were theirs, not mine. But they should not keep these prizes, I said; some, all, I would wrest from them. Just how I would do it I could never decide: by reading law, by healing the sick, by telling the wonderful tales that swam in my head, — some way. With other black boys the strife was not so fiercely sunny: their youth shrunk into tasteless sycophancy, or into silent hatred of the pale world about them and mocking distrust of everything white; or wasted itself in a bitter cry, Why did God make me an

W. E. B. Du Bois was an American sociologist, historian, civil rights activist, and author. This excerpt is taken from his 1903 work *The Souls of Black Folk*.

outcast and a stranger in mine own house? The shades of the prison-house closed round about us all: walls strait and stubborn to the whitest, but relentlessly narrow, tall, and unscalable to sons of night who must plod darkly on in resignation, or beat unavailing palms against the stone, or steadily, half hopelessly, watch the streak of blue above.

After the Egyptian and Indian, the Greek and Roman, the Teuton and Mongolian, the Negro is a sort of seventh son, born with a veil, and gifted with second-sight in this American world,—a world which yields him no true self-consciousness, but only lets him see himself through the revelation of the other world. It is a peculiar sensation, this double-consciousness, this sense of always looking at one's self through the eyes of others, of measuring one's soul by the tape of a world that looks on in amused contempt and pity. One ever feels his twoness,—an American, a Negro; two souls, two thoughts, two unreconciled strivings; two warring ideals in one dark body, whose dogged strength alone keeps it from being torn asunder.

Reading, Writing, and Discussion Questions

1. What kind of figurative language does W. E. B. Du Bois use in his opening paragraph? What tone does his language set?
2. Analyze the language in paragraph 2. How does Du Bois use personification to talk about the strife that he and other black boys felt?
3. What metaphor does Du Bois introduce in paragraph 3? Is the metaphor effective?

Concrete and Abstract Language

Unlike **concrete words**, which point to real objects and real experiences, **abstract words** express qualities apart from particular things and events.

Concrete	*Abstract*
Velvety, dark red roses	Beauty
Returning money found in the street to the owner, although no one has seen the discovery	Honesty

Although they also rely on the vividness of concrete language, arguments use abstract terms far more extensively than other kinds of writing. Using abstractions effectively, especially in arguments of value and policy, is important for two reasons:

1. Abstractions represent the qualities, characteristics, and values that the writer is explaining, defending, or attacking.
2. Abstractions enable the writer to make generalizations about his or her data.

Abstractions tell us what conclusions we have arrived at; details tell us how we got there. Look at the following paragraph by Michael Pollan.

> Domestication is an evolutionary, rather than a political, development. It is certainly not a regime humans somehow imposed on animals some ten thousand years ago. Rather, domestication took place when a handful of especially opportunistic species discovered, through Darwinian trial and error, that they were more likely to survive and prosper in an alliance with humans than on their own. Humans provided the animals with food and protection in exchange for which the animals provided the humans their milk, eggs, and—yes—their flesh. Both parties were transformed by the new relationship: The animals grew tame and lost their ability to fend for themselves in the wild (natural selection tends to dispense with unneeded traits) and the humans traded their hunter-gatherer ways for the settled lives of agriculturists. (Humans changed biologically, too, evolving such new traits as the ability to digest lactose as adults.)[9]

Taken by itself, Pollan's first sentence (or topic sentence) is a bit general, relying heavily on the abstract word *evolutionary* to describe *domestication*. The rest of the paragraph, however, supports the first sentence with concrete details. Just as definitions are needed for vague or ambiguous terms (see Chapter 11), an arguer must use concrete language to provide readers with a clear understanding of an abstract concept.

A common problem in using abstractions is omission of details. Either the writer is not a skilled observer and cannot provide the details, or the writer believes that such details are too small and quiet compared to the grand sounds made by abstract terms. These grand sounds, unfortunately, cannot compensate for the lack of clarity and liveliness. Lacking detailed support, abstract words may be misinterpreted. They may also represent ideas that are so vague as to be meaningless.

Practice: Concrete and Abstract Language

Write three to five specific details to support one of these topic sentences that use abstract language.

1. College students often live with a lot of stress.
2. Much of the coursework in college is not relevant to students' future plans.
3. Bipartisanship has hampered the passage of legislation that would improve the quality of life of the average American.
4. Our campus should work toward sustainability.
5. Social networking encourages relationships that are very superficial.
6. Shoppers have to admit that healthy food choices are available if they take the time to look for them.

[9] Michael Pollan, *The Omnivore's Dilemma* (New York: Penguin, 2006), 320.

Shortcuts

Shortcuts are abbreviated substitutes for argument that avoid the hard work necessary to provide facts, expert opinion, and analysis of warrants. Even experts, however, can be guilty of using shortcuts, and the writer who consults an authority should be alert to that authority's use of language. Two of the most common uses of shortcuts are clichés and slogans.

Clichés

A cliché is an expression or idea grown stale through overuse. Clichés in language are tired expressions that have faded like old photographs; readers no longer see anything when clichés are placed before them. Some phrases are so obviously clichés and so old-fashioned that you are not likely to use them in your writing:

Thick as thieves	As old as the hills
Opposites attract	Time heals all wounds
Read between the lines	Live and learn
Age before beauty	Avoid like the plague
Dry as a bone	Fit as a fiddle
All bets are off	All bent out of shape
Caught me off guard	Clean bill of health
Take it from me	Takes its toll on you
Par for the course	Pass the buck
Fall through the cracks	Make a federal case of it
First things first	Made of money
More than meets the eye	A half-baked idea

Others are a bit more likely to slip into your writing because they are almost filler in sentences, empty words:

All in due time	The bottom fell out
Back against the wall	By the book
Boils down to	Call the shots
Business as usual	Cut your losses
Call it a day	From day one
Go downhill	Hit the fan
In this day and time	Raise the bar
A bad call	

Another category of phrases has been labeled *thought-terminating clichés*. These clichés represent ready-made answers to questions, stereotyped solutions to problems, "knee-jerk" reactions:

God moves in mysterious ways.
You don't always get what you want.
To each his own.

We will have to agree to disagree.
Because that is our policy.
I'm the parent, that's why.
There's no silver bullet.
You're either with us or against us.

Certain cultural attitudes encourage the use of clichés. The liberal American tradition has been governed by hopeful assumptions about our ability to solve problems. A professor of communications says that "we tell our students that for every problem there must be a solution."[10] But real solutions are hard to come by. In our haste to provide them, to prove that we can be decisive, we may be tempted to produce familiar responses that resemble solutions. All reasonable solutions are worthy of consideration, but they must be defined and supported if they are to be used in a thoughtful, well-constructed argument.

Attitudes toward certain cultures also encourage the use of clichéd language and thought. When we accept a worn-out and overused perception of an ethnicity, nationality, or any other group, we are viewing individuals as **stereotypes**. Avoid stereotypes in your writing, and be wary of other writers who employ them to further an argument.

Slogans

Slogans, like clichés, are short, undeveloped arguments. They represent abbreviated responses to often complex questions. As a reader, you need to be aware that slogans merely call attention to a problem; they cannot offer persuasive proof for a claim in a dozen words or less. As a writer you should avoid the use of slogans that evoke an emotional response but do not provide a reason for that response.

Advertising slogans are the most familiar. These may give us interesting and valuable information about products, but most advertisements give us slogans that ignore proof—shortcuts substituting for argument.

Walmart: Save money. Live better.
FedEx: When there is no tomorrow.
Red Cross: The greatest tragedy is indifference.
PlayStation: Live in your world. Play in ours.
Disneyland: The happiest place on earth.
Ajax: Stronger than dirt.
IBM: Solutions for a small planet.
McDonald's: i'm lovin' it.
Hallmark: When you care enough to send the very best.
De Beers: A diamond is forever.
Levi's: Quality never goes out of style.
Subway: Eat fresh.

---

[10] Malcolm O. Sillars, "The New Conservatism and the Teacher of Speech," *Southern Speech Journal*, 21 (1956), 240.

The persuasive appeal of advertising slogans heavily depends on the connotations associated with products. In Chapter 7, we discussed the way in which advertisements promise to satisfy our needs and protect our values (see "Appeals to Needs and Values," p. 214). Wherever evidence is scarce or nonexistent, the advertiser must persuade us through skillful choice of words and phrases (as well as pictures), especially those that produce pleasurable feelings. "Let it inspire you" is the slogan of a popular liqueur. It suggests a desirable state of being but remains suitably vague about the nature of the inspiration. Another familiar slogan—Coca-Cola's "Taste the Feeling"—also suggests a sensation that that we might approve of, but what exactly is this feeling and how do we taste a feeling? Since the advertisers are silent, we are left with warm feelings about the words and not much more. What feelings are evoked by the slogans listed on the previous page?

Advertising slogans are persuasive because their witty phrasing and punchy rhythms produce an automatic *yes* response. We react to them as we might react to the lyrics of popular songs, and we treat them far less critically than we treat more straightforward and elaborate arguments. Still, the consequences of failing to analyze the slogans of advertisers are usually not serious. You may be tempted to buy a product because you were fascinated by a brilliant slogan, but if the product doesn't satisfy, you can abandon it without much loss. However, ignoring ideological slogans coined by political parties or special-interest groups may carry an enormous price, and the results are not so easily undone.

Ideological slogans, like advertising slogans, depend on the power of connotation, the emotional associations aroused by a word or phrase. American political history is, in fact, a repository of slogans:

1864	Abraham Lincoln	Don't Swap Horses in the Middle of the Stream
1900	William McKinley	A Full Dinner Pail
1916	Woodrow Wilson	He Kept Us Out of War
1924	Calvin Coolidge	Keep Cool with Coolidge
1928	Herbert Hoover	A Chicken in Every Pot and a Car in Every Garage
1964	Lyndon B. Johnson	The Stakes Are Too High for You to Stay at Home
1980	Ronald Reagan	Are You Better Off Than You Were Four Years Ago?
1988	George Bush	A Kinder, Gentler Nation
1992	Bill Clinton	Putting People First
2000	George W. Bush	Leave No Child Behind
2008	Barack Obama	Change We Can Believe In
2016	Donald Trump	Make America Great Again

Over time, slogans, like clichés, can acquire a life of their own and, if they are repeated often enough, come to represent an unchanging truth we no longer need to examine. "Dangerously," says Anthony Smith, "policy makers become prisoners of the slogans they popularize."[11]

Slogans also have numerous shortcomings as substitutes for the development of an argument:

First, their brevity presents serious disadvantages. Slogans necessarily ignore exceptions or negative instances that might qualify a claim. They usually speak in absolute terms without describing the circumstances in which a principle or idea might not work. Their claims therefore seem shrill and exaggerated. In addition, brevity prevents the sloganeer from revealing how he or she arrived at conclusions.

Second, slogans may conceal unexamined assumptions. When Japanese cars were beginning to compete with American cars, the slogan "Made in America by Americans" appeared on the bumpers of thousands of American-made cars. A thoughtful reader would have discovered in this slogan several implied assumptions: *American cars are better than Japanese cars; the American economy will improve if we buy American; patriotism can be expressed by buying American goods.* If the reader were to ask a few probing questions, he or she might find these warrants unconvincing.

Silent assumptions that express values hide in other popular and influential descriptors. "Pro-life," the description and slogan of those who oppose abortion, assumes that the fetus is a living being entitled to the same rights as individuals already born. "Pro-choice," the identifier of those who favor access to abortion, suggests that the freedom of the pregnant woman to choose is the foremost or only consideration. The words *life* and *choice* have been carefully selected to reflect desirable qualities, but the words are only the beginning of the argument.

Third, although slogans may express admirable sentiments, they often fail to tell us how to achieve their objectives. They often address us in the imperative mode, ordering us to take an action or refrain from it. But the means of achieving the objectives may be nonexistent or very costly. If sloganeers cannot offer workable means for implementing their goals, they risk alienating the audience. Sloganeering is one of the recognizable attributes of propaganda. Propaganda for both good and bad purposes is a form of slanting, of selecting language and facts to persuade an audience to take a certain action. Even a good cause may be weakened by an unsatisfactory slogan. If you assume that your audience is sophisticated and alert, you will probably write your strongest arguments devoid of clichés and slogans.

ARGUMENT ESSENTIALS

Evaluating Language

- The writer's choice of words should advance the writer's argument.
- Emotive language may be used appropriately to express and arouse emotions.
- Words with positive and negative connotations should be used with care.
- Avoid using one-sided and prejudicial language.
- Words that produce images in the mind of the reader can heighten the impact of the message.
- Use concrete language to support abstract language.
- Clichés and slogans are no substitutes for facts, expert opinion, and analysis.

---

[11] "Nuclear Power—Why Not?" *The Listener*, October 22, 1981, 463.

Evaluating Language

Strategies for Evaluating Word Choice and Choosing Your Words Carefully

READ: Evaluating Word Choice

- Consider whether the writer's word choices create a voice that is appropriate for the intended audience. Will the style and tone convince the audience? Does the author seem authoritative and credible?

- Consider whether the author has used language that may be misinterpreted. Do certain words have connotations that will make the intended audience respond positively? negatively?

- Consider whether the author uses slanted language. If so, does it strengthen his or her argument? weaken it? Will it alienate readers?

- Note any use of figurative language. Is it appropriate for the argument? Is it effective for the intended audience? What images or emotions does it evoke?

- Look for concrete language and abstract language. Is abstract language explained clearly with specific details? Are there places where the author needs more concrete language to support an idea?

- Note any clichés or slogans. Are they lazy and unoriginal? Do they effectively convey the author's ideas? What language should the author have used instead?

WRITE: Choosing Words with Care

- Strive for a voice that is appropriate for your intended audience. Following the rest of these suggestions will help you achieve that goal. Think about the type of *ethos* you want to present to your readers by means of the language you use.

- Avoid language with connotations that might produce a negative reaction in your audience. Even if you do not agree with your audience, you want your case to be heard. Let your ideas speak for you, and don't let your word choice alienate your audience.

- If you have used slanted language, consider whether it will advance or weaken your argument. Your argument will be an opinion. You don't want to seem so opinionated that no one will listen.

- Use figurative language where appropriate for your purposes. It can produce images in the minds of audience members and can arouse emotion when doing so is appropriate.

- Support abstract language with concrete language. Concrete details can convey to your readers exactly what you have in mind much more precisely than abstract language.

- Edit out any clichés or slogans from your early drafts. Clichés and slogans are stale, unoriginal language or catchphrases that are too brief to convey complex ideas.

READING ARGUMENT

Seeing Language

The following selection incorporates all of the aspects of language discussed in this chapter. As you read it, consider connotation, slanting, figurative language, concrete versus abstract language, and shortcuts. After reading the selection and the accompanying annotations, answer the questions that follow.

Selfie: The Revolutionary Potential of Your Own Face
RACHEL SYME

1

Simile

Shot One: Open on a woman snapping a picture of herself, by herself. Maybe she is sitting at an outdoor cafe, her phone held out in front of her like a gilded hand mirror, a looking glass linked to an Instagram account. Maybe she tilts her head one way and then another, smiling and smirking, pushing her hair around, defiantly staring into the lens, then coyly looking away. She takes one shot, then five, then 25. She flips through these images, appraising them, an editrix putting together the September issue of her face; she weighs each against the others, plays around with filters and lighting, and makes a final choice. She pushes send and it's done. Her selfie is off to have adventures without her, to meet the gazes of strangers she will never know. She feels excited, maybe a little nervous. She has declared, in just a few clicks, that she deserves, in that moment, to be seen. The whole process takes less than five minutes.

Metaphor

Personification

Shot Two: Zoom in on a group of people watching this woman, one table over. They are snickering, rolling their eyes, whispering among themselves. Maybe they are older than she is, making jokes about Narcissus and the end of civilization as we know it. Maybe they are all men, deeply affronted by a woman looking at herself with longing, a woman who is both the see-er and the seen, the courier of her own message. Maybe they are a group of chattering women, who have internalized a societal shame about taking pleasure in one's face in public, who have learned to be good girls, to never let their self-regard come off as a threat. Maybe they are lonesome and hungry for connection, projecting their own lack of community onto this woman's solo show, believing her to be isolated rather than expansive. They don't see where her image is headed, where it will take up space in the infinite. This is scary for them, this lack of control, this sense that her face could go anywhere, pop up anywhere. This is why they sneer at her like she is masturbating. This is why they believe that no selfie could ever mean anything other than vanity. This is why they think selfies are a phase, something they can wish away. Whoever they are, and for whatever reason they hate selfies, they are wrong.

Metaphor

Rachel Syme writes a regular column for the *New Yorker* and writes often for a variety of other publications on fashion, consumer culture, women's lives, history, and fame. This excerpt comes from "Selfie: The Revolutionary Potential of Your Own Face, in Seven Chapters," which was published on Matter, an award-winning publication on Medium, on November 19, 2015.

2

Whenever I think about selfies, I think about the women who came before. I think about the ones who never got to use front-facing cameras, that technological ease and excess that we have so quickly taken for granted.

I think about Julia Margaret Cameron, who got her first camera as a gift, in 1863, when she was 48 years old. Her daughter gave it to her, a toy to stave off the solitude of aging. The machine must have felt electric in her hands. See, Julia wasn't really a head-turner. We know this from her great-niece, Virginia Woolf, who wrote that Julia was an ugly duckling in a family full of cameo complexions; her nickname was "Talent," where her sisters got to be called "Beauty." Cameron became instantly obsessed with photography and dove into her second act. She made hundreds of silver albumen prints, practicing and practicing in a kind of fever dream until she had created a unique method of applying a soft, dewy focus to her portraits of British celebrities. In front of her lens, Cameron made everyone look gauzy, beautiful, ethereal. She copyrighted her technique, sold prints to museums, and wrote myth-making prose about her process in her memoirs:

> I longed to arrest all beauty that came before me, and at length the longing has been satisfied.

Julia Margaret Cameron. A self-portrait of the British pioneer of photography. Julia Margaret Cameron/Getty Images

Syme announces her focus for this second part.

Metaphor

Cliché

Julia took only a few pictures of herself, and in them she looks far less   5
imposing than her subjects, who were usually stoic, grizzled male intellectuals or creamy-cheeked actresses and debutantes. In her own portraits, she
looks glum, dejected, staring at the ground or into the lens with a withering
squint, as if she cannot believe she is doing this. Her self-portraits contain
sighs. Vintage cameras had long exposure times, requiring the sitter to hold
the same expression forever. I don't know why Julia chose to glower, but if
I had to guess, I would think she knew she could grimace for a full hour.
It was an expression she was used to. The type of camera Julia used wasn't
made for experiments; each snap was a big commitment. We aren't bound
by her constraints now, with our ability [to] flood our clouds with unlimited
smirks, kissy pouts, tongue waggles, goofy winks, and come-hither stares.
When we can take endless shots from endless angles, we start to discover
dimensions of ourselves we never even knew were there. That girl in the
park taking selfie after selfie after selfie? She's investigating her own silhou-
ette. She's figuring out which parts of her face she loves; she's doing confidence fact-finding. Sometimes it takes a hundred selfies to capture the one
that rings out with recognition: this, *this* is who I am. Julia didn't have the
bandwidth to focus on herself until she felt like she could smile. But we do.

I think about Marian Hooper Adams, who went by Clover, the society
doyenne of post–Civil War D.C. Clover and her husband, writer Henry
Adams, lived across from the White House in a grand, creaky manse, where

Marian Hooper Adams, circa the
1860s. Wikimedia Commons

Emotive language
Personification

Emotive language

she played hostess to intellectuals and diplomats as they came through town. In their sitting room, Henry was king, while Clover played subservient wife, as women of the time were expected to do. No matter that she was extremely educated, the daughter of a prominent doctor and a Transcendental poetess. She was expected to stay quiet and erase herself, a smiling woman with a polished silver tray.

Metaphor and also emotive language

But upstairs, in her little room, she worked with colloidal silver, and there, Clover was queen of her domain. She started taking photographs as a side hobby in 1883 (Henry would never let her go pro with it), collecting pictures of her friends and family and the politicians that flowed through her house, the ones she wasn't really supposed to talk to all that much. Instead, she used her photographs to communicate, to make some sense of her surroundings, to speak about her isolation. She wrote extremely technical notes about her work; her avocation became her calling. She took a devastating portrait of her in-laws, who barely spoke to her, their scowls barely concealing their grumpy disdain. Whenever she shot herself, she blocked out her face with a giant hat or some other prop; sometimes she was just a blurry smudge darting across the frame. I think even in these moments of silent communion with the camera, Clover was trying to grapple with how unseen she was, how little she felt she deserved to show herself. For a socialite, she didn't have much of a social network of her own. She had no one to share her face with, and so she kept it to herself like a secret.

Emotive language

One day, two years after she started taking pictures, Clover killed herself in front of her bedroom fire. She was only 42. She swallowed potassium cyanide, the agent she used to develop her photographs.

After her death, Henry would destroy all of Clover's letters and write her out of his autobiography; he almost managed to make her disappear. But somehow, her photographs survived. If I could go back and climb upstairs to her studio, I would tell her to show her face. If you ever feel scared to take your portrait and push it out to your feed, let me urge this: don't focus on your anxiety, focus on all the Clovers, on all the women who felt the heat of a camera in their hands but were cut off from sharing with the world, who burned silently and alone for the chance to connect.

10   I think about Francesca Woodman; the lovely, doomed Francesca, the daughter of two bohemian artists, a plaintive blonde who spent summers in Italy and learned to take photographs of herself in an old farm house. She started noodling around with a camera when she was only 14 in 1972, fully committing herself to her work when she went off to study at RISD three years later. She sent her shots to fashion houses and magazines, but couldn't really get much traction; she applied for grants and residencies with mixed

Simile

results. She was in such a rush to become a success that any slowness in the process felt like a deep insult. Her depression rolled in like an unshakable fog. She tried to kill herself once, then again, and in 1981, when she was only 22, she succeeded by leaping out of a window of a building on the East Side of Manhattan.

What made Francesca different than Clover—give or take a hundred years—was that she actively inserted her own face and nakedness into her work, she made over 10,000 negatives demanding to be seen by someone, anyone. Looking at her work is like seeing someone discover and then delight in her own body, how far she could push it, how weird she could get, alone in a room with a roll of film. Sometimes Francesca shot herself as drowning in a river like a wet rat, or screaming, or holding a sharp knife while she bared one breast to the camera. Sometimes she showed herself disfigured by tight clothing, sometimes she bounced around in oversized dresses, exploring the space of a giant, empty, room. She played with exposure times—at the end of her life she was playing with such a slow shutter speed that she had to sit in front of her lens for hours—she was interested in her body as a vessel of both life and decay, of something vitally here and then suddenly gone. She sometimes referred to her work as "ghost pictures."

Concrete details

Since her work came back in vogue—a documentary, a book, an exhibition, a feminist re-appraisal—many are quick to view Francesca's work in light of her death, to say that she was actively trying to cancel herself out by isolating parts of her body in the frames, that her self-portraits were angry momento mori. This is likely a mistake: those who knew her described Francesca as extremely ambitious; she wrote in her journals in the third person, she saw herself from the outside as someone heading for greatness. She was doing that thing that makes women fearsome: she was trying to make art that mattered.

Metaphor

Syme's claim

Consider this: maybe a woman—or really any person—who takes and publishes many pictures of herself is simply ambitious. She wants people to recognize her image-making ability, her aesthetic boldness, her bravery for stepping into the frame and clicking send. When you tell someone that they have sent too many images of themselves into their feeds, when you shame them with cries of narcissism and self-indulgence, when you tell them that they are taking up too much virtual space (space that is at present, basically limitless, save for the invented boundaries of taste): you need to question your motives. Are you afraid of a person's ambition to be seen? Where does that come from?

If you take nothing else away from this historical detour, remember this: These women didn't have the ability to take and post their own images to thousands of people at once. And they were still the lucky ones, the ones with cameras. So many women's stories were erased (and will never be recovered) because they didn't have access to private image-making. Virginia Woolf knew this: "[The history of most women is] hidden either by silence, or by flourishes and ornaments that amount to silence." The same could be said for not just women but anyone living on the margins of race, gender, or class. The human longing to be seen and appraised has existed for centuries, but only a few had the technological power (and the distribution channels) to control it. Selfies are just one way of making up lost time, all of that yearning and desire that we never got to see because the powerless didn't have their own cameras and printing presses. Types of people who never got to be looked at before are getting looked at, and are creating entire communities surrounding that looking, and these communities are getting stronger and stronger every day.

Practice: Examining Language

Use the questions following this excerpt from a speech by Barack Obama to guide your analysis of its author's use of language.

Remarks at Memorial Service for Fallen Dallas Police Officers, July 12, 2016
BARACK OBAMA

Like police officers across the country, these men and their families shared a commitment to something larger than themselves. They weren't looking for their names to be up in lights. They'd tell you the pay was decent but wouldn't make you rich. They could have told you about the stress and long shifts, and they'd probably agree with Chief Brown when he said that cops don't expect to hear the words "thank you" very often, especially from those who need them the most.

No, the reward comes in knowing that our entire way of life in America depends on the rule of law; that the maintenance of that law is a hard and daily labor; that in this country, we don't have soldiers in the streets or militias setting the rules. Instead, we have public servants—police officers—like the men who were taken away from us.

And that's what these five were doing last Thursday when they were assigned to protect and keep orderly a peaceful protest in response to the killing of Alton Sterling of Baton Rouge and Philando Castile of Minnesota. They were upholding the constitutional rights of this country.

Barack Obama served as president of the United States from 2009 to 2017. He made this speech at a memorial service for five Dallas police officers gunned down during a protest of the shooting of black men by police officers.

For a while, the protest went on without incident. And despite the fact that police conduct was the subject of the protest, despite the fact that there must have been signs or slogans or chants with which they profoundly disagreed, these men and this department did their jobs like the professionals that they were. In fact, the police had been part of the protest's planning. Dallas PD even posted photos on their Twitter feeds of their own officers standing among the protesters. Two officers, black and white, smiled next to a man with a sign that read, "No Justice, No Peace."

5   And then, around nine o'clock, the gunfire came. Another community torn apart. More hearts broken. More questions about what caused, and what might prevent, another such tragedy.

I know that Americans are struggling right now with what we've witnessed over the past week. First, the shootings in Minnesota and Baton Rouge, and the protests, then the targeting of police by the shooter here — an act not just of demented violence but of racial hatred. All of it has left us wounded, and angry, and hurt. It's as if the deepest fault lines of our democracy have suddenly been exposed, perhaps even widened. And although we know that such divisions are not new — though they have surely been worse in even the recent past — that offers us little comfort.

Faced with this violence, we wonder if the divides of race in America can ever be bridged. We wonder if an African-American community that feels unfairly targeted by police, and police departments that feel unfairly maligned for doing their jobs, can ever understand each other's experience. We turn on the TV or surf the Internet, and we can watch positions harden and lines drawn, and people retreat to their respective corners, and politicians calculate how to grab attention or avoid the fallout. We see all this, and it's hard not to think sometimes that the center won't hold and that things might get worse.

I understand. I understand how Americans are feeling. But, Dallas, I'm here to say we must reject such despair. I'm here to insist that we are not as divided as we seem. And I know that because I know America. I know how far we've come against impossible odds. (Applause.) I know we'll make it because of what I've experienced in my own life, what I've seen of this country and its people — their goodness and decency — as President of the United States. And I know it because of what we've seen here in Dallas — how all of you, out of great suffering, have shown us the meaning of perseverance and character, and hope.

When the bullets started flying, the men and women of the Dallas police, they did not flinch and they did not react recklessly. They showed incredible restraint. Helped in some cases by protesters, they evacuated the injured, isolated the shooter, and saved more lives than we will ever know. (Applause.) We mourn fewer people today because of your brave actions. (Applause.) "Everyone was helping each other," one witness said. "It wasn't about black or white. Everyone was picking each other up and moving them away." See, that's the America I know.

10   The police helped Shetamia Taylor as she was shot trying to shield her four sons. She said she wanted her boys to join her to protest the incidents of black men being killed. She also said to the Dallas PD, "Thank you for being heroes." And today, her 12-year old son wants to be a cop when he grows up. That's the America I know. (Applause.)

In the aftermath of the shooting, we've seen Mayor Rawlings and Chief Brown, a white man and a black man with different backgrounds, working not just to restore order and support a shaken city, a shaken department, but working together to unify a city with strength and grace and wisdom. (Applause.) And in the process, we've been reminded that the Dallas Police Department has been at the forefront of improving relations between police and the community. (Applause.) The murder rate here has fallen. Complaints of excessive force have been cut by 64 percent. The Dallas Police Department has been doing it the right way. (Applause.) And so, Mayor Rawlings and Chief Brown, on behalf of the American people, thank you for your steady leadership, thank you for your powerful example. We could not be prouder of you. (Applause.)

These men, this department — this is the America I know. And today, in this audience, I see people who have protested on behalf of criminal justice reform grieving alongside police officers. I see people who mourn for the five officers we lost but also weep for the families of Alton Sterling and Philando Castile. In this audience, I see what's possible — (applause) — I see what's possible when we recognize that we are one American family, all deserving of equal treatment, all deserving of equal respect, all children of God. That's the America that I know.

Reading, Writing, and Discussion Questions

1. In paragraph 6, Barack Obama makes use of the term *fault lines*. How is that term an example of figurative language?

2. What examples of figurative language do you see in the final paragraph?

3. How would you summarize some of the main points that Obama is trying to make?

4. How effective do you feel that Obama was in his choice of language to make his points, considering the context in which he spoke? Do you find many words with either positive or negative connotations? What sort of tone does the language create? Is that tone appropriate for the situation?

Assignments for Language

Reading and Discussion Questions

1. Choose a popular slogan from advertising or politics, and explain how it appeals to needs and/or values.

2. Look back at the company slogans on page 288, and explain what each means.

3. Examine a few periodicals from fifty or more years ago. Select either an advertising or a political slogan in one of them, and relate it to beliefs or events of the period. Alternatively, tell why the slogan is no longer relevant.

4. Make up a slogan for a cause that you support. Explain and defend your slogan.

5. In watching television dramas about law, medicine, or criminal or medical investigation, do you find that the professional language plays a positive or negative role in your enjoyment of the show? Explain your answer.

Writing Suggestions

1. Analyze a print ad of your choosing, explaining how text and visuals work together to support a claim. Your essay can be analytical or evaluative.

2. Write two paragraphs about your roommate, a family member, or a former teacher, making one balanced and the other either negatively slanted or positively slanted. Make the two distinctive through the facts you choose to include or omit, not the words you choose.

3. Write two paragraphs, one a positive and one a negative description of either a fictional person or someone you know. The facts should be essentially the same, but use charged words to make the difference.

4. Locate a speech by Martin Luther King Jr. such as "I Have a Dream" (choose a short one), and write an essay analyzing its use of figurative language. You'll need a thesis that holds your examples together.

5. Explain in an essay why shortcuts are a natural result of our technological age, especially in language.

6. Analyze a presidential or other debate using some of the terms discussed in this chapter.

RESEARCH ASSIGNMENT ▶   **Evaluating Language**

In the following passages, locate words with negative connotations, inflammatory language, language that builds on hidden assumptions, or offensive language.

Passage 1

Until we have universal background checks, better reporting from the states, and more—just more safety across the board, maybe a presence in schools is worth considering. I know that there is a police presence in the new location of the Sandy Hook school, and it certainly does reassure me.

— Veronique Pozner, mother of one of the children killed at Sandy Hook Elementary

(Source: *Anderson Cooper 360 Degrees*, "Guns under Fire Town Hall." CNN, January 31, 2013.)

Passage 2

I have even been the subject of an eighteen and a half minute rant by Rachel Madcow on MSNBC, and the current attorney general of the United States knows—and despises—me by name because of the Fast and Furious scandal that . . . I broke the news of on the Internet.

— Speech at a Hartford firearm rights rally, April 20, 2013

(Source: Mike Vanderboegh, "My Name Is Mike Vanderboegh & I Am an Arms Smuggler," sipseystreetirregulars.blogspot.com, April 20, 2013.)

Passage 3

The rapidity of change and the speed with which new situations are created follow the impetuous and heedless pace of man rather than the deliberate pace of nature. Radiation is no longer merely the background radiation of cosmic rays, the ultraviolet of the sun that have existed before there was any life on earth; radiation is now the unnatural creation of man's tampering with the atom. The chemicals to which life is asked to make its adjustment are no longer merely the calcium and silica and copper and all the rest of the minerals washed out of the rocks and carried in rivers to the sea; they are the synthetic creations of man's inventive mind, brewed in his laboratories, and having no counterparts in nature.

— Rachel Carson, marine biologist and nature writer
(Source: Rachel Carson, *Silent Spring*, "The Obligation to Endure" [New York: Houghton Mifflin, 1962], 7.)

Definition

The Purposes of Definition

Arguments often revolve around definitions of crucial terms. Consider the following examples. In the gun control debate, there is disagreement over what an assault weapon is. In the debate over euthanasia, it makes a difference whether the issue is passive or active euthanasia. When planning the prosecution of an alleged criminal, whether the accused is defined as an enemy combatant or not determines how he will be tried. In the publicity surrounding the death of Trayvon Martin, it made a difference whether George Zimmerman was viewed as a neighborhood watch leader or as a vigilante. The CHANGE Act proposed in 2019 would replace the phrases *alien* and *illegal alien* in all federal laws with *foreign national* and *undocumented foreign national*.

A corrupt use of definition can be used to distort reality. But even where there is no intention to deceive, the snares of definition are difficult to avoid. For example, after Hurricane Katrina moved through New Orleans in 2005, a pair of pictures circulated on the internet. One showed a white couple wading through the flood waters carrying groceries. The caption read, "Two residents wade through chest-deep flood water after *finding* bread and soda from a local grocery store after Hurricane Katrina came through" (italics added). A similar picture showed a young black man in a similar situation, but the caption this time read, "A young man walks through chest-deep water after *looting* a grocery store in New Orleans on Tuesday, August 30, 2005" (italics added). There was such an outcry online that Yahoo! offered this statement: "Yahoo! News regrets that these photos and captions, viewed together, may have suggested a racial bias on our part. We remain committed to bringing our readers the full collection of photos as transmitted by our wire service partners."

How do you define *abortion*? Is it "termination of pregnancy"? Or is it "murder of an unborn child"? During a celebrated trial of a physician who performed an abortion and was accused of manslaughter, the prosecution often used the word *baby* to refer to the fetus, but the defense referred to "the products of conception." These definitions of *fetus* reflected the differing judgments of those on opposite sides. Not only do judgments create definitions, but definitions also influence judgments.

Definitions can indeed change the nature of an event or a "fact." How many farms are there in the United States? The answer to the question depends on the definition of *farm*. For example, in the following excerpt, the writer shows that re-defining the term immediately led to a 20 percent drop in the number of farms in New York state, and that a business may be called a farm in the United States for producing goods amounting to only $1,000, a relatively small amount:

> An operation could be considered a farm for growing 4 acres of corn, a tenth of an acre of berries, or for owning one milk cow. Consequently, most U.S. establishments classified as a farm produce very little, while most agricultural production occurs on a small number of much larger operations. . . .[1]

A change in the definition of *poverty* can have similar results. An article in the *New York Times*, under the headline "A Revised Definition of Poverty May Raise Number of U.S. Poor," makes this clear. The article first establishes the current definition:

> The official definition of *poverty* used by the Federal Government for three decades is based simply on cash income before taxes.

Then, the article contrasts the definition with a new proposal, put forth by a team of experts that Congress brought together:

> The Government should move toward a concept of poverty based on disposable income, the amount left after a family pays taxes and essential expenses.[2]

The differences are wholly a matter of definition. But such differences can have serious consequences for those being defined, most of all in the disposition of billions of federal dollars in aid of various kinds.

In fact, local and federal courts almost every day redefine traditional concepts that can have a direct impact on our lives. The definition of *family*, for example, has undergone significant changes that acknowledge the existence of new relationships. In January 1990, the New Jersey Supreme Court ruled that a family may be defined as "one or more persons occupying a dwelling unit as a single nonprofit housekeeping unit, who are living together as a stable and permanent living unit, being a traditional family unit or the

---

[1] Erik O'Donoghue, "Changing the Definition of a 'Farm' Can Affect Federal Funding," *Amber Waves*, Dec. 2009, 7.

[2] *New York Times*, April 10, 1995, A1.

ARGUMENT ESSENTIALS
Purposes of Definition

- Controversy often revolves around definitions of crucial terms.
- Effective communication between writer and reader is not possible if they do not have in mind the same definition of a key term.
- Negotiating a definition that all parties can agree on is the starting point to resolving conflict.

functional equivalent thereof" (italics for emphasis added). This meant that ten Glassboro State College students, unrelated by blood, could continue to occupy a single-family house despite the objection of the borough of Glassboro.[3] Even the legal definition of *maternity* has shifted. Who is the mother—the woman who contributes the egg or the woman who bears the child (the surrogate)? Several states, acknowledging the changes brought by medical technology, now recognize a difference between the birth mother and the legal mother.

READING ARGUMENT

Seeing the Purposes of Definition

The following selection illustrates how definition can aid argumentation. After she defines the term *cisgender*, Sunnivie Brydum explains that it is not surprising that cisgendered individuals do not feel the need to be so categorized because their identity as it conforms to their biological gender at birth is something they take for granted. What to them is so obviously the "norm" does not need a label. It is only in contrast to its opposite—*transgender*—that *cisgender* becomes a useful, or indeed a necessary, term. Just as heterosexuals do not feel the need to "come out" as straight, neither do cisgendered individuals feel that need. Defining these terms is essential to establish Brydum's argument that the concepts exist in conflict.

The True Meaning of the Word "Cisgender"
SUNNIVIE BRYDUM

Let's get one thing straight: The *Oxford English Dictionary* describes the word "cisgender" as an adjective and defines it as "Denoting or relating to a person whose self-identity conforms with the gender that corresponds to their biological sex; not transgender."

Beginning a feature with the "dictionary definition" of a subject goes against every lesson drilled into a prospective journalist's head in J-school, but in this instance, it's necessary. Because alongside the stratospheric rise in media visibility for transgender people comes the all-too-predictable pushback from those who are uncomfortable with change or those who claim the term is yet another unnecessary label that only serves to divide us, spotlighting our differences.

With such phenomena as angry hashtags on the fringes of social media proclaiming

Sunnivie Brydum, an award-winning journalist, is editorial director at YES! Media and former managing editor at the *Advocate*. She covers the politics of equality and telling the stories of the LGBTQ community. Her essay was posted on the *Advocate* on July 31, 2015.

[3] *New York Times*, February 1, 1990, B5.

#DieCisScum and passionate op-eds defiantly declaring "I Am NOT Cisgendered," the cisgender population seems to be having an identity crisis. Perhaps that's because for many of us, "cisgender" is a new identity, a new label, that many people may not have even realized has applied to our lived experience all along.

But it has existed all along. Or at least since the mid-1990s, explains K. J. Rawson, a transgender scholar and assistant professor of English and women's and gender studies at College of the Holy Cross, who earned his Ph.D. in composition and cultural rhetoric from Syracuse University.

5   "The term is typically credited to biologist Dana Leland Defosse, who used 'cisgender' in 1994," explains Rawson. "Like most subcultural terms, I would guess that it was being used informally with increasing frequency, but the print literature we have available is slightly behind in representing that."

From an epistemological standpoint, the word is essentially a straightforward antonym of "transgender." Both words share Latin roots, with "trans" meaning "across, beyond, or on the other side of" and "cis" meaning "on this side of."

Add the suffix "gender" onto either word, and both terms emerge as strictly descriptive adjectives . . .

As for those who argue that labeling them "cisgender" is forcing an unwelcome label on their own, hard-fought identity, Rawson has a powerful parallel:

> Is "heterosexual" a slur? No. It describes an identity and experience. Because straight folks don't typically experience their heterosexuality as an identity, many don't identify as heterosexual — they don't need to, because culture has already done that for them. Similarly, cisgender people don't generally identify as cisgender because societal expectations already presume that they are. . . .

It's an incredible and invisible power to not need to name yourself because the norms have already done that for you. You don't need to come out as heterosexual or cisgender because it is already expected. Since it isn't a derogatory term, those who take exception to it may be uncomfortable with trans issues or perhaps they are unwilling to confront their own privilege.

Practice: The Purposes of Definition

Read the following essay, and answer the questions that follow it.

Twitter Bans Dehumanization
LUCAS WRIGHT

Earlier this week, Twitter announced a new rule against language that dehumanizes others on the basis of religion. This change is a step in the right direction, but in order to truly mitigate offline harms, the company must define dehumanizing speech by its likely effect on others in addition to the literal content of the speech.

This new rule represents an important shift in how Twitter administrators think about

Lucas Wright is a graduate student at Oxford University studying the ethics and politics of internet regulation and was previously a researcher at the Dangerous Speech Project in Washington, D.C. His article was published on the Dangerous Speech Project website on July 12, 2019.

harm. Until now, the company has focused on regulating speech that leads to harm for individuals on Twitter—like harassment targeted at a specific person. This new rule, which has been in development since last August, acknowledges that speech on Twitter which targets groups can lead to harm offline as well. Dehumanization, which is one of the hallmarks of Dangerous Speech, is a good place to start for such a shift because the potential for offline harm is fairly intuitive, but the way Twitter defines dehumanization will determine the effectiveness of the new rule.

For now, the rule is limited to religious dehumanization, but Twitter administrators have said that they will expand it to include other groups. This is important, as many non-religious groups also face dehumanizing rhetoric.

Twitter has also limited the new rule in another way. Based on the examples that Twitter shared in their announcement to illustrate the new rule, the company is defining dehumanization as explicit comparisons of someone to an animal or non-human object. This definition and the focus on religion appear to be an intentional response to public concern that a rule against dehumanization broadly defined would restrict too much speech, like calling someone a "kitten" or "monster" in an endearing way. While dehumanization should be defined narrowly to prevent the term from coming to stand in for any form of harmful speech, Twitter's approach limits the enforcement of the new rule to the most literal cases.

5   Yet dehumanization can also take place though implicit comparisons. For example, as Dr. Anna Szilagyi wrote on our blog last year, a speaker can dehumanize a group using coded language—in such a way that they don't literally call that group subhuman and yet the audience still understands that this is the meaning of words. She writes:

> [Polish politician] Jaroslaw Kaczynski argued in a campaign speech that the refugees from the Middle East bring "very dangerous diseases long absent from Europe" and carry "all sorts of parasites and protozoa, which [...] while not dangerous in the organisms of these people, could be dangerous here." While he could claim that he was merely pointing to potential health risks, his implication that refugees constituted a "disease" was obvious to his listeners.

Even if Twitter administrators expand the new rule to include protections for refugees, it seems unlikely that they would call Kaczynski's speech dehumanization since it doesn't literally call refugees a disease.

This false negative is the inverse of Twitter's fear of false positives when people call others "kittens" and "monsters." If Twitter content moderators considered the likely effect of a tweet in addition to its literal meaning, they would see that Kaczynski's speech is likely to have a harmful, dehumanizing effect whereas, "All [religious group] are kittens," is not. This is similar to how we determine whether an expression is Dangerous Speech—by considering the context of an expression, not just the content, in order to determine the likely effect of the speech.

The public was right to point out to Twitter that there are times when it is acceptable to use language that, when read literally, might be taken as dehumanizing. Twitter's response to such concerns should be to incorporate context into their decision making. This is a challenge, especially when moderators have to make a quick decision about whether a tweet is allowed. It is also much more difficult for speech detection algorithms to determine context and likely effect than it is for them to identify literal comparisons to subhuman objects or animals. But incorporating context is a critical step if Twitter wants effective policies against dehumanization that also allow for innocuous tweets that meet the literal criteria of dehumanization.

Reading, Writing, and Discussion Questions

1. What specific type of speech had Twitter just banned when the article was written?
2. According to Lucas Wright, why is it not enough to judge speech by its literal meaning? What else must be considered?
3. What does Wright mean by the terms *false positive* and *false negative*?
4. How could Wright's claim about definition be applied to terms other than *dehumanization*?

Defining the Terms in Your Argument

An argument can end almost before it begins if writer and reader cannot agree on definitions of key terms. While clear definitions do not guarantee agreement, they do ensure that all parties understand the nature of the argument. In the Rogerian approach to argumentation, discussed in Chapter 5, negotiating a definition that all parties can accept is the starting point to resolving conflict.

The Limitations of Dictionary Definitions

Reading a dictionary definition is the simplest and most obvious way to learn the basic definition of a term. An unabridged dictionary is the best source because it usually gives examples of the way a word can be used in a sentence; that is, it furnishes the proper context.

In many cases, the dictionary definition alone is not sufficient. It may be too broad or too narrow for your purpose. Suppose, in an argument about pornography, you want to define the word *obscene*. *Webster's New International Dictionary* (3rd edition, unabridged) gives the definition of *obscene* as "offensive to taste; foul; loathsome; disgusting." But these synonyms do not tell you what qualities make an object or an event or an action "foul," "loathsome," and "disgusting." In 1973 the Supreme Court, attempting to narrow the definition of *obscenity*, ruled that obscenity was to be determined by the community in accordance with local standards. One person's obscenity, as numerous cases have demonstrated, may be another person's art. The celebrated trials in the early twentieth century about the distribution of novels regarded as pornographic—D. H. Lawrence's *Lady Chatterley's Lover* and James Joyce's *Ulysses*—emphasized the problems of defining obscenity.

Another dictionary definition may strike you as too narrow. *Patriotism*, for example, is defined in one dictionary as "love and loyal or zealous support of one's country, especially in all matters involving other countries." Some readers may want to include an unwillingness to support government policies they consider wrong.

These limitations illustrate why opening an essay with a dictionary definition is often not a very effective strategy, although many beginning writers use it. In order to initiate the effective discussion of a key term, you should be able to define it in your own words.

Stipulation and Negation: Stating What a Term *Is* and *Is Not*

Since definitions can vary so much and well-meaning writers want their readers to understand their arguments, it is often necessary to establish from the beginning what definition a writer is using for the purposes of a particular argument. That means writers may **stipulate** the definition that they are using, knowing that other people in other contexts may define the term differently. In some cases, one way to clarify how a term is being used is to stipulate what it is not. This is called **negation**.

In stipulating the meaning of a term, the writer asks the reader to accept a definition that may be different from the conventional one. The writer does this to limit or control the argument. A term like *national security* can be defined by a nation's leaders in such a way as to sanction persecution of citizens and reckless military actions. Likewise, a term such as *liberation* can be appropriated by terrorist groups whose activities often lead to oppression rather than liberation.

Even the word *violence,* which the dictionary defines as "physical force used so as to injure or damage" and whose meaning seems utterly clear and uncompromising, can be manipulated to produce a definition different from the one that most people normally understand. Some pacifists refer to conditions in which "people are deprived of choices in a systematic way" as "institutionalized quiet violence." Even where no physical force is employed, this lack of choice in schools, in the workplace, in black neighborhoods is defined as violence.[4]

A writer and an audience cannot agree on a solution to a problem if they cannot even agree on what they are talking about. Carl Rogers's advice applies here: Listen to how your audience defines a key term. Make clear how you define it. Then work from there toward a definition that you can stipulate as the agreed-upon definition that you will use as you move toward resolution.

---

[4] Newton Garver, "What Violence Is," in James Rachels, ed., *Moral Choices* (New York: Harper & Row, 1971), 248–49.

In *Through the Looking-Glass*, Alice asked Humpty Dumpty "whether you can make words mean so many different things."

"When *I* use a word," Humpty Dumpty said scornfully, "it means just what I choose it to mean—neither more nor less."[5]

A writer, however, is not free to invent definitions that no one will recognize or that create rather than solve problems between writer and reader.

To avoid confusion, it is sometimes helpful to tell the reader what a term is *not*. In discussing euthanasia, a writer might say, "By euthanasia I do not mean active intervention to hasten the death of the patient." Another example: "Patients are diagnosed with PDD-NOS (Pervasive Developmental Disorder-Not Otherwise Specified) if they have some behaviors seen in autism but do not meet the full criteria for having an autistic disorder." A negative definition may be more extensive, depending on the complexity of the term and the writer's ingenuity.

Defining Vague and Ambiguous Terms

You will need to define other terms in addition to those in your claim. If you use words and phrases that have two or more meanings, they may appear vague and ambiguous to your reader. In arguments of value and policy, abstract terms such as *freedom of speech*, *justice*, and *equality* require clarification. Despite their abstract nature, however, they are among the most important in the language because they represent the ideals that shape our laws. When conflicts arise, the courts must define these terms to establish the legality of certain practices. Is the Ku Klux Klan permitted to make disparaging public statements about ethnic and racial groups? That depends on the court's definition of *free speech*. Can execution for some crimes be considered cruel and unusual punishment? That, too, depends on the court's definition of *cruel and unusual punishment*.

Consider the definition of *race*, around which so much of U.S. history has revolved, often with tragic consequences. Until recently, the only categories listed in the census were white, black, Asian-Pacific, and Native American, "with the Hispanic population straddling them all." But rapidly increasing intermarriage and ethnic identity caused a number of political and ethnic groups to demand changes in the classifications of the Census Bureau. Some Arab Americans, for example, prefer to be counted as "Middle Eastern" rather than white. Not all children of black-white unions or Asian-white unions identify—or are identified—in the same ways. Research has been conducted to discover how people feel about the terms that are used to define them.

---

[5] Lewis Carroll, *Alice in Wonderland* and *Through the Looking-Glass* (New York: Grosset & Dunlap, 1948), 238.

As one anthropologist pointed out, "Socially and politically assigned attributes have a lot to do with access to economic resources."[6]

"Socially and politically assigned attributes" can also be the basis for judging others. The definition of *success*, for example, varies among social groups as well as among individuals within the group. So difficult is the formulation of a universally accepted measure for success that some scholars regard the concept as meaningless. Nevertheless, we continue to use the word as if it represents a definable concept because the idea of success, however defined, is important for the identity and development of the individual and the group. It is clear, however, that when crossing subcultural boundaries, even within a small group, we need to be aware of differences in the use of the word. If contentment — that is, the satisfaction of achieving a small personal goal — is enough, then a person making a minimal salary but doing work that he or she loves may be a success. But you should not expect all your readers to agree that these criteria are enough to define *success*.

Abstract terms can be one source of vagueness in writing. Concrete examples usually help to define an abstraction. Abstract and concrete terms are treated more fully in Chapter 10, Language (p. 285-86).

RESEARCH SKILL ▶ Using Encyclopedias to Find Definitions

When there is disagreement about the definition of a term, you may need more than a dictionary definition to clarify the points on which the disagreement occurs. Often an encyclopedia can give a much fuller discussion of the complexities of defining terms that defy simple, clear-cut definitions. The more specialized the encyclopedia, the more useful the information — unless it uses so much jargon that it is useful only to specialists.

For example, *abortion* is defined in the *Encyclopedia Britannica Online* like this:

Abortion — the expulsion of a fetus from the uterus before it has reached the stage of viability (in human beings, usually about the 20th week of gestation). An abortion may occur spontaneously, in which case it is also called a miscarriage, or it may be brought on purpose-fully, in which case it is often called an induced abortion.

A specialized encyclopedia may provide more detailed information by discussing different positions in the debate for or against abortion. What follows is only a portion of an article from the *Encyclopedia of Philosophy*, which also includes a list of works cited that leads to other possible sources:

The claims to which partisans on both sides of the "abortion" issue appeal seem, if one is not thinking of the abortion issue, close to self-evident, or they appear to be easily defensible. The case against abortion (Beckwith 1993) rests on the proposition that there is a very strong presumption that ending another human life is seriously wrong. Almost everyone who is not thinking about the abortion issue would agree. There are good arguments for the view that fetuses are both living and human. ("Fetus" is generally used in the philosophical literature on abortion to refer to a human organism from

---

[6] *Wall Street Journal*, September 9, 1995, B1.

the time of conception to the time of birth.) Thus, it is easy for those opposed to abortion to think that only the morally depraved or the seriously confused could disagree with them. Standard pro-choice views appeal either to the proposition that women have the right to make decisions concerning their own bodies or to the proposition that fetuses are not yet persons. Both of these propositions seem either to be platitudes or to be straightforwardly defensible. Thus, it is easy for pro-choicers to believe that only religious fanatics or dogmatic conservatives could disagree. This explains, at least in part, why the abortion issue has created so much controversy. The philosophical debate regarding abortion has been concerned largely with subjecting these apparently obvious claims to the analytical scrutiny philosophers ought to give to them.

Consider first the standard argument against abortion. One frequent objection to the claim that fetuses are both human and alive is that we do not know when life begins. The reply to this objection is. . . .

You may find that your library has a database — such as Gale Virtual Reference Library — that lets you search a number of different encyclopedias at the same time. Just the first six entries from the list generated by that database lead to a range of encyclopedias you can investigate:

1. Abortion: I. Medical Perspectives. Allan Rosenfield, Sara Iden, and Anne Drapkin Lyerly. *Encyclopedia of Bioethics*. Ed. Stephen G. Post. Vol. 1. 4th ed. New York: Macmillan Reference USA, 2014.

2. Abortion. Menachem Elon. *Encyclopaedia Judaica.* Ed. Michael Berenbaum and Fred Skolnik. Vol. 1. 2nd ed. Detroit: Macmillan Reference USA, 2007. pp. 270–73.

3. Abortion. Don Marquis. *Encyclopedia of Philosophy*. Ed. Donald M. Borchert. Vol. 1. 2nd ed. Detroit: Macmillan Reference USA, 2006. pp. 8–10.

4. Abortion. *National Survey of State Laws*. Ed. Richard A. Leiter. 7th ed. Detroit: Gale, 2016.

5. Abortion. *West's Encyclopedia of American Law*. Ed. Shirelle Phelps and Jeffrey Lehman. Vol. 1. 2nd ed. Detroit: Gale, 2005. pp. 13–26.

6. Abortion. Mark R. Wicclair and Gabriella Gosman. *Encyclopedia of Science, Technology, and Ethics*. Ed. Carl Mitcham. Vol. 1. Detroit: Macmillan Reference USA, 2005. pp. 1–6.

Note: Wikipedia is a convenient source that often appears as the first source listed in the results from an online search, but it should be used with caution, if at all, for serious research. The information it contains can be written by anyone, no matter what their credentials may be. However, it may serve as a good source of references and links to more reputable sources.

Definition by Example

One of the most effective ways of defining terms in an argument is to use examples. Both real and hypothetical examples can bring life to abstract and ambiguous terms. The writer in the following passage defines *cognate* in the first two sentences through negation and then defines it by means of examples:

At some colleges and universities, a cognate is a personalized alternative to a minor. Where a minor is a cluster of courses from one department that a student takes in addition to a major as a secondary emphasis area, a cognate lets a student, with the approval of an advisor, choose a cluster

ARGUMENT ESSENTIALS

Defining the Terms in Your Argument

- You and your reader must agree on definitions of key terms if your argument is to be effective.

- In most cases, a dictionary definition is not sufficient.

- Stipulate the definition of key terms that you are using because other people in other contexts may define the term differently.

- In some cases, you may clarify a term by stipulating what it is not, or by negation.

- Avoid vague and ambiguous terms, or take the time to explain which of two or more possible meanings is the one you intend.

- Use examples, real or hypothetical, to clarify abstract or ambiguous terms.

of courses from different departments that serve as a secondary emphasis area to complement his or her minor. For example, a film studies major might take a course in the Foreign Languages department about how foreign cultures are represented through film, a course in the anthropology department focusing on anthropology in film, a course in the English department about film adaptation of novels, and a course in the psychology department on the representation of abnormal psychology in film. A student interested in the environment might major in biology and put together a cognate from courses in law, economics, geography, and history.

Extended Definitions

When we speak of an extended definition, we usually refer not only to length but also to the variety of methods for developing the definition. The argumentative essay can take the form of an extended definition. This type of definition essay is appropriate when the idea under consideration is so controversial or so heavy with historical connotations that even a paragraph or two cannot make clear exactly what the arguer wants his or her readers to understand. For example, if you were preparing a definition of *patriotism*, you would probably use a number of methods to develop your definition: personal narrative, examples, stipulation, comparison and contrast, and cause-and-effect analysis.

READING ARGUMENT

Seeing an Extended Definition

The excerpt below is the first two paragraphs of an extended definition essay. At the end of the full essay, the author concludes with what he would do, faced with the sorts of decisions he describes in the essay: "I expect that I will be able to take a step back and fully take on the mantle of the physician and act for the good of my patients, respecting their values as well as medical evidence, never putting my own interests before those of my patients."

Conscientious Objection in Medicine: A Moral Dilemma
ISHMEAL BRADLEY

Consider this: what would you do if a patient with terminal pancreatic cancer told you, his primary care doctor of twenty years, that he wanted your help to end his life? Or, what if a woman in her first trimester who contracted an infection that threatened the health of her fetus asked you, her obstetrician, to perform an abortion? Ethical questions like these are encountered not infrequently today. However, they can pose a moral dilemma for the physician. Where are the boundaries between professional obligations and personal morality? Can personal morality override professional duty when it comes to patient care?

Conscientious objection in medicine is the notion that a health care provider can abstain from offering certain types of medical care with which he/she does not personally agree. This includes care that would other-wise be considered medically appropriate. An example would be a pro-life obstetrician who refuses to perform abortions or sterilizations. On the one hand, there is the argument that physicians have a duty to uphold the wishes of their patients, as long as those wishes are reasonable. On the other is the thought that physicians themselves are moral beings and that their morality should not be infringed upon by dictates from the legislatures, medical community, or patient interests.

> Bradley opens with examples of moral dilemmas doctors face.

> Here Bradley most directly states his definition of conscientious objection in medicine.

> Conscientious objection in medicine is so controversial because of the conflict between personal morality and the law or medical standards.

Practice: Extended Definition

In the United States, terrorism has received unprecedented attention since the tragic events of September 11, 2001. You may be surprised to learn that the essay that follows was written in May of that year, *before* planes crashing into the World Trade Center, the Pentagon, and a field in Pennsylvania gave the term new meaning for Americans forever. Just as the problem of terrorism has not yet been solved, the problem of defining terrorism remains unsolved as well. Like most extended definitions, the definition of *terrorism* in the essay below uses several of the means of defining a term that this chapter has covered. Which of them do you see, and where? Read the essay, and answer the questions that follow it.

Ishmeal Bradley is a doctor of internal medicine at CHRISTUS St. Vincent in New Mexico. This article was posted in full on May 28, 2009, on *Clinical Correlations: The NYU Langone Online Journal of Medicine.*

The Definition of Terrorism

BRIAN WHITAKER

Decide for yourself whether to believe this, but according to a new report there were only 16 cases of international terrorism in the Middle East last year.

That is the lowest number for any region in the world apart from North America (where there were none at all). Europe had 30 cases—almost twice as many as the Middle East—and Latin America came top with 193.

The figures come from the U.S. State Department's annual review of global terrorism, which has just been published on the Internet. Worldwide, the report says confidently, "there were 423 international terrorist attacks in 2000, an increase of 8% from the 392 attacks recorded during 1999."

No doubt a lot of painstaking effort went into counting them, but the statistics are fundamentally meaningless because, as the report points out, "no one definition of terrorism has gained universal acceptance."

5   That is an understatement. While most people agree that terrorism exists, few can agree on what it is. A recent book discussing attempts by the UN and other international bodies to define terrorism runs to three volumes and 1,866 pages without reaching any firm conclusion.

Using the definition preferred by the state department, terrorism is: "Premeditated, politically motivated violence perpetrated against noncombatant* targets by subnational groups or clandestine agents, usually intended to influence an audience." (The asterisk is important, as we shall see later.)

"International" terrorism—the subject of the American report—is defined as "terrorism involving citizens or the territory of more than one country."

The key point about terrorism, on which almost everyone agrees, is that it's politically motivated. This is what distinguishes it from, say, murder or football hooliganism. But this also causes a problem for those who compile statistics because the motive is not always clear—especially if no one has claimed responsibility.

So the American report states—correctly—that there were no confirmed terrorist incidents in Saudi Arabia last year. There were, nevertheless, three unexplained bombings and one shooting incident, all directed against foreigners.

Another essential ingredient (you might think) is that terrorism is calculated to terrorize the public or a particular section of it. The American definition does not mention spreading terror at all, because that would exclude attacks against property. It is, after all, impossible to frighten an inanimate object.

Among last year's attacks, 152 were directed against a pipeline in Colombia which is owned by multinational oil companies. Such attacks

10

Brian Whitaker is the former Middle East editor of the British newspaper the *Guardian* and author of *Arabs without God: Atheism and Freedom of Belief in the Middle East*. This article was published May 7, 2001, in the daily online version of the *Guardian*.

are of concern to the United States and so a definition is required which allows them to be counted.

For those who accept that terrorism is about terrorizing people, other questions arise. Does it include threats, as well as actual violence? A few years ago, for example, the Islamic Army in Yemen warned foreigners to leave the country if they valued their lives but did not actually carry out its threat.

More recently, a group of Israeli peace activists were arrested for driving around in a loudspeaker van, announcing a curfew of the kind that is imposed on Palestinians. Terrifying for any Israelis who believed it, but was it terrorism?

Another characteristic of terrorism, according to some people, is that targets must be random — the intention being to make everyone fear they might be the next victim. Some of the Hamas suicide bombings appear to follow this principle but when attacks are aimed at predictable targets (such as the military) they are less likely to terrorize the public at large.

15   Definitions usually try to distinguish between terrorism and warfare. In general this means that attacks on soldiers are warfare and those against civilians are terrorism, but the dividing lines quickly become blurred.

The state department regards attacks against "noncombatant* targets" as terrorism. But follow the asterisk to the small print and you find that "noncombatants" includes both civilians and military personnel who are unarmed or off duty at the time. Several examples are given, such as the 1986 disco bombing in Berlin, which killed two servicemen.

The most lethal bombing in the Middle East last year was the suicide attack on USS *Cole* in Aden harbor which killed 17 American sailors and injured 39 more.

As the ship was armed and its crew on duty at the time, why is this classified as terrorism? Look again at the small print, which adds: "We also consider as acts of terrorism attacks on military installations or on armed military personnel when a state of military hostilities does not exist at the site, such as bombings against U.S. bases."

A similar question arises with Palestinian attacks on quasi-military targets such as Israeli settlements. Many settlers are armed (with weapons supplied by the army) and the settlements themselves — though they contain civilians — might be considered military targets because they are there to consolidate a military occupation.

If, under the state department rules,   20 Palestinian mortar attacks on settlements count as terrorism, it would be reasonable to expect Israeli rocket attacks on Palestinian communities to be treated in the same way — but they are not. In the American definition, terrorism can never be inflicted by a state.

Israeli treatment of the Palestinians is classified as a human rights issue (for which the Israelis get a rap over the knuckles) in a separate state department report.

Denying that states can commit terrorism is generally useful, because it gets the U.S. and its allies off the hook in a variety of situations. The disadvantage is that it might also get hostile states off the hook — which is why there has to be a list of states that are said to "sponsor" terrorism while not actually committing it themselves.

Interestingly, the American definition of terrorism is a reversal of the word's original meaning, given in the *Oxford English Dictionary* as "government by intimidation." Today it usually refers to intimidation of governments.

The first recorded use of "terrorism" and "terrorist" was in 1795, relating to the Reign of Terror instituted by the French government. Of course, the Jacobins, who led the government at the time, were also revolutionaries and gradually "terrorism" came to be applied to violent revolutionary activity in general. But the use of "terrorist" in an anti-government sense is not recorded until 1866 (referring to Ireland) and 1883 (referring to Russia).

25   In the absence of an agreed meaning, making laws against terrorism is especially difficult. The latest British anti-terrorism law gets round the problem by listing 21 international terrorist

organizations by name. Membership of these is illegal in the UK.

There are six Islamic groups, four anti-Israel groups, eight separatist groups, and three opposition groups. The list includes Hizbullah, which though armed, is a legal political party in Lebanon, with elected members of parliament.

Among the separatist groups, the Kurdistan Workers Party—active in Turkey—is banned, but not the KDP or PUK, which are Kurdish organizations active in Iraq. Among opposition groups, the Iranian People's Mujahedeen is banned, but not its Iraqi equivalent, the INC, which happens to be financed by the United States.

Issuing such a list does at least highlight the anomalies and inconsistencies behind anti-terrorism laws. It also points toward a simpler—and perhaps more honest—definition: terrorism is violence committed by those we disapprove of.

Reading, Writing, and Discussion Questions

1. Even the U.S. State Department reports that its carefully compiled statistics on terrorism are meaningless. Why?
2. Where in the essay does Brian Whitaker use examples to try to explain the definition of terrorism?
3. Where does Whitaker try to explain terrorism by what it is *not*?
4. Having read Whitaker's essay, how would you summarize the difficulties of defining the term *terrorism*? What other terms can you think of that are similarly difficult to define?

Strategies for Writing a Definition Essay

1. **Choose a term that needs definition** because it is controversial or ambiguous, or because you want to offer a personal definition that differs from the accepted interpretation. Explain why an extended definition is necessary. Or choose an experience that lends itself to treatment in an extended definition. One student defined *culture shock* as she had experienced it while studying abroad in Hawaii among students of a different ethnic background.

2. **Decide on the thesis** — the point of view you wish to develop about the term you are defining. If you want to define *heroism*, for example, you may choose to develop the idea that this quality depends on motivation and awareness of danger rather than on the specific act performed by the hero.

3. **Distinguish wherever possible between the term you are defining and other terms with which it might be confused.** If you are defining *love*, can you make a clear distinction between the different kinds of emotional attachments that the word conveys?

4. **Try to think of several methods of developing the definition** using examples, comparison and contrast, analogy, cause-and-effect analysis. However, you may discover that one method alone — say, use of examples — will suffice to narrow and refine your definition.

5. **Arrange your supporting material** in an order that gives emphasis to the most important ideas.

Assignments for Definition

Reading and Discussion Questions

1. Why is definition such a crucial element in argumentation? In what ways can it help resolve issues? How can it lead to problems?

2. Who has the power to stipulate how a term is defined? The government? the media? society in a broader sense? Where have you seen examples of each in the readings in this chapter?

Writing Suggestions

1. Narrate an experience you have had in which you felt either aided or hindered by being defined as a member of a specific group. It could be a group defined by gender, race, religious affiliation, or membership on a team or in a club.

2. Would adoption at the state level of a policy prohibiting classifying people by race, color, ethnicity, or national origin be beneficial or pernicious for the individual and for society? In other words, what is good or bad about classifying people?

3. Find a subject for which definition is critical to how statistics are interpreted and for which you can make a successful argument in a 750- to 1,000-word paper. Your essay should provide proof for a claim.

4. Write about an important or widely used term whose meaning has changed since you first learned it. Such terms often come from the slang of particular groups: drug users, rock music fans, musicians, athletes, computer programmers, or software developers.

5. Write an essay in which you provide specific examples of how government officials sometimes use euphemisms and other careful word choices to disguise the truth.

RESEARCH ASSIGNMENT ▸ **Using Encyclopedias**

1. Find out what encyclopedias your library has to offer. A librarian may be able to give you a list. Some may be in print and others online. If there is no list, you can search under "encyclopedia" and scan the list for relevant titles.

2. Choose one of the controversial subjects listed below, or another of your choice, and investigate what you can learn about it from three different encyclopedias. Do not use more than one general encyclopedia. Cut, paste, and print; photocopy; or take notes on the three sources and be prepared to discuss what you found. One question you should consider is how useful each encyclopedia would be to a researcher.

   ■ Solar power
   ■ Undocumented workers
   ■ Current legal status of gender-neutral bathroom bills
   ■ Sexual harassment

Logic

Throughout the book, we have pointed out the weaknesses that cause arguments to break down. In the vast majority of cases, these weaknesses represent breakdowns in logic or the reasoning process. We call such weaknesses **fallacies**, a term derived from Latin. Sometimes these false or erroneous arguments are deliberate; in fact, the Latin word *fallere* means "to deceive." But more often these arguments are either carelessly constructed or unintentionally flawed. Thoughtful readers learn to recognize them; thoughtful writers learn to avoid them.

As discussed in Chapter 5, the reasoning process was first given formal expression by Aristotle. In his famous treatises, he described the way we try to discover the truth—observing the world, selecting impressions, making inferences, generalizing. In this process, Aristotle identified two forms of reasoning: induction and deduction. Both forms, he realized, are subject to error. Our observations may be incorrect or insufficient, and our conclusions may be faulty because they have violated the rules governing the relationship between statements. Induction and deduction are not reserved only for formal arguments about important problems; they also represent our everyday thinking about the most ordinary matters. As for the fallacies, they, too, unfortunately, may crop up anywhere, whenever we are careless in our use of the reasoning process.

In this chapter, we examine some of the most common fallacies. First, however, a closer look at induction and deduction will make clear what happens when fallacies occur.

Induction

Induction is the form of reasoning in which we come to conclusions about the whole on the basis of observations of particular instances. For example, two friends decided to do some price comparisons.[1] They went to four

---

[1] Amanda Miller, "Shop-o-nomics: 'Which Grocery Store Has the Lowest Prices?'" Get Out of Debt Guy, September 20, 2010, http://getoutofdebt.org/21926/shop-o-nomics-which-grocery -store-has-the-lowest-prices.

popular stores, and at each one they checked the prices of the same four items: Sunbeam Giant Bread, Charmin Ultra Strong 9 Pack Mega Roll toilet paper, a gallon of store-brand whole milk, and a 12-pack of Cherry Coke Zero.

These shoppers were using the inductive method to determine which store is the least expensive. They studied the prices of individual items at individual stores and used that information to arrive at a generalization. They were moving from specifics—the prices of specific items at specific stores—to general observations. They compared the prices at the four stores and concluded that Walmart is the least expensive.

They were using induction, but how accurate was their conclusion? In inductive reasoning, the reliability of your conclusion depends on the quantity and quality of your observations. Were four items out of the thousands available at these four stores a sufficiently large sample? Would the friends' conclusion have been the same if they had chosen fifty items? One hundred? Even without pricing every item in all four stores, you would be more confident of your generalization as the quality and quantity of your samples increased.

In June of 2019, the blog LendEDU compared the online cost of fifty nearly identical items in five different categories from Amazon, Walmart, and Target.[2] In this study, the team compared prices on fifty similar items, a more convincing sample size than in our previous example. In other words, there were more specific pieces of information to put together in reaching a generalization. If you bought all fifty items, Walmart was 1.73 percent cheaper than Amazon while Target was 1.24 percent more expensive than Amazon. Walmart, however, averaged 5.50 percent more expensive per item than Amazon, while Target averaged 1.24 percent more expensive per item than Amazon. How can that be? One analyst explains, "The only category where both Walmart and Target beat out Amazon on price was in the Food & Beverage group, by 4.61 percent and 7.30 percent respectively. The main section that makes Walmart cheaper in total was Technology & Entertainment, where it was 4.19 percent cheaper." The process represents inductive reasoning because the researchers moved from specifics to generalizations, but the details reveal how closely you must look at the numbers in order to be sure your conclusions are valid. In this case, the specifics of what you were buying were more relevant to where you should shop than simply the total cost of all items.

Generalizations can also be complicated by other factors. Walmart recently aired television commercials citing specific items to prove that its prices on groceries are better than those at Publix. A blogger on Iheartpublix.com responded with her own list of prices on fifty-three items, showing that

---

[2] Ted McCarthy, "Amazon vs. Walmart vs. Target Price Comparison," LendEDU, Shop Tutors, June 25, 2019, https://lendedu.com/blog/amazon-walmart-target-price-comparison/.

Publix prices are better.[3] How can both be true? The blogger acknowledges that her prices were drawn from Publix's weekly ads. In other words, she compared Publix's sale prices with Walmart's everyday prices. (Her argument was that at least some of the Walmart items in the commercial were on sale and that smart shoppers buy when an item is on sale.)

Later in the chapter, we will discuss a fallacy called *hasty generalization* that occurs when a generalization is based on too little evidence.

In some cases, you can observe all the instances in a particular situation. For example, by acquiring information about the religious beliefs of all the residents of a dormitory, you can arrive at an accurate assessment of the number of Buddhists. But since our ability to make definitive observations about everything is limited, we must make an inductive leap about categories of things that we ourselves can never encounter in their entirety. We make a leap when we have to accept less than absolute certainty or complete data and conclude that we have enough information on which to generalize. It is too much of a leap to conclude from a study of four items that one store is less expensive than another. It is less of a leap to conclude on the basis of fifty items.

In other cases, we may rely on a principle known in science as "the uniformity of nature." We assume that certain conclusions about oak trees in the temperate zone of North America, for example, will also be true for oak trees growing elsewhere under similar climatic conditions. We also use this principle in attempting to explain the causes of behavior in human beings. If we discover that the institutionalization of some children from infancy results in severe developmental delay, we think it safe to conclude that under the same circumstances all children would suffer the same consequences. As in the previous example, we are aware that certainty about every case of institutionalization is impossible. With rare exceptions, the process of induction can offer only probability, not certain truth.

Keep in mind that induction is a reasoning process, not an organizational pattern for academic essays. An author may make use of inductive reasoning to arrive at a generalization that then becomes the thesis of an essay. It may not always be obvious that the author used induction to arrive at his or her thesis, but in the following essay, author Steven Doloff describes the inductive process he used.

> **ARGUMENT ESSENTIALS**
> ## Induction
>
> - Induction is the process of arriving at a generalization based on the observation of a number of particular instances.
> - The accuracy of the generalization depends on the quantity and quality of the particular instances observed.
> - In most cases, the generalization will be a probability, not a certainty.
> - Arriving at a generalization based on too few particular instances is a logical fallacy called "hasty generalization."

---

[3] Michelle, "See the Real Difference—Publix vs. Walmart Shopping," I Heart Publix, June 16, 2012, https://www.iheartpublix.com/2012/07/see-the-real-difference-publix-vs-walmart -shopping-comparision/.

READING ARGUMENT

Seeing Induction

The following essay has been annotated to show inductive reasoning.

Greta Garbo, Meet Joan Rivers . . . (Talk amongst Yourselves)
STEVEN DOLOFF

Doloff used the inductive process 25 years ago to see what conclusions he could draw about how men and women were represented differently in featured obituaries. This sets up a comparison with his more recent analysis.

Twenty-five years ago, I examined the gender breakdown of the featured obituaries in *The New York Times* for a week, from April 13–19, 1990. I found fifty-three deceased men rated essay-long obituaries, but only one woman — Greta Garbo, the long retired movie actress from the 1920s and 30s. And in an issue of this journal, *Women and Language* (XV.2, 1992), I lamented that retrospective disregard that added the insult of oblivion to the injury of devaluation, so long inflicted upon the experience of women's lives. In a footnote to my piece, the editor of *W & L* urged its readers to prod their local media outlets to correct for this sexist bias.

Doloff repeated the inductive process but with a larger sample in 2014.

So here we are, a quarter of a century later, and how far have we come in rectifying this journalistic prejudice? Well, I repeated my survey of *The New York Times'* featured obituary essays in 2014, this time expanding my sample to cover not one, but five weeks (September 1–October 5, 2014), and I discovered . . . some progress. Within this thirty-five day period, "The Gray Lady" (a nickname for the paper based on its historically higher-than-normal copy-to-graphics ratio) ran a hundred and four obituary essays: eighty-four for men, and twenty for women — that's just short of 24 percent women, or roughly four men to one woman. And the most prominent eulogized woman, by far, was the comedienne Joan Rivers, who died last year from a botched medical procedure.

Doloff generalizes that there was progress in equality in 25 years, but not enough.

Now 24 percent is a big jump from the 1.8 percent I found in 1990 — that's true — but it nevertheless demonstrates the same ongoing bias: that lives of men still count for more than the lives of women. Actually, my updated statistical findings closely resembled a similar obituary review, nine years ago, of another big city daily, the *Chicago Tribune*, self-reported on by that paper's own "public editor," Timothy McNulty ("Gender gap, even in death," November 13, 2006). He found 73 percent of the *Tribune's*

Another similar study supported his generalization.

Steven Doloff is professor of Humanities and Media Studies at Pratt Institute. He writes about culture and education for such publications as the *New York Times*, the *Washington Post*, and the *Chronicle of Higher Education*. This essay appeared in 2015 in *Women and Language*, a peer-reviewed journal that focuses on issues of communication, language, and gender.

obituaries were of men, and that that same percentage breakdown, give-or-take, matched those in major newspapers all over the country.

And what was McNulty's opinion on the cause of this "lopsided" state of affairs? He believed that the heavy preponderance of past and present male corporate leaders simply monopolized the most journalistically recognized field of human accomplishment, "business."

5   "Though women are increasingly reaching high levels of business in the society," he acknowledged, "those on contemporary obituary pages are more likely to have had one of the traditional roles: teacher, nurse, nun, mother of a large family, social worker, and very active volunteer." McNulty also postulated that because women live longer than men, and thereby often well after their most publicly active years, they're more prone to being forgotten. Finally, he observed that since many women in retirement are likely to relocate "to follow their . . . children and grandchildren," they may move away from the place where they would otherwise be publicly remembered for their achievements. Hmmm.

Aside from the comparable gender statistics themselves, my more recent perusal of *The New York Times* obituary page revealed something other than what McNulty proposes. I found a fairly broad range of professional achievements that proved print-worthy of the eighty-four deceased men. While only five seemed categorically distinguished as corporate magnates, most were not, and included a variety of sports figures, diplomats, journalists, academics, politicians, scientists, military heroes, inventors, and creative and performing artists of every stripe. Also noted were the deaths of the sons of Bernie Madoff and Victor McLaglan, a police informer, an exonerated state prisoner, and two cartoonists. The range of distinctions among the twenty deceased women was much narrower. Fifteen were from the arts and performance fields, accompanied by an epidemiologist, a pilot, a duchess, a woman who, as a child, refused to stand up for the pledge of allegiance in her school, and a transgender advocate. No nuns, no nurses, no social workers, and not one celebrated for the size of her family.

So why is there still this skew towards the encomia of male experience, even in the nation's most highly regarded "paper of record"? Is it really, as McNulty presents it, just a matter of waiting for more women, who now comprise 47 percent of the American work force, to elbow their way further up the same competitive ladders built by men, and so "win" better percentages on the *Times* obit page?

Well, McNulty might be right, even if a recent and lengthy front-page article in the *NYT* seems to suggest that the promise of competitively

---

The other researcher, McNulty, tries to explain why fewer women are represented in the obituary essays. He is examining the cause/effect relationship behind the numbers.

Doloff offers his rebuttal.

McNulty predicts it is just a matter of time before women work their way up to obituary equality.

achieved, top-tier professional gender equality may still be a ways off. Jodie Kantor, in "A Gender Gap More Powerful than the Internet" (*NYT*, December 23, 2014, A1, A18, A19), reported on the 20th reunion of the 1700-person Stanford University class of 1994. Back in the 90s, she points out, Stanford, "already the most powerful incubator in Silicon Valley," had adopted a diversity policy designed to pump representative numbers of women and minorities into the new era of cyber technology and entrepreneurship.

Yet Kantor discovered, through extensive interviews, that even though the class of 94 had participated in a Stanford campus "gone computer science crazy, with the majority of students taking programming courses," still it was primarily from the male half of the graduates (with some female exceptions, here and there) that the most recognizable movers, shakers, and earners of the current internet age emerged. She surmised that the high-wire financial ambiance of the internet industry, capitalized by "mostly male-run venture funds," somehow induced otherwise totally techno-capable female members of the class into opting for "safe jobs in and out of technology," or more conventional careers in law, finance, medicine.

This may seem like disheartening news for the cause of obituarial gender 10 equality. And it would be, if we accept that the public sphere reflected by newspapers like *The New York Times* is, in fact, as it is and all there is, and that newspapers are and will continue to be the defining medium for that sphere. But if we consider that such selectively highlighted corporate rungs and ladders (even those extending into cyberspace) are not the only indicators of social contributions, a far more equitable gender achievement horizon appears. Nor do we need to wait for women to build their own ladders to competitively ascend, as there are already countless women's lives full of notable virtue and accomplishment.

As Gloria Steinem put it, women "have always been an equal part of the past . . . [they] just haven't been a part of history." And it is the internet (not newspapers), despite any cyber-mogul gender gap, that is correcting this discrepancy—if not from the top down in corporate figureheads, then from the bottom up in revelatory and substantive content. Simply scan the constantly expanding library of MAKERS.com, the online digital and video platform launched in 2012, that has been accumulating thousands of women's stories, in both original interview and archival film and photo format. In 2013, its documentary "MAKERS: Women Who Made America" was watched by over four million viewers on PBS stations around America, and in 2014, PBS further aired MAKERS' six-week series: Women in Space,

---

Kantor's research, however, suggests progress is coming more slowly than might have been hoped, even at Stanford, where diversity was stressed early.

Doloff has generalized about what the numbers meant in the past; now he focuses on what they mean for the future: very little once we recognize that popular newspapers don't have to be the "defining medium" for achievement.

Doloff claims that it is the internet that is correcting the discrepancy between how men's and women's lives are valued.

Women in Hollywood, Women in Comedy, Women in Business, Women in War, and Women in Politics. Also last year, MAKERS began compiling an archive of hitherto insufficiently credited female achievement in the STEM fields (science, technology, engineering, and mathematics). It's just a matter of impartially looking.

So here's my two-part prediction: first, we will never see gender equality on the obituary pages of printed "major" daily newspapers. And, second, that's okay. Why never? Because, I believe, they will probably stop printing newspapers in any really significant numbers before the particular bias skewing those pages truly dissipates. And why is that okay? Because the decline in newspapers' social impact as a winnowing medium of popular history is already happening. As advertising dollars are increasingly and inevitably redirected into the endlessly inclusive medium of the internet, with its far larger and more diversified audience, newspaper size and circulation proportionally (and, again, inevitably) diminish. And while newspapers aren't dead yet, their prospective demise is a common editorial chew toy — their own obit, as it were, a work-in-progress.

First prediction: before the skewing can be corrected, newspapers will have lost their social impact.

Let me finally prognosticate that there will probably never be an uber-narrative of history published anywhere reflecting perfect gender equality. But at least in the budding, pluralistic cyber universe, it would appear the more egalitarian pixels "of record" will fall, to quote James Joyce, equally "upon all the living and the dead" of both sexes.

Second prediction: there will never be a published history in which men and women share gender equality, but the cyber world is more egalitarian, and there they can.

So if Garbo does happen to bump into Rivers in the hereafter, and they do talk, let's hope it gets recorded, because I'm sure it will make for a hilarious conversation.

Reading, Writing, and Discussion Questions

1. How much progress did Steven Doloff find in the treatment of women on the obituary page between his original study and the more recent one?
2. What is McNulty's explanation for the discrepancy that still exists between men and women when it comes to obituary essays? What is Doloff's response to McNulty's explanation?
3. How does Doloff's essay illustrate the use of inductive reasoning?
4. Do you feel that Doloff effectively supports his main claim? Why, or why not?
5. Doloff concludes that women have a better chance of having their accomplishments recognized as equivalent to those of men on the internet than in newspapers. Consider the many women who have recently entered national politics. Write an essay in which you explain whether you feel the extensive online coverage of these women has helped or hurt them as candidates.

Deduction

It is useful to think of deduction as working in the opposite direction from induction. With deductive reasoning, an arguer essentially starts with a general statement that would apply to a number of specific situations. Then the arguer applies that generalization to one specific instance. Unlike the conclusions from induction, which are only probable, the conclusions from **deduction** are certain. The simplest deductive argument consists of two premises and a conclusion. Outlined in the form of a **syllogism**, the classic form of deductive reasoning, such an argument looks like this:

> **Major premise:** All students with 3.5 averages and above for three years are invited to become members of Kappa Gamma Pi, the honor society.
>
> **Minor premise:** George has had a 3.8 average for over three years.
>
> **Conclusion:** Therefore, he will be invited to join Kappa Gamma Pi.

This deductive conclusion is *valid*, or logically consistent, because it follows necessarily from the premises. No other conclusion is possible. **Validity**, however, refers only to the form of the argument. The argument itself may not be satisfactory if the premises are not true — if Kappa Gamma Pi has imposed other conditions or if George has only a 3.4 average. The difference between truth and validity is important because it alerts us to the necessity for examining the truth of the premises before we decide that the conclusion is sound. To be **sound**, an argument must be valid and all of its premises must be true.

One way of discovering how the deductive process works is to look at the methods used by Sherlock Holmes, that most famous of literary detectives, in solving his mysteries. On one occasion, Holmes observed that a man sitting opposite him on a train had chalk dust on his fingers. From this observation, Holmes deduced that the man was a schoolteacher. If his thinking were outlined in a syllogism, it would take this form:

> **Major premise:** All men with chalk dust on their fingers are schoolteachers.
>
> **Minor premise:** This man has chalk dust on his fingers.
>
> **Conclusion:** Therefore, this man is a schoolteacher.

The major premise offers a generalization about a large group or class. This generalization has been arrived at through inductive reasoning, or observation of particulars. The minor premise makes a statement about a specific member of that group or class. The third proposition is the conclusion, which links the other two propositions, in much the same way that an assumption links support and a claim.

But although the argument may be logical and *valid*, it is faulty. A deductive argument is only as strong as its premises. In this case, the major premise, the generalization that all men with chalk dust on their fingers are schoolteachers, is not true, so the argument is not *sound*. Perhaps all the men with dusty fingers

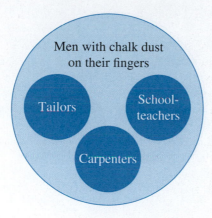

whom Holmes had so far observed had turned out to be schoolteachers, but his sample was not sufficiently large to enable him to conclude that all dust-fingered men are teachers. In Holmes's day, draftsmen or carpenters or tailors might have had fingers just as white as those of schoolteachers. Sometimes it is helpful to draw a Venn diagram, circles representing the various groups in their relation to the whole.

If the large circle above represents all those who have chalk dust on their fingers, we see that several different groups may be contained in this universe. To be safe, Holmes should have deduced that the man on the train *might have been* a schoolteacher; he was not safe in deducing more than that. Obviously, if the inductive generalization or major premise is false, the conclusion of the particular deductive argument is also false or invalid.

The deductive argument may also go wrong elsewhere. What if the *minor* premise is untrue? Could Holmes have mistaken the source of the white powder on the man's fingers? Suppose it was not chalk dust but flour or confectioner's sugar or talcum or heroin. Any of these possibilities would weaken or invalidate Holmes's conclusion.

Another example, closer to the kinds of arguments you will examine in your academic work, reveals the flaw in the deductive process.

Major premise: All Communists oppose organized religion.
Minor premise: Robert Roe opposes organized religion.
Conclusion: Therefore, Robert Roe is a Communist.

The fact that two things share an attribute does not mean that they are the same thing. The following diagram (p. 328) makes clear that Robert Roe and Communists do not necessarily share all attributes. Remembering that Holmes may have misinterpreted the signs of chalk on the traveler's fingers, we may also want to question whether Robert Roe's opposition to organized religion has been misinterpreted.

Some deductive arguments give us trouble because one of the premises, usually the major premise, is omitted. As in the assumptions we examined in Chapter 8, a failure to evaluate the truth of an unexpressed premise may lead to an invalid conclusion. When only two parts of a syllogism appear, we call the resulting form an **enthymeme**. Suppose we overhear the following bit of conversation:

"Did you hear about Jean's father? He had a heart attack last week."
"That's too bad. But I'm not surprised. I know he always refused to go for his annual physical checkups."

The second speaker has used an unexpressed major premise, the cause-and-effect assumption *If you have annual physical checkups, you can avoid heart attacks.* He does not express it because he assumes that it is unnecessary to do so. The first speaker recognizes the unspoken assumption and may agree with it. Or the first speaker may produce evidence from reputable sources that such a generalization is by no means universally true, in which case the conclusion of the second speaker is suspect.

A knowledge of the deductive process can help guide you toward an evaluation of the soundness of your reasoning in an argument you are constructing. A syllogism is often clearer than an outline in establishing the relations between the different parts of an argument.

Setting down your own or someone else's argument in this form will not necessarily give you the answers to questions about how to support your claim, but it should clearly indicate what your claims are and, above all, what logical connections exist between your statements.

ARGUMENT ESSENTIALS
Dection

- Deduction is the process of applying a generalization to a particular instance.
- The simplest deductive argument consists of two premises and a conclusion — a syllogism.
- The conclusions from deduction are certain if both premises are true.

READING ARGUMENT

Seeing Deduction

The following essay has been annotated to show deduction.

Are We Living Too Long?

SEAMUS O'MAHONY

Rolf Zinkernagel, a Swiss immunologist who won the Nobel Prize in Physiology or Medicine in 1996, believes that the lifespan of human beings has far exceeded what it was intended to be: "I would argue that we are basically built to reach 25 years of age. All the rest is luxury." Wealthy older people spend a lot of time and money maintaining their health and postponing death. Dinner-party conversations center on colonoscopies, statins (drugs which reduce blood cholesterol), and new diets. Many Americans who are not doctors subscribe to the *New England Journal of Medicine*. I have noticed a similar trend in well-off, older acquaintances of mine: health, and its maintenance, has become their hobby.

O'Mahony generalizes about how the wealthy view aging.

A restatement of the generalization

All quite laudable, but let's take this trend to its logical conclusion. What are the consequences for society if average life expectancy rises to 100 years, or even more? We face the prospect of an army of centenarians cared for by poorly paid immigrants. The children of these centenarians can expect to work well into their 70s, or even 80s. The world of work will alter drastically, with diminishing opportunities for the young.

O'Mahony now takes that generalization and applies it.

Long working lives spent caring for the elderly would be the effect on the lives of specific, real people.

What if powerful new therapies emerge which can slow down the aging process and postpone death? Undoubtedly it will be the rich and powerful who will avail themselves of them. Poor people in Africa, Asia, and South America will continue to struggle for simple necessities, such as food, clean water, and basic healthcare. There will be bitter debates about whether the state should fund such therapies. The old are a powerful lobby group and, compared to the young, are far more likely to vote, and thus hurt politicians at the ballot box. Politicians and policymakers mess with welfare provision for the old at their peril. The baby boomers of rich Western countries are now in their 60s and 70s and are aiming for a different kind of old age than

Again, O'Mahony applies a generalization to specific realities. This time the generalization is specifically about the development of life-extending therapies.

His major premise applied to baby boomers in the West

Seamus O'Mahony is a consultant gastroenterologist at Cork University Hospital in Ireland, associate editor for medical humanities of the *Journal of the Royal College of Physicians of Edinburgh*, and author of *The Way We Die Now* (2016) and *Can Medicine Be Cured? The Corruption of a Profession* (2019). His essay appeared in the *Saturday Evening Post* on April 30, 2019.

their parents. They demand a retirement that is wellfunded, active, and packed with experience. They are unfettered by mortgage debt and are the last generation to receive defined benefit pensions. The economic downturn of the last several years has only strengthened their position. They are passionate believers in the compression of morbidity.

Major premise: Wealthy older people want a different kind of old age than their parents.

Minor premise: Many will spend their final years in nursing homes.

Conclusion: Their vision of aging is "wishful thinking," or improbable.

But this vision of aging is wishful thinking. Many now face an old age in which the final years are spent in nursing homes. There are several societal reasons for this: increased longevity, the demise of the multi-generational extended family, and the contemporary obsession with safety. None of us wants to spend the end of our life in a nursing home; they are viewed (correctly) as places which value safety and protocol over independence and living.

What are we to do? We will not see a return of the preindustrial extended family; the future is urban, atomized, and medicalized. The bioethicist Ezekiel Emanuel outraged the baby boomers with his 2014 essay for the *Atlantic*, "Why I Hope to Die at 75." He attacked what he called the *American immortal*: "I think this manic desperation to endlessly extend life is misguided and potentially destructive. For many reasons, 75 is a pretty good age to aim to stop. Americans may live longer than their parents, but they are likely to be more incapacitated. Does that sound very desirable? Not to me."

5

The downside of living too long

Auberon Waugh (who died aged 61), son of Evelyn Waugh (who died aged 62), once remarked, "It is the duty of all good parents to die young." Montaigne put it like this: "Make room for others, as others have made room for you."

A dystopian view of living too long

Charles C. Mann wrote an essay in 2005 for the *Atlantic* called "The Coming Death Shortage," which envisaged a future "tripartite society" of "the very old and very rich on top, beta-testing each new treatment on themselves; a mass of ordinary old, forced by insurance into supremely healthy habits, kept alive by medical entitlement; and the diminishingly influential young."

I am broadly in agreement with Mann that ever-increasing longevity is bad for society, but the problem is this: Given the opportunity of a few extra years, would I take them? Of course I would. There is an old joke: "Who wants to live to be 100? A guy who's 99."

Medicine has taken much of the credit, but longevity in developed countries has increased owing to a combination of factors, which include not only organized healthcare, but also improved living conditions, disease prevention, and behavioral changes, such as reductions in smoking.

10   Interestingly, the maximum human lifespan has remained unchanged
at about 110–120 years; it is average longevity which has increased so
dramatically. Where do we draw the line and call "enough"? We can't.
John Gray has eloquently argued that although scientific knowledge has
increased exponentially since the Enlightenment, human irrationality
remains stubbornly static. Science is driven by reason and logic, yet our
use of it is frequently irrational. Does this phenomenon have any relevance
to my daily work as a doctor? Well yes, it does. Irrationality pervades all
aspects of medicine, from deluded, internet-addled patients and relatives,
to the overuse of scans and other diagnostic procedures, to the widespread use of drugs of dubious benefit and high cost. Cancer care has been
described as "a culture of medical excess." Overuse and futile use is driven
by patients, doctors, hospitals, and pharmaceutical companies. The doctor
who practices sparingly and judiciously has little to gain either professionally or financially.

Major premise: People can now know what diseases they might get.

Minor premise: They are worried before they are even sick.

Conclusion: Spending on medicine may cause more harm than good.

Many within medicine view with alarm the direction modern healthcare
has taken — that spending on medicine in countries like the U.S. has passed
the tipping point where it causes more harm than good. We have seen the
rise in the concept of disease "awareness," promoted, not infrequently, by
pharmaceutical companies. Genetics has the potential to turn us all into
patients by identifying our predisposition to various diseases. Guidelines
from the European Society of Cardiology on treatment of blood pressure
and high cholesterol levels identified 76 percent of the entire adult population of Norway as being "at increased risk." This ruse of "disease mongering"
(driven mainly by the pharmaceutical industry) has identified the worried
well, rather than the sick, as their market.

Major premise: When the pursuit of health is obsessive, it impoverishes us spiritually and financially.

Minor premise: The wealthy elderly are obsessed with health.

Conclusion: The wealthy elderly are impoverished spiritually and financially.

We cannot, like misers, hoard health; living uses it up. Nor should we
lose it like spendthrifts. Health, like money, is not an end in itself; like
money, it is a prerequisite for a decent, fulfilling life. The obsessive pursuit
of health is a form of consumerism and impoverishes us not just spiritually,
but also financially. Rising spending on healthcare inevitably means that we
spend less on other societal needs, such as education, housing, and transport.
Medicine should give up the quest to conquer nature, and retreat to a core
function of providing comfort and succor.

O'Mahony's overall conclusion: Let medicine do what it is intended to do, offer comfort and succor, not conquer nature.

Practice: Deduction

The following excerpt exemplifies former secretary of state Hillary Clinton's
frequent use of deduction. Read the excerpt, and answer the questions that
follow it.

Remarks at the Asia Pacific Economic Cooperation Women and the Economy Summit

HILLARY CLINTON

Integrating women more effectively into the way businesses invest, market, and recruit also yields benefits in terms of profitability and corporate governance. In a McKinsey survey, a third of executives reported increased profits as a result of investments in empowering women in emerging markets. Research also demonstrates a strong correlation between higher degrees of gender diversity in the leadership ranks of business and organizational performance. The World Bank finds that by eliminating discrimination against female workers and managers, managers could significantly increase productivity per worker by 25 to 40 percent. Reducing barriers preventing women from working in certain sectors would lower the productivity gap between male and female workers by a third to one half across a range of countries.

Hillary Clinton served as secretary of state for then president Barack Obama from 2009 to 2013. The speech was given in September 2011.

Reading, Writing, and Discussion Questions

1. What is the major premise in this passage from Clinton's speech?
2. What is the relationship between the first sentence and the rest of the paragraph?

Common Fallacies

In this necessarily brief review it would be impossible to discuss all the fallacies listed by logicians, but we can examine the ones most likely to be found in the arguments you will read and write. Fallacies are difficult to classify, first, because there are literally dozens of systems for classifying, and second, because under any system there is always a good deal of overlap. It's helpful to remember that even if you cannot name the particular fallacy, you can learn to recognize it and not only refute it in the arguments of others but avoid it in your own as well.

> **RESEARCH SKILL** | **Structuring Your Research with Generalizations and Specifics**
>
> Whether you approach the subject of your research inductively or deductively, you will need to be aware throughout the research process of the relationship between generalizations and specifics. You may start with an idea that you want to support (a working thesis for deductive arguments), or you may do research to arrive at a general conclusion (induction). You do yourself a disservice, however, and risk producing a flawed argument, if you view research as a quest for specific information that will support that stand. You have to be open to information that you come across that does not fit neatly under your thesis, since the whole point of deductive research is to link specifics with the generalizations they support or, on the other inductive hand, to adapt generalizations to match what your research reveals. That does not mean ignoring what doesn't fit.
>
> If you approach your research inductively, you may be more flexible about considering all of the specific information you come across. That doesn't mean that you have no idea where your research might lead — although it could — but it means, again, being open to what you find and willing to adapt your thesis as you go through the research process.
>
> Whether you start with the big idea and apply it to specifics or build from the specifics toward a generalization, the relationships between general and specific can give a very natural structure to your writing. Your broadest generalization or conclusion will be your thesis, and the specifics will be your supporting paragraphs. Within paragraphs, the specifics will support topic sentences that together support your thesis. This very basic structure for an essay grew out of the fact that linking the general and the specific inductively and deductively is the way that the human mind naturally works.

Hasty Generalization

Many of our prejudices are a result of **hasty generalization**. A prejudice is literally a judgment made before the facts are in. On the basis of experience with two or three members of an ethnic group, for example, we may form the prejudice that all members of the group share the characteristics that we have attributed to the two or three in our experience.

Superstitions are also based in part on hasty generalization. As a result of a very small number of experiences with black cats, broken mirrors, Friday the thirteenth, or spilled salt, some people will assume a cause-and-effect relation between these signs and misfortunes. *Superstition* has been defined as "a notion maintained despite evidence to the contrary." The evidence would certainly show that contrary to the superstitious belief, in a lifetime, hundreds of such "unlucky" signs are not followed by unfortunate events. To generalize about a connection is therefore unjustified.

Any generalization based on too few particular instances is a hasty generalization. Since we seldom have the chance to observe every possible instance before arriving at a generalization, we have to interpret what "too few" means in a particular context. Here are some examples of hasty generalizations:

- I got a parking ticket for parking on the street before I got my permit and another ticket for parking facing the wrong way on the street. These police in Columbia are just out to make money off of college students!
- That elderly driver cut me off. Old people shouldn't be allowed to drive.
- I studied for my first two statistics tests and still failed. I'm not going to even bother to study for the final because I'm going to fail it anyway.
- I've got to wear my lucky Clemson shirt! We never lose when I wear it!
- It made me really nervous having that family of Muslims on my flight.

Faulty Use of Authority

The use of authority—the attempt to bolster claims by citing the opinions of experts—was discussed in Chapter 7. Experts are a valuable source of information on subjects we have no personal experience with or specialized knowledge about. Properly identified, they can provide essential support. The **faulty use of authority** occurs when individuals are presented as authorities in fields in which they are not. An actor who plays a doctor on television may be hired to advertise the latest sleep medicine but actually has no more expertise with medications than the average consumer. The role that he plays may make him appear to be an authority but does not make him one. No matter how impressive credentials sound, they are largely meaningless unless they establish relevant authority.

Vintage ads are a rich source of false use of authority:

- More doctors smoke Camels than any other cigarettes. (1949)
- For Sun Giant Raisins: Horror film star Vincent Price says, "Around my kitchen this is raisin time of year . . . because raisins are good, and good for you." (1974)

- The Soda Pop Board of America claimed that laboratory tests have proven that babies who start drinking soda early have a much higher chance of gaining acceptance and "fitting in" during the preteen years. (2002 parody)

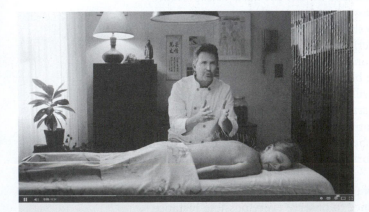

FIGURE 12.1   Holiday Inn Express commercial

In a series of popular television commercials for Holiday Inn Express that ran for eleven years starting in 1998 and then were started again in 2013, ordinary people step in to perform the role of professionals. (See Fig. 12.1.) When it is discovered that they are not professionals as others assumed, the retort is always the same: "But I stayed at a Holiday Inn Express last night." In one of the ads a woman relaxes under what she assumes to be the talented hands of a skilled acupuncturist, only to find that his sole claim to authority is what hotel he stayed at the night before.

Post Hoc or Doubtful Cause

The entire Latin term for this fallacy is *post hoc, ergo propter hoc*, meaning, "After this, therefore because of this." The arguer infers that because one event follows another event, the first event must be the cause of the second. But proximity of events or conditions does not guarantee a causal relation, as you can see from the following examples of the post hoc fallacy:

- The rooster crows every morning at 5:00 and, seeing the sun rise immediately after, decides that his crowing has caused the sun to rise.
- A month after A-bomb tests are concluded, tornadoes damage the area where the tests were held, and residents decide that the tests caused the tornadoes.
- After the school principal suspends daily prayers in the classroom, acts of vandalism increase, and some parents are convinced that failure to conduct prayer is responsible for the rise in vandalism.

In each of these cases, the fact that one event follows another does not prove a causal connection. The two events may be coincidental, or the first event may be only one—and an insignificant one—of many causes that have produced the second event. The reader or writer of causal arguments must determine whether another more plausible explanation exists and whether several causes have combined to produce the effect. Perhaps the suspension of prayer was only one of a number of related causes: a decline in disciplinary action, a relaxation of academic standards, a change in school administration, and changes in family structure in the school community.

In the social sciences, cause-and-effect relations are especially susceptible to challenge. Human experiences can seldom be subjected to laboratory conditions. In addition, the complexity of the social environment makes it difficult, even impossible, to extract one cause from among the many that influence human behavior.

False Analogy

Many analogies are merely descriptive and offer no proof of the connection between the two things being compared. An analogy is called a **false analogy** when two things are compared to each other on the basis of superficial similarities while significant dissimilarities are ignored. Some examples:

- Bill Clinton had no experience of serving in the military. To have Bill Clinton become president, and thus commander-in-chief of the armed forces of the United States, was like electing some passerby on the street to fly the space shuttle.

- Students should be allowed to look at their textbooks during examinations. After all, surgeons have X-rays to guide them during an operation; lawyers have briefs to guide them during a trial; carpenters have blueprints to guide them when building a house. Why, then, shouldn't students be allowed to look at their textbooks during an examination?
- Education cannot prepare men and women for marriage. Trying to educate them for marriage is like trying to teach them to swim without allowing them to go into the water. It can't be done.
- People are like dogs. They respond best to clear discipline.

Ad Hominem

The Latin term *ad hominem* means "against the man" and refers to an attack on the person rather than on the argument or the issue. The assumption in such a fallacy is that if the speaker proves to be unacceptable in some way, his or her statements must also be judged unacceptable. Attacking the author of the statement is a strategy of diversion that prevents the reader from giving attention where it is due — to the issue under discussion.

You might hear someone complain, "What can the priest tell us about marriage? He's never been married himself." This ad hominem accusation ignores the validity of the advice the priest might offer. In the same way, a patient might reject advice on diet by an overweight physician. In politics, it is not uncommon for antagonists to attack each other for personal characteristics that may not be relevant to the tasks they will be elected to perform. They may be criticized for infidelity to their partners, age, atheism, or a flamboyant social life. Even if certain assertions should be proved true, voters should not ignore the substance of what politicians do and say in their public offices.

Some examples of ad hominem assertions:

- I wouldn't vote for Higgins because he left his wife and three kids to run off with his secretary.
- The CEO of that company is too young, so I wouldn't buy its products.
- She shouldn't serve on the school board; she has two children and has never been married!

Ad hominem accusations against the person do *not* constitute a fallacy if the characteristics under attack are relevant to the argument. If the politician is irresponsible and dishonest in the conduct of his or her personal life, we may be justified in thinking that the person will also behave irresponsibly and dishonestly in public office.

False Dilemma

As the name tells us, the **false dilemma**, sometimes called the "black-white fallacy," poses an either-or situation. The arguer suggests that only two alternatives exist, although there may be other explanations of or solutions to the

David Frent/Getty Images

problem under discussion. The false dilemma reflects the simplification of a complex problem. Sometimes it is offered out of ignorance or laziness, sometimes to divert attention from the real explanation or solution that the arguer rejects for doubtful reasons.

You may encounter the either-or situation in dilemmas about personal choices. "At the University of Georgia," says one writer, "the measure of a man was football. You either played it or worshipped those who did, and there was no middle ground."[4] Clearly, this dilemma—playing football or worshiping those who do—ignores other measures of manhood.

Politics and government offer a wealth of examples:

- U.S.A.: Love it or leave it.
- If we don't end our dependence on oil, we will destroy our children's future.
- Either you are with us, or you are with the terrorists.

In an interview with the *New York Times* in 1975, the Shah of Iran was asked why he could not introduce into his authoritarian regime greater freedom for his subjects. His reply was, "What's wrong with authority? Is anarchy better?"

Slippery Slope

If an arguer predicts that taking a first step will lead inevitably to a second, usually undesirable step, he or she must provide evidence that this will happen. Otherwise, the arguer is guilty of a **slippery-slope** fallacy.

Predictions based on the danger inherent in taking the first step are commonplace. In a speech to Congress on October 27, 1999, Independent

---

[4] Phil Gailey, "A Nonsports Fan," *New York Times Magazine*, December 18, 1983, 96.

presidential candidate Ron Paul said, "I am strongly pro-life. I think one of the most disastrous rulings of this century was *Roe versus Wade*. I do believe in the slippery-slope theory. I believe that if people are careless and casual about life at the beginning of life, we will be careless and casual about life at the end. Abortion leads to euthanasia. I believe that." Here are other examples:

- The Connecticut law allowing sixteen-year-olds and their parents to divorce each other will mean the death of the family.
- If we ban handguns, we will end up banning rifles and other hunting weapons.

Slippery-slope predictions are simplistic. They ignore not only the dissimilarities between first and last steps but also the complexity of the developments in any long chain of events.

Begging the Question

If the writer makes a statement that assumes that the very question being argued has already been proved, the writer is guilty of **begging the question**. In a letter to the editor of a college newspaper protesting the failure of the majority of students to meet the writing requirement because they had failed an exemption test, the writer said, "Not exempting all students who honestly qualify for exemption is an insult." But whether the students are honestly qualified is precisely the question that the exemption test was supposed to resolve. The writer has not proved that the students who failed the writing test were qualified for exemption. She has only made an assertion *as if* she had already proved it.

Circular reasoning is an extreme example of begging the question: "Women should not be permitted to join men's clubs because the clubs are for men only." The question to be resolved first, of course, is whether clubs for men only should continue to exist.

Other examples:

- I hate soccer because it's a sport I just don't like.
- The reason these clubs are in such demand is that everyone wants to get in them.
- Freedom of speech is important because people should be able to speak freely.

Straw Man

The **straw-man** fallacy consists of an attack on a view similar to but not the same as the one your opponent holds. It is a familiar diversionary tactic. The name probably derives from an old game in which a straw man was set up to divert attention from the real target that a contestant was supposed to knock down.

Notice how in the following passage about New York mayor Michael Bloomberg's proposed 2012 ban on the sale of sugary drinks larger than sixteen ounces, conservative pundit George Will shifts the focus from that proposed restriction to global warming:

> "Liberals are so enamored over the issue of climate change," Will continued. "They say all our behaviors in some way affect the climate, therefore, the government—meaning, we liberals, the party of government—can fine tune all your behavior right down to the light bulbs you use."[5]

Red Herring

Another diversionary tactic is the **red herring**. The straw man is an attempt to draw an opponent's attention to an issue similar to but not exactly what the opponent was talking about that the speaker or writer can better address. A red herring is an attempt to divert attention away from the subject at hand to *any* other subject, not just one related to the original subject.

An outstanding example of the red herring fallacy occurred in the famous Checkers speech of Senator Richard Nixon. In 1952, during his vice-presidential campaign, Nixon was accused of having appropriated $18,000 in campaign funds for his personal use. At one point in the radio and television speech in which he defended his reputation, he said:

> One other thing I probably should tell you, because if I don't they will probably be saying this about me, too. We did get something, a gift, after the election.
>
> A man down in Texas heard Pat on the radio mention the fact that our two youngsters would like to have a dog, and, believe it or not, the day before we left on this campaign trip we got a message from Union Station in Baltimore saying they had a package for us. We went down to get it. You know what it was?
>
> It was a little cocker spaniel dog, in a crate that he had sent all the way from Texas, black and white, spotted, and our little girl, Tricia, the six-year-old, named it Checkers.
>
> And, you know, the kids, like all kids, loved the dog, and I just want to say this, right now, that regardless of what they say about it, we are going to keep it.[6]

Of course, Nixon knew that the issue was the alleged misappropriation of funds, not the ownership of the dog, which no one had asked him to return.

---

[5] David Edwards, "George Will Uses Bloomberg's Soda Ban to Blast Climate Change Laws," *Raw Story*, June 3, 2012, http://www.rawstory.com/2012/06/george-will-uses-bloombergs-soda-ban-to-blast-climate-change-laws/.
[6] Radio and television address of Senator Nixon from Los Angeles on September 23, 1952.

Two Wrongs Make a Right

The **two-wrongs-make-a-right** fallacy is another example of the way in which attention may be diverted from the question at issue.

After President Jimmy Carter in March 1977 attacked the human rights record of the Soviet Union, Russian officials responded:

> As for the present state of human rights in the United States, it is characterized by the following facts: millions of unemployed, racial discrimination, social inequality of women, infringement of citizens' personal freedom, the growth of crime, and so on.

The Russians made no attempt to deny the failure of *their* human rights record; instead they attacked by pointing out that the Americans are not blameless either.

Other examples:

- Anyone who killed those innocent children deserves the death penalty.
- It's okay to use chemical weapons against the U.S. since the U.S. used them against Vietnam.
- I had every right to take his Xbox. He broke mine!

Non Sequitur

The Latin term *non sequitur*, which means "it does not follow," is another fallacy of irrelevance. An advertisement for a book, *Worlds in Collision*, whose

theories about the origin of the earth and evolutionary development have been challenged by almost all reputable scientists, states:

> Once rejected as "preposterous"! Critics called it an outrage! It aroused incredible antagonism in scientific and literary circles. Yet half a million copies were sold and for twenty-seven years it remained an outstanding bestseller.

We know, of course, that the popularity of a book does not bestow scientific respectability. The number of sales, therefore, is irrelevant to proof of the book's theoretical soundness—a *non sequitur*.

Other examples sometimes appear in comments by politicians and political candidates. In June 2010, President Obama said, "After all, oil is a finite resource. We consume more than 20 percent of the world's oil, but have less than 2 percent of the world's oil reserves."[7] This is a non sequitur because the relevant relationship would be between the U.S. percentage of world *population* (not oil reserves) and the U.S. percentage of world oil consumption.

Ad Populum

Arguers guilty of the **ad populum** fallacy make an appeal to the prejudices of the people (*populum* in Latin). They assume that their claim can be adequately defended without further support if they emphasize a belief or attitude that the audience shares with them. One common form of *ad populum* is an appeal to patriotism, which may enable arguers to omit evidence that the audience needs for proper evaluation of the claim. In the following advertisement, the makers of Zippo lighters made such an appeal in urging readers to buy their product:

> It's a grand old lighter. Zippo—the grand old lighter that's made right here in the good old U.S.A.
>
> We truly make an all-American product. The raw materials used in making a Zippo lighter are all right from this great land of ours.

Other examples:

- But you have to let me go to the party! *Everyone* will be there!
- Everybody drives a little over the speed limit. If I drove the speed limit, I would get rear-ended!
- Lipton Ice Tea. Join the Dance.

---

[7] Glen Kessler, "U.S. Oil Resources: President Obama's 'Non Sequitur Facts,'" *Washington Post*, March 15, 2012, http://www.washingtonpost.com/blogs/fact-checker/post/us-oil-resources -president-obamas-non-sequitur-facts/2012/03/14/gIQApP14CS_blog.html.

Appeal to Tradition

In making an **appeal to tradition**, the arguer assumes that what has existed for a long time and has therefore become a tradition should continue to exist *because* it is a tradition. If the arguer avoids telling his or her reader *why* the tradition should be preserved, he or she may be accused of failing to meet the real issue.

The following statement appeared in a letter defending the membership policy of the Century Club, an all-male club established in New York City in 1847 that was under pressure to admit women. The writer was a Presbyterian minister who opposed the admission of women.

> I am totally opposed to a proposal which would radically change the nature of the Century. . . . A club creates an ethos of its own over the years, and I would deeply deplore a step that would inevitably create an entirely different kind of place.[8]

Numerous activities continue "because it's always been done that way." They range from debutante balls that may seem out of sync with modern times to football traditions. Texas A&M students were so devoted to the massive bonfire that marked the approach of their game with rival University of Texas that it was continued off campus, unsanctioned by the school, even after eleven students and one former student died during a collapse of the stacked wood in 1999. Tradition in and of itself is not a bad thing, but discrimination, injustice, and unsafe behaviors have often been prolonged in the name of tradition.

Strategies for Uncovering Logical Fallacies

1. If your source is making use of induction — that is, drawing a conclusion based on a number of individual examples — ask yourself if it has enough examples with variety to justify the conclusion. In other words, will your readers be able to make the inductive leap from examples to the conclusion you are asking them to make?

2. If your source is making use of deduction, is its conclusion a logical one based on the premises underlying it? To be sure, write out its argument in the form of a syllogism, and confirm that both the major and the minor premises are true.

3. Avoid sources that word their thesis statements in absolute terms like *all, every, everyone, everybody,* and *always.*

4. Use the list of fallacies in this chapter as a checklist while you read each of your sources with a critical eye, looking for any breakdown in logic.

---

[8] David H. C. Read, letter to the *New York Times,* January 13, 1983, 14.

Practice

Decide whether the reasoning in the following examples is faulty. Use the common fallacies presented in the previous pages to explain your answers.

1. The presiding judge of a revolutionary tribunal, being asked why people are being executed without trial, replies, "Why should we put them on trial when we know that they're guilty?"

2. The government has the right to require the wearing of helmets while operating or riding on a motorcycle because of the high rate of head injuries incurred in motorcycle accidents.

3. Children who watch game shows rather than situation comedies receive higher grades in school. So it must be true that game shows are more educational than situation comedies.

4. The meteorologist predicted the wrong amount of rain for May. Obviously, the meteorologist is unreliable.

5. Women ought to be registered in the Selective Service System. Why should men be the only ones to face death and danger?

6. If Michelle Obama uses Truvia, it must taste better than Splenda.

7. People will gamble anyway, so why not legalize gambling in this state?

8. Because so much money was spent on public education in the last decade while educational achievement declined, more money to improve education can't be the answer to reversing the decline.

9. He's a columnist for a campus newspaper, so he must be a pretty good writer.

10. We tend to exaggerate the need for Standard English. You don't need much Standard English for most jobs in this country.

11. It's discriminatory to mandate that police officers must conform to a certain height and weight.

12. A doctor can charge for a missed appointment, so patients should be charged less when a doctor keeps them waiting.

13. Because this soft drink contains so many chemicals, it must be unsafe.

14. Core requirements should be eliminated. After all, students are paying for their education, so they should be able to earn a diploma by choosing the courses they want.

15. We should encourage a return to arranged marriages in this country since marriages based on romantic love haven't been very successful.

16. I know three redheads who have terrible tempers, and since Annabel has red hair, I'll bet she has a terrible temper, too.

17. Supreme Court Justice Byron White was an all-American football player while in college, so how can you say that athletes are dumb?

18. Benjamin H. Sasway, a student at Humboldt State University in California, was indicted for failure to register for possible conscription. Barry Lynn, president of Draft Action, an antidraft group, said, "It is disgraceful that this

administration is embarking on an effort to fill the prisons with men of conscience and moral commitment."

19. James A. Harris, former president of the National Education Association: "Twenty-three percent of schoolchildren are failing to graduate and another large segment graduates as functional illiterates. If 23 percent of anything else failed—23 percent of automobiles didn't run, 23 percent of the buildings fell down, 23 percent of stuffed ham spoiled—we'd look at the producer."

20. A professor at Rutgers University: "The arrest rate for women is rising three times as fast as that of men. Women, inflamed by the doctrines of feminism, are pursuing criminal careers with the same zeal as business and the professions."

21. Physical education should be required because physical activity is healthful.

22. George Meany, former president of the AFL-CIO, in 1968: "To these people who constantly say you have got to listen to these younger people, they have got something to say, I just don't buy that at all. They smoke more pot than we do and if the younger generation are the hundred thousand kids that lay around a field up in Woodstock, New York, I am not going to trust the destiny of the country to that group."

23. That candidate was poor as a child, so he will certainly be sympathetic to the poor if he's elected.

24. When the federal government sent troops into Little Rock, Arkansas, to enforce integration of the public school system, the governor of Arkansas attacked the action, saying that it was as brutal an act of intervention as Russia's sending troops into Hungary to squelch the Hungarians' rebellion. In both cases, the governor said, the rights of a freedom-loving, independent people were being violated.

25. Governor Jones was elected two years ago. Since that time, constant examples of corruption and subversion have been unearthed. It is time to get rid of the man responsible for this kind of corrupt government.

26. Are we going to vote a pay increase for our teachers, or are we going to allow our schools to deteriorate into substandard custodial institutions?

27. You see, the priests were right. After we threw those virgins into the volcano, it quit erupting.

28. The people of Rome lost their vitality and desire for freedom when their emperors decided that the way to keep them happy was to provide them with bread and circuses. What can we expect of our own country now that the government gives people free food and there is a constant round of entertainment provided by television?

29. From Mark Clifton, "The Dread Tomato Affliction" (proving that eating tomatoes is dangerous and even deadly): "Ninety-two point four percent of juvenile delinquents have eaten tomatoes. Fifty-seven point one percent of the adult criminals in penitentiaries throughout the United States have eaten tomatoes. Eighty-four percent of all people killed in automobile accidents during the year have eaten tomatoes."

30. From Galileo, *Dialogues Concerning Two New Sciences*: "But can you doubt that air has weight when you have the clear testimony of Aristotle affirming that all elements have weight, including air, and excepting only fire?"

31. Robert Brustein, artistic director of the American Repertory Theater, commenting on a threat by Congress in 1989 to withhold funding from an offensive art show: "Once we allow lawmakers to become art critics, we take the first step into the world of Ayatollah Khomeini, whose murderous review of *The Satanic Verses* still chills the heart of everyone committed to free expression." (The Ayatollah Khomeini called for the death of the author Salman Rushdie because Rushdie had allegedly committed blasphemy against Islam in his novel.)

READING ARGUMENT

Seeing Logical Fallacies

The following essay has been annotated to point out places where the author finds logical fallacies with cyclists' demands for road privileges. Annotations also note logical problems with the author's argument.

Drivers Get Rolled
CHRISTOPHER CALDWELL

Late last August, along the coast of New Hampshire, Kevin Walsh, police chief in the town of Rye, got a lecture on law enforcement from a bunch of grown-up bicyclists. Local law requires bikers to ride single-file when there is traffic. But this day, a pack of a dozen or so bikers were racing down Ocean Boulevard, at high speed, up to five abreast, according to an interview the chief later gave. Walsh decided to flag them down and tell them what they were doing was unsafe, "out of control," and "an accident waiting to happen." He stood in the middle of Ocean Boulevard and signaled them to stop. The bikers blew past him in a whoosh! of Lycra, sweat, and profanity. Walsh got in his cruiser and cut off the bikers four miles up the road. When he stopped them, they began to chew him out. "You almost killed somebody back there, standing in the middle of the road," one of them screamed at the cop. "Do you understand we can't stop? Do you understand we can't stop like a car?"

The bikers are setting up a straw man to divert blame from themselves.

Christopher Caldwell is a journalist and former senior editor at the *Weekly Standard*, where this article appeared on November 18, 2013. He has also written frequently for the *Wall Street Journal*, the *New York Times*, and the *Washington Post*, among many other publications.

Shows the false analogy:
If they can't stop like a car,
they shouldn't expect the
rights of drivers.

Like many episodes in the world of adult recreational cycling, this one breaks new ground in the annals of chutzpah. Few non-cyclists would think to scold a law enforcement official for having nearly been run over by them. Fewer still would release to the news media a video of the incident—which came from a camera mounted on the handlebars of one of the bikers—in the almost demented belief that it constituted a vindication rather than an incrimination. And yet you can see it online.

Incidents like this now happen every day. Laws governing bikes on roads have never been crystal-clear, and have always been marked by a degree of common sense and compromise. An increase in racing and commuting bikers has altered what passes for common sense. Cyclists like the ones in New Hampshire, whose reckless riding and self-righteousness have earned rolled eyes nationwide and the nickname of "Lycra louts" in England, have tested the public's willingness for compromise. As bicyclists become an ever more powerful lobby, ever more confident in the good they are doing for the environment and public health, they are discovering—to their sincere surprise—that they are provoking mistrust and even hostility among the public.

Transported

When there are more bicyclists on the road, when most bicyclists are no longer children and teens, and when well-built bikes can easily descend a hill at 50 miles an hour, new questions come up. The first is how we are to think of bikes. Are they like really fast pedestrians? Or like cars with a lower maximum speed? The law's general view is that they are vehicles. But what the law really means is not that bikes are exactly like cars but that they are analogous. You don't need to get a license to ride a bike, you don't need your vehicle inspected to put it on the road, and you aren't charged tax for the upkeep of highways. There is considerable ambiguity here, and activist bikers, with lawyerly sophistication, almost unfailingly claim the best of both worlds. Consider the guy we mentioned above who insisted police chief Walsh give him all the rights of the road for a vehicle he claimed to be unable to stop. Bicyclists are exactly like cars when it suits them—as when they occupy the middle of a lane in rush hour. But they are different when it suits them—going 18 mph in that very same lane even though the posted speed is 45, riding two abreast, running red lights if there's nothing coming either way, passing vehicles on the right when there's a right turn coming up. This makes bikes a source of unpredictability, frustration, and danger.

Shows why the analogy
between cars and bikes
works only part of the time

This should not alarm us unduly. Bicyclists sometimes do require the middle of the roadway, and do need special consideration. The rightmost

5

part of the road is often punctuated with old-fashioned sewer grates that will swallow a tire whole and fling you over the handlebars. There are broken bottles, dropped hypodermic needles, oil slicks that have drained off the road's crown, and places where the road is frittered away. The right side of the road is also where passenger doors get flung open, sometimes suddenly, and one piece of bad timing will send you to kingdom come. Almost 700 cyclists died on the road in the United States in 2011. Let us not forget the environmental, aesthetic, and health benefits of cycling over driving, which are obvious and undeniable.

A reminder of the dangers of bicycling

The problem is that our transportation network, built at the cost of trillions over the decades, is already over capacity, as the Obama administration was fond of reminding us when arguing for the 2009 stimulus package. It is not so easily rejiggered. Unquestionably we have misbuilt our transport grid. It makes us car-dependent. It should better accommodate bikers and walkers. But for now it can't. Unless you want to cover much more of the country in asphalt — which is far from the professed wishes of bikers — lane space is finite. There are few places in America where public transportation can serve as a serious alternative to driving. In only five metropolitan areas — Boston, New York, Washington, Chicago, and San Francisco — do as many as 10 percent of commuters take public transportation.

A simple if unfortunate fact: Our transportation network was not built to accommodate bicycles.

So, except in a few spots where roads were built too wide and can now accommodate bike paths, adding bicycles to the mix means squeezing cars. Bike-riders don't "share" the road so much as take it over. Their wish is generally that the right-hand lane of any major or medium-sized road be turned into a bike lane or, at best, a shared-use lane. This would place drivers in a position of second-class citizenship on roads that were purpose-built for them. There are simply not enough cyclists to make that a reasonable idea. What is going on is the attempt of an organized private interest to claim a public good. Cyclists remind one of those residents in exurban subdivisions who, over years, allow grass and shrubbery to encroach on dirt public sidewalk until it becomes indistinguishable from their yards, and then sneakily fence it in.

False dilemma: Private interest and public good do not have to be mutually exclusive.

Our numbers about how many people bike and how often are relatively imprecise. The best estimates come from counting commutes and accidents. According to the U.S. census, 120 million people drive to work every weekday, and 750,000 bike. In other words, there are 160 drivers for every biker. Bike use is growing — but even at 40 times the present level it would still not be sensible public policy to squander a quarter, a third, or half of the lane space on a busy rush-hour artery for a bike lane.

Bike riding could be the wave of the future, or it could be a sports fad, the way tennis was in the 1970s or skateboarding in the 1980s or golf in the 1990s. It is hard to tell, since bike riding is now the beneficiary of vast public and private subsidies and massive infrastructure projects, from Indianapolis's $100 million plan to add bike lanes and other nonauto byways to Citibank's underwriting of the New York City bike-share program. "Subsidize it and they will come," could be the motto. Drivers are being taxed to subsidize their own eviction.

High Rollers

There are a number of internationally recognized signals through which   10
bicyclists convey their intentions to drivers. The raised left hand means a right turn, the dropped left hand means slowing down, and so on. I have never seen either of these gestures used. Instead, cyclists tend to communicate with motorists through a simpler, all-purpose gesture, the raised middle finger.

Hasty generalization: Not all bikers are rude.

The self-righteousness, the aplomb, of bicyclists is their stereotypical vice and quirk, like the madness of hatters, the drunkenness of poets, and the communism of furriers.

The attitude was nicely captured in a pro-biking letter to the editor in the *Brookline TAB*, the community paper for Boston's richest neighborhoods: "Whenever someone bikes or walks to the store or to work," the writer began, "he or she is taking one automobile off the road and making a significant contribution both to Brookline's safety and to reducing the carbons so dangerous to life on earth." You see? It only looks like I'm having a midlife crisis—I'm actually on a rescue mission! The question of what courtesy the cyclist owes the community is immediately taken off the table, replaced by the question of what the community can possibly do to repay its debt to the cyclist.

The virtues of biking are irrelevant to the issue of biking safely.

All of us who care about the environment have a sense—even a conviction—that biking is more virtuous than driving. What distinguishes the biking enthusiast is that he is just as convinced that biking is more virtuous than walking: "While riding," another *TAB* correspondent wrote, "I have encountered pedestrians who are texting. They are a danger to themselves and others, because they sometimes make erratic movements and often ignore requests to step to the side so a bicycle can pass." By "request," the writer probably means a barked command of "On your right!" or "On your left!" made by a cyclist approaching from behind at 30 mph.

If bicyclists have a more highly developed sense that they can boss others around, this is because they disproportionately belong to the classes from which bosses come. They are, to judge from their blogs, more aggrieved by delivery trucks parked in bike lanes than drivers are by delivery trucks parked in car lanes. This may be because proportionately fewer of them have ever met a person who drives a delivery truck. The 2011 accident data of the National Highway Traffic Safety Administration give us a hint that ardent bicycling is not, for the most part, a youthful avocation, as those whose biking days ended in the 1970s or '80s might assume. The average age of those killed cycling—presumably a rough proxy for those doing the most grueling road riding—has been rising by close to a year annually. In 2003 it was 36; in 2011 it was 43. Cyclists are heavily weighted towards the baby boom generation. The group involved in the most fatal accidents in 2011 is ages 45–54, followed by ages 55–64. The two cohorts make up those born between 1947 and 1966.

This generation is at the height of its earning power, and bikers are drawn from the very richest part of it. Shortly after Birmingham, England, got almost $30 million from the government to make itself more bike-friendly, the *Birmingham Post* researched who was building bike spaces in London. Topping the list were the Gherkin, the ghastly Norman Foster–designed skyscraper in the financial district that houses a lot of London's financial-services industry; Goldman Sachs's Fleet Street headquarters; and London Wall Place, a high-end office building slated for construction in the City. This helps explain why Portland, Oregon, is so proud of its status as the country's most "bicycle-friendly" city, and why Las Vegas, Louisville, and other places are vying to outdo it. City officials want to be "bicycle-friendly" for the same reason they want to be "gay-friendly" or "internet-friendly," and for the same reason they built opera houses in the nineteenth century and art museums in the twentieth—it is a way of telling investors: "Rich people live here."

15   Once you understand that bicycling is a rich person's hobby, you can understand the fallacy that *Slate* editor David Plotz, an ardent bicyclist, committed when he asked why such a large number of dangerous drivers he encountered while cycling to work drove the same make of car. Of the twenty scares he's had in his life, ten came from BMWs. "In other words," Plotz wrote, "the BMW, a car that has less than 2 percent market share in the United States, was responsible for 50 percent of the menacing." Why, he wondered? Was it a sense of entitlement, or were BMW-drivers just "assholes"? Probably neither—it is that luxury-car-driving and bike-commuting are heavily concentrated in the same very top sliver of the American class hierarchy. The percentage of BMWs driving between where the average cyclist

Doubtful cause: Is that why cities want to be bicycle friendly?

False dilemma: Feeling entitled and being assholes are not the only alternatives.

lives to where the average cyclist works is a heck of a lot higher than 2 percent. It may not be 50 percent—the Help, after all, needs to use these roads, too—but it is high.

Wheel Estate

If bike-friendly areas are rich neighborhoods, they are a particular kind of rich neighborhood. They are college towns, or at least "latte towns," to use the term David Brooks coined in these pages. The top cities for cycling commuters, according to the U.S. census, are Corvallis and Eugene in Oregon, Fort Collins and Boulder in Colorado, and Missoula, Montana. The census notes that Portland, Oregon, is the only metropolitan area in which at least 2 percent of commutes are by bike.

Its concentration in cultural hubs has consequences. Bicycling's apostles have behind them not just the economic and lobbying power of the "One Percent," but also the cultural and intellectual power of its most sophisticated members. The idea that there might be alternative social goods competing with cycling, or any reason not to offer cyclists as much leeway and indulgence as they might demand, seems scarcely to have occurred to anybody who discusses it in public. That, surely, is why a cyclist might think that posting a video of a cyclist scolding a well-meaning New Hampshire police chief might help the cycling cause. The promotion of cycling is open to discussion as to means, but not as to ends. The question is how, not whether, to build more bike infrastructure; and how, not whether, to educate motorists about their responsibilities to bikers. It is never about educating bicyclists on how to find alternative modes of transport.

Leaders of the biking community, though, most often try to cast themselves as an underprivileged minority. Ian Walker, a "traffic psychologist" from the University of Bath, describes cyclists as a "minority outgroup"—they suffer in a society that "views cycling as anti-conventional and possibly even infantile." In an August editorial calling for an end to "anti-cyclist bias," the *San Francisco Bay Guardian* opined: "To focus exclusively on the behavior of cyclists is like blaming a rape victim for wearing a short skirt."

As is not uncommon when progressive utopias are being constructed, there are a number of informal activist groups for enforcing opinion. The Twitter feed CycleHatred was founded in Britain to expose those who wrote negative things about cyclists, although recent press reports have implicitly questioned whether such exposure might do the anti-cycling cause more good than harm. The cycling journalist Peter Walker of the *Guardian* commented on a Tweet

Bicyclists expect privileges.

False analogy

(probably good-humored) attacking Britain's Olympic gold medalist Bradley Wiggins for having made cycling popular ("If Wiggins came in here, I'd give him a piece of my mind"). Ian Walker responded:

> This is a fantastic example of what is sometimes called the "cyclists should get their house in order" argument—that people who have nothing in common except choosing cycling as one of their several regular forms of transport are nonetheless necessarily defined by it, and are somehow responsible for the worst actions by others on bikes.

Walker points out the hasty generalization.

20   But this is a category error. That our road system cannot provide the resources to support cyclists in the style to which they would like to become accustomed is a matter of policy and limited resources, not of civil rights and prejudice. An action that is ignorable at the individual level—such as cycling down the middle of the street at high speed—can become a problem when the masses do it. That is why, for instance, people have been forbidden to burn leaves in their backyard for the past half-century. One pile of leaves is a beautiful smell. Several are a pollution problem, or so they tell us. Right or wrong, those who consider leaf burning a problem are not making a bigoted assessment of the personalities of the individual leaf-burners.

Bikers' unmet needs, in terms of both infrastructure and law, are limitless. A common trope is to compare America's spending on bikes with that of the Netherlands. Amsterdam spends $39 per resident on bike trails, laments the *Boston Globe*, while Boston spends under $2. Until we shell out as much as the Dutch, there can be no such thing as misspent money. Pointing to areas, mostly poor, in which Washington, D.C.'s Capital Bikeshare program has failed to win a following, the director of the program assured the *Washington Post* that "those areas where the bike community is not yet self-sustaining" are "precisely where the District Department of Transportation needs to double its efforts."

The analogy is incomplete unless the number of bikers is also compared.

The bicycle agenda is coming to resemble the feminist agenda from the 1970s, when previously all-male universities went co-ed. Everything that was ever off-limits to the aggrieved minority must be opened up, while sancta established for the minority in the old days must be preserved, and new ones founded. So bikers must have access to roads and hiking trails, but also get their own new "bike boulevards." Having a special bike-friendly highway, such as Route 9W, west of the Hudson River, does not mean that certain other highways will ever be closed off to bikes in the interest of efficiency or fairness.

The analogy is not clear.

While it is wrong to call bicyclists a downtrodden minority, they are a minority in one sense. They are one of those compact, issue-oriented small groups that, as the economist Mancur Olson warned in his classic *The Logic of Collective Action* (1965), generally take unmotivated majorities to the cleaners. There are probably a million dedicated cyclists in this country, bent on taking over a quarter or a third of the nation's road space, built at the price of, let us repeat, trillions. They are ranged against the 200 million drivers who have a vague sense they are being duped. But this sense is only vague, and because motorists, like other American voters, have developed the habit of being talked into giving up what is theirs, any wise person would bet on the bicyclists' winning all they ask for. A small collection of elite hobbyists will continue, as Tacitus might have put it, to make a traffic jam and call it peace.

Reading, Writing, and Discussion Questions

1. Explain why the anecdote in the first paragraph is an example of the straw man fallacy.
2. Explain one or more of the examples of false analogy in the article.
3. How convincing is Christopher Caldwell's argument that bicyclists are among our richest citizens? Does your experience seem to support that claim? Explain.
4. Have you experienced or witnessed the sorts of problems between bikers and drivers that Caldwell describes? If so, give an example.
5. In spite of the focus in the annotations on logical fallacies, what strengths does the article have?

Practice: Uncovering Logical Fallacies

Read the following court decision, and answer the questions that follow. It will be useful to keep in mind that the plaintiff, Homer Plessy, although a Creole who could easily have passed for white, was legally "colored" according to the law of that day because he had one eighth African blood. He chose not to deny his African heritage when asked and expected to be arrested or at least to be removed from the train car for whites for which he had bought a ticket.

Plessy v. Ferguson: The Opinion of the Court
HENRY BILLINGS BROWN, U.S. SUPREME COURT

This case turns upon the constitutionality of an act of the general assembly of the state of Louisiana, passed in 1890, providing for separate railway carriages for the white and colored races. Acts 1890, No. 111, p. 152.

The first section of the statute enacts "that all railway companies carrying passengers in their coaches in this state, shall provide equal but separate accommodations for the white, and colored races, by providing two or more passenger coaches for each passenger train, or by dividing the passenger coaches by a partition so as to secure separate accommodations: provided, that this section shall not be construed to apply to street railroads. No person or persons shall be permitted to occupy seats in coaches, other than the ones assigned to them, on account of the race they belong to."

By the second section it was enacted "that the officers of such passenger trains shall have power and are hereby required to assign each passenger to the coach or compartment used for the race to which such passenger belongs; any passenger insisting on going into a coach or compartment to which by race he does not belong, shall be liable to a fine of twenty-five dollars, or in lieu thereof to imprisonment for a period of not more than twenty days in the parish prison, and any officer of any railroad insisting on assigning a passenger to a coach or compartment other than the one set aside for the race to which said passenger belongs, shall be liable to a fine of twenty-five dollars, or in lieu thereof to imprisonment for a period of not more than twenty days in the parish prison; and should any passenger refuse to occupy the coach or compartment to which he or she is assigned by the officer of such railway, said officer shall have power to refuse to carry such passenger on his train, and for such refusal neither he nor the railway company which he represents shall be liable for damages in any of the courts of this state." . . .

The information filed in the criminal district court charged, in substance, that Plessy, being a passenger between two stations within the state of Louisiana, was assigned by officers of the company to the coach used for the race to which he belonged, but he insisted upon going into a coach used by the race to which he did not belong. Neither in the information nor plea was his particular race or color averred.[1]

The petition for the writ of prohibition averred that petitioner was seven-eighths Caucasian and one-eighth African blood; that the mixture of colored blood was not discernible in him; and that he was entitled to every right, privilege, and immunity secured to citizens of the United States of the white race; and that, upon such theory, he took possession of a vacant seat

5

The case of *Plessy v. Ferguson* was a landmark case decided by the Supreme Court in 1896 that established "separate but equal" justification for racial segregation. The plaintiff in error — the person who had brought the case against the railroad and was now appealing the verdict — was Homer Plessy, a resident of Louisiana. The defendant was the Honorable John H. Ferguson, judge of the criminal District Court for the parish of Orleans, where the case was originally heard. Henry Billings Brown was the United States Supreme Court justice who wrote the opinion of the majority of the court.

[1] Alleged as a fact in support of a plea. — EDS. [All notes are the editors'.]

in a coach where passengers of the white race were accommodated, and was ordered by the conductor to vacate said coach, and take a seat in another, assigned to persons of the colored race, and, having refused to comply with such demand, he was forcibly ejected, with the aid of a police officer, and imprisoned in the parish jail to answer a charge of having violated the above act.

The constitutionality of this act is attacked upon the ground that it conflicts both with the Thirteenth Amendment of the Constitution, abolishing slavery, and the Fourteenth Amendment, which prohibits certain restrictive legislation on the part of the states.

1. That it does not conflict with the Thirteenth Amendment, which abolished slavery and involuntary servitude, except as a punishment for crime, is too clear for argument. Slavery implies involuntary servitude, a state of bondage; the ownership of mankind as a chattel, or, at least, the control of the labor and services of one man for the benefit of another, and the absence of a legal right to the disposal of his own person, property, and services. This amendment was said in the Slaughter-House Cases, 16 Wall. 36, to have been intended primarily to abolish slavery, as it had been previously known in this country, and that it equally forbade Mexican peonage or the Chinese coolie trade, when they amounted to slavery or involuntary servitude, and that the use of the word "servitude" was intended to prohibit the use of all forms of involuntary slavery, of whatever class or name. It was intimated,[2] however, in that case, that this amendment was regarded by the statesmen of that day as insufficient to protect the colored race from certain laws which had

been enacted in the Southern states, imposing upon the colored race onerous disabilities and burdens, and curtailing their rights in the pursuit of life, liberty, and property to such an extent that their freedom was of little value; and that the Fourteenth Amendment was devised to meet this exigency.

So, too, in the Civil Rights Cases, 109 U.S. 3, 3 Sup. Ct. 18, it was said that the act of a mere individual, the owner of an inn, a public conveyance or place of amusement, refusing accommodations to colored people, cannot be justly regarded as imposing any badge of slavery or servitude upon the applicant, but only as involving an ordinary civil injury, properly cognizable[3] by the laws of the state, and presumably subject to redress[4] by those laws until the contrary appears. "It would be running the slavery question into the ground," said Mr. Justice Bradley, "to make it apply to every act of discrimination which a person may see fit to make as to the guests he will entertain, or as to the people he will take into his coach or cab or car, or admit to his concert or theater, or deal with in other matters of intercourse or business."

A statute which implies merely a legal distinction between the white and colored races— a distinction which is founded in the color of the two races, and which must always exist so long as white men are distinguished from the other race by color—has no tendency to destroy the legal equality of the two races, or re-establish a state of involuntary servitude. Indeed, we do not understand that the Thirteenth Amendment is strenuously relied upon by the plaintiff in error in this connection.

---

[2] Hinted or suggested.

[3] Within the jurisdiction of.

[4] Remedy or compensation for a wrong or grievance.

10 2. By the Fourteenth Amendment, all persons born or naturalized in the United States, and subject to the jurisdiction thereof, are made citizens of the United States and of the state wherein they reside; and the states are forbidden from making or enforcing any law which shall abridge the privileges or immunities of citizens of the United States, or shall deprive any person of life, liberty, or property without due process of law, or deny to any person within their jurisdiction the equal protection of the laws.

The proper construction of this amendment was first called to the attention of this court in the Slaughter-House Cases, 16 Wall. 36, which involved, however, not a question of race, but one of exclusive privileges. The case did not call for any expression of opinion as to the exact rights it was intended to secure to the colored race, but it was said generally that its main purpose was to establish the citizenship of the negro, to give definitions of citizenship of the United States and of the states, and to protect from the hostile legislation of the states the privileges and immunities of citizens of the United States, as distinguished from those of citizens of the states. The object of the amendment was undoubtedly to enforce the absolute equality of the two races before the law, but, in the nature of things, it could not have been intended to abolish distinctions based upon color, or to enforce social, as distinguished from political, equality, or a commingling of the two races upon terms unsatisfactory to either. Laws permitting, and even requiring, their separation, in places where they are liable to be brought into contact, do not necessarily imply the inferiority of either race to the other, and have been generally, if not universally, recognized as within the competency of the state legislatures in the exercise of their police power. The most common instance of this is connected with the establishment of separate schools for white and colored children, which have been held to be a valid exercise of the legislative power even by courts of states where the political rights of the colored race have been longest and most earnestly enforced.

One of the earliest of these cases is that of Roberts v. City of Boston, 5 Cush. 198, in which the supreme judicial court of Massachusetts held that the general school committee of Boston had power to make provision for the instruction of colored children in separate schools established exclusively for them, and to prohibit their attendance upon the other schools. "The great principle," said Chief Justice Shaw, "advanced by the learned and eloquent advocate for the plaintiff [Mr. Charles Sumner], is that, by the constitution and laws of Massachusetts, all persons, without distinction of age or sex, birth or color, origin or condition, are equal before the law. . . . But, when this great principle comes to be applied to the actual and various conditions of persons in society, it will not warrant the assertion that men and women are legally clothed with the same civil and political powers, and that children and adults are legally to have the same functions and be subject to the same treatment; but only that the rights of all, as they are settled and regulated by law, are equally entitled to the paternal consideration and protection of the law for their maintenance and security." It was held that the powers of the committee extended to the establishment of separate schools for children of different ages, sexes, and colors, and that they might also establish special schools for poor and neglected children, who have become too old to attend the primary school, and yet have not acquired the rudiments of learning, to enable them to enter the ordinary schools. Similar laws have been enacted by congress under its general power of legislation over the District of Columbia (sections 281–283, 310, 319, Rev. St. D. C.), as well as by the legislatures of many of the states, and have been generally, if not uniformly, sustained by the courts. . . .

Laws forbidding the intermarriage of the two races may be said in a technical sense to interfere with the freedom of contract, and yet have been universally recognized as within the police power of the state. State v. Gibson, 36 Ind. 389.

While we think the enforced separation of the races, as applied to the internal commerce of the state, neither abridges[5] the privileges or immunities of the colored man, deprives him of his property without due process of law, nor denies him the equal protection of the laws, within the meaning of the Fourteenth Amendment, we are not prepared to say that the conductor, in assigning passengers to the coaches according to their race, does not act at his peril, or that the provision of the second section of the act that denies to the passenger compensation in damages for a refusal to receive him into the coach in which he properly belongs is a valid exercise of the legislative power. Indeed, we understand it to be conceded by the state's attorney that such part of the act as exempts from liability the railway company and its officers is unconstitutional. The power to assign to a particular coach obviously implies the power to determine to which race the passenger belongs, as well as the power to determine who, under the laws of the particular state, is to be deemed a white, and who a colored, person. This question, though indicated in the brief of the plaintiff in error, does not properly arise upon the record in this case, since the only issue made is as to the unconstitutionality of the act, so far as it requires the railway to provide separate accommodations, and the conductor to assign passengers according to their race.

It is claimed by the plaintiff[6] in error that, in a mixed community, the reputation of belonging to the dominant race, in this instance the white race, is "property," in the same sense that a right of action or of inheritance is property. Conceding this to be so, for the purposes of this case, we are unable to see how this statute deprives him of, or in any way affects his right to, such property. If he be a white man, and assigned to a colored coach, he may have his action for damages against the company for being deprived of his so-called "property." Upon the other hand, if he be a colored man, and be so assigned, he has been deprived of no property, since he is not lawfully entitled to the reputation of being a white man.

In this connection, it is also suggested by the learned counsel for the plaintiff in error that the same argument that will justify the state legislature in requiring railways to provide separate accommodations for the two races will also authorize them to require separate cars to be provided for people whose hair is of a certain color, or who are aliens, or who belong to certain nationalities, or to enact laws requiring colored people to walk upon one side of the street, and white people upon the other, or requiring white men's houses to be painted white, and colored

15

_____

[5] Restricts.

_____

[6] The person who brings legal action against another (the *defendant*).

men's black, or their vehicles or business signs to be of different colors, upon the theory that one side of the street is as good as the other, or that a house or vehicle of one color is as good as one of another color. The reply to all this is that every exercise of the police power must be reasonable, and extend only to such laws as are enacted in good faith for the promotion of the public good, and not for the annoyance or oppression of a particular class. . . .

So far, then, as a conflict with the Fourteenth Amendment is concerned, the case reduces itself to the question whether the statute of Louisiana is a reasonable regulation, and with respect to this there must necessarily be a large discretion on the part of the legislature. In determining the question of reasonableness, it is at liberty to act with reference to the established usages, customs, and traditions of the people, and with a view to the promotion of their comfort, and the preservation of the public peace and good order. Gauged by this standard, we cannot say that a law which authorizes or even requires the separation of the two races in public conveyances is unreasonable, or more obnoxious to the Fourteenth Amendment than the acts of Congress requiring separate schools for colored children in the District of Columbia, the constitutionality of which does not seem to have been questioned, or the corresponding acts of state legislatures.

We consider the underlying fallacy of the plaintiff's argument to consist in the assumption that the enforced separation of the two races stamps the colored race with a badge of inferiority. If this be so, it is not by reason of anything found in the act, but solely because the colored race chooses to put that construction upon it. The argument necessarily assumes that if, as has been more than once the case, and is

not unlikely to be so again, the colored race should become the dominant power in the state legislature, and should enact a law in precisely similar terms, it would thereby relegate the white race to an inferior position. We imagine that the white race, at least, would not acquiesce in this assumption. The argument also assumes that social prejudices may be overcome by legislation, and that equal rights cannot be secured to the negro except by an enforced commingling of the two races. We cannot accept this proposition. If the two races are to meet upon terms of social equality, it must be the result of natural affinities, a mutual appreciation of each other's merits, and a voluntary consent of individuals. As was said by the court of appeals of New York in People v. Gallagher, 93 N. Y. 438, 448: "This end can neither be accomplished nor promoted by laws which conflict with the general sentiment of the community upon whom they are designed to operate. When the government, therefore, has secured to each of its citizens equal rights before the law, and equal opportunities for improvement and progress, it has accomplished the end for which it was organized, and performed all of the functions respecting social advantages with which it is endowed." Legislation is powerless to eradicate racial instincts, or to abolish distinctions based upon physical differences, and the attempt to do so can only result in accentuating the difficulties of the present situation. If the civil and political rights of both races be equal, one cannot be inferior to the other civilly or politically. If one race be inferior to the other socially, the Constitution of the United States cannot put them upon the same plane. . . .

The judgment of the court below is therefore affirmed.

Reading, Writing, and Discussion Questions

1. How is Justice Henry Billings Brown's argument in paragraphs 4–5 an example of begging the question?

2. Why does Brown say that it is "too clear for argument" that the actions of the railroad did not violate the Thirteenth Amendment (para. 7)? Why did "statesmen of that day" feel that the Thirteenth Amendment was not enough, leading them to push for the passage of the Fourteenth?

3. Consider Brown's position in paragraph 8 about "ordinary civil injury" such as deciding whom to entertain and whom to rent a room to. What is the legal stance today toward such decisions made by individuals? Can you name (or find) any more recent examples of events or court cases to support your answer?

4. Paraphrase paragraph 11, which gets to the heart of the argument that the case is most famous for.

5. Paragraph 12 compares the case to a case of Boston public schools. What is the fallacy (or fallacies) at work in this paragraph?

6. Evaluate the logic of paragraph 15 and its interpretation of the Fourteenth Amendment's reference to "life, liberty, or property." What logical fallacies are at play? Where does the logic falter?

7. Evaluate the analogy in paragraph 16. Is it logical? Why or why not? What does the tone suggest about Brown's attitude toward those who are not white?

8. How does paragraph 17 illustrate the fallacy called appeal to tradition?

9. Brown opens paragraph 18 by saying that the argument of the plaintiff's counsel is fallacious in that if a "badge of inferiority" exists as a result of separating the races, it exists only in the minds of people of color. How does Brown contradict his own argument by the end of the paragraph?

10. What has happened to the legal concept of "separate but equal" since 1896?

Assignments for Logic

Reading and Discussion Questions

1. How do the inductive and deductive reasoning processes relate to the scientific method?

2. Why is it sometimes difficult to read an essay and tell whether the writer approached the topic through induction or deduction?

3. Look at a product review in *Consumer Reports* or a similar publication or website. Pick a general category like laptop computers, SUVs, or smartphones. Explore how the researchers arrive at their recommendations. Do they use induction or deduction?

4. Locate print ads to illustrate some of the fallacies covered in this chapter.

Writing Suggestions

1. Write an essay in which you analyze one or more fallacies in a single print ad or use several ads to illustrate logical fallacies.

2. Seamus O'Mahony makes this statement: "Irrationality pervades all aspects of medicine, from deluded, internet-addled patients and relatives, to the overuse of scans and other diagnostic procedures, to the widespread use of drugs of dubious benefit and high cost." He adds that "spending on medicine in countries like the U.S. has passed the tipping point where it causes more harm than good." Write an essay in which you argue whether you agree or disagree with O'Mahony's view of medicine.

3. According to Anup Gampa, a researcher from the University of Virginia, and Sean Wojcik, a researcher from the University of California, Irvine, "being able to hear the other side can open us up to our own flawed arguments."[9] Write an essay either agreeing or disagreeing with Gampa and Wojcik's statement, supporting your views with examples from contemporary political or campus issues.

RESEARCH ASSIGNMENT

1. Go to Google or another general search engine that you are familiar with. Do a search for a subject you're interested in or a current issue discussed in class. Choose a current controversial issue from class discussion or from recent headlines. Consider the topic, and decide if you want to research through an inductive or deductive process. Write a paragraph to explain your choice. Outline a plan for your inductive or deductive research process. Think about the relationship between generalizations and specifics. What sort of information would you need for your research to produce that would bridge the gap between the two? If you research deductively, what working thesis will you use to guide your research? What resources will you use to find sources, and what keywords and subject terms will guide your research?

2. Search for sources and gather at least ten potential sources. Pause and reevaluate. Based on what you have collected, do you need to adjust your working thesis at all? Do you have a sense of the generalization you will draw? (An annotated bibliography can be an especially helpful tool for this exercise. See "MLA-Style Annotated Bibliography" in Chapter 15, p. 437.)

3. Write a paragraph or two explaining how your research process led you to adjust your working thesis or shaped your conclusion. If you did not adjust your thesis at all, reexamine it to ensure it is of an appropriate scope (not too narrow or broad) and is debatable.

---

[9] James Murray, "Logical Reasoning: An Antidote or a Poison for Political Disagreement?," *Net News Ledger*, April 18, 2019, http://www.netnewsledger.com/2019/04/18/logical-reasoning-an-antidote-or-a-poison-for-political-disagreement/.

Incorporating
RESEARCH

Planning and Research

By now, you should be fairly adept at supporting claims. The next step is to apply your skills to writing an argument of your own on a subject of your choice or one assigned to you that requires research.

In this chapter, we move through the various stages involved in preparing to write a researched argument: choosing a topic, locating and evaluating sources, and taking notes. We have introduced various Research Skills throughout the earlier chapters of the book, since research happens in multiple stages, at different times during the writing process, and depending on your writing situation. Here is a list to remind you of the topics that we have covered:

Finding an Appropriate Topic

To write an argument, you first must identify your topic. This is a relatively easy task for someone writing an argument as part of his or her job—a lawyer defending a client, for example, or an advertising executive presenting a campaign. For a student, however, it can be daunting. Which of the many ideas in the world worth debating would make a good subject?

Several guidelines can help you evaluate the possibilities. Perhaps your assignment limits your choices. If you have been asked to write a research paper, you obviously must find a topic on which research is available. You need a topic that is worth the time and effort you expect to invest in it, and your subject should be one that interests you. Don't feel you have to write about what you know—very often, finding out what you don't know will turn out to be more satisfying. You should, however, choose a subject that is familiar enough for you to argue about without fearing you're in over your head.

In this chapter, we will follow a student, Anna, who has been assigned a research paper for her first-year English class. This is the assignment that Anna must complete:

> Choose an argumentative topic related in some way to a campus issue or an issue in the national headlines. Your thesis should be either a claim of value or a claim of policy. Your essay should be 5–7 double-spaced pages and must use at least six sources. There should be some variety in type of sources—books, articles, electronic journals, etc. Use MLA guidelines for documentation.

Invention Strategies

As a starting point, think of conversations you've had in the past few days or weeks that have involved defending a position. Is there some current political issue you're concerned about or some dispute with friends that would make a valid paper topic? One of the best sources is controversies in the media. Keep your project in mind as you watch TV or news clips, read print or online sources, or listen to the radio or podcasts. You may even run into a potential subject in your course reading assignments or classroom discussions. Fortunately for the would-be writer, nearly every human activity includes its share of disagreement.

As you consider possible topics, write them down. One that looks unlikely at first glance may suggest others or may have more appeal when you come back to it later. Further, simply putting words on paper has a way of stimulating the thought processes involved in writing. Even if your ideas are tentative, the act of converting them into phrases or sentences can often help in developing them.

When student researcher Anna began thinking about her research assignment, she made the following entry in her journal:

> Since I can relate to college campus life and am interested in campus culture, I am thinking about a topic that relates to trigger warnings and/or safe spaces on college campuses. I need to look closely at the relationship between these two topics. I know that students and faculty on my campus are concerned about both, so I will start my research on these areas.

Evaluating Possible Topics

As you consider possible topics, you must, of course, follow any guidelines provided by your instructor. Not every topic is appropriate for an argumentative essay. Some would be difficult or impossible to find support for; others would make your job as a researcher more difficult than it has to be. The Strategies for Identifying Effective Research Paper Topics box (p. 366) describes some characteristics of effective research paper topics.

Even if you start out with a topic that does not meet the criteria in the Strategies box, you can use that as a starting point and move toward one that does, as in the examples. Don't discard a topic that you are interested in until you have tried reworking and improving it. A topic that is too broad can be narrowed down; one that is too narrow can become part of a larger argument. A shift in focus can sometimes make a topic that is not debatable or interesting into one that is.

At this preliminary stage, don't worry if you don't know exactly how to word your thesis. It's useful to write down a few possible phrasings to be sure your topic is one you can work with, but you need not be precise. The information you unearth as you do research will help you to formulate your ideas. Also, stating a thesis in final terms is premature until you know the organization and tone of your paper. Student researcher Anna focused her initial topic idea like this:

> To narrow my topic, I'm interested in the ways in which spaces that attempt to foster a sense of safety pertain to both college campuses and the workplace. I think I would like my claim to be that all college campuses should offer safe spaces to the students who wish to use them, but I need to first try to find sources that define these spaces and identify why they improve the happiness and well-being of college students.

Strategies for Identifying Effective Research Paper Topics

Keep the following points in mind when settling on a topic for your research paper.

■ **Interesting.** Your topic must interest your audience. Who is the audience? For a lawyer, it is usually a judge or jury; for a columnist, anyone who reads the newspaper in which his or her column appears. For the student writer, the audience is to some extent hypothetical. You should assume that your paper is directed at readers who are reasonably intelligent and well informed, but who have no specific knowledge of the subject. It may be useful to imagine you are writing for a local or school publication.

Less Interesting	*More Interesting*
The popularity of e-cigarettes	The cause of recent vaping deaths
College bowl games	The debate over whether there should be an eight-game instead of a four-game college football playoff

■ **Debatable.** The purpose of an argument is to defend or refute a thesis, so you should choose a topic that can be seen from more than one perspective. In evaluating a subject that looks promising, ask yourself: can a case be made for other views? If not, you have no workable ground for building your own case.

Less Debatable	*More Debatable*
Shoplifting (Nobody would disagree that it is wrong.)	The increased use of security cameras in public spaces
Popularity of meditation apps (Nobody would disagree that these have become enormously popular.)	The effects of meditation on grades in college coursework

■ **Not Too Broad.** Consider how long your paper will be and whether you can do justice to your topic in that amount of space. Your essay will not be very effective if you are able to cover your subject in only a general way with no specifics. As a general rule, the more specific your topic, the better the resulting essay.

■ **Not Too Narrow.** In contrast, if you can cover your subject in a paragraph or even in a single page, it clearly is too narrow to be the subject for an argumentative essay.

Too Broad	*Too Narrow*	*Appropriate*
Nuclear energy around the world	Why a hybrid car made sense to me	Why United States homeowners should consider solar energy as an alternative power source

■ **Not Too Unconventional.** When offering an explanation, especially one that is complicated or extraordinary, look first for a cause that is not too difficult to accept — one that doesn't strain credibility. A reasonable person interested in the truth would search for more conventional explanations before accepting the bizarre or the incredible. Looking for a supernatural explanation for the disappearance of ships in the Bermuda Triangle or a new conspiracy theory to explain the assassination of John F. Kennedy is probably not the best use of your research time and would lead to a claim that would be difficult if not impossible to support.

Initiating Research

The success of any argument, short or long, depends in large part on the quantity and quality of the support behind it. Research, therefore, can be crucial for any argument outside your own experience.

Keeping Research on Track

You should prepare for research by identifying potential resources and learning how they work. Here are some guidelines for tracking your research throughout your project:

- Make sure you know how to use the library's catalog and other databases available either in the library or through the campus network.
- For each database that looks useful, explore how to execute a subject search, how to refine a search, and how to save, print out, or download results.
- Make sure you know how to find books, relevant reference materials, and journals.
- Find out whether interlibrary loan is an option and how long it takes.
- If you plan to use government publications, find out if your library is a depository for federal documents.
- Finally, discuss your topic with a librarian at the reference desk to make sure you haven't overlooked anything.

RESEARCH SKILL ▶ What Is Common Knowledge?

Common knowledge is information so widely known that you do not need to identify a source. How do you decide?

- One rule that some writers follow is to classify information as common knowledge if at least three to five general reference works such as dictionaries or encyclopedias provide the same information. A more general guideline is to consider it common knowledge if the average reader would be familiar with it.

- It is not necessary to document common knowledge because it is readily available information.
- If you are in doubt as to whether certain information is common knowledge, it is better to identify your source.

Sketching a Preliminary Outline

An outline is usually not written in complete sentences, but some instructors prefer complete sentences, so check your assignment. If your outline is written in sentence form, it will pretty closely match the topic sentences in your body paragraphs. If not, the ideas in the outline will provide the organization of the ideas in your paper. Ideas represented by Roman numerals are parallel in signif-icance; the same is true for items represented by *A*, *B*, *C*, and so on. You would never have a *I* without a *II*. The same is true at the next level: you wouldn't have

Strategies for Keeping Your Research on Track

1. **Focus your investigation on building your argument,** not merely on collecting information about the topic. Do follow any promising leads that turn up from the sources you consult, but don't be diverted into general reading that has no direct bearing on your thesis.

2. **Look for at least two pieces of evidence to support each point you want to make.** If you cannot find sufficient evidence, you may need to revise or abandon the point.

3. **Use a variety of sources.** Seek evidence from different kinds of sources (books, magazines, websites, government reports, even personal interviews with experts) and from different fields.

4. **Be sure your sources are authoritative.** Articles and essays in scholarly journals are more authoritative than articles in college newspapers or in magazines. Authors whose credentials include many publications and years of study at reputable institutions are probably more reliable on their specialized topics than newspaper columnists and the so-called man in the street. However, you can judge reliability much more easily if you are dealing with facts and inferences than with values and emotions.

5. **Be sure your sources are appropriate.** A nonacademic source may be perfectly appropriate, depending on the subject you are researching, particularly if the subject is a fast-breaking news story and not one that takes specialized knowledge to write about. If timeliness is of the essence, you may want to seek out articles from such respected outlets as the *New York Times* or the *Wall Street Journal* because of the speed with which these sources can break a story. There may even be times

that a social media post is appropriate if you are making a point about social media and not looking for the most authoritative source on a subject. A tweet, for example, can reveal a great deal about the person posting it — often more than about the subject of the tweet.

6. **Don't let your sources' opinions outweigh your own.** Your paper should demonstrate that the thesis and ideas you present are yours, arrived at after careful reflection and supported by research. The thesis need not be original, but your paper should be more than a collection of quotations or a report of the facts and opinions you have been reading.

7. **Don't ignore information that opposes the position you plan to support.** Your argument is not strengthened by pretending such information does not exist. You may find that you must revise or qualify your position based on what your research reveals. Your readers may be aware of other positions on the issue and may judge you to be unreliable, careless, or dishonest if you do not acknowledge them. It is far better to fairly summarize opposing arguments and refute them than to ignore them.

8. **Be sure to use the right number of sources.** Review your assignment to see if the instructor has provided guidelines. Eight sources is about right for a 1,500-word paper, unless your assignment states otherwise. That means sources that you actually use, not ones that you examine but never use ideas or wording from. You want to have enough sources, but not too many. Don't place so much weight on any single source that your paper seems to be mostly a rehash of one author's ideas.

an *A* without a *B*. The logic behind that guideline is that there is no reason for breaking a category into only one subordinate category. If your outline needs to be more detailed, *A*, *B*, *C* levels are broken down using *1*, *2*, *3*, and so on. Those can be further broken down into *a*, *b*, *c* levels if necessary. You will most likely not need that level of specificity in your outline unless your instructor requires it.

One approach is to save the Roman numeral levels for the major divisions of your paper and use the *A*-level for paragraph-level ideas. Make the wording of each level as nearly parallel as possible, as in the following preliminary outline:

Thalidomide: Changing a Drug's Reputation

I. Thalidomide's history: a promising drug but a medical nightmare
   A. Explain how drug was developed
   B. Explain the medical disaster it caused
II. New look at thalidomide: its potential to effectively treat cancer and other diseases
   A. Discuss how it first worked to treat leprosy
   B. Support how it can treat cancer
   C. Support how it can treat other diseases
III. Conclusion

Now you are ready to begin the search for material that will support the argument you have outlined. Remember that your plan for your paper may change depending on what your research reveals. Be prepared to change your outline as necessary so that the outline you turn in with your final draft matches the paper you eventually write.

Student researcher Anna's preliminary outline looked like this:

With the two academic sources I currently have, I think I have enough information to begin a simple outline for my essay. As I gather more sources, perhaps from reputable news sources or books on the subject of safe spaces, I expect my thesis may have to change.

Safe Spaces on College Campuses

I. The history and evolution of safe spaces on college campuses
   A. What safe spaces are
   B. Why students, their families, and faculty want safe spaces
   C. Why other students and faculty are opposed to safe spaces
II. The benefits of safe spaces for college students
   A. On mental health and happiness
   B. On the college community and experience as a whole
   C. On members of marginalized groups
III. Suggested implementation
IV. Conclusion

Types of Sources

There are two principal ways of gathering supporting evidence for your argument—primary research and secondary research.

Primary Research

Primary sources are firsthand information. By *firsthand* we mean information taken directly from the original source, including field research (interviews, surveys, personal observations, or experiments). If your topic relates to a local issue involving your school or community, or if it focuses on a story that has never been reported by others, field research may be more valuable than anything available in the library. However, the library can be a source of firsthand information. Memoirs and letters written by witnesses to past events, photographs, contemporary news reports of historical events, or expert testimony presented at congressional hearings are all primary sources that may be available in your library.

The internet, too, can be a source of primary data. A discussion forum, newsgroup, or social media organization focused on your topic may give you a means to converse with activists and contact experts. Websites of certain organizations provide documentation of their views, unfiltered by others' opinions. The text of laws, court opinions, bills, debates in Congress, environmental impact statements, and even selected declassified FBI files can be found through government-sponsored websites. Other sites present statistical data or the text of historical or political documents. Be aware that primary sources do not have to be print sources. Photographs, posters, advertisements, videos, and other visuals can also serve as raw material to be interpreted.

Student researcher Anna came up with the following list of possible primary sources:

I want to find at least two additional items to serve as my primary sources. Here are some possibilities:

> Website with campus policy or documentation on safe spaces
> Interview with college students
>
> Interview with parent
>
> Interview with college advisor, counselor, or therapist
>
> Reports and statistics about student mental health
>
> Reports and statistics about students in marginalized groups
>
> Letters to the editor

One of the rewards of primary research is that it often generates new information, which in turn produces new interpretations of familiar conditions. It is a favored method for anthropologists and sociologists, and most physical and natural scientists use observation and experiment at some point as essential tools in their research.

The information gleaned from primary research can be used directly to support your claim, or it can provide a starting point for secondary research.

Secondary Research

Secondary sources provide commentary on and analysis of a topic. In addition to raw evidence found in primary sources, secondary sources provide a sense of how others are examining the issues and can yield useful information and analysis. Secondary sources may be written for a popular audience, ranging from news coverage, to popular explanations of research findings, to social analysis, to opinion pieces. Or they may be scholarly publications—journals in which experts present their research and theories to other researchers. (For more on popular and scholarly sources, see the Research Skill: Popular vs. Scholarly Articles box below.) These sources might also take the form of analytical reports written to untangle possible courses of action, such as a report written by staff members for a congressional committee or an analysis of an issue by a think tank that wants to use the evidence it has gathered to influence public opinion.

You can find both primary and secondary sources in your school library and online. For example, you can find journal articles in a library database and statistics on a government website.

RESEARCH SKILL ▶ Popular vs. Scholarly Articles

Popular Articles (Magazines, Newspapers, and Online Publications)

- Often written by journalists or professional writers for a general audience
- Use language easily understood by the general public
- Rarely give full citations for sources; in online publications, references to sources may rely solely on hyperlinks
- Tend to be shorter than journal articles
- May be reviewed by an editor or fact-checker, but not always, especially for online-only publications that are not sponsored by a major organization that will be held accountable

FIGURE 13.1 Popular magazines. RICHARD B. LEVINE /Newscom/Levine Roberts Photography/NEW YORK/NY/USA

Scholarly Articles (Journals)

- Written by and for faculty, researchers, or scholars (chemists, historians, doctors, artists, etc.)
- Use scholarly or technical language

- Tend to be longer articles about research
- Include full citations for sources
- Often available in print as well as online, especially through your college or university library's databases

continued

- Often refereed or peer-reviewed (articles are reviewed by an editor and other specialists before being accepted for publication)
- Book reviews and editorials are not considered scholarly articles, even when found in scholarly journals.

Some Points to Remember

- Both magazine and journal articles can be good sources for your work.
- When selecting articles, think about how you intend to use the information:
    - Do you want background on a topic that is new to you? (use popular periodicals or reliable websites)
    - Did your instructor say to cite scholarly resources? (use journals)
- Often a combination of the two will be most appropriate for undergraduate research.

The American Economic Review

ARTICLES

JAMES HECKMAN, RODRIGO PINTO, AND PETER SAVELYEV
  Understanding the Mechanisms Through Which an Influential Early Childhood Program Boosted Adult Outcomes

DAMON CLARK AND HEATHER ROYER
  The Effect of Education on Adult Mortality and Health: Evidence from Britain

DAVID H. AUTOR, DAVID DORN, AND GORDON H. HANSON
  The China Syndrome: Local Labor Market Effects of Import Competition in the United States

AMIT K. KHANDELWAL, PETER K. SCHOTT, AND SHANG-JIN WEI
  Trade Liberalization and Embedded Institutional Reform: Evidence from Chinese Exporters

ERICA FIELD, ROHINI PANDE, JOHN PAPP, AND NATALIA RIGOL
  Does the Classic Microfinance Model Discourage Entrepreneurship Among the Poor? Experimental Evidence from India

NICO VOIGTLÄNDER AND HANS-JOACHIM VOTH
  How the West "Invented" Fertility Restriction

MICHAEL J. ROBERTS AND WOLFRAM SCHLENKER
  Identifying Supply and Demand Elasticities of Agricultural Commodities: Implications for the US Ethanol Mandate

KLAUS DESMET AND ESTEBAN ROSSI-HANSBERG
  Urban Accounting and Welfare

JIN LI AND NIKO MATOUSCHEK
  Managing Conflicts in Relational Contracts

PHILIPPE GAGNEPAIN, MARC IVALDI, AND DAVID MARTIMORT
  The Cost of Contract Renegotiation: Evidence from the Local Public Sector

GIACOMO CALZOLARI AND VINCENZO DENICOLÒ
  Competition with Exclusive Contracts and Market-Share Discounts

MARCIN PĘSKI AND BALÁZS SZENTES
  Spontaneous Discrimination

PAOLO BUONANNO AND STEVEN RAPHAEL
  Incarceration and Incapacitation: Evidence from the 2006 Italian Collective Pardon

ARTHUR CAMPBELL
  Word-of-Mouth Communication and Percolation in Social Networks

LEVON BARSEGHYAN, FRANCESCA MOLINARI, TED O'DONOGHUE, AND JOSHUA C. TEITELBAUM
  The Nature of Risk Preferences: Evidence from Insurance Choices

SHORTER PAPERS: J. A. Parker, N. S. Souleles, D. S. Johnson, and R. McClelland; S. Dhingra; E. E. Schlee; A. Kurmann and C. Otrok; A. Ziegelmeyer, C. March, and S. Krügel

OCTOBER 2013

FIGURE 13.2 Scholarly journal
American Economic Association

Finding Sources

The nature of your topic will determine which route you follow to find good sources. If the topic is current, you may find it more important to use articles than books and might bypass the library catalog altogether. If the topic has to do with social policy or politics, government publications may be particularly useful, though they would be unhelpful for a literary paper. If the topic relates to popular culture, the internet may provide more information than more traditional publications. Consider what kinds of sources will be most useful as you choose your strategy. If you aren't certain which approaches fit your topic best, consult with a librarian at the reference desk.

Databases

You will most likely use one or more databases (online catalogs of reference materials) to locate books and articles on your topic. The library catalog is a database of books and materials owned by the library; other databases may cover articles in popular or specialized journals and may even provide the full text of articles. Some databases may be available only in the library; others may be accessible all over campus.

To search for books, videos, or periodical publications, use the library catalog. For every book in the library, there is an entry in the catalog that gives the book's author, title, publisher, date, length, and subject headings and perhaps some notes about its contents. The catalog entry also gives the call number or location on the shelf and may offer some indication as to the book's availability. Remember when searching the catalog, though, that entries are for whole books and not specific parts of them. If you use search terms that are too narrow, you may not find a book that has a chapter on exactly what you are looking for. Plan to browse the shelves and examine the tables of contents of the books that you find through the catalog to see which ones, in fact, are most helpful for your topic.

Student researcher Anna searched the keywords "safe spaces" on her college's catalog.

FIGURE 13.3 A university catalog search

With the information listed here, Anna could view several e-books, go to the shelves and use the call numbers to locate the books to see if they would be helpful for her research, or navigate to a website with a film. The advanced search allows you to narrow down the types of sources you want to search for—if you wanted to find only print books in the library, for example.

To search for articles, use a generalized database of periodicals. Online indexes such as *EBSCO Multiple Database Search*, *Academic OneFile*, *Readers' Guide Full Text Mega*, and *ProQuest* may include citations, citations with abstracts (brief summaries), or the entire text of articles. Ask the librarian what is available in your school's library. Student researcher Anna's database search is included below:

> I knew that our college library has a database of books and scholarly articles I can search through OneSearch, so I started there. I searched for "safe spaces" in the database first and got over 2.5 million results. Before I began to narrow down my search, I explored some of the options that appeared at the top of the results list. These first two results were both e-books, but for my paper, I'd like to begin pulling information from more concise and focused articles.

Databases have features that can save time and help to narrow the focus of your research. This section identifies some common features.

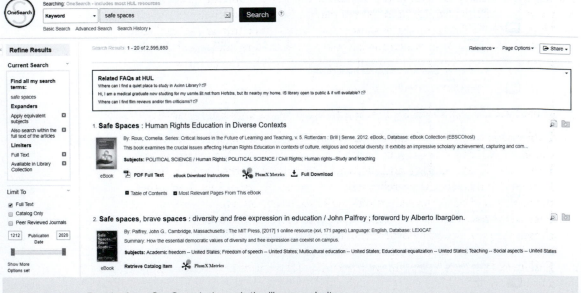

FIGURE 13.4 Results from OneSearch through the library website

Keyword or Subject Searching

You might have the option of searching a database by *keyword*—using the words that you think are most relevant to your search—or by subject. Typically, a keyword search will locate any occurrence of your search term in titles, notes, or the descriptive headings provided by database catalogers or indexers. The advantage to keyword searching is that you can use terms that come naturally to mind so that you cast your net as widely as possible. The disadvantage is that there may be more than one way to express your topic and you may not capture all the relevant materials unless you use the right keywords.

With *subject searching*, you use search terms from a list of subject headings (sometimes called *descriptors*) established by the creators of the database. To make searching as efficient as possible, they choose one word or phrase to express a subject. Every time a new source is entered into the database, the indexers describe it using words from the list of subject headings: when you use the list to search the database, you retrieve every relevant source. You might find that a database lists these subject headings through a thesaurus feature. The sophisticated researcher will always pay attention to the subject headings or descriptors generally listed at the bottom of a record for clues to terms that might work best and for related terms that might be worth trying.

Searching for More Than One Concept

Most database searches allow you to combine terms using the connectors *and, or,* and *not.* These connectors (also known as *Boolean operators*) group search terms in different ways. If you search for "zoos *and* animal rights," for example, the resulting list of sources will include only those that deal with both zoos and animal rights, leaving out any that deal with only one subject and not the other. If you connect terms with *or,* your list will contain sources that deal with either concept: a search for "dogs *or* cats" will create a list of sources that cover either animal. *Not* excludes concepts from a search. A search for "animal rights *not* furs" will search for the concept animal rights and then cut out any sources that deal with furs.

Limiting a Search

Most databases have options for limiting a search by a number of variables:

- **Publication date.** If you want the most recent information you can find, you can indicate that you want your search results to start with the newest items.
- **Language.** This is a quick and easy way to eliminate works not in English.
- **Format.** Many database searches will sort the results according to whether the results are books, journal articles, newspaper articles, etc.
- **Peer-reviewed.** This option limits your search results to scholarly works chosen for publication by other scholars and thus some of the most authoritative specialized works you can find.
- **Full-text.** Practically, you will want access to full articles instead of simply a brief abstract.
- **Includes images.** The presence of images may or not be important to the topic you are researching, but this can be a useful tool for some subjects.

Truncating Search Terms with Wild Cards

At times, you will search for a word that has many possible endings. A wild card is a symbol that, placed at the end of a word root, allows for any possible ending for a word. For example, *animal** will allow a search for *animal* or *animals*.

Saving Records

You may have the opportunity to print, download, or email to yourself the citations you find in a database. Many databases have a feature for marking just the records you want so you save only those of interest.

Anna did an advanced search on Academic OneFile (Gale) with the keywords "safe space" and "colleges." She asked for only full-text articles, not simply titles or abstracts (see Fig. 13.5). Two of the results were magazine articles, from *Modern Age* and *Spectator*.

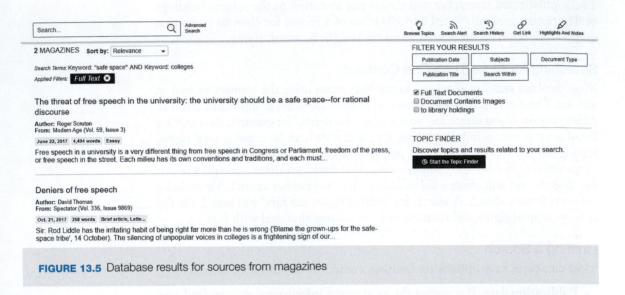

FIGURE 13.5 Database results for sources from magazines

Anna could use the library catalog to locate the hard copy periodicals on the shelves or the online versions to investigate whether any of the titles prove to be useful. The first few words from the article appear in the list of results and will help her decide which are worth investigating.

Another category of results were articles from academic journals. Figure 13.6 shows the first few of eleven scholarly articles found. Again, Anna could use the catalog to locate where the periodicals were on the library shelves or online. If she had not selected "full text" in her advanced search, she may have gotten more results since some journals—especially older sources—are only available to the library in hard copy, bound volumes. Even though it may not be as convenient as accessing an article from the comfort of your room, don't discount the sources that appear on your library's shelves; they may be just what you're looking for and worth the trip to the stacks.

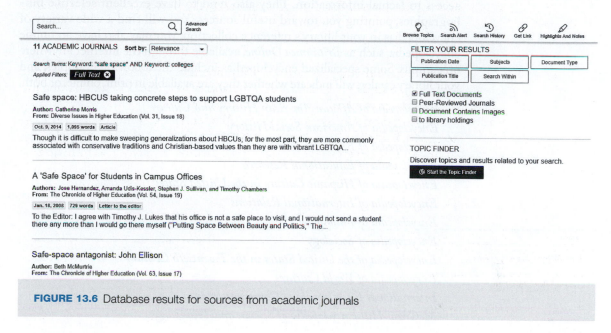

FIGURE 13.6 Database results for sources from academic journals

The largest number of articles found through Anna's search were from newspapers. Figure 13.7 shows only a few of the 106 news articles her search produced through the Academic OneFile database:

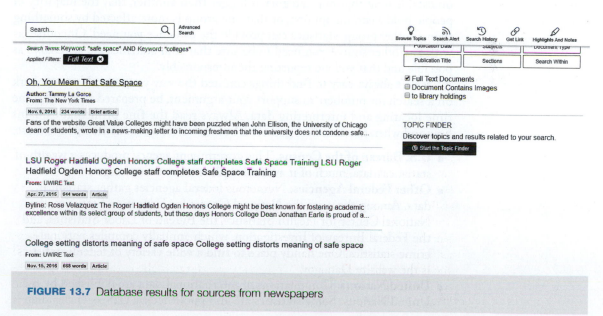

FIGURE 13.7 Database results for sources from newspapers

Encyclopedias

General and specialized encyclopedias offer quick overviews of topics and easy access to factual information. They also tend to have excellent selective bibliographies, pointing you toward useful sources. You will find a wide variety of encyclopedias in your library's reference collection; you may also have an online encyclopedia, such as *Britannica Online*, available through the internet anywhere on campus. Some specialized encyclopedias include the following examples, and your library catalog will indicate whether they are available in print, online, or both.

Encyclopedia of African American History and Culture

Encyclopedia of American Social History

Encyclopedia of Bioethics

Encyclopedia of Educational Research

Encyclopedia of Hispanic Culture in the United States

Encyclopedia of International Relations

Encyclopedia of Philosophy

Encyclopedia of Sociology

Encyclopedia of the United States in the Twentieth Century

Encyclopedia of World Cultures

International Encyclopedia of Communications

McGraw-Hill Encyclopedia of Science and Technology

Statistical Resources

Often statistics are used as evidence in an argument. If your argument depends on establishing that one category is bigger than another, that the majority of people hold a certain opinion, or that one group is more affected by something than another group, statistics can provide the evidence you need. Of course, as with any other source, you need to be sure that your statistics are as reliable as possible and that you are reporting them responsibly.

It isn't always easy to find things counted the way you want. If you embark on a search for numbers to support your argument, be prepared to spend some time locating and interpreting data. Always read the fine print that explains how and when the data were gathered. Some sources for statistics include these:

- **U.S. Bureau of the Census.** This government agency produces a wealth of statistical data, much of it available online at www.census.gov.
- **Other Federal Agencies.** Numerous federal agencies gather statistical data. Among these are the National Center for Education Statistics, the National Center for Health Statistics, the Bureau of Labor Statistics, and the Federal Bureau of Investigation, which annually compiles national crime statistics. One handy place to find a wide variety of federal statistics is the website Data.gov.
- **United Nations.** Compilations of international data are published by the United Nations. Some statistics are also published by U.N. agencies such

as the Food and Health Organization. Some are available from the U.N. website at un.org.

- **Opinion Polls.** Several companies conduct opinion polls, and some of these are available in libraries. One such compilation is the Gallup Poll series, which summarizes public opinion polling from 1935 to the present. Another valuable source of data is think tanks such as the Pew Research Center. Other poll results are reported by the press. Search a database that covers news publications by using your topic and "polls" as keywords to locate some summaries of results.

Government Resources

Beyond statistics, government agencies compile and publish a wealth of information. For topics that concern public welfare, health, education, politics, foreign relations, earth sciences, the environment, or the economy, government documents may provide just the information you need.

The U.S. federal government is the largest publisher in the world. Its publications are distributed free to libraries designated as document depositories across the country. If your library is not a depository, chances are there is a regional depository somewhere nearby. Local, state, and foreign governments are also potential sources of information.

Federal documents distributed to depository libraries are indexed in print versions of *The Monthly Catalog of U.S. Government Documents* through December 2004, and online in the Catalog of U.S. Government Publications. These include congressional documents such as hearings and committee reports, presidential papers, studies conducted by the Education Department or the Centers for Disease Control, and so on. If you learn about a government publication through the news media, chances are you will be able to obtain a copy at the website of the sponsoring agency or congressional body. In fact, government publications are among the most valuable of resources available online because they are rigorously controlled for content. You know you are looking at a U.S. federal government site when you see the domain suffix *.gov* in the URL.

Online Sources

The internet is an important resource for researchers. It is particularly helpful if you are looking for information about organizations, current events, political debates, popular culture, or government-sponsored research and activities. It is not an especially good place to look for literary criticism, historical analysis, or scholarly research articles, which are still more likely to be published in traditional ways. Biologists reporting on an important experiment, for example, are more likely to submit an article about it to a prestigious journal in the field than simply post their results online.

Because anyone can publish whatever they like online, searching for good information can be frustrating. Search engines operate by means of automated programs that gather information about sites and match search terms to whatever is out there, regardless of quality. A search engine may locate thousands of online documents on a topic, but most are of little relevance and dubious quality. The key is to know in advance what information you need and who might have produced it. For example, if your topic has to do with some aspect of free speech and you know that the American Civil Liberties Union is involved in the issue, a trip to the ACLU home page may provide you with a wealth of information, albeit from a particular perspective. If your state's pollution control agency just issued a report on water quality in the area, you may find the report published at the agency's website or the email address of someone who could send it to you. The more you know about your topic before you sit down to search online, the more likely you will use your time productively.

If you have a fairly specific topic in mind or are looking for a particular organization or document, a search engine can help you find it. Google is the most common. As with databases, there are usually ways to refine a search and improve your results. Many search engines offer an advanced search option that may provide some useful options for refining and limiting a search. Google Scholar is a good resource for narrowing results to academic sources, but many of the sources that appear will still not be available to you in full text through your browser, and you will need to search for full text versions while logged in to your library.

Because publishing and transmitting texts online are relatively easy, it is becoming more common for libraries to subscribe to databases and electronic journals that are accessed through a web browser. You may have *Wall Street Journal* archives as an option on your library's home page. However, the contents of those subscriptions will be available only to your campus community and will not be searched by general search engines.

Anna explains her general online search on the topic "safe spaces":

To find more sources, I decided to explore articles that I may not have easily found within the scope of my university's databases. I would like my paper to have a strong foundation of supporting facts and statistics, and I thought a report would provide some useful graphs that may reveal trends surrounding the rise of safe spaces and their relationship to the college student experience.

Using Google, I searched for "mental health report college students." To gauge credibility, I looked at the URL suffixes of the topmost results. Most of the results were maintained by companies and organizations, but the first result was for a university: an annual report on collegiate mental health published by Penn State University. This source might provide the numbers and statistics I'm looking for, since it has a .edu domain. The link took me to a page that provided a brief overview of the report, which, according to Penn State's website, presents research about mental health trends over an eight-year period.

Google | mental health report college students 🎤 🔍

Q All | 📰 News | 🖼 Images | ▶ Videos | 🏷 Shopping | ⋮ More | Settings | Tools

About 300,000,000 results (0.54 seconds)

Annual collegiate mental health report examines trends and ...
https://news.psu.edu › story › 2019/01/16 › academics › annual-collegiate-... ▾
Jan 16, 2019 - The 2018 Center for Collegiate **Mental Health** (CCMH) Annual **Report**, found that
college students seeking treatment (and the professionals who treat them) continue to identify
anxiety and depression as the most common concerns for seeking treatment, among dozens of
other concerns.

People also ask

What percent of college students have a mental illness?	⌄
What causes mental illness in college students?	⌄
What causes anxiety in college students?	⌄
What is the most common mental illness among college students?	⌄

Feedback

College Student Mental Health and Well-Being: A Survey of ...
https://www.higheredtoday.org › 2019/08/12 › college-student-mental-hea... ▾
Aug 12, 2019 - Headlines in newspapers across the country are **reporting** that a **mental health**
crisis exists at U.S. **colleges** and universities, and that it is ...

Top 5 Mental Health Challenges Facing College Students
https://www.bestcolleges.com › resources › top-5-mental-health-problems-... ▾
Jun 26, 2019 - This online resource for **college students** seeking **mental health** wellness ...
According to the organization's **report**, anxiety disorders affect 40 ...
Depression · Anxiety · Suicide

Study: College Presidents Prioritizing Student Mental Health
https://www.insidehighered.com › news › 2019/08/12 › college-presidents-... ▾
Aug 12, 2019 - As cases of **student** anxiety and depression skyrocket, top **university** officials are
focusing more on these issues, according to a new **report**.

FIGURE 13.8 Google search results

Multimodal Sources

Since the internet is a world of images as well as words, it may give you ideas for
livening up your own work with all sorts of visuals—if your instructor allows it.
(In "Online Sources," pp. 379–81, Anna looked for graphs that she could use in
her paper to support her argument and appeal to her audience.) You may also
find useful visuals in the books and articles that you read. Don't forget, though,
that you are obligated to give credit to the source of your visuals along with the
ideas and words that you use. A graph or chart may provide just the sort of statistical support that will make a key point in your argument, and it can be easily cut
and pasted into your electronic text, but you must document that graph or chart
as you would text. You should acknowledge the location where you found the

visual and as much information as is provided about who produced it. You must seek permission to use visuals that you intend to publish in print or electronic form. (For more help with documenting sources, see Chapter 15.)

Evaluating Sources

When you begin studying your sources, read first to acquire general familiarity with your subject. Make sure that you are covering all sides of the question as well as facts and opinions from a variety of sources. As you read, look for what seem to be the major issues. Record questions as they occur to you in your reading. It may be useful to review Chapters 2 and 3 for more help with reading critically.

Relevance

The sources you find provide useful information that you need for your paper and help you support your claims. One key to supporting claims effectively is to make sure you have the best evidence available. It is tempting when searching a database or the internet to take the first sources that look good, print them or copy them, and not give them another thought until you are sitting down to compose your argument — only to discover that the sources aren't as valuable as they could be. Sources that looked pretty good at the beginning of your research may turn out to be less useful once you have learned more about the topic. And a source that seems interesting at first glance may turn out to be a rehash or digest of a much more valuable source, something you realize only when you sit down and look at it carefully.

To find the right material, be a critical thinker from the start of your research process. Scan and evaluate the references you encounter throughout your search. As you examine options in a database, choose sources that use relevant terms in their titles, seem directed to an appropriate audience, and are published in places that will look credible in your Works Cited list. For example, a Senate Foreign Relations Committee report will carry more weight as a source on global politics than a comparable article in *Good Housekeeping*. An article from the scholarly journal *Foreign Affairs* will carry more clout than an article from *Reader's Digest*, even if they are on the same subject. (For more on popular versus scholarly sources, see the Research Skill: Popular vs. Scholarly Articles box on pp. 371–72.)

Skim and quickly evaluate each source that looks valuable.

- Is it relevant to your topic?
- Does it provide information you haven't found elsewhere?
- Can you learn anything about the author, and does what you learn inspire confidence?

As you begin to learn more about your topic and revise your outline as necessary, you can use sources to help direct your search. If a source mentions an organization, for example, you may use that clue to run an online search for that organization's home page. If a newspaper story refers to a study published in a scientific journal, you may want to seek out that study to see the results of the research firsthand. And if you have a source that includes references to other publications, scan through them to see which ones might also prove helpful to you.

When you first started your research, chances are you weren't quite sure what you were looking for. Once you are familiar with your topic, you need to concentrate on finding sources that will best support the claims you want to make, and your increasing familiarity with the issue will make it easier to identify the best sources. That may mean a return trip to the library. Keep in mind, too, that as you learn from your research, sources you identified may no longer be as relevant as they once were to your project; for that reason, you should always identify more sources to evaluate than you think you may need (or than the assignment calls for) so you can use only the sources that support your ideas best in writing.

READING ARGUMENT

Seeing Relevance

Through her journal entries, you can trace Anna's thought process as she evaluates some of the sources she found:

> In my database search, I found two scholarly articles that seem promising. One is called "Safe Spaces" by Alicia Oglesby. Skimming the article, I gathered that Oglesby believes safe spaces to be crucial to the physical, mental, and emotional well-being of marginalized groups.

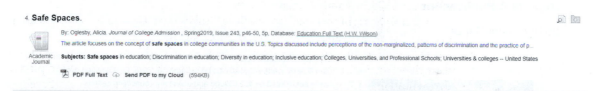

4. **Safe Spaces**.

By: Oglesby, Alicia. *Journal of College Admission* , Spring2019, Issue 243, p46-50, 5p, Database: Education Full Text (H.W. Wilson)

The article focuses on the concept of **safe spaces** in college communities in the U.S. Topics discussed include perceptions of the non-marginalized, patterns of discrimination and the practice of p...

Subjects: Safe spaces in education; Discrimination in education; Diversity in education; Inclusive education; Colleges, Universities, and Professional Schools; Universities & colleges -- United States

PDF Full Text   Send PDF to my Cloud   (594KB)

FIGURE 13.9 Close-up of single journal article in results list

> The second article is called "From Infantilizing to World Making: Safe Spaces and Trigger Warnings on Campus" by Katie Byron. This article seems to highlight safe spaces and trigger warnings as consequences of sexual violence that foster negative environments on college campuses. The author also references a few statistics about marginalized groups, the college campus experience, and how safe spaces relate to those experiences.
>
> The last piece of source material I felt was missing from my topic was a piece in opposition to my argument—one that attempts to discredit the use of safe spaces and trigger warnings on college campuses. To find this source, I did another Google search using the phrase "safe spaces bad for mental health." The first few results were

actually articles in favor of safe spaces and trigger warnings, although this may be attributed to Google's algorithm and the keyword "safe spaces" in my query. The fifth result was an essay by Greg Lukianoff and Jonathan Haidt titled "The Coddling of the American Mind." I skimmed the essay and felt it was a good counterargument.

In particular, the Oglesby article and the one by Lukianoff and Haidt seem to highlight both sides of the issue of safe spaces and trigger warnings on campus. From my own experience, I know that students and faculty both have strong opinions about the meaning and impact of these concepts, which should make it a good controversy.

My Google search also turned up a link to a Penn State report. I found statistics that suggest a rise in the number of mental health issues and the frequency with which college students seek out professional counseling resources that will support my argument in favor of safe spaces.

PennState Student Affairs

Counseling & Psychological Services
Center for Collegiate Mental Health (CCMH)

| CAPS | Home | About | Join | Reports & Publications | SDS & CCAPS | Data | Member Information | Webinars | FAQ | Contact |

Reports & Publications

2018 Annual Report

The 2018 Annual Report summarizes data contributed to CCMH during the 2017-2018 academic year, closing on June 30, 2018. De-identified data were contributed by 152 college and university counseling centers, describing 179,964 unique college students seeking mental health treatment; 3,723 clinicians; and over 1,384,712 appointments.

The 2018 Report examined the impact of two different center-level policy decisions, 8-year mental health trends, the most common mental health concerns for students, reasons why students terminate treatment, and much more.

Previous Annual Reports:

2017
2016
2015
2014
2013
2012
2011
2010
2009

BRINGING SCIENCE AND PRACTICE
Together.

FIGURE 13.10 Useful website found through general search engine

Practice: Evaluate Sources for Relevance

Look at the following two charts about trauma experienced by college students that Anna found through the Penn State website as part of her online search. Answer the questions that follow to consider the relevance of her findings to her research project, which you have read about throughout this chapter.

COLLEGE STUDENTS' ANSWERS TO MENTAL HEALTH HISTORY ITEMS

Experienced a traumatic event that caused you to feel intense fear, helplessness, or horror (how many times)

	Overall (%) n=116,485	Female (%) n=74,732	Male (%) n=39,353	Transgender (%) n=776	Self-Identify (%) n=1,624
Never	59.4	56.2	66.4	45.9	42.6
1 time	17.2	18.7	14.4	15.2	17.0
2-3 times	13.8	15.0	11.3	17.0	18.3
4-5 times	2.4	2.6	1.9	4.1	5.2
More than 5 times	7.2	7.5	5.9	17.8	16.8

This question is from the Standardized Data Set Question #86

Experienced a traumatic event that caused you to feel intense fear, helplessness, or horror (the last time)

	Overall (%) n=42,553	Female (%) n=29,556	Male (%) n=11,747	Transgender (%) n=375	Self-Identify (%) n=875
Never	0.2	0.1	0.2	0.0	0.3
Within the last 2 weeks	10.0	9.5	11.6	7.7	5.4
Within the last month	7.0	6.9	7.6	4.3	4.2
Within the last year	22.7	23.0	22.1	18.4	22.6
Within the last 1-5 years	36.9	38.1	33.3	42.4	43.1
More than 5 years ago	23.2	22.3	25.2	27.2	24.3

This question is from the Standardized Data Set Question #87

FIGURE 13.11 Data charts from Penn State report

Reading, Writing, and Discussion Questions

1. Do the two tables help a researcher know how the number of students affected by trauma has changed over time?
2. How is the information presented in the two charts different? Is one more useful than the other in establishing a need for safe spaces on campuses? Explain.
3. Does the fact that the responses are broken down by gender add any useful information for someone researching safe spaces on college campuses? Explain.

4. This information was found at a website for Penn State Student Affairs, Counseling & Psychological Services, Center for Collegiate Mental Health. It is part of an annual report published by the center. Evaluate the author of this report for relevance. Is the authoring center relevant to the paper? What do you know, or what could you find out about the author? Would a different author be more relevant?

Reliability

Once you have selected some useful sources to support your claims, it is time to make a more in-depth evaluation to be sure each source is reliable.

- Is the source current enough? Have circumstances changed since this text was published?
- Is the author someone you would want to call on as an expert witness? Does the author have the experience or credentials to make a solid argument that will carry weight with your readers?
- Is it reliable information for your purposes? It may be highly opinionated, but are the basic facts it presents confirmed in other sources? Is the evidence presented in the text convincing?

These questions are not always easy to answer. In some cases, articles will include some information about the author, such as where he or she works. In other cases, no information or even an author's name is given. In that case, it may help to evaluate the publication and its reputation. If you aren't familiar with a publication and don't feel confident making your own judgment, see if it is described in *Magazines for Libraries*, which evaluates the reputation and quality of periodicals.

Websites pose challenges and offer unique opportunities for researchers. When evaluating a website, first examine what kind of site you are reading.

- Is the web page selling or advertising goods or services (a business site)?
- Is it advocating a point of view (an advocacy site) or providing relatively neutral information (an informative or educational site)?
- Is the website addressing the interests of people in a particular organization or with common interests (an information-sharing site)?
- Is it reporting up-to-the-minute news (a news site) or appealing to some aspect of an individual's life and interests (a personal site)?
- Does it reflect a clear bias — political or religious, for example — that you can identify from the name of the site or from the subject matter or the contributors?

Useful information for a research paper may be obtained from any of these kinds of websites, but it is helpful to know what the main purpose of the site is — and who its primary audience is — when determining how productive it will be for your research.

As you weigh the main purpose of the site, evaluate its original context. Does the site originate in a traditional medium, such as a print journal or an encyclopedia? Is the site part of an online journal, in which case its material had to go through a screening process? Or is the site the product of one individual's or

> **RESEARCH SKILL** Evaluating Multimodal Sources
>
> Whether you find them in print or online, sources that include a mix of images, audio, video, and even text require special attention. Keep the following questions in mind.
>
> - **Audio.** How does the sound affect what is being shown or spoken? Is there a speaker? Would the use of audio enhance what you have written? How?
> - **Images.** What effect does the image have on the message? Does the image serve a rhetorical purpose? What effect does the composition as a whole have (cropping, focus, angle, etc.)? Does it advance the point you are trying to make?
> - **Film/Video.** Is the production of good quality? Is the perspective of the film appropriate for the points you are trying to make? Is the time it would take to show the film or video worthwhile in making your argument? Will it be clear to your audience why you included the film? Does your audience feel like a participant in the action or a viewer? How does the use of close-ups, long shots, color, lighting, and other visual effects affect the mood? How does sound affect the mood?
> - **Other Multimodal Sources.** Consider the mood or tone that the creator is trying to achieve through sound, pictures, and video. Think about pace, volume, and imaging. Do your multimodal sources elicit emotions — fear, humor, guilt, or sadness — that advance your argument rather than merely eliciting an emotional response?

organization's desire to create a website or blog, which means the work may not have been screened or evaluated by any outside agency? In that case, the information may still be valuable, but you must be even more careful when evaluating it.

To determine if an online source is reliable, make a brief overview of the site itself by looking, for example, at the clues contained in the URL. That is, *.com* in the address often means a business or commercial site; *.edu* is a site sponsored by a university or college; *.k12* is a site associated with a primary or secondary school; *.gov* indicates that the state or federal government sponsored the site; and *.org* suggests that the site is part of a nonprofit or noncommercial group. Sites originating outside the United States have URLs that end with a two-letter country abbreviation, such as *.uk* for United Kingdom. Although these address clues can reveal a great deal about the origins and purposes of a website, remember that personal websites may also contain some of these abbreviations. Institutions such as schools and businesses sometimes sponsor individuals' personal websites (which are often unscreened by the institution) as well as official institutional sites. If you are unsure of the sponsoring organization of a page, try erasing all the information in the URL after the first slash (/) and pressing the "Enter" key. Doing so often brings you to the main page of the organization sponsoring the website.

Many sites will have a link to an organization's mission statement or a link labeled "About" or "Who We Are." Clicking on those links can give you additional information about who is behind the site and what they are seeking to accomplish. The ads on a site can also give you insight into its focus; the more ads, the more the website is trying to sell you something (or keep itself funded) than it is trying to provide you with good facts and reporting.

ARGUMENT ESSENTIALS

Evaluating Sources

Check All Sources for Relevance

- Be critical of your sources from the beginning of your research. Look for the best sources, not the first ones you can locate.
- Look for sources that use relevant terms in their titles, are directed to an appropriate audience, and are published in reputable places.
- Skim possible sources for relevance to your topic, usefulness (not information you already have), and informative value.
- Let your sources lead you to other possible sources.

Check All Sources for Reliability

- Check each source for **currency**. Is the information recent (unless there is a reason for using a source from an earlier period)? You do not want to build your case on information that has been superseded by more recent sources.
- Check the **authority** of the author(s). Is the author an expert in the field or otherwise qualified through experience to write about the subject? Be wary of a source if no author is listed.
- Check the **accuracy** of the information. Does the support the author offers for his or her ideas convince you that the major ideas expressed are valid and accurate? Factual information can often be checked by finding another source that provides the same information.
- Check for **objectivity**; subjectivity gets in the way of reliability. Does the author reveal bias that could keep the content from being reliable? You do not want to build your case on someone else's unsupported opinion.
- Check for adequate **coverage** of the subject. Does the author provide enough information about the subject, in enough detail, to be useful for your purposes? If not, you might find other sources to be more useful.

Use Special Care with Online Sources

- Consider what type of site it is. Is it trying to sell something, advocating a point of view, providing information, reporting the news?
- Consider its original context. Is it, for example, a journal article available through a database? A site created and maintained by a single person?
- Consider the sponsor or creator of the site. Do they have a clear and potentially biased mission or agenda? Is it a *.gov*, *.com*, *.edu*, or *.org* site? What does that tell you?

Consider Multimodal Sources

- Consider livening up your work with visuals if your instructor allows it.
- Be sure to give your source for information in modes other than text just as conscientiously as you would for text.

Practice: Evaluate Sources for Reliability

Look at the entries from a Google search of the terms "competitive foods" and "school." Use the questions that follow to consider how reliable these potential sources might be.

FIGURE 13.12 Google search results for "competitive foods" and "school"

Reading, Writing, and Discussion Questions

1. The first entry is a publication of the CDC and has a *.gov* URL. What is the CDC, and what does that suggest to you about how reliable the source might be?

2. The fifth entry is also a *.gov* source, although from a state government rather than the federal government. What does *SDE* stand for? What does that suggest about the reliability of the source?

3. There are two sources here that are from organizations' sites. Go online to find the articles, and see what you can determine about the organizations that would suggest they are trustworthy sources.

4. What kind of source does the final link lead to? How do you know? Does it look reliable?

Taking Notes

While everyone has methods of taking notes, here are a few suggestions that should be useful to research writers who need to read materials quickly, comprehend and evaluate the sources, use them as part of a research paper assignment, and manage their time carefully. If you need more detailed help with summarizing, paraphrasing, and quoting, review "Providing Support" in Chapter 4, pages 95-99.

When taking notes from a source, summarize instead of quoting long passages. Summarizing as you read saves time. If you feel that a direct quote is more effective than anything you could write and provides crucial support for your argument, copy the material word for word. Leave all punctuation exactly as it appears, and insert ellipsis points (. . .) if you delete material. Enclose all quotations in quotation marks, and copy complete information about your source, including the author's name, the title of the book or article, the journal name if appropriate, page numbers, and publishing information. If you quote an article that appears in an anthology, record complete information about the book itself.

If you aren't sure whether you will use a piece of information later, don't copy the whole passage. Instead, make a note of its bibliographic information or copy and save the link to an online source so that you can find it again if you need it. Taking too many notes, however, is preferable to taking too few, a problem that will force you to go back to the source for missing information.

One of the most effective ways to save yourself time and trouble when you are ready to write your research paper is to document your research as you go along. That way, when the time comes to create your Works Cited page, you will be ready to put the works you used in alphabetical order — or let your computer do it for you — and provide a list of those works at the end of your paper. Some instructors may require a bibliography, or a list of all of the works you consulted, but at a minimum you will need a Works Cited or References page. As that title indicates, the list will include only those works that you quote, paraphrase, or summarize directly in your paper.

Once you are fairly certain that you will use a certain source, go ahead and put its information in proper bibliographic form. That way, if the citation form is complicated, you can look it up or ask your instructor before the last minute. Also, you will realize immediately if you are missing information required by the citation and can record it while the source is still at hand. See Chapter 15, Documenting Sources, for complete details about what information you will need and the proper form for it.

Note Taking and Prewriting

Use the note-taking process as a prewriting activity. Often when you summarize an author's ideas or write down direct quotes, you see or understand the material in new ways. Freewrite about the importance of these quotes, paraphrases, or summaries, or at least about those that seem especially important. If nothing else, take a minute to justify in writing why you chose to record the notes. Doing so will help you clarify and develop your thoughts about your argument.

Taking this prewriting step seriously will help you analyze the ideas you record from outside sources. You will then be better prepared for the more formal (and inevitable) work of summarizing, paraphrasing, and composing involved in thinking critically about your topic and writing a research paper. Maybe most important, such work will help with that moment all writers face when they realize they "know what they want to say but can't find the words to say it." Overcoming such moments does not depend on finding inspiration while writing the final draft of a paper. Instead, successfully working through this common form of writer's block depends more on the amount of prewriting and thoughtful consideration of the notes done early in the research process.

Working with Your Outline

As you take notes, also remember to refer to your outline to ensure that you are acquiring sufficient data to support all the points you intend to raise. Of course, you will be revising your outline during the course of your research as issues are clarified and new ideas emerge, but the outline will serve as a rough guide throughout the writing process. Keeping close track of your outline will also prevent you from recording material that is interesting but not relevant. It may help to label your notes with the heading from the outline to which they are most relevant.

Relying on the knowledge of others is an important part of doing research; expert opinions and eloquent arguments help support your claims when your own expertise is limited. But remember, this is *your* paper. Your ideas and insights into other people's ideas are just as important as the information you uncover at the library or through reputable online sources. When writing an argument, do not simply regurgitate the words and thoughts of others in your essay. Work to achieve a balance between providing solid information from expert sources and offering your own interpretation of the argument and the evidence that supports it.

Managing and Documenting Sources

Using word-processing software can invigorate the processes of note taking and of outlining. Taking notes using a computer gives you more flexibility than using pen and paper alone. For example, you can save your computer-generated notes and your comments on them in numerous places (on your personal computer, in the cloud, on internet-based documents that you can modify from anywhere, even your phone); you can cut and paste the text into various documents; you can add to the notes or modify them and still revert to the originals with ease.

You can also link notes to background material online that may be useful once you begin writing drafts of your paper. For example, you could create links to an author's website or to any of his or her other works published online. You could create a link to a study or an additional source cited in your notes, or you could link to the work of other researchers who support or argue against the information you recorded.

Because you can record information in any number of ways on a computer, your notes act as tools in the writing process. One of the best ways to start is to open a file or page for each source; enter the bibliographic information; directly type into the file a series of potentially useful quotations, paraphrases, and summaries; and add your initial ideas about the source. (For each entry, note the correct page references as you go along, and indicate clearly whether you are quoting, paraphrasing, or summarizing.) You can then use the capabilities of a computer to aid you in the later stages of the writing process. For example, you can collect all your research notes into one large file in which you group similar sources, evaluate whether you have too much information about one issue or one side of an argument, or examine sources that conflict with one another. You can imagine various organizational schemes for your paper based on the central themes and issues of the notes you have taken, and you can more clearly determine which quotes and summaries are essential to your paper and which ones may not be needed.

When you're ready to begin your first draft, you can readily integrate material from your source notes into your research paper by cutting and pasting, thus eliminating the need to retype and reducing the chance of error. Be sure, though, that cutting and pasting do not lead you to plagiarize inadvertently. Any wording taken from your sources that you use in your paper must be placed in quotation marks and attributed to the source. You can also combine all the bibliographic materials you have saved in separate files and then use the computer to alphabetize your sources for your final draft.

Although taking notes on the computer does not dramatically change the research process, it does highlight the fact that taking notes, prewriting, drafting a paper, and creating a Works Cited page are integrated activities that should build from one another. When you take notes from a journal, book, or website, you develop your note-taking abilities so that they help with the entire writing process.

ARGUMENT ESSENTIALS
Taking Notes

- Summarize instead of quoting long passages.

- If you do quote a passage, copy it word for word in quotation marks, using ellipsis points (. . .) to indicate any words that you left out (but only if the omission does not change the essential meaning of the passage).

- Write down all the bibliographic information (in proper form) that you will need for your Works Cited or References page. (See Chapter 15 for details.)

- Jot down a few notes to yourself about why these notes are important.

- Label notes according to the part of your rough outline they support.

- When taking notes on your computer, start a new file for each potential source.

- When cutting and pasting information from a source, be sure not to plagiarize unintentionally.

READING ARGUMENT

Seeing How to Take Notes

Read the following essay, and then read student researcher Anna's notes following it as an example of how to take notes on your reading.

Safe Spaces
ALICIA OGLESBY

Safe spaces within college communities isn't a new concept. The term derives from the idea that marginalized and oppressed communities need a place to get away from those who or that which marginalizes and/or oppresses. Just as most people typically don't subject themselves to various degrees of perpetual abuse, safe spaces are typically physical areas that a person can enter or leave by choice.

An extreme example of a safe space is a domestic violence shelter. A less extreme example is a classroom where the professor welcomes trans students by calling them by their chosen name and correct pronoun. The idea of feeling safe is a basic need on the Maslow Hierarchy of Needs Scale and can quickly and succinctly be distinguished from discomfort.

The 40-foot border wall, travel bans from majority-Muslim countries, and state violence against descendants of enslaved black people, only scratch the surface of why we need safe spaces for marginalized students' mental and emotional health. In fact, the needs among students are going to increasingly grow more diverse. To truly help all students succeed, we need to have these kinds of supports in place and constantly strategize new ones.

Perceptions of the Non-Marginalized

Flemming Rose, a *Huffington Post* contributor, wrote an article in 2017, "Safe Spaces on College Campuses Are Creating Intolerant Students." The first paragraph sets readers up to identify safe spaces as a place where students are "protected from ideas and speakers they don't like." This is an incorrect definition of safe spaces. I didn't read beyond the first paragraph. Maybe I should have. Maybe he mentions more helpful ways of exploring safe spaces. But I couldn't get past the first paragraph's inherent fallacy — he didn't recognize that for marginalized groups these spaces are sacred, necessary, and life-saving.

"The Coddling of the American Mind" by Greg Lukianoff and Jonathan Haidt goes into great detail about how safe spaces, trigger warnings, and "safetyism" lead to anxious and incapable young people. This is surely not a one-size-fits-all American experience. Here we have white men looking through their own eyes, but the white American experience certainly is not synonymous or interchangeable with the black American experience. The same goes for heterosexual colleagues not recognizing the perceptions of LGBTQ colleagues and students. Middle class vs. low-income; private independent

5

Alicia Oglesby is a high school counselor in the Washington, D.C. area. She is coauthor, with Rebecca Atkins, of *Interrupting Racism: Equity and Social Justice in School Counseling* (2018). Her article appeared in the *Journal of College Admissions* in 2019.

vs. public schools—the list of privileged groups misunderstanding less privileged groups goes on and on.

To clarify, safe spaces and healthy growth from experiencing emotional, intellectual, physical and emotional discomfort can and should exist together. We need places where we can gain nourishment. We also need to be respectfully challenged by our educators who have our personal growth in mind.

As you read articles or participate in online forums, make it a point to note the race, gender, and other characteristics of the authors and ask yourself if they are able to see their own limitations. You'll find that those who argue against safe spaces belong to groups that historically have not been threatened. Absorb that reflective practice into your conversation, interactions, and thoughts about how to better support students who may not be exactly like you.

The Reality

Patterns of discrimination and the practice of pushing marginalized students farther toward the edge are happening all around us:

- Black students often don't feel safe at predominantly white institutions (PWIs) because they are surrounded by white students and professors who can and do call campus police on them.
- Low-income students are lumped in with other students who can easily call home for money, afford spring break trips, don't have to worry about tuition being paid so they can register for next semester.
- LGBTQ students are not included when there are no unisex bathrooms, changing rooms, or clear standards and policies about anti-discrimination.

- Trans students feel excluded or unsafe in high schools when, during active shooter drills, they are uncomfortable with or unclear on which locker room they are allowed to shelter in.
- According to the Southern Poverty Law Center, 25 percent of hate crimes nationally occur in schools, from kindergarten through college.

The reality is that these experiences are psychologically, intellectually, emotionally, and economically traumatic. To function—and to thrive—these groups need the respite found in safe spaces.

As marginalized students start thinking about going to college, (hopefully) they'll bring their concerns to your office. I am the assistant director of school and college counseling at Bishop McNamara High School in Prince George's County, Maryland.

Our school is an anomaly—Catholic and majority black. As a black woman, I feel especially proud to be among students like myself.

I talk ad nauseam about college, but I do a lot of listening. I want my office to be a safe space, where students can share with me their fears, hopes, and plans. Here are some of the things they've revealed:

10

"I'm not going to a white school. They will wind up putting me in the dorm with the white girl who pours bleach in my Gatorade. Nah. You won't catch me there." This student is referring to an incident highlighted in the news where a white female roommate attempted to poison her black female roommate by spitting in her food products and rubbing used tampons on her belongings. The white female student was charged with criminal mischief and a

hate crime. The white female student was appropriately expelled but served no time for her crimes.

"I don't mind going to a white school, but it can't be too white (laughter)." My college counseling program often includes specific racial breakdowns about who is on campus. Our "sweet spot" is at least half and half (half white, half students of color). Keep in mind, some of my students of color feel comfortable attending PWIs—those that have strong diversity, equity and inclusion programs, such as a Filipino Student Association.

"If I can't be 'gay-gay' on campus then take it off my list because I just got to the point where I can truly be me." It is difficult for my gay students to be fully out at our Catholic school. I try to be as supportive as possible and encourage them to apply to colleges that will continue that support, affirmation, and love.

"It would be hard for me to connect with them because I would always have to wonder if they really want to be my friend or if I'm their token Latina friend or if they are working out their Trump issues on me. It's weird. I just don't want to have to worry about that AND study." Because of the current political landscape and the history of oppression in communities of color and Spanish-speaking communities, there is a shared distrust that must be intentionally resolved.

For students to successfully transition to higher education, we need all parties creating these spaces. Everyone's office should be a safe space, but beyond that, what spaces can we offer on campus? How can we guide students toward them? We have to continually assess our own privileges and marginalizations as we talk about and build safe spaces.

For example, even with our challenges, my students and I have our own privileges. We belong to multiple groups of both privileged and oppressed identities, which puts us in a unique position to talk about safe spaces. I feel especially compelled to write about safe spaces as a Howard University (DC) alumna. Howard, for me, was a safe space because I am black. I'm not first-generation college and I come from a middle-class background. But, I have also attended PWIs and have experienced blatant racism from white male professors.

Inform Students and Your Office

Students who feel supported by diversity, equity, and inclusion efforts are more likely to feel safe. But because the majority often takes safety for granted, these efforts must be intentional, systemic, and honest.   15

How do we create this scenario? Start with the student perspective:

- How can I learn about programs that come alongside safe spaces I need every day?
- How are you attracting marginalized students to apply?
- Are admission counselors and deans of admission visiting public urban and rural high schools?
- Are admission counselors and deans of admission attending community events within city limits?
- How many of the students who attend your visit programs are offered admission?
- What aspects of the visit program mimic what happens on campus during a typical school year?

I often use Swarthmore College (PA) as an example because of the opportunities they create for non-white, non-affluent students. My high school counselor colleagues offer Pomona College (CA), Carleton College (MN), Rice University, Vanderbilt University (TN), University of Vermont, Radford University (VA), Baldwin Wallace University (OH), University of North Carolina–Greensboro, and Elon University (NC) as other PWIs creating safe spaces for marginalized students.

As you work to create safe space on your campus, don't reinvent the wheel, find out what others are doing and adjust it to your school's community and mission. Read up on the experts who support safe spaces:

- *Meaningful LGBTQ Inclusion in Schools: The Importance of Diversity Representation and Counterspace* by Alison Cerezo & Jeannette Bergfeld;

- *The African American Student Network: Creating Sanctuaries and Counterspaces for Coping With Racial Microaggressions in Higher Education Settings* by Tabitha L. Grier-Reed;

- *Racial and Gender Microaggressions on a Predominantly-White Campus: Experiences of Black, Latina/o and White Undergraduates* by Janice McCabe.

There are countless experts, articles, books, lesson plans, and information if you choose to explore.

As our country continues to become more diverse in every way, we are behind the curve if we haven't adapted the ways in which we educate, include, discuss, engage, and involve. Now that we know better, we owe it to our students to do better.

20

Oglesby, Alicia. "Safe Spaces." *The Journal of College Admissions*, 2019. OneSearch, pp. 48–50.

PWI—Predominantly white institutions

Safe Spaces—Marginalized/oppressed students have a space to escape the people or situations that make them feel that way (48)

The college experience is varied and complex; a system in which under-privileged groups are misunderstood and oppressed by privileged groups (48)

Marginalized groups include black, low-income, LGBTQ, and other minority students (48)

"Students who feel supported by diversity, equity, and inclusion efforts are more likely to feel safe. But because the majority often takes safety for granted, these efforts must be intentional, systemic, and honest" (49).

Create spaces of inclusivity, healing, and open communication by learning about similar programs and supporting marginalized students in the application process. (50)

"Here we have white men looking through their own eyes, but the white American experience certainly is not synonymous or interchangeable with the black American experience" (48).

After reviewing my notes, I see that marginalization plays a key role in the establishment of safe spaces and trigger warnings. I think I should tie marginalized groups to my explanation of how safe spaces and trigger warnings aim to be inclusive of all students.

Practice: Taking Notes

Using Anna's notes as a model, take notes on the following essay.

Why "Safe Spaces" Are Important for Mental Health—Especially on College Campuses

MEGAN YEE

For the better half of my undergraduate years, nearly everyone seemed to have something to say about "safe spaces." Mentioning the term had the potential to elicit heated reactions from students, politicians, academics, and anyone else remotely interested in the topic.

Headlines about safe spaces and their relevance to free speech on college campuses flooded the editorial sections of news outlets. This occurred, in part, as a result of widely publicized incidents regarding safe spaces at universities across the country.

In the fall of 2015, a series of student protests over racial tension erupted at the University of Missouri over safe spaces and their impact on freedom of the press. Weeks later, a controversy at Yale over offensive Halloween costumes escalated into a fight over safe spaces and students' rights to freedom of expression.

In 2016, the dean of University of Chicago wrote a letter to the incoming class of 2020 stating that the university didn't condone trigger warnings or intellectual safe spaces.

Some critics suggest that safe spaces are a direct threat to free speech, foster groupthink, and limit the flow of ideas. Others accuse college students of being coddled "snowflakes" who seek protection from ideas that make them uncomfortable.

What unites most anti–safe space stances is that they focus almost exclusively on safe spaces in the context of college campuses and free speech. Because of this, it's easy to forget that the term "safe space" is actually quite broad and encompasses a variety of different meanings.

5

Megan Yee is a freelance writer for Healthline Media. Her article appeared on Healthline.com on June 3, 2019, and the byline included a note that it was "medically reviewed by Timothy J. Legg, PhD, PsyD."

What Is a Safe Space?

On college campuses, a "safe space" is usually one of two things. Classrooms can be designated as academic safe spaces, meaning that students are encouraged to take risks and engage in intellectual discussions about topics that may feel uncomfortable. In this type of safe space, free speech is the goal.

The term "safe space" is also used to describe groups on college campuses that seek to provide respect and emotional security, often for individuals from historically marginalized groups.

A "safe space" doesn't have to be a physical location. It can be something as simple as a group of people who hold similar values and commit to consistently provide each other with a supportive, respectful environment.

The Purpose of Safe Spaces

It's well-known that a little anxiety can boost our performance, but chronic anxiety can take a toll on our emotional and psychological health.

Feeling like you need to have your guard up at all times can be exhausting and emotionally taxing.

10   "Anxiety pushes the nervous system into overdrive which can tax bodily systems leading to physical discomfort like a tight chest, racing heart, and churning stomach," says Dr. Juli Fraga, Psy.D.

"Because anxiety causes fear to arise, it can lead to avoidance behaviors, such as avoiding one's fears and isolating from others," she adds.

Safe spaces can provide a break from judgment, unsolicited opinions, and having to explain yourself. It also allows people to feel supported and respected. This is especially important for minorities, members of the LGBTQIA community, and other marginalized groups.

That said, critics often redefine the concept of a safe space as something that's a direct attack on free speech and only relevant to minority groups on college campuses.

Perpetuating this narrow definition makes it difficult for the general population to understand the value of a safe space and why they can benefit all people.

Using this constricted safe space definition   15 also limits the scope of productive discussions we can have regarding the topic. For one, it prevents us from examining how they relate to mental health — an issue that's just as relevant, and arguably more urgent, than free speech.

Why These Spaces Are Beneficial for Mental Health

Despite my background as a journalism student, racial minority, and native of the ultra-liberal Bay Area, I still had difficulty understanding the value of safe spaces until after college.

I was never anti–safe space, but during my time at Northwestern I never identified as someone who *needed* a safe space. I was also wary of engaging in discussions about a topic that could ignite polarizing debates.

In hindsight, however, I've always had a safe space in one form or another even before I started college.

Since middle school, that place was the yoga studio in my hometown. Practicing yoga and the studio itself was so much more than downward dogs and handstands. I learned yoga, but more importantly, I learned how to navigate discomfort, learn from failure, and approach new experiences with confidence.

20   I spent hundreds of hours practicing in the same room, with the same faces, in the same mat space. I loved that I could go to the studio and leave the stress and drama of being a high schooler at the door.

For an insecure teenager, having a judgment-free space where I was surrounded by mature, supportive peers was invaluable.

Even though the studio fits the definition nearly perfectly, I had never thought of the studio as a "safe space" until recently.

Redefining the studio has helped me see how focusing solely on safe spaces as a barrier to free speech is unproductive because it limits people's willingness to engage with the topic as a whole — namely, how it relates to mental health.

Drafting, Revising, and Presenting Arguments

Chapter 13 discusses the planning of an argumentative paper and the process involved in researching topics that require support beyond what the writer knows firsthand. This chapter discusses moving from the planning and researching stage into the actual writing of the paper or presentation.

Reviewing Your Research

Making a preliminary outline before you conduct any needed research gives direction to your research and helps you to organize your own thoughts on the subject. Preliminary outlines can change, however, in the process of researching and writing the paper. As you begin drafting the paper, be sure you have a solid thesis and strong and plentiful evidence for each topic in your preliminary or revised outline.

Once you are satisfied that you have identified all the issues that will appear in your paper, you should begin to determine what kind of organization will be most effective for your argument. Now is the time to organize the results of your thinking into a logical and persuasive form, which may be determined by your assignment requirements, your genre, your audience, or your purpose. (As a reminder of the different ways and approaches to organizing your paper, see Part Two, "Writing Argument," and especially Chapter 5, "Approaches to Argument," and Chapter 9, "Structuring the Argument.") If you have read about your topic, answered questions, and acquired some evidence, you may already have decided on ways to approach your subject. If not, you should look closely at your outline now, recalling your purposes when you began your investigation, and develop a strategy for using the information you have gathered to achieve those purposes.

As you did in Chapter 9 in writing arguments not based on independent research, be mindful of the context in which the argument is taking place, and try this procedure for tackling the issues in any controversial problem.

1. Raise the relevant issues, and omit those that would distract you from your purpose. Plan to devote more time and space to issues you regard as crucial.
2. Produce the strongest evidence you can to support your factual claims, knowing that the opposing side or critical readers may try to produce conflicting evidence.

3. Defend your value claims by finding support in the fundamental principles with which most people in your audience would agree.

4. Explain as specifically as possible what you want your audience to think or do when you are arguing a policy claim.

5. Argue with yourself. Try to foresee what kinds of refutation are possible. Try to anticipate and meet the opposing arguments.

6. Consider the context in which your argument will be read, and be sensitive to the concerns of your audience.

Student researcher Anna applied the six steps in the review process to her topic like this:

1. The relevant issue for my thesis is that marginalized college students are experiencing more mental health issues every year, and safe spaces are a tool that can be used to support these students. I need to establish that there has been a steady rise in the number of students experiencing mental health issues as a result of trauma, which is a claim of fact. However, I don't need to spend too much time on the state of mental health in college. Instead, my essay will focus on why safe spaces specifically are necessary in order to solve the issue of mental health on college campuses.

2. I can draw my support for the claim of fact that more students are experiencing mental health issues primarily from the Penn State article, pointing out that they draw their data from dozens of different schools.

3. Culturally, I believe the nation is steadily gaining in social awareness regarding issues of mental health and depression at large. Most people, especially college students and parents with college-aged children, should agree that mental illness is harmful and should be combated.

4. I want universities across the country to maintain safe spaces for students in conjunction with further programming supporting students with mental health issues or those that are experiencing the effects of trauma.

5. One of the strongest points of the opposition is that allowing students to "escape" from the more difficult realities of American social, academic, professional, and political life provides too much hand-holding and encourages hyper-sensitivity, making students incapable of engaging with the world around them.

6. College administrators, students, and parents should be concerned about the mental well-being of student bodies. My argument is further supported by the increased awareness of mental health issues at large, as more organizations are speaking out in participation of Mental Health Awareness Month and similar movements.

RESEARCH SKILL ▶ Reviewing Your Research

- Is your thesis the right scope — not too broad or too narrow?
- Does your working outline show any gaps in your argument?
- Does your research show enough counterarguments? If not, your thesis may not be debatable and may need to be changed.
- Does your research show strong counterarguments that might make you want to change your thesis or shift the perspective of your argument?
- Have you identified the assumptions linking your claim with data and ensured that these assumptions, too, are adequately documented?

- Have you found sufficient data to support your claim?
- Is your research varied enough and not too reliant on one source or source type? Have you met your instructor's guidelines for number and type of sources?
- Do your notes include exact copies of all statements you may want to quote and paraphrased or summarized versions of material that does not need to be quoted directly? Do your notes include complete references?
- Have you answered all the relevant questions that have come up during your research?
- Do you have enough information about your sources to document your paper?

Avoiding Plagiarism

Plagiarism is the use of someone else's words or ideas without adequate acknowledgment—that is, presenting such words or ideas as your own. Putting something into your own words is not in itself a defense against plagiarism; the source of the ideas must be identified as well. Giving credit to the sources you use serves three important purposes:

1. It reflects your own honesty and seriousness as a researcher.
2. It enables the reader to find the source of the reference and read further, sometimes to verify that the source has been correctly used.
3. It adds the authority of experts to your argument.

Plagiarism is nothing less than cheating, and it is an offense that deserves serious punishment. You can avoid accidentally slipping into plagiarism if you are careful in researching and writing your papers.

Taking care to document sources is an obvious way to avoid plagiarism. You should also be careful in taking notes and, when writing your paper, indicating where your ideas end and someone else's begin. When taking notes, make sure either to quote word for word or to paraphrase—one or the other, not both mixed together. If you quote, enclose any language that you borrow from other sources in quotation marks. That way, when you look back at your notes days or weeks later, you won't mistakenly assume that the language is your own. If you know that you aren't going to use a particular writer's exact words, then take the time to summarize that person's ideas right away. That will save you time and trouble later.

> **ARGUMENT ESSENTIALS**
> Avoiding Plagiarism
>
> - Take notes with care.
> - Be clear in your writing where another person's words and ideas begin and end.
> - Either quote word for word or paraphrase, not a mixture of both.
> - Document your use of sources, whether you are quoting, paraphrasing, or summarizing.

When using someone else's ideas in your paper, always let the reader know where that person's ideas begin and end. Here is an example from a paper that uses APA style:

> When zoo animals do mate successfully, the offspring is often weakened by inbreeding. According to geneticists, this is because a population of 150 breeder animals is necessary in order to "assure the more or less permanent survival of a species in captivity" (Ehrlich & Ehrlich, 1981, p. 211).

The phrase "according to geneticists" indicates that the material to follow comes from another source, cited parenthetically at the end of the borrowed material. If the writer had not included the phrase "according to geneticists," it might look as if she only borrowed the passage in quotation marks, and not the information that precedes that passage.

Building an Effective Argument

In general, the writer of an argument using research follows the same rules that govern any form of expository writing. (Writing arguments is covered in detail in Part Two, "Writing Argument.") Your organization should be logical, your style clear and readable, your ideas connected by transitional phrases and sentences, your paragraphs coherent. The main difference between an argument and expository writing is the need to persuade an audience to adopt a belief or take an action. You should assume your readers will be critical rather than neutral or sympathetic. Therefore, you must be equally critical of your own work. Any apparent gap in reasoning or ambiguity in presentation is likely to weaken the argument.

For help with your organization, look back at the organizational patterns discussed in "Organizing the Argument" in Chapter 9 on pages 249–62:

- Defining the thesis
- Refuting an opposing view
- Finding the middle ground
- Presenting the stock issues

You may also want to review what Chapter 9 says about writing introductions and conclusions. The style and tone you choose depend not only on the nature of the subject but also on how you can best convince readers that you are a credible source. **Style** in this context refers to the elements of your prose—simple versus complex sentences, active versus passive verbs, metaphors, analogies, and other literary devices. It is usually appropriate in a short paper to choose an expository style, which emphasizes the elements of your argument rather than your personality. You can discover some helpful pointers on essay style by reading the editorials in newspapers such as the *New York Times*, the *Washington Post*, and the *Wall Street Journal*. The authors are typically addressing a mixed audience comparable to the hypothetical readers of your own paper. Though their approaches vary, each writer is attempting to portray himself or herself as an objective analyst whose argument deserves careful attention. **Tone** is the approach you take to your topic—solemn or humorous, detached or sympathetic. Style and tone together compose your **voice** as a writer.

Remember too that part of establishing your credibility as a writer is to document your sources with care. You will need to use a combination of quotations, paraphrases, and summaries to support your points. See "Providing Support" in Chapter 4 (pp. 95–99) for guidance on how to incorporate these elements into your paper. See Chapter 15 for advice on how to cite these sources.

ARGUMENT ESSENTIALS
Checklist for Effective Arguments

- Interesting and debatable thesis
- All claims supported with documented evidence
- No unsupported controversial warrants
- Appropriate organization
- Opposing arguments refuted

Using Sentence Forms to Write Arguments

Since you will be making use of others' ideas in supporting your own, you need to be respectful of what others say and write, and you need to account for their positions accurately. You'll want to be sure to clearly summarize other authors' ideas when you write about them.

When you present a negative evaluation of an argument, it is important to clearly explain how the previous writer approached the topic, and then explain how your view differs. Sometimes the points of difference are large, sometimes small. But in writing for college, it is crucial that you explain your own understanding of a situation *and* that you express your own point of view.

It is easier to think about how you might summarize the argument of others and present your own if you have a model from which to work. This kind of model is called a *sentence form*, and we showed you a few examples in Chapter 9. Sentence forms can help you to organize the presentation of others' views and your own responses to them. Following are some basic sentence forms for this kind of work.

(Keep in mind that a parenthetical citation comes at the end of information borrowed from a source; for more details on how to cite sources correctly, see Chapter 15.)

Presenting Another's View

In _____, X claims that _____.

X's conclusion is that _____.

On the topic of _____, X attempts to make the case that

_____.

These sentence forms are useful for presenting a brief summary of another's views on an issue. Note that the final sentence form implies that the writer has failed to make a convincing argument. (You would then go on to explain X's failure.)

Presenting Another's View Using Direct Quotations

In _____, X writes, "_____."

After discussing the topic of _____, X's conclusion is that

"_____."

X attempts to make the case that "_____."

Quotations are a powerful way to present another's views when the language is particularly striking, clear, and succinct. (For more on using quotations, including a list of alternatives to the verb "writes," see "Research Skill: Incorporating Quotations into Your Text" on pp. 98–99.) These sentence guides help you to employ a key skill in making an argument: showing the work others have done on the issue. The next step is to introduce your own voice.

Presenting Another's View and Responding to It

She claims _____. It is actually true that _____.

In his essay _____, X writes that _____. However,

_____.

X attempts to make the case that "_____."

In her essay, X implies _____. However, careful consideration

shows that _____.

The formula for this kind of template introduces what the author has to say and then has you take your turn with your own view of the matter.

When you agree with some of what a writer says, but not all of it, you must distinguish between the parts you think are correct and those parts that are not. Sentence forms for this kind of response include the following.

Agreeing in Part

Although most of what X writes about _____ is true, it is not

true that _____.

X is correct that _____. But because of _____ it is actually

true that _____.

X argues that _____. While it is true that _____ and

_____ are valid points, _____ is not. Instead, _____.

These sentence templates ask you to identify those parts of the argument that are valid. Keep in mind that it is rare to disagree totally with every view expressed in an argument. A careful arguer will separate out what is correct and what is not. The writer can then focus energy on showing why these parts are not correct.

At times, you'll need to correct a distortion or misstatement of fact. Statistics, for instance, can be and often are manipulated to present the arguer's viewpoint in the best light. You may wish to propose an alternative interpretation or set the statistics in a different context, one more accurate and favorable to your own point of view. Of course, you'll want to be certain that you do not distort statistics. (For more on the importance of using statistics fairly, see the full discussion in the section "Statistics" in Chapter 7, on pp. 195–97.) Here's a sentence form for correcting factual information in an argument.

Correcting a Factual Mistake

While X claims _____, it is actually true that _____.

Although X states _____, a careful examination of _____

and _____ indicates that _____.

These sentence guides allow you to identify a mistaken claim of fact in an argument and present evidence opposing it.

More often, rather than correcting clear mistakes of fact, you'll need to refine the argument of a writer. You may find that much of the argument makes sense to you, but that the writer does not sufficiently anticipate important objections. In those cases, a sentence form such as one of the following can help you refine the argument to make a stronger conclusion.

Refining Another's Argument

Although it is true, as X shows, that _____, the actual result is

closer to _____ because _____.

While X claims _____ and _____, he fails to consider the

important point _____. Therefore, a more accurate conclusion is

_____.

Such sentence forms enable you to clarify and amplify an argument.

At times, you'll need to distinguish between the views of two different writers and then weigh in with your own assessment of the situation. When two authors write on the same topic, they will most likely share similar views on some of the points. They will, however, disagree on other points. Similarly, you may find that you agree with some of what each writer has to say, but disagree with some other parts. Your job is to identify the points of contrast between the two authors and then explain how your own position differs from one or both. In those cases, you may find the following sentence forms helpful.

Explaining Contrasting Views and Adding Your Position

X says _____. Y says _____. However, _____.

On the topic of _____, X claims that _____.

In contrast, _____.

Y argues that _____. However,

_____.

A careful writer makes sure the reader understands fine distinctions. The forms above help make those distinctions clear.

While sentence forms may be rather simple — perhaps even simplistic — good writers use them all the time. Once you have tried them out a few times, you'll begin to use them automatically, perhaps without even realizing it. They are powerful tools for incorporating others' views into your own work and then helping you to make careful distinctions about various parts of arguments.

> **ARGUMENT ESSENTIALS**
> Addressing Opposing Arguments Using Sentence Forms
>
> Before you analyze or evaluate another's argument, you must first be sure that you understand it. Then you can show where it is weak and how your view is different by using some of the sentence forms in this section:
>
> - Presenting another's view
> - Presenting another's view using direct quotations
> - Presenting another's view and responding to it
> - Agreeing in part
> - Correcting a factual mistake
> - Refining another's argument
> - Explaining contrasting views and adding your position

Revising

The final stage in writing an argument is revising. The first step is to read through what you have written to be sure your paper is complete and well organized. Have you omitted any of the issues, warrants, or supporting evidence on your outline? Is each paragraph coherent in itself? Do your paragraphs work together to create a coherent paper? All the elements of the argument—the issues raised, the underlying assumptions, and the supporting material—should contribute to the development of the claim in your thesis statement. Any material that is interesting but irrelevant to that claim should be cut.

Next, be sure that the style and tone of your paper are appropriate for the topic and the audience. Remember that people choose to read an argument because they want the answer to a troubling question or the solution to a recurrent problem. Besides stating your thesis in a way that invites the reader to join you in your investigation, you must retain your audience's interest through a discussion that may be unfamiliar or contrary to their convictions. The outstanding qualities of argumentative prose style, therefore, are clarity and readability. In addition, your paper should reach a clear conclusion that reinforces your thesis.

Style is obviously harder to evaluate in your own writing than organization. Your outline provides a map against which to check the structure of your paper. Clarity and readability, by comparison, are somewhat abstract qualities. Two procedures may be helpful. The first is to read two or three (or more) essays by authors whose style you admire and then turn back to your own writing. Awkward spots in your prose are sometimes easier to see if you get away from it and respond to someone else's perspective than if you simply keep rereading your own writing.

The second method is to read aloud. If you have never tried it, you are likely to be surprised at how valuable this can be. Again, start with someone else's work that you feel is clearly written, and practice until you achieve a smooth, rhythmic delivery that satisfies you. And listen to what you are reading. Your objective is to absorb the patterns of English structure that characterize the clearest, most readable prose. Then read your paper aloud, and listen to the construction of your sentences. Are they also clear and readable? Do they say what you want them to say? How would they sound to a reader? According to one theory, you can learn the rhythm and phrasing of a language just as you learn the rhythm and phrasing of a melody. And you will often *hear* a mistake or a clumsy construction in your writing that has escaped your eye in proofreading.

Use the spell-check and grammar-check functions of your word-processing program, but keep in mind that correctness depends on context. A spell-check will not always flag a real word that is used incorrectly, such as the word *it's* used where the word *its* is needed. Also, a grammar-check function lacks the sophistication to interpret the meaning of a sentence and may flag as incorrect a group of words that is indeed correct while missing actual errors. It is ultimately up to you to proofread the paper carefully for any mistakes and to correct the errors.

Oral Arguments and Presentations

You will often be asked to make oral presentations in your college classes. Many jobs, both professional and nonprofessional, will call for speeches to groups of fellow employees or prospective customers, to community groups, and even to government officials. Wherever you live, there will be controversies and public meetings about schooling and political candidates, about budgets for libraries and road repairs and pet control. The ability to rise and make your case before an audience is one that you will want to cultivate as a citizen of a democracy.

Some of your objectives as a writer will also be relevant to you as a speaker: making the appropriate appeal to an audience, establishing your credibility, finding adequate support for your claim. But other elements of argument will be different: language, organization, and the use of visual and other aids.

The Audience

Most speakers who confront a live audience already know something about the members of that audience. They may know why the audience is assembled to hear the particular speaker, their vocations, their level of education, and their familiarity with the subject. They may know whether the audience is friendly, hostile, or neutral to the views that the speaker will express. Analyzing the audience is an essential part of speech preparation.

In college classes, students who make assigned speeches on controversial topics are often encouraged to first survey the class. Questionnaires and interviews can give the speaker important clues to the things he should emphasize or avoid: They will tell him whether he should give both sides of a debatable question, introduce humor, use simpler language, and bring in visual or other aids.

If you know something about your audience, ask yourself what impression your clothing, gestures and bodily movements, voice, and general demeanor might convey. Make sure, too, that you understand the nature of the occasion—is it too solemn for humor? too formal for personal anecdotes?—and the purpose of the meeting, which can influence your choice of language and the most effective appeal.

Credibility

Credibility, as you learned in Chapter 5, is another name for *ethos* (the Greek word from which the English word *ethics* is derived) and refers to the honesty, moral character, and intellectual competence of the speaker.

Public figures, whose speeches and actions are reported in the media, can acquire (or fail to acquire) reputations for being endowed with those characteristics. And there is little doubt that a reputation for competence and honesty can incline an audience to accept an argument that would be rejected if offered by a speaker who lacks such a reputation.

How, then, do speakers who are unknown to the audience or who boast only modest credentials convince listeners that they are responsible advocates? From the moment the speaker appears before them, members of the audience begin to make an evaluation based on external signs such as clothing, mannerisms, and body language. But the most significant impression of the speaker's credibility will be based on what the speaker says—and how. Does the speaker give evidence of knowing the subject? of being aware of the needs and values of the audience? Especially if arguing an unpopular claim, does the speaker seem modest and conciliatory?

Unknown speakers are often advised to establish their credentials in the introduction to their speech, to summarize their background and experience as proof of their right to argue the subject they have chosen.

Speakers often use an admission of modesty as proof of an honest and unassuming character, presenting themselves not as experts but as speakers well aware of their limitations. Such an appeal can generate sympathy in the audience (if they believe the speaker) and a sense of identification with the speaker.

Organization

A well-planned speech has a clearly defined beginning, middle, and end. The beginning, which offers the introduction, can take a number of forms, depending on the kind of speech and its subject. Above all, the introduction must win the attention of the audience, especially if they have been required to attend, and encourage them to look forward to the rest of the speech. The authors of *Principles of Speech Communication* suggest seven basic attention-getters:

- referring to the subject or occasion
- using a personal reference
- asking a rhetorical question
- making a startling statement of fact or opinion
- using a quotation
- telling a humorous anecdote
- using an illustration[1]

The middle or body of the speech is, of course, the longest part. It is devoted to development of the claim that appears at the beginning. The length of the speech and the complexity of the subject determine how much support you provide. Some points are more important than others and should therefore receive more extended treatment. Unless the order is chronological, it makes sense for the speaker to arrange the supporting points in emphatic order, that is, the most important at the end because this may be the one that listeners will remember.

The conclusion should be brief; some rhetoricians suggest that the ending should constitute 5 percent of the total length of the speech. For speeches that contain several main points with supporting data, you may need to summarize. Or you may return to one of the attention-getters mentioned earlier.

The speaker must also ensure the smooth flow of argument throughout. **Coherence**, or the orderly connections between ideas, is even more important in speech than in writing because the listener cannot go back to uncover these connections. The audience listens for expressions that serve as guideposts—words,

---

[1] Bruce E. Gronbeck et al., *Principles of Speech Communication*, 13th brief ed. (New York: Longman, 1998), 243–47.

phrases, and sentences to indicate which direction the argument will take. Words such as *next, then, finally, here, first of all, whereas, in addition, second, in fact, now,* and *in conclusion* can help the listener to follow the argument's development.

Language

> It should be observed that each kind of rhetoric has its own appropriate style. That of written prose is not the same as that of spoken oratory.
>
> —Aristotle

In the end, your speech depends on the language you use. No matter how accurate your analysis of the audience, how appealing your presentation of self, how deep your grasp of the material, if the language does not clearly and emphatically convey your argument, the speech will probably fail. Fortunately, the effectiveness of language does not depend on long words or complex sentence structure—quite the contrary. Most speeches, especially those given by beginners to small audiences, are distinguished by an oral style that respects the rhythms of ordinary speech and sounds spontaneous.

- Use words that both you and your listeners are familiar with, language that convinces the audience you are sharing your knowledge and opinions, neither speaking down to them nor talking over their heads. You never want to use language that makes the audience appear ignorant or unreasonable.
- Make sure that the words you use will not be considered offensive by some members of your audience. Today we are all sensitive, sometimes hypersensitive, to terms that were once used freely if not wisely. One word, improperly used, can cause some listeners to reject the whole speech. This is particularly true of terms that suggest bias based on gender, race, or sexual orientation.
- Consider whether the subject is one that the particular audience you are addressing is not likely to be familiar with. If this is the case, then explain even the basic terms. In one class, a student who had chosen to discuss a subject about which he was extremely knowledgeable, betting on horse races, neglected to define clearly the words *exacta, subfecta, trifecta, parimutuel,* and others, leaving his audience fairly befuddled.
- Wherever it is appropriate, use concrete language with details and examples that create images and cause the listener to feel as well as think. One student speaker used strong words to good effect in providing some unappetizing facts about hot dogs: "In fact, the hot dog is so adulterated with chemicals, so contaminated with bacteria, so puffy with gristle, fat, water, and lacking in protein, that it is nutritionally worthless."[2]
- Because the audience must grasp the grammatical construction without the visual clues of punctuation available on the printed page, use short,

---

[2] Donovan Ochs and Anthony Winkler, *A Brief Introduction to Speech* (New York: Harcourt, Brace, Jovanovich, 1979), 74.

direct sentences. Use subject-verb constructions without a string of phrases or clauses preceding the subject or interrupting the natural flow of the sentence. Use the active voice frequently.

- Consider a popular stylistic device—repetition and balance, or parallel structure—to emphasize and enrich parts of your message. Almost all inspirational speeches, including religious exhortation and political oratory, take advantage of such constructions, whose rhythms evoke an immediate emotional response. It is one of the strengths of Martin Luther King Jr.'s "I Have a Dream" speech, which you can read and listen to online. Keep in mind that the ideas in parallel structures must be similar and that, for maximum effectiveness, they should be used sparingly in a short speech. Not least, the subject should be weighty enough to carry this imposing construction.

Support

The support for a claim is essentially the same for both spoken and written arguments. Factual evidence, including statistics and expert opinion, as well as appeals to needs and values, is equally important in oral presentations. But time constraints will make a difference. In a speech, the amount of support that you provide will be limited by the capacity of listeners to digest and remember information that they cannot review. This means that you must choose subjects that can be supported adequately in the time allotted.

While both speakers and writers use logical, ethical, and emotional appeals in support of their arguments, the forms of presentation can make a significant difference. The reasoning process demanded of listeners must be relatively brief and straightforward, and the supporting evidence readily assimilated. The ethical appeal or credibility of the speaker is affected not only by what is said but also by the speaker's appearance, bodily movements, and vocal expressions. And the appeal to the sympathy of the audience can be greatly enhanced by the presence of the speaker. Take the example of former U.S. congresswoman Gabrielle Giffords, shot in the head in 2012 and slowly recovering movement and speech. Written descriptions of pain and heartbreak are very moving, but place yourself in an audience, looking at Giffords and imagining her suffering. No doubt the effect would be deep and long-lasting, perhaps more memorable even than the written word.

Because the human instrument is so powerful, it must be used with care. You have probably listened to speakers who used gestures and voice inflections that had been dutifully rehearsed but were obviously contrived and worked, unfortunately, to undermine rather than support the speaker's message and credibility. If you are not a gifted actor, you should avoid gestures, body language, and vocal expressions that are not truly authentic.

Some speeches, though not all, can be enhanced by visual and other aids: charts, graphs, maps, models, objects, handouts, recordings, and computerized images. These aids, however, no matter how visually or aurally exciting, should not overwhelm your own oral presentation. The objects are not the stars of the show. They exist to make your spoken argument more persuasive.

Presentation Aids

Charts, Graphs, Handouts

Charts and graphs, large enough and clear enough to be seen and understood, can illuminate speeches that contain numbers of any kind, especially statistical comparisons. You can make a simple chart yourself to be projected or to be printed for presentation to an audience. Enlarged illustrations or a model of a complicated machine — say, the space shuttle — would help a speaker to explain its function. You already know that photographs or videos are powerful instruments of persuasion, above all in support of appeals for humanitarian aid or conservation efforts, for both people and animals.

The use of a handout also requires planning. It's probably unwise to put your speech on hold while the audience reads or studies a handout that requires time and concentration. Confine the subject matter of handouts to material that can be easily grasped as you discuss or explain it, or to handouts that encourage the audience to listen and take notes.

Audio

Audio aids may also enliven a speech or even be indispensable to its success. One student played a recording of a scene from *Romeo and Juliet*, spoken by a cast of professional actors, to make a point about the relationship between the two lovers. Another student chose to define several types of popular music, including rap, goth, heavy metal, and house music. But he used only words, and the lack of any musical demonstration meant that the distinctions remained unclear.

Video

With sight, sound, and movement, a video can illustrate or reinforce the main points of a speech. A speech warning people not to text while driving will have a much greater effect if enhanced by a video showing the tragic and often gruesome outcome of car accidents caused by distracted driving. Schools that teach driver's education frequently rely on these bone-chilling videos to show their students that getting behind the wheel is a serious responsibility, not a game. If you want to use video, check to make sure that a computer and projector are available to you. Most schools have an audio-visual department that manages the delivery, setup, maintenance, and return of all equipment.

Multimedia

Multimedia presentations enable you to combine several different media such as text, charts, sound, and still or moving pictures into one unit. In the business world, multimedia presentations are commonly used in situations where there is a limited amount of time to persuade or teach a fairly large audience.

Though effective when done well, technically complicated presentations require careful planning. First you need to familiarize yourself with the program.

Most presentation software programs come equipped with helpful tutorials. If the task of creating your own presentation from scratch seems overwhelming, you can use one of the many preformatted presentation templates: You will simply need to customize the content.

You also need to make sure the equipment you need (computer, projector, connection cords, etc.) will be available. Robert Stephens, founder of the Geek Squad, a Minneapolis-based business that provides on-site emergency response to computer problems, gives tips for multimedia presentations, including always having a backup (preferably in a different format, such as a flash drive), and assuming that the internet will fail or be too slow to work properly (and if you must use it, again, have a backup!). He sums up his advice: "In the end, technology cannot replace creativity. Make sure that you are using multimedia to reinforce, not replace, your main points."[3]

If you have never used the devices you need for your presentation, practice using them before the speech. Few things are more disconcerting for the speechmaker and the audience than a speaker who is fumbling with his or her materials, unable to find the right picture or to make a machine work.

READING ARGUMENT

Examining a Speech

Read the following excerpts from a speech by Jimmy Carter, thirty-ninth president of the United States of America, to get a better understanding of audience, credibility, organization, language, and support.

Why I Believe the Mistreatment of Women Is the Number One Human Rights Abuse

JIMMY CARTER

Credibility: Carter establishes his former position of authority as president.

Thinking about my career since I left the White House, I'm reminded of a cartoon I saw in the *New Yorker* a couple of years ago. This little boy is looking up at his father and says, "Daddy, when I grow up, I want to be a former president."

Jimmy Carter was the thirty-ninth president of the United States, serving from 1977 to 1981. In 1982 he and his wife Rosalynn founded the Carter Center, a nonpartisan and nonprofit institute that works to advance human rights and democracy and to fight disease throughout the world. He and his wife have devoted their time and prestige to Habitat for Humanity well into their 90s. Carter received the Nobel Peace Prize in 2002.

---

[3] Robert Stephens as paraphrased by Eric Matson, "When Your Presentation Crashes . . . Who You Gonna Call?," *Fast Company*, February/March 1997, 130.

Well, as a former president, I have been blessed to have access that very few other people in the world have had to get to know so many people around this whole universe. Not only am I familiar with the fifty states in the United States, but also my wife and I have visited more than 145 countries in the world, and the Carter Center has had full-time programs in eighty nations. A lot of times when we go into a country, we not only meet the king or the president, but we also meet the villagers who live in the most remote areas.

Our overall commitment at The Carter Center is to promote human rights, and knowing the world as I do, I can tell you without any equivocation that the number-one abuse of human rights on Earth, strangely not addressed quite often, is the abuse of women and girls.

There are a couple of reasons for this that I'll mention to begin with. First of all is the misinterpretation of religious scriptures — holy scriptures in the Bible, Old Testament, New Testament, Quran, and so forth — and these have been misinterpreted by men who are now in the ascendant positions in the synagogues and the churches and in the mosques. And they interpret these rules to make sure that women are ordinarily relegated to a secondary position compared to men in the eyes of God.

5   This is a very serious problem, which usually is not addressed. A number of years ago, in the year 2000, I had been a Southern Baptist for seventy years — I still teach Sunday school every Sunday — but the Southern Baptist Convention in the year 2000 decided that women should play a secondary position, a subservient position to men. So they issued an edict, in effect, that prevents women from being priests, pastors, deacons in the church, or chaplains in the military. If a woman teaches a classroom in a Southern Baptist seminary, they cannot teach if a boy is in the room, because you can find verses in the Bible — there are over 30,000 of them — that say that a woman shouldn't teach a man, and so forth. But the basic thing is the scriptures are misinterpreted to keep men in an ascendant position. That is an all-pervasive problem, because men can exert that power, and if an abusive husband or an employer, for instance, wants to cheat women, they can say that if women are not equal in the eyes of God, why should I treat them as equals myself? Why should I pay them equal pay for doing the same kind of work?

The other very serious blight that causes this problem is the excessive resort to violence, and that is increasing tremendously around the world. In the United States of America, for instance, we have had an enormous increase in abuse of poor people, mostly black people and minorities, by putting them in prison. When I was governor of Georgia, one out of every

Credibility: His good works have extended beyond his years in office.

Claim

Support: He presents errors in interpretation as a matter of fact, not a matter of faith.

Audience: Identifies with the everyday person who might be listening and as someone with religious values and a spirit of care and service.

Support: Uses rhetorical question to apply God's view of women to the workplace and to marriage.

Support: Establishes a logical cause/effect relationship and offers statistical support for his claim that the abuse of the poor has increased.

1,000 Americans was in prison. Nowadays, 7.3 people per 1,000 are in prison. That's a sevenfold increase. And since I left the White House, there's been an 800 percent increase in the number of women who are black who are in prison. We also are one of the only developed countries on Earth that still has the death penalty. And we rank right alongside the countries that are most abusive in all elements of human rights in encouraging the death penalty. We're in California now, and I figured out the other day that California has spent $4 billion dollars in convicting thirteen people for the death penalty. If you add that up, that's $307 million it costs California to send a person to be executed. Nebraska this week just passed a law abolishing the death penalty, because it costs so much. (Applause) So the resort to violence and abuse of poor people and helpless people is another cause of the increase in abuse of women.

Let me just go down a very few abuses of women that concern me most, and I'll be fairly brief, because I have a limited amount of time, as you know.

One is genital mutilation. Genital mutilation is horrible and not known by American women. But in some countries, many countries, when a child is born that's a girl, very soon in her life, her genitals are completely cut away by a so-called cutter who has a razor blade and, in a non-sterile way, removes the exterior parts of a woman's genitalia. And sometimes, in more extreme cases but not very rare cases, they sew the orifice up so the girl can just urinate or menstruate. And then later, when she gets married, the same cutter goes in and opens the orifice up so she can have sex. This is not a rare thing, although it's against the law in most countries. In Egypt, for instance, 91 percent of all the females that live in Egypt today have been sexually mutilated in that way. In some countries, it's more than 98 percent of the women are cut that way before they reach maturity. This is a horrible affliction on all women that live in those countries.

Another very serious thing is honor killings, where a family through misinterpretation, again, of a holy scripture — there's nothing in the Quran that mandates this — will execute a girl in their family if she is raped or if she marries a man that her father does not approve, or sometimes even if she wears inappropriate clothing. This is done by members of her own family, so the family becomes murderers when the girl brings so-called disgrace to the family. An analysis was done in Egypt not so long ago by the United Nations, and it showed that 75 percent of these murders of a girl are perpetrated by the father, the uncle, or the brother, but 25 percent of the murders are conducted by women.

Audience: The cruelty of the procedure, and the lack of clean conditions, arouses sympathy.

Audience: Carter hopes to arouse sympathy due to the reasons women are killed and the fact that family members kill them. Although he mentions the Quran, he does not specifically label these families as Muslims, which might have aroused bias in some listeners.

10   Another problem that we have in the world that relates to women particularly is slavery, or human trafficking, as it's called nowadays. There were about 12.5 million people sold from Africa into slavery in the New World back in the nineteenth century and the eighteenth century. There are 30 million people now living in slavery. The U.S. Department of State now has a mandate from Congress to give a report every year, and the State Department reports that 800,000 people are sold across international borders every year into slavery, and that 80 percent of those are women sold into sexual slavery. In the United States right this moment, 60,000 people are living in human bondage, or slavery. In Atlanta, Georgia, where The Carter Center is located and where I teach at Emory University, there are between two hundred and three hundred women sold into slavery every month, making it the number-one place in the nation for sex trafficking. Atlanta has the busiest airport in the world, and they also have a lot of passengers that come from the Southern Hemisphere. If a brothel owner wants to buy a girl that has brown or black skin, they can do it for $1,000. A white-skinned girl brings several times more than that, and the average brothel owner in Atlanta and in the United States now can earn about $35,000 per slave. The sex trade in Atlanta, Georgia, exceeds the total drug trade in the city. So this is another very serious problem, and the basic problem is prostitution, because there's not a whorehouse in America that's not known by the local officials, the local policemen, or the chief of police, or the mayor and so forth.

And this leads to one of the worst problems, and that is that women are bought increasingly and put into sexual slavery in all countries in the world.

Sweden has a good approach to it. About fifteen to twenty years ago, Sweden decided to change the law, and women are no longer prosecuted if they are in sexual slavery, but the brothel owners and the pimps and the male customers are prosecuted, and — (Applause) — prostitution has gone down. In the United States, we take just the opposite position. For every male arrested for illegal sex trade, twenty-five women are arrested in the United States of America. Canada, Ireland, I've already said Sweden, France, and other countries are moving now towards this so-called Swedish model. That's another thing that can be done.

We have two great institutions in this country that all of us admire: our military and our great university system. In the military, they are now analyzing how many sexual assaults take place. According to the last report I got, there were 26,000 sexual assaults that took place in the military — 26,000. Only 3,000, not much more than 1 percent, are actually prosecuted, and the reason is that the commanding officer of any

Organization: Carter helps his audience follow his argument by using signal phrases such as "another."

Audience: Carter's audience consists primarily of American citizens, and it is probably shocking to most Americans to think of slavery existing in today's Atlanta.

Support: Cause/effect. Prostitution will be a problem as long as law enforcement officials know about it and do nothing.

Organization: Carter builds his argument from least to most serious problems.

Support: Carter uses statistics to convince his audience.

organization—a ship like my submarine, a battalion in the Army, or a company in the Marines—the commanding officer has the right under law to decide whether to prosecute a rapist or not, and of course, the last thing they want is for anybody to know that under their command, sexual assaults are taking place, so they do not do it. That law needs to be changed.

About one out of four girls who enter American universities will be sexually assaulted before she graduates, and this is now getting a lot of publicity, partially because of my book, but also other things, and so eighty-nine universities in America are now condemned by the Department of Education under Title IX because the officials of the universities are not taking care of the women to protect them from sexual assault. The Department of Justice says that more than half of the rapes on a college campus take place by serial rapists, because outside of the university system, if they rape somebody, they'll be prosecuted, but when they get on a university campus, they can rape with impunity. They're not prosecuted. Those are the kinds of things that go on in our society.

Another thing that's very serious about the abuse of women and girls is   15
the lack of equal pay for equal work, as you know. (Applause) And this is sometimes misinterpreted, but for full-time employment, a woman in the United States now gets 23 percent less than a man. When I became president, the difference was 39 percent. So we've made some progress, partially because I was president and so forth,—(Applause) (Laughter)—but in the last fifteen years, there's been no progress made, so it's been just about 23 or 24 percent difference for the last fifteen years. These are the kinds of things that go on. If you take the Fortune 500 companies, twenty-three of them have women CEOs, out of five hundred, and those CEOs, I need not tell you, make less on an average than the other CEOs. Well, that's what goes on in our country.

Another problem with the United States is we are the most warlike nation on Earth. We have been to war with about twenty-five different countries since the Second World War. Sometimes, we've had soldiers on the ground fighting. The other times, we've been flying overhead dropping bombs on people. Other times, of course, now, we have drones that attack people and so forth. We've been at war with twenty-five different countries or more since the Second World War. There were four years, I won't say which ones, where we didn't—(Applause)—we didn't drop a bomb, we didn't launch a missile, we didn't fire a bullet. But anyway, those kinds of

Credibility. He establishes his qualifications to discuss this topic because his book helped publicize the problem of sexual assault on campus.

Language: Carter downplays his role in high office to be more approachable, but still acknowledges his influence to improve pay for women.

Organization/language: Carter repeats this fact to emphasize his point. The number would surprise many and arouse an emotional response (*pathos*).

things, the resort to violence and the misinterpretation of the holy scriptures are what causes, are the basic causes, of abuse of women and girls.

There's one more basic cause that I need not mention, and that is that in general, men don't give a damn. (Applause) That's true. The average man that might say, "I'm against the abuse of women and girls," quietly accepts the privileged position that we occupy, and this is very similar to what I knew when I was a child, when separate but equal had existed. Racial discrimination, legally, had existed for one hundred years, from 1865 at the end of the War Between the States, the Civil War, all the way up to the 1960s, when Lyndon Johnson got the bills passed for equal rights. But during that time, there were many white people that didn't think that racial discrimination was okay, but they stayed quiet, because they enjoyed the privileges of better jobs, unique access to jury duty, better schools, and everything else, and that's the same thing that exists today, because the average man really doesn't care. Even though they say, "I'm against discrimination against girls and women," they enjoy a privileged position. And it's very difficult to get the majority of men who control the university system, the majority of men that control the military system, the majority of men that control the governments of the world, and the majority of men that control the great religions—to act for change.

So what is the basic thing that we need to do today? I would say the best thing that we could do today is for the women in the powerful nations like this one, and where you come from, Europe and so forth, who have influence and who have freedom to speak and to act, to take the responsibility on yourselves to be more forceful in demanding an end to racial discrimination against girls and women all over the world. The average woman in Egypt doesn't have much to say about her daughters getting genitally mutilated and so forth. I didn't even go into detail about that. But I hope that out of this conference, all the women here will get your husbands to realize that these abuses on the college campuses and the military and in the future job market and so forth are happening, and they need to protect your daughters and your granddaughters.

I have four children, twelve grandchildren, and ten great-grandchildren, and I think often about them and about the plight that they will face—whether they live in America or Egypt or another foreign country—in having equal rights. I hope that all of you will join me in being a champion for women and girls around the world and protect their human rights. Thank you very much.

Language: After all of the proof of abuse, Carter here places the blame squarely on men, using firm and strong language for emphasis.

Organization: Carter ends with a cause-and-effect argument that is also a call to action: change will require the work of women in positions of power and women influencing their husbands.

Language/Audience: The use of the 2nd person (*you*) makes the proposal to act personal to arouse emotion.

Credibility/Audience: He can relate because he has children, grandchildren, and great-grandchildren himself.

Practice: Examining a Speech

Read the following speech given at Georgetown University on May 18, 2012, by U.S. Department of Health and Human Services Secretary Kathleen Sebelius, and answer the questions that follow it.

Remarks to Georgetown University's Public Policy Institute

KATHLEEN SEBELIUS

Dean Montgomery, members of the faculty, family, friends, and graduates: It's an honor to be with you this morning. And let me start with some well-earned congratulations. Last weekend, on Mother's Day, I was at the University of Kansas when my younger son received his Master's degree. So I know the hard work and effort that got you here today.

I married a Georgetown law graduate and am a Hoya Mom — the mother of a double Georgetown graduate. So in my family, Hoya Saxa comes second only to Rock Chalk Jayhawk.

And I was especially pleased to be invited to speak to you, the public policy graduates. Having spent my entire life in public service, I believe you've chosen the most challenging, frustrating, exciting, consequential, and rewarding career there is. And today, I want to share a few lessons from my career that I hope will be useful as you begin yours.

I started out as an "unpaid volunteer." My dad got into politics when I was five, so for most of my childhood, I spent my fall days putting up yard signs and going door to door.

5   Actually, the more accurate term might be forced labor. There wasn't a lot of choice in the matter. (It was only later that I discovered that other families were going to football games and picnics while I was attending political rallies.)

But what I got from those fall outings, and from our conversations around our dinner table, was a deep belief in the value of public service. And throughout my career, it's been that unwavering belief that's carried me to my highest points — and gotten me through my lowest.

I know you share that belief. If you didn't, you wouldn't be here today. You wouldn't have suffered through regression analysis. You wouldn't have passed up bigger salary possibilities in other fields.

So my first hope for you today is that you always hold on to your commitment to work for the common good. If you let that focus guide you, you will never go off course.

I learned the second lesson when I came to Washington in the late 60s to attend Trinity College. Those were tumultuous times in our nation's history, and DC was right in the middle of it. During my college years, the draft was reinstated, as the government ramped up the war in Vietnam. Racial tensions, that had been smoldering, erupted after the assassination of Martin Luther King Jr., and neighborhoods in DC were burned to the ground.

What was striking at the time is how young   10 people were driving these national debates. There was a feeling not just that young people could change the world — but that we had to.

Kathleen Sebelius served as governor of Kansas from 2003 to 2009 and as secretary of the U.S. Department of Health and Human Services from 2009 to 2014.

Robert Kennedy spoke about those times in a famous speech. He said: "This world demands the qualities of youth. Not a time of life, but a state of mind, a temper of the will, a quality of the imagination, a predominance of courage over timidity, of the appetite for adventure over the life of ease."

As you set out on your careers, you may find yourselves tempted to defer to those who are older or have more experience. And on behalf of the parents in the audience, I want to be clear that even though we may not know who Kim Kardashian is, or why everyone is always so angry about her, we do still have some wisdom to share. You still need to call your mom! (In fact, after this ceremony ends, the first thing you should do is thank the parents, teachers, mentors, and friends who supported your journey to this graduation day.)

But the truth is, wisdom isn't the only thing that comes with age. Growing older can also bring complacency and cautiousness.

I know Georgetown hasn't trained you to sit on the sidelines. You've studied under leading policy-makers. You've proven your skills, not just on tests and papers, but in the real world through programs like Project Honduras.

15 So my second piece of advice is: Don't wait. Go ahead and do it yourself—because if you don't, it might never happen.

Now, I wish I could give you a roadmap for exactly how to do that. But the truth is that career paths are usually only visible looking backwards, like the tracks we make in the snow.

I'm an accidental feminist who learned that girls can do anything by attending an all-girls school where we had to do everything. I ended up in Kansas because that's where my husband grew up. I began my political career because our part-time legislature was a better fit for me,

as a mother with two young children, than the 60-hour-a-week job I had.

As I moved along, I sought out opportunities to learn new skills and new subject areas. I started out working in corrections. Later, I worked on everything from education, to children and family issues, to the budget, to jobs and economic development, to rural challenges.

One of the issues I kept coming back to was health care, culminating in my current position. And now, I have the extraordinary opportunity to help implement legislation that is finally, after seven decades of failed debate, ensuring that all Americans have access to affordable health coverage.

But I never would have been here if I hadn't 20 taken some chances. For me, the biggest risk was running for Kansas Insurance Commissioner. The indicators were not promising. The statewide office had never been held by a woman or a Democrat. The previous three commissioners had close ties to the insurance industry and had served nearly fifty years combined. And it was 1994, when running for office as a Democrat was the basic equivalent of wearing a Georgetown jersey in the Syracuse student section.

But I went for it and won. And I ended up not just getting an incredible opportunity to make a difference, but also gaining invaluable experience for the job I have now. (Who knew?)

All of you are going to face similar choices in your careers. It might be taking a more senior position at a much smaller organization. It might be moving abroad to work. It might be going from running a campaign to becoming a candidate.

And when you do encounter these opportunities, I encourage you take a deep breath and seize them.

And that brings me to the final lesson I want to leave with you today, which is that no matter what path you choose, it's going to be hard.

25   Ultimately, public policy is about making difficult choices. Today, there are serious debates under way about the direction of our country—debates about the size and role of government, about America's role as a global economic and military leader, about the moral and economic imperative of providing health care to all our citizens. People have deeply held beliefs on all sides of these discussions, and you, as public policy leaders, will be called on to help move these debates forward.

These are not questions with quick and easy answers. When I was in junior high, John Fitzgerald Kennedy was running for president. I wasn't old enough to vote, but it was the first national campaign I really remember. Some of then-Senator Kennedy's opponents attacked him for his religion, suggesting that electing the first Catholic president would undermine the separation of church and state, a fundamental principle of our democracy. The furor grew so loud that Kennedy chose to deliver a speech about his beliefs just seven weeks before the election.

In that talk to Protestant ministers, Kennedy talked about his vision of religion and the public square, and said he believed in an America, and I quote, "where no religious body seeks to impose its will directly or indirectly upon the general populace or the public acts of its officials—and where religious liberty is so indivisible that an act against one church is treated as an act against us all."

Kennedy was elected president on November 8, 1960. And more than fifty years later, that conversation, about the intersection of our nation's long tradition of religious freedom with policy decisions that affect the general public, continues.

Contributing to these debates will require more than just the quantitative skills you have learned at Georgetown. It will also require the ethical skills you have honed—the ability to weigh different views, see issues from other points of view, and in the end, follow your own moral compass.

These debates can also be contentious. But   30
this is a strength of our country, not a weakness. In some countries around the world, it is much easier to make policy. The leader delivers an edict and it goes into effect. There's no debate, no criticism, no second guessing.

Our system is messier, slower, more frustrating, and far better. It requires conversations that can be painful, and it almost always ends in compromise. But it's through this process of conversation and compromise that we move forward, together, step by step, toward a "more perfect union."

Looking out on you this morning, I feel very optimistic about the future of that union. If you hold on to your idealism, resist complacency, take chances, and engage thoughtfully with the difficult challenges of our time, you will succeed. And I can't wait to see what you will accomplish.

Congratulations and good luck!

Reading, Writing, and Discussion Questions

1. How does Sebelius attempt to relate to audience members and thus draw them into her speech?

2. What did Sebelius learn from her early involvement in her father's campaigns? How does that relate to her audience on this occasion?

3. What advice does she offer the graduates?

4. Why does she feel that the jobs the graduates will enter will require ethical skills? Does she come across as an ethical person herself? Why, or why not?

Documenting Sources

As you write your paper, any time that you make use of the wording or ideas of one of your sources, you must document that use. Two of the most common methods of crediting sources are the Modern Language Association (MLA) and American Psychological Association (APA) systems. Each system consists of two main components: the in-text citations and the list of Works Cited or References.

MLA In-Text Citations

The following guidelines cover common scenarios where you will need to use in-text citations in MLA format, but you may encounter other variations. For more help, consult the *MLA Handbook*, 8th edition (2016).

In the text of your paper, immediately after any quotation, paraphrase, or idea you need to document, simply insert a parenthetical mention of the author's last name and the page number(s) on which the material appears. You don't need a comma after the author's name or an abbreviation of the word *page* or *p.*

> Although both "are intended to mitigate the harm caused to trauma-tized students engaging in sensitive materials," trigger warnings are written texts and are relatively easy to implement while safe spaces "are characterized by the physical location and by the community that gathers there" (Byron 119).

The parenthetical reference tells the reader that the information in this sentence came from pages of the book or article that appears in the Works Cited at the end of the paper. The complete reference on the Works Cited page provides all of the information readers need to locate the source:

> Byron, Katie. "From Infantilizing to World Making: Safe Spaces and Trigger Warnings on Campus." *Family Relations*, vol. 66, no. 1, Fall 2017, pp. 116–25. *Wiley Online Library*, doi:10.1111/fare.12233.

If the author's name is mentioned in the same sentence, it is also acceptable to place only the page numbers in parentheses; it is not necessary to repeat the author's name. For example:

> In her article "From Infantilizing to World Making: Safe Spaces and Trigger Warnings on Campus," Katie Byron distinguishes between trigger warnings and safe spaces. Although both "are intended to mitigate the harm caused to traumatized students engaging in sensitive materials," trigger warnings are written texts and are relatively easy to implement while safe spaces "are characterized by the physical location and by the community that gathers there" (119).

Remember, though, that a major reason for using qualified sources is that they lend authority to the ideas expressed. The first time an author is mentioned in the paper, he or she — or they — should be identified by full name and by claim to authority:

> According to Dr. Heather Hartline-Grafton, Senior Nutrition Policy Analyst for the Food Research and Action Center (FRAC), although there are nutritious competitive options, those do not sell as well as the ones high in sugar, salt, and calories (2–3).

A last name and page number in parentheses do not carry nearly the same weight as a full name and credentials. You should save the former for subsequent citations once the author has been fully identified. If more than one sentence comes from the same source, you do not need to put parentheses after each sentence. One parenthetical citation at the end of the material from a source is enough if it is clear from the way you introduce the material where the source's ideas begin and end:

> Alicia Oglesby, the assistant director of school and college counseling at Bishop McNamara High School in Prince George's County in Maryland, highlights the personal, academic, and professional struggles that face marginalized groups as they attempt to consider the challenge of navigating the confusing and overwhelming college experience for the first time. In her article "Safe Spaces," Oglesby identifies three groups that could benefit from the support of safe spaces in academic settings: low-income students, LGBTQ students, and students of color (48).

If you are using more than one work by the same author, you will need to provide in the parentheses the title or a recognizable shortened form of the title of the particular work being cited. If the author's name is not mentioned in the sentence, you should include in parentheses the author's last name, the title, and the page number, with a comma between the author's name and the title. If both the author's name and the title of any work being cited are mentioned in the sentence, the parentheses will include only the page number.

Had two works by Hartline-Grafton been listed in the Works Cited of an essay, information from one of the two would have been cited like this:

> Although there are nutritious competitive options, those do not sell as well as the ones high in sugar, salt, and calories (Hartline-Grafton, "How Competitive Foods" 2–3).

If there is more than one author, don't forget to give credit to all. Two authors are acknowledged by name in the parentheses if not in your own sentence: (Hacker and Sommers 23). With three or more authors, use "et al.," the Latin term for "and others": (Braithwaite et al. 137).

Some sources do not name an author. To cite a work with an unknown author, give the title, or a recognizable shortened form, in the text of your paper. If the work does not have numbered pages, which is often the case in web pages or nonprint sources, do not include page numbers. For example:

> In some cases Sephardic Jews, "converted" under duress, practiced Christianity openly and Judaism in secret until recently ("Search for the Buried Past").

Direct quotations should always be introduced or worked into the grammatical structure of your own sentences. When introducing your sources with signal phrases, MLA suggests the use of present tense. For example,

> Helme discovers . . .

> Helme suggests . . .

If you need help introducing quotations, refer to the Strategies for Summary, Paraphrase, and Quotation box (p. 99) in Chapter 4. Remember, however, that you need to provide parenthetical documentation not only for every direct quotation but also for every paraphrase or summary. Document any words or ideas that are not your own.

As a general rule, you cannot make any changes in a quotation. Two exceptions must be clearly marked when they occur. At times, you may use brackets to make a slight change that does not alter the meaning of the quotation. For example, a pronoun may need to be replaced by a noun in brackets to make its reference clear. Or a verb tense may be changed and bracketed to make the quotation fit more smoothly into your sentence. An ellipsis (. . .) is used when you omit a portion of the quotation that does not change the essential meaning of the quote. You do not need to use ellipses at the beginning or end of a direct quotation. If the omitted portion includes the end of one sentence and the beginning of another, there should be a fourth period (. . . .).

> The reason for this, as Helme points out, is that until that time, "the FDA [did] not require it without a showing of adverse health effects" (363).

> As seen in Europe and noted by Helme, "When coupled with a negative perception of GMOs . . . mandatory labeling can push genetically modified (GM) food out of the market" (380).

If a quotation is more than four typed lines long, it needs to be handled as a block quotation. A block quotation is usually introduced by a sentence followed by a colon. The quotation itself is indented one-half inch from the left margin. No quotation marks are necessary since the placement on the page informs the reader that it is a quotation. The only quotation marks in a block quotation would be ones copied from the original, as in dialogue. If a paragraph break is required within a block quotation, add an additional indent for the first line of the new paragraph. The parenthetical citation is the same as with a quotation run into your text, but the period appears before the parenthesis.

> Oglesby highlights the ability of safe spaces to ease the transition for these marginalized students from the first academic year between their high school graduation to the first day their college classes:
>
> > Here we have white men looking through their own eyes, but the white American experience certainly is not synonymous or interchangeable with the black American experience. The same goes for heterosexual colleagues not recognizing the perceptions of LGBTQ colleagues and students. Middle class vs. low-income; private independent vs. public schools—the list of privileged groups misunderstanding less privileged groups goes on and on. (48)

With print sources in particular, you will often need to cite one work that is quoted in another or a work from an anthology. For the former, the parenthetical documentation provides the name and page number of the source you actually used, preceded by the words "qtd. in":

> The National School Lunch Program has been in existence since 1946 "as a measure of national security, to safeguard the health and well-being of the Nation's children and to encourage the domestic consumption of nutritious agricultural commodities and other food" (qtd. in Center for Science 230).

A work in an anthology, which includes this book, is cited parenthetically by the name of the author of the work, not the editor of the anthology: (Thunberg 22).

The list of Works Cited includes all material you have used to write your research paper. This list appears at the end of your paper and always starts on a new page. Center the title Works Cited, double-space between the title and the first entry, and begin your list, which should be arranged alphabetically by author. Each entry should start at the left margin; indent all subsequent lines of the entry one-half inch. Number each page, and double-space throughout.

One more point: *information notes*, such as footnotes and endnotes, which provide additional information not readily worked into a research paper, are indicated by superscript numbers. Footnotes appear at the bottom of a page, and endnotes are included on a Notes page before the list of Works Cited.

MLA Works Cited Entries

Following are examples of the citation forms you are most likely to need as you document your research. In general, for both books and magazines, information should appear in the following order: author, title, and publication information. Each item should be followed by a period. In citing the publication information, provide the whole name of the publisher, but you may use the abbreviation "P" for "Press" and "U" for "University" and leave off articles and company abbreviations such as "Inc." and "Co." When you are citing an article, a chapter, or anything else shorter than a book-length work, give the page number range for the whole article, chapter, or short work rather than the single page number from which a quotation, paraphrase, or summary is drawn. When using as a source an essay that appears in this book, follow the citation model for "A Work in an Anthology," unless your instructor indicates otherwise. Consult the *MLA Handbook*, 8th edition (2016), for other documentation models.

Directory of MLA Works Cited Entries

Print Sources

1. A Book by a Single Author

Edsel, Robert M. *Saving Italy: The Race to Rescue a Nation's Treasures from the Nazis*. W. W. Norton, 2013.

2. Two or More Works by the Same Author or Authors

Rashid, Ahmed. *Pakistan on the Brink: The Future of America, Pakistan, and Afghanistan*. Penguin Books, 2012.

For the second and subsequent books by the same author, replace the author's name with three hyphens, followed by a period and the title.

---. *Taliban: The Power of Militant Islam in Afghanistan and Beyond*. 2nd ed., Yale UP, 2008.

3. A Work with Two Authors

Stiglitz, Joseph E., and Bruce C. Greenwald. *Creating a Learning Society: A New Approach to Growth, Development, and Social Progress*. Columbia UP, 2015.

This form is followed even for two authors with the same last name, but only the first author's name is inverted.

Engler, Mark, and Paul Engler. *This Is an Uprising: How Nonviolent Revolt Is Shaping the Twenty-First Century*. Bold Type Books, 2016.

4. A Work with Three or More Authors

Fry, Tony, et al. *Design and the Question of History*. Bloomsbury Academic Press, 2015.

If there are more than two authors, name only the first and add "et al." (meaning "and others").

The Elements of Citation

BOOK (MLA)

When you cite a book using MLA style, include the following:

1 Author   **3** Publisher

2 Title and subtitle   **4** Date of publication

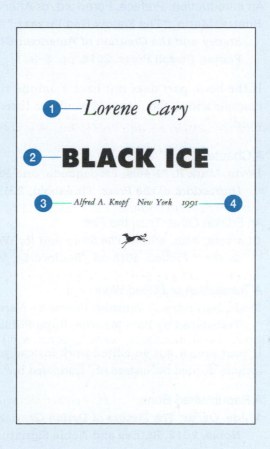

1 *Lorene Cary*

2 BLACK ICE

3 *Alfred A. Knopf*   *New York*   *1991*   **4**

Works Cited entry for a book in MLA style

┌──── 1 ───┐ ┌── 2 ──┐ ┌──────── 3 ────────┐ ┌─ 4 ─┐

Cary, Lorene. *Black Ice*. Alfred A. Knopf, 1991.

5. An Anthology or a Compilation

Dark, Larry, editor. *Prize Stories 1997: The O. Henry Awards*.
Anchor Books, 1997.

6. A Work in an Anthology

Sayrafiezadeh, Saïd. "Paranoia." *New American Stories*, edited
by Ben Marcus, Vintage Books, 2015, pp. 3–29.

7. An Introduction, Preface, Foreword, or Afterword

Buatta, Mario. "The Fellow Had Pizzazz." Foreword. *George
Stacey and the Creation of American Chic*, by Maureen
Footer, Rizzoli Press, 2014, pp. 8–9.

If the book part does not have a unique title, omit the title. In the
example above, the foreword would be listed as "Buatta, Mario. Foreword. . . ."

8. A Chapter

Levin, Mark R. "News, Propaganda, and Pseudo-Events."
Unfreedom of the Press. Threshold, 2019, pp. 117–44.

9. An Edition Other Than the First

Charters, Ann, editor. *The Story and Its Writer: An Introduction
to Short Fiction*. 10th ed., Bedford/St. Martin's, 2019.

10. A Translation or Edited Work

Modi, Narendra. *A Journey: Poems by Narendra Modi*.
Translated by Ravi Mantha, Rupa Publications, 2014.

If your source was an edited work instead of a translation, you would
include "Edited by" instead of "Translated by."

11. A Republished Book

Wilde, Oscar. *The Picture of Dorian Gray*. 1891. Barnes and
Noble, 2012. Barnes and Noble Signature Editions.

The only information about original publication you need to provide is the
publication date, which appears immediately after the title.

12. An Article from a Journal

Manzi, Jim. "The New American System." *National Affairs*,
vol. 1, no. 19, Spring 2014, pp. 3–24.

13. An Article from a Newspaper

Doctorow, E. L. "Quick Cuts: The Novel Follows Film into a World of Fewer Words." *The New York Times*, 15 Mar. 1999, p. B1+.

14. An Article from a Magazine

Sanneh, Kelefa. "Skin in the Game." *The New Yorker*, 24 Mar. 2014, pp. 48–55.

15. An Anonymous Work

Keep Walking, This Doesn't Concern You: The Internet's Favourite Memes. Ebury Press, 2016.

"The March Almanac." *The Atlantic Monthly*, Mar. 1995, p. 20.

16. A Review

Jackson, Lawrence. "The Vampire: The Fickle Career of Carl Van Vechten." Review of *The Tastemaker: Carl Van Vechten and the Birth of Modern America*, by Edward White. *Harper's Magazine*, Apr. 2014, pp. 89–94.

17. An Article in a Reference Work

"Child Abuse." *Mosby's Medical Dictionary*, 10th ed., Elsevier, 2017.

A reference work could refer to a dictionary, encyclopedia, or similar source. When articles in an encyclopedia or similar reference work are listed alphabetically, a page number is not necessary.

18. A Government Publication

United States, Congress, Committees on Foreign Relations of the U.S. Senate and the International Relations of the U.S. House of Representatives. *Annual Report on International Religious Freedom: 2000*. Government Printing Office, 2000.

19. An Editorial or Letter to the Editor

Starr, Evva. "Local Reporting Thrives in High Schools." *The Washington Post*, 4 Apr. 2014. Letter.

20. A Cartoon or a Comic Strip

Ziegler, Jack. "Tai Chi vs. Chai Tea." *The New Yorker*, 14 Apr. 2014, p. 51. Cartoon.

Online Sources

21. A Website

Glazier, Loss Pequeño, director. *Electronic Poetry Center*. State U of New York at Buffalo, 2017, epc.buffalo.edu/.

Include the name of the author or editor of the website when this information is available; otherwise, begin the entry with the name of the website in italics, followed by a period; the name of the sponsor or publisher, followed by a comma; the date of publication or last update; and the URL, without http://, followed by a period. If the website does not have an update date or publication date, include your date of access at the end (see the second example in item 22).

22. A Short Work from a Website

Enzinna, Wes. "Syria's Unknown Revolution." *Pulitzer Center on Crisis Reporting*, 24 Nov. 2015, pulitzercenter.org/projects /middle-east-syria-enzinna-war-rojava.

Bali, Karan. "Kishore Kumar." *Upperstall*, upperstall.com/profile /kishore-kumar/. Accessed 15 Jan. 2020.

23. An Online Book

Euripides. *The Trojan Women*. Translated by Gilbert Murray, Oxford UP, 1915. Internet Sacred Text Archive, 2011, www .sacred-texts.com/cla/eurip/troj_w.htm.

In this case, the book had been previously published, and information about its original publication was included at the site.

24. An Article from an Online Journal

Butler, Janine. "Where Access Meets Multimodality: The Case of ASL Music Videos." *Kairos*, vol. 21, no. 1, Fall 2016, kairos .technorhetoric.net/21.1/topoi/butler/index.html.

In this case, the journal is published solely online. For an article found online that was originally (or also) published in print, see entry 25.

25. An Article from a Database

Coles, Kimberly Anne. "The Matter of Belief in John Donne's Holy Sonnets." *Renaissance Quarterly*, vol. 68, no. 3, Fall 2015, pp. 899–931. JSTOR, doi:10.1086/683855.

If the Digital Object Identifier (DOI) is not available, use the permalink (stable URL) or the full URL for the article.

The Elements of Citation

ARTICLE FROM A WEBSITE (MLA)

When you cite a brief article from a website using MLA style, include the following:

1 Author

2 Title of work

3 Title of website

4 Sponsor or publisher of the site (If the site title and the sponsor/publisher are the same, omit the sponsor/publisher.)

5 Date of publication or latest update (If a site has no update date, give your date of access at the end.)

6 URL

₁
Brooks, Cornell W., et al. "NAACP & Partners Standing for Civil Rights against New Threats." NAACP, ^{3, 4}

₅ ₆
15 November 2016, www.naacp.org/latest/naacp-partners-standing-civil-rights-new-threats/.

26. An Abstract

Olsson, Jan. "Pressing Matters: Media Crusades before the
Nickelodeons." *Film History*, vol. 27, no. 2, 2015, pp. 105–39.
Abstract. *JSTOR,* doi:10.2979/filmhistory.27.2.105.

Note: MLA does not officially cover this type of source, as it is best
to read critically the full article and engage with your source's main
text. We include it here as a likely result in your database searches.

27. An Article from an Online Reference Work (Including a Wiki)

"Adscititious." *Merriam-Webster*. 5 Sept. 2019, www
.merriam-webster.com/dictionary/adscititious.

"Behaviorism." *Wikipedia*, 11 Oct. 2019, en.wikipedia.org
/w/index.php?title=Behaviorism&oldid=915544724.

28. A Personal Email Communication

Franz, Kenneth. "Re: Species Reintroduction." Received by
Selena Anderson, 18 Sept. 2017.

29. A Social Media Post

kevincannon. "Portrait of Norris Hall in #Savannah, GA—home
(for a few more months, anyway) of #SCAD's sequential art
department." Instagram, Mar. 2014, www.instagram.com
/p/lgmqk4i6DC/.

@grammarphobia (Patricia T. O'Conner and Steward Kellerman).
"Is 'if you will,' like, a verbal tic? http://goo.gl/oYrTYP
#English #language #grammar #etymology #usage #linguistics
#WOTD." Twitter, 14 Mar. 2016, 9:12 a.m., twitter.com
/grammarphobia.

Treat these as short works from a website. List the poster's handle as
the author name, and include the poster's real name in parentheses, if
available. Use the text accompanying the post as the title, in quotation
marks, if such text is available. If the post has no title or text, use the
label *Post*.

30. An Online Video

Nayar, Vineet. "Employees First, Customers Second." *YouTube*,
9 June 2015, www.youtube.com/watch?v=cCdu67s_C5E.

The Elements of Citation

ARTICLE FROM A DATABASE (MLA)

When you cite a brief article from a database using MLA style, include the following:

1 Author

2 Title of article

3 Title of periodical, volume, and issue numbers

4 Date of publication

5 Inclusive pages

6 Name of database

7 DOI (or URL, if DOI is unavailable)

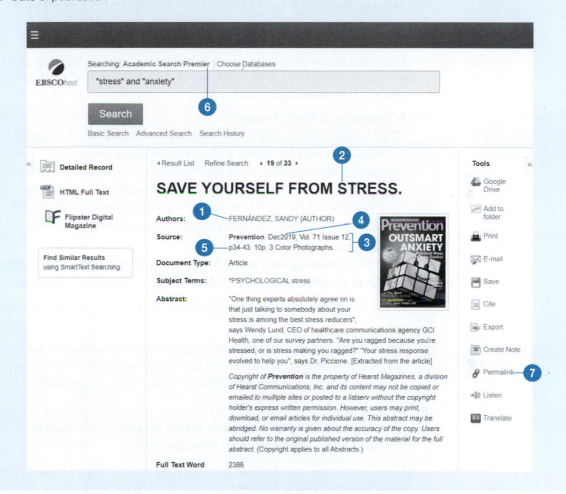

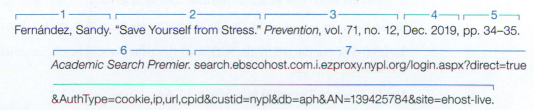

Works Cited entry for an article from a database in MLA style

Fernández, Sandy. "Save Yourself from Stress." *Prevention*, vol. 71, no. 12, Dec. 2019, pp. 34–35.

Academic Search Premier. search.ebscohost.com.i.ezproxy.nypl.org/login.aspx?direct=true

&AuthType=cookie,ip,url,cpid&custid=nypl&db=aph&AN=139425784&site=ehost-live.

Other Sources

31. A Lecture

Grant, Adam. 92Y Talks. "Giving: The Secret of Getting
Ahead." 92nd Street Y, New York, NY, 16 Apr. 2014.

32. A Film or Video

Bale, Christian, performer. *The Big Short*. Directed by Adam
McKay, Paramount Pictures, 2015.

Jenkins, Barry, director. *Moonlight.* Performances by Trevante
Rhodes, André Holland, Naomie Harris, Janelle Monáe, and
Mahershala Ali, A24, 2016.

Begin your entry with the person or element you are emphasizing in your
work, such as an actor, director, or the entire film or video (in which case
you would begin with the title).

33. A Television or Radio Program

"The London Season." *Downton Abbey*, performances by Shirley
MacLaine and Elizabeth McGovern, PBS, 23 Feb. 2014.

"Obama's Failures Have Made Millennials Give Up Hope." *The Rush
Limbaugh Show*, narrated by Rush Limbaugh, Premiere Radio
Networks, 14 Apr. 2014, www.rushlimbaugh.com/daily/2014/04
/14/obama_s_failures_have_made_millennials_give_up_hope.

34. A Podcast

Raz, Guy. "Peering into Space" *TED Radio Hour*, NPR, 3 Jan. 2020.
Spotify, open.spotify.com/show/1vfOw64nKjQ8LzZDPCfRaO.

In this case, the podcast was accessed through a streaming platform, Spotify.

35. A Performance

Piano Concerto no. 3. By Ludwig van Beethoven, conducted by
Andris Nelsons, performances by Paul Lewis and Boston Symphony Orchestra, Symphony Hall, Boston, MA, 9 Oct. 2015.

36. An Interview

Bacharach, Sam. "Where Money Meets Morale." Interview by
Alexa Von Tobel. *Inc.*, Apr. 2014, pp. 48–49.

If the interviewer's name is not given or if there is no title to the interview,
these elements may be left out.

A broadcast interview would be documented as follows:

Hines, Gregory. Interview by Charlie Rose. *Charlie Rose*, PBS, 30 Jan. 2001.

An interview conducted by the author of the paper would be documented
as follows:

Akufo, Dautey. Personal interview. 11 Apr. 2016.

MLA-Style Annotated Bibliography

An annotated bibliography is a list of sources that includes the usual bibliographic information followed by a paragraph describing and evaluating each source. Its purpose is to provide information about each source in a bibliography so that the reader has an overview of the resources related to a given topic.

For each source in an annotated bibliography, the same bibliographic information included in a Works Cited list (or References, if using APA style) is provided, alphabetized by author. Each reference also has a short paragraph that describes the work, its main focus, and, if appropriate, the methodology used in or the style of the work. An annotation might note special features such as tables or illustrations. Usually an annotation evaluates the source by analyzing its usefulness, reliability, and overall significance for understanding the topic. An annotation might include some information on the credentials of the author or the organization that produced it.

A Sample Annotation Using the MLA Citation Style

Warner, Marina. "Pity the Stepmother." *New York Times*, 12 May 1991, www.nytimes.com/1991/05/12/opinion/pity-the -stepmother.html.

The author asserts that many fairy tales feature absent or cruel mothers, transformed by romantic editors such as the Grimm brothers into stepmothers because the idea of a wicked mother desecrated an ideal. Warner argues that figures in fairy tales should be viewed in their historical context and that social conditions often affected the way that motherhood figured in fairy tales. Warner, a novelist and author of books on the images of Joan of Arc and the Virgin Mary, writes persuasively about the social roots of a fairy-tale archetype. This article provides useful historical background for my topic and will support the analysis of motherhood in fairy tales.

MLA-Style Paper Format

Print your essay on one side of 8½-by-11-inch white computer paper, double-spacing throughout. Leave 1-inch margins on all sides, and indent each paragraph one-half inch or five spaces. Unless a formal outline is part of the paper, a separate title page is unnecessary. Instead, beginning about one inch from the top of the first page and flush with the left margin, type your name, the instructor's name, the course title, and the date, each on a separate line; then double-space and type the title, capitalizing the first letter of the words of the title except for articles, prepositions, and conjunctions. Double-space and type the body of the paper.

Number all pages at the top-right corner, typing your last name before each page number in case pages are mislaid. If an outline is included, number its pages with lowercase roman numerals.

MLA-Style Sample Research Paper

Harvin 1

Anna Harvin
Dr. Winchell
ENGL 5789
26 September 2019

The Place for a Safe Space: Mental Health and
the College Student Experience

For the current generation of college students, it has grown increasingly difficult to walk across campus without being exposed to conversations surrounding trigger warnings, safe spaces, comfort zones, and inclusivity circles. Just as students are made aware of the protections these services offer, they are also made to consider the opposition—that safe spaces attack free speech and encourage a new generation of "snowflakes," a group unable to cope with the harsh realities of life within academic, social, and professional circles. Indeed, the debate over whether such safe spaces should be advertised— or permitted at all—on college campuses has grown with the rise of social justice movements and difficult conversations about race, religion, nationality, and the human experience as a whole. Students are bombarded with opinions, some aligned with their own beliefs and inclinations as well as others that seem to directly challenge their fundamental understanding of the ways in which we interact with the world around us and with one another—both professionally and personally. Should these students have the option of embracing a space on campus dedicated to fostering an environment that is safe, secure, and understanding? The opinions differ greatly, but more than the sanctity of free speech may be at stake.

In her article "From Infantilizing to World Making: Safe Spaces and Trigger Warnings on Campus," Katie Byron

---

MLA-style header

Title is centered, one line space below header and one line space above the first paragraph.

Anna ends her introduction with a question and suggestions but does not explicitly state her thesis.

Harvin 2

distinguishes between trigger warnings and safe spaces. Although both "are intended to mitigate the harm caused to traumatized students engaging in sensitive materials," trigger warnings are written texts and are relatively easy to implement while safe spaces "are characterized by the physical location and by the community that gathers there" (119). However, according to Angela M. Carter, author of "Teaching with Trauma: Trigger Warnings, Feminism, and Disability Pedagogy," it is a mistake to use the word "triggered" to refer simply to anything that makes an individual uncomfortable; in fact, "disagreements about the classroom as a 'safe space' often divert the conversation away from any real discussion of pedagogy and access in higher education." Carter continues:

> When presented as an access measure, it becomes evident that trigger warnings do not provide a way to "opt out" of anything, nor do they offer protection from the realities of the world. Trigger warnings provide a way to "opt in" by lessening the power of the shock and the unexpectedness, and granting the traumatized individual agency to attend to the affect and effects of their trauma. Traumatized individuals know that trigger warnings will not save us. Such warnings simply allow us to do the work we need to do so that we can participate in the conversation or activity. They allow us to enter the conversation, just like automatic doors allow people who use wheelchairs to more easily enter a building.

A look at some statistics reveals the need that exists among college students for the sort of accommodation that trigger warnings and safe spaces provide. According to the 2018 annual report on the mental health of college students published by the Center for Collegiate Mental Health at Penn State University, "counseling center utilization increased by an average of 30–40 percent, while enrollment increased by only 5 percent" between Fall 2009 and Spring 2015 (2018 Annual Report 4). Such increases in the demand for services reflect the startling reality of the college student experience in relation to mental health and well-being. As students battle with the ramifications of mental illness, their ability

Because the author's name is clear from Anna's sentence, it does not need to appear in the parenthesis with the page number.

Again, the author is clearly indicated, along with her authority as a published author on the subject of trigger warnings.

A block quotation because it is more than four typed lines. No quotation marks because the indention indicates it is a quotation. There is no page number for this online source, but it is clear which information comes from Carter's article.

Since there is no author, the parenthesis provides title of the work and the page number.

Harvin 3

to excel in the classroom is compromised, emphasizing the inaction on behalf of universities to properly address issues of mental health and stability in relation to hostile campus environments and interactions. The report highlights a growing dependence on campus resources currently in place for situations requiring "rapid access," such as emergency counselling: "Between Fall 2010 and Spring 2016, counseling center resources devoted to 'rapid access' services increased by 28 percent on average, whereas resources allocated to 'routine treatment' decreased slightly by 7.6 percent" (4). Even more concerning, the report indicates a nine percent rise in the number of students who have experienced a traumatic event that caused intense fear, helplessness, or horror from 2012 to 2018, and the number of students who have attended counseling for mental health concerns has risen seven percent in the same period (10). These numbers reveal a growing student desire for programming and resources dedicated to fostering academic and social spheres that alleviate trauma within and around the American college campus. In moments when trauma resurfaces, a safe space becomes necessary—if not vital—to the emotional stability and academic success of students.

Opponents of the implementation of safe spaces and trigger warnings cite the threat to the American right to free speech. Further, they express an overwhelming concern for the fostering of a new generation of college graduates unable to cope with ideas and opinions that differ from their own—that safe spaces "prepare them poorly for professional life, which often demands intellectual engagement with people and ideas one might find uncongenial or wrong" (Lukianoff and Haidt). Throughout their essay "The Coddling of the American Mind," Greg Lukianoff and Jonathan Haidt assert that safe spaces and trigger warnings foster anxiety and hyper-sensitive college students, rendering them incapable of coping with the reality of differing opinions and political incorrectness: "When the ideas, values, and speech of the other side are seen not just as wrong but as willfully aggressive toward innocent victims, it is hard to imagine the kind of mutual respect, negotiation, and compromise that

A direct quotation introduced by a complete sentence, followed by a colon. Since the source is clear from the context, the parenthesis provides only the page number.

The page number reference indicates the information in this sentence is summarized from the source.

Anna offers a rebuttal to her opposition.

Because there are two authors, both are acknowledged in the citation.

Harvin 4

are needed to make politics a positive-sum game." Generally speaking, this opposition may highlight a legitimate concern for the ability of safe spaces and trigger warnings to work for students with different opinions . . . but at what benefit? Safe spaces offer an opportunity for marginalized students to combat their trauma head-on and without the fear of judgment or scrutiny from their peers and professors, allowing them to work through emotional damage or discomfort in a way that will better equip them for future engagements and difficult conversations with others.

    Safe spaces and trigger warnings are a tool for success— not an effort to coddle or encourage hyper-sensitivity. Clinical social worker and therapist Megan Yee emphasizes the ability of safe spaces to improve communication skills and foster a community of healing: "Safe spaces can provide a break from judgment, unsolicited opinions, and having to explain yourself. . . . This is especially important for minorities, members of the LGBTQIA community, and other marginalized groups."

    Perhaps the strongest misconceptions about the intent of safe spaces and trigger warnings revolve around whom they are meant to protect and why. Alicia Oglesby, the assistant director of school and college counseling at Bishop McNamara High School in Prince George's County in Maryland, highlights the personal, academic, and professional struggles that face marginalized groups as they attempt to consider the challenge of navigating the confusing and overwhelming college experience for the first time. In her article "Safe Spaces," Oglesby identifies three groups that could benefit from the support of safe spaces in academic settings: low-income students, LGBTQ students, and students of color (48). While attempting to navigate the college experience, marginalized groups are affected by the weighty, powerful influence of administration and faculty, often older, middle-class white men. Indeed, the support of safe spaces and trigger warnings should, in theory, provide emotional and academic stability throughout their college career whenever trauma resurfaces. Oglesby highlights the ability of safe spaces to ease the transition for these

Anna concedes the opposition's point but says it isn't enough.

Anna establishes the author's claim to authority. There is no page number at the end of the sentence because this is an online source with no page numbers.

Author and claim to authority established in text, so page number only in parenthesis. The page number at the end of the passage indicates that the ideas are paraphrased from the source.

marginalized students from the first academic year between their high school graduation to the first day their college classes:

> Here we have white men looking through their own eyes, but the white American experience certainly is not synonymous or interchangeable with the black American experience. The same goes for heterosexual colleagues not recognizing the perceptions of LGBTQ colleagues and students. Middle class vs. low-income; private independent vs. public schools — the list of privileged groups misunderstanding less privileged groups goes on and on. (48)

These students and their experiences reveal a deeply ingrained campus culture of intolerance, aggression, and misunderstanding that seeps into professional environments — a consequence of a politically charged academic space that should aim to foster civil conversation rather than fuel hatred and miscommunication. Racial, sexual, and class issues have the ability to stimulate meaningful conversations about our students' differences and how they can overcome them. Instead, these issues become inflamed as a result of minority groups not having access to spaces in which they can explore and learn to cope with the very real and debilitating traumas inflicted overwhelmingly by a cis white upper-class majority that has dominated higher education for generations.

When considering what should be the true aim behind higher education, the preservation of the young American future seems as though it should be at the forefront of administrations' agendas. Why, then, are college students so depressed — more of them succumbing to the effects of mental illness every year? The answer may very well lie in the lack of substantial, preventative resources for combatting traumas that inhibit students from succeeding inside the college classroom and out. In order to facilitate healing and the building of stronger communication skills and mental well-being, schools must take action and create safe spaces to make

With a block quotation, the period goes before the parenthesis.

Anna's thesis

Harvin 6

marginalized students feel safe as well as protect the student body at large from content that could trigger a negative response. The encouragement and implementation of safe spaces and trigger warnings does less to inhibit the flow of free speech and more to foster environments of healing and the free flow of ideas. This helps universities and colleges uphold the integrity and true mission of the college experience in the United States: to build a stronger, more empathetic, more capable, and more understanding generation of Americans to lead the country forward.

Harvin 7

Works Cited

2018 Annual Report. Center for Collegiate Mental Health, Penn State U, 27 Sept. 2019, ccmh.psu.edu /files/2019/09/2018-Annual-Report-9.27.19-FINAL.pdf.

Byron, Katie. "From Infantilizing to World Making: Safe Spaces and Trigger Warnings on Campus." *Family Relations*, vol. 66, no. 1, Fall 2017, pp. 116–25. *Wiley Online Library*, doi:10.1111/fare.12233.

Carter, Angela M. "Teaching with Trauma: Trigger Warnings, Feminism, and Disability Pedagogy." *Disability Studies Quarterly*, vol. 35, no. 2, 2015, dsq-sds.org/article/view /4652/3935.

Lukianoff, Greg, and Jonathan Haidt. "The Coddling of the American Mind." *The Atlantic*, 31 July 2017, www .theatlantic.com/magazine/archive/2015/09/the-coddling -of-the-american-mind/399356/.

Oglesby, Alicia. "Safe Spaces." *The Journal of College Admission*, no. 243, Spring 2019, pp. 46–50. *Academic Search Premier*, http://search.ebscohost.com.i.ezproxy.nypl.org/login .aspx?direct=true&AuthType=cookie,ip,url,cpid&custid =nypl&db=aph&AN=136025367&site=ehost-live.

Yee, Megan. "Why 'Safe Spaces' Are Important for Mental Health—Especially on College Campuses." *Healthline*, 3 June 2019, www.healthline.com/health/mental-health /safe-spaces-college#1.

APA In-Text Citations

Instructors in the social sciences might prefer the citation system of the American Psychological Association (APA), which is used in the sample paper on GMOs (genetically modified organisms) (p. 457). Like the MLA system, the APA system calls for a parenthetical citation in the text of the paper following any quotations from your sources. The APA only recommends that page numbers be included for paraphrases or summaries, but it is a good practice to provide page numbers for these anyway unless your instructor advises you that they are not necessary. The following guidelines cover common scenarios where you will need to use in-text citations in APA format, but you may encounter other variations. For more help, consult the *Publication Manual of the American Psychological Association*, 7th edition (2020).

In the text of your paper, immediately after any quotation, paraphrase, or idea you need to document, insert a parenthetical mention of the author's last name and the page number on which the material appears. The APA system also includes the year of publication in the parenthetical reference, using a comma to separate the items within the citation and using "p." or "pp." before the page number(s) in books and articles; citations for newspaper articles include only the page number, not "p." or "pp.". Even if the source has a month of publication, only the year is included in the parenthetical citation. Here is an example:

> If large agricultural states such as California implemented statewide labeling standards, nearly twelve percent of the food market within the United States would be affected. In turn, companies would have to weigh the cost of changing their labels for one state to the cost of avoiding California as a whole (Helme, 2013, p. 372).

The parenthetical reference tells the reader that the information in this sentence comes from page 372 of the 2013 work by Helme that appears on the References page at the end of the paper. The complete publication information that a reader would need to locate Helme's work will appear on the References page:

> Helme, M. A. (2013). Genetically modified food fight: The FDA should step up to the regulatory plate so states do not cross the constitutional line. *Minnesota Law Review, 98*(1), 356–384.

If the author's name is mentioned in the same sentence in your text, the year in which the work was published follows it, in parentheses, and the page number only is placed in parentheses at the end of the sentence:

> According to Helme (2013), if large agricultural states such as California implemented statewide labeling standards, nearly twelve percent of the food market within the United States would be affected (p. 372).

When introducing your sources with signal phrases, APA requires the use of past tense or present perfect tense. For example,

> Helme (2013) discovered . . .

> Helme (2013) has suggested . . .

In the APA system, it is appropriate to include only the last name of the author unless you have more than one author with the same name in your list of references, in which case you would include the first initial of the author.

If your list of references includes more than one work written by the same author in the same year, cite the first work as "a" and the second as "b." For example, Helme's second article of 2013 would be cited in your paper like this: (Helme, 2013b).

If a work has two authors, list both in your sentence, using "and" between them, or in the parentheses, using an ampersand (&) between them. In these examples, there is no page number because the source is a short work from a website:

> Yoest and Yoest (2002) recalled the Fall 2000 suggestion from DACOWITS for a possible recruiting slogan: "A gynecologist on every aircraft carrier!"

> The Fall 2000 suggestion from DACOWITS included a possible recruiting slogan: "A gynecologist on every aircraft carrier!" (Yoest & Yoest, 2002).

If there are three to five authors, which is often the case in the sciences and social sciences, list them all by the last name of the first author and the term "et al." (meaning "and others" in Latin): therefore, a 2001 article from Sommers, Mylroie, Donnelly, and Hill would be listed as "Sommers et al. (2001)" within the sentence or "(Sommers et al., 2001)" at the end of the sentence.

If no author is given, use the name of the work where you would normally use the author's name, placing the names of short works in quotation marks and italicizing those of book-length works.

> As a result of changes in the city's eviction laws, New York's eviction rate dropped by over a third from 2013 to 2018 ("Pushed Out," 2019).

Titles that are part of in-text citations are set in *title case*, which means you should capitalize the first and last words of a title and subtitle, all significant words, and any words of four letters or more. For long works like books or films, italicize the title, and for articles and pieces of larger works like chapters, use quotation marks around the title, as in the example above.

If you consulted a reprinted, republished, or translated work, include both the date of original publication and the date of the version you used, and separate the dates with a slash: (Padura, 2009/2014). When using electronic sources, follow as much as possible the rules for parenthetical documentation of print sources, though note some differences. For example, for titles of websites, use quotation marks around the site title. If no author's name is given, cite by the title of the work. If no date is given, use instead the abbreviation "n.d.", which should also be included in the source's listing on the References page. For a long work, if there are no page numbers, as is often the case with electronic sources, give paragraph numbers if the work has numbered paragraphs, or, if the work is divided into sections, the paragraph number within that section:

> Jamison (1999) warned about the moral issues associated with stem cell research, particularly the guilt that some parents felt about letting their children's cells be used (Parental Guilt section, para. 2).

Remember that the purpose of parenthetical documentation is to help a reader locate the information that you are citing.

At times, you will need to cite one work that is quoted in another or a work from an anthology. The parenthetical documentation provides author's name, year of publication, and page number of the source you actually used, preceded by the words "as cited in":

> One reviewer commended the author's "sure understanding of the thoughts of young people" (Brailsford, 1990, as cited in Chow, 2019, para. 9).

A work in an anthology is cited parenthetically by the name of the author of the work, not the editor of the anthology.

Personal communications, such as emails or interviews you conducted, should only be included as in-text citations; they should not be included in the References list.

> A researcher studying the effect of the media on children's eating habits has argued that advertisers for snack foods should be required to design ads responsibly for their younger viewers (F. Johnson, personal communication, October 20, 2019).

For any specific section in a source, such as an introduction, dedication, or foreword, include the full source in your References list, but identify the specific section within the text itself.

> In a dedication written while he was in hiding, Salman Rushdie (1991) included an acrostic of his son's name: SAFAR.

APA List of References

Following are examples of the bibliographical forms you are most likely to employ if you are using the American Psychological Association (APA) system for documenting sources. If you need the format for a type of publication not listed here, consult the *Publication Manual of the American Psychological Association,* 7th edition (2020). If you are citing a work in this textbook, use the form for "A Work in an Anthology." When you are citing an article, a chapter, or anything else shorter than a book-length work, give the page range for the whole article, chapter, or short work rather than the single page number from which a quotation, paraphrase, or summary is drawn.

If you are used to the Modern Language Association (MLA) system for documenting sources, take a moment to notice some of the key differences: in APA style, all authors and editors are listed last name first, followed by initials rather than full names, and the year comes immediately after the author's or editor's name instead of at or near the end of the entry. Titles in general are capitalized in *sentence case*, which means that only the first word of the title, the first word of the subtitle, and any proper nouns are capitalized. The overall structure of each entry, however, will be familiar: author, title, publication information.

Directory of APA Reference Entries

Print Sources

1. A Book by a Single Author

Isreal, J. (2012). *Democratic enlightenment: Philosophy, revolution, and human rights, 1750–1790*. Oxford University Press.

2. Multiple Works by the Same Author in the Same Year

Gardner, H. (1982a). *Art, mind, and brain: A cognitive approach to creativity*. Basic Books.

Gardner, H. (1982b). *Developmental psychology: An introduction* (2nd ed.). Little, Brown.

Insert lowercase letters following the year in the order in which the sources appear. If they are works that are the same type (for instance, two books), list them in alphabetical order. Otherwise, works that include only the year (such as articles in scholarly journals) should appear before works that include a specific month or day (such as popular magazine articles).

3. A Work by Two Authors or Editors

Lester, D., & Rogers, J. R. (2012). *Crisis intervention and counseling by telephone and the internet* (3rd ed.). Charles C. Thomas.

4. A Work by Three to Twenty Authors or Editors

Wiegand, I., Seidel, C., & Wolfe, J. (2019). Hybrid foraging search in younger and older age. *Psychology and Aging*, 34(6), 805–820.

For up to twenty authors, list the names of *all* the authors or editors, last name first then first initial and a period, with an ampersand (&) before the last author.

5. A Work by Twenty-One or More Authors

Sharon, G., Cruz, N. J., Kang, D.-W., Gandal, M. J., Wang, B., Kim, Y.-M., Zink, E. M., Casey, C. P., Taylor, B. C., Lane, C. J., Bramer, L. M., Isern, N. G., Hoyt, D. W., Noecker, C., Sweredoski, M. J., Moradian, A., Borenstein, E., Jansson, J. K., Knight, R., . . . Mazmanian, S. K. (2019). Human gut microbiota from autism spectrum disorder promote behavioral symptoms in mice. *Cell*, 177(6), 1600–1618.e17.

For twenty-one or more authors, list the first nineteen authors followed by an ellipsis (three spaced dots), and then list the last author's name. In these citations, there is no ampersand before the last author.

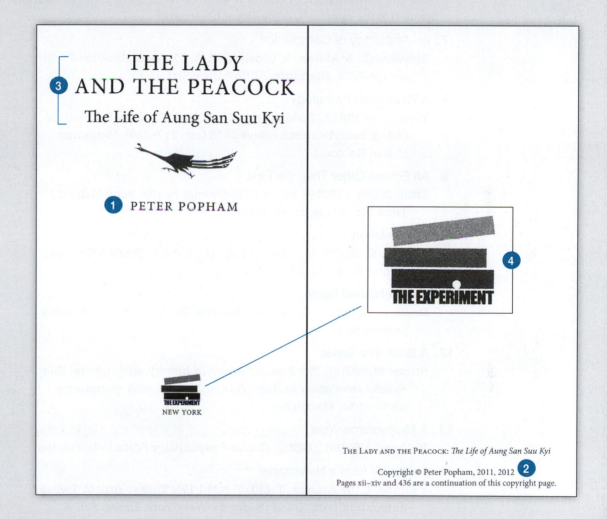

The Elements of Citation

BOOK (APA)

When you cite a book using APA style, include the following:

1 Author

2 Date of publication

3 Title and subtitle

4 Publisher

3 THE LADY AND THE PEACOCK

The Life of Aung San Suu Kyi

1 PETER POPHAM

4 THE EXPERIMENT

THE EXPERIMENT
NEW YORK

THE LADY AND THE PEACOCK: *The Life of Aung San Suu Kyi*

Copyright © Peter Popham, 2011, 2012 **2**
Pages xii–xiv and 436 are a continuation of this copyright page.

Reference list entry for a book in APA style

Popham, P. (2011/2012). *The lady and the peacock: The life of Aung San Suu Kyi.*

The Experiment.

6. A Work by a Corporate Author or Organization

Congressional Quarterly (2014). *Issues for debate in American public policy: Selections from* CQ Researcher (14th ed.).

If author and publisher are the same (as occurs sometimes with a corporate author), omit the publisher. Omit business terms such as *Ltd.* or *Inc.* In the example above, the "Inc." was removed from the corporate name, and the publisher "CQ Press" was omitted from the end of the citation since it is the same as "Congressional Quarterly."

7. An Anthology or Compilation

Strayed, C., & Atwan, R. (Eds.). (2013). *The best American essays 2013.* Houghton Mifflin Harcourt.

8. A Work in an Anthology

Yang, V. W. (2013). Field notes on hair. In J. C. Oates & R. Atwan (Eds.), *Best American essays 2013* (pp. 217–224). Houghton Mifflin Harcourt.

9. An Edition Other Than the First

Litin, S. (Ed.). (2009). *Mayo Clinic family health book* (4th ed.). Time Inc. Home Entertainment.

10. A Translation

Khalifa, K. (2008). *In praise of hatred* (L. Price, Trans.). Thomas Dunne Books-St. Martin's Press.

11. A Republished Book

Dickens, C. (2013). *Great expectations.* Penguin. (Original work published 1861)

12. A Book in a Series

Stone, M. (2013). *The Bedford series in history and culture: The Fascist revolution in Italy: A brief history with documents.* Bedford/St. Martin's.

13. A Multivolume Work

Helfgott, J. B. (Ed.). (2013). *Criminal psychology* (Vols. 1–4). Praeger.

14. An Article from a Newspaper

Yeginsu, C., & Arango, T. (2014, April 17). Turkey greets Twitter delegation with list of demands. *New York Times,* A6.

15. An Article from a Magazine

McWilliams, J. (2014, Spring). Loving animals to death. *The American Scholar,* 18–30.

16. An Article from a Journal

Purchase, H. C. (2014). Twelve years of diagrams research. *Journal of Visual Languages & Computing, 25*(2), 57–75.

17. An Article in a Reference Work

Chichinguane (2014). In P. Monaghan, *Encyclopedia of goddesses and heroines* (p. 6). New World Library.

18. A Government Publication

Federal Emergency Management Agency (2009, August). *Flood insurance claims handbook* (FEMA F-687). U.S. Department of Homeland Security. Government Printing Office.

If no author is listed, include the agency or department that produced the document in the "author" position, and include the broader organization as the publisher.

19. An Abstract

Brey, E., & Pauker, K. (2019, December). Teachers' nonverbal behaviors influence children's stereotypic beliefs [Abstract]. *Journal of Experimental Child Psychology, 188.*

When the dates of the original publication and of the abstract differ, give both dates separated by a slash: Fritz, M. (1990/1991).

20. An Anonymous Work

The status of women: Different but the same. (1992–1993). *Zontian, 73*(3), 5.

21. A Review

Huff, T. E. (2013). Why some nations succeed. [Review of the book *Why nations fail: The origins of power, prosperity & poverty*, by D. Acemoglu & J. A. Robinson]. *Contemporary Sociology, 42*(1), 55–59.

Start with the author of the review, followed by the year and the title (if any). Provide the title of the book or film being reviewed in brackets, along with the title of the book or the year of the film.

22. An Editorial or Letter to the Editor

Pritchett, J. T., & Kellner, C. H. (1993). Comment on spontaneous seizure activity [Letter to the editor]. *Journal of Nervous and Mental Disease, 181*, 138–139.

23. Proceedings of a Meeting, Published

Guerrero, R. (1972/1973). Possible effects of the periodic abstinence method. In W. A. Uricchio & M. K. Williams (Eds.), *Proceedings of a Research Conference on Natural Family Planning* (pp. 96–105). Human Life Foundation.

If the date of the symposium or conference is different from the date of publication, give both, separated by a slash. If the proceedings are published annually, treat the reference like a periodical article.

Online Sources

24. An Article from an Online Periodical

> Chattopadhyay, P. (2003). Can dissimilarity lead to positive outcomes?
> The influence of open versus closed minds. *Journal of Organiza-
> tional Behavior, 24,* 295–312. https://doi.org/10.1002/job.118

If the article duplicates the version that appeared in a print periodical, use the
same basic primary journal reference. See "An Article from a Newspaper," "An
Article from a Magazine," or "An Article from a Journal." Some online articles
have a "digital object identifier" (DOI), which APA recommends using whenever possible, using a link format—https://doi.org/—followed by the DOI
numbers. If the article does not have a DOI, use the URL at the end of the
entry. Lengthy DOIs and URLs may be shortened using sites such as bitly.com.

> Riordan, V. (2001, January 1). Verbal-performance IQ discrep-
> ancies in children attending a child and adolescent psychi-
> atry clinic. *Child and Adolescent Psychiatry On-Line.* Priory
> Lodge Education. http://www.priory.com/psych/iq.htm

If the site is one that will be updated regularly, include "Retrieved from"
before the URL.

25. A Website

> Munro, K. (2001, February). *Changing your body image.* http://
> www.kalimunro.com/article_changing_body_image.html

In general, follow this format: author's name, the date of publication (if no
publication date is available, use "n.d."), the title of the document in italics,
and the source's URL.

26. A Document or Section of a Website

> Fister, B. (2019, February 14). Information literacy's third wave.
> *Library Babel Fish.* https://www.insidehighered.com/blogs
> /library-babel-fish/information-literacy%E2%80%99s-third-wave

27. An Online Reference Work (Including a Wiki)

> Merriam-Webster. (n.d.). Adscititious. In *Merriam-Webster.com
> dictionary.* Retrieved September 5, 2019, from https://www
> .merriam-webster.com/dictionary/adscititious

If a source is intended to be updated regularly, include a retrieval date.

> Behaviorism. (2019, October 11). In *Wikipedia.* https://en.wikipedia
> .org/w/index.php?title=Behaviorism&oldid=915544724

Since Wikipedia makes archived versions available, you need not include
a retrieval date. Instead, include the URL for the version you used, which
you can find by clicking on the "View history" tab on the site.

The Elements of Citation

ARTICLE FROM A WEBSITE (APA)

When you cite an article from a website using APA style, see first if it falls into other categories, such as "article from a newspaper" or "blog post" (which we used here). For a section of an article, the website name follows the title. Include the following:

1 Author

2 Date of publication (if you cannot find one, use "n.d." for "no date")

3 Title and subtitle of article

4 Title of website

5 URL or DOI (APA suggests shortening lengthy URLs via a service like bitly.com. (Include "Retrieved [month day, year] from" before the URL only if a site will be updated regularly, which is not the case with this article.)

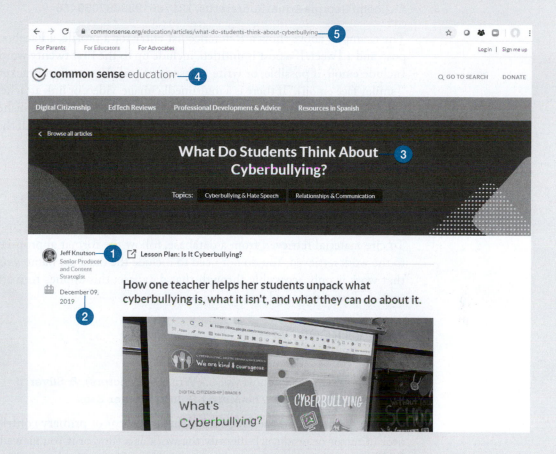

Reference list entry for a brief article from a website in APA style

└─1─┘ ┌──2───┐ ┌────────3────────┐ ┌──────4──────┐
Knutson, J. (2019, December 9). What do students think about cyberbullying? *Common Sense Education*.

┌──────────────5──────────────┐
http://commonsense.org/education/articles/what-do-students-think-about-cyberbullying

28. A Social Media Post

Georgia Aquarium. (n.d.). *Home* [Facebook page]. Facebook. Retrieved October 15, 2019, from https://www.facebook .com/GeorgiaAquarium/

Georgia Aquarium. (2019, October 10). *Meet the bigfin reef squid* [Video]. Facebook. https://www.facebook.com /GeorgiaAquarium/videos/2471961729567512/

Georgia Aquarium [@GeorgiaAquarium]. (2020, January 16). *We're proud to partner with @zoos_aquariums to help and house #corals in the path of a stony disease tissue outbreak . . .* [Image attached] [Tweet]. Twitter. https://twitter .com/GeorgiaAquarium/status/1217861923687059456

The examples above show a Reference list entry for a profile, a Facebook post, and a Tweet. If a post is untitled, include up to the first twenty words. Include emoji, if possible, or write a description of the emoji in brackets: "[smiley face emoji]." If there is a multimedia image, video, or link attached, identify it in brackets. Identify the social media website as the publisher. Care should be taken when citing electronic discussions. In general, they are not scholarly sources.

29. An Article from a Database

Le Texier, T. (2019). Debunking the Stanford Prison Experiment. *American Psychologist, 74*(7), 823–839. https://doi.org/10.1037 /amp0000401

To cite material retrieved from a database, follow the format appropriate to the work retrieved. You do not need to include the database name *unless* that work is only accessible through that database; this applies to works such as dissertations and certain archives.

Other Sources

30. A Film

Wachowski, L., & Wachowski, L. (Writers/Directors), & Silver, J. (Producer). (1999). *The Matrix* [Film]. Warner Bros.

Include the name and the function of the originator or primary contributor (director or producer). Identify the work as a film, or if you viewed a DVD, include the appropriate label in brackets. If the film has multiple production companies, separate the production companies by semicolons.

31. A Television or Radio Program

Waller-Bridge, P. (Writer), & Bradbeer, H. (Director). (2019, March 18). The provocative request (Season 2, Episode 3) [TV series episode]. In P. Waller-Bridge, H. Williams, & J. Williams (Executive Producers), *Fleabag*. Two Brothers Pictures; BBC.

The Elements of Citation

ARTICLE FROM A DATABASE (APA)

In APA style, omit the database name you used to access an article — and a URL to the article on the database — *unless* that work is only accessible through that database or has limited circulation (this is uncommon). In other words, cite it just like you would an article in print or online, if there is a DOI. Include the following:

1 Author
2 Date of publication
3 Title of article

4 Title of periodical, volume, and issue numbers
5 Inclusive pages
6 URL

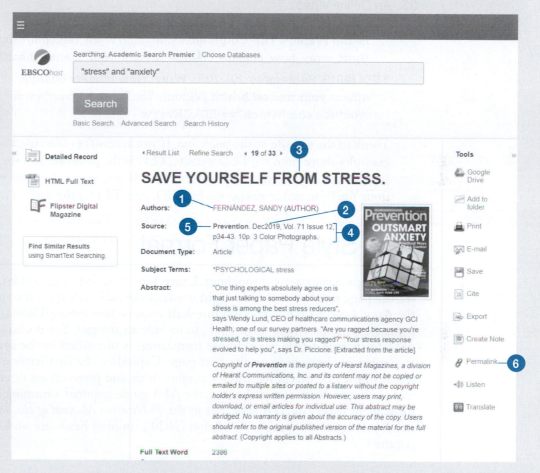

Reference list entry for an article from a database in APA style

|—— 1 ——| |—— 2 ——| |——— 3 ———| |—— 4 ——| |— 5 —|

Fernández, S. (2019, December). Save yourself from stress. *Prevention*, *71*(12), 34–43.

|——— 6 ———|

search.ebscohost.com.i.ezproxy.nypl.org/login.aspx?direct=true&AuthType=cookie,

ip,url,cpid&custid=nypl&db=aph&AN=139425784&site=ehost-live

If referencing the full series, not a single episode, use only the second half of the citation above, beginning after "In" and identify in brackets the type of program after the title: *Fleabag* [TV series].

32. A Podcast

Raz, Guy. (Host). (2020, January 3). Peering into Space [Audio podcast episode]. In *TED radio hour*. NPR. https://www.npr .org/2013/02/15/172136499/peering-into-space?showDate =2020-01-03

33. An Online Video

Wray, B. (2019, May). *How climate change affects your mental health* [Video]. TED Conferences. https://www.ted.com/talks /britt_wray_how_climate_change_affects_your_mental_health

TED. (2019, September 20). *Britt Wray: How climate change affects your mental health* [Video]. YouTube. https://www .youtube.com/watch?v=-IlDkCEvsYw

Think of the website as the publisher. If you access the video used in the examples above from the TED website, TED is the publisher and the person giving a talk in the video is the author. If you access the same video from YouTube, and it was posted by TED, then TED is the author.

APA-Style Paper Format

Double-space your essay throughout. Leave 1-inch margins on all sides, and set the page number at the top right corner, one-half inch from the top of the page. Indent each paragraph one-half inch or five spaces. Unless your instructor requires it, you do not have to include an abstract. You do, however, need to include a title page, whose formatting is identified in the sample student paper beginning on the next page. Capitalize the first letter of the words of the title except for articles, conjunctions, and prepositions three letters or shorter. Note that in the past, the APA guide required a running head for student papers in APA style, but in the *Publication Manual of the American Psychological Association*, 7th edition (2020), running heads are no longer required.

APA-Style Sample Research Paper

The following essay was written using APA style guidelines by Daniel M. Weinzapfel when he was a student at the University of Findlay; it was published in 2017 in *Inquiries Journal*, *9*(2). We have formatted it as a student paper to illustrate APA style.

1

The Economic Argument for Expanding GMO Regulation in America

Daniel M. Weinzapfel

Department of English, University of Findlay

ANSC 110: First-year Experience for Animal Science Majors

Dr. Jane Smith

April 7, 2015

Title centered, boldface, 3–4 lines below the top margin of the page. If the title is longer than one line, it should be double spaced.

After one space, the following information on individual lines:

- Author's name (the "byline")
- The department and school
- The course number and course title
- The instructor's name
- The due date

2

Abstract

The necessity to grow crops faster and more efficiently has long been a goal for the agriculture industry. Now, through the development of GMOs, this goal is being achieved. However, many critics doubt the reputation of GMOs, instead arguing that we must be more wary of the relatively new science. Overall, the general trend among scholarly authors is that GMOs should be regulated more strictly, as the benefits of increased GMO regulation outweigh the state of the current system. Most scholarly discussions have moved past the perspective that GMOs should be regulated because of health concerns and instead, cultivate the idea that GMOs should be regulated based on economic factors. Because of this, in conducting my research I have chosen to focus mainly on the economic risks GMOs pose to the economy as opposed to the health concerns commonly discussed among GMO critics. By taking a look at how scholars address issues such as the state of the current GMO regulatory system, how GMOs agitate a fragile international trade market, and how GMOs have the potential to upset interstate commerce, it is easy to see that GMOs need to be regulated more strictly.

Keywords: agriculture, food production, genetically modified organisms, GMOs, international trade

APA guidelines do not require abstracts in student papers. However, if your instructor requires one, follow the professional style guidelines: set it with the title "Abstract" in boldface at the top of the page.

If your instructor requires an abstract, follow professional style guidelines by including keywords.

3

The Economic Argument for Expanding GMO Regulation in America

For thousands of years, nature has controlled the success of the agriculture industry. However, within the past several decades, modern technology has begun to wean the world's agriculture industry off its dependence on the cooperation of nature. One of the largest recent innovations has been the development of genetically modified organisms, or GMOs. GMOs are plants which have been genetically modified to tolerate conditions or chemicals which would normally be detrimental to their survival. However, many opponents of GMOs disapprove of their widespread use, arguing that because of insufficient government regulations GMOs have the potential to do more harm than good. The federal government should more strictly regulate GMOs because of confusion between regulatory bodies, how GMOs affect international trade and how they carry the risk of disrupting commerce within the United States.

GMOs should be regulated more strictly because the current system contains many overlaps and gaps and cannot efficiently monitor the thriving industry of genetic engineering. Rebecca Bratspies (2013) addressed these shortcomings in her article "Is Anyone Regulating? The Curious State of GMO Governance in the United States" when she said, "At least ten different laws and numerous agency regulations and guidelines are pressed into service to regulate GE [Genetically Engineered] plants, animals, and microorganisms. Each of these laws predates the advent of biotechnology, and they reflect widely different regulatory approaches and procedures" (p. 931).

As Bratspies showed, the current agencies which oversee U.S. GMO regulation are outdated and no longer directly relate to the regulation of GMOs. With the responsibilities allocated out between multiple agencies, no comprehensive method of assessment and regulation exists.

Repeat the title, in boldface, on the first text page of the paper. Center it and set it one inch from the top of the page.

Daniel defines the key term in his essay.

Daniel's thesis statement

Author and year correctly identified in the text; page number only in parentheses

Signal phrases use the past tense to identify ideas or information from sources.

4

As a result, the regulatory framework surrounding GMOs is imbalanced. In its infancy, the GMO industry was small, manageable and its effects could not be seen or felt by the public.

However, thirty years later, its billion-dollar footprint is seen on nearly every store shelf and in countless agriculture sectors. The current system is flawed, requiring broader and stricter regulation to ensure that the rapidly expanding genetic engineering industry is receiving the attention it requires. As GMOs begin to slip through the cracks in the regulatory bureaucracy, the imperfections of the current system come to light through the harms seen by many farmers.

Regulation of GMOs should be tightened because due to the gaps in the regulatory process environmental problems have arisen as a result of GMO integration into the agricultural market. Rebecca Bratspies (2013) has again been quoted saying, "The United States regulatory system for genetically engineered crops is riddled with major gaps and omissions. Omitted from the regulatory inquiry are systemic environmental issues" (pp. 955–956). Here, Bratspies again reinforces the fact that there is little organized regulation of genetically modified crops and that environmental issues are not addressed through current regulation schemes. Bratspies concluded,

> As a result, the United States is in the process of reaping a harvest of environmental harms associated with uncontrolled planting of GE crops including: contamination of conventional and organic crops; an explosion of herbicide-resistant weeds; and a massive overall increase in herbicide use. (p. 925)

Without consistent and effective regulation, GMOs have spread throughout American agriculture, polluting the environment and causing unforeseen damages. These damages could have been prevented had the regulatory agencies been more thorough in their investigation before releasing them for agricultural use. However, in the wake of the discrepancies in regulation, new problems have been cultivated which are

Signal phrase in the past perfect tense

Block quotation used for a passage 40 words or longer. No quotation marks. Period before parenthesis.

5

damaging to the environment. These concerns are not limited strictly to American soil, though; the contamination of GMO crops with conventional crops is beginning to have international consequences as well.

Steven Mufson (2013), a writer for the *Washington Post*, reported how in 2013, the United States agriculture market was dealt a tremendous blow when Japan and South Korea suspended wheat imports from the United States (para. 4). This decision was made in the wake of the discovery that GMO crops had been found contaminating regular crops. The suspension marked an enormous setback not only for the wheat industry but American agriculture as a whole. This lapse in oversight severely damaged American agriculture's international reputation. Following the discovery, the European Union urged its members to closely monitor their imports for contamination and American exports were closely scrutinized on an international stage. This is only one example of GMOs affecting the international economy, which in total has cost billions of dollars by throwing international agriculture markets into disarray.

GMOs carry enormous risks to America's international agriculture trade, and because current regulations do not adequately contain the production of GMOs to within the United States, they deserve stricter regulation. The United States is one of a handful of countries that argue the safety of GMOs and, as a result, are relatively tolerant of GMOs. Most other countries, however, do not share America's opinion. Consequently, international policies are generally much more stringent. Kyndra Lundquist (2015) in her article "Unapproved Genetically Modified Corn: Its What's for Dinner" outlined the risks when she said, "GMOs also have the potential to affect the global economy, largely because there are several sectors of the world's population who are opposed to GMOs, and GMOs, like all plants, do not respect borders, having the potential to spread or cross-contaminate with other plants" (p. 828). Because of the international community's opinion toward GMOs, they pose a significant threat to the global economy.

Here Daniel makes the transition to his second supporting point: the effect of GMOs on international trade.

The author is associated with a reputable publication. Since the article was accessed online, there is no page number. The parenthesis gives the paragraph number instead to help readers locate the article.

6

Author and year identified in text, so only page number is necessary in parenthesis.

This is largely the result of how plants behave naturally through processes such as pollination. Because of these natural interactions, crops can be difficult to contain to a single field and may possibly contaminate bordering fields that are destined for foreign markets. This is exactly what occurred in the case of Japan and South Korea. This idea was built upon by Arne Holst-Jenson (2008) in her article "GMO Testing— Trade, Labeling or Safety First?" when she warned of the dangers of unapproved GMOs by saying, "Unauthorized GMOs altogether pose a significant socioeconomic risk through their potential effects on trade and trust in industry and authorities"(p. 858).

When genetically engineered plants that have not been approved for sale, or have avoided inspections altogether, enter the market accidentally, the risk for how these GMOs may affect trade with other countries becomes a concern. Because of the strict regulations seen in other countries, regulation agencies must be very cautious to be sure the products being exported are not contaminated with GMOs. As seen in the case of Japan, a slip-up will cause unknown amounts of damage to both the pocket and face of the agriculture industry. As the world's leading agricultural exporter, America's standards for GMO regulation should be thorough and above reproach; however, this is not the case.

It is imperative that the United States more closely regulate agriculture exports because of the negative effects shown through historical precedent; however, the United States fails to address these concerns with their current regularity approach. The idea that current regulation does not adequately address the effects GMO contamination has on a foreign market is shown in the article "Unapproved Genetically Modified Corn: It's What's for Dinner" when author Kendra Lundquist (2015) stated, "The current U.S. regulatory scheme for unapproved GM products is weak because it fails to adequately address the ability of GM products, unlike their natural counterparts, to disrupt global markets [and] cause

7

farmers economic loss" (p. 836). When genetic engineering first began, instead of creating an entirely new organization for the regulation of a relatively new science, the duties of regulation were divided among the most relevant preexisting administrations. While this may have been sufficient three decades ago, today, exports to foreign countries, where GMOs are considered as unsafe, are not required to undergo more strenuous tests to ensure that what is exiting the country is not tainted with GMOs.

As made clear through the occurrence with Japan, many gaps exist in America's regulation process and must be addressed by regulatory agencies. Later in her article, Lundquist (2015) supported the notion of tightening regulation by pointing out, "The United States can avoid the economic costs that GM escapes cause in the domestic and international agriculture markets as well as litigation arising from these incidents through improved oversight" (p. 851). Here, the author argued that increased federal oversight through regulation will alleviate the concerns of economic damages by more strictly monitoring the production of products leaving the country. With so much of the world opposed to GMOs, America's indiscreet attitude toward regulation should be concerning. A continuation of current regulatory practices is only setting America up for another economic trade blow, and it is only a matter of time before the recent history with Japan is repeated. Under-regulation of GMOs poses a distinct threat to the foreign economy of American agriculture; however, the effects of GMO regulatory deficiencies may soon be felt within the domestic sphere of the United States as well.

Many Americans have long argued for the mandatory labeling of GMO products, and, as a result of public opinion, many states have recently pushed for the regulation of GMOs within their state. As documented by Morgan Helme (2013) in her article "Genetically Modified Food Fight: The FDA Should Step Up to the Regulatory Plate so States Do Not Cross the Constitutional Line" as many as twenty-five states have considered labeling

The transition to Daniel's third supporting point: that GMOs "carry the risk of disrupting commerce within the United States."

An example of a direct quotation worked smoothly into the author's own sentence. The brackets indicate the slight change from a capital letter to a lowercase one.

requirements for products containing GMOs; however, no state has been able to pass measures that would implement GMO labeling (p. 358). The federal government has long maintained the position that GMOs do not require extensive regulation. The reason for this, as Helme (2013) pointed out, is that "[d]espite consumer support for GMO labeling, the FDA does not require it without a showing of adverse health effects" (p. 363). However, many states relentlessly advocate the labeling of GMO products. If the states are successful in their push for individual regulation, a variety of issues would arise that would be damaging to the economy of the United States.

Cooperation between states is vital for commerce to freely flow from one state to another. Individual state regulations which differ from one state to another have the potential to affect certain economies within interstate commerce. To avoid this, the federal government should unilaterally regulate the labeling of all GMO products within the United States. While commenting on Vermont's action to introduce mandatory GMO labeling laws, Jim Kling (2014), author of "Labeling for Better or Worse," commented, "Companies would have to choose between dropping the Vermont market, developing a Vermont-only label for thousands of products or changing labels nationwide. Companies argue that the latter two choices would be burdensome to interstate commerce" (p. 1180). When an individual state requires special labeling, it is no longer conducive or profitable for food producers to market to that state. This is because the cost of modifying the current infrastructure to align with the mandated segregation of GMO crops would significantly increase production costs for producers. In essence, by adding select requirements for GMO business within an individual state, most producers are discouraged from business interactions with that state because the cost is simply too high.

Many states control huge percentages of production in select agricultural products and when prominent production

9

states regulate themselves any adverse effects would rebound across the entire market. According to Helme (2013), if large agricultural states such as California implemented statewide labeling standards, nearly twelve percent of the food market within the United States would be affected. In turn, companies would have to weigh the cost of changing their labels for one state to the cost of avoiding California as a whole (p. 372). Changes in regulation of states that lead America in the production of agricultural commodities would have national implications and the increased complexity of interstate commerce might result in untold economic weakening. Remarking on this idea of state regulation, Helme (2015) furthered the argument by stating, "The impact may be magnified if multiple states pass different labeling requirements, which would require packaging to contains several variously worded GMO warnings in order to comply with all regulations" (p. 373).

A paraphrase, generally preferred in APA style over direct quotations

If each state were to regulate individually, much confusion would be generated between the states due to differing or contradictory regulations. When multiple states create individual regulations, the issue of interstate regulation complication is compounded, and food producers would be put in an increasingly tighter situation. Producers would have to create individual labels to correlate with specific state regulations, resulting in previously unnecessary expenditures for producers. Ultimately, because of increased costs, producers may decide to terminate business to specially regulated states. Such terminations would damage that state's economy. Overarching government implemented standards, providing voluntary regulation, would satisfy states' appeals for regulation and would alleviate potential confusion among producers as well as maintain the economic balance between states.

The European Union (EU) has long held the opinion that GMOs should be regulated because they are harmful; however, in the United States the call for regulation does not stem from fear. Rather, it originates simply from the desire to know what is in the food people consume. Prior to the mandatory

Paraphrase. Since
neither author nor
title is mentioned
in the text, both
appear along with
the page number in
the parenthesis.

regulation of GMOs in the European Union, genetically
modified food faced a barrage of public criticism and, upon
its mandatory labeling, GMO products nearly became extinct
in European countries (Helme, 2013, p. 374).

Agencies should implement regulations on a voluntary
basis to prevent an attitude of fear toward GMOs and to help
avoid the alienation of GMOs on the agriculture market in the
United States. In most regards, the American public is very
subdued in their criticism of GMO products and they do not
share the paranoia seen in Europe. With the American public
still moderately tolerant of GMO products, regulatory agencies
should introduce voluntary labeling to avert the catastrophe
following European regulation. As seen in Europe and noted
by Helme (2013) in her article, "When coupled with a negative
perception of GMOs . . . mandatory labeling can push genetically
modified (GM) food out of the market" (p. 380). Helme echoed
this later when she explained how mandatory labeling in
Europe effectively barred GMO food products out of the
European market (p. 381).

Fear and speculation can be powerful motivators and under
their influence the European public distanced themselves from
GMO products and drove them off the shelves. These actions
ended any future for the GMO market in Europe. American
agriculture is overwhelmingly dominated by genetic engineering,
and traces of GMO products can be seen in thousands of
products. Essentially, GMOs are the bread and butter of
American agriculture. If Americans were to respond in the
same way as seen in Europe, the agriculture industry would
likely lose billions of dollars, causing incalculable damage to
the American economy. By responding to Americans' call for
GMO labeling with unilateral federal regulation, situations
such as those seen in Europe can be avoided.

Not everyone agrees that GMOs should be regulated
however. Some proponents of genetic engineering argue that
GMOs have not been found to genetically alter plants, which
would result in hazardous crops; therefore, GMOs do not

11

require extensive regulation. Authors Alan McHughen and Stuart Smyth (2008) advocated the safety of genetically engineered crops in their article "US Regulatory System for Genetically Modified [Genetically Modified Organism (GMO), rDNA or Transgenic] Crop Cultivars" when they related that the incidences of hazardous crops being created by unexpected genetic changes was extremely low (p. 3). GMOs have not been found to be inherently harmful and cases of harmful GMOs occurring naturally in the environment are very uncommon.

This apparent safety has resulted in regulatory agencies placing an unusual amount of trust in producers to identify and report problems to the appropriate authorities. Commenting on this process, McHughen and Smyth (2008) noted that it is "a system that has worked remarkably well considering the lack of hazards reported for new crop cultivars over the years" (p. 3). According to the authors, this system of checks and balances is an effective preventative measure against potential harms associated with genetically modified organisms. The problem with this approach, however, is that the regulatory agencies have failed to consider what motivation producers would have to report incidences of hazardous crops.

Regulatory agencies have essentially given producers the power to regulate themselves. This may be the reason hazards of genetic engineering have not appeared in recent years. Producers could be protecting their business by ignoring concerns they are supposed to report. Bratspies (2013) commented on the effects of a leniently regulated market when she said, "Private actors, motivated by short-term interests, are able to engage in conduct that imposes risks on wider society without any democratic consideration of the acceptability of those risks" (p. 926).

Producers eliminate the possibility of regulating themselves because increased regulation surrounding their business may cut into their profits. Bratspies continued, saying, "It is precisely because individuals make decisions based on individual

Daniel correctly gives credit to both authors.

12

and short-term considerations that environmental regulation is necessary" (p. 943). Producers trying to make a profit cannot be trusted with the safety of the products they produce. Because individuals often act in response to personal interests, the notion that they would purposely report situations that could hurt their business is an irrational conclusion. As such, regulation should be controlled by a separate, unbiased organization such as the federal government.

In this conclusion, Daniel reiterates his thesis and his first two supporting points.

GMOs should be more closely regulated by federal agencies because current standards do not address a variety of concerns seen in the status quo. Although further investigation into the necessity for stricter GMO regulation is required, many issues have been addressed which together suggest that the regulatory processes surrounding GMOs are in desperate need of improvement and strengthening. First, regulatory agencies overlooking GMOs are ineffective and outdated. Because of this they are no longer capable of effectively monitoring the rapidly expanding industry of genetic engineering and many environmental problems have begun to arise. Additionally, existing regulations fail to address the effect GMOs play in international trade and, as seen through past precedent, the potential for economic damage to occur should never be underestimated.

His third supporting point

Finally, commerce between states has the potential to be damaged if the regulation of GMOs is not strengthened through federally mandated unilateral regulation. Genetically modified organisms have repeatedly been shown to possess substantial potential to cause damage to the economy of the United States and, in light of these dangers, Americans should push for a comprehensive and effective federal regulation scheme which protects the future of American agriculture.

13

References

Bratspies, R. M. (2013). Is anyone regulating? The curious
state of GMO governance in the United States. *Vermont
Law Review, 37*(4), 923–956.

Helme, M. A. (2013). Genetically modified food fight: The FDA
should step up to the regulatory plate so states do not
cross the constitutional line. *Minnesota Law Review,
98*(1), 356–384.

Holst-Jensen, A. (2008). GMO testing—trade, labeling or
safety first? *Nature Biotechnology, 26*(8), 858–859.

Kling, J. (2014). Labeling for Better or Worse. *Nature
Biotechnology, 32*(12), 1180–1183.

Lundquist, K. A. (2015). Unapproved genetically modified corn:
It's what's for dinner. *Iowa Law Review, 100*(2), 825–851.

McHughen, A., & Smyth, S. (2008). US regulatory system
for genetically modified [genetically modified organism
(GMO), rDNA or transgenic] crop cultivars. *Plant
Biotechnology Journal, 6*(1), 2–12.

Mufson, S. (2013, May 30). Unapproved genetically
modified wheat from Monsanto found in Oregon field.
The Washington Post. https://www.washingtonpost.com
/business/economy/unapproved-genetically-modified
-wheat-from-monsanto-found-in-oregon-field/2013/05/30
/93fe7abe-c95e-11e2-8da7-d274bc611a47_story.html

An article in a journal

Source with two
authors

Article from
a newspaper,
published online

Acknowledgments

Ben Adler, "Banning Plastic Bags Is Great for the World, Right? Not So Fast," *Grist*, June 2, 2016. Copyright © 2016 by Grist. Used with permission.

Stefan Andreasson, "Fossil Fuel Divestment Will Increase Carbon Emissions, Not Lower Them — Here's Why," *The Conversation*, November 25, 2019. https://theconversation.com/fossil-fuel-divestment-will-increase-carbon-emissions-not-lower-them-heres-why-126392.

Jessica Andrews, "How to Avoid Cultural Appropriation at Coachella," *Teen Vogue*, April 13, 2018. © Conde Nast. Reprinted by permission.

Sharon Astyk and Aaron Newton, "The Rich Get Richer, the Poor Go Hungry" from Sharon Astyk and Aaron Newton, *A Nation of Farmers*. (Originally published in *The Utne Reader*, September/October 2010). Reprinted by permission of New Society Publishers.

Jack Beyrer, "Innovative Gun Control Idea Gains Support," *Real Clear Politics*, June 22, 2019. Used with permission.

Mel Bondar, "The Financial Case for Trade School Over College," *US News & World Report*, April 12, 2016. Copyright © 2016 by US News & World Report. Used with permission.

Ishmeal Bradley, "Conscientious Objection in Medicine: A Moral Dilemma." *Clinical Correlations*, May 28, 2009. Reprinted by permission of Ishmeal Bradley, MD, MPH.

Sunnivie Brydum, "The True Meaning of the Word 'Cisgender'," *Advocate*, July 31, 2015. Copyright © 2015, Pride Publishing. Reprinted by permission.

Christopher Caldwell, "Drivers Get Rolled," *The Weekly Standard*, November 8, 2013. © The Weekly Standard. Reprinted with permission.

Jimmy Carter, "Why I Believe the Mistreatment of Women Is the Number One Human Rights Abuse," *TED Conference*, May 2015. Copyright © 2015 by Jimmy Carter. Used with permission from The Carter Center.

Samuel Chi, "The NFL's Protest Crisis," *CNN*, September 16, 2016. Copyright © 2016 by Turner Broadcasting Systems, Inc. All rights reserved. Used under license.

College Board, from "Inside the Test: SAT® Essay," https://collegereadiness.collegeboard.org/sat/inside-the-test/essay. Reprinted by permission of The College Board.

Steven Doloff, "Greta Garbo, Meet Joan Rivers . . . (Talk amongst Yourselves)," *Women & Language* 38.2, Fall 2015, 137–42. Copyright © 2015 by Women & Language. Used with permission.

Christopher Elliott, "The Insider: A Tale of Two Airlines," *National Geographic Traveler*, December 2012/January 2013. Reprinted by permission.

Amy Froide, "Spinster, Old Maid or Self-partnered—Why Words for Single Women Have Changed through Time," *The Conversation*, December 1, 2019. https://theconversation.com/spinster-old-maid-or-self-partnered-why-words-for-single-women-have-changed-through-time-126716.

Ronald M. Green, "Building a Baby from the Genes Up," *The New York Times*, April 13, 2008. Reprinted by permission of the author.

Sarah Griffiths, "Why Having a Crush Is Good for You," *Medium.com*, December 3, 2018. Reprinted by permission of the author.

Jennifer Grossman, "Food for Thought (and for Credit)," *The New York Times*, Sept. 2, 2003, p. 23, col. 1. Copyright © 2003 by Jennifer Grossman. Reprinted by permission of the author.

Elisha Dov Hack, "College Life Versus My Moral Code," *The New York Times*, September 9, 1997. Reprinted by permission of the author.

Pamela Powers Hannley, "Bathroom Politics: Preserving the Sanctity of the 'Ladies' Room'," *tucson-progressive.com*, May 6, 2014. Used with permission of the author.

Odie Henderson, "Black Panther," Ebert Digital LLC, February 15, 2018. Copyright © 2018 by Ebert Digital LLC. Used with permission.

James W. Ingram III, "Electoral College Is Best Way to Choose U.S. President," *San Diego Union-Tribune*, January 13, 2017. Used with permission from the author.

Left, Right and Center, "Recession fears, immigration rules and 'electability'." Prepared and published by KCRW, August 16, 2019. Reprinted by permission of KCRW.

Sid Kirchheimer, "Are Sports Fans Happier?" from *The Saturday Evening Post*, March 2012. Copyright © SEPS licensed by Curtis Licensing, Indianapolis, IN. All rights reserved. Reprinted by permission.

John R. Koza, "States Can Reform Electoral College—Here's How to Empower Popular Vote," *TheHill.com*, November 10, 2016. Reprinted by permission of Featurewell.com, Inc. on behalf of Capitol Hill Publishing Corporation.

Mark R. Levin, excerpt from UNFREEDOM OF THE PRESS. Copyright © 2019 by Mark R. Levin. Reprinted with the permission of Threshold Editions, a division of Simon & Schuster, Inc. All rights reserved.

Michael Levin, "The Case for Torture." Originally published in *Newsweek*, June 7, 1982. Copyright © 1982 by Michael Levin. Reprinted by permission of the author.

Liza Long, "I Am Adam Lanza's Mother" published by *The Blue Review*. Reprinted with permission of The Blue Review.

Brian Whitaker, "The Definition of Terrorism," *The Guardian Unlimited*, May 7, 2001. Copyright Guardian News & Media Ltd 2017. Reprinted by permission.

Lucas Wright, "Twitter Bans Religious Dehumanization," *Dangerous Speech Project*, July 12, 2019. Copyright © 2019 by Dangerous Speech Project. Used with permission.

Megan Yee, "Why 'Safe Spaces' Are Important for Mental Health—Especially on College Campuses." Reprinted by permission of Healthline Media, Inc.

Glossary

Abstract language: language expressing a quality apart from a specific object or event; opposite of *concrete language*

Ad hominem: "against the man"; attacking the arguer rather than the *argument* or issue

Ad populum: "to the people"; playing on the prejudices of the *audience*

Analogy: a complex comparison between two things similar in some ways but dissimilar in others, often used to explain the less familiar in terms of the more familiar

Anecdotal evidence: stories or examples used to illustrate a *claim* but that do not prove it with scientific certainty

Annotate: to mark a text as a means of understanding it more fully, using underlining, highlighting, and/or marginal notes

APA: the American Psychological Association, a scientific and professional organization that represents psychologists in the United States

Appeal to needs and values: an attempt to gain assent to a *claim* by showing that it will bring about what your *audience* wants and cares deeply about

Appeal to tradition: a proposal that something should continue because it has traditionally existed or been done that way

Argument: a statement or statements providing *support* for a *claim*

Argumentation: a process of reasoning and advancing proof about issues on which conflicting views may be held

Aristotelian rhetoric: the approach to oral persuasion espoused by Aristotle (384 BCE–322 BCE) and used to shape school curricula well into the nineteenth century; a rhetorical theory based on using a combination of *logos*, *ethos*, and *pathos* to move an audience to a change in thought or action

Assumption: a *general principle* that establishes a connection between the *support* and the *claim*; see also *warrant*

Audience: those who will hear an *argument*; more generally, those to whom a communication is addressed

Backing: the assurances on which an *assumption* is based

Begging the question: making a statement that assumes that the issue being argued has already been decided

Charged words: words that present a subject favorably or unfavorably

Claim: the conclusion of an *argument*; what the arguer is trying to prove

Claim of fact: a *claim* that asserts something exists, has existed, or will exist, based on facts or data that the *audience* will accept as objectively verifiable

Claim of policy: a *claim* asserting that specific courses of action should be instituted as solutions to problems

Claim of value: a *claim* that asserts some things are more or less desirable than others

Cliché: a worn-out expression or idea, no longer capable of producing a visual image or provoking thought about a subject

Coherence: orderly and consistent connection between ideas

Common ground: used in *Rogerian argument* to refer to any concept that two opposing parties agree on and that can thus be used as a starting point for negotiation

Concession: acceptance of a point made by an opposing view or counterargument, but usually not the entire argument

Conclusion: the closing of an argument; in a *syllogism*, a statement that is a logical assertion based on the preceding *major premise* and *minor premise*

Concrete language: language that describes specific, generally observable, persons, places, or things; in contrast to *abstract language*

Confirmation bias: the tendency to look for and interpret information in such a way as to reinforce existing beliefs

Connotation: the overtones that adhere to a word through long usage

Credibility: the audience's belief in the arguer's trustworthiness; see also *ethos*

Critical reading: an approach to a text that goes beyond reading for understanding to analyze, interpret, and evaluate it

Data: facts or figures from which a conclusion may be inferred; see *evidence*

Deduction: reasoning by which we establish that a conclusion must be true because the statements on which it is based are true; see also *syllogism*

Definition: an explanation of the meaning of a term, concept, or experience; may be used for clarification, especially of a *claim*, or as a means of developing an *argument*

Emotive language: language that expresses and arouses emotions

Empirical evidence: *support* verifiable by experience or experiment

Enthymeme: a *syllogism* in which one of the premises is implied

Ethos: the qualities of character, intelligence, and goodwill in a writer or speaker that contribute to an *audience's* acceptance of the *claim*

Euphemism: a pleasant or flattering expression used in place of one that is less agreeable but possibly more accurate

Evaluation: a reader's reaction to or critical judgment of an *argument*

Evidence: *facts* or opinions that support an issue or *claim*; may consist of statistics, reports of personal experience, or views of experts

Extended definition: a *definition* that uses several different methods of development

Fact: something that is believed to have objective reality; a piece of information regarded as verifiable

Factual evidence: *support* consisting of *data* that are considered objectively verifiable by the *audience*

Fallacy: an error of reasoning based on faulty use of *evidence* or incorrect *inference*

False analogy: assuming without sufficient proof that if objects or processes are similar in some ways, then they are similar in other ways as well

False dilemma: simplifying a complex problem into an either/or dichotomy

Faulty emotional appeals: basing an *argument* on feelings, especially pity or fear—often to draw attention away from the real issues or conceal another purpose

Faulty use of authority: failing to acknowledge disagreement among experts or otherwise misrepresenting the trustworthiness of sources

Figurative language: phrasing that goes beyond the literal meaning of words, often to produce images in the minds of the *audience*

General principles: broad assumptions shaped by your observations, your personal experience, and your participation in a culture that can be applied in a number of different circumstances

Hasty generalization: drawing conclusions from insufficient *evidence*

Induction: reasoning by which a general statement is reached on the basis of particular examples

Inference: an interpretation of the *facts*

Logos: an appeal to logic and reason

Main claim: the *thesis*, or the single statement that summarizes the main point of an essay

Major premise: see *syllogism*

Metaphor: a comparison that does not make use of *like* or *as*

Minor premise: see *syllogism*

MLA: the Modern Language Association, a professional organization for college teachers of English and foreign languages

Motivational appeal: an attempt to reach an *audience* by recognizing their *needs* and *values* and how these contribute to their decision making

Multimodal: a combination of modes—such as visual and aural—in addition to, or other than, text that is used to create and convey a message; often used in presentations and digital media

Multimodal argument: words in combination with another medium or an *argument* in a mode other than the printed word: photographs, illustrations, audio, video, or digital media, for example

Need: in the hierarchy of Abraham Maslow, whatever is required, whether psychological or physiological, for the survival and welfare of a human being

Negation: classification of a term by stipulating what it is not

Non sequitur: "it does not follow"; using irrelevant proof to buttress a *claim*

Parallel order comparison: an organizational pattern that focuses fully on one subject to discuss points made in an *argument*, then fully on another subject; in a comparison/contrast essay with two subjects, the pattern focuses roughly half the essay on Subject A and then the other half on Subject B, with the points made in each half being parallel and presented in the same order

Paraphrase: a restatement of the content of an original source in your own words

Pathos: an appeal to the emotions

Personification: giving human attributes to the nonhuman

Persuasion: the use of a combination of *logos*, *ethos*, and *pathos* to move an *audience*

Plagiarism: the use of someone else's words or ideas without adequate acknowledgment

Point-by-point comparison: an organizational pattern that focuses on each point made in an *argument*, considering all subjects being compared under each point; in a comparison/contrast essay with two subjects, the pattern addresses the point about Subject A and Subject B together before moving on to the second and following points

Policy: a course of action recommended or taken to solve a problem or guide decisions

Post hoc: mistakenly inferring that because one event follows another they have a causal relation; from *post hoc ergo propter hoc* ("after this, therefore because of this"); also called "doubtful cause"

Premise: an assertion or proposition from which a *conclusion* is drawn

Primary source: firsthand information taken directly from the original source, including field research (interviews, surveys, personal observations, or experiments), memoirs, letters, photographs, contemporary news reports, court documents, and texts of laws or bills

Proposition: see *claim*

Purpose: the occasion or situation that motivates a writer to write; the reason behind undertaking the writing

Qualifier: a restriction placed on the *claim* to indicate that it may not always be true as stated

Quote: to repeat exactly words from a printed, electronic, or spoken source

Red herring: an attempt to divert attention away from the subject at hand

Referential summary: a summary that focuses on the author's ideas rather than on the author's actions and decisions

Refutation: an attack on an opposing view to weaken it, invalidate it, or make it less credible

Reservation: a restriction placed on the *assumption* to indicate that unless certain conditions are met, the assumption may not establish a connection between the *support* and the *claim*

Rhetoric: the art of effective or persuasive speaking or writing

Rhetorical situation: the context, *purpose*, and *audience* for a speech or written text

Rhetorical summary: a condensation of a passage in the writer's own words that stresses the author's decisions as a writer

Rogerian argument: a rhetorical theory based on the counseling techniques of Carl Rogers (1902–1987) that emphasizes a search for *common ground* that would allow two opposing parties to start negotiations

Secondary source: texts that provide commentary on and analysis of a topic or of *primary sources*

Simile: a comparison using *like* or *as*

Slanting: selecting *facts* or words with *connotations* that favor the arguer's bias and discredit alternatives

Slippery slope: predicting without justification that one step in a process will lead unavoidably to a second, generally undesirable step

Slogan: an attention-getting expression used largely in politics or advertising to promote support of a cause or product

Sound: an *argument* that is valid and in which all of its *premises* are true

Spin: slanting information in favor of or against one position over others

Stasis theory: a set of four questions for exploring argumentative topics, developed by the ancient Greek philosophers Aristotle and Hermagoras

Statistics: information expressed in numerical form

Stereotype: overgeneralized perception of an ethnic group, nationality, or any other group

Stipulative definition: a *definition* that makes clear that it will explore a particular area of meaning of a term or issue

Straw man: disputing a view similar to, but not the same as, that of the arguer's opponent

Style: choices in words and sentence structure that make a writer's language distinctive

Summary: a condensation of a passage into a shorter version in the writer's own words

Support: any material that serves to prove an issue or *claim*; in addition to *evidence*, it includes appeals to the *needs* and *values* of the *audience*

Syllogism: a formula of deductive *argument* consisting of three propositions: a major premise, a minor premise, and a logical *conclusion*

Synthesis: the bringing together and analyzing of ideas to formulate opinions

Thesis: the main idea of an essay, often expressed in a clear sentence or two as a *thesis statement*, especially in academic writing

Tone: the approach taken toward a topic—solemn or humorous, detached or sympathetic, for example—often established through language and word choice

Toulmin model: a conceptual system of *argument* devised by the philosopher Stephen Toulmin; the terms *claim*, *support*, *assumption* (often called *warrant*), *backing*, *qualifier*, and *reservation* are adapted from this system

Two wrongs make a right: diverting attention from the issue by responding to an accusation with a counteraccusation that makes no attempt to refute the first accusation

Validity: logical consistency in a deductive *conclusion* that follows necessarily from the *major* and *minor premises*

Values: conceptions or ideas that act as standards for judging what is right or wrong, worthwhile or worthless, beautiful or ugly, good or bad

Voice: the combination of style and tone in a text

Warrant: see *assumption*

Index